# Society,
## Crime, and
### Criminal
### Careers

# Society, Crime

# and
# Criminal
# Careers

## An Introduction to Criminology

DON C. GIBBONS
*San Francisco State College*

PRENTICE-HALL, INC.                    Englewood Cliffs, New Jersey

Society, Crime, and Criminal Careers:
An Introduction to Criminology
Don C. Gibbons

© 1968 by PRENTICE-HALL, INC.
*Englewood Cliffs, New Jersey*

PRENTICE-HALL INTERNATIONAL, INC., *London*
PRENTICE-HALL OF AUSTRALIA, PTY. LTD., *Sydney*
PRENTICE-HALL OF CANADA, LTD., *Toronto*
PRENTICE-HALL OF INDIA PRIVATE LTD., *New Delhi*
PRENTICE-HALL OF JAPAN, INC., *Tokyo*

Current printing (last digit):

10   9   8   7   6   5   4   3

Library of Congress Catalog Card Number: 68-11341

PRINTED IN THE UNITED STATES OF AMERICA

# Preface

The problem of crime and what to do about it promises to be one of the central concerns of citizens in the second half of the twentieth century. Already the belief is widespread that criminality in the United States has increased in recent decades far more than has population. Coupled with this view is the commonly-held opinion that lawbreaking has recently taken on a more vicious and aggressive form. The report of the President's Commission on Law Enforcement and Administration of Justice, published in 1967, represents an attempt to respond to these endemic fears about ominous trends in modern society.

When one wishes to become informed on crime trends, crime causation, and related matters, he quickly finds that the truth is exceedingly difficult to discover. The student of criminality quickly learns that criminal statistics must be treated gingerly and with a good deal of skepticism, in view of the way in which they are compiled. Perhaps much of the assumed rise in lawbreaking in recent decades is nothing more than a statistical artifact—in other words, a reflection of improvements in crime reporting. Then too, part of the upsurge of offenders could be the consequence of heightened attention to criminality. Conceivably, criminal deviants may not be much more common now than they were in earlier times, but because contemporary American society is paying more attention to them they seem more numerous.

*Society, Crime, and Criminal Careers* is a typologically-oriented work: Its basic premise is that progress in explaining lawbreaking behavior or in correcting that conduct demands that the heterogeneous assortment of criminal roles be sorted out into homogeneous patterns for study. This book is an endeavor to throw light upon the complexities of criminality, crime causation, and reactions to offenders. The reader will be continually confronted with evidence that lawbreaking is complex and difficult to comprehend. For one thing, the forms of criminality are so extremely varied that no single explanatory formula will make sense of this behavior. Moreover, these various kinds of illegality are so complexly bound

v

up into the structure of modern societies that to unravel crime one must also unravel the fabric of social organization.

The reader will discover that this work is unlike its predecessors in several ways. Of the twenty-one chapters, fourteen deal with causation, whereas the remaining seven discuss societal reactions to offenders, including correctional processes that attempt to convert these persons into lawabiding citizens. However, this text departs from the format of most criminology books, which usually contain two general and quite separate parts—one dealing with etiology and the other with corrections or penology. Most of those books imply that causation has little to do with correctional responses directed at lawbreakers and devote a large number of pages to descriptive details of administrative processes in corrections. *Society, Crime, and Criminal Careers*, however, deals with the workings of police agencies, prosecuting attorneys, judges, juries, and other administrative structures and persons that convert "suspects" into "criminals" in Chapters 3 and 4, rather than at the back of the book as in other texts. Also, it attempts to identify some of the ways in which correctional reactions may inadvertently contribute to causal processes: For example, those persons who are sent to penal institutions may encounter liabilities stemming from their status as "ex-cons" that make it very difficult for them to adopt lawabiding behavior patterns. The latter part of the text shows how effective correctional practices which try to convert deviants into conformists, demand a body of sound behavioral theory derived from the study of causation. No attempt has been made here to provide a compendium of penological details. In these and other ways, this text is designed as a single book, rather than as two works under a single cover.

A number of persons have helped in preparing this book for publication. All of my colleagues in sociology at San Francisco State College have provided advice and encouragement at various steps in its development. Mr. James Clark of Prentice-Hall, Inc. had much to do with my decision to embark upon this project, and he supplied a good deal of further help on the book. Professor Herbert Blumer made a number of incisive and valuable suggestions regarding the contents of the text. My wife and children cheered me on throughout the writing of the manuscript. Finally, several student "slaves" were of invaluable aid to me, including Mr. David Roth. In particular, Miss Valerie Field carried out a large number of the less exciting but important tasks that were involved in getting the manuscript in shape for publication. Of course, none of these individuals bears any responsibility for defects in the book. Any defects or errors are to be blamed on the author, although if I had a co-author, I would surely blame them on him!

DON C. GIBBONS

*San Francisco, California*

# Contents

# 9    Causal Analysis: The Social-Psychology of Criminal Careers

# 10    Causal Analysis: The Study of Role-Careers

# 11    Introduction to Property Offender Careers

# 12    Additional Property Offender Careers

# Society,
## Crime, and
### Criminal
### Careers

# 1

# Crime and Criminology

## INTRODUCTION

The various "bad guys" in modern societies, including criminals, juvenile delinquents, drug addicts, and homosexuals, are the subject of continuous and intense discussion in all sorts of places by many kinds of individuals. Much of this commentary seems motivated by a kind of envy of the deviant who dares to engage in the pursuit of bizarre, peculiar, or ecstatic experiences. Reading of the exploits of some notorious law violator enables us to participate vicariously in forbidden behavior, so it is said. At any rate, most of the mass media attention directed at "outsiders," men and women who have been fenced off from conventional society because of behavior which has been reacted to as "bad" or deviant, is sensationalistic in form.[1] This material is little interested in explanation of the behavior in question, or dispassionate presentation of the facts of deviation. Instead, dramatic, exceptional instances of noncomformity are emphasized, while more usual, mundane cases of misconduct are ignored. Overly simple, often erroneous notions are put forward as explanations of deviant conduct, rather than the complex and sophisticated propositions required to account for criminality and other forms of disapproved conduct.

The list of simple, and sometimes simple-minded, hypotheses about criminality is extensive. At various times, hereditary taint, bad companions, or wicked parents have been identified as the culprits responsible for crime. These arguments have also included the view that lawbreakers are the result of comic books, television programs, or other mass media influences. It has been claimed that crime is the by-product of societal breakdown, in which citizens have turned away from God. All of these theories are naive, for they are vastly oversimplified. For example, it may be that modern societies have suffered an increase in crime due to growing secularization of human affairs. However, the drift of societal changes has been far more complex than is suggested in popular

[1] Howard S. Becker, *Outsiders* (New York: Free Press of Glencoe, Inc., 1963).

notions about burgeoning wickedness and the rejection of religious thought.

However, not all of the attention directed at criminality and criminals is of the above kind. A field of study called *criminology*, which is concerned with the objective analysis of crime as a social phenomenon, has grown up in western societies. Criminology includes within its scope inquiry into the processes of making laws, breaking laws, and reacting to the breaking of laws.

The terms *criminology* and *criminologist* are not used in a consistent manner by everyone. Criminology is sometimes employed as a label for the scientific techniques of law enforcement and detection. In this usage, criminologists are persons who work in police laboratories and are involved in the collection and analysis of evidence concerning crimes. Additionally, lay persons who write essays or novels concerning crime are sometimes labeled as criminologists, as are psychiatrists or psychologists who concern themselves with various facets of criminality. But the most common use of these labels is with regard to the subfield of sociology, in which criminality is studied as a form of social behavior. Those sociologists who specialize in this substantive topic are called criminologists. Criminology and criminologist are used in this last sense in this book. In short, this text is a statement of sociological propositions and research evidence about criminality which have been developed, for the most part, by sociologists interested in the study of law violation as social behavior. It should be pointed out that most of the theorizing and research regarding criminality has been the work of sociologists.

## PROBLEMS OF EXPLANATION

The study of crime and criminals involves so many topics or questions that criminological analysis represents a large and continuing responsibility of sociologists. Some order can be imposed upon the diverse interests of criminologists by sorting them into half a dozen major categories. These are: *a*) definition of *crime* and *criminals,* *b*) origins of criminal law, *c*) epidemiology of crime, *d*) the sociology of criminality, *e*) social-psychology of criminal careers, and *f*) societal reactions to crime. Let us look at what is involved in each of these areas of interest.

### Definition of Crime and Criminals

Speaking on the general topic of deviant behavior, of which criminality is one form, Cohen has declared: "The most pressing problem in the field of social disorganization and deviant behavior is to define these terms. If we cannot agree on what we are talking about, we cannot agree on what is relevant, much less on what is important." [2] Just as the first step in the analysis of deviance is defining the phenomenon of attention, the first stage in the study of criminality and criminals centers about explicit specification of the scope and meaning of these labels. What do we mean by criminality? What is a criminal or a noncriminal? Who and what is to be included or excluded from criminological scrutiny?

Does everyone agree upon the meaning of crime and criminals, so that explicit definitions are not required? The answer is emphatically negative, for considerable controversy has raged in criminology over questions of this kind. Some authorities have suggested that the proper subject matter encompasses only those persons convicted in a criminal court of criminal violations of law, while other criminologists would include within the population of criminals persons who have been arrested but not convicted. Still others would study "white collar criminals," who have violated criminal laws but have been processed informally or through civil courts. Probably the majority of students of criminality would focus upon all those individuals who have violated criminal laws, whether or not they have been apprehended. Finally, a few persons contend that the proper area of inquiry would be the study of "norm violations" and "norm violators," of which criminal acts and violators of criminal law constitute only a part.

Clearly, the definitional task is more complicated than first appearances suggest. Moreover, it is a task having priority over all others, for all succeeding steps in criminological analysis hinge upon clear and valid initial definitions of the phenomena of study. A major part of Chapter Two is concerned with the explication of a criminological frame of reference, and will present the various perspectives that have been put forth on the question of the scope of criminological inquiry, along with our own judgment regarding the proper subject matter of investigation.

## The Origins of Criminal Law

In the last analysis, society "creates" crime through processes in which acts are singled out as "bad" and "criminal." By "society" is meant groups of persons who manage to get some act included within a set of statutes that declare certain behaviors criminal in form. Crime is not inherent in the nature of behavior; somebody has to identify acts of one kind or

[2] Albert K. Cohen, "The Study of Social Disorganization and Deviant Behavior," in *Sociology Today*, ed. Robert K. Merton, Leonard Broom, and Leonard S. Cottrell, Jr. (New York: Basic Books, Inc., 1959), p. 461.

another as criminal. For behavior to become criminal, someone's conception of an act as criminal must get widespread adoption. Legislatures must pass laws which publicly assert that crimes have been defined.

The social character in conceptions of crime can be seen in the fact that the number of acts regarded as crimes has steadily increased over the past several hundred years as lawmaking bodies have created more and more criminal statutes. Definitions of criminal acts are subject to variations from place to place. Within the United States, marked variations occur from one state to another in both the language and content of criminal codes, so that no uniform set of criminal laws exists in this country. Crime is not an invariant and universal phenomenon, consistently the same in all places and at all times.

The processes of lawmaking constitute social behavior. Particular criminal laws have identifiable antecedents—there are reasons for the emergence of laws at some particular time or in some specific place. Moreover, statutes are created by real persons whose actions can and should be made the subject of sociological attention. But relatively little is known about the development of criminal laws and the variables which account for these origins, for this has been a neglected area of inquiry until recently. However, in Chapter Two, we will examine a number of theories which have been put forth regarding the genesis of criminal laws, along with several pieces of research evidence on the development of theft laws, vagrancy statutes, and several other kinds of criminal laws.

### The Epidemiology of Crime

The term epidemiology is usually associated with public health studies of the extent, distribution, and characteristics of various forms of physical illness or disease, so that the epidemiology of tuberculosis concerns facts about the number of tubercular persons in the population, their social characteristics, and so forth. The term has been used in criminology in reference to the facts regarding the number, location, and social characteristics of criminals. Epidemiological data are needed prior to any endeavor to explain criminality. A clear and detailed picture of the phenomenon to be explained is prerequisite to causal inquiry.

If a definition of criminality were employed which restricted the scope of that term to persons convicted of criminal offenses in criminal courts, the matter of epidemiology would be relatively simple. One could glean the facts of crime from records of court proceedings. However, if a broader definition of crime is utilized, in which commission of illegal acts would be required for an individual to be termed a criminal, but in which

conviction in a court (or police apprehension) is not required, epidemiological problems of some complexity arise to plague the student of
criminology.

The broader conception of criminality is used in this book. We intend
to examine the actions of persons who violate criminal laws, only a
fraction of whom are apprehended and subsequently convicted of such
offenses. As a result, we have to assemble a picture of crime in American
society which will clarify the size and characteristics of various components of the offender universe. For example, we will need to inquire
as to the proportion of all lawbreakers represented by those individuals
who have been reported to the police. In addition, we will want to discover whether some kinds of violators are more likely to be reported to
the police than are others. Do variables such as social class backgrounds,
racial characteristics, and offender-victim relationships influence police
referral policies? Throughout Chapter Five, the task of epidemiological
presentation will be complicated by the grossly inadequate state of the
basic statistical data regarding crime in the United States. Much more
reliable and detailed statistics are maintained on such things as professional baseball behavior than upon social bookkeeping regarding deviants.

## The Sociology of Criminality

Discovery of the causes of crime (and juvenile delinquency) is the
principal business of the criminologist sociologist. His major aim is to
develop a body of generalizations or propositions accounting for criminality. This task is many-faceted, but there are two main components of the
explanatory job. These are closely related, but are analytically separate
problems. The first has to do with the development of explanations for
the *kinds and amounts of criminality* observed in a society, while the
other centers about discovery of the processes involved in the *acquisition
of criminal behavior patterns by specific individuals*. Cressey has had
this to say about these two problems of analysis:

> ... a theory explaining social behavior in general, or any specific kind of
> social behavior, should have two distinct but consistent aspects. First, there
> must be a statement that explains the statistical distribution of the behavior in
> time and space (epidemiology), and from which predictive statements about
> unknown statistical distributions can be derived. Second, there must be a state-
> ment that identifies, at least by implication, the process by which individuals
> come to exhibit the behavior in question, and from which can be derived pre-
> dictive statements about the behavior of individuals.[3]

[3] Donald R. Cressey, "Epidemiology and Individual Conduct: A Case From Criminology," *Pacific Sociological Review*, III (Fall 1960), 47.

Investigators have not always kept the distinction between these two queries clear. As Cohen has indicated:

Much that travels under the name of sociology of deviant behavior or of social disorganization is psychology—some of it very good psychology, but psychology. For example, Sutherland's theory of differential association, which is widely regarded as preeminently sociological, is not the less psychological because it makes much of the cultural milieu. It is psychological because it addresses itself to the question: How do people become the kinds of individuals who commit criminal acts? A sociological question would be: What is it about the structure of social systems that determines the kinds of criminal acts that occur in these systems and the way in which such acts are distributed within the systems? In general, a sociological field is concerned with the structure of interactional systems, not with personalities, and the distribution and articulation of events within these systems.[4]

Sutherland's theory of differential association, alluded to by Cohen, is an argument which we shall examine in some detail in Chapter Nine, for it represents the most sophisticated attempt to date by a sociologist to account for the development of criminality in individuals. In brief, that theory argues that persons learn criminal attitudes and behavior through a process of differential association or interaction with carriers of criminal culture.

If Sutherland's theory is not directed to the sociology of crime, what would such a theory be like? Let us examine a hypothetical illustration. Suppose that an epidemiological study of lawbreaking patterns within a particular city shows that certain forms of gang delinquency on the part of juveniles and certain kinds of property crime carried on by adults are heavily concentrated in slum areas and uncommon elsewhere in the city. The focus of attention here ought to be upon questions of the sort, "Why are these kinds of crime so common in some areas and virtually nonexistent in others?" or "Is there something about community social organization, such as social class patterns existing in different areas, which results in these observed patterns of delinquency and crime?" These are questions primarily concerned with the explanation of *rates*. Some particular criminologist might come forward with hypotheses alleging that variations in neighborhood social structure and differences in expectations of material success in American society which exist between lower and middle class citizens are responsible for the widely divergent rates of deviation. To test such claims, data would have to be gathered to provide indices of neighborhood social organization, differential social class values, and so on. In turn, these hypotheses would be confirmed or disproved to the degree that correlations or covariations

4 Cohen, op. cit., p. 462.

were observed between crime rates and the measures of social organization. Insofar as those areas with high crime rates are also the most disorganized, and to the degree that low crime neighborhoods are the most cohesive, the hypotheses would be verified.

Another illustrative case falling within the sociology of crime is found in comparative figures for the United States and certain European nations which seem to indicate that American society is the most ridden with criminality. A sociological hypothesis commonly advanced to account for this contrast holds that American society is more "criminalistic" or "criminogenic" than the others because of such things as inordinate emphasis upon material success and endemic disrespect for law and order in American values and beliefs. Although an adequate test of these claims has not been made, and such research would be difficult to carry out, the kinds of evidence called for are relatively clear. Crime rates would have to be assembled in order to rank societies in terms of criminality, while indices of cultural values, attitudes toward materialism, law enforcement, and so on would be required in order to test causal propositions.

The chapters to follow will be concerned with a number of theories and pieces of evidence that are centered about differentials in crime rates and explanations for such variations.

### The Social-Psychology of Criminal Careers

Etiological or causal analysis in criminology involves both explanation of differentials in crime rates *and* exploration of the processes by which specific individuals acquire criminal attitudes and behavior patterns. The latter is what Cohen has identified as a psychological issue. Our preference is for the term *social-psychology of criminal careers*, in that social-psychology is that discipline which is concerned with *socialization* —the processes through which individuals learn to behave in a human fashion. Thus we speak of the socialization of children in reference to those experiences which create humans out of the biological raw material represented by the neonate. The term is also utilized to direct attention at learning experiences through which mature individuals come to acquire new behavior patterns, such as the socialization of the medical student, the worker, or the homosexual. The roles of physician, automobile worker, homosexual, or criminal are all learned patterns of behavior.

The difference between social-psychological propositions regarding criminal careers and the sociology of crime can be clarified through our earlier example of different crime and delinquency rates in a specific city. Suppose we have noticed, in addition to the facts already specified, that there are several different patterns of behavior among juveniles in the high delinquency area. Some boys have high occupational aspirations, are highly motivated in school, and are conformist in behavior. Other juveniles are "corner boys," not heavily involved in delinquency, but neither are they intensely meshed in patterns of mobility-striving or achievement. They are unmotivated, conformist juveniles whose actions center about short-run hedonism. A third group of juveniles contains boys heavily caught up in delinquent activities, whose major social role is that of "tough kid" and "delinquent." One social-psychological problem in this case has to do with the discovery of factors that led these specific youths into several different behavioral careers. The kinds of candidate hypotheses on this matter that might be entertained would include the proposition that the delinquent boys may be the ones with more personality problems than conformist, working-class boys. Perhaps the delinquents are from more lax or criminalistic family backgrounds than are the nondelinquents, or, additionally, differential association in conformist or delinquent peer groups may be a factor of considerable importance.

Other examples of explanatory problems concerned with deviant socialization patterns and the development of criminal role patterns, rather than rates, are easily identified. Some study has been made of the impact of being apprehended and processed as a lawbreaker. It appears that these events sometimes contribute to encouragement of a role in deviation, while in some other cases the experiences act to deter the individual from further involvement in deviance. In the same vein, some attention has been given to the developmental processes by which embezzlers manage to rationalize deviant acts in advance of carrying out defalcations. Some work has been carried out on the question of variations in behavior among different juveniles in high delinquency areas. These and other cases are more clearly concerned with social-psychological matters than anything else.

At this point, someone might object to these distinctions on the grounds that truly adequate causal analysis ought to explain both variations in rates of criminalistic deviance and variations in involvement in criminality or law-abiding behavior on the part of individuals in particular neighborhoods, social classes, or other settings. It should be noted that many specific instances of criminological theory and/or research are, in fact, jointly concerned with these two problems. Nevertheless, it makes sense to keep these two matters analytically separate.

Much of the ambiguity and confusion in contemporary theorizing and commentary regarding criminality can be traced, in part, to the failure at defining clearly the explanatory problem being addressed. Take those psychiatric hypotheses which allege that offenders are pathological persons suffering from various psychological impairments. Are such claims intended to account for variations in rates of criminality, as among different social class groups? Do they imply that much larger numbers of working class individuals, criminals and conformists alike, suffer from personality problems as compared to members of other social classes? That is the inference that follows if psychogenic hypotheses are put forth as an explanation of rate variations. On the other hand, psychiatric arguments which are advanced to account for the development of deviant or nondeviant careers on the part of certain individuals *within* a social class group leave the matter of rate variations an open question. As an explanation of career development, the personality pathology framework is logically compatible, at least, with a sociological explanation of rate variations which emphasizes such variables as differences in neighborhood organization. Conceivably, high crime rates which are compounded out of specific criminal careers might be most commonly found in those social areas with community influences conducive to criminality, and where, in addition, relatively large numbers of persons with personality problems are located and serve as candidates for criminality. Conversely, in neighborhoods more cohesive in character, individuals with personality aberrations may be prone to behavior of a noncriminal kind.

All of this discussion merely serves as a hypothetical illustration, rather than an exposition of the version of etiological theory preferred by us and to be introduced later. The empirical accuracy of these notions is not an issue here.

### Societal Reactions to Crime

There are myriad forms of reactions to such deviant behavior as criminality in complex societies such as the United States. Some kinds of crime are rarely reported to any social control agency, such as the police. Other instances of deviation are reacted to with police arrest or court action in some cases but not in others, depending upon such contingencies as variations in social class backgrounds of the offenders and the amount of incriminating evidence that can be assembled against the lawbreaker. In addition, those violators who are processed in the social control machinery to the point of court trial are subjected to a variety of subsequent experiences. Some are placed on probation, others incarcerated in jails, and still others sentenced to penal institutions of various types. The social events that occur to deviants which constitute societal reactions are the consequence of a number of factors, some of which are only slightly understood at present. In any event, the elaborate pattern of social control devices and experiences undergone by law violators as they are processed through this machinery represent basic topics for study by the criminologist. Indeed, it might be argued that the major business of the sociologist-criminologist ought to be investigation of the workings of social control patterns and structures. In modern societies, control, repression, or alteration of deviants has been formalized and given over to several special occupational groups. As a result, the sociological analysis of social control machinery ranks in importance with the study of social stratification, family behavior, or certain other "core" institutions of modern society. Elaborate social inventions for the control of deviants represent prominent social organizations in modern societies.

One major point to be developed in later chapters is that the societal reactions to offenders at any point in time in a particular society reflect other characteristics of that social organization. Actions taken against law violators in different historical periods have changed over time, in the general direction of treatment or rehabilitative orientation and away from punitive actions. Societal reactions are a part of ongoing social structure, so as social conditions change, reactions to deviants become altered. One of the tasks of the criminologist is to develop generalizations to account for the historical trends which have been observed in societal reactions.

The emerging therapeutic or treatment orientation toward offenders in the United States (and elsewhere) is a relatively new development.[5] As a result, the social control devices now employed in contemporary America constitute a not entirely harmonious mixture of rehabilitative approaches, punitive devices, and other reactions. The matter of contradictory correctional goals is something that subsequent chapters will examine in detail, for the present schizoid character of the sum of reactions to deviants poses severe obstacles to efforts to change lawbreakers into conforming citizens.

## THE ROLE-CAREER PERSPECTIVE

The principal distinguishing feature of this text is its emphasis upon criminal role-careers. This book argues that criminological attention must turn away from the study of crime and criminals to the examination of various types or role-careers in criminality. We aver that the situation of

[5] For a detailed discussion of treatment theory and the deficiencies of that material, along with the statement of treatment theory based on offender role-careers, see Don C. Gibbons, *Changing the Lawbreaker* (Englewood Cliffs, N.J.: Prentice-Hall, Inc., 1965).

criminology is similar to that of medicine—there is not one form of sickness, there are many. There is not one cause of illness, there are a number of causes, each related to a particular form of sickness. So it is with criminality, for that rubric is a broad one indeed, containing under it a very large number of behavioral forms having little in common with each other. If this is so, then it is doubtful that a general theory of criminal etiology can be discovered which will explain all of the disparate forms taken by criminality. Instead, specific theories or subtheories are required in order to account for different criminal role-careers.

This is not the first criminology text to acknowledge the importance of differentiation of offender types or the need to develop propositions specific to the types. Several other recent works have given some recognition to this general point.[6] Indeed, it would be hard to imagine anyone being able to ignore the obvious differences among such kinds of criminals as violent rapists, professional thieves, white collar offenders, and prostitutes. But it is one thing to acknowledge the fact of differences among offenders, and another to develop a systematic analysis of criminality oriented around the study of criminal role-careers. Among other things, types of offenders must be identified by the sociologist, for they are not readily apparent from direct observations of offenders. That is, the sociologist often demonstrates the existence of types by pointing to similarities among offenders which may have gone unnoticed by both the lawbreakers and the citizens concerned about them. The criminologist's activities are parallel to those of the policeman, who also sorts offenders into types. The case of burglary serves as an illustration, in that among citizens, burglars and burglaries are viewed as all pretty much alike. However, the policeman speaks of "cat burglars" and of "regular burglars." He applies the "cat burglar" label to those persons who burglarize dwelling units while the occupants are on the premises. These individuals differ in criminal techniques from "regular burglars," who take special pains to make sure that no one is at home during the time they are engaged in their crimes. In the policeman's view, "cat burglars" are thought to differ in psychological makeup from other burglars. "Cat burglars" or "hot prowlers" are suspected of aberrant motives and are viewed as "weirdos" who get "kicks" from their crimes, unlike the utilitarian, businesslike, run-of-the-mill burglars. The point

[6] See Richard R. Korn and Lloyd W. McCorkle, *Criminology and Penology* (New York: Holt, Rinehart and Winston, Inc., 1959), pp. 142–56; Paul W. Tappan, *Crime, Justice and Correction* (New York: McGraw-Hill Book Co., Inc., 1960), pp. 215–34; Walter C. Reckless, *The Crime Problem* (4th ed.; New York: Appleton-Century-Crofts, Inc., 1967), pp. 185–373; Herbert A. Bloch and Gilbert Geis, *Man, Crime, and Society* (New York: Random House, Inc., 1962), pp. 191–445; Marshall B. Clinard and Richard Quinney, *Criminal Behavior Systems* (New York: Holt, Rinehart and Winston, Inc., 1967).

of all this is that policemen and the rest of us see "cat burglars" in the population of offenders only after we have developed observational concepts which tell us to look for certain recurrent features of behavior on the part of some lawbreakers.

How are law violators to be sorted into types or role-careers? How are etiological variables to be organized and brought to bear upon the study of role-careers? These are the kinds of theoretical and conceptual issues that must be addressed if the study of role-careers is to bring about improvements in criminological knowledge. Many of the subsequent chapters endeavor to work out these theoretical problems of criminology. It might be noted in advance that our view is that types of offenders can be observed when lawbreakers are examined in terms of a few major variables or dimensions. Two of these have to do with offense behavior, described in ways which differ from criminal statute definitions of offenses, and with the situational context within which criminality occurs. Two other major dimensions, social-psychological in form, are self-concept and attitudinal patterns. In this perspective, an offender type such as the professional "heavy" criminal is comprised of individuals who engage in similar patterns of criminality and exhibit common social-psychological characteristics. Much of the remainder of this text will be devoted to showing that persons who fall into one of the role-careers defined in this way also exhibit common etiological or causal background experiences.

## SUMMARY

This introductory chapter has noted that the question of the proper subject matter for study has been a controversial one about which authorities have disagreed. We have seen that attention must be given to the complexities of criminal law. Criminologists also have the task of investigating the origins of criminal statutes so as to throw light upon the factors implicated in lawmaking as a form of social behavior. The study of criminal law also requires that the sociologist assess the extent to which particular criminal codes at any particular time are congruent with social sentiments, so as to place the law within the larger system of social order.

This chapter has also enumerated the major questions involved in the explanation of criminality as a form of deviant behavior. The criminologist has the job of unraveling the contributions which various strands of the social fabric make to patterns and rates of criminality. We need to strive to comprehend the variety of social influences which operate in the acquisition of criminal rules by various kinds of lawbreakers. Finally, criminology seeks to reveal the workings of the social control machinery as it attempts to convert offenders into law-abiding citizens.

The thrust of this brief chapter is that criminality is an exceedingly complex matter which is unlikely to be understood in terms of simple explanations holding that offenders are the product of defective heredity, psychological aberrations, or a few abnormal and atypical features of society. In the same way, the control of crime is not likely to be accomplished through the application of a few simple panaceas. Instead, if we are to make sense of criminality, we must grapple with a host of complicated questions. It is to the first of these, the nature of laws and definitions of criminality, that our attention turns in Chapter Two.

# 2

# Definition
## Origin
## and Trends
## in Criminal Law

## INTRODUCTION

Chapter One identified the definitional task as the first order of business in the study of criminal behavior. Unless criminologists can first agree upon the nature and scope of the phenomena they are to study, little or no progress can be made in the understanding of crime and criminal behavior. Chapter One also noted that consensus does not now exist regarding the proper subject matter of criminology. Instead, various arguments have been advanced to the effect that the concept of crime should be broadened to include more than that behavior identified by criminal statutes. This matter of definition is addressed in this chapter; several issues centering around definitional problems will be discussed in the sections to follow.

Whatever final decision the investigator of criminology makes regarding the appropriate subject matter of criminology, his starting point must necessarily be with the criminal laws. These statutes specify the nature of the legal entity, "crime"; they identify the constituent elements of action which must occur in order for an individual to acquire the legal identity of "criminal"; and they specify the attendant penalties invoked against "criminals." If the criminologist is to investigate a body of subject matter different from that identified by the criminal laws, he must be prepared to indicate the points of divergence of his definitions from legal ones, and to defend his departure from convention. Conversely, if the criminologist is to adopt a legalistic posture regarding the proper scope of inquiry, he must possess some understanding of the nature of criminal laws. The section to follow discusses some of the major features of criminal law as distinct from other social control inventions or bodies of normative prescriptions.

The second part of this chapter concerns the sociology of criminal law, and will explore the origins of the criminal law in some detail. We will take note of a variety of theories which have been advanced to account for the development of legal norms, along with several investigations which have been made of the social sources of certain criminal

17

laws. Another aspect of this matter concerns the extent to which criminal laws are supported by social sentiments, so we will look at several studies which illuminate this question. Finally, the last portion of the chapter grapples with the issue of whether a legalistic or some other perspective should be taken by the criminologist regarding crime. Should "antisocial" persons be the focus of attention? Should the criminologist study all norm violations, or should he restrict his attention to violations of criminal laws? In summary, this chapter lays the definitional ground work for the analysis of crime and criminal behavior.

## ELEMENTS OF CRIMINAL LAW

### Law and Social Control

The first thing to be said about criminal laws is that they represent only one of a number of devices intended to accomplish the goal of social control. The term social control designates those social arrangements which have been contrived in order to promote predictability of behavior and social regularity. Social control stands in contrast to *personal* control, which refers to those mechanisms inside the actor which constrain behavior. The latter consist of internalized or introjected norms, along with such internal or psychological mechanisms of control as feelings of guilt. A major share of the predictability of human behavior is the result of personal control, rather than external coercion. In turn, a central task of the socialization process centers about the inculcation of mechanisms of personal control. Personal and social control are not entirely independent phenomena, but social control develops to take care of behavioral instances in which personal control has broken down. In brief, social control is brought into play when the individual fails to be "his own policeman"—when he fails to curtail his deviant impulses.

The forms of social control are rich and varied, so that criminal laws comprise only one kind of social control. On this point, Clinard has observed that all groups and societies contrive ways of dealing with unusual behavior that falls outside of their norms. "Negative sanctions" in the way of penalties are imposed on those who violate norms, while "positive sanctions" such as praise or recognition are bestowed on exemplary persons. These positive and negative sanctions are forms of social control. Some types of social control are "formal" or official, while others are "informal" or unofficial in character, such as gossip and ridicule. Formal controls are exercised by some official apparatus established for that purpose. In the case of the criminal laws, enforcement and implementation rests with an elaborate machinery of law enforcement, judicial, and correctional structures.[1]

The formalization of bodies of law, including criminal statutes, is a relatively recent development in human history. For many centuries, men restrained themselves and other persons from some actions by various informal procedures and through unwritten, informal norms, often called *folkways* and *mores* by sociologists. Moreover, the accretion of modern law made up of formalized norms and sanctions has been uneven throughout the world. The law has flourished in urbanized, western nations, while there are some contemporary societies in which laws are still relatively undeveloped and traditional informal controls still dominant.

The distinctive features of law as a form of social control have been identified by Llewellyn and Hoebel.[2] They note that laws are a part of the normative structure of a society, that is, they constitute one set of definitions of obligatory or forbidden actions. Laws involve sanctions, so they are accompanied by penalties or punishments invoked in instances in which they are disobeyed. A third characteristic of laws is that in cases of conflict with other interests, laws must be followed, even in violation of other norms. The laws must prevail over other injunctions. Finally, laws are part of a larger legal *system* which includes a relatively explicit underlying rationale or philosophy, a set of procedures for applying and enforcing laws, and a body of recognized officials delegated the responsibility of carrying out legal procedures. Each of these four characteristics must be present in order for a normative system to be considered legal.

Although *criminal* law exhibits the characteristics identified above, it is at the same time only one of a number of legal systems. The criminal law possesses distinctive features setting it off from other bodies of law. Let us examine the nature of criminal law more closely.

### Ingredients of Criminal Law

Broadly speaking, criminal laws are those rules which prohibit or compel instances of conduct held to be important for the welfare of society or the state. Criminal laws exist in contradistinction to civil laws, which are regarded as a body of legal rules governing the conduct of individual persons in their private lives. The wrongs identified by civil

---

[1] Marshall B. Clinard, *The Sociology of Deviant Behavior* (rev. ed.; New York: Holt, Rinehart and Winston, Inc., 1963), pp. 148–49.

[2] Karl N. Llewellyn and E. Adamson Hoebel, *The Cheyenne Way* (Norman: University of Oklahoma Press, 1941).

law are considered to be private ones, rather than as wrongs against the State. A "tort" is a violation of civil law, or an offense against an individual. The injured individual must set the court machinery in operation, and he is the recipient of redress from the offender. But a crime is a violation of criminal law and an offense against the State. The State acts as the plaintiff, initiates the action against the offender, and exacts the punishment assigned the offender.

Sutherland and Cressey have identified the essential characteristics of criminal law as involving *politicality, specificity, uniformity,* and *penal sanction.*[3] These are the components identified in legal theory; in other words, they are the elements of criminal law which would be present in a completely rational, ideal system of criminal statutes. The law in practice can and does depart from these characteristics. Also, the differences between criminal laws and other bodies of conduct regulations are sometimes less clear-cut than these rubrics imply.

*1.* Politicality means that the criminal laws originate through the actions of the State rather than some private organization or group. Only those rules promulgated by legislatures of the State and its subdivisions constitute criminal laws, so that regulations of labor unions, social fraternities, college faculties, and so on, do not qualify as criminal statutes, even though they often show some similarity to the rules created by legislative processes.

*2.* Specificity as a characteristic of the criminal law means that criminal statutes provide strict definitions of particular acts which constitute crimes. In turn, those acts not clearly and unmistakably included in descriptions of crimes within the statutes are not to be labeled as crimes. However, in practice, specificity is a matter of degree, for some laws are relatively broad and general in language, such as those defining vagrancy, disorderly conduct, or omnibus clauses in definitions of juvenile delinquency which list "immorality" and "ungovernability" as forms of delinquent behavior. Societies have sometimes adopted broadly worded statutes which depart markedly from the principle of specificity. Thus in Nazi Germany, the German Act of 1935 provided that persons could be tried for acts analogous to, but not identical with, those acts proscribed in existing statutes. Similar laws were enacted in the Soviet Union in 1926.[4]

*3.* Uniformity as a feature of criminal acts refers to the effort to specify crimes and invoke sanctions against offenders in an even-handed fashion. Criminal laws do not contain exclusionary provisions allowing some

---

[3] Edwin H. Sutherland and Donald R. Cressey, *Principles of Criminology* (7th ed.; Philadelphia: J. B. Lippincott Co., 1966), pp. 5–9.

[4] Jerome Hall, *General Principles of Criminal Law* (Indianapolis: Bobbs-Merrill Co., Inc., 1947), p. 42.

categories of individuals to be dealt with differently than other groups who have committed similar law violations. Instead, criminal liability is supposed to be uniform for all, irrespective of social background or social status. However, the principle of uniformity breaks down in practice at several points. Law enforcement processes are not always uniformly administered, nor are judicial decisions always free from theoretically extraneous or irrelevant considerations of background variations or social influence.

4. Penal sanctions as an aspect of criminal law means that penalties are specified for violation of the statutes. Laws declare that certain acts are forbidden or required, and that violators of the law will be punished in some way. The latter half of this book is concerned with the detailed study of penal sanctions in operation.

The foregoing elements of criminal codes are essentially *external* characteristics, for they indicate the outward ingredients of the criminal law. Criminal statutes are created by political bodies and involve penalties when they are violated. A number of authorities have attempted to identify the *differentiae of crime*, that is, those elements of behavior which must occur in order for certain actions to be properly brought within the criminal law.[5] The differentiae of crime are those characteristics of the behavior of an individual which must be present for that behavior to constitute criminal conduct.

The first requirement of crime is that the behavior constitute a "harm." The act must result in visible, external consequences which are regarded as detrimental to social interests. Insofar as an act is held to result in injuries only to the parties immediately concerned in the act, that behavior does not qualify as a crime. Private injuries are civil offenses, not criminal acts.

In order for an act to be identified as a crime, that act must be legally forbidden. In other words, antisocial conduct is not criminal until it has been specifically proscribed in the body of criminal law. In the proceedings against a person, careful attention is usually paid to the question of whether or not an act has been explicitly forbidden. It is not enough that the behavior in question be reasonably similar to actions proscribed by law. Instead, it must be demonstrated that the instance at hand clearly fits within an existing category of forbidden conduct. Moreover, an elaborate appeal system has been contrived as a safeguard against misapplication of laws, so detailed scrutiny is often given to alleged acts of unlawful conduct.

[5] Sutherland and Cressey, op. cit., pp. 12–15; Richard R. Korn and Lloyd W. McCorkle, *Criminology and Penology* (New York: Holt, Rinehart and Winston, Inc., 1959), pp. 102–106; Hall, op. cit., pp. 19–20.

In addition to the foregoing, "conduct" must occur for a crime to take place. It must be demonstrated that intentional behavioral events took place, resulting in some harmful consequence. For instance, in order to convict an individual of murder, it must be proven that the person actually pulled the trigger of a gun or behaved in some other fashion which led directly to the death of the victim. It is not enough to show by a chain of circumstantial reasoning that a particular harmful consequence *probably* ensued from some illegal actions of a suspect. In order to convict an alleged offender of murder, more would be required than simply a demonstration that the weapon used to kill a person was owned by the suspect, for someone else might have utilized the gun and committed the murder.

A fourth and critical element in crime is that of *mens rea*, literally "evil mind" or "guilty mind." *Mens rea* refers to *intent*, rather than to *motivation*. In order to demonstrate *mens rea*, it must be shown that an actor intended or calculated to behave in a manner defined as illegal. Thus, for example, an individual is guilty of arson if he deliberately or intentionally sets a fire in a dwelling, with the result that the house burns to the ground. If a fire occurs as a result of an accidental action by the actor, the crime of arson has not occurred.

A guilty individual may have engaged in a line of conduct or formed criminal intent out of various reasons or motives, but his reasons or motives are not directly relevant to the question of *mens rea*. For example, a person who, out of feelings of compassion, deliberately kills an invalid spouse suffering from an incurable and painful disease is equally guilty of a crime as is a professional killer who murders someone in "cold blood" and for pay. *Mens rea* would be present in both cases. Of course, the penalty handed out to each of these murderers may be considerably different, and the professional killer might receive a decidedly more punitive sentence than the other murderer. Variations in sentences which are a function of social background differences among offenders, differences in motivation, and so on, are commonplace in the workings of the legal machinery. However, the basic point remains that "good" motives are not taken into account in the determination of whether or not a crime has occurred, at least in legal theory.

The notion of *mens rea* is basic to the plea of insanity as extenuating in criminal court trials. In brief, the claim that an individual was insane at the time that a harmful act took place, if successfully sustained, relieves that person of culpability of a criminal act. The actor is held to be guiltless because of an incapacity to form criminal intent, from the absence of *mens rea*.

Other elements of crime include the requirement that there be a fusion of *mens rea* and conduct, or that they occur together in order to result in a crime. For example, a crime has not taken place in the instance of an intended but abortive attempt by A to murder B, followed by a somewhat later event in which B dies through the unintended negligence of A, who has left a gas stove turned on but unlighted, resulting in B's death from gas poisoning.

Another requirement is that there be a causal relationship between someone's voluntary misconduct and the legally forbidden harm. In other words, it must be shown that the harm was a direct consequence of the misconduct, rather than an indirect one or due to some other antecedent events. An obvious illustration of the causal connection would be an instance of homicide in which a drunken driver runs over a pedestrian having the right-of-way in a crosswalk, and the pedestrian dies immediately after being hit by the car. A not-so-clear instance might be the case of an abortion in which the aborted female receives medical care in a hospital, recovers from the infection resulting from the abortion, but then succumbs to another disease contracted while in the hospital. In the latter case, the accused abortionist could plead not guilty of homicide by reason of a lack of causal connection between his illegal acts and the death of the victim. The abortionist would be guilty of abortion, but not of the death of his customer.

The final element of crime is that the forbidden act must carry a legally prescribed punishment. The voluntary conduct of the violator must be punishable by law.

The criminal law in practice shows discrepancies from these criteria of crimes. In particular, the requirement of *mens rea* is not part of the so-called strict liability offenses. That is, there are certain kinds of offenses in which the intent of the actor is not considered, so that certain actions and consequences constitute crimes even though the harmful consequences were unintended by the perpetrator. "Statutory rape" and "contributing to the delinquency of a minor" are cases in point, as are certain automobile violations. In the instance of contributing to the delinquency of a minor, an individual can be held liable for law violation for a number of acts carried on with a minor female (or male) in which no criminal conduct was intended. Similarly, an actor can be convicted and punished for statutory rape if he has sexual intercourse with a minor female, even though he went through elaborate efforts to determine her age and was completely convinced that the girl was above the age of consent. In these cases, it is enough that the actor engaged in some line of conduct; his intentions are legally irrelevant.

## THE SOCIAL SOURCES OF CRIMINAL LAW

### The Problem

The immediate answer to the question, "Where do criminal laws come from?" is that they are produced by individuals acting as members of state legislatures. But such a brief answer is unsatisfactory. Criminal laws do not encompass all antisocial or harmful acts, and at the same time they include some acts that many would claim are not antisocial or social harms, such as homosexual acts between consenting partners or the use of various narcotic drugs. Moreover, criminal laws have varied from place to place and from one time period to another. Contemporary criminal codes contain many more acts specified as illegal than the criminal laws of a century or two ago. Lawmaking is a continuous process, and exists as a response to social influences operating in societies at different points in time. In short, the making of criminal laws represents a fundamental social process which ought to attract the attention of the sociologist.[6]

Selznick has described the sociological study of law as "an attempt to marshal what we know about the natural elements of social life and to bring that knowledge to bear on a consciously sustained enterprise, governed by special objectives and ideals. Thus understood, legal sociology follows a pattern similar to that of industrial sociology, political sociology, and educational sociology."[7] In this same discussion, Selznick suggests that the sociological study of law has not developed much beyond an earlier stage of relative immaturity and general neglect.[8] In a similar vein, one criminologist has recently argued that American criminology has been restricted almost entirely to the study of criminal behavior, rather than to "crime."[9] He points out that behavior is not inherently criminal, but becomes so through social processes in which it is defined as criminal. Yet the major thrust of sociological attention has centered about the processes by which persons become individuals who act out or behave in ways that have already been defined as illegal, rather than on the social processes leading to the creation of criminal laws. On this

[6] A recent casebook on criminal law which places issues in contemporary criminal law in their social contexts is Richard C. Donnelly, Joseph Goldstein, and Richard D. Schwartz, *Criminal Law* (New York: Free Press of Glencoe, Inc., 1962).
[7] Philip Selznick, "The Sociology of Law," in *Sociology Today*, ed. Robert K. Merton, Leonard Broom, and Leonard S. Cottrell, Jr. (New York: Basic Books, Inc., 1959), p. 116.
[8] *Ibid.*, pp. 115–27.
[9] Clarence R. Jeffery, "The Structure of American Criminological Thinking," *Journal of Criminal Law, Criminology and Police Science*, XLVI (January–February 1956), 658–72.

point, Jeffery is quite right in claiming that little attention has been paid to the social conditions which explain the emergence of criminal codes.

It is readily apparent that formalized bodies of criminal law, including mechanisms for the implementation of codes, represent a relatively recent human invention. For much of human history, behavior has been controlled by personal controls and informal social control devices, as we have already noted. But as western societies have grown in size, complexity, and impersonality, the folkways and mores have become inadequate for the task of maintaining social stability. Consequently, the legal institutions have developed to buttress or shore up the more traditional forms of control. In this sense, lawmaking is the behavior of desperate men trying to reverse the deterioration of informal norms. A microcosmic illustration of this development can be seen in Eaton's study of social changes among the Hutterites, a contemporary North American religious sect practicing an Anabaptist faith coupled with a socialistic economy.[10] As this group was drawn into more intense contacts with the surrounding social organization of non-Hutterites, many of the unwritten customs of the group were challenged. In response to these perceived breakdowns, the elders of the group were moved to formalize previously informal norms and to create specific punishments for rule violations.

At least in general terms, it is clear that the development of criminal codes of various sorts and at various points in time is related to conditions of general social structure. Criminal statutes that have sprung up reflect basic interests and values in the societies in which they are found. Western, capitalistic societies are characterized by a large number of criminal laws surrounding property rights with the protection of law, because of the central place of private property values and emphasis on acquired wealth in western nations. In the same way, many other criminal norms in force at some point in time can be taken as a crude index of the core interests held in common by large and important segments of the population. However, it would be an error to assume that all criminal laws reflect cultural consensus on values. Some of them grow out of special interests of particular groups in the population, and may well be resisted and resented by other segments of the society.

A number of more specific theories have been advanced regarding the origins of criminal law.[11] In the classical view, criminal norms were seen as originating in torts or private wrongs, from which the state eventually came to redefine some private injuries as social ones. However, there are several defects in this theory, one being that the process by which

10 Joseph W. Eaton, "Controlled Acculturation: A Survival Technique of the Hutterites," American Sociological Review, XVII (June 1952), 331–40.
11 Sutherland and Cressey, op. cit., pp. 9–12.

private harms were converted into public or social ones has been left largely unspecified.

Some authorities have held that criminal laws arise as expressions of rational processes which take place as societies become unified. This line of argument claims that, as societies emerge out of earlier states of disunity in which the area has been divided up into independent fiefs, tendencies toward the development of uniform behavioral codes, including criminal laws, develop. There is still another contention, the converse of this one, holding that the enactment of law is a somewhat irrational, emotional response to social problems. The claims advanced by foreign visitors to the United States that this nation places undue and somewhat unthinking faith in the power of legislation to eradicate social problems is illustrative of this hypothesis. Thus it is sometimes said that Americans pass laws first, and only later make effective efforts to understand or solve problems against which they have already legislated.

Another theory on the origin of criminal laws asserts that they are an outgrowth or product of the mores. In this view, statutes represent an attempt to codify the mores and develop a coherent supportive rationale for the body of formalized mores. We have noted a somewhat different contention regarding the relation between custom and law, namely that the latter grows up in response to perceived shortcomings in the mores or their implementation. Finally, it has been suggested that some criminal norms are the consequence of conflicts of interest between different power groups, so that they symbolize the victory of one faction over another. Certain criminal laws represent devices created to serve some special interest group in its effort to dominate another group.

Each of these theories may explain the genesis of some criminal laws, but fail to account for other statutes. Moreover, little systematic and detailed evidence exists concerning the social origins of particular criminal laws. Specific studies of particular criminal laws, designed to collect evidence which would confirm and clarify the applicability of one or another of these general theories, are needed in considerable quantity. However, some data are already at hand concerning the rise of particular criminal laws, and it is to this material that the discussion below turns.

### Some Studies of Criminal Laws

Chambliss has examined the origins of vagrancy laws in England and the United States and the shifts in their nature since their creation.[12] He notes that the first vagrancy statute was enacted in England in 1349,

[12] William J. Chambliss, "A Sociological Analysis of the Law of Vagrancy," *Social Problems,* XII (Summer 1964), 67–77.

in which the giving of alms to any unemployed person of sound mind and body was made a crime. This law was the indirect result of the Black Death, which struck England about 1348 and had the effect of decimating the English labor force. It has been estimated that half of the English population died during the plague epidemic. As a result, the supply of cheap labor was severely reduced precisely at a time when serfdom was beginning to break down and peasants began to flee from the manors. Landowners had begun to experience great difficulties in the maintenance of their holdings. According to Chambliss, "It was under these conditions that we find the first vagrancy statutes emerging. There is little question but that these statutes were designed for one express purpose: to force laborers (whether personally free or unfree) to accept employment at a low wage in order to insure the landowner an adequate supply of labor at a price he could afford to pay." [13] In effect, the vagrancy laws were an attempt to sustain conditions of serfdom after the breakdown of the serf-manor system had already begun.

For most of the period after their enactment in 1349 to the sixteenth century, vagrancy laws remained a dormant statutory device. They were not utilized because the conditions which spurred their development had disappeared. However, about 1530 the statutes were revised in language and restored to use. The new phraseology focused attention on criminals rather than upon unemployed persons. In effect, these revamped vagrancy codes were intended to provide the control of persons suspected of being robbers or other sorts of criminals, but had not been apprehended for some specific violation of law. Chambliss accounts for these changes as a social response to the growth of commerce and industry in England. The large number of foreign merchants abroad in England in the sixteenth century were subject to frequent attacks by robbers. We shall see later, in Hall's study of the origin of theft laws, that the same concern for the regulation and protection of commerce and merchants in England provided the source of early statutes identifying theft as a crime.

Further elaborations and changes in vagrancy laws have occurred over the past several hundred years. However, the general trend has been to broaden the range of kinds of individuals who come within the definition of vagrant. A mechanism has been devised which provides police agencies with broad powers to "clear the streets" of various sorts of "suspicious" and "undesirable" persons. Accordingly, vagrancy laws are frequently a means of controlling the denizens of such city areas as Skid Road. As Chambliss notes, the individual states in the United States borrowed the

[13] *Ibid.,* 69.

eighteenth century English vagrancy laws substantially *in toto,* so that the laws in both countries are relatively similar.

Chambliss argues that the creation of vagrancy laws, and the subsequent changes in the language of these statutes and their interpretation or implementation, represent one case consistent with the interest group theory regarding the origin of criminal codes. The vagrancy statutes were contrived and later altered in order to protect the interests of such specific groups as landowners and merchants.

A second, well-known study of the development of law is Jerome Hall's investigation of the growth of modern theft laws.[14] Hall traces the growth of property and theft statutes back to the Carrier's Case of 1473. In this case, a defendant had been charged with a felony because he failed to carry out properly an assignment from a merchant. The carrier had been hired to carry certain bales to Southampton, England, but instead had absconded with them, broken them open, and taken the contents. In the deliberations which ensued, some of the judges argued that no felony had been committed, and that the carrier could not steal that which he already had in his possession. This line of argument was in accord with decisions previously rendered in the most common kinds of property crimes occurring up to this point, thefts of cattle. There the taking of property meant literally the physical removal of it. No such act had occurred in the Carrier's Case. Nonetheless, the defendant was ultimately found guilty on the grounds that he had broken open and taken the contents of the bales. While he had possession of the bales, he did not have possession of their contents. Hall asserted that this case laid the foundation for an emerging distinction between *custody* of goods and *possession* of them that was to become the basis for succeeding elaborations of theft law. In short, Hall's study shows that existing legal rules were revised by the judiciary in order to solve a social control problem posed by the carrier and his actions.[15]

According to Hall, the social conditions that gave rise to the creation of new legislative interpretations beginning with the Carrier's Case are these:

With the growth of manufacturing in the fifteenth century came marked changes in the manorial system and numerous departures from its mediaeval form. Came also the decay of serfdom and the rise of a new class of tenants whose rights were gradually recognized by the courts. But most important of all is the fact that during this period the older feudal relationships gave way before a rising middle class which owed its influence to the development of a rapidly expanding industry and trade. For example, in the middle of the four-

14 Jerome Hall, *Theft, Law and Society* (2nd ed.; Indianapolis: Bobbs-Merrill Co., Inc., 1952).
15 *Ibid.,* pp. 4–33.

teenth century there were only 169 important merchants, but at the beginning of the sixteenth century there were more than 3,000 merchants engaged in foreign trade alone. . . .

The great forces of an emerging modern world, represented in the above phenomena, necessitated the elimination of a formula which had outgrown its usefulness. A new set of major institutions required a new rule. The law, lagging behind the needs of the times, was brought into more harmonious relationship with the other institutions by the decision rendered in the Carrier's Case.[16]

The remainder of Hall's analysis is concerned with subsequent elaborations of modern theft law up to the present. The major conclusion drawn from the Carrier's Case which germinated this process was that new laws governing property rights emerged correlative with the emergence of commerce and industrialization in the Western world. Thus Hall and Chambliss both show the linkages between certain laws, the Industrial Revolution, and the growth of the market place.

An investigation of more recent developments in criminal law is to be found in the massive study by Radzinowicz of changes in English law, police systems, and criminal policy between 1750 and 1833.[17] One volume of this study is concerned with historical analysis of the shift in English criminal law from the situation current in 1750, when capital offenses were numerous and executions commonplace even for what would presently be regarded as petty offenses, toward a reduction in the number of capital crimes and executions under the laws. According to Radzinowicz, the development of a more rational and humane system of correctional control was impeded by many factors. He declared that, "among the effects of the Industrial Revolution were the emergence of great urban agglomerations and industrial regions, the formation of a large and mobile class of wage earners, the disintegration of some of the ancient orders of society, and the rapid accumulation of wealth by some sections of the community coinciding with the spread of poverty and economic instability, the evils of which were accentuated by the lack of a protective social policy. . . . England was in a state of transition and it is a truism that in such periods of social tension the Legislature becomes overridingly preoccupied with the strengthening of the State against the danger of an anticipated wave of lawlessness, inclined to lay stress on the deterrent function of criminal law and to oppose any attempt to change the established system of criminal justice, particularly if it would entail the relaxation of severity." [18]

[16] Reprinted from *Theft, Law and Society*, by Jerome Hall, Copyright 1935, 1952 by the Bobbs-Merrill Co., Inc. Reprinted by permission. All rights reserved.

[17] Leon Radzinowicz, *A History of English Criminal Law and its Administration from 1750*, 3 vols. (New York: The Macmillan Co., 1948–1957).

[18] *Ibid.*, Vol. 1, pp. 351–52.

Radzinowicz's analysis traces the emergence of a more equitable, humane, and less punitive system of legislation and correctional machinery from the writings of Beccaria and Jeremy Bentham. His study also shows the growth of modern metropolitan police systems during the latter part of the eighteenth century out of an earlier pattern of conflicting, overlapping police systems in which officers were employed part-time.[19] To a marked degree, the legislative, penal, and law enforcement reforms studied by Radzinowicz laid the foundation for contemporary systems of criminal justice.

The significance of Radzinowicz's arguments for the contemporary scene ought to be acknowledged. Some striking parallels can be drawn between the punitive sentiments of eighteenth century England and those insistent demands heard in the United States today for more repressive responses to offenders as a way of turning back the tide of lawlessness. One of the sentiments called out from citizens over the matter of racial turmoil in American cities has been the proposal that the police "get tough" with those involved in racial incidents. In the same way, longer and harsher penalties have been advocated for drug users and several other kinds of criminals. The sense of all these recommendations is that, if the responses to criminality are harsh enough, individuals will be deterred from such behavior. European experience suggests that the application of brutal punishments to large numbers of lawbreakers did little to curtail this behavior. Thus the chances are not great that these measures will prevent those who have long-standing grievances against society from expressing them in militant and sometimes criminal ways.

A more recent inquiry into the social factors implicated in the development of criminal statutes is to be found in the work of Sutherland, concerning sexual psychopath laws.[20] The first of these originated in Illinois in 1938, followed in rapid succession by sexual psychopath laws in other states. In nearly every case, their enactment followed a few dramatic, well-publicized sexual attacks in the state in question, so these laws represent a legislative reflex action. Sutherland points out that these laws are hopelessly ambiguous, usually defining a sexual psychopath as someone who has demonstrated an inability to control his sexual urges. These statutes are based upon a number of faulty or erroneous assumptions, not the least of which is the belief that such a clinical entity as a sexual psychopath exists in identifiable form. It seems clear that this particular legislative device represents an attempt to ameliorate a behavioral prob-

19 Ibid., Vol. 3, "Cross-Currents in the Movement for the Reform of the Police."
20 Edwin H. Sutherland, "The Sexual Psychopath Laws," Journal of Criminal Law and Criminology, XL (January–February 1950), 543–554; Sutherland, "The Diffusion of Sexual Psychopath Laws," American Journal of Sociology, LVI (September 1950), 142–48.

lem through legislation, in advance of the requisite knowledge of the basic dimensions of the problem. For all of these reasons, sexual psychopath laws are essentially inoperable.

Our final piece of evidence regarding the backgrounds of particular laws comes from Becker's study of the development of criminal norms designed to repress the use of marijuana.[21] Becker notes that the Marijuana Tax Act of 1937 had forerunners in earlier criminal statutes designed to suppress the pursuit of vices and ecstatic experiences, such as the Volstead Act (alcohol) and the Harrison Act (opium and derivatives). The Narcotics Bureau of the Treasury Department was unconcerned with marijuana in its earlier years, arguing instead that the regulation of opiates was the real problem. However, in the several years before 1937, the Narcotics Bureau came to redefine the matter of marijuana use as a serious problem. As a consequence, this agency acted in the role of *moral entrepreneur*, in which it attempted in several ways to create a new definition of marijuana use as a social danger. For example, the bureau provided information to mass media systems on the dangers of marijuana, including "atrocity stories" which detailed the gruesome features of marijuana smoking. Finally, in 1937, the Marijuana Tax Act was passed, ostensibly as a taxation measure but with the real purpose of preventing persons from marijuana smoking. One revealing sidelight on this legislation is that this bill encountered some strenuous objections from users of hempseed oil and the birdseed industry, which held that hemp seeds constituted a vital ingredient in various bird seed mixtures. These objections stalled the bill temporarily, but were finally satisfied through changes in the act which exempted hemp seeds from control. This modification highlights interest group involvement in the passage of criminal laws.

These few studies indicate some of the factors which give rise to various criminal laws. They are all illustrative of the kind of research into the social sources of criminal law which is needed in greater quantity.

## CRIMINAL LAW AND SOCIAL SENTIMENTS

As we have seen, a criminal statute may be born out of widely shared social sentiments, or it may have only a narrow base of public support. Criminal laws which once received general approval may fall into disfavor as they become out of tune with social values. In the same way, actions taken by the courts and correctional agencies with respect to violators of different laws are sometimes highly congruent with citizen

[21] Howard S. Becker, *Outsiders* (New York: Free Press of Glencoe, Inc., 1963), pp. 121–46.

preferences, while at other times significant discrepancies exist between correctional practices and the attitudes of the citizenry. In this sense, criminal laws and correctional practices mirror social values, but sometimes in a distorted manner. In the extreme case, when laws or practices depart too far from public preferences, pressures for revisions or modifications in laws develop. This matter of social sentiments toward the law and its implementation has not been given much attention. But some studies are available which do illuminate these concerns.

Rose and Prell conducted a study of lay attitudes toward forms of lawbreaking and the punishments thought to be appropriate to them, in which 13 minor felonies in California state law, which provided nearly equal minimum and maximum penalties, were selected for analysis.[22] Students at the University of Minnesota were asked to choose the most serious offenses among these crimes, which included child-beating, assault with a deadly weapon, and issuing fictitious checks. A pronounced rank order of judgments was found, in which child-beating and assault with a deadly weapon were held to be the most serious offenses, while unlawful manufacture, sale, or possession of weapons was judged to be least serious. These opinions about crimes seemed unrelated to the sentencing policies of the courts in California, in that inmates in a California prison who had been convicted of child-beating received considerably shorter sentences than did those involved in crimes judged as less important.

In a second investigation of this kind, carried on in the San Francisco area, a number of citizens were asked to complete a questionnaire which inquired about the kind of knowledge they had of criminality, correction, and kindred matters.[23] The principle of "out of sight, out of mind" described the responses, for most of the persons knew about a few flamboyant or bizarre cases of criminality, but few had any detailed knowledge of the workings of the law enforcement, judicial, or correctional systems.

Rooney and Gibbons conducted an inquiry into citizen views regarding "crimes without victims,"[24] in which a group of San Francisco area residents were questioned about policies which they felt should be pursued in cases of abortion, homosexuality, and drug addiction.[25] The respondents agreed generally that the laws regarding the legal grounds for abortions

[22] Arnold M. Rose and Arthur E. Prell, "Does the Punishment Fit the Crime? A Study in Social Valuation," *American Journal of Sociology*, LXI (November 1955), 247–59.

[23] Don C. Gibbons, "Who Knows What About Correction?" *Crime and Delinquency*, IX (April 1963), 137–44.

[24] Edwin M. Schur, *Crimes Without Victims* (Englewood Cliffs, N.J.: Prentice-Hall, Inc., 1965).

[25] Elizabeth A. Rooney and Don C. Gibbons, "Social Reactions to 'Crimes Without Victims,'" *Social Problems*, XIII (Spring 1966), 400–10.

should be liberalized. For example, 79 per cent of them held that women should be allowed to obtain therapeutic (legal) abortions if they have contacted German measles early in their pregnancy, while 83.6 per cent agreed that a pregnancy resulting from rape or incest should be allowable grounds for an abortion. At the time of the study, the legal fact was that in California, as in over half of the other states, the only condition under which an abortion could legally be carried out was if the life of the woman was imperiled by the pregnancy. Obviously, current abortion laws have not kept pace with changing social values. It seems apparent that legislators will come under increased pressure to liberalize abortion statutes as this gap between what the law permits and what people are willing to tolerate grows.[26] Indeed, California statutes were modified early in 1967.

The citizens in this research investigation were much less sympathetic to proposed reforms in the laws which would ignore voluntary acts of homosexuality. Instead, they generally opted for a continuation of policies which treat consenting homosexual conduct as criminal. Finally, most of the respondents were quite antagonistic to any changes in statutes which would result in drug users being dealt with outside the framework of the criminal law.

In another study to be mentioned in this review, closely related to the Rose and Prell investigation, San Francisco citizens indicated the degree of punishment which they deemed appropriate for a wide range of crimes.[27] The criminal acts were described in some detail, so as to elicit responses to run-of-the-mill or usual instances of these offenses. The respondents selected that disposition they thought most fitting from among a series of choices ranging from execution to no penalty.

The severest penalties were selected for cases of murder, robbery, rape, and certain other "garden variety" crimes. Also, a good many persons offered some penalty other than the ones included in the questionnaire for certain offenses. Nearly all of those for rape, narcotics use, child-molesting, and exhibitionism centered about psychiatric care for persons involved in that conduct. As a way of summarizing the findings, the penalty choices on the questionnaire were treated as a crude scale, with a score of 8 given to execution, a score of 1 to "other," a score of 0 to no penalty, and scores of from 7 to 2 for intervening choices. Mean

---

[26] Alice Rossi has reported a National Opinion Research Center study of a national sample of 1,484 persons, in which 71 per cent approved of abortions when the mother's health is endangered and about half favored abortions in cases of rape and in instances in which birth defects are probable. Only 20 per cent of the respondents approved of abortions for reasons of low income, illegitimate, or unwanted pregnancy. See Alice S. Rossi, "Abortion Laws and Their Victims," *Trans-action*, III (September–October 1966), 7–12.

[27] Don C. Gibbons, "Crime and Punishment: A Study in Social Attitudes," unpublished paper.

scores on offenses for the total sample and for males and females in the sample are shown in Table 1.

## TABLE 1
### Mean Penalty Scores, Total Sample and by Sex

| OFFENSE | TOTAL SAMPLE | MALES | FEMALES |
|---|---|---|---|
| Murder, second degree | 6.6 | 6.6 | 6.5 |
| Robbery | 6.3 | 6.3 | 6.5 |
| Manslaughter | 6.3 | 6.2 | 6.7 |
| Burglary | 6.2 | 6.2 | 6.2 |
| Rape | 6.0 | 6.0 | 5.8 |
| Embezzlement | 5.3 | 5.3 | 5.6 |
| Antitrust | 4.6 | 4.6 | 4.5 |
| Auto theft | 4.2 | 4.2 | 4.4 |
| Child-molesting | 4.3 | 4.1 | 4.5 |
| Check forgery | 3.7 | 3.6 | 4.1 |
| Narcotics | 3.9 | 3.8 | 3.9 |
| Assault | 3.4 | 3.4 | 3.5 |
| Misrepresentation in advertising | 3.2 | 3.4 | 2.8 |
| Draft evasion | 3.0 | 3.2 | 2.6 |
| Marijuana | 2.8 | 2.8 | 2.8 |
| Exhibitionism | 2.9 | 2.9 | 3.0 |
| Drunk driving | 2.9 | 2.9 | 2.9 |
| Tax evasion | 1.9 | 2.0 | 1.7 |
| Statutory rape | 2.1 | 2.2 | 1.9 |
| Homosexuality | 1.9 | 1.9 | 1.9 |

The rank order of scores in Table 1 indicates that the harshest penalties were chosen for five offenses which are included within the F.B.I. classification of index offenses (serious crimes), so that criminal acts which are highly visible and often involve coercive attacks upon property are the ones which citizens would have heavily punished. These are the crimes which often do result in long prison sentences for the perpetrators. However, several offenses which now tend to receive relatively lenient penalties are also deemed quite serious by these citizens, for over half of them elected sentences of a year or more in prison for embezzlers and antitrust violators.

There are a good many cases of criminal law and practice in which the level of public support is currently unclear. The area of "white collar crime" is a case in point, for the character of citizen sentiments regarding business crimes is open to conjecture and speculation. Some light is shed on this question through an investigation by Newman concerning violations of the Federal Food, Drug and Cosmetic Act, revised 1938.[28] He asked a sample of about 175 adults to indicate the degree of punishment they thought appropriate for cases of product misbranding and food adulteration selected from the files of a federal district attorney. These choices were then compared with the sentences actually imposed. About 78 per cent of the citizens felt that the penalties should be more severe than the actual court decisions. However, nearly all of the respondents selected punishments which are currently within the maximum allowable by law. Thus, public disapproval in this instance was centered on the administration of food and drug laws rather than upon the laws themselves. Finally, the penalties chosen by the citizens were not as severe as those sanctions imposed upon such run-of-the-mill offenders as thieves and burglars.

## CRIMINOLOGY, CRIME, AND CRIMINALS

### Legal Versus "Sociological" Crime

We have seen in an earlier section that crime consists of certain conduct norms possessing a specified character. Similarly, a criminal, from a legalistic viewpoint, is an individual who has behaved in ways which diverge from the prohibitions or injunctions in the criminal law.

Now, it is obvious that criminal law in any country has changed over time, so that it does not represent a body of stable behavioral norms. Similarly, in a single nation such as the United States, variations are seen from one jurisdiction to another in both the content and language of criminal codes. In short, that which is crime in one area may not have been crime at an earlier time or in another place. Since the criminal codes are far from entirely capricious in character, much of the criminal law of Western societies is concerned with the regulation or repression of many common forms of behavior. Still, the lack of consistency in statutes has led a number of students of crime to suggest that criminology should abandon legalistic definitions of its field of inquiry in favor of some other units of study which are universal and unchanging. Jeffery has summarized a number of these "sociological" approaches to crime which eschew legalistic definitions of the phenomena of study in favor of conduct norms and the violations of them.[29] Sutherland and Cressey have

28 Donald J. Newman, "Public Attitudes Toward a Form of White Collar Crime," *Social Problems*, IV (January 1957), 228–32.
29 Jeffery, *op. cit.*, 660–63.

also discussed a number of these views.[30] Similarly, Bloch and Geis have commented on approaches to criminology which would substitute the study of such phenomena as moral aberrance, parasitism, or deviancy for the investigation of legally defined crime.[31] The rationale for these definitional innovations is that criminology ought to concern itself with the study of antisocial conduct, whether or not that activity happens to be included within the criminal law. According to this view, criminology would be directed at the study of a homogeneous body of subject matter, rather than at a heterogeneous mixture of behavior haphazardly singled out by the criminal laws, which at the same time ignore other forms of sociological crime. Bloch and Geis quite properly criticize these concepts of moral aberrance, parasitism, or deviancy as little more than figures of speech which are devoid of specific meaning. To substitute these for a legalistic definition of the field of inquiry would mean that criminology would be mired in even more terminological and definitional confusion than would result from use of a legalistic criterion of crime.

One of the best known attempts to devise a substitute for a legalistic definition of crime is to be found in the work of Sellin, concerning "conduct norms." [32] Sellin suggested that criminology should study the violations of such norms, and declares: "These facts lead to the inescapable conclusion that the study of conduct norms would afford a sounder basis for the development of scientific categories than a study of crime as defined in the criminal law. Such study would involve the isolation and classification of norms into universal categories, transcending political and other boundaries, a necessity imposed by the logic of science." [33]

At first glance, these recommendations might appear as appealing solutions to the definitional difficulties imposed by legal definitions of crime. However, the study of conduct norms is still only in its infancy. We are a distance away from any sort of inventory of conduct norms, even within the United States. The development of cross-cultural listings of conduct standards is an even more distant goal, however laudable it might be as an end to pursue. Moreover, even if such inventories of conduct definitions were available, they would not accomplish the results Sellin sees for them. The shortcomings of social norms as the unit of study have been identified by Sutherland and Cressey in their critique of Sellin. They argue: "In this respect crime is like all other social phenomena, and the possibility of a science of criminal behavior is similar to the pos-

---

[30] Sutherland and Cressey, op. cit., pp. 15–16.

[31] Herbert A. Bloch and Gilbert Geis, Man, Crime, and Society (New York: Random House, Inc., 1962), pp. 10–13.

[32] Thorsten Sellin, Culture Conflict and Crime (New York: Social Science Research Council, 1938).

[33] Ibid., p. 30.

sibility of a science of any other behavior. Social science has no stable unit, for all social sciences are dealing with phenomena which involve group evaluations. Consequently the methodological problems are by no means solved when crime is redefined as a violation of any conduct norm." [34] Conduct norms are no more stable, universal, or unchanging than legal norms, and they are a good deal more ephemeral in character. Conduct norms vary over time and from place to place, so that little is to be gained (and much perhaps to be lost) by employing them rather than legal norms in the definitions of the boundaries of inquiry.

There is yet another point to be made about those arguments which would replace the study of legally defined crime with social norms and their violation. If the concept of *deviance* current in sociology is employed, in which deviance is seen as behavior which departs from some conduct norm and is reacted to by some significant number of other individuals, the field of study becomes heroic in proportion. Deviance is a label for diverse kinds of behavior, ranging from violations of small group norms in work settings and other relatively primary relationships to instances of such societally disapproved forms of conduct as certain types of criminality. It is unlikely that much progress is going to be made on the study of deviance as a subject matter. Instead, development of more valid generalizations about deviant behavior is probably contingent upon the discovery of confirmatory evidence regarding theories and hypotheses specific to particular, relatively homogeneous forms of deviant conduct. The criminologist would do well to carve out the area of legally proscribed behavior as his subject matter, and would profit as well from an approach to legally defined crime in which different orders of criminality are made the focus of theoretical and research attention.

A final remark on the matter of variability of criminal codes, and hence of crime, is that this variability presents the investigator with a problem for investigation, rather than with an obstacle to be circumvented by redefinition of the field. Criminal laws do vary temporally and from place to place, but, as suggested earlier, the study of social origins and influences in criminal law should be a major subject of sociological attention. As part of this inquiry, the sociologist of law should attempt to pinpoint the factors responsible for particular statutory variations in criminal law.

### Who is the Criminal?

The search for extra-legal definitions of crime has been accompanied by related efforts to articulate a sociologically meaningful conception of

[34] Sutherland and Cressey, op. cit., p. 21.

the criminal. Indeed, the conduct norm position on crime contains obvious parallel views on criminals, so that the latter group is comprised of all violators of social norms. However, the controversy over the proper meaning of criminal has been more complex than simply a quarrel as to whether norm violators are to be considered criminals.

If a legalistic posture is taken on the meaning of criminal, a criminal becomes some individual who has violated a criminal law. But there are some who find this definition objectionable. One of these counter positions has been advanced by Burgess, who would narrow the focus of attention to only a portion of those individuals engaged in violations of criminal law. He declares: "A criminal is a person who regards himself as a criminal and is so regarded by society. He is the product of the criminal-making process." [35] These remarks were made by Burgess in conjunction with a discussion of a study by Hartung of violations of O.P.A. regulations in Detroit during World War II. Burgess claims that, while such activities may legally constitute criminal conduct, they are not "sociologically" classifiable as criminal.

We submit that these claims by Burgess are not well thought out. If his recommendations were followed, many inmates in prison would be excluded from study on the grounds that they do not define themselves as criminals! Additionally, the notion of societal condemnation of crime implies the dubious presumption that uniform societal reactions can be discerned. We agree that criminals are the product of the criminal-making process, so that only those persons who have violated criminal laws should be identified as criminals. But the varied self-definitions of offenders and the divergent societal reactions to criminal acts represent phenomena to be studied, rather than criteria for assigning boundaries to the field of study. Criminologists should be attentive to variations in self-image on the part of different law violators. Similarly, variations in societal reactions to different kinds of criminality form an important substantive topic for investigation. But to identify these as critical items for inquiry is different from including them as definitional criteria, as does Burgess.

Our position on the question of who is or is not a criminal is close to that of Tappan. In one well-known essay on this question, "Who is the Criminal?" Tappan offered some trenchant criticism of those views which would equate the study of criminals with the study of violators

---

[35] Ernest W. Burgess, "Comment" on Frank E. Hartung, "White-Collar Offenses in the Wholesale Meat Industry in Detroit," *American Journal of Sociology*, LVI (July 1950), 32–33; see also Hartung, *op. cit.*, pp. 25–32; "Rejoinder," *loc. cit.*, pp. 33–34; Burgess, "Concluding Comment," *loc. cit.*, p. 34.

of conduct norms.[36] He also attacks the use of the label "white collar crime" to cover those myriad instances of antisocial or "sharp" business practices or other occupational behavior not specifically included within some body of criminal statutes. In another place, Tappan has offered a definition of crime (and, implicitly, of criminals) with which we agree. He says: "What then is the legal definition of crime as it has been employed in practice not only in our courts of law, but in criminology as well? *Crime is an intentional act or omission in violation of criminal law (statutory and case law), committed without defense or justification, and sanctioned by the state as a felony or misdemeanor*" (emphasis in the original).[37] Tappan does not demand that the terms crime or criminal be restricted to acts which have resulted in court conviction or to persons adjudicated as criminals by a court. In an earlier essay, he did quite properly suggest that the legal tag of criminal be restricted to persons so adjudicated, apparently to emphasize that the legal status of criminal is different from that of noncriminal, in that the former carries a number of penalties with it, such as loss of civil rights and restrictions upon movement, which are not imposed on nonadjudicated offenders.[38] Acquisition of the legal status of criminal also results in social stigma being attached to the actor, in addition to the penalties and deprivations authorized in the criminal law. Thus to be a criminal is to acquire a negative public identity of more than slight importance.[39]

There is much merit to the demand that we keep clearly in mind the special legal status occupied by individuals who have been adjudged to be criminals. The term criminal should not be indiscriminately used without distinguishing between those who occupy the legal status as a result of being processed through a court and those who do not, because they have escaped detection or prosecution. At the same time, the demand, sometimes insistently put forward, that criminologists study only those persons who have acquired legal identity as criminals should be rejected. Criminology should concern itself with the study of criminalistic *behavior*, rather than the related but separate matter of judicial processing. Differentials in the correctional process do exist in which some offenders do not become "known" or reported while others are

[36] Paul W. Tappan, "Who is the Criminal?" *American Sociological Review,* XII (February 1947), 96–103.

[37] Paul W. Tappan, *Crime, Justice and Correction* (New York: McGraw-Hill Book Co., Inc., 1960), p. 10.

[38] Tappan, "Who is the Criminal?" 100–103.

[39] One revealing study of the stigmatizing consequences of being convicted of a criminal offense (and even of being acquitted of crime!) can be found in Richard D. Schwartz and Jerome H. Skolnick, "Two Studies of Legal Stigma," in *The Other Side,* ed. Howard S. Becker (New York: Free Press of Glencoe, Inc., 1964), pp. 103–17.

reported to the police, in which some reported offenders are apprehended and others are not, in which some are prosecuted while others are not, or in which some receive penalties not handed out to others. Such differentials depend upon a number of variables, including differences in the kinds of criminal behavior which occur, differences in police policies from one area to another, and social background variations among offenders. This eminently sociological phenomenon of differential outcomes of criminal acts at various stages of the societal reaction process has not received the attention it deserves.[40] However, the point is simply that the criminologist takes, as his primary data, lawbreaking behavior, or, in Sutherland's words, "Behavior which would raise a reasonable expectancy of conviction if tried in a criminal court or substitute agency."[41] Those differential experiences which occur to criminal deviants are important topics for his concern, but he should not restrict his attention to those deviants who reach the adjudication stage in the correctional process.

Korn and McCorkle have advanced a position on the definitional question of the scope of criminology identical to the one in this book. They point out, as did Tappan, the necessity to distinguish *criminals-by-adjudication* from *undetected offenders-in-fact* who have not been processed through the court machinery.[42] They go on to suggest that criminology be concerned with the broader class of offenders. Four categories and a number of subtypes of actual and/or convicted offenders are identified, including persons who have commited offenses but are not known to the police, either because the offense was undiscovered, unreported, or the offender not identified. A second category consists of those who committed actual offenses and have become known, but are unpunished due to the failure of the prosecutor to indict them, the inability of the court to obtain a conviction, or the failure of the conviction to be sustained on appeal. The third class of law violators consists of those persons who have actually engaged in offenses and have been convicted and punished, while the final category involves those who have been convicted and punished for offenses which they did not, in fact, commit.[43]

[40] For an attempt to amalgamate a large body of bits and pieces of data on differential correctional reactions to juvenile and adult offenders, see Paul S. Fong, *Social and Legal Factors in the Differential Societal Reactions to Offenders* (Master's thesis, San Francisco State College, 1964).

[41] Edwin H. Sutherland, "White-Collar Criminality," *American Sociological Review*, V (February 1940), 6.

[42] Korn and McCorkle, *op. cit.*, p. 45.

[43] *Ibid.* These distinctions are specific cases of Becker's four categories of "deviants." See Becker, *Outsiders*, pp. 19–22.

If we adopt a legalistic conception of crime, we must attend to all instances of behavior which fit that definition. This means that we need to examine a number of forms of lawbreaking which are now given scant attention. In particular, Ross has drawn attention to traffic law violations as a case of "folk crime."[44] These offenses are violations of laws introduced to solve problems arising out of the increased complexity and division of labor in modern societies. Traffic law violations, "chiseling" on unemployment compensation, and violation of regulatory statutes governing business and commerce are instances of folk crime. Most of these offenses involve a low degree of social stigma, persons of high social status are involved in them, and they are dealt with in a variety of administrative ways. Traffic violation cases are disposed of through violations bureaus, bail forfeiture, and in other ways outside of courts. As Ross notes, modern societies have given rise to a large number of folk crimes which merit sociological attention. These offenses make up a goodly share of the stuff of modern day criminality, so they cannot be ignored or dismissed as "not really crime."

### Felonies, Misdemeanors, and the Classification of Offenders

A brief statement of the orienting framework of this book was put forward in Chapter One, to the effect that a *role-career* perspective on crime and criminals offers the most promise for progress in the study of crime causation. In other words, a clean break must be made with the tradition that studies criminals and delinquents as though these were homogeneous categories of behavior. Instead, specific theories related to particular types of criminality must be developed.

The complex question of how offenders are to be meaningfully classified into types is addressed at some length in Chapter Ten. However, one aspect of the taxonomic problems of criminological classification should be taken up here. This is the issue of the extent to which the criminologist should base his classificatory efforts upon existing legal categories.

The body of conduct definitions and attendant penalties for their violation contains several systems of classification within it. One of these is the sorting of offenses into felonies and misdemeanors. The former are those crimes thought to be most serious or heinous, and carry maximum penalties of death or imprisonment in a state prison. Misdemeanors, on the other hand, are regarded as relatively petty acts of lesser significance.

[44] H. Laurence Ross, "Traffic Law Violation: A Folk Crime," *Social Problems*, VIII (Winter 1960–1961), 231–41.

They are punishable by county jail terms of less than a year, or fines. Although criminal codes in all of the states distinguish between the two categories of offenses, the specific misdemeanor-felony distinctions are not uniform from one jurisdiction to another. In one state the felony of grand larceny involves theft of goods valued at over $25.00, while in another state grand larceny is defined as any theft involving a loss of more than $50.00. Accordingly, behavior which is a misdemeanor in one area is a felony in another.

As the discussion of specificity as an element of the criminal law indicated, and as is relatively apparent to all adult citizens, the criminal code of any jurisdiction consists of a body of specific prohibitions against various forms of conduct. Thus the body of criminal laws is composed of a set of definitions of acts identified as burglary, arson, murder in the first degree, statutory rape, sodomy, grand larceny, larceny by bailee, and so forth. However, these specific acts, as with felony-misdemeanor distinctions, are subject to jurisdictional variations in definition.

Statistical tabulations on criminal behavior, research studies, and other reports on criminality commonly employ legal felony-misdemeanor distinctions or offense labels for purposes of classifying offenses or offenders. As a consequence, these materials are of reduced significance, certainly insofar as these reports are utilized in generalizations regarding causation of criminality. Legal labels are inadequate as a basis for etiological classification of crimes or criminals, for several reasons. They reveal nothing about such important elements of criminal acts as offender-victim relationships or the social context of the deviant act, which are probably of considerable importance in the understanding of different patterns of criminality. To illustrate, criminologists would probably profit from an approach to the analysis of criminality in which cases of burglary involving "cat burglars" or "hot prowlers" (acts of burglary involving only a single burglar and carried on in a dwelling occupied by the tenants at the time of the burglary) are singled out for attention from the general class of all burglary. Similarly, persons involved in the burglary of unoccupied dwellings and who carry out their deviant acts with confederates in a gang should be studied as another class of offenders.

Legal offense labels are deficient as the basis for classification in another way, too. Criminal actors who are classified at one point in time as "assaultists" do not engage only in that single offense. Thus, if careers in criminality or behavioral types are to be studied by the criminologist, he will have to contrive schemes for classifying lawbreakers in which a variety of different acts are included within the sociological type.

The foregoing discussion implies that legal labels attached to offenders are accurate, but are deficient for other reasons. Actually, one other major problem is that the legal tag attached to an offender at the terminal end of the legal operation, after he has been processed through the office of prosecutor or through a court, is very frequently a label different from the one initially assigned the offender at the stage of apprehension. Also, the latter more commonly comes closer to accurately describing the offender. This discrepancy between behavior and legal label comes about through a process usually termed "pleading guilty for consideration," or, in the argot of offenders and law enforcement workers, "copping out" or "plea copping." That is, the suspect is often offered a "deal" by the prosecutor, taking the form of an agreement to reduce the charge against him in return for a plea of guilty on his part. This is a *quid pro quo* arrangement, profitable to both the prosecutor and the offender. The former is assured a successful outcome to the case in the form of an automatic conviction, and at the same time the workload of the court is relieved because a trial is not required in the instance of a "guilty" plea. The offender receives a lesser sentence than he would if his plea of "not guilty" to the more serious offense is not sustained in court.

For all of these reasons, legal offense labels are eschewed as the basis for etiological classification of crimes and offenders. Instead, the position to be covered in some detail in Chapter Ten is one in which the criminologist takes as his primary data proscribed acts included within the body of criminal laws, and persons who have engaged in these forbidden activities. But the criminologist should be free to contrive his own classifications of offenders or of crimes which cut across existing legal labels, combine several specific legally defined offenses into a single category, sort some offenders charged with a specific offense into a category which includes other persons charged with a related but different offense, or define careers in criminality by assembling particular offenses into *patterns of conduct*. The approach we advocate is similar to the position advanced by Cressey some years ago,[45] and which can be seen in application in some research by Roebuck.[46]

[45] Donald R. Cressey, "Criminological Research and the Definition of Crimes," *American Journal of Sociology,* LVI (May 1951), 546–51; Cressey, *Other People's Money* (New York: Free Press of Glencoe, Inc., 1953).

[46] Julian B. Roebuck and Mervyn L. Cadwallader, "The Negro Armed Robber as a Criminal Type: The Construction and Application of a Typology," *Pacific Sociological Review,* IV (Spring 1961), 21–26; Roebuck, "The Negro Drug Addict as an Offender Type," *Journal of Criminal Law, Criminology and Police Science,* LIII (March 1962), 36–43; Roebuck and Ronald Johnson, "The Negro Drinker and Assaulter as a Criminal Type," *Crime and Delinquency,* VIII (January 1962), 21–33; Roebuck and Johnson, "The Jack-of-all-Trades Offender," *Crime and Delinquency,* VIII (April 1962), 172–81; Roebuck, "The Negro Numbers Man as a Criminal Type: The Construction and Application of a Typology," *Journal of Criminal Law, Criminology and Police Science,* LIV (March 1963), 48–60; Roebuck and Johnson, "The 'Short Con' Man," *Crime and Delinquency,* X (July 1964), 235–48.

## SUMMARY

This chapter has examined a number of facets of criminal law, including the distinguishing characteristics of criminal statutes, the social origins of laws, and the meshing of criminal codes with other social sentiments. The criminal laws define the boundaries of the category of "offenders." This collectivity includes all those who breach the law, and it is with this population that criminology is primarily concerned. However, one segment of this group is made up of criminals, in other words, offenders who have been apprehended and processed through the legal machinery. The next three chapters are devoted to the workings of the legal apparatus as it grinds out criminals. Chapter Three takes up the police; Chapter Four deals with procedures from arrest to trial; while Chapter Five discusses the epidemiological facts resulting from these processes.

# 3

# Becoming a "Criminal"
## The
## Police

## INTRODUCTION

Where do criminals come from? The citizen, the psychiatrist, and the sociologist have usually given roughly similar answers to this question. Depending upon one's theoretical preferences, lawbreakers have been seen as willfully deciding to violate the law, as driven into deviance by urges from deep within the psyche, or as impelled toward criminality by adverse social circumstances.

These views assign police agencies a minor role in crime causation. The police are thought of as reacting *after* crime has broken out but playing no part in the etiology of criminality. Given these presuppositions, it is no wonder that chapters dealing with law enforcement agencies are normally tucked into the back pages of criminology textbooks.

In the view of this text, police organizations deserve much more attention than they have traditionally received, if for no other reason than their omnipresent character in modern life. Formalized police agencies have grown rapidly in size and number from their beginnings in the 1800's. Police agencies were initially restricted to nighttime activity carried on by citizen volunteers, but eventually gave way to organized, full-time police systems. The London metropolitan police force was created in 1829, while the first day and night, "professional" police force in the United States originated in New York City in 1844.

We challenge the notion that the police exercise a minor or insignificant influence upon criminality, and that their role is restricted to responding to law violation. To begin with, individuals may get involved in actions which are forbidden in criminal law as a result of a variety of influences. Some of them become officially designated as criminals, while others remain as covert or hidden deviants. In this discussion of the police and throughout this book, we wish to assert emphatically the possibility that the experience of being apprehended by the police may be an important causal one. Briefly stated, this hypothesis contends that those offenders who fall into the hands of the police may find it unusually difficult to withdraw from criminal careers. Being singled out publicly

47

as a criminal may operate as a career contingency which serves to cut the individual off from nondeviant pathways. Indeed, this may be a more important factor in criminal recidivism than many of the variables to which criminologists have usually attended. If this notion is plausible, study of the police ought to be elevated to major status in criminological inquiry. We shall have much more to say about the etiological effects of social and legal reactions upon law violators in Chapters Nine and Ten.

How do some violators fall into the hands of the police while others remain undetected? Complaints of misbehavior against persons originate from a variety of sources, but it is usually the policeman who effects an arrest of a miscreant. The private citizen's authority to arrest individuals is rarely invoked.

Law enforcement officials are not apprised of a vast amount of offender behavior occurring in modern societies because this activity is not reported to them. Prostitutes and their clients, addicts and drug peddlers, and kindred souls frequently manage to avoid the scrutiny of the police, for their behavior involves no victim who complains to the police. In addition, much of the criminality that is reported to the police fails to result in apprehension of the actors responsible for the lawbreaking, largely due to the obstacles to efficient police work inherent in modern societies. That is, many burglaries, robberies, and so on, go unsolved because the criminals are highly mobile in their operations and skilled in the practice of crime. The police have few tools with which to deal with this kind of criminality. Much of the crime known to the police is handled in informal and discretionary ways, as, for example, when the authorities "wink at" gambling or minor traffic offenses. In other cases, law enforcement agents deal out warnings and admonitions instead of arresting offenders. Finally, some of the individuals known to the police are arrested and started on their way through the legal machinery which tags them as criminals.

We ought to know a good deal about the activities of police agencies, the contingencies which determine whether offenses become known to the police, and the variables which influence the differential handling of cases of which the police are apprised. Yet police agencies have been little studied by social scientists. The reasons for this inattention are several, but a major one has to do with rapport problems which would be involved in efforts to study law enforcement agencies. Policemen are the targets of a good deal of public hostility, and they reciprocate these feelings. A sociologist would get an especially cold reception in many police stations, for he would be suspected of having a major interest in exposing the police to further public condemnation.

For reasons of this sort, a large share of the commentary on police by social scientists has had to do with relations of police agencies to the "host" society, including such factors as public hostility toward them. Investigations of the internal workings of police systems are few in number. However, some important studies have been made in recent years by Banton [1] and by Skolnick.[2] Banton has provided descriptions of the workings of the police in "Carolina City," a community of 200,000 population, "Georgia City," a city of 500,000 population, and "Felsmere City," a town of 60,000 population in Massachusetts. Skolnick's investigation was conducted in Oakland, California.

Much of the commentary on law enforcement organizations has dealt with municipal police systems. A major reason for this concentration is that city policemen are responsible for the largest portion of arrests in the United States. However, it should be noted that American society is characterized by a large number of police agencies of different forms.

One of these is the sheriff system found in nearly every county in the United States. County sheriff departments in metropolitan areas are often quite large, for they are responsible for law enforcement in all of the unincorporated parts of the county. The sheriff system is an anomaly in contemporary America, for the sheriff is an elected official who usually comes to office without any special training in policework. The job of sheriff involves rapid turnover of personnel, in that the incumbent is often defeated when he runs for reelection. In many sheriff's departments, the deputy officers obtain their positions as political favors. For reasons of this nature, sheriff's departments are particularly vulnerable to corrupt practices.

Federal police of several kinds represent another major group of law enforcement personnel in the United States. The most famous federal police agency is, of course, the Federal Bureau of Investigation. However, there are eight national police organizations in all, including the Bureau of Narcotics, the Secret Service, and Post Office inspectors.

Still another collection of law enforcement groups is found at the state level. The best known state policing agency is identified variously as the State Police or the State Highway Patrol. These organizations are normally restricted largely to enforcement of motor vehicle laws. In addition, most states also have state narcotics bureaus, tax enforcement organizations, game wardens, liquor inspectors, and other police groups.

A final form of police organization is represented by private police of various kinds. Such places as suburban shopping centers frequently

[1] Michael Banton, *The Policeman in the Community* (New York: Basic Books, Inc., 1964).

[2] Jerome H. Skolnick, *Justice Without Trial* (New York: John Wiley and Sons, Inc., 1966); David J. Bordua, ed., *The Police: Six Sociological Essays* (New York: John Wiley and Sons, Inc., 1967).

employ police officers who are paid by the merchants, although the agent has certain law enforcement powers. Store detectives and hotel protective personnel constitute another kind of private police agency.

The pages to follow will have more to say about municipal police systems than about these other organizations. The chapter will generally be divided between commentary regarding the relations of police agencies to the "host" society and remarks concerning the internal workings of police departments. In the plan of the chapter, we shall touch upon a number of things not specifically connected with the work of the police in apprehending offenders. That is, the intent of the chapter is to provide a discussion of police structures as social organizations. Throughout this chapter, a major thread of emphasis will have to do with the ways in which structural features of the society in which the police operate tend to determine the central dimensions of law enforcement practice. Our view differs from the laymen's, which often interprets police activity in terms of assumed stupidity or venality on the part of policemen. We agree with Skolnick, who holds that:

> It is rarely recognized that the conduct of police may be related in a fundamental way to the character and goals of the institution itself—the duties police are called upon to perform, associated with the assumptions of the system of legal justice—and that it may not be men who are good or bad, so much as the premises and design of the system in which they find themselves.[3]

This will not be a chapter on "police administration." It will deal with the police as they actually operate, rather than with law enforcement as it is supposed to be conducted. Operating standards and procedures for efficient, "professional" police work have been discussed in great detail by such individuals as the distinguished police administrator, O. W. Wilson.[4]

## THE POLICE AND SOCIETY

### Public Hostility Toward the Police

Policemen have probably been the targets of negative responses from citizens from nearly the beginnings of organized law enforcement. The United States has always been a nation in which the idea of individual liberty and freedom from external interference has been a central

---

[3] Skolnick, op. cit., pp. 4–5.
[4] O. W. Wilson, Police Administration (2nd ed.; New York: McGraw-Hill Book Co., Inc., 1963).

theme. Accordingly, in the eyes of many, the less the police intrude into their affairs, so much the better.

Antagonistic perspectives on the police have been fed by another source as well in American history. Urban law enforcement agencies have frequently been linked with organized criminals and corrupt city officials in the operation of vice of various kinds.[5] In this arrangement, city police have often operated as regulators of prostitution, gambling, and other forbidden activities, and have shared in the division of spoils from these enterprises. Although prostitution and gambling depend for their support upon a public which presses for provision of illicit services, this fact has not prevented a good many citizens from venting their indignation upon the police, particularly on the occasion of recurrent exposés of police corruption reported in urban newspapers.

A third source of citizen dissatisfaction with law enforcement agencies has grown from use by the police of various illegal or questionable enforcement procedures. There is abundant testimony concerning the practice in many police stations of the "third degree," by which officers have physically coerced confessions from suspects. Other instances of gratuitous use of force by policemen can be found in mob control, as well as cases of entrapment and "man-hunting." These incidents have encouraged the spread of public notions that the police department is a haven for incompetents and sadists. Whether or not such images square with the facts, they have contributed to the low esteem in which policemen are held in this society.

The other side of the coin of public hostility concerns the antagonism of police toward the citizenry. American law enforcement agencies have often assumed many characteristics of a "secret society." They have adopted the posture that they are besieged by enemies of all kinds, including most members of the general public. As a consequence, these organizations have closed ranks to prevent disclosure of any information about their internal workings. At the same time, they have gone to great lengths to throw up protection around even the most deviant and lawless officer on the force. The tension between the police and the society which employs them can be seen in the former's response to efforts to create civilian review boards to "police the police." Suggestions of that kind have frequently been violently opposed by the department in question.

---

[5] Journalistic accounts of police corruption can be found in Albert Deutsch, The Trouble with Cops (London: ARCO Publishers, Ltd., 1955); Ralph Lee Smith, The Tarnished Badge (New York: Thomas Y. Crowell Co., 1965).

### Limitations on Police Powers

Law enforcement agents are expected to bring about near total repression of criminality, or at the very least they are charged by citizens
with the responsibility of apprehending all lawbreakers reported to them.
At the same time, they labor under a variety of restraints upon police
practice in the way of rules of arrest, evidence, and so on, which render
this task impossible of accomplishment. For example, an officer who
arrested an individual who had been detained for a misdemeanor by a
citizen would be guilty of illegal arrest, and could be sued by the person
arrested, if the officer did not observe the misdemeanor being committed.
Law enforcement agencies are placed in a situation of great strain in
that they are given a mandate to promote social order at the same time
that they are circumscribed by a variety of restraints upon police practice. Modern societies are a far cry from "police states," in which the
police have such virtually unlimited powers that technical efficiency is
the only limit upon tactics which they can employ. Skolnick has presented a succinct but incisive discussion of the inherent conflict between the goals of social order and rule of law to be observed by
policemen.[6] He has noted that:

> The police in democratic society are required to maintain order and to do
> so under the rule of law. As functionaries charged with maintaining order, they
> are part of the bureaucracy. The ideology of democratic bureaucracy empha-
> sizes initiative rather than disciplined adherence to rules and regulations. By
> contrast, the rule of law emphasizes the rights of individual citizens and con-
> straints upon the initiative of legal officials. This tension between the opera-
> tional consequences of ideas of order, efficiency, and initiative, on the one hand,
> and legality, on the other, constitutes the principle problem of police as a
> democratic legal organization (emphasis in the original).[7]

Skolnick has observed that another ingredient in the conflict between
social order and rule of law derives from the fact that there are varied
conceptions of order in modern society. Some persons would applaud
the police for harassing transients, homosexuals, or some other group,
but other individuals would contend that these matters are not the business of the police.[8]

According to Skolnick, the police bitterly resent the legal restrictions
imposed upon them. They see themselves as craftsmen, skilled in the

6 Skolnick, op. cit., pp. 1–22.
7 Ibid., p. 6.
8 Ibid., pp. 10–12.

work of crime detection and law enforcement. They view the world in probabilistic terms, and contend that when their observations lead them to suspect someone of wrongdoing, they are nearly always correct in their suspicions. From this perspective, procedural rules are often regarded as obstacles which prevent the officer from doing his job to the extent of his capabilities.[9]

The case for restraints upon the police to prevent infringement of civil rights has been stated many times. One well-known expression of this preference was made by Justice Oliver Wendell Holmes, Jr. in 1928, when he declared: "We have to choose, and for my part, I think it is less evil that some criminals should escape than that the government should play an ignoble part."

The citizen in American society enjoys freedom from improper police actions through the guarantees of the Bill of Rights, specifically the first eight Amendments. These are designed to protect the citizen from illegal searches, from being compelled to testify against himself, and so on. However, over the history of the United States, the Supreme Court has been reluctant to extend the provisions of the Bill of Rights beyond instances of federal cases. For decades, the police in various states have not felt themselves to be under any obligation to desist from searches without warrants or the use of other indefensible tactics.

Police work in city police departments has included the third degree, that is, the use of force to coerce confessions from suspects. Policemen have engaged in searches without warrants, suspects have been interrogated for unduly long periods of time, and a variety of other expedient techniques, such as the use of informants, have been employed in order to make arrests. Thus, historically, the police have promoted social order by circumventing or ignoring the procedural rules which are supposed to control their activities.[10]

Over the past two decades, the police have come under greater pressure to conform to the rule of law. The Supreme Court, in a series of decisions extending over this period, has moved to sharpen the conflict over social order versus rule of law. The nature of the changes wrought by the Supreme Court has been summarized by Packer:

[9] *Ibid.*, pp. 182–203.

[10] One discussion of the ways in which policemen employ informants in detective work, and of the reciprocity between the police and the informants, can be found in *ibid.*, pp. 122–38. The use of informants is *not* an illegal police procedure. Moreover, most policemen argue that informants are vital to successful law enforcement. See Skolnick's discussion, *ibid.*, pp. 139–63, for a report on narcotics enforcement patterns and the use of informants. He notes that unlike routine narcotics work or "good pinches," "big cases" provide policemen with the conditions under which constitutional standards of legality can best be met. For example, officers do not labor under the same time pressures in "big cases" as they do in others.

The choice, basically, is between what I have termed the Crime Control and the Due Process models. The Crime Control model sees the efficient, expeditious and reliable screening and disposition of persons suspected of crime as the central value to be served by the criminal process. The Due Process model sees that function as limited by and subordinate to the maintenance of the dignity and autonomy of the individual. The Crime Control model is administrative and managerial; the Due Process model is adversary and judicial. The Crime Control model may be analogized to an assembly line, the Due Process model to an obstacle course.

What we have at work today is a situation in which the criminal process as it actually operates in the large majority of cases probably approximates fairly closely the dictates of the Crime Control model. The real-world criminal process tends to be far more administrative and managerial than it does adversary and judicial. Yet, the officially prescribed norms for the criminal process, as laid down primarily by the Supreme Court, are rapidly providing a view that looks more and more like the Due Process model. The development, with which everyone here is intimately familiar, has been in the direction of "judicializing" each stage of the criminal process, of enhancing the capacity of the accused to challenge the operation of the process, and of equalizing the capacity of all persons to avail themselves of the opportunity for challenge so created.[11]

The older "hands off" policy of the Supreme Court, as concerned with the abridgment of constitutional guarantees by local police, is illustrated in the *Wolf* decision handed down in 1949. In that case, the court exempted the states from the exclusionary rule which disallowed use of evidence obtained through illegal search or seizure. The court voiced reluctance to intrude in that instance into a situation of long standing, in which state courts had been accepting evidence obtained illegally.

One of the first signs of court movement toward what Packer calls the Due Process model came in the 1947 case of *Adamson*. In that appeal, the court debated the question of whether the states must be bound by the provisions of the Fifth Amendment concerning the right of the accused to remain silent and to refuse to testify against himself. Although four of the justices took the affirmative view in this case, the five-man majority ruled that the states would violate due process only by action that "shocks the conscience." Somewhat later, in the case of *Mallory* heard in 1952, the court ruled that a person under arrest in a federal case must be taken "without unnecessary delay" before a federal commissioner to be apprised of his rights to silence and legal counsel. Then in 1961, in the *Mapp* decision, the court ruled that the states must enforce the Fourth Amendment guarantee against unreasonable search and

11 Herbert L. Packer, "The Courts, The Police, and the Rest of Us," *Journal of Criminal Law, Criminology and Police Science,* LVII (September 1966), 239; see this entire issue for a series of papers presenting discrepant views of the correctness and significance of these decisions.

seizure. The exclusionary rule was thus extended to the states, compelling the police to have valid search warrants before seizing evidence.

The *Gideon* decision of 1963 represents another landmark in the rise of the Due Process model, for in that case the court extended the Sixth Amendment guarantee of legal counsel to all serious crimes. This decision has meant that an indigent accused will be said to have been deprived of a fair trial unless he has been provided with adequate legal assistance.

The most controversial actions of the Supreme Court have occurred in the past few years, beginning with the *Escobedo* decision in 1964. In that case, the court voided a murder confession because the accused, Danny Escobedo, had been prevented from seeing his lawyer, who was present in the police station house. Since the *Escobedo* decision, a series of other cases, including *Miranda*, have been decided which have had the effect of making it mandatory that the police inform any person whom they detain or take into custody of his right to remain silent. As illustrative of the consequences which these decisions have had upon police practice, the San Francisco Police Department now equips all officers with warning and waiver cards. These cards inform suspects that: "1. You have the right to remain silent. 2. Anything you say can and will be used against you in a court of law. 3. You have the right to talk to a lawyer and have him present with you while you are being questioned. 4. If you cannot afford to hire a lawyer one will be appointed to represent you before any questioning, if you wish one." This same card contains two questions which ask the suspect if he wishes to waive his right to silence, and it provides space for the accused to sign this waiver of rights.

These decisions have been surrounded by a great deal of heated controversy and acrimonious comment. Those who support these court actions argue that all the decisions do is extend protections to accused individuals which have been standard in England for a long time. Moreover, these persons contend that the recent rulings will have the salutary effect of correcting laziness among policemen. These rulings will make it difficult for them to depend solely upon confessions in order to obtain convictions, and will force them to work harder at building a strong framework of evidence obtained through diligent detective work to support accusations against suspects. Those who take a different view of these matters contend that these rulings against interrogation will further tie the hands of the police, who have already been rendered relatively impotent by court rulings at the very time that crime is increasing dramatically.

Many angry words have been exchanged in this controversy, but little real evidence has been assembled. Data concerning the effects of these rulings on police practice are needed. However, Souris has reported one instance which appears to indicate that the post-*Escobedo* period has not been one of law enforcement breakdown.[12] He observed that the Detroit police reported that in 1961 confessions were obtained in 60.8 per cent of the criminal cases in that city, and were deemed essential to conviction in 13.1 per cent of the cases. In 1965, the Detroit police claimed that confessions were obtained in 58 per cent of the offenses, and were critical in leading to conviction in 11 per cent of those cases.

Whatever the end result of Supreme Court decisions, the police will continue to face the dilemma of contradictory expectations. They will be held responsible for the repression of crime at the same time that they are expected to behave with scrupulous attention to individual rights. The solution to this problem will come only when it is recognized that both of these goals cannot be realized. If we are to have police agencies which respect individual rights, we shall have to become reconciled to the situation in which a good many persons escape the law enforcement machinery.

### The Police and Discretionary Action [13]

Although police chiefs can often be found publicly asserting that their departments enforce all laws equally, the fact is that police everywhere go about selective enforcement of criminal laws. This discretionary and selective enforcement is of two kinds. In one case, certain statutes are not attended to at all. In many localities, archaic laws which were designed for earlier social conditions remain in force but are ignored by the police. Some laws go unenforced by the police even though the conditions these statutes attempt to regulate do exist in the community. Rules against various forms of gambling represent a case in point, for in many areas the police have evolved tolerance policies which allow such statutes to be violated with impunity. The second general form of discretionary activity by the police centers about the differential application of laws to different individuals. That is, the police often apprehend some, but not all, of the persons whom they observe violating some statute.

The usual defense for discretionary actions revolves about the claim that total enforcement would almost immediately bring the judicial

---

[12] Theodore Souris, "Stop and Frisk or Arrest and Search—the Use and Misuse of Euphemisms," *Journal of Criminal Law, Criminology and Police Science*, LVII (September 1966), 251–64.

[13] A detailed discussion of arrest procedures used by police, along with reports on police discretionary behavior, drawn from a study of police in Kansas, Michigan, and Wisconsin, can be found in Wayne LaFave, *Arrest, The Decision to Take a Suspect Into Custody* (Boston: Little, Brown and Co., 1965).

machinery to a halt, jails and prisons would overflow, and chaos would result. The argument has also been advanced that judicious enforcement of laws is needed to keep petty offenders out of the legal machinery at the same time that intractable or difficult lawbreakers receive intensive attention and handling. According to this view, the interests of society are best served by selective law enforcement rather than by legal intervention applied indiscriminately. However, the problem with this perspective comes when efforts are made to implement basic policies of police discretion. The danger is that what begins as selective enforcement might degenerate into discriminatory law enforcement.

What principles guide the police in their exercise of discretionary powers? According to Banton, the police are attuned to notions of popular morality. They endeavor to take official action in cases where even the people who suffer from this intervention will be compelled to concede that the police are morally right in their activity. In short, Banton maintains that policemen are much like other citizens in certain ways, and are sensitive to many widely held cultural values.[14]

Goldstein has provided one of the most incisive discussions of the problems inherent in use of discretion by the police.[15] He maintains that selective enforcement represents low-visibility interaction between individual officers and various citizens. The exercise of discretion is not guided by clear policy directives, nor is it subject to administrative scrutiny. For reasons of this sort, selective enforcement can easily deteriorate into police abuse and discriminatory conduct. In Goldstein's view, the decisions as to which laws should be enforced should be scrutinized by an impartial civilian body. In that way, discretionary conduct would become more visible and might result in selective law enforcement which would then become a subject for open public dialogue.

Several pieces of information are at hand regarding the exercise of discretion by the police, although most of these have to do with juvenile rather than adult offenders. One report concerned a census of cases of known delinquency in Washington, D.C.[16] That study showed that only a fraction of the delinquency cases known to the police and other public agencies resulted in juvenile court referral. Also, the percentages of juveniles referred to the court varied from one offense to another. Most known

---

[14] Banton, op. cit., pp. 127–55.

[15] Joseph Goldstein, "Police Discretion Not to Invoke the Criminal Process: Low Visibility Decisions in the Administration of Criminal Justice," Yale Law Journal, LXIX (March 1960), 543–94.

[16] Edward E. Schwartz, "A Community Experiment in the Measurement of Juvenile Delinquency," National Probation Association Yearbook, 1945 (New York: National Probation Association, 1945), pp. 157–81.

thieves ended up in the court, while almost none of the truancy cases were handled in that way.

Another investigation of this kind was conducted by Goldman in Allegheny County, Pennsylvania.[17] That study, carried on in 1950, was located in a small mill town, an industrial center, a trade center, and an upper class residential area. The data indicated that 64 per cent of the juveniles apprehended by the police were released without court referral. The police took 91 per cent of the auto thieves they encountered to court, while they reported only 11 per cent of the mischief cases. A major differential in the reporting practices of the police was that 65 per cent of the Negro offenders were taken to court, in marked contrast to the 34 per cent of the white juveniles so handled.[18]

This matter of differentials in handling racial groups is fairly complex in character. Goldman indicated that the referral rate was about the same for white and Negro youths involved in serious offenses. But Negroes apprehended for minor delinquencies were much more likely to be taken to juvenile court than were their white counterparts. Much the same observation was made by Axelrad concerning Negro and white training school wards.[19] The Negro boys were younger and less delinquent, and had been placed on probation fewer times than the white youths. Axelrad maintained that these actions are taken against the Negro boys because of their inadequate social backgrounds, rather than as a result of prejudicial attitudes on the part of the police and court officials.

Some of Goldman's other findings included the observation that males and females were reported to the court in about the same proportions, while referrals increased with the age of offenders.[20] Somewhat surprisingly, the upper class residential area had the highest arrest rate of the four communities. But the communities with the lowest arrest rates, "Trade City" and "Steel City," had the highest proportion of arrests for serious offenses. The sorts of complaints leading to juvenile arrests in the upper class area and the mill town were generally ignored by citizens and police in "Trade City" and "Steel City." In short, the police in the latter communities apparently found themselves engaged in more serious business than responding to juvenile peccadilloes.[21]

Goldman gathered some interview material from Allegheny County

[17] Nathan Goldman, *The Differential Selection of Juvenile Offenders for Court Appearance* (New York: National Council on Crime and Delinquency, 1963).

[18] *Ibid.*, pp. 35–47.

[19] Sidney Axelrad, "Negro and White Male Institutionalized Delinquents," *American Journal of Sociology,* LVII (May 1952), 569–74.

[20] Goldman, *op. cit.,* pp. 44–47.

[21] *Ibid.*, pp. 48–92.

police regarding the factors influencing their decisions about juvenile offenders. The officers showed a good deal of variability in the criteria employed, but several variables seemed to loom large in their actions. The police were influenced by the seriousness of the offenses. They were also affected by their views of the juvenile court, those who thought the court had deleterious effects upon youths referred few of them. The officers also gave a good deal of emphasis to the demeanor of the juveniles, so that those who were surly or defiant were more likely to be referred than were those youngsters who were polite or contrite.[22]

A recent inquiry by Piliavin and Briar is congruent with that of Goldman.[23] These investigators studied the behavior of policemen in a large California city and reported that discretion was widely used in police dealings with juveniles. Most of those youngsters apprehended by the officers for serious forms of lawbreaking were subsequently referred to the juvenile court. However, the less serious cases were differentially reported, with some youngsters turned loose with admonitions to behave themselves, while others were taken to court. These discretionary judgments were arrived at in terms of a few, readily observable cues. Officers made such decisions in terms of the general demeanor of the youngsters. Those who seemed to be members of gangs, who were Negroes, who dressed like "cats," or who were flippant in manner were the ones who ended up at the juvenile hall.[24]

All of the studies above have to do with discretionary activities concerning juvenile offenders. One could assemble a large amount of impressionistic evidence suggesting that the police commonly engage in selective law enforcement with adults as well. One piece of evidence on this point comes from Skolnick's study.[25] He indicated that the Oakland officers make discretionary decisions in their traffic warrant enforcement operation. Some offenders who have traffic fines outstanding are arrested for nonpayment, and other individuals are allowed to remain at liberty while they arrange to pay these fines. Proportionately more Negroes than whites are arrested instead of being dealt with more leniently, but not because of racial factors per se. According to Skolnick, the police are about as biased in their attitudes toward Negroes as citizens generally, customarily referring to Negroes in uncomplimentary terms and showing other signs of prejudicial attitudes. However, the reason they arrest more Negroes is because these persons are more likely to be

[22] Ibid., pp. 93–124.

[23] Irving Piliavin and Scott Briar, "Police Encounters with Juveniles," American Journal of Sociology, LXX (September 1964), 206–14.

[24] Another study reporting much the same thing is George W. Mitchell, Youth Bureau: A Sociological Study (Master's thesis, Wayne State University, 1958).

[25] Skolnick, op. cit., pp. 71–90.

unemployed, so that they have difficulty in satisfactorily settling their affairs with the warrant bureau. Skolnick maintains that the police manage to keep their anti-Negro sentiments from intruding upon their work in warrant bureau operations, even though these prejudices do enter into other aspects of police relations with minority group members.

The evidence above suggests some of the major dimensions involved in selective law enforcement. However, it must be clear that more investigation of this activity is in order, particularly with regard to discretionary actions concerning adult offenders. One aspect of this matter which needs more study is the process by which officers learn how to practice discretion in law enforcement. The police are not generally empowered to enforce laws selectively, so this feature of law enforcement is not usually articulated in the formal socialization of recruits in police academies. Instead, norms governing discretion are probably acquired through informal socialization in a squad car, in which an older, more experienced officer relates "the facts of life" to the rookie patrolman.

### New Tasks for the Police

It is likely that many citizens think of the police in stereotyped images which portray their main business as the pursuit of violent and dangerous criminals. Actually, the police officer's job resembles many other occupations in that much of the work is tedious, routine, and unglamorous. Much of the routine character of police work in American society stems from the delegation of a great many responsibilities as peace officers, in addition to tasks of crime detection and repression. That is, American police are held responsible for the maintenance of orderly social life. They spend much of their time patrolling Skid Road to make certain that the vagrants remain out of the vision of other citizens. They give over time to regulating the flow of traffic throughout the city, supervising the movements of pedestrians, and taking care of a host of other regulatory functions which have come to them by default. In many cities, the police have been put in charge of all licensing functions. They are usually the persons appealed to when a citizen perceives that someone he associates with has begun to act "crazy," thus the police routinely process referrals to psychiatric wards of county hospitals. There are myriad other chores of this kind which the police handle, most of them relatively distinct from crime repression or prevention.

Documentation of the extent of peace officer activities of the police can be found in a study by Cumming, Cumming, and Edell.[26] They recorded

[26] Elaine Cumming, Ian Cumming, and Laura Edell, "Policeman as Philosopher, Guide and Friend," *Social Problems*, XII (Winter 1965), 276–86.

the nature of police calls coming into the complaint desk of an American city. Over half of these calls dealt with appeals for assistance or support regarding personal or interpersonal problems, rather than matters of crime. These data suggest that although policemen may not always be admired by citizens, they are the first persons who come to mind when members of the general public are casting about for someone to rescue them from the complexities of urban life.

Some further insight into the peace keeping roles of American police-men comes from a study of law enforcement practices on Skid Road.[27] Bittner reports that patrolmen assigned to this section of the city see themselves not as "law officers," but rather as mainly concerned with keeping order. They receive few explicit directives from their superiors as to how they are to keep the peace. Thus, as craftsmen, they contrive their own techniques and procedures.

Skid Road officers seek to accumulate a rich supply of information on area residents and such community operations as flophouses and missions. As they go about their peace keeping, they are relatively unconcerned with strict notions of culpability and evidential standards. Instead, they tend to ignore fine distinctions between "offenders" and "victims," and act toward Skid Road denizens as though all were lawbreakers. More-over, policemen make arrests as a way of solving immediate problems of order. They handle many cases informally, even though they could arrest persons for illegal acts. In short, decisions to use force or to refrain from coercion, to arrest or not to arrest, and other choices, are made with an eye toward maintenance of order. Their behavior is less a response to lawbreaking than it is to the aim of peace keeping.

Bittner has also provided some data concerning order keeping en-deavors of policemen concerned with the mentally ill.[28] Urban law enforcement persons are routinely involved in large numbers of cases where complaints have been made that someone is mentally ill. The officer in these cases must act the role of quasi-psychiatrist. He must decide whether or not to make an emergency apprehension of a person to be held for psychiatric examination. Bittner suggests that emergency apprehensions are most common in instances of attempted suicide, ex-treme agitation, or serious disorientation on the part of the person. On the other hand, informal dispositions of complaints occur most often when the officer is able to find someone who will take charge of the dis-turbed individual.

The principal problem of this trend which would make the police

[27] Egon Bittner, "The Police in Skid-Row: A Study of Peace Keeping," unpublished.

[28] Egon Bittner, "Police Discretion in Emergency Apprehension of Mentally Ill Persons," *Social Problems*, XIV (Winter 1967), 278–92.

serve as a "jack-of-all-trades" organization is that budgets have often failed to increase at the same rate as additions to responsibilities. As a result, the police in various municipalities frequently engage in chronic appeals to the city government for more funds and personnel. The addition of peace maintenance tasks to the traditional responsibilities of the police further complicates their law enforcement activities. Critics who would have them make large numbers of arrests often fail to take into account both the procedural restrictions and the manpower limitations under which the police function.

### Social Structure and Police Efficiency

The contention that the Federal Bureau of Investigation is a highly efficient, "professional" police force from which offenders rarely escape would usually go unchallenged, as would the contrasting claim that city police forces are marked by inefficiency, laxness, and poor performance.[29] Nevertheless, there are those who aver that much of this adulatory picture of the F.B.I. is a carefully constructed myth.[30] But let us assume that the municipal police do solve fewer crimes than do the federal police, even though the disparity in performance may not be as great as sometimes thought. Such an assumption is probably a correct one. How are we to account for this difference? One possible explanation is that the F.B.I. recruits intelligent agents while the city police attract dullards and incompetents. Doubtless there are those who favor such an explanation. However, a more likely hypothesis is that the kinds of criminality with which these agencies deal, and the circumstances surrounding them, play a major determining role in police practice. In short, the municipal police may be faced with offenders who are less "catchable" than those whom the federal authorities encounter.

Consider the following case as an example of the effects of social circumstances and patterns of criminality upon law enforcement.[31] Some years ago, the city newspapers in Vancouver, B.C., Canada, became greatly alarmed about a "crime wave" of robberies of grocery stores, particularly because several of the proprietors had been shot by the criminals when they interfered with the offenders. The newspapers alleged that police were doing less than they might have done to repress these robberies. A check upon robberies known to the police in Seattle, a city of size nearly equal to Vancouver's, revealed that there were many more of these offenses occurring in Vancouver. However, a tabulation of

29 This view is seen in Don Whitehead, The FBI Story (New York: Random House, Inc., 1965).
30 Fred J. Cook, The FBI Nobody Knows (New York: The Macmillan Co., 1964).
31 The facts in this case were gathered by the author.

the number of small grocery stores (through the telephone directories of these two communities) also revealed that there were approximately twice as many such places in Vancouver as in Seattle. In part, then, the crime wave was simply a function of greater opportunities for robbery in Vancouver. These small stores constituted attractive "marks" or victims, for most of them were manned by a single individual, were without alarm systems, and were widely scattered throughout the city. These stores could be speedily robbed and the offenders melt into the night before the police could be summoned. The difficulties the police might encounter in trying to anticipate the scene of future robberies so as to lie in wait for the culprits involved can easily be imagined. A postscript to this incident is that the robbers were eventually captured, but in connection with another crime. While in custody awaiting trial for that offense, they confessed to the grocery store robberies. The solution to the robberies came about more by luck than by dint of detective work!

Some of the structural conditions influencing police practice have been discussed by Stinchcombe.[32] He has pointed out that "private places" can be distinguished from "public" ones. The police do not have access to the former without warrants, while they can freely enter public settings. Some crimes normally occur in private places while others usually take place in public ones, and they vary along other dimensions as well, so that some involve violence while others are free from violence. Following these distinctions, Stinchcombe has identified a number of different patterns of criminality, along with their law enforcement consequences. Coercion in private life is one of these, involving wife-beating and similar actions which occur in private places. These cases are usually reported to the police but infrequently result in convictions. The complainants tend to be reluctant to testify against the accused persons. Wives who have been beaten do not wish to have their spouses prosecuted, for fear this will bring about a permanent rupture in their marriage.

Another form of criminality centers about illegitimate businesses and "dangerous" organizations. Prostitution, gambling, and traffic in drugs are cases in point. Some of these activities occur in public places while others take place in private situations. In either event, these offenses are victimless because they have to do with illicit commodities which are widely desired. The participants are motivated to keep their conduct secret from the police, so there is no one to act as a complainant. As a result, the police are put in a position where they must "drum up their

---

[32] Arthur L. Stinchcombe, "Institutions of Privacy in the Determination of Police Administrative Practice," *American Journal of Sociology*, LXIX (September 1963), 150–60.

own business" by means of undercover agents, informants, and other techniques which they do not employ in other kinds of criminality.

Still another general form of lawbreaking has to do with invasion of private places by criminals, of which burglary would be an example. This kind of crime is usually reported to the police, but it infrequently results in apprehension of the responsible parties. These offenses are carried on with stealth, few clues are provided for the police, and the culprits are highly mobile and exceedingly difficult to intercept. Finally, disorders and nuisances in public places constitute a form of criminality which is easily observed and successfully processed by the police and courts.

If we now return to the original question about the performance of federal and municipal police, the analysis above would suggest that the large number of crimes unsolved by the city police stems from the fact that many of these are offenses difficult to observe or solve. The federal law enforcement business more commonly involves such criminal actions as tax evasion, in which incriminating evidence against offenders is easily gathered through perusal of tax records or kindred enforcement techniques.

## SOCIAL ORGANIZATION OF THE POLICE

In the past several decades, sociological inquiry has concentrated heavily upon the study of complex social organizations. Industrial settings, welfare agencies, educational institutions, correctional facilities, and a number of other kinds of organizational structures have been extensively studied. However, police departments represent important organizations which, for the most part, have escaped the attention of sociologists. In the past few years, this gap in the data has begun to be corrected through the accumulation of some studies of police forces as organizations. Let us examine some of this material in the remainder of this chapter.

### The Social Role of Policemen

The notion that a man's occupation determines many of the features of his personality and social life is familiar to sociologists. They often assert that the varied conditions under which men earn a living in complex societies heavily influence their general perspectives on life and their modes of social participation. On this point, Skolnick has sketched some features of the policeman's "working personality." [33] According to Skolnick, the elements of danger and authority, which are central to police work, lead law enforcement persons to develop certain common personality characteristics. One of these is suspiciousness, another is conservatism. Policemen come to be especially attentive to unusual situations, for the unpredictable is also likely to be dangerous. The police are cast as defenders of the status quo, so they come to prefer stability and lack of rapid social change. The dangerous aspects of their work, and the fact that policemen are engaged in compelling others to obey laws, many of which are unpopular with citizens, give rise to police solidarity and social isolation from nonpolicemen. Skolnick presents evidence to show that the police he studied were involved in more off-the-job interaction with each other than most other occupational groups.

The thrust of these observations by Skolnick, and of the parallel report on American police by Banton,[34] is that there is indeed a "cop mentality," as claimed by laymen. The difference between the views of Skolnick or Banton and the views of laymen is that the former suggest that it is the nature of the job which produces the personality elements, while the latter imply that certain personalities seek out police work. It should be clear enough that the first view is favored in this book.

### Police Bureaucracies

Metropolitan police organizations are structured along the lines of complex bureaucracies or formal organizations. There are a variety of specific organizational tables or patterns which describe the way the police divide up their tasks, but in every case a formalized and highly complex division of labor characterizes these systems.[35] Most police departments are placed under administrative surveillance of a police commission which is supposed to "police the police," but the control exercised through this device is often minimal. In most cases, the real power and leadership of the department emanates from the office of the Chief of Police.

Police bureaucracies usually involve a group of deputy chiefs immediately under the control of the chief. These administrative persons are responsible for the major divisions of the departmental organization, supervising the patrol, crime prevention, juvenile services, traffic management, detective services, and other major tasks of the police force. These

---

[33] Skolnick, op. cit., pp. 42–70.
[34] Banton, op. cit., pp. 110–26.
[35] See Wilson, op. cit., for a detailed discussion of police organizational patterns.

officials are housed in a Hall of Justice or other headquarters facility located in the city center, and are held responsible for the city-wide supervision of the police force. Also located downtown are those police workers who perform such staff functions as planning and research, the detectives whose work takes them throughout the city, crime prevention personnel, and clerical workers. These headquarters personnel are arranged into a vertical hierarchy of ranks, so that some are captains, others lieutenants, sergeants, or patrolmen.

City departments are further segmented through the precinct pattern of operation. Most large municipalities are divided into police districts or precincts, with district police stations out of which the patrolmen operate. These police stations are organized in hierarchical fashion, headed by a captain assisted by lieutenants and sergeants.

One of the features of police activity about which little is known at present concerns occupational mobility within departments. City police organizations are usually included within a civil service system; entry into the department is by means of standardized recruiting procedures, testing, and other regularized practices. Advancement from the rank of patrolman upward is governed by civil service regulations, with standard examinations used for selection of sergeants and more advanced ranks. This aspect of occupational mobility in police departments is the familiar one of bureaucratic progression through stages of the occupational system.

Those factors which operate as determinants of job assignments within the department are much less evident. Nearly all officers start with the department as patrolmen, but some move into police jobs coveted by nearly all, such as detective assignments. These jobs often put the incumbents in line for advancement into the administrative hierarchy. Other police officers remain in precinct patrol work and never rise beyond the rank of sergeant in the system. Finally, some officers receive distasteful assignments, such as "fixed post" jobs directing traffic at downtown street intersections. The assignments received by officers are not governed by civil service procedures. Individual policemen account for assignment practices through a variety of informal processes which they sum up by such expressions as "clout" and "juice." These terms refer to interpersonal influence which results in desirable assignments for certain officers. There are several forms of "clout," so that in different departments ethnic background, kinship ties to high officials, a record of having made a number of dramatic "big pinches," or other variables contribute to "juice."

There is little question that informal factors are implicated in mobility patterns in police departments, just as it is apparent that these considerations are often found in other bureaucratic organizations. The formal organization in which all events are governed by explicit rules does not exist, except in the abstract formulations of sociologists. However, the nature of these unwritten norms and influences in police mobility needs further study, for little investigation of this topic has been conducted.

Another general observation about police bureaucracies has to do with ecological peculiarities in these organizations. Many formal organizations are located in a single place, such as a college, a prison, or a factory. Control of individuals is made easier by virtue of the visual surveillance which can be maintained over them. But the police organization is scattered about the community in headquarters and precinct stations. It is further scattered due to the fact that the largest single group of police employees are the patrolmen, most of whom are in patrol cars and not at the station house at all. These conditions make it difficult for police officials to conduct systematic evaluations of job performance of the workers, save through such devices as recording the number of arrests made by officers. The ecological structure of police work also creates difficulties in the way of control over deviant workers. Many of the deviant acts in which policemen sometimes engage, such as drinking on the job, are extremely difficult for administrators to observe. The spatial peculiarities of police systems probably go some way toward explaining the persistence of corrupt practices in the face of reform efforts occurring on the occasion of police scandals.[36]

### Police Violence

We have already noted that one of the chronic complaints lodged against policemen in American cities has dealt with gratuitous use of force. The observation has repeatedly been made that the police have engaged in the use of force to extract confessions from suspects. Additionally, innumerable cases have come to light in which the police have assaulted suspects or physically abused other citizens. In recent years, criticism of the police over illegal use of violence has been most apparent in the area of civil rights demonstrations and racial disturbances. While some of these recent charges may have been exaggerated, there can be little doubt that law enforcement officers have often utilized force in their dealings with citizens in which the violence clearly exceeded the demands of the situation.

Westley has made the most detailed study of the use of violence by

[36] One discussion of police control systems can be found in David J. Bordua and Albert J. Reiss, Jr., "Command, Control, and Charisma: Reflections on Police Bureaucracy," American Journal of Sociology, LXXII (July 1966), 68–76.

police officers.[37] He argues that the police lean to the view that any technique which will help them make arrests are acceptable, so that force is justified on expedient grounds. In particular, police values uphold the use of force if it contributes to the making of "good pinches," that is, arrests in well-publicized and serious criminal cases. Along the same line, many policemen regard violence as particularly useful in handling such cases as sex offenses, where prosecutions are difficult to obtain. They argue that application of a beating to a sex offender operates as a deterrent to future episodes of such conduct on his part.

Westley asked a number of officers in a city department to indicate those circumstances in which they deemed violent techniques appropriate. The largest number of responses centered about the use of force to obtain respect from hostile or defiant persons. Over one-third of the officers said that they regarded force as appropriate in these cases.

In recent years, police departments have come under increasing criticism for the use of violence, particularly as directed at minority groups. No doubt this criticism, along with the growing "professionalization" of law enforcement, will serve eventually to reduce the use of undue force. Still, progress in this area may be relatively slow and undramatic. In 1967, one of the task forces of the President's Commission on Law Enforcement and Administration of Justice reported that its studies indicated that brutality, intimidation, and dishonesty remain as common features in many American police departments. As a consequence, police relations with minority groups are at explosive levels in a number of cities, including Washington, Baltimore, Detroit, Newark, St. Louis, New Orleans, Atlanta, Memphis, Chicago, Cleveland, Philadelphia, and Cincinnati.[38]

### Racial Attitudes in Police Departments

Let us take up the matter of racial attitudes in police departments in a bit more detail. The most revealing study on this subject is Kephart's investigation into the Philadelphia police force.[39] Among other things, he found in interviews with patrolmen in that department that 91 per cent of them overestimated the number of Negroes on the police force.[40] He presents a good deal of evidence showing that Negro officers in that organization were discriminated against, for they received the least

[37] William A. Westley, "Violence and the Police," *American Journal of Sociology,* LIX (July 1953), 34–41.

[38] The President's Commission on Law Enforcement and Administration of Justice, *Task Force Report: The Police* (Washington, D.C.: U.S. Government Printing Office, 1967), pp. 144–207.

[39] William M. Kephart, *Racial Factors and Urban Law Enforcement* (Philadelphia: University of Pennsylvania Press, 1957).

[40] *Ibid.,* p. 93.

desirable assignments.[41] The commanding officers of the department contended that no conflict existed between Negro and white officers and
that, generally, race played no part in the operations of that department.[42]
At the same time, nearly 60 per cent of the patrolmen interviewed by
Kephart maintained that they would object to a patrol car assignment in
which their partner was a Negro officer.[43] It seems apparent that the
commanding officers chose not to believe or acknowledge unpleasant
facts about the department.

The patrolmen in this study also exhibited a common set of attitudes
toward Negro citizens. Three-fourths of the officers overestimated the
proportion of the arrests in their areas in which Negroes were involved.[44]
Over one-half of the officers claimed that they had found it necessary to
be more strict with Negro offenders than with white lawbreakers.[45]
Finally, the majority of the police felt that Negro offenders were generally
more difficult to deal with than white criminals.[46]

It is probably true that Negro citizens, particularly in slum areas, are
somewhat more hostile toward policemen than are white groups. The
hardening of racial sentiments in both whites and Negroes in the United
States in the past decade has probably heightened the antagonistic views
toward the police held by minority group members. The other side of
the coin is that anti-Negro sentiments in the police may have become
intensified too, as the police have been subjected to more and more
troublesome experiences in slum areas.[47]

Several devices have been created in various parts of the United States
as techniques for reducing the friction between minority groups and the
police. One of these, the police review board, involves citizens and police
officials who jointly consider complaints of improper behavior by the
police. Another effort to control racial antagonisms is community relations bureaus within the police department, which have the responsibility
of dealing with minority groups and of improving police-community
relations. Finally, race relations materials have been injected into the
curriculum of police academies in an effort to create objective attitudes
on the part of law enforcement workers.

[41] *Ibid.,* pp. 26–56.
[42] *Ibid.,* pp. 57–74.
[43] *Ibid.,* p. 78.
[44] *Ibid.,* pp. 88–89.
[45] *Ibid.,* p. 81.
[46] *Ibid.,* p. 64.
[47] One recent report of law enforcement agencies and racial problems is Paul Jacobs, "The
Los Angeles Police," *Atlantic,* CCXVIII (December 1966), 95–101.

## SUMMARY

This chapter has considered a number of facets of police behavior in the United States, with particular emphasis upon the variables which result in persons being apprehended or individuals escaping from police attention. In this discussion, our interest has centered upon the ways in which offenders are started on their way to becoming criminals by police action. But this is only half of the story. We also need to examine the workings of the legal machinery as it takes persons who have been arrested and turns out various products from this human material. This is the topic of Chapter Four, where we shall consider the various things that happen to different individuals who have been apprehended by the police.

# 4

# Becoming a "Criminal" From Arrest to Trial

## INTRODUCTION

The purpose of this chapter is to trace out the sorts of things which can happen to a person who has been identified as an accused or a suspect. In Chapter Three, we saw that the police dispose informally of a great many cases which they learn about, exercising discretion in moving persons into the official legal machinery. What happens to those individuals whom the police start on their way through this processing? What events ensue when citizens take complaints to a district attorney? These are the matters with which this chapter is concerned. We shall begin with a brief examination of the major elements of state and federal legal systems. This discussion will be followed by a more detailed look at the workings of various parts of these systems.

## ELEMENTS OF THE LEGAL SYSTEM

### State Systems

The chief legal officer in state criminal systems is the county prosecuting attorney (district attorney). This elected official, along with his deputy prosecutors in larger counties, is responsible for representing "the state" in criminal actions against accused individuals. The prosecutor's adversaries, whose task is to represent and defend the accused, consist of criminal attorneys hired by the accused, lawyers provided the indigent by a legal aid society, or legal counsel supplied through a public defender's office. Another set of functionaries in the legal system consists of the personnel who maintain the county jail or lockup in which persons awaiting trial are held. Certain private citizens are systematically involved in the handling of persons caught up in this machinery. The chief group of these is the bail bondsmen who arrange bail for accused individuals.

The state courts, which constitute the central component of the legal operation, are diverse in character throughout the United States.[1] Nonetheless, a general pattern of court structure can be discerned indicating two basic forms of courts, trial courts and appellate courts. Trial courts are, in turn, divided into several levels.

One group of trial courts consists of inferior courts, which are variously termed justice of the peace courts or municipal courts. In urban areas, these courts are presided over by elected officials who are full-time, qualified judges with legal training. These magistrates hold court in municipal courts and other court-like surroundings. In rural areas, on the other hand, the municipal courts are more likely to be controlled by relatively unqualified magistrates and conducted in out-of-the-ordinary circumstances. The business of inferior courts centers about the processing of minor civil cases, adjudication of such minor criminal cases as misdemeanor charges, and preliminary hearings regarding serious criminal cases.

The higher trial courts in the various states are usually organized on a county basis. These courts deal with serious felony cases and are variously called circuit courts, superior courts, county courts, or district courts. In some states, these courts have general jurisdiction, hearing criminal, civil, matrimonial, and probate matters all in the same court. In other states, the courts are fragmented so that each handles only one of these matters.[2]

Appellate courts on the state level are usually called supreme courts. The main business of these courts is hearing appeals, in which they review the proceedings of trial courts in order to determine whether errors have occurred in the trial of an individual which would require reversal of judgment or a new trial. Appellate courts also have the responsibility of scrutinizing the constitutionality of new legislation.

### The Federal System [3]

The legal officers and courts of the federal government have jurisdiction over those offenders who commit ordinary crimes on federal reservations or against federal instrumentalities. Thus, although there is no federal law prohibiting murder, homicides occurring on military posts or

[1] Delmar Karlen, The Citizen in Court (New York: Holt, Rinehart and Winston, Inc., 1964), pp. 3–7.

[2] The backgrounds and activities of judges in the United States have received relatively little research attention. For two studies of the sort which are needed, see Shirley D. McCune and Daniel L. Skoler, "Juvenile Court Judges in the United States, Part I: A National Profile," Crime and Delinquency, XI (April 1965), 121–31; Regis H. Walther and Shirley D. McCune, "Juvenile Court Judges in the United States, Part II: Working Styles and Characteristics," Crime and Delinquency, XI (October 1965), 384–93.

[3] Karlen, op. cit., pp. 14–23.

similar places fall within federal court jurisdiction. However, the largest group of lawbreakers with whom the federal machinery is concerned consists of persons who violate federal laws.

Although the federal criminal code runs to almost 2500 sections, federal concern with criminality is considerably narrower than that of the individual states. The federal criminal code grows out of the legislative powers accorded Congress.[4] Congress is empowered to regulate interstate and foreign commerce, establish post offices, declare war and maintain order, and organize armed forces. Congress also has jurisdiction over counterfeiting and piracy, naturalization procedures, and rules on bankruptcy, patents, and copyrights. Finally, Congress is authorized to make all laws "necessary and proper" to executing its powers. Federal criminal law centers about these matters; for example, the Mann Act deals with interstate traffic in prostitution, while the Dyer Act is directed at transportation of stolen vehicles across state lines.

The federal court system consists of three kinds of courts: district courts, courts of appeals, and the Supreme Court. The 91 district courts are trial courts which have control over federal offenses in all or part of a single state. The 11 appellate courts receive appeals from district courts and from federal administrative agencies. Lastly, the Supreme Court takes up questions of constitutionality.

One should not suppose that state and federal courts have an equal share of the criminal workload. While there are about 400 federal judges, there are eight times that number of state magistrates in New York State alone. Even when justices of the peace are excluded from this comparison, New York judges are still twice as numerous as their federal counterparts.[5]


## PROCESSING THE SUSPECT THROUGH THE LEGAL MACHINERY [6]

Let us examine the flow of business through the state courts, for this pattern is closely paralleled in federal courts. The criminal processing machinery is usually set into motion by the arrest of an individual by the police, who take him into custody. However, in some cases a preliminary investigation by the district attorney or the grand jury leads to a formal accusation against an individual, followed by issuance of a warrant for

[4] *Ibid.*, pp. 7–8.
[5] *Ibid.*, pp. 23–35.
[6] *Ibid.*, pp. 38–57; see also The President's Commission on Law Enforcement and Administration of Justice, *Task Force Report: The Courts* (Washington, D.C.: U.S. Government Printing Office, 1967).

his arrest. Embezzlement is one of the offenses in which preliminary investigation is commonly carried on prior to arrest. A third means of entry into this system is through citizen complaints to the prosecuting attorney. Common cases of this type are bad checks and other improper business conduct, nonsupport and other domestic quarrels, borderline offenses against the person, such as negligent homicide, and obscene literature and other borderline offenses against morality. Many of the cases in this latter group are dealt with informally by the prosecutor, and are not moved further along. For example, district attorneys often endeavor to settle bad check complaints without prosecution by sending letters to the offender which direct him to settle his financial affairs with the complaining citizen. If the check forger complies, the case is then terminated by the district attorney.[7]

After an individual has been apprehended by the police, he is supposed to be taken almost immediately before a magistrate of an inferior court. In the instance of petty misdemeanor offenses, a formal accusation called a *complaint* is made against the person by a police officer or private citizen. These petty cases are normally dealt with quite swiftly, usually through a plea of guilty entered by the accused individual. In felony charges, appearance before a magistrate is for the purpose of setting bail and arranging for a *preliminary hearing*. This hearing, also before a magistrate, is an inquiry designed to determine whether there is "probable cause," that is, enough evidence against an individual to warrant holding him for prosecution. Normally, only the prosecutor presents evidence at a preliminary hearing, and then only the minimum necessary to establish "probable cause." If the preliminary hearing results in the judgment that "probable cause" has been demonstrated, a formal accusation is made against the accused. In about half of the states, a *grand jury* made up of citizens chosen by judges hears testimony in secret and draws up a formal accusation called an *indictment*, while in other states the prosecutor formulates the accusation, called an *information*, without going through grand jury hearings. The general trend in the United States in recent decades has been to by-pass the grand jury. In California, as one example, less than 10 per cent of the felony cases proceed through the grand jury.[8]

At the point where a preliminary hearing has resulted in the holding of an accused individual for prosecution, a critical juncture has been reached by the suspect in his travel through the machinery. This is the

[7] Frank W. Miller and Frank J. Remington, "Procedures Before Trial," *Annals of the American Academy of Political and Social Science*, CCCXXXIX (January 1962), 111–24.

[8] Herbert A. Bloch and Gilbert Geis, *Man, Crime, and Society* (New York: Random House, Inc., 1962), pp. 481–82.

point at which he may be offered a "deal" by the prosecutor, so that if
he agrees to plead guilty, he will be allowed to plead to a reduced
charge. In the offender's terminology, he is given an opportunity to "cop
out" to a "knocked-down" charge. If the accused agrees to this arrangement, an indictment will be drawn up alleging that he committed a
different and less serious offense than the one for which he was originally
apprehended. We shall return to this bargaining process later in this
chapter.

The next step in the criminal process in felony cases is *arraignment*,
which takes place in the court empowered to try the case. At arraignment,
the accused is read the indictment or information and asked how he
pleads to the charge. If he pleads guilty, which occurs in three-fourths or
more of the cases, he will then be sentenced by the judge. If he contends
that he is not guilty, he will be held for trial before a judge or a *petit jury*
(trial jury). The usual outcome of a trial is that the accused is found
guilty, eventually receiving a sentence from the judge. The end product
ground out by this machinery is a legal entity, "the criminal," who becomes, among other things, a statistic in crime reports. He also becomes
a target for correctional activities which attempt to change him from a
"bad guy" into a "good guy."

The criminal justice system goes into operation at the point that crimes
occur, for these are the events which set the police to work. From that
point onward, a large number of subsequent actions and dispositions are
made of criminal cases. Figure 1 shows a general view of the parts of
the legal machinery in terms of the flow of cases through that apparatus.

Figure 1 outlines the elements of the criminal justice system and of the
juvenile system as well. On the whole, the juvenile justice structure follows the form of the criminal system, but has tended toward informality
and less concern for "due process" than the criminal courts. However,
recent thinking has moved in the direction of modifications in juvenile
justice designed to restore "due process" to accused juveniles. Thus, in
some places, attorneys have been provided to charged juveniles, more
attention has been paid to due process for youths, and court proceedings
have become more legalistic.

## SOME PROBLEMS OF CRIMINAL COURTS

Recent reports of The President's Commission on Law Enforcement and
Administration of Justice make it abundantly clear that many American
courts fall far short of ideal in operation.[9] Lower or inferior courts in

[9] The President's Commission on Law Enforcement and Administration of Justice, op. cit., passim.

# FIGURE 1

## A General View of the Criminal Justice System

This chart seeks to present a simple yet comprehensive view of the movement of cases through the criminal justice system. Procedures in individual jurisdictions may vary from the pattern shown here. The differing weights of line indicate the relative volumes of cases disposed of at various points in the system, but this is only suggestive since no nationwide data of this sort exists.

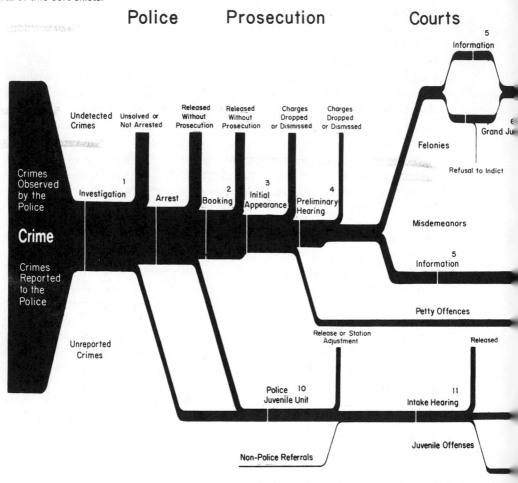

1  May continue until trial.

2  Administrative record of arrest. First step at which temporary release on bail may be available.

3  Before magistrate, commissioner, or justice of peace. Formal notice of charge, advice of rights. Bail set. Summary trials for petty offenses usually conducted here without further processing.

4  Preliminary testing of evidence against defendant. Charge may be reduced. No separate preliminary hearing for misdemeanors in some systems.

5  Charge filed by prosecutor on basis of information submitted by police or citizens. Alternative to grand jury indictment; often used in felonies, almost always in misdemeanors.

6  Reviews whether Government evidence sufficient to justify trial. Some States have no grand jury system; others seldom use it.

78

This chart is taken from pp. 8–9 of The President's Commission on Law Enforcement and Administration of Justice, *The Challenge of Crime in a Free Society* (Washington: U.S. Government Printing Office, 1967).

# Corrections

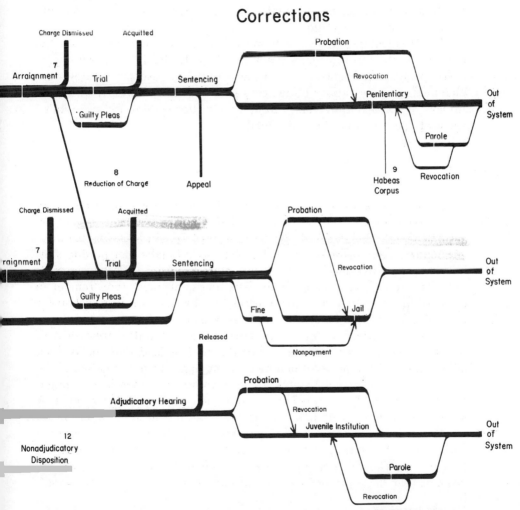

7 Appearance for plea; defendant elects trial by judge or jury (if available); counsel for indigent usually appointed here in felonies. Often not at all in other cases.

8 Charge may be reduced at any time prior to trial in return for plea of guilty or for other reasons.

9 Challenge on constitutional grounds to legality of detention. May be sought at any point in process.

10 Police often hold informal hearings, dismiss or adjust many cases without further processing.

11 Probation officer decides desirability of further court action.

12 Welfare agency, social services, counselling, medical care, etc., for cases where adjudicatory handling not needed.

particular turn out to be inferior in a number of ways.[10] According to the commission, many of the lower courts are nearly swamped with impressively large workloads. They are staffed by ill-trained personnel. Little or no screening or investigation of cases occurs. Assembly line justice is dispensed to the misdemeanants who appear there. In the case of justice of the peace courts, the commission indicated that in three states the justice still receives payment only when he convicts and collects his fee from the defendant, a practice the U.S. Supreme Court ruled unconstitutional 40 years ago! [11]

The President's Commission found other reasons to quarrel with the current situation in the courts. Lack of adequate defense counsel for accused persons, deficiencies in bail and pretrial release procedures were identified, as were various bottlenecks jamming up the orderly and careful flow of accused individuals through the justice system. Let us examine some of these matters in more detail.

## BAIL

As we have already observed, one of the concerns in preliminary hearings has to do with the setting of bail. Bail is a sum of money, determined by the judge, which the accused must post in order to guarantee his appearance in court at a later date. The individual either produces his own money as bail or obtains it from a bail bondsman. If the person is not allowed bail, or cannot obtain bail funds, he must then remain in jail until his trial. In a good many cases he may languish in a lockup for a number of months before his trial takes place.

The bail practices of American courts have received a great deal of negative commentary.[12] Among other things, it is said that the bail set at preliminary hearings is often unreasonably high. An investigation of the accused person's financial status, social stability, or other factors might lead to a low bail figure being set, but such inquiry is rarely held. A second complaint about bail practices is that the ultimate decision on whether an accused awaits trial in jail rather than in the community rests with a private citizen, the bail bondsman, rather than with a court functionary. Finally, bail practices are vulnerable to criticism on the grounds that those persons held in jail unnecessarily suffer severe handi-

[10] *Ibid.*, pp. 29–36.
[11] *Ibid.*, p. 34.
[12] Charles Ares and Herbert Sturz, "Bail and the Indigent Accused," *Crime and Delinquency*, VIII (January 1962), 12–20.

caps as a result. They do not have easy access to lawyers, their entrance into the court in the company of a guard may bias their case with a jury, and, in the event of acquittal, they have undergone incarceration without being guilty of a crime.

Two studies of the operation of the bail process have been reported by Foote.[13] These investigations took place in Philadelphia in 1953 and New York City in 1957. The major findings from these projects indicated that many defendants were unable to furnish bail even when the amount set was nominal. In the Philadelphia experience, almost one-half of the accused individuals could not post bail and were detained from 50 to 100 days before trial.[14] Furthermore, as the amount of bail increased beyond $1000, decidedly fewer persons managed to secure pretrial release. Foote notes that bail was usually set at such a high figure in serious felony cases that most defendants could not obtain bail. While some 10 to 20 per cent of those defendants confined in jail before trial were not convicted, on the whole, jailed defendants were more likely to be convicted and also received more severe sentences than counterparts who had been free on bail. Finally, these studies indicated that bail was often used for purposes other than to insure court appearance by the defendant. For example, persons who had been accused of attacks upon policemen either were not offered bail or had an excessive bail figure set in their cases.

One response to these criticisms of bail procedures has taken the form of efforts to have defendants released on their "own recognizance," that is, without posting bail. One of these projects is the Manhattan Bail Project, started in 1961 in New York City.[15] A group of New York University law students interviewed indigent defendants and in many cases were able to secure their release on parole pending trial. The unnecessary character of bail in many cases is apparent in the finding that only three of the 275 persons paroled on the basis of information provided by the bail project failed to appear in court.[16]

A parallel project to that in New York was conducted in a U.S. district court in Michigan, where about 72 per cent of the defendants were released on their "own recognizance." No difference was observed in ab-

[13] Caleb Foote, "The Bail System and Equal Justice," *Federal Probation*, XXIII (September 1959), 43–48.

[14] Caleb Foote, "Compelling Appearance in Court: Administration of Bail in Philadelphia," *University of Pennsylvania Law Review*, CII (June 1954), 1031–79.

[15] Ares and Sturz, *op. cit.*; see also Frederic Suffet, "Bail Setting: A Study of Courtroom Interaction," *Crime and Delinquency*, XII (October 1966), 318–31.

[16] Herbert Sturz, "An Alternative to the Bail System," *Federal Probation*, XXVI (December 1962), 49–53.

sconding by bonded and nonbonded persons. In all, only 12 of 12,400 defendants failed to appear in court.[17] A number of other projects of this kind, designed to obtain pretrial release for indigent accused persons, have been conducted in widely separated parts of the nation in recent years.[18]

## "PLEA COPPING": PLEADING GUILTY FOR CONSIDERATIONS

Many citizens probably carry around a view of the legal machinery based on movie and television portrayals. This picture characterizes the legal process as usually culminating in a jury trial of the accused person, who has pleaded not guilty. In point of fact, most criminal cases end with guilty pleas by offenders, so trials are the exception rather than the rule. Skolnick reports that 86 per cent of the cases in federal courts between 1960 and 1963 were settled by guilty pleas, while such pleas were only slightly less frequent in state courts.[19]

Newman has conducted a detailed study of guilty pleas in felony cases in a Wisconsin county in which he found that over 90 per cent of the offenders had been sentenced on a guilty plea, although about a third of them had originally entered pleas of not guilty.[20] In nearly every case, the offense to which an offender pleads guilty is lesser than or different from the original charge (or charges).

The incentive to the prosecutor for accepting a guilty plea is readily apparent, for this arrangement allows the state to avoid a costly and lengthy court trial. But what does the accused receive in exchange for a guilty plea? Newman indicated that there were four kinds of bargains offered the offender. Some had reduced charges placed against them, while about half of the offenders received a "deal" in the form of a reduction in sentence for pleading guilty. A third group got concurrent sentences rather than separate ones for each offense committed. Finally, some suspects had some charges dropped in exchange for a guilty plea.

[17] Talbot Smith, "A New Approach to the Bail Practice," Federal Probation, XXIX (March 1965), 3–6.

[18] A summary of these can be found in Dorothy C. Tompkins, Bail in the United States, A Bibliography (Berkeley, Cal.: Institute of Governmental Studies, 1964).

[19] Jerome H. Skolnick, Justice Without Trial (New York: John Wiley & Sons, Inc., 1966), pp. 12–15; see also The President's Commission on Law Enforcement and Administration of Justice, op. cit., p. 9. The commission report indicates that negotiated pleas of guilty were responsible for convictions in between 66 and 96 per cent of the cases in a sample of different state jurisdictions for which information was available.

[20] Donald J. Newman, "Pleading Guilty for Considerations: A Study of Bargain Justice," Journal of Criminal Law, Criminology and Police Science, XLVI (March–April 1956), 780–90.

Some further detail on guilty pleas and allied matters is reported in a study by Sudnow.[21] This investigation was carried on in a public defender's office in a metropolitan community in California. The public defender is an employee of the county whose job it is to defend indigent accused persons in criminal trials. The public defender system has grown as a replacement for legal aid societies and as a device to insure that low-income persons will not be deprived of legal counsel.

Sudnow's discussion includes the distinction between "necessarily-included-lesser-offenses" and "situationally-included-lesser-offenses." Assault is an example of the first category. It must occur prior to battery in that assault refers to menacing gestures, such as verbal threats, while battery consists of carrying out the threats. Similarly, second-degree homicide is necessarily included in first-degree murder because the latter involves premeditation, along with all of the other ingredients of second-degree homicide. Situationally included offenses are those crimes which usually occur in company with another violation of law, even though the one is not incorporated in the other in the criminal statutes. Drunkenness as an accompaniment of vehicular homicides would illustrate this category.

At first glance, it might be supposed that most reduced charges against offenders would involve necessarily included or situationally included lesser offenses. But this is not the case, at least in the situation observed by Sudnow. Instead, both the prosecutor and the public defender act out their roles with a shared conception of "normal crimes." For example, both of them perceive that most rapes grow out of flirtations between persons who have been drinking and have engaged in sexual byplay. These generalizations about the way offenses usually occur constitute a classification of "normal crimes."

When the prosecutor and public defender are bargaining about a "normal crime," they cast about for a reduced charge which will meet the ends of justice and provide an incentive to the accused to plead guilty. Quite often the offense they eventually settle upon is neither situationally or necessarily included in the crime with which the person was originally charged. Sudnow notes that both the prosecutor and the public defender strive to obtain a guilty plea wherever possible so as to avoid a trial. But each party is concerned that the defendant "receive his due" in the way of a penalty. The reduced charge must be of such a nature that the offender will plead guilty to it, but it must also lead to a sentence which the person "deserves."

[21] David Sudnow, "Normal Crimes: Sociological Features of the Penal Code in a Public Defender Office," *Social Problems*, XII (Winter 1965), 255–76.

The day-to-day operations of the public defender system and the prosecutor's office depart markedly from the image of the combative struggle between the state and the counsel for the accused. Sudnow observed that the public defender views his interests as close to those of the prosecutor—to move offenders in an orderly fashion through the legal machinery. The public defender assumes at the outset that the persons he serves are guilty. His interviews with his clients are designed to determine whether the person's offense is a "normal" one so that a bargain can be reached with the prosecutor. In most "normal" cases, the accused individuals are persuaded by the public defender to plead guilty. It is important to note, however, that guilty pleas are not solicited or accepted by the prosecutor from those lawbreakers who have engaged in crimes which are atypical and not "normal."

## TRIAL BY JURY

### *The Structure of Jury Trials* [22]

The right to jury trial is Constitutionally guaranteed in all states in cases of serious crimes, and in some states for minor crimes. Although a jury trial can be waived in favor of trial before a judge, relatively few defendants exercise this option.

The trial jury (or *petit jury*) of 12 citizens is drawn from a larger panel or group of potential jurors previously selected for jury duty by a jury commissioner or court clerk. In principle, jury duty is an obligation of all citizens who meet some minimal qualifications, such as citizenship and literacy. Conversely, Negroes or other groups of persons are not supposed to be excluded from jury duty, for juries are intended to be representative of the larger community. A specific jury is assembled out of a panel of potential jurors through a selection process in which both the prosecutor and defense attorney participate. Both are allowed to "challenge for cause" prospective jurors thought to be unfit for jury duty. Potential jurors are challenged on such grounds as being related to the defendant or having already formed an opinion of the guilt or innocence of the accused. These persons are excused from jury duty by the presiding judge, as are those potential jurors who have been the target of *peremptory challenges.* Both the prosecutor and defense attorney have a limited number of these challenges, for which no reason has to be stated.

[22] Karlen, op. cit., pp. 48–54.

The completion of jury selection is followed by the opening statement by the prosecutor, in which he outlines the evidence he expects to introduce against the accused, and usually by opening remarks of the defense as well. Following these, the prosecutor presents the state's evidence, while the defense attorney cross-examines witnesses. When the prosecution has completed its case, the accused may make a motion for acquittal on the grounds of insufficient evidence. If the judge deems the evidence sufficient to proceed, the defense then has its opportunity to present evidence to undermine the state's case. After the case for the accused has been presented, the defense may move for a directed verdict of acquittal by the judge.

If the judge does not direct a verdict of acquittal, the trial moves to final arguments to the jury by both sides. The judge gives his instructions to the jury and the jury retires behind closed doors for secret deliberations. If the jury brings in a verdict of not guilty, the case is closed forever. But if the accused is found guilty, his attorney may move for a new trial, arguing that the trial proceedings erred at some point. If this motion is not granted, the defendant is sentenced and becomes the legal entity, a criminal.

### Research on Jury Behavior

The research literature on the workings of various segments of the law enforcement and correctional machinery has recently been enriched by the jury study conducted by the University of Chicago Law School.[23] The volume which resulted from this investigation is a goldmine of information concerning the behavior of criminal trial juries in the United States. Kalven and Zeisel note that the jury system has been surrounded by controversy almost from its inception. On the negative side, critics have argued that the process of jury selection works to load juries with ignorant persons incapable of making sound judgments. The spokesmen for the jury system have been equally emphatic in asserting that juries act as a check upon judges who might otherwise apply the law in a heavy-handed fashion. However, most of this debate has consisted of opinion rather than hard facts.[24] The Kalven and Zeisel research has gone some distance toward illuminating this quarrel with empirical findings.

How frequent are jury trials? Kalven and Zeisel estimate that there were about 60,000 trials carried through to a verdict in the United States

[23] Harry Kalven, Jr., and Hans Zeisel, *The American Jury* (Boston: Little, Brown and Co., 1966).
[24] *Ibid.*, pp. 3–11.

in 1955, with an additional group of 20,000 jury trials begun but not carried to a jury verdict. While these figures indicate that jury trials are numerous, they are nonetheless relatively uncommon occurrences. As noted earlier in this chapter, guilty pleas represent the most usual ending of charges against an individual. Similarly, Kalven and Zeisel note that 75 per cent of the cases of major crimes in the United States terminate with guilty pleas, while 10 per cent result in bench trials (trial before a judge) and 15 per cent eventuate in jury trials. A second observation is that jury trials are largely an American device, for it appears that over 80 per cent of the criminal jury trials in the world take place in this country. However, jury trials do not occur at the same rate in all of the 50 states. In states such as Connecticut, where jury trials are allowed only in cases of major crimes, the number of jury trials is quite small, while in jurisdictions where jury trials are available in a wide variety of offenses they occur much more commonly.[25]

The evidence which Kalven and Zeisel assembled on jury behavior came from questionnaires completed by a sample of 555 judges from throughout the United States. These judges provided information on 3576 trials over which they had presided.[26] The investigators asked a large number of questions concerning the judges' evaluations of the outcomes of these trials. For the most part, these queries had to do with whether the judge was in accord with the decision of the jury; if not, the reasons for his disagreement were sought.

One major finding of this research centered about the convergence of jury decisions with the views of judges. The pattern of jury-judge verdicts can be seen in Table 2. The statistics in that table, along with other findings of this research, strongly indicate that juries do usually render sound and reasonable verdicts.

### TABLE 2[27]
### Verdict of Jury and Judge

|  |  | JURY VERDICT RENDERED | | |
|---|---|---|---|---|
|  |  | ACQUITS | CONVICTS | HANGS |
| Judge's Decision | Acquits | 13.4% | 2.2% | 1.1% |
|  | Convicts | 16.9% | 62.0% | 4.4% |

[25] Ibid., pp. 12–32.
[26] Ibid., pp. 33–44.
[27] Ibid., p. 56.

As can be seen in Table 2, the judges contended that they would have rendered the same decision as the jury in over 75 per cent of the cases. It is also readily apparent that the instances of disagreement are heavily in one direction, with juries acting in a more lenient fashion than judges. There were few instances where judges would have acquitted persons convicted by juries.

Judges may dispute the decisions of juries in ways additional to the matter of guilt or innocence. Kalven and Zeisel note that the judges in the study sometimes disagreed with the juries on the charge for which a person was convicted or the penalty handed down. These instances of disagreement, when added to discordant views on guilt or innocence, brought the proportion of disagreements between judge and juries to 33.8 per cent.[28]

What are the issues over which judges and juries disagree? Kalven and Zeisel discovered a large number of specific reasons for disagreements which can be grouped into five major categories: disagreements centered about sentiments on the law, sentiments on the defendant, issues of evidence, facts only the judge knew, and disparity of counsel. Disagreements revolving about the law had to do with instances of the sort where juries took into account contributory negligence on the part of the victim, even though the law makes no such allowance. Rape cases illustrate this point nicely, in that the rape victim has often behaved in a manner which provoked the offender into sexual aggressiveness. Similarly, sentiments about defendants concerned characteristics of these persons which influenced judge or jury opinions. Disparity of counsel refers to cases in which the superiority of either the prosecutor or defense attorney contributed to a trial outcome. Kalven and Zeisel indicate that issues of evidence are at the heart of about half the judge-jury disagreements, while 29 per cent of them were based on sentiments on the law. Sentiments about defendants, facts known only to the judge, and disparity of counsel entered into only a few of the disagreements.[29]

The phenomenon of judge-jury disagreement on evidential grounds is complicated. According to Kalven and Zeisel, judges and juries disagree infrequently when evidence alone is at issue; rather, they disagree when evidential questions occur accompanied by sentiments. They aver that: "The sentiment gives direction to the resolution of the evidentiary doubt; the evidentiary doubt provides a favorable condition for a response to the sentiment." [30]

[28] *Ibid.*, pp. 59–62.
[29] *Ibid.*, pp. 104–17.
[30] *Ibid.*, p. 165.

Throughout the detailed report of findings by Kalven and Zeisel, juries come off remarkably well. When disagreements arise on questions of evidence, the views of juries are reasonable. On the whole, judges rarely characterized juries as gullible.[31] Juries are occasionally willing to entertain greater "reasonable doubt" about cases than are judges, but the magistrates do not view the juries as having excessively loose standards.[32]

Juries bring to bear a variety of sentiments about the legal codes as they go about their decision-making. In some instances, they incorporate into their decisions considerations about self-defense which are not found in the statutes. Thus they sometimes acquit individuals who have harmed persons who had earlier acted violently toward them, even though the offender's actions were retaliatory rather than in self-defense.[33] Juries also condition their evaluation of evidence when they perceive contributory negligence on the part of the victims, even though the law makes no such allowance.[34] Juries sometimes acquit individuals when the evidence demonstrates their guilt because the jury regarded the offense as too trivial to be punished.[35] One such case would be that of indecent exposure before an adult female, where the jury finds it difficult to perceive real social harm in the misbehavior. Other kinds of jury sentiments which intrude into decision-making include the matter of unpopular laws, such as game laws, where juries are loath to convict offenders. Juries also occasionally bring in verdicts that do not accord with the evidence when they think that the defendant has already received an adequate measure of punishment of some sort, or regard the threatened punishment as out of keeping with the act.[36]

A final matter regarding the Kalven and Zeisel research is the "cross-over phenomenon." This is their term for those infrequent instances in which judges would have acquitted persons whom juries had convicted. These cases appeared to involve such factors as the unattractiveness of the accused person, to which the jury attended but the judge ignored. Cross-overs were sometimes attributable to the jury placing less faith in the credibility of the accused person's testimony than did the judge.[37]

These paragraphs do not exhaust the material in this jury research volume. The reader is advised to study this rich source of data on his own. The Kalven and Zeisel study is truly an important one in advancing our comprehension of the social workings of the legal apparatus.

[31] *Ibid.*, pp. 168–81.
[32] *Ibid.*, pp. 182–90.
[33] *Ibid.*, pp. 221–41.
[34] *Ibid.*, pp. 242–57.
[35] *Ibid.*, pp. 258–85.
[36] *Ibid.*, pp. 286–312.
[37] *Ibid.*, pp. 375–94.

## SUMMARY

This chapter concludes our overview of the workings of the parts of the law enforcement machinery through which individuals come to be tagged as criminals. In the next chapter, we turn to the epidemiological facts generated by this enforcement structure, as well as to some data concerning those persons who commit offenses but manage to stay undetected by the police.

# 5

# Epidemiology

## INTRODUCTION

The opening remarks in Chapter One indicated that the study of criminality must address itself to epidemiological questions at an early point. We want to identify the number of offenders in society, the various forms their offenses take, their social characteristics, and other features of law-breaking and lawbreakers. Chapter Five is concerned with matters of this sort.

It ought to be acknowledged at the outset that epidemiological ventures are inevitably frustrating and unsatisfactory. For one thing, the agencies which process known violators have often been more interested in distorting the epidemiological facts than in reporting them accurately. However, the basic problem which confronts those who would amass statistical facts on criminality is that most lawbreakers take pains to keep their violations secret. Estimates of the extent of illegal behavior must be made from data on those offenses known to the authorities. This is but a small and perhaps biased sample of total crime, and it is exceedingly difficult to gauge the relationship between the two.[1]

This chapter is centered exclusively on epidemiological observations, but material concerning the facts of crime distribution will also be taken up in a number of the chapters which follow. In particular, Chapters Twelve, Thirteen, and Sixteen will examine some statistics on forms of lawbreaking which are rarely reported to the police, such as gambling and "white collar crime."

---

[1] Other general summaries of crime rates and allied matters can be found in Edwin H. Sutherland and Donald R. Cressey, *Principles of Criminology* (7th ed.; Philadelphia: J. B. Lippincott Co., 1966), pp. 27–52; Cressey, "Crime," in *Contemporary Social Problems,* ed. Robert K. Merton and Robert A. Nisbet (2nd ed.; New York: Harcourt, Brace and World, Inc., 1966), pp. 141–60; The President's Commission on Law Enforcement and Administration of Justice, *The Challenge of Crime in a Free Society* (Washington, D.C.: U.S. Government Printing Office, 1967), pp. 17–53.

## SOURCES AND PROBLEMS OF CRIMINOLOGICAL DATA

### Sources of Information

Criminological investigators have on a few occasions endeavored to discover the extent of criminality in American society through self-reports of citizens. In these studies, which we will utilize later in this chapter, the researchers have asked citizens to acknowledge the illegal acts they have performed. However, the more common index used to estimate the magnitude of crime in society has been constructed from statistics concerning crimes reported to the police, persons arrested, and other reports of this sort.

Official figures and reports are of several kinds. National statistics on juvenile delinquents are gathered by the Children's Bureau of the U.S. Department of Health, Education and Welfare. Since 1955, this bureau has collected data on juveniles reported to juvenile courts from a national sample of such courts. Figures regarding the number of individuals incarcerated in prisons each year are compiled by the Federal Bureau of Prisons within the U.S. Department of Justice. These data are reported in the publication, *National Prisoner Statistics*. Additionally, the National Office of Vital Statistics collects information on homicides through the records of coroners in the United States, reporting these in *Vital Statistics in the United States*. A number of state agencies gather and publish data on criminality which are used by criminologists. The state of California has the best developed social bookkeeping system of this kind, and material from publications of statistical agencies in that state will be used throughout this book.

The most widely-used data on American criminality is that gathered by the Federal Bureau of Investigation and reported annually in *Uniform Crime Reports for the United States*. The Federal Bureau of Investigation compiles statistics on· "crimes known to the police" for seven major offenses which, taken together, comprise the bureau's Crime Index. Reports from about 8000 towns and cities in the United States are collated to provide Crime Index information. In 1965, the *Uniform Crime Reports* data on index crimes included information about nearly 92 per cent of the total population. In addition to figures on index crimes known to the police, the F.B.I. also gathers and publishes information regarding arrests for nonindex crime.[2]

[2] A history and critique of the *Uniform Crime Reports* can be found in Marvin E. Wolfgang, "Uniform Crime Reports: A Critical Appraisal," *University of Pennsylvania Law Review*, CXI (April 1963), 708–38.

## Problems of Official Data

Crime statistics are among the most unreliable and questionable social facts, as has been pointed out by a number of authorities. For example, Sutherland and Cressey have indicated that crimes known to the police constitute only a fraction of all offenses. Moreover, the ratio of illegal acts known to the authorities to criminal acts committed varies from offense to offense. Variations in legal codes from one jurisdiction to another reduce the possibility of meaningful statistical comparisons between areas and communities. Sutherland and Cressey also note that police agencies have not always behaved honestly with respect to statistical reporting. They cite the case of Chicago, in which robberies reported by the police increased from 1263 in 1928 to 14,544 in 1931, while burglaries jumped from 879 to 18,689 within the same period. Clearly, these changes were due more to alterations in reporting practices than anything else.[3]

Some more recent evidence on police tampering with statistics can be found in the report of the President's Commission on Law Enforcement and Administration of Justice. An instance in Philadelphia in 1953 is discussed there, in which the police reported 28,560 index crimes, negligent manslaughter offenses, and cases of larceny under 50 dollars. This figure represented an increase of 70 per cent over that for 1951, but the sudden jump was due to modifications in reporting procedures rather than an increase in crime. An even more dramatic case of reporting problems had to do with Chicago, which from 1935 to 1950 reported many more burglaries and robberies than did New York City, even though it had only about one-half the population of New York.[4]

The President's Commission report discusses in some detail the factors implicated in variations in crime reporting practices. The commission suggests that relatively more offenses are now being subjected to official attention, so they turn up in official statistics more often than was formerly the case. The changing expectations of slum area citizens may have made them less tolerant of lawbreaking and more likely to complain of it to the police. In turn, the professionalization of police agencies may make them more likely to take official actions against offenders rather than to handle violators informally.[5] Citizens may be quicker to inform the

---

[3] Sutherland and Cressey, op. cit., pp. 29–32.

[4] The President's Commission on Law Enforcement and Administration of Justice, op. cit., pp. 24–27.

[5] Precisely this difference was reported by Wilson for two juvenile operations in separate police departments. In one the juvenile officers were well-trained, and in the other the officers were untrained in juvenile work. In the professionalized department, more juveniles were processed officially than in the less professional force. Wilson asserts that the professional training of

police of thefts than they once were, due to beliefs that theft insurance policies require that offenses be reported to law enforcement authorities. On the other side of the coin, the commission avers that police manipulation of crime statistics continues to create problems in the interpretation of official data. According to the commission report:

> The reporting problem arises at least in part from the tendency of some cities, noted in 1931 by the Wickersham Commission, to "use these reports in order to advertise their freedom from crime as compared with other municipalities." This tendency has apparently not yet been fully overcome. It sometimes arises from political pressure outside the police department and sometimes from the desire of the police to appear to be doing a good job of keeping the crime rate down. Defective or inefficient recording practices may also prevent crimes reported by citizens from becoming a part of the record.[6]

Those who would generalize about the total population of offenders on the basis of official statistics have usually taken a pessimistic view toward these data. However, some investigators have argued that official statistics ought to be studied in their own right for what they tell us about the processes and procedures of official labelling agencies in the correctional apparatus.[7] In this view, the official statistics are not a defective and biased representation of "true crime," but are accurate indicators of the workings of official agencies which go about isolating and labelling some individuals as deviants and lawbreakers. Stated differently, the real deviants and criminals in modern societies are those who have been identified as such by enforcement and control organizations. Similarly, this argument holds that sociological attention ought to be concentrated heavily upon the activities of these agencies, including the business of how these structures go about identifying and processing their clientele.

Skolnick has recently provided an illustration of the sociological analysis of statistics-making. He points out that the clearance rate concerning offenses which the police solve is subject to a good deal of manipulation. Of the offenses reported to them, policemen can classify a number as "unfounded," thereby increasing the percentage of offenses which are

---

the officers made them more likely to be stringent with the offenders than were the untrained officers. Also, in the professionalized department, the juvenile bureau was centered at headquarters rather than being dispersed in precincts. The effect of this arrangement was to encourage policemen to take official action. See James Q. Wilson, "The Police and the Delinquent in Two Cities," in *Controlling Delinquents*, ed. Stanton Wheeler (New York: John Wiley and Son, Inc., 1967).

[6] The President's Commission on Law Enforcement and Administration of Justice, *op. cit.*, p. 27.

[7] John I. Kitsuse and Aaron V. Cicourel, "A Note on the Uses of Official Statistics," *Social Problems*, XI (Fall 1963), 131–39.

cleared. Also, clearance of a case may mean that the police have arrested someone, or it may mean that the officers have persuaded an offender apprehended for another crime to "cop out" to a series of hitherto unsolved cases.[8]

There is considerable merit to the suggestion that the sociologist treat crime and delinquency statistics as primary sociological phenomena for study. However, criminologists will probably also continue to grapple with the problem of gauging the extent of total crime from the data on offenses known to authorities. In short, the study of statistics-making should go hand-in-hand with efforts to assess the magnitude of criminal acts, including those known to agencies and those which are unreported and undetected.

## SOME DIMENSIONS OF KNOWN CRIME

### The Extent of Known Crime

As indicated earlier, the F.B.I. Crime Index is made up of seven major felonies; the F.B.I. collects information regarding the number of these offenses known to the police. These seven felonies were chosen to comprise the crime index because they are all serious, major law violations, and because they are types of criminality likely to be reported to the police when they occur. The numbers of these index crimes reported in 1965 are shown in Table 3.

### TABLE 3
### Index of Serious Crimes, 1965 [9]

| OFFENSE | NUMBER KNOWN TO THE POLICE |
|---|---|
| Murder, non-negligent manslaughter | 9,850 |
| Forcible rape | 22,467 |
| Robbery | 118,916 |
| Aggravated assault | 206,661 |
| Burglary | 1,173,201 |
| Larceny, $50 and over | 762,352 |
| Motor vehicle theft | 486,568 |
| Total, crimes against the person | 357,894 |
| Total, property crimes | 2,422,121 |

[8] Jerome H. Skolnick, *Justice Without Trial* (New York: John Wiley and Sons, Inc., 1966), pp. 164–81.

[9] The President's Commission on Law Enforcement and Administration of Justice, *op. cit.*, p. 8.

The President's Commission on Law Enforcement and Administration of Justice has provided some further evidence regarding the nature and extent of serious crimes in the United States. The commission's report indicates that a survey of 297 robberies in Washington, D.C., showed that injury was inflicted upon the victims in about one-fourth of the cases. Injuries were caused to victims in large proportions of other cases, too. The commission concluded that the likelihood of serious personal attack on any American in a given year is about one in 550. In the view of the commission, the risk of a personal attack is high enough to warrant concern on the part of all Americans.[10]

Remember that the F.B.I. collects nationwide statistics on arrests, rather than on crimes known to the police, for nonindex crimes. These two kinds of data are difficult to match up, in that the ratios between crimes known to the police and arrests vary. About 90 per cent of known murders culminate in arrests, while only about 20 per cent of the known larcenies are solved by arrests. The F.B.I. indicates that, in 1965, 91 per cent of all known murders were cleared by arrest, while the figure for negligent manslaughter was 85 per cent. Forcible rapes were cleared in 64 per cent of the cases, 73 per cent of the aggravated assaults were cleared, 38 per cent of the robberies, 25 per cent of the burglaries and auto thefts, and 20 per cent of the larcenies.[11]

## TABLE 4
### Numbers and Rates of Arrests
### for the Ten Most Frequent Offenses, 1965 [12]

| OFFENSE | NUMBER | RATE PER 100,000 POPULATION | PER CENT OF TOTAL ARRESTS |
|---|---|---|---|
| Drunkenness | 1,535,040 | 1144.7 | 31.0 |
| Disorderly conduct | 570,122 | 425.2 | 11.5 |
| Larceny (over and under $50) | 385,726 | 286.2 | 7.7 |
| Driving under the influence | 241,511 | 180.1 | 4.9 |
| Simple assault | 207,615 | 154.8 | 4.2 |
| Burglary | 197,627 | 147.4 | 4.0 |
| Liquor laws | 179,219 | 133.7 | 3.6 |
| Vagrancy | 120,416 | 89.8 | 2.4 |
| Gambling | 114,294 | 85.2 | 2.3 |
| Motor vehicle theft | 101,763 | 75.9 | 2.1 |

[10] *Ibid.*

[11] Federal Bureau of Investigation, U.S. Department of Justice, *Uniform Crime Reports for the United States, 1965* (Washington, D.C.: U.S. Government Printing Office, 1966), p. 18.

[12] The President's Commission on Law Enforcement and Administration of Justice, *op. cit.*, p. 20.

One thing clear regarding F.B.I. statistics on nonindex crimes is that they far outnumber index offenses. Table 4 shows the numbers and rates of arrests for the ten most frequent offenses in the United States in 1965. As can be seen, drunkenness arrests and other "peace keeping" matters occupy much of the time and attention of the police.

Another category of criminal acts not discussed in F.B.I. reports concerns federal crimes. According to the President's Commission report, the federal cases filed in court in 1966 included seven antitrust offenses, 350 food and drug violations, 863 income tax evasion cases, 2729 liquor law violations, 2293 narcotics cases, and 3188 immigration crimes.[13] These figures suggest that federal crimes are relatively few in number. However, we shall see in Chapter Thirteen that "white collar" violations of regulatory statutes are much more frequent than implied by the above data.

### The Victims of Crime

The recently published report of the President's Commission contains considerable information on the topic of victims, a matter which has received little attention in the past.[14] One set of data comes from a survey undertaken for the commission by the National Opinion Research Center. That study asked a representative sample of 10,000 American citizens whether they had been the victims of a crime in the previous year. Table 5 shows the rates of victimization, that is, the number of victimized

### TABLE 5
### Victimization by Income [15]
### (rates per 100,000 population)

|  | INCOME | | | |
|---|---|---|---|---|
|  | $0–2999 | 3000–5999 | 6000–9999 | 10,000 and over |
| Total | 2369 | 2331 | 1820 | 2237 |
| Forcible rape | 76 | 49 | 10 | 17 |
| Robbery | 172 | 121 | 48 | 34 |
| Aggravated assault | 229 | 316 | 144 | 252 |
| Burglary | 1319 | 1020 | 867 | 790 |
| Larceny ($50 and over) | 420 | 619 | 549 | 925 |
| Motor vehicle theft | 153 | 206 | 202 | 219 |

[13] Ibid., p. 20.
[14] Ibid., pp. 38–43.
[15] Ibid, p. 38.

persons per 100,000 citizens, classified by income. Although these rates show a mixed pattern, it is apparent that low income persons are the most frequent targets of rape, robbery, and burglary. Other observations of the President's Commission note that nonwhites are victimized relatively more often than are whites by all index crimes except grand larceny. Men are the victims of crime about three times more frequently than women.[16]

What are the relationships between offenders and victims? The President's Commission report observes that homicides occur most commonly among offenders and victims known to each other. Similarly, findings from a crime commission survey in Washington, D.C., indicated that about two-thirds of the rape victims are assaulted by someone they know, at least casually. That same study noted that aggravated assaults usually occur among individuals acquainted with each other. Finally, materials from Chicago reveal that assaultive crimes are usually intraracial, rather than between persons of different races.[17]

### The Economic Costs of Crime

The President's Commission report includes some estimates of the economic costs of crime, along with the other matters discussed there.[18] According to the commission, crimes against persons cost about $815,000,000 per year through losses of earnings, hospitalization, and so on. Crimes against property cause annual costs to the public of around $3,932,-000,000. Index crimes contribute only about $600,000,000 in economic costs to this figure, unreported commercial thefts are thought to cost about $1,400,000,000 annually, while embezzlement results in losses of about $200,000,000 per year. Frauds are estimated to involve economic losses of around $1,350,000,000 yearly, while forgeries cost $82,000,000 and arson and vandalism result in losses of about $300,000,000. Clearly, such garden-variety property offenses as larceny and burglary are economically less costly than a variety of "white collar" and "hidden" crimes.

The President's Commission sets the annual cost of crimes involving illegal goods and services, such as prostitution, gambling, and other forms of organized crime, at $8,075,000,000. The economic costs of law enforcement and criminal justice operations is estimated to be about $4,212,000,000 annually, comprised of $2,792,000,000 in police expenses, $261,000,000 in court costs, $125,000,000 in prosecution and defense

16 *Ibid.*, p. 39.
17 *Ibid.*, pp. 39–41.
18 *Ibid.*, pp. 31–35.

counsel expenses, and $1,034,000,000 for the operation of correctional services.

The usual comments about the costs of crime made by citizens and social critics emphasize the costs of ordinary crime. However, these figures of the President's Commission make it clear that the major economic consequences stem from organized crime and certain forms of "hidden" or unreported criminality. Further, these figures suggest that a dramatically sudden reduction of crime in the United States would have major consequences, some of which would be disruptive in nature. The reduction of crime would alter the economic workings of society and probably produce revenue which could be used for more positive ends. But a major reduction in criminality would also result in employment dislocations, rendering goodly numbers of social control agents idle. In this sense at least, crime is functional in American society in that it produces employment opportunities in some quantity.

### Spatial Distribution of Crime

Crime rates vary markedly from one state to another. The rates for index crimes known to the police in 1965 show that Alabama had the highest murder and nonnegligent manslaughter rate, 11.4 per 100,000 population. Georgia, South Carolina, Florida, and Mississippi all had high rates, while the lowest rates were found in Wisconsin, Utah, Minnesota, Iowa, North Carolina, and Vermont. Aggravated assaults were also most frequent in the southern states of North Carolina, Florida, Maryland, Alabama, and Georgia, while the lowest rates were in Vermont, New Hampshire, Iowa, North Dakota, and Delaware. California had the highest rate of forcible rape, 21.2, followed by Michigan, Missouri, Alaska, and Arizona. The lowest rate of forcible rape was Hawaii, with .8 per 100,000 population. Low rates were also observed in New Hampshire, Wisconsin, Rhode Island, and Maine. Illinois and California had the highest robbery rates, while Maine and Vermont had the lowest figures. California and Florida led the nation in burglaries, while South Dakota, West Virginia, and North Dakota had the lowest rates. Nevada and California showed the highest rates of larceny over $50, while Massachusetts and California had the highest automobile theft rates.[19] The major pattern revealed in these figures centers about the high rates of crimes against persons in the southern part of the United States.

Crimes also vary considerably within urban areas. Table 0 shows rates for index crimes for the 15 largest standard metropolitan areas in 1965.

[19] Federal Bureau of Investigation, op. cit., pp. 52–55.

## TABLE 6
### Crime Rates, Standard Metropolitan Areas, 1965 [20]
### (rates per 100,000 population)

| | MURDER, NONNEGLI- GENT MAN- SLAUGHTER | FORCIBLE RAPE | ROBBERY | AGGRA- VATED ASSAULT | BURGLARY | LARCENY OVER $50 | AUTO THEFT |
|---|---|---|---|---|---|---|---|
| Baltimore | 8.7 | 18.0 | 125.6 | 233.6 | 676.5 | 625.0 | 401.2 |
| Boston | 2.8 | 5.0 | 53.0 | 54.1 | 563.4 | 340.1 | 691.1 |
| Chicago | 6.9 | 21.6 | 244.3 | 188.4 | 638.3 | 417.3 | 532.1 |
| Cleveland | 5.7 | 8.9 | 101.0 | 81.9 | 546.6 | 144.6 | 301.0 |
| Detroit | 6.2 | 26.8 | 178.4 | 150.6 | 840.4 | 508.1 | 488.9 |
| Houston | 10.7 | 11.8 | 95.5 | 172.8 | 941.8 | 379.4 | 278.8 |
| Los Angeles | 6.1 | 32.9 | 189.1 | 229.7 | 1564.4 | 917.0 | 627.4 |
| Minneapolis | 2.1 | 9.0 | 84.5 | 71.7 | 894.7 | 530.4 | 366.2 |
| Newark | 4.6 | 13.2 | 109.4 | 153.4 | 872.3 | 436.1 | 405.9 |
| New York | 6.1 | 11.3 | 83.9 | 154.2 | 584.5 | 780.5 | 361.0 |
| Philadelphia | 5.5 | 15.9 | 82.9 | 126.6 | 530.1 | 247.4 | 287.2 |
| Pittsburgh | 3.5 | 10.3 | 76.4 | 72.3 | 482.4 | 285.8 | 373.1 |
| St. Louis | 7.9 | 20.7 | 130.2 | 136.1 | 915.0 | 337.7 | 368.9 |
| San Francisco | 4.3 | 13.7 | 130.4 | 132.5 | 1171.4 | 569.0 | 518.0 |
| Washington | 8.2 | 14.2 | 153.2 | 212.6 | 891.3 | 496.1 | 395.7 |

Los Angeles had the highest rates for three of the seven offenses, but generally the rates are not consistently higher in one community than another. What is most apparent from Table 6 is that crime rates for the index crimes are of quite different magnitudes within the 15 areas, so that, for example, robbery rates range from 53.0 to 244.3 per 100,000 population.

How do crime rates for standard metropolitan statistical areas compare with those for other portions of the nation? Index crime rates are shown in Table 7 for standard metropolitan areas, other cities, and rural parts of the country.

In that the majority of the American population lives in metropolitan areas, we should not be surprised to find that most crimes occur there. But Table 7 also indicates that the *relative* occurrence of crime is less in rural areas; metropolitan areas show high rates of crime, as well as large numbers of offenses. Table 7 also shows that homicide rates are nearly equal in metropolitan and rural areas and that forcible rapes are nearly equal in all areas. The pronounced contrast of rates is found in robbery, burglary, larceny, and auto theft. The high rates of property

[20] *Ibid.,* pp. 71–89.

## TABLE 7
### Crime Rates, Metropolitan Areas, Other Cities, and Rural Areas, 1965 [21]
(rates per 100,000 population)

| | TOTAL | MURDER, NONNEGLI-GENT MAN-SLAUGHTER | FORCIBLE RAPE | ROBBERY | AGGRA-VATED ASSAULT | BURGLARY | LARCENY $50 AND OVER | AUTO THEFT |
|---|---|---|---|---|---|---|---|---|
| U.S. total | 1434.3 | 5.1 | 11.6 | 61.4 | 106.6 | 605.3 | 393.3 | 251.0 |
| Standard metro-politan areas | 1781.5 | 5.4 | 13.7 | 85.2 | 122.4 | 736.6 | 483.1 | 335.1 |
| Other cities | 995.7 | 3.5 | 5.4 | 18.2 | 84.0 | 448.4 | 301.6 | 134.7 |
| Rural areas | 567.8 | 5.1 | 8.3 | 9.7 | 69.0 | 272.3 | 156.0 | 47.4 |

crime in urban areas are probably explained in terms of the loosened social bonds, lack of legitimate opportunities, and other concomitants of urbanization. We shall have more to say about differential social organization in cities and its link to criminality in later chapters.

The relationship of crime and urbanization is also revealed in crime rates for cities of different size. Table 8 shows rates for index crimes known to the police for 1965, arranged by size of community.

Although the patterns in Table 8 are somewhat mixed, it can be seen that crime rates generally decrease as we move from the largest cities to smaller ones.

## CHARACTERISTICS OF KNOWN OFFENDERS

### Age Variations

In 1960, 44.5 per cent of the total population of 179,325,675 Americans were under 25 years of age. Persons 15 to 25 years old made up 13.4 per cent of the population. However, the 15 to 25 year old group was involved in criminality far out of proportion to its numbers in the population. Conventional crime is heavily concentrated within this group, although there are variations from crime to crime in the contribution made by young persons. Table 9 shows the arrest figures for 1965 by age.

Table 9 indicates that persons under 25 years of age accounted for 42.2 per cent of all arrests. However, these individuals were particularly implicated in those serious property crimes which occur frequently and

[21] Ibid., p. 51.

# TABLE 8
## Crime Rates by City Size, 1965 [22]
### (rates per 100,000 population)

| | WILLFUL HOMICIDE | FORCIBLE RAPE | ROBBERY | AGGRAVATED ASSAULT | BURGLARY | LARCENY, $50 AND OVER | MOTOR VEHICLE THEFT |
|---|---|---|---|---|---|---|---|
| Cities over 1,000,000 | 10 | 26 | 221 | 246 | 930 | 734 | 586 |
| 500,000—1,000,000 | 10 | 20 | 165 | 182 | 1009 | 555 | 640 |
| 250,000—500,000 | 7 | 15 | 122 | 142 | 1045 | 550 | 468 |
| 100,000—250,000 | 6 | 11 | 73 | 151 | 871 | 556 | 353 |
| 50,000—100,000 | 4 | 8 | 49 | 85 | 675 | 492 | 297 |
| 25,000—50,000 | 3 | 6 | 33 | 71 | 562 | 443 | 212 |
| 10,000—25,000 | 2 | 6 | 19 | 67 | 462 | 309 | 141 |
| Under 10,000 | 2 | 5 | 12 | 62 | 369 | 236 | 99 |
| Rural | 4 | 9 | 10 | 58 | 308 | 176 | 51 |
| Suburban area | 3 | 10 | 28 | 66 | 545 | 359 | 160 |
| All places | 5 | 12 | 61 | 107 | 605 | 420 | 251 |

[22] The President's Commission on Law Enforcement and Administration of Justice, op. cit., p. 28.

## TABLE 9
### Total Arrests of Persons Under 25 Years of Age, 1965 [23]

| OFFENSE CHARGED | TOTAL | NUMBER OF PERSONS ARRESTED UNDER 25 | PERCENTAGE UNDER 25 |
|---|---|---|---|
| Total | 5,031,393 | 2,124,100 | 42.2 |
| Criminal homicide | | | |
| (a) Murder and nonnegligent manslaughter | 7,348 | 2,594 | 35.3 |
| (b) Manslaughter by negligence | 2,815 | 1,204 | 42.8 |
| Forcible rape | 10,734 | 6,897 | 64.3 |
| Robbery | 45,872 | 31,600 | 68.9 |
| Aggravated assault | 84,411 | 35,011 | 41.5 |
| Burglary—breaking or entering | 197,627 | 158,140 | 80.0 |
| Larceny—theft | 383,726 | 291,363 | 75.9 |
| Auto theft | 101,763 | 89,957 | 88.4 |
| Other assaults | 207,615 | 86,282 | 41.6 |
| Arson | 6,187 | 4,901 | 79.2 |
| Forgery and counterfeiting | 30,617 | 13,023 | 42.5 |
| Fraud | 52,007 | 13,949 | 26.8 |
| Embezzlement | 7,674 | 2,142 | 27.9 |
| Stolen property: buying, receiving, etc. | 19,060 | 12,398 | 65.0 |
| Vandalism | 89,668 | 80,277 | 89.5 |
| Weapons: carrying, possessing, etc. | 53,585 | 27,133 | 50.6 |
| Prostitution and commercial vice | 33,987 | 16,098 | 47.4 |
| Sex offenses (except forcible rape and prostitution) | 58,205 | 29,189 | 50.1 |
| Narcotic drug laws | 46,069 | 22,869 | 49.6 |
| Gambling | 114,294 | 17,845 | 15.6 |
| Offenses against family and children | 60,981 | 15,882 | 26.0 |
| Driving under the influence | 241,511 | 39,576 | 16.4 |
| Liquor laws | 179,219 | 131,970 | 73.6 |
| Drunkenness | 1,535,040 | 197,319 | 12.9 |
| Disorderly conduct | 570,122 | 249,268 | 43.7 |
| Vagrancy | 120,416 | 39,231 | 32.6 |
| All other offenses (except traffic) | 531,970 | 296,526 | 55.7 |
| Suspicion | 76,346 | 48,932 | 64.1 |
| Curfew and loitering law violations | 72,243 | 72,243 | 100.0 |
| Runaways | 90,281 | 90,281 | 100.0 |

about which the community is most concerned. Thus, 68.9 per cent of robberies, 80 per cent of burglaries, 75.9 per cent of larcenies, and 88.4 per cent of auto thefts were carried out by persons under 25 years of age. Persons over 25 years of age are the ones most frequently involved in

[23] Federal Bureau of Investigation, op. cit., p. 114.

fraud, embezzlement, gambling, drunkenness, vagrancy, and offenses against the family.

### Sex Variations

One of the most striking features of known crime in the United States is that it is mainly the work of males. Males are arrested for index offenses plus larceny under $50 nearly seven times more frequently than are women. In 1965, the arrest rate for these crimes for males was 1097 per 100,000, as contrasted with 164 per 100,000 population for females. However, the difference in rates has diminished in the past decade, for while the male arrest rate increased between 1960 and 1965 from 926 to 1097 arrests per 100,000 population, female arrest rates increased from 101 to 164 per 100,000 population. In other words, the male rate increased by 18 per cent in this period, while the female rate grew by 62 per cent.[24]

Women are not equally involved in all forms of crime. In 1965, females accounted for 77.5 per cent of prostitution and commercial vice arrests, 20.3 per cent of fraud arrests, and 22.1 per cent of larceny arrests. On the other hand, women accounted for only 4.2 per cent of auto thefts, 3.7 per cent of burglaries, 5.2 per cent of robberies, and 6.3 per cent of arrests for driving under the influence.[25] Reports for individual states contain much the same information. In California in 1965, females were involved in 10.6 per cent of all felony arrests. Women were implicated in 21.9 per cent of the forgery and checks arrests, 15.9 per cent of the homicide arrests, but only 1.7 of the "other sex offenses" arrests and 0.1 per cent of the rape arrests. Similarly, women were involved in 33.5 per cent of the misdemeanor arrests for thefts but only 7.3 per cent of the misdemeanor assaults.[26]

What is the explanation for the disproportionate contribution of males to criminality? Perhaps there is something about female roles in American society which deters women from lawbreaking. However, another thesis has been advanced, principally by Pollak, in which it is argued that women are really as criminally involved as men.[27] Pollak's argument is that the sex-role socialization which women experience leads them to act deviously and cunningly. As a result, they commit a variety of crimes which remain "hidden" and unreported. They carry on surreptitious poisonings which result in homicides, shoplift, and engage in other un-

---

[24] The President's Commission on Law Enforcement and Administration of Justice, op. cit., p. 44.

[25] Federal Bureau of Investigation, op. cit., p. 115.

[26] State of California, Crime and Delinquency in California, 1965 (Sacramento: Bureau of Criminal Statistics, 1966), pp. 43–49.

[27] Otto Pollak, The Criminality of Women (Philadelphia: University of Pennsylvania Press, 1950).

recognized deviations. Pollak has marshaled some evidence of uneven quality which he believes demonstrates that true rates of female crime equal those for men. Our assessment of this argument and the evidence adduced for it is that it is overstated. Females do engage in some kinds of crime which have a low probability of being detected or reported, thus the male and female rates of crime are probably closer together than revealed by arrest statistics. Yet males are also probably more criminally involved than females, due to the different social experiences they have undergone and the greater opportunities they have for lawbreaking.

### Racial Variations

The major concern of those curious about racial characteristics of lawbreakers centers about the extent of involvement of Negroes in criminality. Negroes comprised slightly over 10 per cent of the American population in 1960, so that they represent the major racial group other than Caucasians in the country.

Negroes are apparently strongly overrepresented in crime. In 1965, the arrest rate for Negroes for index crimes plus larceny under $50 was 1696 per 100,000 population, as contrasted with the white rate of 419. The murder rate among whites was 2.5, while the Negro rate was 24.1, nearly ten times higher. The Negro burglary arrest rate was 378, while the white rate was 107 arrests per 100,000 population. In general, Negro arrest rates for property crimes were three times those for whites.[28]

The data in Table 10 indicate the number of Negro and white arrests in 1965 for a wide variety of crimes. As can be seen in that table, Negroes contribute most heavily to arrests for homicides, robberies, assaults, weapons charges, prostitution, and gambling, while they are infrequently involved in fraud, embezzlement, and liquor violations. In general, the high crime pattern for Negroes is comprised of incidents of unskilled personal assaults or property crimes.

The thrust of these arrest statistics is to suggest two factors which may account for these patterns. First, Negroes are probably overrepresented in criminality in part through differential law enforcement. That is, these arrest figures reflect the policies of the police, who sometimes deal officially with Negro offenses which would be handled informally if they had been the work of Caucasians. Secondly, these figures are to be explained in terms of the criminogenic social experiences to which many Negroes are subjected in American society. If racial characteristics per se influenced criminality, one would expect to find crime rates for

---

[28] The President's Commission on Law Enforcement and Administration of Justice, op. cit., pp. 44–45.

## TABLE 10
### Total Arrests by Race, 1965 [29]

| OFFENSE CHARGED | WHITE | NEGRO | NEGRO PERCENTAGE OF TOTAL |
|---|---|---|---|
| Criminal homicide | | | |
|   (a) Murder and nonnegligent manslaughter | 2,675 | 3,704 | 58.1 |
|   (b) Manslaughter by negligence | 1,883 | 541 | 22.3 |
| Forcible rape | 4,485 | 4,665 | 51.0 |
| Robbery | 16,586 | 22,546 | 57.6 |
| Aggravated assault | 32,539 | 36,558 | 52.9 |
| Burglary—breaking or entering | 118,167 | 59,673 | 33.6 |
| Larceny—theft | 247,606 | 109,792 | 30.7 |
| Auto theft | 64,200 | 26,372 | 29.1 |
| Other assaults | 116,734 | 73,284 | 38.6 |
| Arson | 4,321 | 1,127 | 20.7 |
| Forgery and counterfeiting | 21,690 | 5,440 | 20.0 |
| Fraud | 40,843 | 8,253 | 16.8 |
| Embezzlement | 5,777 | 966 | 14.3 |
| Stolen property: buying, receiving, | | | |
|   possessing, etc. | 10,120 | 5,463 | 35.1 |
| Vandalism | 65,601 | 16,074 | 19.7 |
| Weapons: carrying, possessing, etc. | 22,695 | 26,226 | 53.6 |
| Prostitution and commercialized vice | 12,643 | 17,598 | 58.2 |
| Sex offenses (except forcible rape and | | | |
|   prostitution) | 38,615 | 13,759 | 26.3 |
| Narcotic drug laws | 18,530 | 12,069 | 39.4 |
| Gambling | 19,842 | 64,135 | 76.4 |
| Offenses against family and children | 39,449 | 19,699 | 33.3 |
| Driving under the influence | 188,159 | 38,966 | 17.2 |
| Liquor laws | 131,452 | 31,929 | 19.5 |
| Drunkenness | 1,070,861 | 354,158 | 24.9 |
| Disorderly conduct | 312,228 | 179,506 | 36.5 |
| Vagrancy | 83,495 | 28,161 | 25.2 |
| All other offenses (except traffic) | 365,869 | 135,946 | 27.1 |
| Suspicion | 53,651 | 21,721 | 28.8 |
| Curfew and loitering law violations | 54,288 | 14,521 | 21.1 |
| Runaways | 70,382 | 15,142 | 17.7 |

different offenses to be relatively uniform. Instead, Negro and white rates alike are quite varied. We shall examine a number of the crimino-genic factors in American social life which are implicated in Negro criminality in some detail in the chapters ahead.

[29] Federal Bureau of Investigation, *op. cit.,* p. 117.

## TRENDS IN CRIME

In the America of the mid-twentieth century, it is fashionable to as-sume that lawlessness is at an unparalleled high point. In recent Presi-dential and gubernatorial elections, much has been made of the apparent breakdown of law and order and consequent increase of lawbreaking.

But hard evidence which conclusively demonstrates this hypothesized upsurge of criminality is hard to come by. Even inadequate statistics of the sort discussed in this chapter have been gathered for only a short time, so long term trends cannot be identified. However, there is some evidence which suggests that America prior to the twentieth century may have been more lawless than it is now.[30]

Crime trends can be studied for short periods in the immediate past, and these data do suggest that criminality has been growing at an accelerated pace in the past decade. Figures 2 and 3, taken from the President's Commission report, show the trends in index crimes known to the police between 1933 and 1965. These two charts indicate that all index crimes have increased between 1960 and 1965 at a much more pronounced rate than they grew over the longer period since 1933. The rates for property crimes have burgeoned most prominently, in that the 1960 to 1965 increase in violent crimes was 25 per cent, while the increase in property offenses was 36 per cent.[31] Nonindex violations also increased prominently during this period from 1960 to 1965.

In the view of the President's Commission, the 1960–1965 statistics re-veal a real increase in criminality. The commission attributes this growth to such factors as the changing age structure of the population, with more persons in the younger, crime-prone age groups; increased urbanization and the criminogenic influences it creates; and the growing affluence of American society, which produces more opportunities for property crimes.[32]

## "HIDDEN" CRIMINALITY

The crime information we have examined to this point concerned offenses that have been reported to the police or resulted in an arrest. What relation does this known criminality bear to the total volume of

[30] Daniel Bell, "Crime as an American Way of Life," *Antioch Review*, XIII (June 1953), 131–54; The President's Commission on Law Enforcement and Administration of Justice, op. cit., pp. 22–23.
[31] The President's Commission on Law Enforcement and Administration of Justice, op. cit., pp. 23–34.
[32] *Ibid.*, pp. 27–31.

## FIGURE 2

## Index Crime Trends, 1933–1965; Reported Crimes Against Property

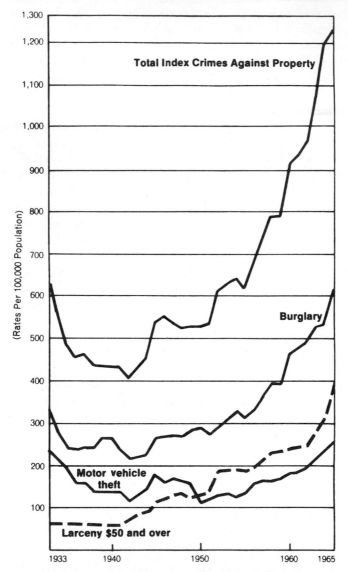

NOTE: The scale for this figure is not comparable with that used in Figure 3.

Source: FBI, Uniform Crime Reports Section; unpublished data.

## FIGURE 3

## Index Crime Trends, 1933–1965; Reported Crimes Against the Person

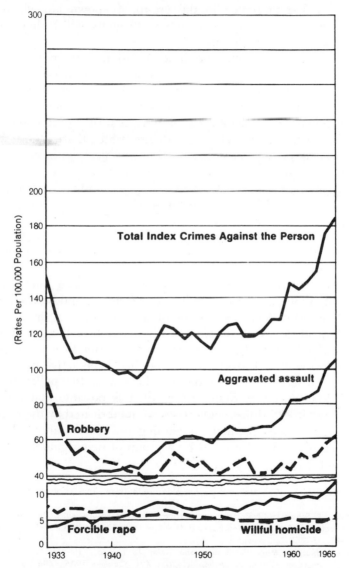

NOTE: Scale for willful homicide and forcible rape enlarged,
to show trend.
Source: FBI, Uniform Crime Reports Section; unpublished data.

lawbreaking? What of deviant behavior that is unreported, unknown by the authorities, and thereby "hidden"? How much of this activity is there? Is known criminality but a small fragment of the body of crime? Is unreported or hidden lawbreaking common among population groups that are underrepresented in the group of known law violators? Are middle class citizens engaged in acts of illegality which they are able to keep from the eyes of the police?

Most of the work done on these questions has concerned juvenile delinquency. Many years ago, Robison observed that the cases of delinquency which had been observed by various public agencies in New York City were much more numerous than those known to the police and juvenile courts.[33] Schwartz conducted a survey of delinquency cases in Washington, D.C., in 1944 which demonstrated that schools, the police, and other social agencies and institutions deal with many cases of juvenile delinquency which do not get referred to the juvenile court.[34] A study in Cambridge and Somerville, near Boston, dramatically indicated that acts of delinquency and misbehavior are much more frequent among youths in high delinquency areas than is revealed in police arrests or court statistics. These data suggest that delinquent conduct is truly a way of life or regularized behavior pattern for many youngsters in urban slum areas.[35]

Delinquency researchers have for some time been interested in the participation of children who live in comfortable, middle class neighborhoods in juvenile lawbreaking. The pioneering study of these youths was by Porterfield, in which he elicited reports from college students about the misbehavior they had been involved in prior to entry into college. Porterfield found that nearly all of them had been active in delinquency, although virtually none had become known to the police or courts.[36] Porterfield's study was quite crude, so it is possible that some of the confessions of peccadilloes and crimes were fabricated by the respondents. However, improved methods of gaining self-reports about delinquency have been devised and utilized by a group of investigators, starting with Short and Nye.[37]

[33] Sophia Robison, Can Delinquency be Measured? (New York: Columbia University Press, 1936).

[34] Edward E. Schwartz, "A Community Experiment in the Measurement of Juvenile Delinquency," National Probation Association Yearbook, 1945 (New York: National Probation Association, 1945), pp. 157–81.

[35] Fred J. Murphy, Mary M. Shirley, and Helen L. Witmer, "The Incidence of Hidden Delinquency," American Journal of Orthopsychiatry, XVI (October 1946), 686–96.

[36] Austin L. Porterfield, "Delinquency and Its Outcome in Court and College," American Journal of Sociology, XLIX (November 1943), 199–208.

[37] F. Ivan Nye and James F. Short, Jr., "Scaling Delinquent Behavior," American Sociological Review, XXII (June 1957), 326–31; Short and Nye, "Extent of Unrecorded Juvenile Delinquency,

The recent collection of studies of hidden delinquency are quite varied, in that they have been conducted in dissimilar communities and with different groups of youngsters. However, they add up to a broad picture of the undetected deviations of youngsters. Most of these children admit that they have engaged in at least one or another delinquent act, but most of the misbehavior they report tends to be relatively innocuous. When undetected delinquents are compared with incarcerated offenders, marked differences between the two groups are noted. The institutionalized delinquents generally admit to a wider variety of offenses, most of which are more serious than those acknowledged by the hidden offenders.

We should hasten to point out that not all of the misbehavior of hidden delinquents is minor in form. Shanley, as well as Karacki and Toby, have discussed groups of juveniles from comfortable economic circumstances who have been implicated in relatively serious kinds of lawbreaking.[38] Nonetheless, much of the hidden misbehavior appears to be hidden and unreported, in part, because it is relatively petty in nature.

Investigations of unreported criminality are few. One study was conducted by Wallerstein and Wyle, who asked a cross-section of the adult population to report upon those acts of law violation in which they had engaged.[39] Most of the respondents admitted one or more deviant act which had gone unreported. Many of these self-reported incidents appear to be relatively harmless ones with which the police do not normally concern themselves. For instance, one woman reported an "assault," by which she meant that she had thrown an ashtray at a suitor. Cases such as this suggest the need for caution lest the conclusion be reached that nearly all citizens are engaged in criminality.

The President's Commission report contains some up-to-date evidence

Tentative Conclusions," *Journal of Criminal Law, Criminology and Police Science*, XLIX (November– December 1958), 296–302; Nye, *Family Relationships and Delinquent Behavior* (New York: John Wiley and Sons, Inc., 1958); Harwin L. Voss, "Socio-Economic Status and Reported Delinquent Behavior," *Social Problems*, XIII (Winter 1966), 314–24; Ronald L. Akers, "Socio-Economic Status and Delinquent Behavior: A Retest," *Journal of Research in Crime and Delinquency*, I (January 1964), 38–46; John P. Clark and Eugene P. Wenninger, "Socio-Economic Class and Area as Correlates of Illegal Behavior Among Juveniles," *American Sociological Review*, XXVII (December 1962), 826–34; Robert A. Dentler and Lawrence J. Monroe, "Social Correlates of Early Adolescent Theft," *American Sociological Review*, XXVI (October 1961), 733–43; William R. Arnold, "Continuities in Research: Scaling Delinquent Behavior," *Social Problems*, XIII (Summer 1965), 59–66.

[38] Larry Karacki and Jackson Toby, "The Uncommitted Adolescent: Candidate for Gang Socialization," *Sociological Inquiry*, XXXII (Spring 1962), 203–15; Fred J. Shanley, "Middle-Class Delinquency as a Social Problem," *Sociology and Social Research*, LI (January 1967), 185–98.

[39] James S. Wallerstein and Clement Wyle, "Our Law-Abiding Lawbreakers," *Probation*, XXV (April 1947), 107–12.

on unreported crime.[40] That report discusses a National Opinion Research Center national poll of 10,000 households, along with detailed surveys which were conducted in Boston, Chicago, and Washington, D.C. The national survey dealt with the extent to which persons had been victims of crimes. The rates of victimization that emerged are compared with F.B.I. rates of crime in Table 11.

### TABLE 11
### Comparison of Survey and UCR Rates [41]
### (rates per 100,000 population)

| INDEX CRIMES | N.O.R.C. SURVEY, 1965–66 | UCR RATE FOR INDIVIDUALS, 1965 | UCR RATE FOR INDIVIDUALS AND ORGANIZATIONS, 1965 |
|---|---|---|---|
| Willful homicide | 3.0 | 5.1 | 5.1 |
| Forcible rape | 42.5 | 11.6 | 11.6 |
| Robbery | 94.0 | 61.4 | 61.4 |
| Aggravated assault | 218.3 | 106.6 | 106.6 |
| Burglary | 949.1 | 299.6 | 605.3 |
| Larceny ($50 and over) | 606.5 | 267.4 | 393.3 |
| Motor vehicle theft | 206.2 | 226.0 | 251.0 |
| Total violence | 357.8 | 184.7 | 184.7 |
| Total property | 1761.8 | 793.0 | 1249.6 |

It is readily apparent from Table 11 that crime touches upon persons in the general population much more frequently than reflected in the official figures. The same conclusion emerges from the observations in three precincts in Washington, D.C., where various crimes were found to be three to ten times more frequent than indicated in police statistics. Similar findings resulted in the Boston and Chicago surveys. In the N.O.R.C. investigation, the most frequent reason given by respondents for not reporting crimes to the police was that they believed the police incapable of dealing with them.

Obviously, the group of offenders which comes to the attention of the authorities represents only a segment of a large collection of criminals. We will have occasion to examine some further evidence on selected forms of unreported crime in chapters to follow. Thus we shall see that "white collar crime," involving violations of business regulations, is widespread in American society.

[40] The President's Commission on Law Enforcement and Administration of Justice, *op. cit.*, pp. 21–22.
[41] *Ibid.*, p. 21.

## SUMMARY

This chapter has identified some of the major dimensions of known crime in American society. In addition, some aspects of hidden criminality have been explored. We have seen that criminality is extremely widespread and costly, and have also observed that lawbreaking is patterned in a variety of ways, so that it is more common in some areas than others. It is also apparent that some individuals, such as those who are male, young, Negro, or from low-income backgrounds, are more likely to be apprehended as criminals than are other persons. These materials provide the beginnings to a study of crime causation, to which our attention now turns. Chapter Six initiates the exploration of etiology by taking up a number of those paths which earlier students of criminality have explored in their search for the causes of lawbreaking.

# 6

# Causal Analysis
## Background
## and History

## INTRODUCTION

The remarks in Chapter One dealing with causal analysis noted that the study of criminal etiology involves three separate but related problems. The first was identified as the epidemiological question, in which "the facts" are at issue. Once the basic facts of criminality have been drawn together, the explanatory job involves: *a*) the sociology of criminality, in which attempts are made to account for rates and patterns of crime, as well as *b*) the social-psychology of criminal careers, in which the analyst endeavors to account for the genesis of criminal role behavior in specific individuals. The preceding chapter was concerned with epidemiology—the facts which must be accounted for by criminological theory. The present chapter takes up some of the theoretical answers to causal questions which criminologists of an earlier generation have regarded as valid. In Chapters Eight through Sixteen, attention will focus upon a variety of contemporary theories and hypotheses regarding criminality.

Man's attention to lawbreaking and deviant conduct of various kinds can be traced back to antiquity. Two general kinds of views of criminality have been advanced, the "demonological" and the "naturalistic" frames of reference.[1] Demonological views entertain the belief in "other world" powers of spirits as being at the root of criminality, while naturalistic theories look for events and characteristics of the directly observable physical and material world as the active agents producing crime. Our concern in this chapter is with naturalistic hypotheses, for these are the only ones with any link to contemporary social science perspectives on deviant behavior.

As we shall see, some of the theoretical assertions examined in this chapter are concerned with rates problems, such as the socialist explanation, while others are designed to account for the process by which

[1] George B. Vold, *Theoretical Criminology* (New York: Oxford University Press, 1958), pp. 4–8. Vold provides a succinct summary and critique of a number of these historically important notions regarding crime.

115

certain persons become criminals. Much of the early work in criminology centers around biogenic propositions, in which biological variables are seen as critical in causation. One other prefatory remark is that this chapter deals with both historically old and historically recent analyses of criminality. For example, socialist views of crime developed around 1850 and were followed by investigations of lawbreaking and economic trends which have continued up to the present. Similarly, biogenic viewpoints originated with Lombroso about 1875, but a long line of biological investigations stemmed from Lombroso's work. Some of these endeavors are going on currently. This chapter will be concerned with these various lines of inquiry, and we shall examine the historical roots and the contemporary manifestations of a number of frames of reference.

## A HISTORY OF ERRORS

What can we learn from the "pioneers in criminology"? [2] The most accurate, brief answer is: "Not a great deal." Probably the most important lesson that the pioneering figures in criminology have to teach us centers about blind alleys which have been explored. Historical efforts in criminology have all too often been fruitless meanderings into theoretical terrain which have failed to account adequately for criminality. There is clearly not an unbroken line of cumulative work on criminality starting a century or so ago. Modern views are not the end product of some multiplicative process, building upon the contributions of the criminological "giants" of the past. Instead, current sociological and psychological viewpoints are relatively unrelated to earlier theorizing regarding criminality. On this point of discontinuity between the past and contemporary efforts in criminology, Vold makes this assessment of those historical searches for evidence that criminals represent a physical type: "Physical type theories turn out to be a more-or-less sophisticated form of shadow-boxing with a much more subtle and difficult to get at problem, namely, that of the constitutional factor in human behavior." [3] Behind this specific evaluation of physical type theories by Vold, and underlying the more sweeping negative judgment regarding historical endeavors as a whole, is the assertion that modern social science puts

[2] This term is taken from a series of articles in the *Journal of Criminal Law, Criminology and Police Science* of a few years ago in which the writings of a number of pioneers or early figures in criminology were examined. See, for example, Elio D. Monachesi, "Pioneers in Criminology: IX-Cesare Beccaria (1738–94)," *Journal of Criminal Law, Criminology and Police Science,* XLVI (November–December 1955), 439–49.

[3] Vold, *op. cit.,* p. 74.

forward an image of man and society which is infinitely more complicated than the representation implied in earlier arguments.

Reduced to barest essentials, modern sociological perspectives on
criminality aver as an article of faith that it is possible to discover
*causal relationships,* that is, some finite or limited number of factors
bearing an invariant or constant relationship to criminality. The social
scientist assumes that statements of the form, "If A, B, and C occur, then
behavior of form X will occur," are discoverable by the methods of
science. There is also general agreement that these causal processes
behind criminality are exceedingly complex. Human behavior in all its
forms is viewed as complicated in character, but this is particularly true
of lawbreaking because there are many divergent forms of behavior included under the terminological umbrella, "crime." A third point of
agreement is that variations in the forms and rates of crime are the
product of basic features of social organization. Crime is no more or
less "normal" than any other kind of behavior, so that modern-day criminologists eschew the "evil causes evil" kind of perspective in which
criminality is attributed to bad homes, inadequate parents, or other
evils. Instead, the modern sociologist is inclined to pay close scrutiny to
social-structural variables included within such broad categories as value
patterns, social stratification influences, differentials in family structure,
or interactions with agencies of social control.

A fourth component of contemporary viewpoints concedes the possibility that certain kinds of personality dynamics and characteristics act
as predisposing conditions leading certain individuals in the direction of
criminal careers. However, the sociologist would argue that most crime is
accomplished by actors lacking in personality pathology, so that the personality dynamics that interact with social or situational influences are
more subtle in character. Also, there are probably different personality
correlates which are influential in the varied forms that criminality takes.
Finally, some present-day students of criminality would concede the
possibility that certain specific biologically related conditions, such as
brain damage, may play a contributory part in particular instances of
deviation, but if so, the relationships involved are complicated ones to
uncover. In summary, modern views on the crime problem involve a
posture of modesty, growing out of the recognition that human behavior
of even a limited and simple kind is rarely the product of some easily
identifiable causal process.

This view of human behavior, in which social action is regarded as a
mysterious but ultimately knowable product of manifold variables in
subtle interaction, is relatively recent. Particularly recent is the body
of behavioral science theory which has begun to spell out some of the

component processes and variables which make up the structure of social action. For most of man's history, simpler and more straightforward beliefs about man and his behavior have been in vogue. In earlier times, the actions of men were believed to be reducible to relatively simple hedonistic pleasure seeking, as activity patterns dictated by the force of biological imperatives of some kind, or as capable of reduction to other simplistic formulas. So it has been with criminological theories too. An examination of the history of criminology turns up a goodly number of viewpoints seen by modern standards as naive, oversimplified, and in other ways inadequate to deal with behavior as it really exists in all its richness and complexity. As one illustration, most of the work that has been done on biological hypotheses in criminality seems clearly defective, apart from the inadequate research methodology of these studies. Nearly all of the biogenic works proceed on the basis of faulty assumptions, one of which is that "nature" and "nurture" (heredity and environment) can be separated from each other and studied in isolation. Another erroneous presupposition which vitiates most biogenic work is that criminality is a constant, unchanging kind of behavior. The fact is that crime is varied from place to place and from time to time, so that there is no such thing as "universal" or timeless crime. Therefore, if there are biological forces involved in criminality, hypotheses which seek to discover them will have to be sufficiently sophisticated to answer the question of how such culturally and temporally variable phenomena as crime could be transmitted genetically. No existing biological theory is equipped to handle this problem.[4]

Doubtless the point should be made that historical efforts in criminology are of considerable value as indicators of theoretical paths that might be bypassed in the search for causes of criminality. Certainly, in this sense, these earlier efforts have much significance for contemporary criminology. The person who would make a diligent attempt to comprehend the nature of crime must begin his labors with an examination of the writings of prior generations of criminologists. But our main point has been that a hiatus exists between contemporary theoretical and empirical work and the endeavors of earlier generations of students of criminal conduct. The substantive body of contemporary criminological theory is more directly allied to concepts and insights from the body of modern behavioral science theory than it is to the works of earlier analysts. Thus we shall see in the pages to follow that many earlier studies of criminality came to abortive conclusions. The generalizations from

---

[4] One incisive critique of theories seeking to find the causes of crime in genetically inherited traits can be found in Richard R. Korn and Lloyd W. McCorkle, *Criminology and Penology* (New York: Holt, Rinehart and Winston, Inc., 1959), pp. 199–204.

these works have not stood the test of time to become building blocks for modern criminological theory.

## THE CLASSICAL VIEW

The classical school refers to the writings of a number of European scholars in the late 1700's, particularly Cesare Beccaria in Italy (1738–1794) and Jeremy Bentham in England (1748–1832).[5] The core concepts of the classical frame of reference are hedonism and free will. Vold notes that all classical theorists accepted as valid, as did most of their lay contemporaries, certain beliefs about human behavior, including the existence of human "will" as a psychological reality. Prevailing opinions of the time agreed that all men, criminals included, act rationally and deliberately in order to avoid pain and encounter pleasure.[6] From these premises, it follows directly that the criminal is a person who makes a deliberate, rational, hedonistically oriented decision to engage in lawbreaking. If this be the case, to deter him or others from crime, an amount and kind of punishment of such magnitude as to counterbalance the pleasure from criminal acts must be swiftly and surely administered to miscreants. In the works of some classical scholars, attempts were made to develop highly detailed scales or hedonistic calculi of punishment, in which specific amounts of pain were identified for each type of lawbreaking. In the criminal codes which grew out of classical writings, constant punishments were decreed for particular violations of law, so the effect of these codes was to render judges as simply instruments for the application of the law. Codes were drafted in such a way as to severely circumscribe the discretionary powers of judges in assigning penalties to offenders.

Early criminologists such as Bentham and Beccaria were not involved in the statement of criminological theories out of any fundamental or overriding interest in the explanation of crime. Instead, the classical version of criminological theory represented a by-product of other kinds of interests. Bentham, Beccaria, and others were social critics and reformers, interested in modifying the social control practices of their native societies. They were concerned about the severe and barbaric punishments commonplace during the late 1700's. Similarly, they were appalled by the existence of tyrannical and capricious judges administering harsh

[5] Vold, op. cit., pp. 14–26, see also Leon Radzinowicz, A History of English Criminal Law and its Administration from 1750, Vol. I (New York: The Macmillan Co., 1948), for a detailed discussion of classical perspectives and the social conditions which gave rise to these notions.

[6] Vold, op. cit., pp. 16–18.

and inequitable punishments to offenders.[7] It was out of these conditions, and a concern for their alleviation, that the classical perspective developed.

Initial attempts to devise specific, detailed, and strict codes following the themes of classical teachings encountered a number of difficulties in practice. As a result, exceptions to penalties were made, and statutes were redrafted giving judges some latitude in application of penalties. Such revisions have continued up to the present, and such developments as the juvenile court movement and the separate, theoretically nonpunitive handling of juvenile lawbreakers, the use of probation and parole, and other innovations have altered the strict form of classical theory and procedure. Nonetheless, it should not be supposed that the classical view of matters has passed from the scene. As we shall see in later chapters of this book, the major outlines of Anglo-Saxon criminal law and procedure are still essentially consistent with classical arguments. Moreover, attempts to deviate from free will premises and from relatively harsh and uniform penalties are usually resisted with considerable fervor by lawyers and citizens alike. For example, recent endeavors to widen the exclusionary operations of courts by freeing mentally disordered individuals from responsibility for their illegal acts represent one prominent case in which modern perspectives on behavior have clashed with the surviving elements of the classical tradition. This battle is not yet won, nor does it yet appear that the classical view will be declared the eventual loser. The prosecutor and the judge are not yet in danger of being replaced by the psychiatrist.

## THE CARTOGRAPHIC SCHOOL

The cartographic or geographic school of criminology pursued the ecological facts of crime, that is, it examined the distribution of forms and rates of criminality among spatial areas.[8] Two of the best-known persons associated with the development of this orientation were Adolphe Quetelet in Belgium and A. M. Guerry in France. Exponents of this approach produced a large series of factual studies of crime and delinquency, many of which have been listed by Lindesmith and Levin.[9]

[7] Radzinowicz has enumerated these practices in great detail. See Radzinowicz, *op. cit.*

[8] Edwin H. Sutherland and Donald R. Cressey, *Principles of Criminology* (7th ed.; Philadelphia: J. B. Lippincott Co., 1966), pp. 55–56.

[9] Alfred Lindesmith and Yale Levin, "The Lombrosian Myth in Criminology," *American Journal of Sociology*, XLII (March 1937), 653–71; see also Levin and Lindesmith, "English Ecology and Criminology of the Past Century," *Journal of Criminal Law and Criminology*, XXVII (March–April 1937), 801–16.

These authors argue that the founding of modern criminology is erroneously attributed to Lombroso, for the cartographic scholars preceded Lombroso's work by 50 years. Moreover, the works of cartographic students have more in common with contemporary criminological efforts than does Lombroso's work.

The cartographic school arose out of the development of systems of social bookkeeping first established in European countries in the 1500's, such as the systematic recording of births and deaths.[10] Quantitative studies of crime began to appear in England and France around 1800. Guerry's ecological study of crime rates in France appeared in 1833, while Quetelet produced an elaborate analysis of crime and social conditions in France, Belgium, Luxembourg, and Holland in 1836.

These early endeavors were forerunners of a long line of studies which have continued to the present. One of these persistent interests has centered about the relationship, if any, between economic conditions and fluctuations in crime and delinquency. Literally hundreds of studies have appeared on this question.[11] Some of the major conclusions from this work are to be discussed in the following section on socialist views, crime, and economic trends.

Another interest stemming from cartographic beginnings is in regional variations in crime. Sutherland and Cressey have enumerated a large number of these investigations which have been carried on since the 1800's.[12] For example, a study by Enrico Ferri showed that homicide convictions varied widely from province to province in major European nations, while another study of major crimes known to the police in England observed that crime rates varied in a relatively stable fashion among regions in that country.[13] As the reader will recall, the commentary in Chapter Five on the epidemiology of crime noted the existence of rural-urban and regional variations in crime rates in the United States. Studies of these patterns by Lottier and Shannon represent relatively modern instances of cartographic investigations.[14]

Another modern version of cartographic interests is to be found in studies of ecological variations in crime and delinquency rates in indi-

---

[10] For a summary of these developments, see Vold, op. cit., pp. 162-65.

[11] Many of these are summarized in Ibid., pp. 165-82.

[12] Sutherland and Cressey, op. cit., pp. 183-87.

[13] Ibid., pp. 183-84.

[14] Stuart Lottier, "Distribution of Criminal Offenses in Metropolitan Regions," Journal of Criminal Law and Criminology, XXIX (May–June 1938), 37–50; Lottier, "Distribution of Criminal Offenses in Sectional Regions," Journal of Criminal Law and Criminology, XXIX (September–October 1938), 329–44; Lyle W. Shannon, "The Spatial Distribution of Criminal Offenses by States," Journal of Criminal Law, Criminology and Police Science, XLV (September–October 1954), 264–73.

vidual cities.[15] The work of Schmid is a notable representative of this kind of activity.[16] In a recent investigation in Seattle, some 35,000 cases of "offenses known to the police" and 30,000 "arrests" were examined from an ecological perspective. Elaborate correlational analyses were undertaken of a number of types of criminal activities and social characteristics of census tracts in Seattle. Among other things, this research showed that certain forms of criminal *acts* are heavily concentrated in the central business district of the city, while others are more common in other parts of the city. Similarly, a variety of concentrations of specific kinds of criminal *persons* is found in different areas in the city. In general, illegal activities and criminal actors are most common in areas of low social cohesion, weak family life, low economic status, physical deterioration of property, high population mobility, and various forms of personal demoralization.

The difficulty with these investigations based on official data is that it is not clear whether they reveal the ecological distribution of criminality, the spatial patterning of police and judicial practices, or some blend of both. The nagging suspicion is that these studies tell us more about law enforcement policies and record keeping than they do about total crime.

Schmid's presentation indicates another characteristic of studies of the cartographic form—the facts do not "speak for themselves." At one time in the development of the behavioral sciences, the naive view was widely held that the job of social science was principally to accumulate a mountain of factual data from which scientific generalizations would automatically emerge. However, we have come to learn that the investigator must speak for the facts—it is his responsibility to interpret empirical observations. In the last section of Schmid's research report, attention is devoted to a *post factum* examination of a number of theories which might account for the results reported. Although studies of the kind carried on by Schmid are important for an understanding of criminality, they do not stand as an equivalent to theory construction and testing. We draw attention to this in order to note a limitation to ecological fact-gathering research endeavors, rather than to indicate a basic flaw in them.

[15] See, as one example, Lyle W. Shannon, "Types and Patterns of Delinquency in a Middle-Sized City," *Journal of Research in Crime and Delinquency*, I (January 1964), 53–66.

[16] Calvin F. Schmid, "A Study of Homicides in Seattle," *Social Forces*, IV (June 1926), 745–56; Schmid, "Urban Crime Areas: Part I," *American Sociological Review*, XXV (August 1960), 527–42; Schmid, "Urban Crime Areas: Part II," *American Sociological Review*, XXV (October 1960), 655–78.

## SOCIALIST VIEWS, CRIME, AND ECONOMIC TRENDS

Socialist explanations of crime grew as an expansion of the economic theory of Karl Marx, first published in 1867.[17] According to socialistic arguments, exploitation of workers in capitalistic societies leads to endemic poverty and misery. In turn, these conditions produce a variety of criminalistic responses, including alcoholism, prostitution, and larceny. The systems of criminal justice prevailing in capitalistic societies protect the exploitive interests of the owner class.[18] Thus prevention of criminality demands reorganization of the economic order along socialist lines.

The most eminent contributor to socialist theories was Dutch sociologist William A. Bonger (1876–1940). He argued that the capitalistic economic system by its very nature encourages *egoism,* that is, the relatively unrestrained pursuit of self-interest.[19] His own summary of his perspective is as follows:

In recapitulating now the egoistic tendencies of the present economic system and of its consequences, we see clearly that they are very strong. Because of these tendencies the social instinct of man is not greatly developed; they have weakened the moral force in man which combats the inclination towards egoistic acts, and hence towards the crimes which are one form of these acts. To mention only the most important things, in a society in which, as in ours, the economic interests of all are in eternal conflict among themselves, compassion for the misfortunes of others inevitably becomes blunted, and a great part of morality consequently disappears. The slight value that is attached to the opinion of others is also a consequence of the strife of economic interests, for we can be responsive to that opinion only when we do not see adversaries in our fellows.[20]

Much of the work of Bonger should have a familiar ring to the modern student of sociology. Bonger's arguments anticipated a host of later sociological analyses of criminality in capitalistic societies, in which a variety of social and economic conditions are held to be involved in the

[17] Karl Marx and Frederick Engels, *Capital* (New York: Random House, Inc., 1906).

[18] For a socialist interpretation of fluctuations in penal policies, see Georg Rusche and Otto Kirchheimer, *Punishment and Social Structure* (New York: Columbia University Press, 1939).

[19] William A. Bonger, *Criminality and Economic Conditions* (Boston: Little, Brown, and Co., 1916); see also William A. Bonger, "The Criminal—A Product of the Capitalistic System," (edited excerpts) in *Criminology,* ed. Clyde B. Vedder, Samuel Koenig, and Robert E. Clark (New York: Dryden Press, 1953), pp. 158–65.

[20] Bonger, in Vedder, Koenig, and Clark, *op. cit.,* p. 164.

genesis of criminality.[21] Bonger's writings bear more than a slight similarity to such recent thinking represented by the delinquency theory of Cloward and Ohlin.[22]

Studies of economic influences on criminality have been numerous since Bonger's early works. In their summary of the principal findings of such inquiries, Sutherland and Cressey note that one conclusion frequently reached is that lower economic class groups have much higher crime rates than upper class groups.[23] A plethora of investigations has been conducted of samples of arrested, convicted, or committed adult or juvenile offenders, all of which show that working class groups are heavily overrepresented in the population of detected lawbreakers. For example, in the Glueck study of 1000 juvenile delinquents in the 1930's, over 70 per cent were found to be from families of marginal or dependent economic status.[24] Ecological studies of the distribution of crime and delinquency rates in cities have repeatedly pointed to the concentration of criminality in lower class neighborhoods.[25] However, Sutherland and Cressey question the validity of the argument that lawbreaking is peculiarly lower class in distribution, on the same grounds as we have earlier challenged this conclusion in Chapter Five. Although it does appear that certain juvenile and adult forms of crime, such as gang delinquency, are disproportionately the activity of working class individuals,[26] the same is not true of "total crime." If statistics were available on white collar offenses and a variety of other kinds of underreported or unreported criminality, the socio-economic picture of illegal conduct might well be quite different.

Studies of fluctuations in crime rates and the business cycle have also been numerous since the days of Bonger.[27] These investigations have been flawed by a variety of theoretical and methodological inadequacies, but taken as a whole they appear to show that serious crimes increase during times of depression, while the general or total crime rate tends not to increase during periods of economic decline. These studies also

21 See, for example, Donald R. Taft and Ralph W. England, Jr., *Criminology* (4th ed.; New York: The Macmillan Co., 1964), pp. 275–79; Robert K. Merton, *Social Theory and Social Structure* (rev. and enl. ed.; New York: Free Press of Glencoe, Inc., 1957), Chaps. 4 and 5.

22 Richard A. Cloward and Lloyd E. Ohlin, *Delinquency and Opportunity* (New York: Free Press of Glencoe, Inc., 1960).

23 Sutherland and Cressey, *op. cit.*, pp. 234–42.

24 *Ibid.*, p. 236.

25 *Ibid.*, p. 239.

26 Albert K. Cohen, *Delinquent Boys* (New York: Free Press of Glencoe, Inc., 1955).

27 Many of these have been summarized in Thorsten Sellin, *Research Memorandum on Crime in the Depression* (New York: Social Science Research Council, 1937); see also Vold, *op. cit.*, pp. 162–81; Sutherland and Cressey, *op. cit.*, pp. 239–41.

suggest that property offenses accompanied by violence increase during depressions, while nonviolent property crimes do not. Drunkenness and crimes against persons do not show any consistent relationship to economic fluctuations, while rates of juvenile delinquency seem to increase during depression periods.

Vold has raised a series of important questions regarding these conclusions. He notes that different assumptions regarding the time interval between the onset of economic changes and alterations in rates of criminality lead to drastically different conclusions from the same basic data.[28] He shows that in a study by Dorothy Thomas of crime rates and economic variations in England and Wales for the period 1857–1913, the correlation coefficient between economic conditions and criminality was −.25 when the crime rates and economic measures for the same years were correlated.[29] However, the correlation between economic conditions for particular years and the crime rates observed *two years later* was +.18. As Vold argues, it makes considerable sense to assume that some time lag is required before economic and business changes have repercussions upon the volume of lawbreaking.

The most sensible conclusion on this issue is equivocal. At best, it appears that the influence of economic changes and business trends upon crime is relatively slight, rather than a markedly strong correlation. The total of criminal behavior is compounded out of many discrete forms of behavior, some of which may be influenced by economic variations, while others may be insensitive to such fluctuations. The causative factors in criminality are doubtless too many and too complex to be easily reflected or measured by the kinds of indices of economic fluctuations that are at hand.

Support for these interpretations can be seen in a recent study of crime trends and economic factors by Glaser and Rice.[30] They found some support for the hypothesis that rates of juvenile delinquency are inversely correlated with unemployment, so that juvenile misconduct is most prominent during times of prosperity. On the other hand, criminality among adults between 18 and 35 years of age seems to be most frequent during periods of widespread unemployment. Glaser and Rice interpret these findings in terms of sociological theories which stress the demoralizing influences of unemployment upon adults.

---

[28] Vold, *op. cit.*, pp. 177–81.

[29] Dorothy Swaine Thomas, *Social Aspects of the Business Cycle* (London: Routledge and Kegan Paul, Ltd., 1925).

[30] Daniel Glaser and Kent Rice, "Crime, Age, and Employment," *American Sociological Review*, XXIV (October 1959), 679–86.

## THE SEARCH FOR BIOLOGICAL TYPES

The central theme of biogenic views is familiar to layman and criminologist alike. The belief that human behavior generally, and criminal behavior specifically, are determined by biological factors is of ancient origins. It is a hypothesis that has been phrased in a variety of ways and which persists in the minds of many citizens today. Vold has identified the core propositions of biological theories as follows: "Back of all physical type theories is the general idea of biological differences in behavior. All biological explanations rest on the basic logic that *structure determines function.* Individuals behave differently owing to the fundamental fact that they are somehow structurally different" (emphasis in the original).[31]

In this section, we shall examine a number of variants upon this common theme. We shall begin with the writings of Lombroso, and follow the elaborations upon biogenic theory and research to the contemporary efforts of Sheldon, directed at the search for temperament and physical type patterns which may be related to criminality. Some of these endeavors can be judged to be preposterous in form, given the benefit of hindsight. Modern behavioral science foundations contradict most of the elements of Lombroso's theories, such as the concept of *atavism* and the hypothesized criminal nature of prehistoric man. But at the time that Lombroso wrote, close on the heels of the appearance of Darwin's evolutionary teachings in *Descent of Man* (1871), claims that criminals constitute evolutionary throwbacks seemed much more plausible. There is a sociology of knowledge, in which particular ideas that develop grow out of social conditions in some era. So it is with criminological views, for they have been the rather natural product of social conditions in different historical periods.

### Lombroso and Positivist Viewpoints

Cesare Lombroso (1835–1909) stands as a giant of criminology, although, as Vold has pointed out, he has often been a misunderstood pioneering figure. Lombroso has often been described as the originator of the theory of atavism and of the criminal as a biological type, without his later, modified views being mentioned, or without recognition of the key role he played in development of the positivist approach to crimi-

---

[31] Vold, *op. cit.*, p. 43.

nality.[32] Positivism refers to an emphasis upon crime as a natural phenomenon, produced by a variety of factors (multiple causation), some of which are biological, others environmental. Lombroso was the original spokesman for a viewpoint which, in broad outlines, is the prevailing criminological opinion of today.

The claims for which Lombroso is most famous center about the notion that the criminal is of different physical type than the noncriminal. According to a frequently told tale, Lombroso, as a physician, was once called upon to perform an autopsy upon a famous Italian brigand. In the course of this autopsy, he discovered a number of physical abnormalities in the brain of the criminal. He was struck by these observations, out of which he formulated the view that criminals are *atavists*, or genetic throwbacks to an earlier kind of human species, *homo delinquens*. Lombroso supposed that modern man, *homo sapiens*, evolved out of this earlier and lower type of human. The earlier species was assumed to be characterized by asocial behavior of various kinds. Accordingly, a contemporary criminal is simply a biological reversion to this primitive form of man. These views were published in *The Criminal Man*, which went through five separate editions. In this book, Lombroso maintained that the degenerate and atavistic criminal type could be identified by a number of characteristics or stigmata, including facial asymmetry, eye defects and peculiarities, ears of unusual size, excessively long arms, and other physical peculiarities.[33]

These are the notions with which Lombroso is usually identified. However, it should be noted that he held that while some offenders were throwbacks, others were not. In the revisions of his book, the manuscript grew in size from several hundred pages to nearly 2000 in length. In the later editions, a host of causal factors were enumerated, in addition to reversion to an earlier biological type. In the mature version of his thinking, Lombroso asserted that there are three major kinds of criminals: (1) *born* criminals, (2) *insane* criminals, and (3) *criminaloids*, who are individuals of normal physical and psychological makeup who commit crimes in unusual circumstances. Less than half of the total population of offenders were asserted to be of the first type.

A mortal assault upon Lombroso's theories of the offender as a physical type was mounted by Charles Goring in the early 1900's.[34] Goring and a number of collaborators undertook a series of careful measurements of

[32] *Ibid.,* pp. 29–32. See Vold's entire discussion of Lombroso, for a detailed and balanced evaluation of Lombroso's place in criminology, pp. 28–32, 50–54.

[33] *Ibid.,* pp. 50–51.

[34] Charles Goring, *The English Convict: A Statistical Study* (London: His Majesty's Stationery Office, 1913). See also Vold, *op. cit.,* pp. 52–55.

approximately 3000 English convicts and large numbers of noncriminals. Almost without exception, the physical anomalies hypothesized by Lombroso were no more common among the prisoners than the nondeviants. In Goring's words, "Our inevitable conclusion must be that *there is no such thing as a physical criminal type*" (emphasis in the original).[35]

The two most famous followers of Lombroso were Enrico Ferri (1856–1928) and Raffaele Garofalo (1852–1934).[36] Ferri was a student under Lombroso who expanded upon the ideas of his teacher, claiming that social, economic, and political factors are involved in crime, as well as the biological causes suggested by Lombroso. Ferri is also recognized for his fourfold classification of offenders as insane, born, occasional, and criminals by passion. These notions are not too different in general form from claims often put forward in contemporary works on criminality.

Garofalo was the third major Italian positivist. Among his other interests, he attempted to formulate a universal definition of "natural" crime, in which he held that the sociological conception of crime refers to offenses that violate the sentiments of probity and pity. In this sense, Garofalo anticipated some of the later concern with such cross-cultural definitions of crime as those of Sellin which we examined in Chapter Two.

Over the years in which positivist perspectives developed, attention veered away from biological hypotheses toward emphasis upon a variety of psychological and sociological dimensions in crime causation. Nonetheless, curiosity regarding biogenic variables continued in a number of forms. This interest was revived most dramatically in the work of Hooton, to which we turn next.

### Hooton's Research

Constitutional or physical type arguments waned in influence for some time following the work of Goring. However, these claims were dramatically resurrected in the work of Harvard physical anthropologist Earnest A. Hooton, published in 1939.[37] This book was the result of a 12-year study of over 13,000 prisoners in ten states, compared with a smaller number of civilian nonoffenders, on some hundred anthropometric measurements. His observations led him to conclude that "the primary cause of crime is biological inferiority."[38] Moreover, Hooton averred that

---

[35] Goring, op. cit., p. 173. Although Goring's conclusion stood almost unchallenged, other investigations in the late 1800's and early 1900's did turn up some apparent physical variations between offenders and nonoffenders. See Vold, op. cit., pp. 55–58.

[36] For a resumé of the works of Ferri and Garofalo, see Vold, op. cit., pp. 32–39.

[37] Earnest A. Hooton, *Crime and the Man* (Cambridge, Mass.: Harvard University Press, 1939).

[38] Ibid., p. 130.

biological inferiority was inherited, so that eugenic programs of sterilization represent the most efficacious solution to criminality. According to Hooton:

... inherently inferior organisms are, for the most part, those which succumb to the adversities or temptations of their social environment and fall into antisocial behavior ... it is impossible to improve and correct environment to a point at which these flawed and degenerate human beings will be able to succeed in honest social competition.[39]

In spite of the impressive number of subjects in this research, Hooton's work was greeted with hostility and criticism by sociologists, criminologists, and anthropologists.[40] The major deficiencies in Hooton's research are clear.[41] His control groups of nonoffenders were small in size and markedly unrepresentative of noncriminal citizens as a whole. The control group of 1976 persons included 146 municipal firemen from Nashville, Tennessee, along with an odd assortment of militiamen, bathhouse patrons, and outpatients from Boston. Some of the subgroups within the control sample differed more from each other than they did from the prisoners. A second defect of Hooton's work was that many of the subsamples on which he based ethnic comparisons between convicts and civilians were extremely small. A third counterargument to Hooton's conclusions is that, even if one assumed that the research techniques in this investigation were adequate, prisoners do not constitute a representative sample of criminals. There are good reasons for supposing that those offenders who fall into the hands of the police, and later into prison, might be in poorer physical shape than those who escape detection. Finally, one of the most devastating criticisms of Hooton's work is that he had no explicit criterion of "biological inferiority." As Vold notes:

His method of translating physical deviations into evidence of inferiority is nowhere made clear. Unless there is independent evidence of the inferiority of certain kinds of physical characteristics, conclusions regarding inferiority must be drawn from the association with criminality—a nice illustration of circular reasoning: use the criminality to discover the inferiority, then turn around and use the inferiority to explain or account for the criminality.[42]

[39] Ibid., p. 388.
[40] Some of these evaluations of Hooton's work are Robert K. Merton and M. F. Ashley Montagu, "Crime and the Anthropologist," American Anthropologist, XLII (July–September 1941), 384–408; James S. Wallerstein and Clement J. Wyle, "Biological Inferiority as a Cause for Delinquency," Nervous Child, VI (October 1947), 467–72; N. S. Timasheff, "The Revival of Criminal Anthropology," University of Kansas Law Review, IX (February 1941), 91–100; William B. Tucker, "Is There Evidence of a Physical Basis for Criminal Behavior?" Journal of Criminal Law and Criminology, XXXI (November–December 1940), 427–37.
[41] Sutherland and Cressey, op. cit., pp. 128–29; Korn and McCorkle, op. cit., pp. 216–19; Vold, op. cit., pp. 59–64.
[42] Vold, op. cit., p. 64.

### Some Other Lines of Activity

The preceding commentary has centered upon some of the more prominent and influential inquiries into biological factors in criminality. However, there are other interests which have been popular at different stages in criminological history. For example, the now discredited phrenological arguments of Franz Joseph Gall (1758–1828) and John Gaspar Spurzheim (1776–1832) were at one time thought to represent powerful explanations of behavior generally and criminality specifically.[43] Persons of phrenological persuasion argued that conformations of the skull reveal "faculties" or propensities to behavior which are the product of biological inheritance. Criminals were held to be deficient in some of the normal faculties influencing behavior.

A related line of analysis, prominent in the past, centered on the hypothesis that tendencies toward criminality are inherited.[44] In this view, "like father—like son," so criminal parents pass on to their offspring genetic tendencies toward lawbreaking. One kind of evidence brought forth to demonstrate the hereditary transmission of deviant tendencies concerns studies of identical (one-egg) and fraternal (two-egg) twins.[45] The logic is that environmental influences are controlled or constant for twins, so if hereditary influences are of importance in behavior, the one-egg twins should show concordance or similar behavior. If one is a criminal, the other should also be a deviant. However, the two-egg twins should show more discordant behavior, for they do not share the same hereditary backgrounds. Those investigations which have made such comparisons have turned up evidence of greater concordance of behavior among one-egg than two-egg twins, hence these analyses seem to constitute proof of hereditary transmission. Yet the assessment of most biologists is that such a conclusion is not in order, in view of some serious defects in these studies. All of them are based on very small samples. Identification of identical twins is fraught with possibilities of error because it rests on observation of external physical characteristics. Insofar as mistakes are made, they tend to be in the direction of misidentification of fraternal twins as identical, so that observations are biased in favor of the hereditary hypothesis. A third point has been raised

43 *Ibid.,* pp. 44–49.

44 These arguments are summarized in Sutherland and Cressey, *op. cit.,* pp. 123–28.

45 A number of these studies are summarized and criticized in M. F. Ashley Montagu, "The Biologist Looks at Crime," *Annals of the American Academy of Political and Social Science,* CCXVII (September 1941), 46–57; a good discussion of these studies can be found in Korn and McCorkle, *op. cit.,* pp. 198–204.

to the effect that environmental influences are not controlled in these comparisons, for identical twins may receive more comparable parental treatment than do two-egg twins. Consequently, whatever concordance of behavior might be observed could be attributable to environmental influences.

There are fundamental difficulties which plague all attempts to discover hereditary influences upon behavior, criminality included. Korn and McCorkle have identified some of the theoretical issues which must be untangled if hereditary influences are to be identified.[46] For one thing, hereditary and environmental influences are in interaction with one another almost from the point of conception of the human organism. As a consequence, it is almost impossible to separate the unique contribution heredity makes to behavior of any kind.

An additional complication facing those who would attribute criminality to hereditary factors is that modern genetic theory indicates that inherited traits are specific in nature, so that a person inherits blue eyes, hair color, and so on. But criminal behavior is not specific, in that it covers a wide gamut of activities. Moreover, many individual criminals engage in an assortment of criminal acts. How can genetic endowment account for this variability? Perhaps offenders inherit general tendencies to break laws. This is a flawed argument, for it runs counter to genetic theory. Also, most criminals obey most laws. Their behavior does not square with any hypothesis of inherited general "badness."

By way of summary on the hereditary transmission theory, Korn and McCorkle have this to say: "The enormous labor expended in the search for hereditary causes of crime illustrates the extent to which research may be diverted into blind alleys by careless definition of terms and by a failure to examine the implications of an underlying point of view." [47]

One final piece of work on biological correlates of criminality is found in the writings of the endocrinologists. Following the arguments of Berman and others in the 1920's on the relationships of glandular processes and personality, several persons attempted to devise theories showing that criminality is due to endocrine malfunctioning.[48] The writings of Schlapp and Smith represent the best-known of such statements, in which extreme and speculative claims were put forth asserting that the explanation of criminality is to be found in glandular malfunctioning.[49] However, in general, careful research which has been carried out has

[46] Korn and McCorkle, op. cit., pp. 202–4.

[47] Ibid., p. 204.

[48] Louis Berman, The Glands Regulating Personality (New York: The Macmillan Co., 1921); Berman, New Creations in Human Beings (New York: Doubleday & Company, Inc., 1938).

[49] Max G. Schlapp and Edward H. Smith, The New Criminology (New York: Boni and Liveright, 1928).

failed to support these claims. The general position of most endocrinologists at present is that not nearly enough is yet known about endocrine functioning for us to be able to identify with accuracy personality consequences of endocrine patterns or connections of endocrine malfunctioning to criminality.[50]

### Body Type, Temperament, and Criminality

When one of Shakespeare's characters uttered the injunction, "Beware yon Cassius for he hath a lean and hungry look, such men are dangerous, they think too much," he was expressing a theme of ancient origin and widespread popularity. This is the thesis that man's behavior is to be explained by his physical structure, so that fat men are also jolly men because corpulence produces a jovial temperament, while slim persons are destined to be introverted. Ideas of this kind have been extended to the area of criminality, and it has sometimes been supposed that deviance is a function of physical structure. Two contemporary versions of this thesis are to be found in the works of Kretschmer and of Sheldon.[51] Kretschmer is a German scholar who produced a book in the 1920's arguing that certain patterns of physical structure lead to particular temperament types, and that, in turn, specific kinds of mental disorder and criminality are related to these somatic and personality structures. Kretschmer and others have reported research findings which suggest a relationship between body type and patterns of criminality, but fail to demonstrate the hypothesized temperament linkages to these patterns.[52]

The most recent version of the body type and temperament argument is to be found in the work of Sheldon and associates.[53] Sheldon has asserted that somatic structure can be classified in terms of the degree to which *endomorphic, mesomorphic,* or *ectomorphic* physical characteristics are most apparent in different individuals. He argues that *viscerotonic, somotonic,* or *cerebrotonic* temperament patterns tend to accom-

[50] R. G. Hoskins, *Endocrinology* (New York: W. W. Norton Co., 1941).

[51] Summaries of the work of Sheldon and Kretschmer can be found in Vold, *op. cit.,* pp. 66–74; Korn and McCorkle, *op. cit.,* pp. 219–23; Sutherland and Cressey, *op. cit.,* p. 130.

[52] For a description of Kretschmer's work, see Vold, *op. cit.,* pp. 68–69; American research following Kretschmer's notions is found in George J. Mohr and Ralph H. Gundlach, "The Relation Between Physique and Performance," *Journal of Experimental Psychology,* X (April 1927), 117–57; Mohr and Gundlach, "A Further Study of the Relations Between Physique and Performance in Criminals," *Journal of Abnormal and Social Psychology,* XXIV (April–June 1929), 91–103.

[53] William H. Sheldon, S. S. Stevens, and W. B. Tucker, *Varieties of Human Physique* (New York: Harper & Row, 1940); Sheldon and Stevens, *Varieties of Temperament* (New York: Harper & Row, 1942); Sheldon, Emil M. Hartl, and Eugene McDermott, *Varieties of Delinquent Youth* (New York: Harper & Row, 1949).

pany certain of the body types. He has developed scales for measuring these dimensions, in which individuals are scored on each component on a range from 1 to 7, with the largest score denoting predominance of that particular somatic pattern. Vold has summarized the characteristics of the somatic and personality patterns: [54]

Sheldon's Basic Types:

| *Physique* | *Temperament* |
|---|---|
| 1. *Endomorphic:* relatively great development of digestive viscera; tendency to put on fat; soft roundness through various regions of the body; short tapering limbs; small bones; soft, smooth, velvety skin. | 1. *Viscerotonic:* general relaxation of body; a comfortable person; loves soft luxury; a "softie" but still essentially an extrovert. |
| 2. *Mesomorphic:* relative predominance of muscles, bone, and the motor-organs of the body; large trunk; heavy chest; large wrists and hands; if "lean" a hard rectangularity of outline; if "not lean" they fill out heavily. | 2. *Somotonic:* active, dynamic person; walks, talks, gestures assertively; behaves aggressively. |
| 3. *Ectomorphic:* relative predominance of skin and its appendages which includes the nervous system; lean, fragile, delicate body; small, delicate bones; droopy shoulders; small face, sharp nose, fine hair; relatively little body mass and relatively great surface area. | 3. *Cerebrotonic:* an introvert; full of functional complaints, allergies, skin troubles, chronic fatigue, insomnia; sensitive to noise and distractions; shrinks from crowds. |

Although it is obvious that individuals come in various shapes and sizes and variations in physique do exist, it is by no means clear that the hypothesized temperament relationships to body structure are correct. Sheldon's research has so far failed to convincingly demonstrate the accuracy of that hypothesis. On the subject of criminality, several attempts have been made to extend the somatotype argument to the area of deviant behavior. In one study of several hundred residents of the Hayden Goodwill Inn in Boston, a specialized rehabilitation home for boys, Sheldon claims to have demonstrated linkages between delinquency and certain body types.[55] However, the critics have not been kind to Sheldon, pointing out that he employed a loose and atypical definition of delinquency, centering around a notion of "disappointing-

[54] Vold, op. cit., p. 71.
[55] Sheldon, Hartl, and McDermott, op. cit.

ness" rather than upon involvement in illegal behavior. His methodological procedures were deficient in other ways, too, so he failed to provide a convincing case for these hypotheses.[56] Another study of this kind was carried on by the Gluecks, who indicate that the delinquent boys in their sample were somewhat more mesomorphic or athletic in bodily structure than were the nondelinquents in this investigation.[57] But there is nothing particularly surprising about such a discovery, for it could be argued that delinquent subcultures recruit new members selectively, placing a premium upon agile, muscular boys because these are characteristics that make for a successful career in delinquent role behavior. Excessively fat or overly thin and sickly youngsters make poor candidates for the rough and tumble world of delinquent behavior, so they are excluded from delinquent peer groups. If so, this is a social process, not a biologically determined pattern of behavior.

## FEEBLEMINDEDNESS AND CRIME

The most popular single theory of crime causation adhered to by laymen, and by many serious investigators as well, is that offenders are defective in some psychological fashion. In this view, the causes of crime and delinquency are "inside the person." An early version of this theme sought for the mainsprings of deviance in feeblemindedness, while later forms of this frame of reference have centered on the search for mental abnormality in the form of psychotic symptoms in offenders. The modern variant of this orientation is concerned with the possibility that lawbreakers are responding to a variety of subtle kinds of emotional problems.[58] This chapter will review the first of these hypotheses, while Chapter Seven will be devoted to a detailed examination of current psychogenic perspectives on criminality.

It will become abundantly apparent in this section and in Chapter Seven that our view is that many psychological claims of one kind or another are clearly erroneous, while others represent gross overstatements. While some lawbreakers may be responding to emotional tensions,

[56] Edwin H. Sutherland, "Critique of Sheldon's Varieties of Delinquent Youth," American Sociological Review, XVI (February 1951), 10–13; S. L. Washburn, "Review of W. H. Sheldon's Varieties of Delinquent Youth," American Anthropologist, LIII (October–November 1951), 561–63.

[57] Sheldon and Eleanor Glueck, Physique and Delinquency (New York: Harper & Row, 1956).

[58] General discussions of the feeblemindedness investigations are contained in Vold, op. cit., pp. 75–89, and Korn and McCorkle, op. cit., pp. 259–67. A useful review of this entire body of inquiry can be found in Lawson G. Lowrey, "Delinquent and Criminal Personalities," in Personality and the Behavior Disorders, II, ed. J. McV. Hunt (New York: The Ronald Press Co., 1944), pp. 794–821.

many of them are not. In all probability, the majority of offenders are no more or less "normal" than are nonoffenders. We agree with Cohen, who has argued that: "A major task before us is to get rid of the notion, so pervasive in sociological thinking, that the deviant, the abnormal, the pathological, and, in general, the deplorable always come wrapped in a single package." [59]

At one time in the history of criminology, the thesis that criminality is the product of low mentality was exceedingly popular. This theory averred that general hereditary degeneracy, including feeblemindedness, leads to criminality in that the physically and intellectually degenerate individual is unable to cope with life circumstances in a normal and satisfactory fashion.

This argument regarding criminality and social deviation grew out of a series of studies of families, disguised by such fictitious names as the Jukes, Kallikaks, and Nams,[60] that came to light in the late 1800's and early 1900's. In each of these, a long family line of social misfits was produced by ancestors who were presumably feebleminded. The conclusion from these observations was that feeblemindedness is inherited and leads to social inadequacy, deviation, and criminality. Subsequent inquiry on the question of low mentality has, of course, indicated that the simple hereditary transmission view of feeblemindedness is in error. It is now clear that the involvement of successive generations of individuals in deviant behavior is probably the result of *social* transmission.

In the early 1900's, the development of intelligence tests led to the application of these measures to samples of offenders. Initial results seemed to confirm the picture of lawbreakers as uncommonly characterized by mental impairment. Thus Goddard reported results of different studies showing that very high percentages of the criminals investigated were feebleminded.[61] Goddard was moved to conclude from these data that: "It can no longer be denied that the greatest single cause of delinquency and crime is low-grade mentality, much of it within the limits of feeble-mindedness." [62]

All of these early studies of the intelligence of criminal persons were carried on without control group comparisons and without knowledge of

[59] Albert K. Cohen, "Social Disorganization and Deviant Behavior," in Sociology Today, ed. Robert K. Merton, Leonard Broom, and Leonard S. Cottrell, Jr. (New York: Basic Books, Inc., 1959), p. 463.

[60] Richard L. Dugdale, The Jukes (New York: Putnam, 1877); Henry H. Goddard, The Kallikak Family (New York: The Macmillan Co., 1912); A. H. Estabrook, The Jukes in 1915 (Washington, D.C.: Carnegie Institute, 1916); A. H. Estabrook and C. B. Davenport, The Nam Family (Lancaster, Pa.: New Era Publishing Co., 1912).

[61] Henry H. Goddard, Feeblemindedness: Its Causes and Consequences (New York: The Macmillan Co., 1914).

[62] Henry H. Goddard, Juvenile Delinquency (New York: Dodd, Mead and Co., 1921), p. 22.

the average mental age of law-abiding citizens. Instead, it was assumed that the average citizen had attained a mental age of 16, that is, that he had a test performance in which he responded correctly to all the questions asked of 16 year old individuals. Measured against this standard, criminals seemed to be markedly deficient in intelligence. The error of these studies came to light with the publication of intelligence test results from the World War I draft experience. The average mental age of adult draftees, presumably a representative sample of law-abiding citizens, turned out to be 13.08, not 16! [63] In short, citizens proved to be less intelligent than had been supposed. When criminal samples were compared to the standard from the army testing, the offenders appeared to be no more defective than the draftees. Thus Sutherland discovered that the average proportion of criminals diagnosed as feebleminded in some 350 studies surveyed was about 50 per cent for the period 1910–1914, but only about 20 per cent for the 1925–1928 period.[64] Systematic comparisons of prisoners and draftees were carried out by Murchison and by Tulchin, showing negligible differences in intelligence between the two groups.[65] In summary, it is now evident that low mentality is not a significant cause of criminality. There are intelligent criminals and stupid ones, just as there are intelligent and stupid nonoffenders, but the proportions of high and low mentality citizens and lawbreakers are approximately equal.

It is quite possible that if the evidence were at hand, it would show one relationship of intelligence variations to criminality. It would not be surprising if prison inmates showed intelligence test scores lower on the average than those of nonincarcerated offenders. It seems likely that one of the contingencies which influences the probability of apprehension, conviction, and incarceration is intelligence. Quite probably, prisons are collection places for the less able among the criminal population, in the same way that unskilled jobs tend to be the occupational niche to which many of the dullards in the general population are allocated.

A second point regarding intelligence patterns is the likelihood that different criminal role patterns are occupied by individuals who vary in mentality. One of the factors which probably helps to determine which offenders become recruits to skilled professional forms of criminality is intelligence. Similarly, one might expect to find that certain kinds of

[63] For a summary of the results of World War I testing, see Vold, op. cit., pp. 82–83.

[64] Edwin H. Sutherland, "Mental Deficiency and Crime," in Social Attitudes, ed. Kimball Young (New York: Holt, Rinehart and Winston, Inc., 1931), pp. 357–75.

[65] Carl Murchison, Criminal Intelligence (Worcester, Mass.: Clark University Press, 1926); Simon Tulchin, Intelligence and Crime (Chicago: University of Chicago Press, 1939); see also Leslie D. Zeleny, "Feeble-mindedness and Criminal Conduct," American Journal of Sociology, XXXVIII (January 1933), 564–76.

criminals, such as embezzlers, abortionists, and white collar offenders, would exhibit higher intelligence than many other kinds of lawbreakers, in that they are occupants of law-abiding occupations which are selective and draw from the college-trained in American society.

There is no systematic body of evidence available on the question of intelligence differences among prisoners and nonincarcerated offenders, or between different criminal types. However, intelligence correlations may well exist. While it is one thing to deny causal significance to feeble-mindedness or low mentality, it is another to claim that there are no intelligence correlations whatsoever. They quite possibly exist.

## SUMMARY

This chapter has dealt with a number of past endeavors to make sense out of criminality. Our evaluation of most of these has been that they have been proved unfruitful. Whatever the explanation of lawbreaking, it is not to be found in defective heredity, biological taint, or in the other formulations presented in this chapter. But what of modern attempts to discover the causal processes in crime? It is to this topic that the next several chapters turn. One of the most widely-held views of crime is that it is the work of individuals with psychological or emotional problems. Chapter Seven is devoted to theories and evidence on psychogenic factors in criminal deviance.

# 7

# Causal Analysis
## Psychogenic
## Approaches

## INTRODUCTION

This chapter continues the overview of basic approaches to causal analysis begun in Chapter Six. This survey is aimed at showing the major directions taken by psychiatric and psychological views. We will comment upon specific psychogenic theories and research as they bear upon offender role patterns in the chapters on specific criminal types, so the present chapter is a general introductory statement.

We noted in Chapter One that the psychogenic approach is devoted predominantly to social-psychological questions regarding criminality and delinquency, so that it attempts to specify the factors which result in lawbreaking by particular actors. The central hypothesis is that the critical causal factors or variables center around personality problems to which criminal deviance is presumed to be a response. Aichhorn, a pioneering figure in the development of this perspective, has declared regarding delinquent behavior: "There must be something in the child himself which the environment brings out in the form of delinquency." [1] Criminals and delinquents behave as they do because they are in some way "sick" or "maladjusted." Aichhorn's statement also indicates a second premise of psychogenic perspectives, that the environment may act as a precipitating but never as a primary force in causation. However, as we shall see in later sections of this chapter, different psychogenic statements accord varying weight to the influences of environmental pressures. Thus psychogenic arguments have given more or less attention to environmental or social factors.

Concentration of effort upon social-psychological types of causal questions has introduced a fundamental ambiguity into psychiatric formulations. These arguments are nearly always mute regarding *rates* of deviance. While it is entirely permissible to concentrate one's energies upon some portion or body of causal questions, and give less emphasis to other explanatory problems, it is necessary in the interest of clarity to identify where partial answers articulate or mesh with hypotheses accounting for

[1] August Aichhorn, *Wayward Youth* (New York: Meridian Books, 1955), p. 30.

other parts of the phenomena to be explained. The issue here is the matter of differential rates of criminality among the different social classes and among other segments of the population. Official data regarding conventional criminality, to which psychogenic propositions are usually applied, suggest that this kind of illegality is heavily concentrated in lower class groups, minority groups, and so forth. How are psychogenic claims, emphasizing personality problems of offenders, to be reconciled with these epidemiological observations?

Several possibilities can be entertained to make psychological hypotheses compatible with epidemiological observations. One proposition would be that personality problems, however widespread or relatively uncommon they might be, are not class-concentrated. These personality pathologies lead to criminality under certain environmental stresses, but eventuate in other responses in different environmental settings. It could be argued that middle class individuals solve their emotional tensions in noncriminal ways. Such a possibility is certainly plausible enough. Perhaps a severe condition of social deprivation is required in order to impel emotionally upset individuals toward criminality, while in a less stressful set of social circumstances emotional tensions can be discharged in noncriminal avenues.

A second argument that would contend with epidemiological observations would hold that personality problems are common at all social class levels. Further, these personality dynamics result in criminality as a common response in all class groups, but differential law enforcement practices result in lower status individuals becoming officially designated as offenders, while middle class persons remain "hidden," undetected criminals. A third proposition might be advanced to the effect that personality problems and criminality are both concentrated in lower class groups, so that middle class persons are both noncriminal in behavior and well-adjusted in terms of mental health.[2]

At this juncture, we are not concerned with adjudicating among these several possibilities. In fact, our bias is toward a fourth possibility, that personality problems are not commonly exhibited by conventional offenders at all. However, the point is simply that most psychiatric formulations have failed to be concerned with epidemiological issues, so they are ambiguous on the question of how such claims fit with the apparent facts of criminality.

[2] Several studies have been conducted on the issue of class linkages and mental disorder, with results that are not entirely clear. See August B. Hollingshead and Fredrick C. Redlich, *Social Class and Mental Illness* (New York: John Wiley and Sons, Inc., 1958); Leo Srole, Thomas S. Langner, Stanley T. Michael, Marvin K. Opler, and Thomas A. C. Rennie, *Mental Health in the Metropolis: The Midtown Manhattan Study* (New York: McGraw-Hill Book Co., Inc., 1962).

The psychogenic perspective, largely the product of psychiatrists, has been a major theme in etiological analysis, with a large number of articles and books presenting causal theories and research in these terms. This approach has been the dominant influence in the development of treatment theories and processes. The rise of the rehabilitative orientation in corrections has centered, for the most part, around the growth of individual treatment policies and theories in which it has been argued that offenders are emotionally "sick." Prison programs, probation services, guidance clinics, juvenile courts, and other treatment agencies have considered the lawbreaker as an emotionally disturbed person in need of psychotherapeutic treatment, almost to the exclusion of any other tactic.[3]

The present chapter will attempt to summarize the basic outlines of the psychogenic perspective. This is no small job, so we need a taxanomic scheme if we are to present a satisfactory resumé and critique of the many variants of psychogenic theory and research endeavors.

## FORMS OF PSYCHOGENIC ANALYSIS

The first matter to be disposed of in a review of psychiatric formulations is the now defunct concern with the hypothesis that criminals are to be explained as sufferers from some form of psychosis or some other marked pattern of mental disorder. This is one of those early ideas which failed to pass the test of evidence. The major portion of this chapter will be devoted to examination of a number of contemporary psychogenic perspectives which, in one form or another, advance the thesis that offenders are to be understood as responding to relatively subtle psychological forces, rather than to some kind of gross pathology. The *psychoanalytic* position is one of these variants, growing out of the framework of psychoanalytic theory developed by Freud and extended to crime and delinquency by Aichhorn, Friedlander, and others. In addition, there are a host of more *general arguments* regarding misbehavior and personality problems which do not stem directly from psychoanalytic thought, such as the work of Healy and Bronner, Hewitt and Jenkins, the Gluecks, and many others. A third argument is that criminal deviance is the product of *psychopathic* or *sociopathic* personality structures.

In the material to follow, psychogenic statements regarding both criminals and delinquents will be noted. There are several reasons for discussing psychiatric claims about juvenile delinquents. Many of the most detailed versions of psychiatric viewpoints have been concerned with

---

[3] One analysis of the theoretical foundations of correctional treatment theory is Don C. Gibbons, *Changing the Lawbreaker* (Englewood Cliffs, N.J.: Prentice-Hall, Inc., 1965).

delinquents. Many psychogenic arguments imply that they hold for adult and juvenile lawbreakers alike. Finally, separation of adult from youthful offenders is often an arbitrary distinction, in that many juvenile delinquents eventually become adult criminals. If personality problems and emotional tensions are involved in juvenile misconduct, they are also indirectly implicated in the causation of adult criminality.

The concluding part of this chapter articulates some psychogenic considerations which must be attended to in the development of etiological theory. Our view is that certain psychological formulations are essential elements of crime causation and cannot be overlooked if criminality is to be explained.[4] There are some kinds of criminal behavior in which emotional tensions play a highly significant causal role. However, as will become clear in the discussions to follow, a number of improvements are needed in psychogenic theory and research before psychogenic formulations can be amalgamated with sociogenic views.

## MENTAL DISORDER AND CRIME

Following the demise of the feeblemindedness theory of criminality, the idea grew that criminality is often attributable to serious forms of mental disorder or impairment. In the early enthusiasm for this view, very large proportions of offenders were diagnosed as suffering from mental pathology. Thus 99.5 per cent of the inmates at the Pontiac Reformatory in Illinois during the decade 1919 to 1929, were classified as psychiatrically abnormal, and most were diagnosed as "psychopathic."[5] A frequently cited study of Sing Sing inmates by Bernard Glueck classified 12 per cent of the prisoners as mentally diseased or deteriorated, along with 19 per cent as "psychopathic personalities."[6] At the same time, a summary of surveys of the incidence of mental disorders among offenders, carried out before 1931, showed wide variations from one jurisdiction to another in the prevalence and forms of pathology reported.[7] A strong impression emerges from this early work that it reveals more about the biases and preconceptions of the psychiatrists and other diagnosticians than it does about the actual characteristics of offenders.

[4] For one comment on this point, see Stanton Wheeler, "The Social Sources of Criminology," *Sociological Inquiry*, XXXII (Spring 1962), 144–45.

[5] Paul W. Tappan, *Crime, Justice and Correction* (New York: McGraw-Hill Book Co., Inc., 1960), p. 117. Tappan has summarized a relatively large body of related studies of criminality and mental disorder in *loc. cit.*, pp. 117–19.

[6] Bernard Glueck, "Concerning Prisoners," *Mental Hygiene*, II (April 1918), 177–218.

[7] Morris Ploscowe, *Some Causative Factors in Criminality*, Vol. 1 of the Reports of the National Commission on Law Observance and Enforcement (Washington, D.C.: U.S. Government Printing Office, 1931).

After the first enthusiasm for the psychopathological hypothesis, inquiries into the extent of psychotic disorders and other gross forms of pathology among criminals involved estimates that these conditions are not much more common in offenders than among law-abiding citizens. One such investigation by the psychiatric clinic of the Court of General Sessions in New York between 1932 and 1935 involved nearly 10,000 felons, of whom only 1.5 per cent were diagnosed as psychotic, 6.9 per cent as psychoneurotic, 6.9 per cent as psychopathic, and 2.4 per cent as feebleminded.[8] Stated differently, 82.3 per cent of the individuals passing through that court were diagnosed as "normal," although they were regarded as exhibiting mild forms of some kind of personality maladjustment. A similar report by Schilder for the same court in 1937 indicated substantially the same thing, classifying 83.8 per cent of the offenders as "normal."[9] Dunham's study of over 500 males committed to the Illinois Security Hospital as criminally insane reached parallel conclusions.[10] According to Dunham, schizophrenia is a negligible factor in the causation of crime, although when criminal behavior and mental disorder are found together in the same person, schizophrenia is more often involved as the form of pathology than are other kinds of disturbance. In turn, schizophrenic disorders are most common in cases of crimes against persons. Results parallel to these were found in another investigation by Erickson.[11]

By now it seems established that few criminals are psychotics. These are two different and independent forms of deviance. As this version of psychopathological theory has proved untenable, interest has shifted toward the hypothesis that offenders are responding to more subtle forms of pathology. One of these modern, currently popular views is the psychoanalytic, to which we now turn.

## PSYCHOANALYTIC THEORIES

A brief summary of Freudian arguments regarding human personality development and criminality is contained in the next several pages, but before we begin this resumé, several disclaimers and cautionary remarks

8 Walter Bromberg and Charles B. Thompson, "The Relation of Psychosis, Mental Defect and Personality Types to Crime," Journal of Criminal Law and Criminology, XXVIII (May–June 1937), 70–89; see also Walter Bromberg, Crime and the Mind (Philadelphia: J. B. Lippincott Co., 1948).

9 Paul Schilder, "The Cure of Criminals and Prevention of Crime," Journal of Criminal Psychopathology, II (October 1940), 152.

10 H. Warren Dunham, "The Schizophrene and Criminal Behavior," American Sociological Review, IV (June 1939), 352–61.

11 M. H. Erickson, "Criminality In a Group of Male Psychiatric Patients," Mental Hygiene, XXII (July 1938), 459–76.

are in order.[12] Without doubt, the psychoanalytic position has been the single most influential nineteenth and twentieth century statement on human behavior.[13] It is an extremely complex body of thought, for the theory originally presented in a number of volumes by Freud has been expanded and modified by psychiatrists and other theorists in a voluminous literature. Similarly, psychoanalytic essays on crime and delinquency are numerous, lengthy, and complex. It would be an impossible goal to try to do justice to either the general theory or applications of it to criminality in a few pages, so what we present here is a necessarily brief and terse summary.[14]

## The Psychoanalytic Argument

Although psychoanalytic thought originated in the writings of Sigmund Freud (1835–1939),[15] there are presently a number of versions of psychoanalytic theory, inasmuch as Freud's original arguments were elaborated and revised by himself and such persons as Carl Jung, Alfred Adler, Wilhelm Reich, Theodore Reik, and Karen Horney, among others. The basic thesis has been changed considerably over time. Some of the present-day versions remain orthodox and similar to the original views of Freud, while others, such as the writings of Horney, represent drastic

[12] A brief outline of psychoanalytic views and the development of this perspective is found in George B. Vold, *Theoretical Criminology* (New York: Oxford University Press, 1958), pp. 114–25; see also Richard R. Korn and Lloyd W. McCorkle, *Criminology and Penology* (New York: Holt, Rinehart and Winston, Inc., 1959), pp. 253–57.

[13] Richard T. LaPiere, *The Freudian Ethic* (New York: Duell, Sloan and Pearce, 1959). LaPiere makes a case for a very pervasive influence of Freudian thought in twentieth-century America which he views as extremely unfortunate. However, the reviewers have not been altogether kindly in their evaluation of this thesis. For example, see the review by Kaspar D. Naegele in *American Sociological Review*, XXV (June 1960), 422–23.

[14] Hakeem has authored several critiques of Freudian notions, along with other psychiatric formulations in criminology. See Michael Hakeem, "A Critique of the Psychiatric Approach," in *Juvenile Delinquency*, ed. Joseph S. Roucek (New York: Philosophical Library, 1958), pp. 79–112; Hakeem, "A Critique of the Psychiatric Approach to Crime and Correction," *Law and Contemporary Problems*, XXIII (Autumn 1958), 650–82.

[15] Sigmund Freud, *The Ego and the Id*, trans. Joan Riviere (London: Hogarth Press, 1927); Freud, *A General Introduction to Psychoanalysis* (New York: Boni and Liveright, 1920); Freud, *Civilization and its Discontents*, trans. Joan Riviere (London: Hogarth Press, 1953); Freud, *The Basic Writings of Sigmund Freud*, trans. and ed. A. A. Brill (New York: The Modern Library, 1938); A. A. Brill, *Freud's Contribution to Psychiatry* (New York: W. W. Norton and Co., 1944); Patrick Mullahy, *Oedipus: Myth and Complex* (New York: Hermitage Press, Inc., 1952); Bartlett H. Stoodley, *The Concepts of Sigmund Freud* (New York: Free Press of Glencoe, Inc., 1959). For a relatively brief but lucid and careful summary of psychoanalytic thought, see Calvin S. Hall and Gardner Lindzey, "Psychoanalytic Theory and its Application in the Social Sciences," *Handbook of Social Psychology*, ed. Gardner Lindzey (Cambridge, Mass.: Addison-Wesley Publishing Co., Inc., 1954), pp. 143–80.

departures from some of the basic postulates.[16] What follows is a version of psychoanalytic theory in the direction of the original views of Freud. This has been the dominant form that has been applied to the explanation of criminal and delinquent behavior.

Three propositions are at the heart of psychoanalytic thought. First, it is held that behavior is largely the product of psychological-biological forces ("drives" or "instincts") which are unconscious in nature and are not directly perceived or understood by the actor. Second, functional behavior disorders, including criminality, arise out of conflicts related to these basic drives. These behavioral pathologies may be the result of the repression of instinctual energy which presses for recognition in disguised form, or they may be the product of inadequate socialization, so that normal control over impulses is lacking. Third, it is argued that in order to modify the undesirable behaviors of a person, he must be guided toward insight into the unconscious roots of his responses so he can develop control over such impulses. This process of gaining insight is by means of psychoanalysis or some variant, in which a skilled psychoanalyst or therapist uncovers the basis of behavior through dream analysis, free associations, and other observations which point to unconscious motivational factors.

According to Freudians, human personality is made up of a trio of provinces or components. Newborn infants enter the world with an energy reservoir of instinctive, biological drives which are uncontaminated by external reality and undifferentiated in terms of object at birth. This component of personality is the *Id,* or instinctual forces, a major but not exclusive part of which centers around sexual drives in a broadly defined sense. At this point, the human organism is prepared to behave only in terms of the *pleasure principle,* toward the discharge of instinctual energy or tension whenever it arises.

However, soon after birth the *Ego* begins to develop. The autistic, self-absorbed infant begins to acquire an awareness of self as distinct from the surrounding environment, and begins to adapt his drives to the exigencies of reality. Expression of instinctual drives may have to be temporarily postponed due to unavailability of a suitable outlet or the wishes of other persons in the immediate environment. The Ego represents that outgrowth of the Id which adapts the instinctual urges to one another and to the demands of reality. As such, the Ego operates as the executive of the personality. Under the influence of the external world, one part of the Id undergoes a special development in order to act as

---

[16] For a summary of the various schools of psychoanalytic thought, see Ruth S. Monroe, *Schools of Psychoanalytic Thought* (New York: Dryden Press, 1955).

intermediary between the Id and the world of reality. This is the Ego, which determines whether an instinct shall be allowed to obtain satisfaction or be suppressed. Decisions of this kind are reached by the Ego in terms of the *reality principle*, in that Ego attempts to allow or postpone instinctual gratification so as to minimize pain. Initially, there is no necessary conflict between the Id and the Ego, for the Ego works under the guidance of the reality principle to get satisfactions for the Id.

The third component of personality, which develops out of Ego in childhood, is called the *Superego*. The Superego is the last part of the personality to be formed and consists in large part of morality or conscience. The Superego is formed out of the Ego from introjected standards and expectations of parents and other authority figures. In essence, the Superego represents the norms, values, and ideals of the society which are internalized by the actor as his own. It functions to make the person his own policeman by laying down rules for the individual to follow, and punishing him for failure to behave properly. This punishment, psychic in nature, consists of guilt feelings and anxiety. The Superego's function is to limit the expression of instinctual energy, not in accordance with the reality principle, but with the perfectionist standards of parents and authority figures.

In a well-balanced personality, these three components work in relative harmony. But in neurotic individuals and other abnormal cases, some imbalance and disharmony occurs. Superego may become dominant, so that a too-powerful and rigid Superego may create guilt feelings about repressed instinctual drives. Or repressed instinctual energy may press for recognition in disguised form, leading to "bizarre" behavior which has quite another meaning from that suggested by surface appearances. In particular, manifestations of the sexual instinct may appear in these forms. Still another possibility is that the Superego may not be sufficiently well-developed, and antisocial behavior engaged in as a consequence of poorly controlled instincts.

By and large, Freudians argue that personality balance or disharmony is produced by parent-child interactions early in life. In particular, variations in the way in which persons go through the stages of sexual development, from the oral stage of infancy, through the anal, phallic, and latency periods to adult heterosexuality have profound consequences for adult behavior. This theme has been summarized by Benedek in the following terms:

The integration of the *sexual drive* from its pre-genital sources to the *genital primacy* and to functional maturity is the axis around which the organization of the personality takes place. From the point of view of personality development, the process of interaction is the same in both sexes. Men and women alike reach their psychosexual maturity through the reconciliation of the sexual drive with the superego and through the adjustment of sexuality to all other functions of the personality.[17]

This paragraph highlights the important place occupied in Freudian thought by instinctual energy of a sexual form. It follows from such emphasis that many of the difficulties identified by psychoanalysts which emerge in personality development center around sexual tensions and problems.

### Psychoanalytic Interpretations of Criminality

Applications of psychoanalytic notions to criminality grow directly out of the general theory. Vold has summarized the psychoanalytic view of criminality in this way:

Criminal behavior, under this general theoretical orientation, is to be understood, simply and directly, as a substitute response, some form of symbolic release of repressed complexes. The conflict in the unconscious mind gives rise to feelings of guilt and anxiety with a consequent desire for punishment to remove the guilt feelings and restore a proper balance of good against evil. The criminal then commits the criminal act in order to be caught and punished. Unconsciously motivated errors (i.e., careless or imprudent ways of committing the crime) leave "clues" so the authorities may more readily apprehend and convict the guilty, and thus administer suitably cleansing punishment.[18]

The earliest important application of psychoanalytic thought to the explanation of criminal behavior is found in the work of August Aichhorn, an Austrian psychiatrist and director of a correctional institution in that country in the early 1900's.[19] Out of his experience, he began applying Freudian theory to analysis of behavior problems of the boys in his institution. Aichhorn's book, *Wayward Youth*, which presented his line of reasoning, became the parent of a long line of psychoanalytic treatises on crime and delinquency. In addition, his work has played a considerable part in generating enthusiasm for psychiatric views among correctional works in the United States and elsewhere.

In Aichhorn's writings, several kinds of delinquents are described. Some are alleged to be similar to neurotic individuals, others are aggressive

[17] T. Benedek, "Personality Development," in *Dynamic Psychiatry*, ed. Franz Alexander and Helen Ross (Chicago: University of Chicago Press, 1952), p. 100. For a concise summary of the stages of psychosexual development, see Alfred R. Lindesmith and Anselm L. Strauss, *Social Psychology* (rev. ed.; New York: Dryden Press, 1956).

[18] Vold, op. cit., p. 119.

[19] Aichhorn, op. cit., passim.

and lacking in Superego development. Some are said to have little capacity for repressing their instinctual drives, while others are believed to have strong, distorted cravings for affection.[20]

We need not consider Aichhorn's theories in great detail here. His work is important now insofar as it has stimulated psychoanalytic analyses of criminality. His writings describe Austrian juveniles who may be quite unlike American youths. His descriptions are from more than 30 years ago, so it cannot easily be argued that his propositions have much contemporary etiological relevance.

A plethora of psychoanalytic writings regarding crime and delinquency has emerged in the past several decades.[21] For example, Kate Friedlander has devoted an entire book to the exposition of this view.[22] In the main, she agrees with Aichhorn that delinquents are persons expressing antisocial impulses which are repressed in normal persons. Unfavorable environments play a part in lawbreaking, but never as a primary cause, only as a precipitating one which calls out antisocial impulses from within the person.[23] In general, she also argues that the difference between neurotic and criminalistic persons is that the former are characterized by overly strict Superegos, while the latter show weak and defective Superegos stemming from early parental deprivations in childhood.[24]

Another example of psychoanalytic theory is represented by the volume *Searchlights on Delinquency*.[25] This book, commemorating the seventieth birthday of Aichhorn, includes an essay by Johnson on the theme of Superego Lacunae, in which it is held that parents frequently encourage delinquent acts by their children in order to gratify their own forbidden

[20] *Ibid.*, p. 115.
[21] Prominent examples of psychoanalytic writings on criminality include David Abrahamsen, *Crime and the Human Mind* (New York: Columbia University Press, 1945); Abrahamsen, *Who Are the Guilty?* (New York: Holt, Rinehart and Winston, Inc., 1952); Abrahamsen, *The Psychology of Crime* (New York: Columbia University Press, 1960); Franz Alexander and William Healy, *Roots of Crime* (New York: Alfred A. Knopf, Inc., 1935); Alexander and Hugo Staub, *The Criminal, the Judge, and the Public*, rev. ed. (New York: Free Press of Glencoe, Inc., 1956); Lucien Bovet, *Psychiatric Aspects of Juvenile Delinquency* (Geneva: World Health Organization, 1951); Kate Friedlander, *The Psychoanalytic Approach to Juvenile Delinquency* (London: Routledge and Kegan Paul, Ltd., 1947); Benjamin Karpman, *The Individual Criminal* (Washington: Nervous and Mental Disease Publishing Co., 1935); Robert M. Lindner, *Rebel Without a Cause* (New York: Grune and Stratton, 1944); Lindner, *Stone Walls and Men* (New York: Odyssey Press, 1946); William A. White, *Crimes and Criminals* (New York: Farrar and Rinehart, 1933); Gregory Zilboorg, *The Psychology of the Criminal Act and Punishment* (New York: Harcourt, Brace and World, Inc., 1954).
[22] Friedlander, *op. cit., passim.*
[23] *Ibid.*, pp. 7–10.
[24] *Ibid.*, pp. 116–17.
[25] K. R. Eissler, ed., *Searchlights on Delinquency* (New York: International Universities Press, Inc., 1949).

impulses.[26] But the most striking impression that emerges from this symposium is of the great amount of disagreement and internal inconsistency among the different contributors; it is a mistake to suppose that there is only one psychoanalytic theory of criminality.

The writings of Abrahamsen constitute a final illustration of modern psychoanalytic commentary.[27] Although he concedes that environmental and social factors play some part in causation, these are dismissed as having only a precipitating, never primary, role in etiology. His theory of causation is indicated in these remarks: "In general we may say that the causes of a child's delinquent behavior may be traced to his parents, particularly to his mother's emotional attitude toward his early instinctual manifestations, which may be partly caused by her own personality makeup or by other elements from his environment. In addition, his antisocial attitude is also accentuated by the particular way his Ego and Superego (conscience) develop." [28] One of Abrahamsen's better known notions is what he terms a mathematical law expressing the relationship between factors in criminality. That "law" takes the form, $C = T + S/R$, in which $C$ stands for crime, $T$ for tendencies, $S$ for the situation, and $R$ for psychological resistances to impulses.[29] This is nothing more than pseudo-mathematical shorthand, for it is doubtful that the significant etiological factors in criminality will ever be reduced to as few as three mathematical terms.

### Criticisms of the Psychoanalytic Position

General psychoanalytic formulations and applications to criminality have not suffered from a lack of criticism.[30] One line of attack centers around the vague, obscure language and circular reasoning at points in the argument which render many of the central propositions within the theory untestable, due to claims about "unconscious" mind and other notions of that kind. For example, Vold has declared: "A methodology (as in psychoanalysis) under which only the patient knows the 'facts' of the case, and only the analyst understands the meaning of those 'facts' as revealed to him by the patient, does not lend itself to external, third

[26] Adelaide M. Johnson, "Sanctions for Superego Lacunae of Adolescents," in Eissler, op. cit., pp. 225–45. For a critique of this argument, see Hakeem, "A Critique of the Psychiatric Approach," loc. cit.

[27] Abrahamsen, op. cit., passim.

[28] Abrahamsen, Who Are the Guilty?, p. 27.

[29] Ibid., pp. 67–72.

[30] For a discussion of some of these criticisms, see Hall and Lindzey, op. cit.; Robert E. L. Faris, Social Psychology (New York: The Ronald Press Co., 1952), pp. 11–33; Korn and McCorkle, op. cit., pp. 253–57; Vold, op. cit., pp. 114–25.

person, impersonal verification or to generalization beyond the limits of any particular case." [31]

Another group of criticisms deals with the substantive content of the theory, that is, the truth claims of psychoanalytic thought. Some of the most frequent and important of these are the following:

1. The theory is in error because it is built upon assumptions of biological motivation, particularly instincts. The evidence on the question of instincts or drives indicates that these do not exist and that human behavior is not the product of biological forces.

2. The argument is defective because it lays undue stress upon the impact of experiences of infancy and early childhood, particularly weaning, toilet training, and so on, for personality development. The data do not bear out these allegations regarding the consequences of early and harsh toilet training and other experiences for later personality formation.[32]

3. The theory is flawed because it minimizes the influence of social factors on human behavior. Personality patterns develop out of variations in socialization experiences among cultures, and within a particular society, so that the influences of culture and social structure represent more than simply precipitating forces in their effects. However, variations exist among psychoanalysts regarding the role assigned to cultural variables in personality development and, in addition, the fact that psychoanalysts do not pay much attention to cultural variables does not by itself invalidate psychoanalytic arguments.

4. The theory overemphasizes sexual aspects of behavior and motivation. It is an error to suppose that most human behavior is linked, directly or indirectly, to erotic sources of motivation. In particular, the Freudian claims regarding infantile sexuality are open to serious question.[33]

These charges against Freudian theory apply both to the general argument and applications of it to criminality. Several specific criticisms of psychoanalytic conceptions of delinquent and criminal behavior have also been offered. As noted at the beginning of this chapter, these theories are not clear on the process by which so-called neurotic, "acting-out" offenders are produced, as opposed to conventional neurotic individuals. Both are alleged to result from the same causal dynamics. If so, why do two outcomes result from the same etiological processes? The conventional

---

[31] Vold, op. cit., p. 125.

[32] This evidence is contained in Harold Orlansky, "Infant Care and Personality," *Psychological Bulletin*, XLVI (January 1949), 1–48; Robert R. Sears, *Survey of Objective Studies of Psychoanalytic Concepts* (New York: Social Science Research Council, 1943); William H. Sewell, "Infant Training and the Personality of the Child," *American Journal of Sociology*, LVIII (September 1952), 150–59.

[33] Faris, op. cit., pp. 25–26.

answer has been that criminal behavior is available in the environment for the "acting-out" offender to take over as a response. But this begs the question, for the existence of lawbreaking traditions in some areas and not in others must be explained.

We are persuaded by these criticisms, so we reject psychoanalytic views of criminality in favor of alternative theories which make better sense of the facts of lawbreaking. There is a possibility that irrational elements sometimes do enter into acts of criminality, and that some offenders are sometimes only dimly aware or totally oblivious of the reasons for their actions. In this sense, it can be said that lawbreaking is "unconsciously" motivated. However, we submit that the particular formulations of unconscious mainsprings of human action found in psychoanalytic theories of criminality are in error. In addition, a major portion of the criminal population involves actors whose behavior is not to be attributed to unconscious elements of personality or personality aberrations of any kind, who are instead normal, well-socialized individuals. We are in agreement with Maurer, who has argued in the following fashion regarding the absence of mental "conflicts" among pickpockets, likening this situation to the Sioux Indians: "I venture to suggest that any psychiatrist who tried to give the participants in the Custer massacre insight into their 'guilt' feelings in connection with this event would have had rough going indeed. Those Sioux who exterminated Custer's force were behaving as they were expected to be in their culture; they enjoyed every bit of it, and derived status from it which they carried to their dying days." [34]

## EMOTIONAL PROBLEMS AND CRIMINALITY

Beginning around 1900, much has been written by psychiatrists and others about personality problems or emotional disturbances and criminality, a great deal of it independent of orthodox Freudian interpretations. The emotional dynamics identified have been of many kinds, and the genesis of these problems has been alleged to involve a large variety of background situations, particularly parent-child tensions and distorted relationships. An essay by Grossbard provides one example of this view.[35] He claims that most delinquents exhibit inefficient or underdeveloped ego mechanisms, so they tend to act out conflicts instead of handling them by rational means or symptom formation, as do nondelinquents. This view

[34] David W. Maurer, *Whiz Mob* (New Haven: College and University Press, 1964), pp. 16–17.
[35] Hyman Grossbard, "Ego Deficiency in Delinquents," *Social Casework*, XLIII (April 1962), 171–78.

owes something to the psychoanalytic position, but it does not follow Freudian theory with strict fidelity.

### Some Early Studies

Burt's allegation that 85 per cent of the delinquents studied by him were emotionally impaired stands as an early example of the general personality problems view.[36] Probably the most influential of the older studies of delinquency and emotional disturbance was the research of Healy and Bronner, comparing 105 delinquents with 105 of their nondelinquent siblings in New Haven, Boston, and Detroit. After examining these children, Healy and Bronner concluded: ". . . it finally appears that no less than 91 per cent of the delinquents gave clear evidence of being or having been unhappy and discontented in their life circumstances or extremely emotionally disturbed because of emotion-provoking situations or experiences. In great contradistinction we found similar evidence of inner stresses at the most in only 13 per cent of the controls." [37]

These are impressive findings indeed. Nevertheless, this investigation has received critical attention as well as acclaim.[38] The critics have pointed out that the differences between the delinquents and nonoffenders were probably exaggerated, because the staff members who reported on personality characteristics of the subjects were psychiatrists and psychiatric social workers, predisposed to the view that the major causal variable in delinquency is emotional disturbance. Also, the clinical assessments were obtained by subjective methods, no attempt being made to conceal the identities of the subjects prior to the psychiatric examinations. The judgments may have been colored by the knowledge of the delinquent-nondelinquent status of the subjects. Moreover, the psychiatric workers were conducting a treatment program with the offenders and were in greater contact with them. The question arises, if they had spent an equivalent amount of time with the nonoffenders, would they have observed emotional problems which were originally overlooked? The critics have built such a damaging case against the Healy and Bronner investigation that the findings of this study cannot be accepted as valid. Other research results give only partial support at best to these psychogenic contentions.

[36] Cyril Burt, *The Young Delinquent* (London: University of London Press, 1938).

[37] William Healy and Augusta F. Bronner, *New Light on Delinquency and its Treatment* (New Haven, Conn.: Yale University Press, 1936), p. 122.

[38] Hakeem, "A Critique of the Psychiatric Approach," *loc. cit.*, pp. 89–95; Edwin H. Sutherland and Donald R. Cressey, *Principles of Criminology* (7th ed.; Philadelphia: J. B. Lippincott Co., 1966), pp. 173–74.

Although not directly relevant to the study of criminality, the research of Hartshorne and May produced results which create grave problems for a simplified psychogenic thesis.[39] These researchers devised objective methods to study such hypothesized personality characteristics as "deceit," but their major finding was negative, to the effect that there apparently are no general traits of this kind. Instead, traits are specific to particular situations—children steal under some circumstances and not others.

Advocates of psychogenic arguments must also contend with the findings of Schuessler and Cressey, who reviewed a large number of studies of personality characteristics of delinquents and criminals. They concluded that: ". . . of 113 such comparisons, 42 per cent showed differences in favor of the noncriminal, while the remainder were indeterminate. The doubtful validity of many of the obtained differences, as well as the lack of consistency in the combined results makes it impossible to conclude from these data that criminality and personality elements are associated." [40]

### Recent Work

Another review of studies has been presented by Hakeem, involving data from surveys of emotional disturbance among cases from an adolescents' court, a psychiatric clinic attached to a juvenile court, and a juvenile correctional institution.[41] The findings show a diversity of diagnostic decisions in each of the studies. One set of diagnostic labels categorized a number of offenders as suffering from psychoneurosis or neurotic character disturbances, while in the other two studies this category did not appear. Immaturity and mental conflict appear in one report but not in the others. In addition, in comparable diagnostic groups in the three investigations, diverse proportions of offenders are found in the separate tabulations. All of this led Hakeem to conclude that the results probably reveal more about biases of the psychiatrists than about characteristics of offenders. It should also be noted that a number of the diagnostic categories in these three studies are of dubious validity. For example, in one of them the diagnosis "conduct disorders" is used to classify about one-third of the cases. The question in this instance is, were any identifiable characteristics of offenders used to recognize conduct disorders apart from the facts of involvement in delinquency? It is quite likely that

[39] H. Hartshorne and M. A. May, *Studies in the Nature of Character*, Vol. I (New York: The Macmillan Co., 1929); Hartshorne, May, and F. K. Shuttleworth, *Studies in the Nature of Character*, Vol. III (New York: The Macmillan Co., 1930).

[40] Karl F. Schuessler and Donald R. Cressey, "Personality Characteristics of Criminals," *American Journal of Sociology*, LV (March 1950), 476 84.

[41] Hakeem, "A Critique of the Psychiatric Approach," *loc. cit.*, pp. 86–89.

a tautological classification was involved, where the delinquent activity of the juvenile was used to indicate the existence of a conduct disorder.

One of the reports cited by Hakeem was the investigation of the Gluecks, *Unraveling Juvenile Delinquency*.[42] The delinquents and controls in this research were subjected to a psychiatric interview and Rorschach tests, a projective instrument designed to measure basic personality traits. The Gluecks report that: "Considering first those traits in which the delinquents as a group significantly exceed the nondelinquents, we observed that they are to a much greater degree socially assertive, defiant and ambivalent to authority; they are more resentful of others, and far more hostile, suspicious and destructive; the goals of their drives are to a much greater extent receptive (Oral) and destructive-sadistic; they are more impulsive and vivacious, and decidedly more extroversive in their behavior trends." [43] A number of the characteristics identified through the Rorschach test as more common among offenders are not clearly signs of maladjustment. Assertiveness, impulsiveness, and vivacity could be held to indicate that the delinquents are better adjusted than the nondelinquents.

Psychiatric diagnoses of the offenders and nondelinquent controls brought out several points.[44] First, the differences between the two groups were not pronounced; about half of both groups showed no conspicuous mental pathology. Second, the delinquents classified as showing mental deviations were seen as exhibiting a variety of disorders, while the disturbed nonoffenders were predominantly neurotic or showing neurotic trends. This finding runs counter to many psychogenic arguments in the criminological literature which suggest that delinquency is a form of neurotic, acting-out behavior.

Another body of research data on the psychogenic thesis comes from studies using the Minnesota Multiphasic Personality Inventory.[45] The

[42] Sheldon and Eleanor Glueck, *Unraveling Juvenile Delinqency* (Cambridge, Mass.: Harvard University Press, 1951).

[43] *Ibid.*, p. 240.

[44] *Ibid.*, pp. 239–43.

[45] Starke Hathaway and Elio D. Monachesi, eds., *Analyzing and Predicting Juvenile Delinquency with the Minnesota Multiphasic Personality Inventory* (Minneapolis: University of Minnesota Press, 1953); Hathaway and Monachesi, "The Minnesota Multiphasic Personality Inventory in the Study of Juvenile Delinquents," *American Sociological Review*, XVII (December 1952), 704–10; Hathaway and Monachesi, *Adolescent Personality and Behavior—MMPI Patterns* (Minneapolis: University of Minnesota Press, 1963); Dora F. Capwell, "Personality Patterns of Adolescent Girls: II. Delinquents and Non-delinquents," *Journal of Applied Psychology*, XXIX (August 1945), 289–97; Elio D. Monachesi, "Some Personality Characteristics of Delinquents and Non-delinquents," *Journal of Criminal Law and Criminology*, XXXVIII (January–February 1948), 487–500; Monachesi, "Personality Characteristics and Socio-Economic Status of Delinquents and Non-delinquents," *Journal of Criminal Law and Criminology*, XL (January–February 1950), 570–83; Monachesi, "Personality Characteristics of Institutionalized and Non-Institutionalized Male Delinquents,"

M.M.P.I. includes eight scales in which certain responses to questions in each scale are indicative of particular personality patterns. For example, persons with high scale points on the Pa, paranoia scale, of the M.M.P.I. give responses similar to those of individuals clinically diagnosed as suffering from paranoia.

One piece of research using this inventory involved its application to over 4000 Minneapolis ninth grade pupils during 1948. In 1950, the same children were traced through the Hennepin County Juvenile Court and the Minneapolis Police Department to determine which had acquired records of delinquency. Of the boys, 22.2 per cent had become delinquent, while 7.6 per cent of the girls had become known to the court or the police. In analyzing the responses of delinquents and nonoffenders, the researchers found such results as these: 27.7 per cent of the boys with high Pd (psychopathic deviate) scale points were delinquent, as were 25.4 per cent with high Pa (paranoia) scale points. Of the boys with "Invalid" responses indicating uncooperativeness, lying, and so on, 37.5 per cent were delinquent. Thus there is some tendency for delinquent boys to show disproportionate numbers in some of the scale areas of the M.M.P.I., while substantially similar results were obtained with girls.

Hathaway and Monachesi are modest in the claims they make on the basis of these data. In the main, they argue only that the inventory possesses some discriminatory power. Nevertheless, critics have noted the problems of interpretation involved in the variability of results, and have pointed out that a number of social factors correlate more highly with delinquency than do M.M.P.I. scores.[46]

Swanson's study is also relevant to the discussion in this section.[47] Swanson examined the emotional stability and family adjustment of children from Pittsburgh areas with varying delinquency rates. He administered tests to school children from a number of high, medium, and low delinquency areas. Two measures were used, the Woodworth-Mathews Personal Data Sheet and the Child-Parents Relationship Scale. If it is true that children from high delinquency areas are emotionally

Journal of Criminal Law and Criminology, XLI (July–August 1950), 167–79; Thomas E. Hannum and Roy E. Warman, "The MMPI Characteristics of Incarcerated Females," Journal of Research in Crime and Delinquency, I (July 1964), 119–26.

[46] Clarence C. Schrag, review of Hathaway and Monachesi, Analyzing and Predicting Delinquency with the Minnesota Multiphasic Personality Inventory, American Sociological Review, XIX (August 1954), 490–91; Sethard Fisher, "The M.M.P.I.: Assessing a Famous Personality Test," American Behavioral Scientist, VI (October 1962), 21–22. Fisher's main point, on which this book concurs, is that the M.M.P.I. is fundamentally inappropriate in the study of deviant roles. Instead, research needs to look for role-specific patterns of social-psychological characteristics.

[47] Guy E. Swanson, "The Disturbances of Children in Urban Areas," American Sociological Review, XIV (October 1949), 676–78.

unstable and dissatisfied with their family relationships, we should expect to find a correlation between rates of misbehavior and unfavorable scores on these two instruments. The higher the delinquency rate of an area, the larger should be the number of children with unfavorable scores. But such was not the case; instead, the correlations actually observed were negligible. Swanson's study does not lend support to the emotional disturbance argument.

One final piece of work on personality characteristics of offenders concerns the Jesness Inventory.[48] This instrument, developed in the California correctional system, involves eight scales and a delinquency prediction score. The eight scales measure defensiveness, value orientation, neuroticism, authority attitude, family orientation, psychoticism, delinquency orientation, and emotional immaturity. Data from the development and validation studies of this inventory indicate that delinquents and nondelinquents do not differ significantly in defensiveness, value orientation, neuroticism, or family orientation. The two groups do vary on authority attitude, with delinquents exhibiting the greater hostility toward authority figures. They also differ on psychoticism, as the offenders are more suspicious and distrustful of other persons. Additionally, the delinquents can be differentiated from nondelinquents on the two empirical scales, delinquency orientation and emotional immaturity. Compared to nonoffenders, institutionalized delinquents are more concerned about being normal, exhibit more marked feelings of isolation, are less mature, lack insight, and tend to deny that they have problems. The delinquency proneness prediction scales built up out of items in the separate scales differentiate the two groups, but with some degree of overlap. Some nonoffenders have scores predictive of delinquency proneness, while some delinquents have scores indicative of nondelinquency.

### Voices of Dissent

The refrain that virtually all criminality and delinquency is the product of emotional disturbances continues unabated in many quarters, in spite of considerable evidence indicating that such claims do violence to the facts. At the same time, some psychiatrists have entertained doubts about the validity of psychogenic assertions. Esman has argued, on the basis

[48] Carl F. Jesness, The Jesness Inventory: Development and Validation, Research Report No. 29 (Sacramento: California Youth Authority, 1962). See also Jesness, Redevelopment and Revalidation of the Jesness Inventory, Research Report No. 35 (Sacramento: California Youth Authority, 1963). The 1963 report presents somewhat different findings from applications of the Jesness Inventory to additional samples. However, the outlines of the Jesness Inventory results from this later study of delinquents and nondelinquents were not materially altered from those of the 1962 report, discussed here.

of impressionistic observations from a child guidance clinic, that there are a number of types of delinquency in the population of official offenders, only some of which fit the simple psychogenic model of the disturbed youngster acting out his problems in an illegal fashion.[49]

One of the most sophisticated versions of psychiatric dissent from simple psychogenic notions is found in the work of Richard L. Jenkins.[50] His arguments are doubly impressive since many of them are solidly anchored in a foundation of careful and objective research, rather than based on clinical impressions. Jenkins and several collaborators have been involved in a series of research investigations of delinquent types, out of which Jenkins has advanced the argument that there are two common forms of misbehavior, adaptive and maladaptive delinquency.[51] Jenkins claims that delinquent misconduct is not a form of neurotic behavior, for neuroticism involves a high level of inhibition, sense of duty, and introjected standards and strict superego control, while delinquency is frequently the direct opposite of such a pattern. Most offenders are less neurotic than nonoffenders, according to Jenkins. In addition, with regard to delinquents, it is only the maladaptive version or the unsocialized offender who has a disturbed personality. This is the aggressive delinquent who is poorly socialized, lacking in internalized controls, antagonistic toward his peers, and generally maladjusted. The more frequently encountered adaptive, or pseudosocial, violator is usually the product of lower class slum areas, and is reasonably well-socialized and "normal" among his peers and parents. He is characterized by attenuated inhibitions; his loyalty and group identification does not extend to the wider community beyond his local area and immediate peers. He engages in depredations against the community with relatively little guilt or concern. From the perspective of agents of law enforcement and social control, such behavior may be defined as abnormal, but in terms of the adaptive

[49] Aaron H. Esman, "Diagnostic Categories of 'Delinquency,'" N.P.P.A. Journal, I (October 1955), 113–17. For some other dissenters within psychiatry, see Hakeem, "A Critique of the Psychiatric Approach," loc. cit., p. 82.

[50] H. Hart, Richard L. Jenkins, Sidney Axelrad, and P. Sperling, "Multiple Factor Analysis of Traits of Delinquent Boys," Journal of Social Psychology, XVII (May 1943), 191–201; Richard L. Jenkins and Sylvia Glickman, "Common Syndromes in Child Psychiatry," American Journal of Orthopsychiatry, XVI (April 1946), 244–61; Jenkins and Glickman, "Patterns of Personality Organization Among Delinquents," Nervous Child, VI (July 1947), 329–39; Lester E. Hewitt and Richard L. Jenkins, Fundamental Patterns of Maladjustment, The Dynamics of Their Origin (Springfield: State of Illinois Printer, 1947); Jenkins and Hewitt, "Types of Personality Structure Encountered in Child Guidance Clinics," American Journal of Orthopsychiatry, XIV (January 1944), 84–94.

[51] Richard L. Jenkins, "Adaptive and Maladaptive Delinquency," Nervous Child, II (October 1955), 9–11; Jenkins, "Motivation and Frustration in Delinquency," American Journal of Orthopsychiatry, XXVII (July 1957), 528–37; Jenkins, Breaking Patterns of Defeat (Philadelphia: J. B. Lippincott Co., 1954).

offender's immediate situation, his activities are rational and goal-directed. His social adjustment, from this perspective, does not justify the judgment that he is maladjusted.

## PSYCHOPATHY AND CRIMINALITY

### What is a Psychopath?

One currently popular psychogenic hypothesis argues that many delinquents and criminals exhibit what is alleged to be a particular form of mental pathology, psychopathic personality (or sociopathic personality). The term psychopath usually refers to a pattern of pathology characterized by egocentricity, asocial behavior, insensitivity to others, hostility, and so on. Actually, the designation is only one of a number of synonymous terms employed at different times, including psychopathic personality, constitutional psychopathic inferior, moral imbecility, semantic dementia, sociopathy, and moral mania.[52]

What is a psychopath? The answer varies from one respondent to another. One definition is provided by Cleckley, who has given a good deal of attention to this disorder. He lists six general symptoms: (1) The psychopath is free from neurosis, psychosis, or mental defectiveness. He knows the consequences of his behavior but seems to have no inner feeling for what he verbalizes so rationally. (2) The psychopath is habitually unable to adjust his social relations satisfactorily. (3) He is undeterred by punishment; instead, he seeks it out. (4) His conduct lacks motivation, or, if motivated, the motivation is not congruent with his behavior. (5) The psychopath expresses normal affective responses but shows a total lack of concern and callous indifference to others. (6) He is characterized by poor judgment and an inability to learn from experience. This is seen in his pathological lying, repeated crime, and other antisocial acts.[53]

Another list of signs of the psychopath has been offered by Gough. These include overevaluation of immediate goals, unconcern for the rights and privileges of others, and impulsive behavior. Further characteristics of the psychopath are poor loyalty and social attachments, poor plan-

---

[52] Lindner, *Rebel Without a Cause*, p. 1.

[53] Hervey Cleckley, *The Mask of Sanity* (St. Louis: C. V. Mosby and Co., 1941); Cleckley, "Psychopathic Personality," in *Encyclopedia of Criminology*, ed. Vernon C. Branham and Samuel B. Kutash (New York: Philosophical Library, 1949), pp. 413–16; Cleckley, "The Psychopath, A Problem for Society," *Federal Probation*, X (October–December 1946), 22–26; see also Ben Karpman, "A Yardstick for Measuring Psychopathy," *Federal Probation*, X (October–December 1946), 26–31.

ning and judgment, no distress over his maladjustment, and projection of blame to others. Finally, Gough lists as common psychopathic patterns meaningless prevarication, lack of responsibility, and emotional poverty.[54] In descriptions by both Cleckley and Gough, a picture emerges of a poorly socialized, indifferent, and uncooperative person.

Attempts to account for the genesis of psychopathic personalities have taken several directions. Some authorities have held that they are the product of genetic factors. However, the most common hypothesis is that the disorder stems from some defect of family relationships.[55]

If such a personality pattern exists, it might bear more than a slight relationship to criminality, for persons showing these traits might be less subject to the demands of society because they are lacking in inner controls and are insensitive to contemporary conduct norms. However, if we are to make any use of the concept of psychopathic personality, we must first develop some means by which to recognize psychopaths. Here is where the difficulty begins—the concept is not defined in a satisfactory manner. Note that the definitions given by Gough and Cleckley indicate a rather general and unspecific symptomology. Yet these are two of the clearer statements in the literature of psychopathy. Preu, in examining the ways this concept has been used in practice, tells us: "The term, 'psychopathic personality' as commonly understood, is useless in psychiatric research. It is a diagnosis of convenience arrived at by a process of exclusion. It does not refer to a specific behavioral entity. It serves as a scrapbasket to which is relegated a group of otherwise unclassified personality disorders and problems . . . delinquency of one kind or another constitutes the most frequently utilized symptomatic basis for the diagnosis of psychopathic personality." [56] There is no reason why the term cannot be used in this way, but if it is to be a synonym for criminality, it cannot be used to explain that same behavior. Other observers have reached much the same conclusion as Preu regarding the concept in practical application, indicating that it has no stable referent and constitutes a psychiatric wastebasket.[57] Lindesmith has pointed out that the

---

[54] Harrison G. Gough, "A Sociological Theory of Psychopathy," *American Journal of Sociology,* LIII (March 1948), 359–66.

[55] Harry R. Lipton, "The Psychopath," *Journal of Criminal Law, Criminology and Police Science,* XL (January–February 1950), 584–96. For a general summary of the psychopath literature and hypothesized causes, see S. Kirson Weinberg, *Society and Personality Disorders* (Englewood Cliffs, N.J.: Prentice-Hall, Inc., 1952), pp. 260–97; William and Joan McCord, *Psychopathy and Delinquency* (New York: Grune and Stratton, 1956).

[56] Paul W. Preu, "The Concept of Psychopathic Personality," in *Personality and the Behavior Disorders,* Vol. II, ed. J. McV. Hunt (New York: The Ronald Press Co., 1944), pp. 922–37.

[57] Oskar Diethelm, "Basic Considerations of the Concept of Psychopathic Personality," in *Handbook of Correctional Psychology,* ed. Robert M. Lindner and Robert V. Seliger (New York: Philosophical Library, 1947), p. 384; Weinberg, *op. cit.*

term is frequently used in opiate addiction arguments as an etiological factor, but narcotic addiction itself is usually the evidence on which such a diagnosis depends.[58]

## Psychopathy and Criminality

The results of investigations on psychopathy and criminality have been extremely confusing. Sutherland and Cressey have reviewed the evidence on this matter and concluded that no relationship has been shown to exist. They note that one psychiatrist at the Illinois State Penitentiary classified 98 per cent of the inmates as psychopaths, while in a similar institution with different psychiatrists, only 5 per cent of the prisoners were so diagnosed. Such variations tell us more about psychiatrists than they do about prisoners.[59] Other criminologists have reached similar conclusions about the uselessness of the psychopathy notion.[60]

On the other hand, a number of authorities accept the argument that psychopaths exist and that they appear in the population of offenders in inordinate numbers. But in none of these cases is any indication given of how common such personality problems might be in the population at large or in the population of offenders.[61]

One recent and rather remarkable piece of research on psychopathy has been produced by Robins.[62] The study traced the adult adjustments of 524 child guidance clinic patients in St. Louis 30 years after they had appeared in the clinic. A comparison group of 100 normal school children was also subjected to follow-up study in adulthood. Most of the guidance clinic juveniles had been sent by the juvenile court, for over 70 per cent had been referred for "antisocial conduct," such as runaway behavior, truancy, and theft. The remarkable feature of this study is that the investigators managed to obtain interviews concerning 82 per cent of those individuals who had lived to age 25, either from themselves or their relatives.

The clinic patients who had been referred for neurotic symptoms

---

58 Alfred R. Lindesmith, *Opiate Addiction* (Bloomington: Principia Press, 1947).

59 Sutherland and Cressey, *op. cit.*, p. 170.

60 Hakeem, "A Critique of the Psychiatric Approach," *loc. cit.*, p. 111. Hakeem's evaluation of McCord and McCord, *Psychopathy and Delinquency*, is that the authors missed the important point that the concept of psychopath is useless for etiological explanation.

61 Walter C. Reckless, *The Crime Problem* (3rd ed.; New York: Appleton-Century-Crofts, Inc., 1961), pp. 292–95; Tappan, *op. cit.*, pp. 137–44; Harry Elmer Barnes and Negley K. Teeters, *New Horizons in Criminology* (3rd ed.; Englewood Cliffs, N.J.: Prentice-Hall, Inc., 1959), pp. 105–11; Herbert A. Bloch and Frank T. Flynn, *Delinquency: The Juvenile Offender in America Today* (New York: Randon House, Inc., 1956), pp. 144–49; Lewis Yablonsky, *The Violent Gang* (New York: The Macmillan Co., 1962).

62 Lee N. Robins, *Deviant Children Grown Up* (Baltimore: The Williams and Wilkins Co., 1966).

turned out to show satisfactory adult adjustments closely resembling those of the control subjects. However, the antisocial juveniles showed adult careers filled with frequent arrests for criminality and drunkenness, numerous divorces, occupational instability, psychiatric problems, and dependency on social agencies. For example, 44 per cent of the male antisocial patients had been arrested for a major crime, but only 3 per cent of the controls had serious criminal records. In short, the clinic subjects exhibited generally messed-up adult lives.

A major part of this research concerned the detailed study of sociopathic personality among the subjects. The diagnosis of sociopathic personality was in terms of adult behavior patterns. To be judged a sociopath, an individual had to exhibit symptoms of maladjustment within at least five of 19 life areas. That is, he had to show some combination of poor work history, financial dependency, use of drugs, sexual misconduct, and so on. The final determination that a subject was sociopathic rested with the psychiatrists, who made clinical judgments from interview material. In all, 22 per cent of the clinic subjects and 2 per cent of the controls were designated as sociopaths.

Those who are skeptical about the sociopath concept will remain unimpressed by this study. Robins asserts that there is some kind of "disease" or personality entity behind the symptoms which produces sociopaths, but no convincing evidence of this elusive entity appears in the report. Instead, the sociopathic argument looks tautological in form. While this study emphatically shows that many youngsters who get into juvenile courts and guidance clinics live fairly disordered lives as adults, making a career out of failure, there is little evidence in this research that these individuals are pathological personalities. Indeed, some of the findings tend to undermine the sociopath concept. For example, the data suggest that those antisocial children who avoided the juvenile court or a training school were less likely to become sociopaths than those who had been through these agencies. Is it perhaps the crude machinery of these organizations which contributes to adult misfortune and botched lives, rather than sociopathy? About a third of the sociopaths were judged to have given up much of their deviant activity by the time of the follow-up investigation. Since sociopaths are supposed to be especially intractable, what happened to these sociopaths?

We regard any attempt to proceed further with the psychopathy-criminality line of inquiry as presently framed a futile business. At present, we cannot answer questions about the relationship of criminality and psychopathy in the terms in which they are conventionally cast. However, there is one exception to all of this in the work of Gough, to which we now turn.

### Gough's Contribution

A singularly novel and fruitful approach to questions about psychopathy is found in the work of Harrison Gough.[63] In a 1948 essay, he identified the major attitudes and characteristics of psychopathic personality and developed a theory to account for emergence of this syndrome. Briefly stated, this is a role-taking theory, in which psychopaths are viewed as critically deficient in the ability to look upon one's self as an object or identify with another's point of view—role-taking ability. Thus the psychopath does not experience social emotions such as embarrassment, contrition, identification, or loyalty. When other persons look at the psychopath, they see him as asocial because he does not play the social game by the conventional rules. He is a "lone wolf," not a "team player." [64]

In subsequent elaborations of his views, Gough has explicitly conceptualized psychopathy as a continuum, rather than dichotomous in nature. Instead of viewing psychopathy as some kind of clinical entity clearly marked off from "normal" individuals, he argues for a socialization continuum. Thus, a representative sample of the population at large would show personality patterns ranging from the exemplary citizen at one extreme, through persons with negative and positive traits, to the markedly asocial individual at the other extreme. These variations, in turn are seen as the product of variations in the role-taking experiences of persons. Finally, Gough argues that correlations should be found when variations in socialization among persons are matched up with social behavior categories in which these persons are placed. We should expect individuals who are relatively asocial to be disproportionately criminals and other deviants, while well-socialized persons should occupy social positions of trust and repute. However, he notes that: ". . . discrepancies are of course to be expected in individual instances between the sociological baseline and the psychological measurement, if for no other reason than that the culture will occasionally make mistakes, in putting some men in prisons and others in positions of trust and responsibility." [65]

Gough has developed measuring techniques and research to investigate this theory. His California Personality Inventory includes a number of scales designed to measure particular personality dimensions. One of

[63] Gough, op. cit.; Gough and Donald R. Peterson, "The Identification and Measurement of Predispositional Factors in Crime and Delinquency," *Journal of Consulting Psychology,* XVI (June 1952), 207–12; Gough, "Theory and Measurement of Socialization," *Journal of Consulting Psychology,* XXIV (February 1960), 23–30.

[64] Gough, "A Sociological Theory of Psychopathy," passim.

[65] Gough, "Theory and Measurement of Socialization," 23.

these, the Socialization (So) Scale, was developed from the psychopathy theory. The kinds of items in this scale are indicated by the following samples:

1. Before I do something I try to consider how my friends will react to it.
2. I often think about how I look and what impression I am making upon others.
3. I would rather go without something than ask for a favor.
4. I find it easy to drop or "break with" a friend.

Taken together, the 54 items in the scale are designed to provide indices of role-taking deficiencies, insensitivity to the effects of one's behavior on others, resentment against family, feelings of despondency and alienation, and poor scholastic achievement and rebelliousness.[66] These are characteristics by which relatively asocial persons are differentiated from relatively well-socialized individuals.

Gough has tested a number of samples of citizens on the So Scale, ranging from "best citizens" in a high school, through various occupational groups, to known delinquents and prison inmates. Clear differences are seen in the mean or average scores exhibited by these groups. The mean scores indicate the average number of positive or "socialized" responses made by members of the different groups. A group of "best citizens" in high school had a score of 39.44, while a group of college students had a score of 37.41, and a collection of Selective Service inductees showed a mean score of 32.83. Various groups of deviants showed mean scores lower than any of the above: county jail inmates turned up with a score of 29.27, California prison inmates had a mean of 27.76, and a group of inmates in a federal reformatory showed a score of 26.23.[67]

These variations between offenders and nonoffenders have been established in other research studies as well.[68] One case is the work of Reckless and associates, devoted to examining the factors which "insulate" some boys who live in high delinquency areas from delinquent involvement. The potential offenders and nondelinquents in these studies differed in terms of So Scale responses in the expected direction.

In our opinion, this research by Gough and companion studies which use Gough's techniques have much promise for the study of personality

---

[66] Gough and Peterson, *The Identification and Measurement of Predispositional Factors in Crime and Delinquency*, 209.

[67] Gough, "Theory and Measurement of Socialization," 25.

[68] Walter C. Reckless, Simon Dinitz, and Barbara Kay, "The Self Component in Potential Delinquency and Potential Non-delinquency," *American Sociological Review*, XXII (October 1957), 566–70; Reckless, Dinitz, and Ellen Murray, "The 'Good' Boy in a High Delinquency Area," *Journal of Criminal Law, Criminology and Police Science*, XLVIII (May–June 1957), 18–25.

problems and criminality. One major implication of Gough's work is that the search for personality variations will only succeed insofar as the measuring instruments used are specifically related to some explicit hypothesis under investigation.

## THE FUTURE OF PSYCHOGENIC HYPOTHESES

What are we to make of this mass of psychogenic material? What are we to conclude from those theories and research findings considered to this point? We have indicated that hypotheses which characterize offenders as suffering from such gross pathologies as psychoses are demonstrably false. It is now abundantly clear that the extent of psychotic disorders among criminals is no greater than among nonoffenders; indeed, psychoses may be less common among offenders. We have also unequivocally rejected conventional psychoanalytic formulations about criminality. These theories of behavior are hopelessly ambiguous, making rigorous scientific tests of the propositions of psychoanalytic thought impossible. Moreover, psychoanalytic hypotheses about criminality, even when liberally interpreted, seem clearly inconsistent with the facts. Most offenders are responding to observable motives of a form different from that suggested by psychoanalysts. We do not deny that some instances of criminal deviation may represent the expression of dimly perceived motivational elements different from surface ones. For example, some cases of arson may be related to certain sexual tensions on the part of the actor. But even here the nature of the motivational pattern, and of the social background from which it arose, differs in important ways from the representations of psychoanalytic theory. More importantly, the vast majority of offenders seem guided in their conduct by observable motivational pressures of which they are at least dimly aware, and which are relatively utilitarian in character. Psychoanalysts are apparently the only ones capable of seeing evidence in support of psychoanalytic hypotheses about criminal motivation, and even they do not uniformly see the same things when looking at individual deviants.

Our evaluation of conventional notions about psychopaths and the extent of psychopathy among offenders was that the psychopath concept is worthless, both in general and in application to criminality. As used in analyses of lawbreakers, the psychopathy formulations represent nothing more than a deceptive form of namecalling. However, we have suggested that Gough's unique treatment of psychopathy is meritorious and that the research resulting from his views has produced noteworthy findings. Along related lines, we indicated that most of the studies of general emotional problems have turned up negative or inconclusive results. Offenders do not differ from nonoffenders in many of the personality dimensions which have been studied. Yet, at the same time, certain of the inquiries into personality dimensions of law violators, such as the research of Hewitt and Jenkins, the Gluecks, and Jesness, have reported positive evidence. It would be premature to dismiss the possibility that certain forms of personality structure do bear a relationship to criminality.

One major point needs to be heavily emphasized regarding the results of the studies of the Gluecks, Jesness, Gough, and others: there is little occasion for surprise when it is discovered that *prison inmates, training school wards,* or other samples of *incarcerated* offenders turn out to differ from ostensibly noncriminal or nondelinquent individuals, particularly in terms of hostility, negativism, and antagonism toward authority figures. Observation of negligible differences would be reason for bemusement, for it is unlikely that the experience of incarceration has neutral effects upon the self-images and attitudes of prisoners. It might be supposed that a common technique for warding off self-condemnatory feelings stemming from the experience of being segregated in an institution with other "bad" people would be to project blame and hostility onto "the system" instead of one's self. A frequent outcome of the experience of "doing time" may well be some deterioration of the actor's self-image as he takes on some of the invidious identity imputed to him by society. In the same way, a plausible case can be made that other experiences with the social control machinery, such as placement on probation, serve to create attitudinal and self-concept changes in individuals who go through this social apparatus. In short, some of the psychological characteristics observed in offenders which differentiate them from nonoffenders may be the *result* of involvement in deviance, rather than a causal ingredient in the genesis of their misbehavior. The usual argument is that emotional factors produce deviance, while the reverse possibility is not so often entertained. Our view is that there is much to be said for the hypothesis that contacts with the "defining agencies"—the social control organizations —contribute to the development of deviant personalities or role-conceptions. We will examine this possibility at length in Chapter Ten.

Even if it is granted that the social-psychological concomitants of deviant behavior may be the product of deviance in some cases, the question still remains: are there predispositional patterns of personality structure which contribute to at least some kinds of criminality? We think that there may be such relationships, but they are much more subtle in character than suggested by psychogenic theories now around. It is probably futile to search for marked variations in emotional adjustment between some sample of officially designated criminals and another sample of presumed noncriminals.

To begin with, the event of acquiring the official label or identity of criminal, or of avoiding such labeling, is often fortuitous. A great many individuals who are criminals in behavior have avoided apprehension, conviction, and detention.[69] Accordingly, comparison of prison inmates, probationers, or some similar group against noncriminals involves a contaminated sample. Even if some way could be found, utilizing novel investigative techniques, to obtain "pure" samples of criminals and noncriminals, marked personality variations still should not be expected between the two groups. The relatively obvious reason for this is that criminality is compounded of a heterogeneous assortment of behavioral forms having little in common other than a shared label. There are good reasons for supposing that a great many "normal" individuals make their way into the criminal group. Some are accidental offenders with no great involvement in lawbreaking, for whom criminality is an isolated and atypical behavioral episode. Other "normal" individuals in the criminal group are persons whose deviant behavior represents a response to organizational strains of some sort, rather than to internal states of affairs. The white collar criminal involved in law violations in the course of business activities is a case in point.

The noncriminal group includes "normal" individuals and others who are not so well-adjusted, some of whom may exhibit personality configurations parallel to those observed among some group of criminals. By way of illustration, it is conceivable that there are individuals who show a personality pattern of excessive dependence. Some of them may be found in the group of naive check forgers, others are noncriminals but involved in alcoholism, while still others are caught up in yet another pattern of adjustment. These varied outcomes in behavior can be explained as the result of variations in "career contingencies" or life experiences which divert some individuals into one line of behavior and direct others along another pathway.[70] Most behavior patterns exhibited by different actors are the combined product of such personality elements as attitudes and self-images, as these interact with, or are conditioned by, differential social experiences. This is as true for deviant as it is for nondeviant roles. It may take both an "addiction-prone" personality pattern and an opportunity structure of learning experiences with drugs, contacts with drug suppliers, and so forth, for an individual to become caught up in the role of drug addict. In the same way, variations in social

---

[69] For a discussion of this point, see Austin T. Turk, "Prospects for Theories of Criminal Behavior," *Journal of Criminal Law, Criminology and Police Science*, LV (December 1964), 454–61.

[70] Howard Becker, *Outsiders* (New York: Free Press of Glencoe, Inc., 1963).

experience may impinge upon individuals who share certain personality elements in common in such a way as to lead variously to deviant and nondeviant outcomes. On this matter of personality considerations, our views are related to those of Inkeles, who has argued:

> Sociologists have traditionally explained the fact that most people fulfill their major social obligations by referring to the system of sanctions imposed on those who fail to meet, and the rewards granted to those who do meet, the expectations of society. Performance is thus seen as largely dependent on factors "outside" the person. The only thing that need be posited as "inside," in this view, is the general desire to avoid punishment and to gain rewards. Important as such "drives" may be, they do not seem sufficient to explain the differences in the way people perform their assigned social roles. While accepting the crucial importance of the objective factors which determine social behavior, we must recognize that recruitment into occupational and other status-positions, and the quality of performance in the roles people are thus assigned, may, to an important degree, be influenced by personal qualities in individuals. It may be assumed, further, that this happens on a sufficiently large scale to be a crucial factor in determining the functioning of any social system. To the degree that this is true, to predict the functioning of a particular institution, of a small- or large-scale system, we need to know not only the system of status-positions but also the distribution of personality characteristics in the population at large and among those playing important roles in the system.[71]

In this excerpt, Inkeles emphasizes the role of personality configurations as they affect the ways in which actors become allocated to positions in the social order. We concur with Inkeles that personality formulations must be articulated with sociological ones, while at the same time we stress the conditioning effects of differential opportunities on the role-allocation processes by which individuals get sorted into social niches.

If the thrust of the foregoing remarks is on the mark, certain new directions are called for regarding psychogenic hypotheses in criminological analysis. More attention is required to the task of explicating hypotheses which spell out the *specific* constellation of personality ingredients assumed to accompany some specific pattern of criminality. The theorist will have to indicate the factors which act upon personality configurations in order to produce deviant or nondeviant outcomes in behavior. As a case in point of what is required, certain notions currently fashionable hold that middle class adolescent male delinquents commonly experience a good deal of anxiety about masculinity, and much of their behavior is to be under-

[71] Alex Inkeles, *What Is Sociology? An Introduction to the Discipline and Profession*, © 1964. Reprinted by permission of Prentice-Hall, Inc., Englewood Cliffs, N.J., p. 57. For commentary on this general issue of psychological elements in behavior, see Chap. 4, pp. 47–61.

stood as a response to masculinity stresses.[72] This is an unverified contention in need of empirical testing, and it is worthy of further exploration. But in order to convert this line of argument into a testable assertion, several theoretical improvements are required. The boundaries of the population to which this condition of masculine stress applies must be carefully delimited. Do all middle class males experience masculinity problems, or are these more common among certain boys? Are middle class delinquents of various kinds, including casual offenders and car thieves, all to be explained in terms of this central variable? These are some of the specific issues involved in the boundary question. In addition, an adequate theory which revolves around masculinity notions must be prepared to identify the various conditions which produce different behavioral outcomes on the part of individuals who exhibit the hypothesized masculinity concerns.

Another illustration of the kind of psychogenic formulations called for can be seen in Lemert's research on "dependency" as a predispositional factor in alcoholism.[73] In that study, Lemert investigated the specific hypothesis that alcoholic individuals are frequently dependent in character prior to the onset of alcoholism. He discovered evidence of several kinds favoring this contention in a sizeable proportion of the cases examined. The criminological significance of this study is that a related, intuitively derived "hunch" frequently advanced by correctional agents is that naive check forgers are dependent individuals. Perhaps there is a personality configuration of dependency which, under different circumstances, leads to these several outcomes. Still other examples of the type of theorizing required to provide a more convincing analysis of the interplay of psychological and social factors in criminality are found in studies of delinquents by Kinch and Fisher [74] and of sex offenders by Toobert and others.[75]

This chapter is not the appropriate place for an extended discussion of the role of personality elements in specific patterns of criminality. That job is to be performed in Chapters Eleven through Sixteen, where specific offender role-careers are the subject of attention. At that point, we shall resume this dialogue on personality elements in criminal deviance of different forms.

---

[72] Talcott Parsons, *Essays in Sociological Theory* (rev. ed.; New York: Free Press of Glencoe, Inc., 1954), pp. 304–5.

[73] Edwin M. Lemert, "Dependency in Married Alcoholics," *Quarterly Journal of Studies on Alcohol*, XXIII (December 1962), 590–609.

[74] John W. Kinch, "Self Conceptions of Types of Delinquents," *Sociological Inquiry*, XXXII (Spring 1962), 228–34; Sethard Fisher, "Varieties of Juvenile Delinquency," *British Journal of Criminology*, II (January 1962), 251–61.

[75] Saul Toobert, Kenwood Bartelme, and Eugene S. Jones, "Some Factors Related to Pedophilia," *International Journal of Social Psychiatry*, IV (Spring 1959), 272–79.

One final observation remains to be made before closing this chapter. As we have indicated, a number of improvements in criminological theory are required before a completely definitive assessment of psychogenic factors can be conducted. Some innovations in research procedure are also demanded.[76] For one thing, the search for psychogenic correlates of offender behavior calls for construction of research instruments specific to the hypotheses under study. Too often in the past, psychogenic students have proceeded in vacuum-cleaner fashion to administer indiscriminately a variety of personality tests to samples of offenders and nonoffenders, in an attempt to discover inductively significant differences between the two groups. Probably a great many of the personality measures utilized bear no relationship to critical personality variations which may exist. For example, there is no reason to suppose that a scale measuring "masculinity-femininity" would differentiate between some group of offenders and another group of law-abiding citizens, or between different types of lawbreakers, because masculinity-femininity is one of those personality dimensions uncorrelated with criminality. If we are to confirm specific psychogenic hypotheses, the instruments we employ must be suitable to the formulation under investigation. In a number of instances, we may find it necessary to contrive instruments because appropriate ones do not exist.

A second innovation in research procedure has been suggested previously. Attempts to investigate psychogenic hypotheses will continue to be vitiated insofar as we fail to expand the samples studied so as to cover offenders-in-fact. Stated another way, researchers are going to have to follow the example of investigators of "hidden delinquency" by extending inquiry to representative cross-sections of the population, and devising means to identify individuals as criminals or noncriminals independent of reliance on official labels. We need to study uncontaminated samples of offenders and nondeviants.

A final modification in current research designs calls for longitudinal studies of lawbreakers. Whenever research focuses upon samples of individuals at some fixed point in time, after those persons have progressed some distance through the social control machinery, the possibility exists that observed differences between them and nonoffenders under investigation could be the consequence of correctional experiences, rather than actual evidence of etiologically significant variations. The most conclusive demonstration that certain personality variables influence the subsequent behavior of individuals would be one in which the persons studied were followed chronologically from a point in time before the onset of deviant

<hr/>

[76] For some commentary related to this point, see Richard Quinney, "A Conception of Man and Society for Criminology," *Sociological Quarterly*, VI (Spring 1965), 115–27.

careers. That kind of study would be costly and time-consuming, but there are means by which individuals can be studied retrospectively, so as to assess the likelihood that observed personality configurations did, in fact, precede the deviant behavior now under observation. At any rate, however accomplished, research is going to have to become more sensitive to untangling the process that generates criminality.

## SUMMARY

This chapter necessarily ends on an inconclusive note. We have seen that the psychogenic theories about criminality which have been put forth are defective in a number of ways, while the research studies on this matter also leave much to be desired. Some basic revisions in theory and innovations in research design are needed if the role of psychological elements in lawbreaking is to be fully revealed. Among other things, psychogenic arguments must be meshed with those perspectives which focus upon social and cultural influences upon criminality. The next two chapters are concerned with these latter formulations, while Chapter Ten brings some of these strands of thought together through the study of role-careers in criminality.

# 8

# Causal Analysis
## The
## Sociology
## of Crime

## INTRODUCTION

We have examined a number of earlier approaches to crime in the form of biological theories, socialist arguments, and other hypotheses. The previous chapter considered a variety of psychogenic viewpoints regarding crime, in which criminals are thought to be pathological individuals. In the present chapter and the one to follow, our attention will turn to an analysis and critique of a variety of sociological perspectives. This chapter shall be concerned with a group of arguments devoted to the *sociology of crime*—the explanation of criminality and crime rate variations. Chapter Nine continues this exploration of explanatory frameworks, with stress upon the *social-psychology of criminal careers*, factors and processes implicated in the development of criminal behavior patterns in specific persons.

These two chapters are concerned with general theories in which attempts are made to account for crime or criminal behavior as a class of phenomena. Arguments of this sort identify some factor or set of conditions which are alleged to produce deviant behavior or criminality, such as "anomie," social disorganization, or value conflicts. These perspectives pay relatively little attention to different orders of deviance or criminality. Consequently, Chapters Eleven through Sixteen will continue the exploration of sociological theories of crime and criminal behavior, but on a more detailed level in which particular forms of behavior are to be the focus of attention.

Consider what a fully developed scientific explanation of human action might look like. It would probably involve a collection of theories arranged on several levels of generality. On the first level, some overarching propositions or "laws" might articulate the "causes" of deviant behavior, allowing key variables involved in every form of deviance to be identified. On a second level, criminological theories might be elaborated upon the base of deviance theory, so that additional factors and interrelationships which explain certain details about criminality would be specified. These criminological propositions would provide detailed and specific explanations of particular forms of criminality. All of these theories would be stated in explicit and rigorous form so they could be subjected to research test. The task of a criminology textbook would be to direct the reader through successively more complex and detailed formulations, starting with deviance theories, moving on to general perspectives on criminality, and ending with accounts of the nature and genesis of particular orders of criminality.

It is no secret that the social sciences are a great distance away from formalized, axiomatic systems of interrelated theory. Existing theories of deviant behavior are incomplete and unfinished, representing what Hempel has termed "explanation sketches." [1] Although they identify a collection of variables that cannot be overlooked in the explanation of some phenomenon, along with some crude propositions linking up certain of the identified factors, they lack the logical rigor of formalized theories. Deviance theories are not clearly meshed with criminological theories, so it is not entirely apparent as to the extent to which the latter are derivations from the former. The most appropriate term describing the existing situation regarding theories of deviance, criminality, and delinquency might be "disjointed."

In the pages to follow, a look at a number of theoretical perspectives having to do with deviant conduct precedes perusal of an assortment of views that have been developed to account for criminality. Most contemporary views regarding deviance represent outgrowths or offshoots from the pioneering works of Durkheim, so it is with his writings that we shall begin, to be followed by subsequent elaborations made by Merton and others.

## THEORIES OF DEVIANT BEHAVIOR

### Durkheim's Contributions [2]

French sociologist Emile Durkheim (1858–1917) was responsible for at least two seminal themes regarding crime and deviance. He was one of

---

[1] For a discussion of this kind of theoretical statement, and for a fuller discussion of Hempel's notions, see William J. Wilson, Nicholas Sofios, and Richard Ogles, "Formalization and Stages of Theoretical Development," *Pacific Sociological Review*, VII (Fall 1964), 74–80.

[2] Emile Durkheim, *Suicide*, trans. J. A. Spaulding and George Simpson (New York: Free Press of Glencoe, Inc., 1951); Durkheim, *The Rules of Sociological Method*, ed. George E. G. Catlin (Chicago: University of Chicago Press, 1938); excerpts from Durkheim's work relevant to the discussion here can be found in Lewis A. Coser and Bernard Rosenberg, eds., *Sociological Theory: A Book of Readings*, 2nd ed. (New York: The Macmillan Co., 1964), pp. 539–48, pp. 584–91;

the first to insist on the "normality" of criminality.[3] He maintained that the "normal" and the "pathological" are not of instrinsically different forms of behavior, but rather are labels standing for social distinctions which men impose upon behavior. Moreover, Durkheim asserted that it is neither possible nor desirable for a society to repress criminality completely. To do so would be to create a situation inimical to innovation and desirable social changes. In this sense, criminality is functional or desirable behavior.

Why is criminality a natural and inevitable feature of social life? Durkheim points out that crimes are matters of social definition. Members of a society focus their condemnation upon behavioral deviations which depart markedly from prevailing norms, singling these out as crimes. The criminal serves as an identifying sign of the limits of permissible behavior. If it were possible to repress these major violations of normative sentiments, men would become sensitive to the less marked deviations which they now overlook, and these acts would be regarded as crimes. In turn, if these were repressed, even slighter deviations would be elevated to the status of crimes, and so on, in an unending process of crime definition.[4] These increasingly intolerable demands for conformity which would then be imposed upon individuals not now thought of as criminal would be detrimental to social progress, for "to make progress, individual originality must be able to express itself. In order that the originality of the idealist whose dreams transcend his century may find expression, it is necessary that the originality of the criminal, who is below the level of his time, shall also be possible. One does not occur without the other."[5]

Durkheim's second and most important contribution to the study of deviant behavior is in the theory of *anomie*, originally developed as an explanation of suicide.[6] According to Durkheim, the social needs or

Emile Benoît-Smullyan, "The Sociologism of Emile Durkheim and His School," in *An Introduction to the History of Sociology*, ed. Harry Elmer Barnes (Chicago: University of Chicago Press, 1948), pp. 499–537; Nicholas S. Timasheff, *Sociological Theory* (rev. ed.; New York: Random House, Inc., 1957), pp. 106–18; Richard A. Cloward, "Illegitimate Means, Anomie, and Deviant Behavior," *American Sociological Review*, XXIV (April 1959), 164–76; Richard R. Korn and Lloyd W. McCorkle, *Criminology and Penology* (New York: Holt, Rinehart and Winston, Inc., 1959), pp. 274–78.

[3] Durkheim, *The Rules of Sociological Method*, pp. 65–75; Coser and Rosenberg, *op. cit.*, pp. 584–91.

[4] Coser and Rosenberg, *op. cit.*, pp. 585–87.

[5] *Ibid.*, p. 588. A somewhat related theme, holding that punishment of crime is functional for the affirmation of social solidarity, can be found in the work of Mead. See George Herbert Mead, "The Psychology of Punitive Justice," *American Journal of Sociology*, XXIII (March 1918), 585–92. For elaborations of this theme regarding functional consequences of deviance, see Lewis A. Coser, "Some Functions of Deviant Behavior and Normative Flexibility," *American Journal of Sociology*, LXVIII (September 1962), 172–81.

[6] Durkheim, *Suicide*, pp. 247–57; Cloward, *op. cit.*, 164–66; Marshall B. Clinard, "The Theoretical Implications of Anomie and Deviant Behavior," in *Anomie and Deviant Behavior*, ed. Clinard (New York: Free Press of Glencoe, Inc., 1964), pp. 3–10.

desires of humans are potentially insatiable, so collective order (social organization) is necessary as an external regulating force to define and control the goal-seeking of men. If the collective order is disrupted or disturbed, men's aspirations may increase to the point of outdistancing all possibilities of fulfillment. It is at this point, when traditional rules have lost their authority over behavior, that a state of deregulation, normlessness, or anomie can be said to exist. Durkheim claimed that the regulatory functions of the collective order most commonly break down upon the occurrence of sudden depression, sudden prosperity, or rapid technological change, when men are misled into aspiring to goals which are extremely difficult if not impossible to achieve. Sudden depressions have this effect because actors are unable to adapt themselves readily to a reduced state of existence, while sudden prosperity is conducive to anomie because it lures some individuals into supposing that they are capable of attaining seemingly limitless wealth and achievement. Much the same effect stems from rapid technological change, which instills in some imagination of boundless possibilities of achievement. These are the conditions which, according to Durkheim, engender pressures toward suicide, particularly in western, industrialized societies.

Durkheim was not concerned about criminality in the theory of anomie, nor is there anything directly implied about lawbreaking in this argument. However, the thesis originally advanced by Durkheim has been modified and elaborated upon by Robert K. Merton in the most widely utilized contemporary theory of deviant behavior. Moreover, that statement by Merton has generated some specific applications to criminal conduct, so it is to these permutations upon Durkheim's views that we now turn.

### Merton and Anomie Theory [7]

The contemporary American sociologist, Robert K. Merton, has developed a rich body of elaborations upon the initial notions of Durkheim

[7] Robert K. Merton, *Social Theory and Social Structure* (rev. and enl. ed.; New York: Free Press of Glencoe, Inc., 1957), pp. 131–94; Merton, "Social Conformity, Deviation, and Opportunity-Structures: A Comment on the Contributions of Dubin and Cloward," *American Sociological Review*, XXIV (April 1959), 177–89; Merton, "The Social-Cultural Environment and Anomie," in *New Perspectives for Research on Juvenile Delinquency*, ed. Helen L. Witmer and Ruth Kotinsky (Washington, D. C.: U.S. Department of Health, Education and Welfare, 1955), pp. 24–50; Merton, "Anomie, Anomia, and Social Interaction: Contexts of Deviant Behavior," in Clinard, *op. cit.*, pp. 213–42; Cloward, *op. cit.*; Robert Dubin, "Deviant Behavior and Social Structure: Continuities in Social Theory," *American Sociological Review*, XXIV (April 1959), 147–64; Albert K. Cohen, "The Study of Social Disorganization and Deviant Behavior," in *Sociology Today*, ed. Robert K. Merton, Leonard Broom, and Leonard S. Cottrell, Jr. (New York: Basic Books, Inc., 1959), pp. 461–66; Cohen, "The Sociology of the Deviant Act: Anomie Theory and Beyond," *American Sociological Review*, XXX (February 1965), 5–14; Clinard, *op. cit.*, pp. 10–23.

regarding the breakdown of regulatory norms and deviant behavior. In turn, these have been added to in important ways by others, principally by Richard A. Cloward. The resulting body of ideas has served as the single most influential formulation in the sociology of deviance over the past 25 years, as attested to by copious citations in sociological textbooks. Merton has continuously enunciated the sociologist's operating premise that "some unknown but substantial proportion of deviant behavior does not represent impulses of individuals breaking through social controls, but, on the contrary, represents socially induced deviations—deviations which the culture and the social organization conjoin to produce." [8] The major thrust of his work has been to sketch out the details of the processes by which societally generated deviance comes about.

In his analysis, Merton distinguishes between two major elements of social and cultural structures, the culturally defined goals that men are enjoined to pursue, and the social structure which regulates and controls the acceptable modes or means for the pursuit of goals and interests. He notes that goals and institutionalized norms may vary independently of each other, sometimes leading to malintegrated states, one extreme being the instance of inordinate stress upon goals with little concern for pre-scribed means. In this case, a condition of "anything goes" prevails, with goal-striving behavior governed only by considerations of technical expediency. Merton cites the example of unethical activities in college athletics, particularly football, as a situation in which institutionalized norms have become attenuated in favor of excessive concern with certain goals. The other polar case of goals-means malintegration involves undue emphasis upon ritualistic conformity to norms. Between these two extremes are societies with a rough balance between accent upon goals and emphasis upon norms, and it is these that constitute relatively stable societies. [9]

Merton maintains that contemporary American society is anomic, for it represents the polar type in which success goals are emphasized without equivalent emphasis upon institutionalized conduct norms. Merton asserts that:

> The emphasis upon this set of culture goals is imperfectly integrated with the organization of our society, which, as a matter of objective and generally recognizable fact, does not provide equal access to those goals for all members of the society. On the contrary, there are heavily graded degrees of access to this, in terms not only of class and ethnic origins, but also in terms of less immediately visible differentials.

Given the composite emphasis of this uniform cultural value of success being

[8] Merton, in Witmer and Kotinsky, op. cit., p. 29.
[9] Merton, Social Theory and Social Structure, pp. 131–36.

enjoined upon all irrespective of origins, and given the fact of a social organization which entails differentials in the availability of this goal, pressure is exerted upon certain classes of individuals to engage in deviant behavior, particularly those classes or strata or groups which have the least direct access to the goal.[10]

Merton's thesis is that the cultural system of American society enjoins all men to strive for success goals by means of certain normatively regulated or approved forms of behavior. Yet, at the same time, opportunities to reach these goals through socially appropriate means are differentially distributed. According to Merton, in situations of this kind, "it is only when a system of cultural values extols, virtually above all else, certain *common* success-goals for the population at large while the social structure rigorously restricts or completely closes access to approved modes of reaching these goals *for a considerable part of the same population,* that deviant behavior ensues on a large scale" (emphasis in the original).[11] Merton identifies five modes of adaptation to the situation of disjunction, labeled *conformity, innovation, ritualism, retreatism,* and *rebellion.* The category of innovation is of particular interest to the criminologist, for this refers to cases in which actors continue to aspire to approved goals, but by means of deviant or illegitimate techniques. In attempting to account for the adaptations or directions taken by different individuals, Merton is led to place strong emphasis upon variations in class-linked patterns of socialization, arguing that innovative responses are most common among relatively imperfectly socialized persons.

Richard A. Cloward has had an important role in the further development of anomie theory, in several different ways. Cloward has directed attention to the fact of differentials in *illegitimate* opportunities, in addition to varied legitimate opportunity structures.[12] He points out that the forms taken by deviant behavior are conditional *both* upon the situation of disjunction *and* the opportunities to engage in deviant conduct. Just as the prospects for achievement of cultural goals through institutionalized means are differentially distributed, so are the opportunities for various kinds of careers in deviant conduct. For example, the use of drugs depends in part upon contacts with suppliers of illicit narcotics. In a similar fashion, development of a career as a professional criminal is partly contingent upon access to contacts with individuals who will induct the actor into this kind of deviant pattern.

Cloward has also been involved in two major applications of anomie theory to specific cases of social deviation. In the first, he studied a

---

[10] Merton, in Witmer and Kotinsky, *op. cit.,* p. 30.
[11] Merton, *Social Theory and Social Structure,* p. 146.
[12] Cloward, *op. cit.*

military prison in which the prisoners were encouraged by their captors to strive for restoration to active duty through certain approved forms of conduct summed up in the injunction, "Do your own time." However, the inmates quickly came to understand that the "open-class" ideology promulgated by the administrators was a deception, for only 6 per cent of the prisoners were actually restored to active duty, and even those individuals were given this status for reasons different from those articulated by the officials. Cloward observed that this situation led to conformist adaptations by some, while others could be described as following the pattern of ritualism or passive noncooperation.[13] In essence, the prison report by Cloward stands as a microcosmic illustration of the societal pattern described by Merton.

The other application of anomie theory is found in the explanation of subcultural delinquency by Cloward and Ohlin,[14] an elaborate formulation which we will examine in some detail in Chapter Eleven. But the essentials of that theory are as follows: lower class boys share a common American value commitment to "success," measured largely in material terms. But unlike middle class youths, they do not have access to legitimate means or avenues to attain these success goals. If they do have access to legitimate means, they perceive their chances of success as limited. Thus, for many lower class boys, a severe gap exists between aspiration levels and expectations. Pressures to engage in deviant behavior are generated by this goals-means disjunction. In turn, the particular deviant adaptation which develops is a function of opportunity structures for deviant behavior, at least in part. Some lower class areas are characterized by integration of criminalistic and conformist patterns of social organization, whereas others are lacking in stable criminalistic patterns. In the organized, criminalistic area, criminalistic gang subcultures develop in which boys are involved in instrumental acts of theft and in careers which often eventually lead to adult criminal behavior. In areas lacking criminalistic traditions, gang delinquency tends to take the form of "conflict" subcultural behavior, in which "bopping" (gang fighting) predominates. Finally, there are some boys, failures in both the legitimate

[13] Witmer and Kotinsky, op. cit., pp. 80–92.

[14] Richard A. Cloward and Lloyd E. Ohlin, Delinquency and Opportunity (New York: Free Press of Glencoe, Inc., 1960). An inventory of empirical and theoretical studies of anomie can be found in Stephen Cole and Harriet Zuckerman, "Appendix: Inventory of Empirical and Theoretical Studies of Anomie," in Clinard, op. cit., pp. 243–313. Many of the cited works are only tangentially linked to the Merton formulation. Ecological studies of delinquency and anomie can be found in Bernard Lander, Toward an Understanding of Juvenile Delinquency (New York: Columbia University Press, 1954); David J. Bordua, "Juvenile Delinquency and 'Anomie': An Attempt at Replication," Social Problems, VI (Winter 1958–1959), 230–38; Roland J. Chilton, "Continuity in Delinquency Area Research: A Comparison of Studies for Baltimore, Detroit, and Indianapolis," American Sociological Review, XXIX (February 1964), 71–83.

and illegitimate opportunity structures, who engage in retreatist behavior and become narcotic users.

The Mertonian schema regarding deviant behavior represents an elegant, plausible, and appealing formulation. It is true that the framework is amenable to, and in need of, further expansion and revision. Cohen has noted a number of points at which elaboration of the perspective is in order.[15] The unfinished nature of the argument is revealed in the fact that, for all of the popularity the theory has enjoyed, remarkably few applications have been made to specific instances of deviance. Instead, the propositions have been employed most commonly as high level explanatory metaphor, with no real attempt to assess their theoretical utility through the formulation of specific hypotheses about forms of deviant conduct. Aside from the two cases of work by Cloward, criminological explanations have been little influenced by Mertonian theory.

Some of the unfinished business relative to anomie theory and deviance centers around the *boundary question*.[16] The argument is not yet sufficiently explicit regarding the scope of the theory. Is anomie to be taken as an explanation of all forms of deviance, or is it relevant to some kinds of noncomformist action but not to others? It is likely that some kinds of deviance are not accounted for by this argument, but the nature of that which is included or excluded from the explanation remains to be spelled out. In a similar vein, more work is in order on the *translation* of the view so as to coordinate the modes of adaptation (innovation, rebellion, retreatism, ritualism, conformity) with the social labels for deviance familiar in everyday life, such as "bums," "hoods," "pimps," "hustlers," "queers," or "beatniks." The empirical indicators of adaptations must be made explicit. In the case of criminality, more attention is called for regarding the boundaries of anomie theory so that forms of lawbreaking not covered by the theory can be distinguished from those which are

---

[15] Cohen, "The Sociology of the Deviant Act." A harsher view of the needed modifications in anomie theory is found in Edwin M. Lemert, "Social Structure, Social Control, and Deviation," in Clinard, op. cit., pp. 57–97.

[16] Scott and Turner have recently discussed some of the problems of Mertonian theory. They point out that the argument is ambiguous at a number of points. For one, "anomie" is not explicitly defined. Also, Merton makes no attempt to ascertain the range and variety of real-life forms of deviation or to fit the theory to these patterns. Instead, he selectively discusses those forms of behavior which intuitively appear to be explained by the means-ends disjunction situation. Scott and Turner also contend that Merton's conception of anomie is actually closer to the ideas of Max Weber than it is to Durkheim's theories. That is, for Durkheim, anomie was the product of periods of rapid social change and dislocation. In Merton's theory, anomie tends to be centered about a relatively permanent state of affairs involving disjunction. Merton's deviants resemble Weber's western men pursuing unlimited goals, while Merton's modes of adaptation parallel Weber's four types of social action. See Marvin B. Scott and Roy Turner, "Weber and the Anomic Theory of Deviance," *Sociological Quarterly*, VI (Summer 1965), 233–40.

included. To a limited extent, the analyses of specific forms of illegality in succeeding chapters will try to clarify this question.

### Other Theories

The brief critique of anomie theory can be extended to other general views on deviance. That sociological theorist among theorists, Talcott Parsons, has devoted a good measure of attention to explanation of non-conformist conduct in a lengthy analysis which parallels much of Merton's commentary, but with ingredients additional to those in anomie theory.[17] No explicit applications of this argument have been made to particular forms of deviance, so while anecdotal reference is made to cases of deviant action, the viewpoint has not been given any specific empirical interpretation. It is an open question as to whether Parsonian insights have any explanatory prowess in application to criminality.

Two other important essays on deviant conduct are found in the work of Lemert [18] and Becker.[19] However, these sociologists are most heavily concerned with the social processes and factors involved in the development of deviant careers, or with social-psychological questions. Consequently, we shall postpone commentary on these contributions until Chapter Nine.

## THEORIES OF CRIMINALITY

Sociologists have put their conceptual tools to work on the question of causal factors in crime and delinquency in countless textbooks on social disorganization, social problems, and criminology. The result is a bewildering accumulation of claims which initially projects a formidable image to the student of criminology. However, nearly all sociological commentators follow some basic assumptions, to the effect that criminality is "normal" in all societies and lawbreaking the product of various organizational features of particular nations.[20] Crime rates vary from country to

[17] Talcott Parsons, *The Social System* (New York: Free Press of Glencoe, Inc., 1951), pp. 249–325; Cohen, "The Study of Social Disorganization and Deviant Behavior," *loc. cit.*, pp. 466–74.

[18] Edwin M. Lemert, *Social Pathology* (New York: McGraw-Hill Book Co., Inc., 1951); see also Lemert, *op. cit.*

[19] Howard S. Becker, *Outsiders* (New York: Free Press of Glencoe, Inc., 1963).

[20] Good summaries of sociological theories regarding crime can be found in Donald R. Cressey, "Crime," in *Contemporary Social Problems*, ed. Robert K. Merton and Robert A. Nisbet (2nd ed.; New York: Harcourt, Brace and World, Inc., 1966), pp. 136–92; Marshall B. Clinard, *The Sociology of Deviant Behavior* (rev. ed.; New York: Holt, Rinehart and Winston, Inc., 1963), pp. 145–203.

country because of variations in the ways in which they are organized or structured. Within a society, specific individuals become criminals or noncriminals as a consequence of their positions in that system, a result of variations in organizational components within societies. Beyond these presuppositions, most sociologists would agree that the causes of criminality are found in value patterns, normative systems and conflicting patterns of conduct standards, social class influences of various kinds, family and peer group influences, and other identifiable social forms and variables.

In the pages to follow, we shall review a generous sample of the general theories regarding criminality which have been advanced by sociologists. However, we will single out those which, in our opinion, are the most significant of these statements, without any attempt to cover the entire list of sociological theories of criminality.

### Social Disorganization and Crime

The concept of social disorganization is one of those hoary notions which have occupied a place of great importance in sociology. The usual definition of social disorganization is that it consists of a breakdown or disruption in the bonds of relationship, coordination, teamwork, and morale among groups of interrelated persons, so as to impair the functions of the society or smaller social organization.[21] In this view, the United States and other western nations are in various stages of disorganization, and their apparent high crime rates (and rates of deviation of other kinds) are to be attributed to that source.

Analysis of criminality from a social disorganization standpoint often begins with systems without serious manifestations of social disorganization, taken as a standard against which to measure the extent of disorganization in industrialized societies. Thus the antithesis of modern, urban, criminalistic societies is the "folk society."

Redfield has described the folk society in terms of small size, isolation from surrounding cultures, nonliterate population, dependence upon folk knowledge for solution of problems, strong group solidarity, little unconventional behavior, homogeneity of personality types, complex kinship relations, dependence upon folkways, and use of informal social controls rather than formal codes of law to control personal behavior.[22] There is little nonconforming behavior because culturally prescribed aspirations

[21] Robert E. L. Faris, *Social Disorganization* (2nd ed.; New York: The Ronald Press Co., 1955), pp. 3–83.
[22] Robert Redfield, "The Folk Society," *American Journal of Sociology*, LII (January 1947), 293–308. For a detailed critique of the folk-urban argument, see Horace Miner, "The Folk-Urban Continuum," *American Sociological Review*, XVII (October 1952), 529–37.

and socially structured ways of realizing them are in tune. Little personal insecurity or confusion is engendered, and there is slight motivation toward deviant behavior. The concept of folk society represents an ideal which various cultures resemble in greater or lesser degree. Faris describes the characteristics of successful social organizations, as opposed to modern, relatively disorganized systems, in much the same terms. He points out that they are characterized by high morale, little personal deviation, and a predominance of integrated customs and folk knowledge, along with informal controls.[23] Redfield and Faris find the closest approximations of folk societies mainly in the underdeveloped, agrarian nations of the world. It is doubtful that American society ever approached the ideal of folk society, but it has become even more unlike this organization with the passing of decades.

Part of the above argument is that in such a well-organized, consistent society, little personal inconsistency of behavior would be found. In comparison with urban society, personal deviation is uncommon. But it should not be supposed that men are uniformly molded in one image even in folk societies, or that deviations from conventional roles are nonexistent. Demerath has reviewed studies of the distribution of schizophrenia among preliterates, and maintains that the early reports by Elsworth Faris and others of an almost total absence of mental disorder are questionable, in light of the defective research methods on which these studies were based. Demerath indicates that studies have uncovered instances of mental disorder of various kinds among primitives. He also suggests that, while the present data are inadequate for any firm conclusions regarding relative incidence of mental disorder in one society or another, mental disorder is quite rare in truly primitive groups but increases with the processes of acculturation. As a formerly isolated folk group undergoes contact with other societies, certain persons react to culture conflict and marginality of status, with a resulting increase of serious mental aberrations.[24]

A recent study of a modern counterpart of the folk society, the Hutterites of North America, reveals that mental disorders are not unheard of there. The Hutterites are an Anabaptist religious sect who live a simple rural life, with a harmonious social organization and considerable economic security. A number of Hutterites had shown symptoms of mental disorder at some point in their lives, so although the authors of the study concluded that mental pathology is relatively rare among the Hutterites, even a

[23] Faris, op. cit., pp. 3–33.

[24] Nicholas J. Demerath, "Schizophrenia Among Primitives," *American Journal of Psychiatry*, XCVIII (March 1942), 703–7; see also Clinard, *The Sociology of Deviant Behavior*, pp. 393–94.

well-organized society does not completely prevent deviant behavior.[25]

In contrast to the folk culture, the United States and other urbanized nations are complex, dynamic, materialistic, impersonal, and characterized by other features conducive to widespread crime and other kinds of deviant behavior. As illustrative of social disorganization arguments, Faris has this to say:

> The essential feature in the social disorganization that underlies criminality appears to be partial failure of the normal mechanisms of social control. In a modern secular civilization this control is not as strong as in isolated and homogeneous primitive or peasant societies, or as in such religious societies as those of rural Quebec or the early Shaker or Mormon communities. In cities, and particularly in urban slums, the weakening of family and neighborhood controls may be so extreme as to constitute complete failure. In such a situation children who have not already acquired life-organizations based on habits of conventional behavior are, though not inevitably delinquent, at least easily subject to the positive influences of the boy gangs, "fences," and the organized rewards of underworld criminal organizations. . . .
>
> Generalized confusion of standards in our changing contemporary society is also a factor in the encouragement of criminal behavior. The underworld organization of professional criminals is provided with important support by the noncriminal citizen who vigorously insists upon his right to consume prohibited beverages or drugs, to engage in illegal gambling, to purchase goods in evasion of rationing and price regulations, and the like. "Rights" of different kinds and of different origins have come into conflict, and no unified code is accepted by the mass of the population. In this confusion it becomes easy to make and to rationalize moral decisions on the basis of individual interest.[26]

Unfortunately for the advancement of understanding in criminology, the concept of social disorganization is itself disorganized. One of the clearest definitions of social disorganization has been provided by Merton, who asserts that: "Social disorganization refers to inadequacies or failures in a social system of interrelated statuses and roles such that the collective purposes and individual objectives of its members are less fully realized than they could be in an *alternative workable system*" (emphasis added).[27] While this is an exceptionally clear definition, it is by no means

[25] Joseph W. Eaton and Robert J. Weil, "The Mental Health of the Hutterites," in *Mental Health and Mental Disorder*, ed. Arnold Rose (New York: W. W. Norton and Co., 1955), pp. 223–37; Eaton and Weil, *Culture and Mental Disorders* (New York: Free Press of Glencoe, Inc., 1955); see also Herbert Goldhamer and Andrew W. Marshall, *Psychoses and Civilization* (New York: Free Press of Glencoe, Inc., 1953).

[26] Faris, *op. cit.*, p. 246.

[27] Robert K. Merton, "Social Problems and Sociological Theory," in Merton and Nisbet, *op. cit.*, p. 800. See the entire discussion, pp. 799–805.

assured that examples of social disorganization are clearly recognizable. Application of this definition to real-life situations assumes that the collective purposes and individual objectives of members of a society are readily apparent to different sociologists. But there are many who would argue that purposes and objectives are themselves problematic and by no means obvious. The question of alternative workable systems would be likely to provide considerable controversy among different observers. In order to classify American society as disorganized, using this definition, some picture of a more harmonious and attainable system must be entertained. Although such an alternative pattern of organization compatible with the major value orientations of American society might be structured, its outlines are certainly not lucidly visible to all. This leads to the conclusion that the concept of social disorganization is far from flawlessly objective.

Critics of social disorganization notions have also suggested that applications of the theory to real-life situations have often been tautological, the same behavior to be explained by disorganization being used to demonstrate the existence of that state of affairs. In a related fashion, Lemert has charged that social disorganization theory has suffered from a poverty of subsidiary hypotheses, so that few specific propositions to account for forms of pathological behavior have been derived from the general theory.[28] Cohen has charged that the concept is almost hopelessly ambiguous, but has gone on to explicate a revised version which scrapes away the ambiguities of the concept, but also drastically restricts the uses to be made of the notion. Cohen's revision has the effect of limiting application to small social systems rather than to the more traditional analyses of societal conditions.[29] McGee has recently authored an essay on social disorganization in which the term is retained while its customary meaning has been jettisoned. In McGee's work, social disorganization turns out to be another label for deviant behavior.[30]

Over the life history of social disorganization formulations, the major objection has been that they are judgmental in character. Nearly all sociologists agree that modern, industrialized societies represent an amalgam of competing value patterns and normative systems, different social strata with varied "life styles," and subcultures and contracultures of one kind or another. There is consensus on the question of "differential social organization"; the diversified character of modern societies is not at issue.

[28] Lemert, Social Pathology, pp. 7–10.
[29] Cohen, "The Study of Social Disorganization and Deviant Behavior," pp. 475–84.
[30] Reece McGee, Social Disorganization in America (San Francisco: Chandler Publishing Co., 1962).

On this point, a number of authorities have argued that many of the conditions earlier labeled as examples of disorganization or unorganization represent, instead, alternative systems of organization yielding satisfactions to the individuals who are their constituents.[31] The consequence is that evaluation of this state of affairs as disorganized involves more than simply an objective report of empirical observations.[32] For reasons of this kind, the drift of thinking in recent decades has been away from disorganization views and toward stress upon complexity and differential social organization.[33]

### Differential Social Organization and Crime

An abundance of examples of differential social organization views applied to criminality can be found. Sutherland and Cressey have employed this perspective as a companion view to their theory of differential association to be examined in the next chapter. They argue that the social changes involved in the Industrial Revolution, with its emphasis upon individualism, have produced conditions conducive to criminality. The social influences that play upon individuals are inharmonious and inconsistent, and many persons become heavily involved in differential association with carriers of criminalistic norms and become criminals as a consequence.[34] Views parallel to these have been advanced by Sellin, with particular emphasis on the clash of cultural values attendant upon immigration and mobility.[35] Milton Barron has aptly expressed the same theme in a textbook on delinquency titled *The Juvenile in Delinquent Society*.[36] Finally, one well-known statement of this position has been made by Taft and England, in which they argue that the value conflicts, impersonality, individualism, disrespect for law and order, exploitiveness, and other ingredients central to the American way of life make widespread criminality an inevitable by-product of that cultural system.[37]

[31] As a case in point, illustrating the functional utility of crime, see Daniel Bell, "Crime as an American Way of Life," *Antioch Review*, XIII (June 1953), 131–54.

[32] Clinard, *The Sociology of Deviant Behavior*, pp. 22–23.

[33] Books reflecting this view of deviant behavior include Clinard, *The Sociology of Deviant Behavior*; Russell R. Dynes, Alfred C. Clarke, Simon Dinitz and Iwao Ishino, *Social Problems* (New York: Oxford University Press, 1964); Harry C. Bredemeier and Jackson Toby, *Social Problems in America* (New York: John Wiley and Sons, Inc., 1960); Merton and Nisbet, *op. cit.*

[34] Edwin H. Sutherland and Donald R. Cressey, *Principles of Criminology* (7th ed.; Philadelphia: J. B. Lippincott Co., 1966), pp. 101–21.

[35] Thorsten Sellin, *Culture Conflict and Crime* (New York: Social Science Research Council, 1938).

[36] Milton L. Barron, *The Juvenile in Delinquent Society* (New York: Alfred A. Knopf, Inc., 1955).

[37] Donald R. Taft and Ralph W. England, Jr., *Criminology* (4th ed.; New York: The Macmillan Co., 1964), pp. 277–79.

### The Multiple-factor Approach

There is another trend of thought on questions of causation which has flourished alongside the theoretical endeavors described above. This is the multiple-factor view, which holds that causal analysis must be eclectic, providing room for a multitude of factors of different kinds, all bearing some relationship to crime and delinquency.[38] Exponents of this view have often taken pride in their avoidance of dogmatism and rigidity and in their willingness to include biological, psychological, and social factors within some kind of explanatory porridge. Advocates of multiple-factor thinking have suggested that the causes of criminality vary from individual to individual, so it is necessary to compile lengthy inventories of these causes in each instance of deviant conduct. According to this line of reasoning, the best that can be accomplished in the form of explanatory systems is the detailing of a very large set of variables or "categoric risks," all bearing some statistical association to criminality. Supporters of this viewpoint maintain that it is not possible to isolate any factor which shows an invariant relationship to criminality.

We reject this kind of causal nihilism. Multiple-factor orientations as now structured are not explanations at all. If there is to be a scientific explanation of criminality, propositions will ultimately have to be developed of the form: "If conditions A, B, C, and D occur, criminality of some kind will also occur (and if these conditions are absent, noncriminality will be observed." Although multiple-factor thinking asserts as an operating principle that such statements are outside the realm of the discoverable, our preference is for the opposite assumption. We agree with Cohen, who has advanced an incisive critique of multiple-factor perspectives. He points out that the supporters of that framework confuse explanation by means of a *single theory* with explanation by means of a *single factor*. Few modern criminologists would hold that criminality is the result of one variable, although many would aver that some large but finite number of factors do combine to produce criminality. Efforts to develop sociological theories of criminality all involve an extensive list of variables considered to play a role in criminal etiology.[39]

---

[38] Examples of this view are Negley K. Teeters and John Otto Reinemann, *The Challenge of Delinquency* (Englewood Cliffs, N.J.: Prentice-Hall, Inc., 1950), pp. 212–14; Harry Elmer Barnes and Negley K. Teeters, *New Horizons in Criminology* (3rd ed.; Englewood Cliffs, N.J.: Prentice-Hall, Inc., 1959), pp. 206–10.

[39] Albert K. Cohen, discussed in Cressey, *op. cit.,* pp. 171–72; see also George B. Vold, *Theoretical Criminology* (New York: Oxford University Press, 1958), pp. 309–10.

## GENERAL THEORIES: AN EVALUATION

The preceding pages enumerated some theories of deviant behavior which were then criticized on the grounds that they are not specific and detailed enough in application to criminality. We looked at social disorganization approaches to crime causation and found them defective in a number of ways. We also examined multiple-factor views, but rejected these as a viable solution to etiological interests because such orientations deny the possibility of causal analysis.

On a more affirmative level, we hold that theories of criminality framed in differential social organization terms represent a valid approach to the explanation of lawbreaking. It is readily apparent that much of the illegality rampant in American society in particular is related to features of social organization, including conflicts in basic values, a variety of social stratification influences including differentials in availability of legitimate means to attainment of cultural goals, widespread disrespect for law and order, the growing bureaucratization and impersonality of "mass society," and the racial and ethnic cleavages of a nominally democratic society. These are the factors which make sense out of criminality.

But at the same time that we assert confidence in a broadly sociological account of crime causation, we hasten to add that these general theories are flawed by the same ambiguity, fuzzy boundary definitions, and other shortcomings enumerated earlier with regard to theories of deviance. The basic problem with theories of criminality is that the forms of conduct included are extremely varied. Consequently, any formulation which purports to explain crime must be more elegant, elaborate, and detailed than any conceptualization now extant. It is not that existing general theories are false. Rather, they are plausible but basically untestable. The criminality they are designed to explain is unidentified. In addition, they are not sufficiently specific in their claims regarding ways in which particular factors conjoin to produce crime of one kind or another.

As an illustration of the deficiencies of current theories of crime, take the matter of social values and criminality. Robin Williams is one who has tried to identify major value patterns, that is, interests or "things" which stand as principles which individuals employ in organizing their conduct. The values of a society are those pervasive interests which men define as worth pursuing. Williams has suggested that American values include emphasis on achievement and success, stress on activity and work, moral orientations, humanitarianism, efficiency and pragmatism, freedom and inequality, external conformity, secular rationality, and several others as well.[40]

If these are in fact dominant values of American society, it is likely that they have something to do with criminality in the United States. But it would not be amiss to suggest that the value commitments that contribute to such activity as white collar crime may be of a somewhat different order than the interests bound up in other forms of illegality. Accordingly, succeeding chapters will endeavor to advance the understanding of the role of cultural values in crime by paying attention to the contribution that particular values make to different kinds of lawbreaking.

Another illustration of the complex formulations required in order to do justice to the multitude of kinds of criminality can be found in masculinity interests. Many commentators on the American scene have suggested that the compulsive enactment of "manly" forms of behavior is endemic to males in the United States, owing to certain patterns of social organization, particularly family structure which creates anxieties about masculinity in many males. This is a hypothesis in need of testing, but assume for a moment that it is correct. If masculinity strivings are commonplace, they may play some role in crime and delinquency. At the same time, there may be some kinds of lawbreaking quite unrelated to this factor and others which are heavily influenced by masculinity concerns. At least two separate relevant hypotheses have been advanced, one suggesting that lower class male delinquents are plagued with masculinity anxiety,[41] another maintaining that this experience is one which troubles middle class delinquents.[42] Perhaps the problem of masculine identity is bound up in both forms of delinquency in somewhat different ways. If so, a complicated kind of theorizing is called for in order to unravel and clarify these causal strands and weave them into a larger etiological fabric.

A third illustration of the complexities facing general theories of crime and delinquency centers on the hypothesized trend of western societies in the direction of increased rates of criminality. The point has been repeatedly advanced by a variety of doomsayers in recent decades that western societies are not only criminalistic, they are becoming even more

[40] Robin M. Williams, *American Society* (2nd ed., rev.; New York: Random House, Inc., 1960), pp. 397–470.

[41] Walter B. Miller, "Lower Class Culture as a Generating Milieu of Gang Delinquency," *Journal of Social Issues,* XIV, No. 3 (1958), 5–19; Miller, "Implications of Urban Lower Class Culture for Social Work," *Social Service Review,* XXXIII (September 1959), 219–36.

[42] Talcott Parsons, "Certain Primary Sources and Patterns of Aggression in the Social Structure of the Western World," *Psychiatry,* X (May 1947), 167–81; Albert K. Cohen, *Delinquent Boys* (New York: Free Press of Glencoe, Inc., 1955), pp. 161–69.

so with the growth of "mass society." Although the epidemiological facts are not adequate to demonstrate conclusively or invalidate such notions, there is some reason to believe that illegal conduct has become somewhat more pervasive in recent times. However, the long-range drift of things might well include countertendencies, with some kinds of deviant conduct becoming attenuated at the same time others are increasing. Certain kinds of organized prostitution, professional theft, and some other forms of lawbreaking apparently have been on the decline in the recent past. If there is a trend toward burgeoning criminality, certain kinds of illegality may have contributed most heavily to this increase. In particular, it may be that gang fighting, along with utilitarian forms of property crime among lower class persons, is on the rise,[43] as is middle class delinquent conduct.[44] Some of the chapters to follow endeavor to throw further light on these questions.

A final piece of business in the development of criminological theory calls for more attention to certain kinds of criminality which are not included at all within existing general formulations. Sex offender behavior is one major case in point. Although sociologists have a potential contribution of great importance to the understanding of sexual deviations, they have not begun to achieve that potential. Most existing arguments by sociologists regarding criminality are written in such a fashion as to systematically ignore sex offenses. The result is theory which is not only overly general and ambiguous, but also truncated in character. Somewhat the same observation can be made regarding organized crime in American society, for sociologists have had surprisingly little to say about that kind of criminality, other than to repeat some naive conspiratorial descriptions of an assumed Mafia or Cosa Nostra organization.[45]

## SUMMARY

This chapter has considered the present status of general sociological theories of crime. Our assessment of these notions is that the differential social organization perspective offers the most promise for criminological progress. However, those explanations which locate the sources of law-

---

[43] See, on this point, Jackson Toby, "The Prospects for Reducing Delinquency Rates in Industrial Societies," *Federal Probation*, XXVII (December 1963), 23–25.

[44] T. R. Fyvel, *Troublemakers* (New York: Schocken Books, 1962); Ralph W. England, Jr., "A Theory of Middle Class Juvenile Delinquency," *Journal of Criminal Law, Criminology and Police Science*, L (March–April 1960), 535–40; Joseph W. Scott and Edmund W. Vaz, "A Perspective on Middle-Class Delinquency," *Canadian Journal of Economics and Political Science*, XXIX (August 1963), 324–35.

[45] One noteworthy exception is found in Bell, *op. cit.*

breaking in features of social structure are going to have to pay attention to the forms taken by criminality. The starting point for theories stressing differential social organization ought to be with the variations of illegal deviance which must be explained. We need theories sensitive to the forms of crime in all their richness and variety, rather than formulations which try to force the facts of criminality into a preconceived scheme of analysis.

The second half of our review of sociological theories of crime concerns those arguments which have attempted to indicate the factors which operate in the development of criminal behavior and attitudes on the part of individuals. It is to these statements concerning the social-psychology of criminal careers that we turn in Chapter Nine.

# 9

# Causal Analysis
## The Social-Psychology of Criminal Careers

## INTRODUCTION

This chapter continues the overview of general theories of crime and criminality begun in Chapter Eight. While the previous chapter was concerned with theories regarding *rates* of crime or the sociology of crime, the present discussion has to do with the social-psychology of criminal careers. As indicated in the opening chapter, that phrase refers to hypotheses about the factors and experiences which lead to development of particular kinds of careers in law-violating deviant behavior on the part of particular actors.

The chapter begins with an inspection of certain frameworks that have been advanced regarding the emergence of, and changes in, patterns of deviant behavior. The views of Lemert, Becker, and other students of deviance provide some useful concepts and viewpoints to be applied to criminality. Ideally, the study of criminal role-careers ought to be a specialized segment of the general exploration of deviant careers. Propositions regarding deviant conduct would be elaborated to account for criminal patterns. Although existing formulations about deviant patterns of action are not too well articulated, they do contain a number of concepts which should be highly useful in criminology.

This chapter also will examine Sutherland's "theory of differential association," an argument which stands as the most significant effort to date by a criminologist to spell out the nature of the learning processes by which criminal behavior is acquired by individuals. The theory is doubly significant, for Sutherland tried to utilize the same variables used in explanations of the development of "normal" behavior. Sutherland believed that the study of criminal behavior belongs within the main body of sociological endeavors, rather than at the periphery of the main currents of sociological thinking.

The last section of this chapter takes up a number of relatively circumscribed views that have been put forth regarding particular factors or sets of variables thought to play a major role in the development of criminal or delinquent careers. For example, certain patterns of family structure, such as broken or unhappy homes, have often been singled out in attempts to specify criminal producing processes. Other notions have assigned etiological importance to the influences of mass media and a host of other specific variables.

## THE DEVELOPMENT OF DEVIANT CAREERS

### Lemert's Contributions

One of the seminal statements in sociology can be found in the work of Edwin M. Lemert, who has written extensively on the nature of the processes by which persons are singled out as deviants, and by which the life-careers of some become organized or individuated around deviant statuses.[1] Lemert's work is properly regarded as social-psychological in character in that his emphasis is upon deviant individuals and their immediate social interactions with others, rather than upon rates of deviance and the larger social structures producing these rates. Lemert's viewpoint is based on the assumption that "behavioral deviations are a function of culture conflict which is expressed through social organization." [2] However, he has less to say about the ways in which social structure operates to generate deviance than about the processes by which actors become caught up in, and committed to, deviant conduct. In this sense, the arguments of Merton and others examined in the previous chapter are complementary to those of Lemert.

Lemert's writings distinguish between several contexts within which deviant conduct can arise. He suggests the categories of *individual, situational,* and *systematic* deviation to stand for these varied sources of origin.[3] Individual deviation refers to deviant acts which emanate from psychic pressures "within the skin," so to speak, while situational deviation is conduct which develops as a function of situational stresses or pressures. Acts of situational deviation are relatively independent of psychic variations among actors, so varied individuals placed in the same stressful setting would be expected to respond in similar deviant ways.

It is possible to observe instances of deviation which approximate the limiting cases identified by Lemert. For example, some kinds of sexual deviation can be explained only as the consequence of the wholly idio-

[1] Edwin M. Lemert, *Social Pathology* (New York: McGraw-Hill Book Co., Inc., 1951); Lemert, "Social Structure, Social Control, and Deviation," in *Anomie and Deviant Behavior,* ed. Marshall B. Clinard (New York: Free Press of Glencoe, Inc., 1964), pp. 57–97; Lemert, *Human Deviance, Social Problems, and Social Control* (Englewood Cliffs, N.J.: Prentice-Hall, Inc., 1967).

[2] Lemert, *Social Pathology,* p. 23.

[3] *Ibid.,* pp. 37–53.

syncratic motives of the offender. Other cases of this kind can be identified, while it is also possible to point to nearly "pure" illustrations of situational deviation. Samples of the latter include the prison guard caught up in discordant role expectations making deviant acts unavoidable for him, the aircraft worker compelled to utilize deviant work practices in order to solve technological problems created by ill-fitting airplane assembly sections,[4] or individuals implicated in situations of cumulative, catastrophic financial stress such that theft appears the only problem-solving pattern of activity open to them.

As Lemert would acknowledge, these two categories represent polar extremes on a causal continuum, and many occurrences of deviant conduct arise as the joint product of pressures of social situations and factors from the inner life of the individual. In many real-life cases, the etiological task is evaluation of the relative contribution that each motivational source makes to the behavioral product under examination. This job is often at the heart of satisfactory explanation; a critical need in many areas of deviant behavior is for theoretical models which clarify and assign specific weights to these two factors. Take the case of deviant conduct engaged in by police officers as illustrative of the substantive problem. The sociologist who would explain these acts would probably have to examine variations in ethical standards, personality structure, and so on, among police recruits, for it is probable that these individuals vary in relevant ways at the time they enter into the social system of the police department. Policemen vary in terms of involvement in deviant acts, partly as a result of personality differences which they bring with them into police work. In addition, explanation of conduct violations among law enforcement persons would also need to examine the normative system of the organization in order to assess the part played in deviance by *organizational tolerance* for being "on the take" (petty graft), employing violence in contacts with citizens, and other infringements. Readers familiar with a different conceptual language will note that the issue in this illustration revolves around the extent to which psychogenic or sociogenic factors enter into acts of deviant conduct. We will have occasion to take up this central issue at a number of junctures later on. For example, in the analysis of embezzlement, we shall suggest that embezzlement is most likely to occur when certain kinds of personalities are collected in particular kinds of organizational structures. Similarly, the discussion of semiprofessional property offenders will endeavor to indicate the nature of some of those influences which deflect different

4 Joseph Bensman and Israel Gerver, "Crime and Punishment in the Factory: The Function of Deviancy in Maintaining the Social System," *American Sociological Review*, XXVIII (August 1963), 588–98.

individuals in stressful, working class neighborhoods into careers as successful offenders, criminal failures, or law-abiding citizens. We will argue that certain of these factors are to be identified as "inside" the psyches of actors.

Lemert employs the term *systematic deviation* to refer to those patterns of deviant behavior which take on the coloring of subcultures or behavior systems. He says: "when such communication [between deviants] carries specific content, when rapport develops between deviants and common rationalizations make their appearance, the unique and situational forms of deviation are converted to organized or systematic deviation." [5] Systematic or organized forms of deviance arise out of cases of deviant conduct which were individual or situational in genesis. Lemert indicates that systematic deviation is most likely to occur in situations when society makes survival as a deviant person problematic for the individual unless he can become absorbed into some kind of protective social system. Accordingly, the existence of homosexual subcultures in American cities is to be explained, at least in part, as a consequence of the harassment and hostility which the identified homosexual encounters in the United States. [6] One of the points Lemert makes with regard to systematic forms of deviant conduct is worth emphasizing. Most deviant subcultures follow a limited or circumscribed set of deviant mores, for most of the values of the members are those of the dominant culture. [7] This means that drug addicts, homosexuals, or other social pariahs tend to hold allegiance to most conventional values of society, their deviant beliefs and conduct being specific and few in number.

Much of the emphasis in Lemert's presentation is upon *processual* aspects of deviant behavior, in which he shows that deviant careers often undergo marked changes over time. It is fair to say that Lemert has occupied a unique niche in the field of deviant behavior analysis as a result of this temporal accent in his work. The more usual model of explanation is of a simple stimulus-response kind, endeavoring to discover some set of influences which antedated the deviant behavior under study, often with a considerable time span separating the causal factors and present behavior. Little attention has been paid to changes in the nature of deviant careers which flow out of the differential experiences the deviant undergoes in his life history.

In Lemert's theorizing, initial acts of deviant behavior are frequently

[5] Lemert, *Social Pathology*, p. 44.

[6] Maurice Leznoff and William A. Westley, "The Homosexual Community," *Social Problems*, III (April 1956), 257–63; William J. Helmer, "New York's Middle-Class Homosexuals," *Harpers* (March 1963), 85–92; Sherri Cavan, "Interaction in Home Territories," *Berkeley Journal of Sociology*, VIII (1963), 17–32.

[7] Lemert, *Social Pathology*, pp. 48–50.

instances of "risk-taking," representing tentative flirtations with proscribed behavior patterns.[8] Whatever the reasons for these actions, many become subjected to societal reactions. The acts are observed by someone else and made the subject of concern. In this view of things, the subsequent career experiences of the deviant may be more heavily influenced by these societal reactions than by anything else that occurred to him prior to his involvement in disapproved conduct. Lemert notes that societal definitions and reactions in complex societies are often heavily *putative*, so that beliefs become attached to deviant persons which have no foundation in their actual behavior. The "drug fiend" mythology which holds that addicts are generally depraved and immoral is a case in point.[9]

One major distinction introduced by Lemert is between *primary* and *secondary* deviation.[10] This pair of concepts reflects his concern with deviance as a social process, and the impact of societal reactions upon persons. He suggests that primary deviation represents that state of affairs in which an individual engages in norm-violating conduct which he regards as alien to his true self. Secondary deviation, on the other hand, involves cases in which the actor reorganizes his social-psychological characteristics around the deviant role. On this point, Lemert declares that: "The deviant individuals must react symbolically to their own behavior aberrations and fix them in their sociopsychological patterns. The deviations remain primary deviations or symptomatic and situational as long as they are rationalized or otherwise dealt with as functions of a socially acceptable role." [11]

Primary deviation sometimes becomes secondary in character, while in other cases it remains primary. Secondary deviation most often arises out of *a*) repeated acts of norm violation, and *b*) the experience of societal reactions. A kind of feedback process often takes place in which repetition of misconduct or deviation triggers societal reactions to the behavior, which then stimulate further deviant acts. According to Lemert, "The sequence of interaction leading to secondary deviation is roughly as follows: (1) primary deviation; (2) social penalties; (3) further primary deviation; (4) stronger penalties and rejections; (5) further deviation, perhaps with hostilities and resentments beginning to focus upon those doing the penalizing; (6) crisis reached in the tolerance quotient, expressed in formal action by the community stigmatizing of the deviant; (7) strengthening of the deviant conduct as a reaction to the stigmatiz-

[8] Lemert, "Social Structure, Social Control, and Deviation."
[9] Lemert, Social Pathology, pp. 55–57.
[10] Ibid., pp. 73–98; Lemert, Human Deviance, Social Problems, and Social Control, pp. 40–64.
[11] Lemert, Social Pathology, p. 75.

ing and penalties; (8) ultimate acceptance of deviant social status and efforts at adjustment on the basis of the associated role." [12]

In his textbook analysis of forms of deviant conduct, Lemert has gone on to show the applicability of these theoretical notions to the varied forms taken by misconduct and pathological behavior. He has also shown some of the ways in which development of deviant status results in a variety of limitations being imposed upon the social participation of the deviant actor, so that his economic activities, mobility experiences, and so on, become markedly circumscribed as he progresses in deviant conduct. Lemert has also applied these insights on deviant behavior to research studies of alcoholic persons,[13] the development of paranoid social patterns,[14] and the genesis of certain forms of criminality.[15]

We regard these concepts and hypotheses of Lemert very highly. The viewpoints appear to have a high degree of explanatory import for a variety of forms of deviant conduct, with much to be gained from applying them to lawbreaking behavior. In the chapters to follow, much use will be made of some of the core ideas in Lemert's framework. We will repeatedly focus our attention on queries involving contexts of criminal action, so that we shall inquire as to whether forms of criminality represent individual, situational, or systematic deviation. We will also want to explore the matter of societal reactions to criminality in a number of places. In particular, Chapter Ten takes up a variant of societal reactions which is labeled "contacts with defining agencies." The commentary in that chapter will aver that the varied experiences of offenders with various social control agencies operate as powerful influences on the course of their deviant careers. Finally, Lemert's distinction between primary and secondary deviation is incorporated into our distinctions among types of offenders. In the typological materials in Chapter Ten and in succeeding sections of the book, role-career patterns among offenders will be distinguished from each other, in considerable measure in terms of attitudinal and self-image variations among these individuals.

### Other Voices

There are some other lines of commentary regarding the development of deviant careers, additional to those of Lemert, to which we should

---

[12] Ibid., p. 77.

[13] Lemert, "Dependency in Married Alcoholics," Quarterly Journal of Studies on Alcohol, XXIII (December 1962), 590–609.

[14] Lemert, "Paranoia and the Dynamics of Exclusion," Sociometry, XXV (March 1962), 2–20.

[15] Lemert, "The Behavior of the Systematic Check Forger," Social Problems, VI (Fall 1958), 141–49; Lemert, "An Isolation and Closure Theory of Naive Check Forgery," Journal of Criminal Law, Criminology and Police Science, XLIV (September–October 1953), 296–307.

give heed. Becker's recent extended essay bears a good deal of similarity to the claims of Lemert.[16] Among other things, Becker points out that there is no automatic, fixed, and invariant relationship between behavioral acts and societal reactions to the conduct as deviant. Instead, the likelihood that behavioral occurrences will be identified publicly as aberrant varies in accordance with the time at which they occur, the place where they transpire, and the individuals who observe the conduct.[17] Becker notes that some individuals are falsely accused as deviants, for although they have been labeled as outsiders, their behavior has actually been conforming in character. Other persons represent secret deviants; although they misbehave, their misconduct does not come to the attention of any significant public. Still other individuals who acquire a public identity as "queer," "crazy," or in some other way deviant behave in ways which warrant this social judgment.

One of Becker's major contributions is in the stress he places upon the temporal patterning of deviant behavior. He suggests that sociologists need to pay attention to *sequential models of deviance,* that is, to orderly changes in the actions of the deviant over time. He offers the concepts of deviant *careers* and *career contingencies* as possessing considerable explanatory utility. A career contingency is a factor or set of influences which results in the movement of a career incumbent from one position to another in a career pattern.[18] We have already incorporated the notion of career into our analysis. Moreover, in Chapter Ten, these ideas will be elaborated at some length as the viewpoint of this book is spelled out more fully. The career orientation to criminality has already been put through a trial run by the author in another work.[19]

Regarding deviant careers, Becker suggests that interest ought to be concentrated upon the processes and variables which sustain a pattern of deviance over a lengthy time period, rather than upon isolated and fugitive deviant escapades. He argues, in a fashion similar to Lemert, that: "One of the most crucial steps in the process of building a stable pattern of deviant behavior is likely to be the experience of being caught and publicly labeled as a deviant. . . . The most important consequence is a drastic change in the individual's public identity."[20]

Other major insights in Becker's work center upon the distinction between *master* and *subordinate* statuses, in which he argues that a particular deviant status, such as that of "hood," "fairy," or "beatnik," may

[16] Howard S. Becker, Outsiders (New York: Free Press of Glencoe, Inc., 1963); see also Becker, ed., The Other Side (New York: Free Press of Glencoe, Inc., 1964).
[17] Becker, Outsiders, pp. 3–22.
[18] Ibid., pp. 22–39.
[19] Don C. Gibbons, Changing the Lawbreaker (Englewood Cliffs, N.J.: Prentice-Hall, Inc., 1965).
[20] Becker, Outsiders, p. 30.

become superordinate over the other statuses occupied by the individual, with the result that the general social relationships of the person become heavily colored by his public identity as a deviant or discredited person.[21] Finally, Becker, like Lemert, regards the development of deviant groups (subcultures or systematic deviation) as of profound importance as a determinant of the course of a deviant career.[22]

Before passing on to other matters, brief mention should be made in this review of theoretical presentations on deviance of Goffman's work on "stigma." [23] In his essay, Goffman takes up the phenomenon of stigma, the assignment of discrediting or unfavorable social evaluations to individuals. His discussion is not directed specifically at criminality, nor is it focused solely upon deviant persons, for individuals may acquire "spoiled" public identities without being classed as deviants. However, the student who seeks to get some sense of the impact of being assigned such a pariah status as "criminal" would do well to study Goffman's remarks, for they reveal a good deal about the ways in which the stigmatized person adjusts to his social defect, or by which he conceals discrediting facts from observation by others. In this respect, Goffman's work is parallel to the contentions of Lemert and Becker regarding deviant processes.

## SUTHERLAND'S THEORY OF DIFFERENTIAL ASSOCIATION

Few scholars have played a more dominant role in a field of study than sociologist Edwin H. Sutherland (1883–1950). Sutherland's best-known endeavors are in a study of professional theft as a behavior system,[24] development of the concept of "white collar crime," along with research studies of this activity,[25] and his "theory of differential association," which he attempted to apply to various kinds of criminality.[26] No major contribution to the sociological study of *adult* criminal behavior

[21] *Ibid.*, pp. 31–34.

[22] *Ibid.*, pp. 36–39.

[23] Erving Goffman, *Stigma* (Englewood Cliffs, N.J.: Prentice Hall, Inc., 1963).

[24] Edwin H. Sutherland, *The Professional Thief* (Chicago: University of Chicago Press, 1937).

[25] Sutherland, *White Collar Crime* (New York: Dryden Press, 1949).

[26] Sutherland and Donald R. Cressey, *Principles of Criminology* (7th ed.; Philadelphia: J. B. Lippincott Co., 1966). See also Albert K. Cohen, Alfred Lindesmith, and Karl Schuessler, eds., *The Sutherland Papers* (Bloomington: Indiana University Press, 1956), for a resumé of the large number of other papers and studies by Sutherland. Other useful comments on differential association theory are found in George B. Vold, *Theoretical Criminology* (New York: Oxford University Press, 1958), pp. 192–202; Donald R. Cressey, "Epidemiology and Individual Conduct: A Case From Criminology," *Pacific Sociological Review*, III (Fall 1960), 47–58.

has been made in the two decades since Sutherland's untimely death, which serves as a testimonial to his signal place in criminology.

The framework called the theory of differential association with which we are concerned in this chapter emerged over an extended period of development. As Sutherland reported the gestation career of this theory, his first ideas regarding criminological theory began to take shape around 1921, but it was not until 1939 that he developed the mature version of differential association theory.[27] His aim in evolving the differential association perspective is stated in this passage: "I reached the general conclusion that a concrete condition cannot be a cause of crime, and that the only way to get a causal explanation of criminal behavior is by extracting from the varying concrete conditions things that are universally associated with crime."[28] In Sutherland's view, differential association is that thing universally linked to criminal action.

We noted in Chapter Eight that Sutherland's arguments regarding crime causation were built from a foundation of notions regarding differential social organization. In his words: "Cultural conflict in this sense is the basic principle in the explanation of crime."[29] The social and economic changes involved in industrialization of the western world are believed to have generated a pervasive individualism and other conditions conducive to criminality. The social influences persons encounter through their lifetimes are inharmonious and inconsistent, so that many individuals become involved in contacts with carriers of criminalistic norms and become criminals as a consequence. This process is known as "differential association."

The elements of differential association theory as stated in 1939 and in subsequent editions of *Principles of Criminology* are as follows:

1. *Criminal behavior is learned*. Negatively, this means that criminal behavior is not inherited, as such; also, the person who is not already trained in crime does not invent criminal behavior, just as a person does not make mechanical inventions unless he has had training in mechanics.

2. *Criminal behavior is learned in interaction with other persons in a process of communication*. This communication is verbal in many respects but includes also "the communication of gestures."

3. *The principal part of the learning of criminal behavior occurs within inti-*

[27] Cohen, Lindesmith, and Schuessler, *op. cit.*, pp. 13–29. This essay by Sutherland is highly recommended as an all too infrequent report on the "sociology of knowledge." In it, Sutherland presents a highly candid and characteristically modest account of the stages of thought through which he progressed and of the influences upon his thinking, as he evolved the differential association view.

[28] *Ibid.*, p. 19.

[29] *Ibid.*, p. 20.

*mate personal groups.* Negatively, this means that the impersonal agencies of communication, such as movies and newspapers, play a relatively unimportant part in the genesis of criminal behavior.

4. *When criminal behavior is learned, the learning includes* (a) *techniques of committing the crime, which are sometimes very complicated, sometimes very simple;* (b) *the specific direction of motives, drives, rationalizations, and attitudes.*

5. *The specific direction of motives and drives is learned from definitions of the legal codes as favorable or unfavorable.* In some societies an individual is surrounded by persons who invariably define the legal codes as rules to be observed, while in others he is surrounded by persons whose definitions are favorable to the violation of the legal codes. In our American society these definitions are almost always mixed, with the consequence that we have culture conflict in relation to the legal codes.

6. *A person becomes delinquent because of an excess of definitions favorable to violation of law over definitions unfavorable to violation of law.* This is the principle of differential association. It refers to both criminal and anti-criminal associations and has to do with counteracting forces. When persons become criminal, they do so because of contacts with criminal patterns and also because of isolation from anti-criminal patterns. Any person inevitably assimilates the surrounding culture unless other patterns are in conflict; a Southerner does not pronounce "r" because other Southerners do not pronounce "r." Negatively, this proposition of differential association means that associations which are neutral so far as crime is concerned have little or no effect on the genesis of criminal behavior. Much of the experience of a person is neutral in this sense, e.g., learning to brush one's teeth. This behavior has no negative or positive effect on criminal behavior except as it may be related to associations which are concerned with the legal codes. This neutral behavior is important especially as an occupier of the time of a child so that he is not in contact with criminal behavior during the time he is so engaged in the neutral behavior.

7. *Differential associations may vary in frequency, duration, priority, and intensity.* This means that associations with criminal behavior and also associations with anti-criminal behavior vary in those respects. "Frequency" and "duration" as modalities of associations are obvious and need no explanation. "Priority" is assumed to be important in the sense that lawful behavior developed in early childhood may persist throughout life, and also that delinquent behavior developed in early childhood may persist throughout life. This tendency, however, has not been adequately demonstrated, and priority seems to be important principally through its selective influence. "Intensity" is not precisely defined but it has to do with such things as the prestige of the source of a criminal or anti-criminal pattern and with emotional reactions related to the associations. In a precise description of the criminal behavior of a person these modalities would be stated in quantitative form and a mathematical ratio be reached. A formula in this sense has not been developed, and the development of such a formula would be extremely difficult.

8. *The process of learning criminal behavior by association with criminal and anti-criminal patterns involves all of the mechanisms that are involved in any other learning.* Negatively, this means that the learning of criminal behavior is not restricted to the process of imitation. A person who is seduced, for instance, learns criminal behavior by association, but this process would not ordinarily be described as imitation.

9. *While criminal behavior is an expression of general needs and values, it is not explained by those general needs and values since non-criminal behavior is an expression of the same needs and values.* Thieves generally steal in order to secure money, but likewise honest laborers work in order to secure money. The attempts by many scholars to explain criminal behavior by general drives and values, such as the happiness principle, striving for social status, the money motive, or frustration, have been and must continue to be futile since they explain lawful behavior as completely as they explain criminal behavior. They are similar to respiration, which is necessary for any behavior but which does not differentiate criminal from non-criminal behavior.[30]

The essence of Sutherland's argument is that criminal behavior is enacted by individuals who have acquired a number of sentiments in favor of law violation, sufficient to outweigh their prosocial or anticriminal conduct definitions. In turn, different actors get their varied congeries of prosocial and procriminal conduct standards through associations with others in their social environment. In general, those contacts or associations which have the greatest impact on persons are ones which are frequent, lengthy, early in point of origin, and most intense or meaningful. Sutherland suggested that: "It is not necessary, at this level of explanation, to explain why a person has the associations he has; this certainly involves a complex of many things." [31] However, he maintained that the state of differential social organization characteristic of modern societies is responsible, in general terms, for the varied associational ties of different persons.

Sutherland's formulation has dominated criminology for two reasons. First, it is the major effort by a sociologist to state a theory regarding criminality in which a set of general propositions are enunciated as sufficient to explain the occurrence (or nonoccurrence) of criminal conduct. The differential association argument stands in great contrast to multiple-factor orientations, for the latter are no more than descriptive inventories of a great list of specific variables bearing some association to criminality, with few if any linkages indicated between them. A second reason for the popularity of differential association claims is that these are stated in terms of a small group of "core" concepts and arguments to

[30] Sutherland and Cressey, op. cit., pp. 81–82.
[31] Ibid , p. 82.

which all sociologists owe allegiance. The "sociological perspective" advances an image of man as the product of his social experiences, which provide him with the definitions or standards of conduct and beliefs which stimulate and sustain his activities. Moreover, the sociological view is that the primary groups to which men belong (Sutherland's "intimate personal groups") exert the strongest influence upon them. The sociologist sees man as driven by a "motor" which the social process has placed inside him. No wonder that Sutherland's formulation won wide acceptance, for it is stated in the rhetoric and terminology of sociology. It includes no alien terminology from the psychologist's or psychiatrist's bag of words.

For all its merits, the theory of differential association is not without faults. As is true of most sociological exposition, this lacks a good deal in clarity and precision. The problem is not that the claims are false, but rather that they are overly ambiguous; they are rendered plausible but essentially untestable. For example, what are we to make of the contention that persons become criminal due to an excess of definitions favorable to law violation over prosocial sentiments? Perhaps some relationship is implied in which the sheer *number* of conduct definitions of one kind or another is the major determinant of conduct, with criminality resulting whenever the ratio of criminalistic attitudes to law-abiding ones held by an individual becomes two to one, or some other ratio. A case could be made that some conduct definitions are more compelling than others, so a few criminalistic attitudes can, under certain circumstances, overpower a large number of conformist preferences. If we cannot agree as to which of these interpretations is correct, and if we cannot spell out more adequately the relationship suggested by the theory, a definitive test of the argument is rendered impossible.

The same point holds for other parts of the Sutherland statement. Are "associations" to be interpreted as identifiable, physical, group contacts in which individuals are enmeshed? The passages from *Principles of Criminology* rather clearly indicate that group associations of the individual are the important forces in behavior. However, some persons have interpreted Sutherland to mean that associations are those collectivities to which actors orient their conduct—their reference groups—so that some individuals are in differential association with social units other than those with which they are in physical contact.[32] But let us retain the interpretation of associations apparently intended by Sutherland. What kinds of associations are "intense" ones? The common-sense ring to the notion of intensity enables us to agree that, somehow or

---

[32] Daniel Glaser, "Criminality Theories and Behavioral Images," *American Journal of Sociology,* LXI (March 1956), 433–444.

another, certain groups to which we belong are more important to us than are others. Yet it is quite another thing to operationalize the concept of intensity by settling upon empirical indicators of it which will provide for measurement of the intensity of different group associations.

The foregoing are suggestive of objections that have been leveled at differential association theory. The dialogue of criticisms and rejoinders has been so massive as to testify to the seminal role of Sutherland's conceptualization in the development of criminological theory. Whatever the final evaluation of this framework, it must be admitted that the perspective has served criminology well in the role of an intellectual "pump primer."

An extremely detailed and incisive résumé of the differential association controversy has been prepared by Cressey.[33] According to Cressey, allegations regarding defects of differential association theory fall into two groups, those based on misinterpretations of the language of the theory or upon ambiguities contained in it, and those directed at substantive claims in the argument.

One erroneous interpretation of the theory holds that it avers that persons who associate with criminals become criminals in turn. But close examination of the argument shows that Sutherland maintained that criminality ensues from an *excess* of criminal associations over noncriminal ones. Another incorrect interpretation asserts that the theory says that criminality results from involvements with criminal persons, while the formulation actually refers to criminal *patterns,* many of which are carried and communicated by persons who are not gangsters or robbers. Other objections have been raised regarding failure of the theory to specify why individuals have the associations they have, even though Sutherland did give much attention to this question at other points in his work. Still another class of erroneous judgments regarding the theory stem from incorrect notions about the nature and role of theoretical frameworks.[34]

Concerning substantive criticisms, Cressey notes that a number of criminologists have asserted that the theory fails to account for certain forms of criminality, but often without identifying the exceptional cases thought to be outside the boundaries of differential association. He notes that differential association has been said not to apply to rural offenders, violators of World War II O.P.A. regulations, naive check forgers, and certain other types of lawbreakers who have been subjected to research investigation.[35]

[33] Cressey, "Epidemiology and Individual Conduct."
[34] Ibid., 48–50.
[35] Ibid., 51.

Differential association theory has also been criticized for ignoring "personality traits" or "psychological variables." As Cressey makes clear, this is an objection with which Sutherland wrestled at length. Sutherland's opinion was that even if some personality traits are associated with forms of criminality (as distinct from being the *result* of deviant careers), so that some kinds of offenders are uncommonly "aggressive," "introverted," or "anxious," differential association still determines which individuals with the personality patterns become criminal and which do not. We can agree that this is a reasonable rejoinder as far as it goes. Still, we are left with a major task in criminology, to specify the linkages between offender patterns and predisposing personality constellations, as well as to isolate and explicate the ingredients of the processes by which individuals of some type get selectively recruited and canalized by social experience along different behavioral paths. This is major unfinished theoretical business for criminology, but Sutherland cannot be held accountable for a failure to solve this question.[36]

Another substantive, conceptual problem with the theory centers around its failure to spell out the effects which experiences of the person at different age periods have upon his behavior at any point in time. It may be that some early life experiences undergone by individuals affect the *meaning* of later ones. They become influential in conditioning subsequent events, persons who have encountered them reacting to certain adult associations and definitions in a significant fashion. At the same time, adult life events may have a neutral or insignificant impact upon persons who have experienced a divergent set of earlier life happenings.[37] These possibilities resemble the statistician's notion of *stochastic processes,* in which the effects of any present experience or variable depend upon what has transpired earlier in the life histories of the subjects under examination. Further, the probabilities of future events are likely to vary among actors, as they encounter variations in experiences that have not yet taken place. This sort of view of deviant behavior is contained in Becker's notions of "sequential models," "careers," and "career contingencies" discussed earlier in this chapter.

Still another contention regarding defects of the theory is to the effect that the ratio of learned behavior patterns used to explain criminality cannot be precisely studied in specific cases. Cressey offers a number of examples in which researchers have found it impossible to

[36] A recent essay which voices this complaint about the absence of a dynamic view of personality in the differential association theory is S. Kirson Weinberg, "Personality and Method in the Differential Association Theory: Comments on 'A Reformulation of Sutherland's Differential Association Theory and a Strategy for Empirical Verification,'" *Journal of Research in Crime and Delinquency,* III (July 1966), 165–72.
[37] Cressey, "Epidemiology and Individual Conduct," 53.

measure accurately definitions favorable, or unfavorable, to violation of law.[38] Finally, a number of critics have averred that the learning process by which criminality or law-abiding behavior is acquired is more complex than indicated by the theory. For example, it does not allow for the possibility that some individuals contrive their criminality apart from contact with criminal associations.[39]

We can find no better summary evaluation of the dialogue on differential association than Cressey's judgment. He says:

On the other hand, it also seems safe to conclude that differential association is not a precise statement of the process by which one becomes a criminal. The idea that criminality is a consequence of an excess of intimate associations with criminal behavior patterns is valuable because, for example, it negates assertions that deviation from norms is simply a product of being emotionally insecure or living in a broken home, and then indicates in a general way why only some emotionally insecure persons and only some persons from broken homes commit crimes. . . . Yet the statement of the differential association process is not precise enough to stimulate rigorous empirical test, and it therefore has not been proved or disproved.[40]

The notion of differential association ought to be acknowledged as a highly valuable point of view which has served as an initial waypoint in the journey toward a mature version of criminological theory. To so describe it is in no sense to denigrate its importance. But the essence of Cressey's evaluation and of our own is that the task ahead is to elaborate upon and revise the etiological beginnings established by Sutherland. The kinds of efforts in order are several. Sutherland and Cressey have indicated one major line of endeavor in their call for studies of "behavior systems" and other specific forms of criminal behavior.[41] They suggest that research and theoretical labors might concentrate more upon study of specific orders or forms of criminality, rather than further elaboration of a general, overarching theory of crime such as differential association. This sort of activity would perhaps begin to separate forms of criminality which arise out of some process akin to differential association from those which do not. Theoretical endeavors of this sort should also introduce some clarity into the general theory of

[38] Ibid., 53.
[39] Ibid., 53–54.
[40] Ibid., 57.
[41] Sutherland and Cressey, op. cit., p. 287. Other detailed remarks on this direction to theoretical activities can be found in Gibbons, op. cit., pp. 21–73; Gibbons and Donald L. Garrity, "Some Suggestions for the Development of Etiological and Treatment Theory in Criminology," Social Forces, XXXVIII (October 1959), 51–58; Gibbons and Garrity, "Definition and Analysis of Certain Criminal Types," Journal of Criminal Law, Criminology and Police Science, LIII (March 1962), 27–35.

differential association by revealing the specific concatenations of variables or factors which are summed up in the general expression. The major need in contemporary criminology is for elaborate formulations which are congruent with the complex character of social interaction as it is played out in real life.

There have been several recent efforts to revise and renovate the differential association theory so as to make it more serviceable. Jeffery has criticized the argument on the grounds that it is not stated in terms of modern learning theory.[42] Burgess and Akers have actually restated the differential association formulation in terms of modern learning theory from psychology.[43] Probably the most significant contribution to development of the theory is in an essay by De Fleur and Quinney.[44] These sociologists, restating Sutherland's views in the language of set theory, have put the argument into a tightly logical form. They turned up several points of ambiguity in the original formulation. The most important conclusion reached by De Fleur and Quinney is that a testable version of differential association would have to be linked to an adequate taxonomy of criminal role-patterns. We would then discover that there are a number of forms of differential association related to different criminal patterns. In short, De Fleur and Quinney concur with the view of this book that differential association is a label for an assortment of factors or experiences implicated in different forms of lawbreaking.

The discussions of different criminal role-patterns in Chapters Eleven through Sixteen hint at the eventual shape which causal theories may take. These will be seen to show unmistakable signs of linkage to Sutherland's pioneering works.


## FAMILY FACTORS AND CRIMINALITY

The opening remarks in this chapter indicated that certain formulations about the influence of single factors or causal patterns in criminality have enjoyed a good measure of popularity. Most have been points of view or lines of emphasis, rather than rigorous instances of theorizing. Doubtless the most important of these orientations has been the one that

[42] C. R. Jeffery, "Criminal Behavior and Learning Theory," Journal of Criminal Law, Criminology and Police Science, LVI (September 1965), 294–300.

[43] Robert L. Burgess and Ronald L. Akers, "A Differential Association-Reinforcement Theory of Criminal Behavior," Social Problems, XIV (Fall 1966), 128–47.

[44] Melvin L. De Fleur and Richard Quinney, "A Reformulation of Sutherland's Differential Association Theory and a Strategy for Empirical Verification," Journal of Research in Crime and Delinquency, III (January 1966), 1–22; also see Donald R. Cressey, "The Language of Set Theory and Differential Association," Journal of Research in Crime and Delinquency, III (January 1966), 22–26.

assigns a crucial etiological role to intra-family experiences. A great many psychiatrists, psychologists, and sociologists are in general agreement that the family dimension is critical in the genesis of patterns of lawbreaking. Beyond this consensus, however, there are a variety of interpretations of the precise significance attached to home factors. Some would claim that the family variable is *the* crucial one, while others take a much more cautious position, arguing that it is only one of a number of important considerations, and not always the most critical.

The rationale behind heavy emphasis upon home factors in criminality is easily stated. Take first the matter of delinquency and the role of parental family processes in it. In almost every society, the family has the most intense and consistent contact with children from infantile dependence through at least the preadolescent stage of life. Even in American society, where other social structures invade the arena of child rearing, no other social institution has the same degree of control over the socialization process as does the family. Thus the behavior of all youngsters, delinquent or nondelinquent, is probably greatly influenced by primary group interaction within family settings. As a consequence, there has been much interest in relationships among home conditions, child rearing practices, and delinquent conduct.

The family is seen as an important force in adult criminality, but for somewhat different reasons. Some forms of adult lawbreaking may flow out of distortions and pathologies in the offender's childhood experiences in his family. But nearly all adult persons eventually leave the family of orientation or parental family situation and move into a marriage, where they become engaged in the creation and maintenance of a new family system. At any point in time, most adult Americans are either married or in transition between marriages. There is a wealth of evidence to indicate that the family is the major anchorage point for most adults; given that an individual is in a stable family unit, his behavior is likely to be conventional. On the other hand, since disruptions of marital relationships often seem implicated in a host of forms of aberrant, deviant, or otherwise unusual behavior, it is easy to suppose that some kinds of criminality may represent responses to distorted family relationships. Examples of father-daughter incest, acts of victim-precipitated homicide carried out on marital partners, and exhibitionism come readily to mind as instances wherein family variables may be importantly involved.

As far as investigations of the role of family dynamics in criminality are concerned, the bulk of research has concentrated upon juvenile delinquents. Regarding such studies, Sutherland and Cressey have summarized the generalizations made involving home conditions and delinquency. They indicate that delinquents tend to come from homes characterized by one or more of the following conditions: *a*) other members of the family are criminal, delinquent, or alcoholic, *b*) one or both parents are absent from the home through divorce, desertion, or death, *c*) the home is marked by a lack of parental control, *d*) home uncongeniality is evidenced by such things as domination by one member, favoritism, oversolicitude, overseverity, neglect, or jealousy, *e*) racial or religious differences in conventions and standards, foster home or institutional home situations, and *f*) economic pressures stemming from unemployment or insufficient income.[45]

The comparative study by the Gluecks of 500 delinquents and 500 nonoffenders represents a major source of data regarding home factors.[46] From this research, they reported that 49.8 per cent of the delinquents but only 28.8 per cent of the nonoffenders were from broken homes.[47] Moreover, 60.4 per cent of the delinquents and 34.2 per cent of the nondelinquents had at some time prior to the study lived in a home broken by separation, divorce, death, or prolonged absence of one parent.[48] The offenders were more commonly from homes in which the parents had a history of serious physical ailments, mental retardation, emotional disturbance, drunkenness, or criminality.

The social climate of the delinquents' homes was wretched in other ways, too. According to the Gluecks, the parents of the delinquents were not good managers of income, they were relatively poor planners of home routine, and they exhibited less self-respect than parents of the nonoffenders. The same parents were less ambitious, had poorer conduct standards, and poorer conjugal relations. The mothers of the delinquents gave poor supervision to their children, and the parents showed less cohesiveness than did those of nondelinquents.[49] Marked differences were seen between the affection exhibited toward children by the parents of delinquents as compared to nondelinquents.[50] The parents of the offenders were also more frequently lax, overstrict, or erratic in disciplining their children than were the parents of the nondelinquents.[51]

This amalgam of factors led the Gluecks to conclude that defective family patterns represent the major causal dimension in delinquency. It would be hard to ignore this generalization, given these supportive find-

[45] Sutherland and Cressey, op. cit., p. 217. See their chapter on family patterns, pp. 216–33, for a discussion of the supportive data behind these contentions.

[46] Sheldon and Eleanor Glueck, Unraveling Juvenile Delinquency (Cambridge, Mass.: Harvard University Press, 1951).

[47] Ibid., p. 88.

[48] Ibid., p. 122.

[49] Ibid., pp. 108–16.

[50] Ibid., pp. 125–26.

[51] Ibid., p. 131.

ings. However, two points come to mind regarding this conclusion. First, it is conceivable that other variables loom equally large in the etiology of delinquency, as other findings of the Gluecks tend to indicate. Peer group relationships represent one set of such added causal agents. Second, very different family relationships among delinquents might be observed if the focus of attention were to shift away from working class, gang delinquents to other types of juvenile offenders. The evidence from studies of middle class offenders and certain other kinds of adolescent lawbreakers points to a different constellation of parent-child relationships.

Broken homes have received a great deal of emphasis as an important variable in delinquency, with much research directed toward discovering the relationship between this factor and juvenile misconduct. Estimates of the proportion of broken homes among delinquents vary from one study to another, but in general they range from 30 to 60 per cent of the offenders, with lesser numbers of broken homes for nondelinquents.[52]

One contrary piece of evidence on broken homes comes from the work of Shaw and McKay. They compared the incidence of broken homes among Chicago schoolboys and male juvenile delinquents and found that the broken home rate of offenders was 42.5 per cent as compared to 36.1 per cent for the nondelinquents, an insignificant difference.[53] However, Toby has recently shown that evaluation of broken homes as inconsequential in delinquency is valid for older male delinquents, but not for male preadolescents or female offenders.[54] He indicates that the Shaw and McKay study did not include girls, and other research shows that female delinquents do come from broken homes in considerable numbers.[55] Furthermore, he shows that the difference between preadolescent delinquents and nondelinquents in terms of broken homes is rather marked; the broken home does have some causal impact upon both girls and preadolescent boys.

The most common research design regarding family variations and delinquent conduct has compared a group of offenders against a sample of

[52] For a discussion of these estimates, see Harry M. Shulman, "The Family and Juvenile Delinquency," The Annals of the American Academy of Political and Social Science, No. 261 (January 1949), pp. 21–31; P. M. Smith, "Broken Homes and Juvenile Delinquency," Sociology and Social Research, XXXIX (May–June 1955), 307–11.

[53] Clifford Shaw and Henry D. McKay, "Social Factors in Juvenile Delinquency," Report on the Causes of Crime, National Commission on Law Observance and Enforcement, Vol. II (Washington, D.C.: U.S. Government Printing Office, 1937), pp. 261–84.

[54] Jackson Toby, "The Differential Impact of Family Disorganization," American Sociological Review, XXII (October 1957), 505–12.

[55] See, for example, Don C. Gibbons and Manzer J. Griswold, "Sex Differences Among Juvenile Court Referrals," Sociology and Social Research, XLII (November–December 1957), 106–10; William Wattenberg and Frank Saunders, "Sex Differences Among Juvenile Offenders," Sociology and Social Research, XXXIX (September–October 1954), 24–31.

nondelinquents. The Glueck study is one example of this kind. In most cases, the results have been somewhat ambiguous, so that a confused picture of family relationships has been discovered both for lawbreakers and for nondelinquents. Perhaps another kind of procedure is in order. If there are a variety of offender behavior patterns in the total population of delinquents (or criminals), it is probably also true that there are assorted constellations of family factors related to them. Several instances of research have generally confirmed this contention. Jenkins and Hewitt studied a group of guidance clinic cases in which three patterns of maladjustment were identified: unsocialized aggressive children, pseudo-social or gang offenders, and over-inhibited youngsters. The investigators found that the aggressive youths were from backgrounds of parental rejection, while pseudosocial offenders were from situations of parental neglect and exposure to delinquency patterns. The pattern of over-inhibition, in which the youngsters were shy and withdrawn, appeared to be the result of situations of parental repression and over-control.[56]

Another investigation by Reiss produced similar results. He examined the social backgrounds of 1110 juvenile court probationers in Cook County, Illinois, who were classified by court workers as relatively integrated delinquents, offenders with defective superego controls, or delinquents with weak ego controls. The study of social correlates of these types indicated a number of differences among them, some of the major ones having to do with family variations.[57]

Our concluding comment on home factors and delinquency is much the same as our summary assessment of a number of other arguments, such as those involving emotional disturbance or deteriorated neighborhoods. The influence of family patterns on delinquent conduct cannot be gainsaid. However, to argue that family variables always have primacy over all others would be to draw a caricature of real life. Claims that some particular family pattern is found in all forms of criminality are equally erroneous. Parental influences may well vary in significance in different types of criminality, just as parental factors or marital relationships important in one type of deviance may not be significant in another. Consequently, such factors need to be examined within the context of specific offender role-careers. In Chapters Eleven through Sixteen, we will explore the place of family factors in the causation of various forms of criminal conduct.

[56] Richard L. Jenkins and Lester E. Hewitt, "Types of Personality Structure Encountered in Child Guidance Clinics," *American Journal of Orthopsychiatry*, XIV (January 1944), 84–94.
[57] Albert J. Reiss, Jr., "Social Correlates of Psychological Types of Delinquency," *American Sociological Review*, XVII (December 1952), 710–18.

## OTHER PARTICULARISTIC HYPOTHESES

By now, we have covered most of the major general and specific lines of theorizing regarding criminality. There are some other particularistic, single-factor arguments that have been made in addition to those enumerated above. For example, some attention has been given to the role of mass media in criminality, parallel to the vulgarized form of this contention popular with the general public. However, the major share of these specific claims are concerned with delinquents rather than adult criminals.

The evaluation to be made of single-variable contentions should be fully apparent. Insofar as individual ones have merit, it is only as components of more complex, multivariate formulations. Stated differently, any narrowly delimited causal variable operates in a complex interrelationship with many others, the theoretical task of the criminologist centering about the explication of these etiological congeries.

The second point regarding particularistic notions is that they need to be narrowed to those types of deviant careers in which they are most influential. The general situation is parallel to that of family factors and criminality, family influences being of different kinds and entering in different ways into forms of criminality. Accordingly, the meaningful approach to particularistic factors directs attention at specific role patterns, which is the procedure in the chapters to come on offender careers.

## SUMMARY

This chapter has concluded the comprehensive probing into the body of existing theoretical formulations on criminality. The judgment has been reiterated that the most fruitful attack upon etiological questions in criminality would be one which pays close attention to the different forms of conduct practiced by the population of lawbreakers. The time has now come for a close look at this orientation to criminology, the subject to which we move in Chapter Ten.

# 10

# Causal Analysis
## The Study
## of
## Role-Careers

## INTRODUCTION

The three preceding chapters have consistently stressed that progress in causal analysis in criminology depends upon a shift of attention toward the study of specific forms of criminality and away from inquiries into "crime" or "delinquency." Chapter Seven contended that offenders are motivated, striving, feeling beings, so that personality dynamics, including varieties of pathological personality structure, are implicated in crime causation. The major thrust of that discussion was to argue that the interlocking patterns of social and personality variables which activate criminal or noncriminal forms of conduct can only be clarified through study of different offender role-careers. Chapter Eight asserted that existing sociological formulations which aim to account for *rates* of criminality are overly broad in statement. Another level of theorizing is required in which generic formulations about crime would be supplemented by middle range theories directed at particular orders of criminality. The Cloward and Ohlin adaptation of anomie theory to working class gang delinquents is one illustration of the kind of explanatory model needed.[1] Chapter Nine concluded on the note that propositions regarding social-psychological processes in deviant and criminal careers are similarly in need of further exposition in which the permutations of these views would be developed for particular forms of criminal role behavior.

The time has arrived for a detailed look at this perspective on criminality which is usually called the "typological" approach. This chapter initiates the presentation by articulating the major outlines of a typological framework.[2] Chapters Eleven through Sixteen will apply these views to the study of particular forms of criminality.

In the plan of this chapter, a glance will first be taken at typological

[1] Richard A. Cloward and Lloyd E. Ohlin, *Delinquency and Opportunity* (New York: Free Press of Glencoe, Inc., 1960).

[2] An earlier, detailed version of the viewpoint laid out in this chapter is in Don C. Gibbons, *Changing the Lawbreaker* (Englewood Cliffs, N.J.: Prentice-Hall, Inc., 1965).

analyses in the criminological literature. Criminological thinking in the past decade or so has taken a decided turn toward description and explanation of specific orders of criminal and delinquent deviation, replacing to a considerable extent a search for unitary and general theories which explain "crime" and "delinquency."

Following the resumé of existing typological works, the commentary turns to some logical and theoretical requirements of an adequate system of offender types. The major point is simply that there are an almost infinite number of ways in which criminals or delinquents might be classified or "typed," but these taxonomies may not all be equally useful for explanatory purposes. For example, one simple scheme for sorting offenders into types would be on the basis of specific legal offenses with which they are charged. However, there are several problems with such a system. Processes such as "plea copping," in which the person pleads guilty to a charge lesser than the one with which he was originally charged, mean that legal categories do not accurately distinguish various offender patterns. Even more important, legal offense categories often fail to reflect significant dimensions or aspects of the social behavior which has been the subject of social control agency attention. The legal category of "rape" includes quite varied patterns of deviant activity, some rape involving violence, force, and unwilling participation by the victim, whereas these elements are missing in other cases.

Another problem with legal offense categories as the basis of classification is that offenders do not, in many cases, consistently commit only a single kind of deviant act; a person labeled a "burglar" today may become a "larcenist" tomorrow. A more serious difficulty is that legal classifications do not identify theoretically significant types. There is little reason to suppose that persons characterized as "burglars" or typed in terms of some other specific legal offense are the product of a uniform etiological process. Accordingly, the study of causal patterns in deviant behavior is not likely to be advanced through such taxonomic schemes. It will be aided only through discovery of classification categories which sort offenders into types in which a single etiological process does characterize the individuals included in a specific type.

Violators can be classified in terms of a multitude of variables: offense, hair color, race, urban-rural residence, *ad infinitum*. The criminologist who hopes to settle upon a causally significant classification of offenders takes a calculated risk. He must choose one system from the many available. Hopefully, his choice will be significant so that when offenders are sorted out in terms of the selected scheme the result will be homogeneous types in which the etiological process is the same for all members of the category. But there is no one obvious or right way to classify violators which jumps out at the observer from the facts of criminality. The decision to sort out deviants by means of variable $X$ rather than variable $Y$ can be made only in terms of some logic or rationale, some argument in defense of a particular choice of variables. It is not possible to be certain, in advance of research test, that a particular classificatory scheme is causally significant. It is this part of taxonomic and other theoretical work which warrants use of the term "calculated risk."

The latter portion of this chapter will put forth a role-career viewpoint regarding classification of offenders According to this view, violators can be meaningfully categorized in terms of certain variables, such as "offense patterns," "interactional setting," "attitudes," and "self-images." Various deviant types, such as the "naive check forger" or "gang delinquent," can be identified on the basis of these dimensions. This book holds that the types which result from use of these classificatory dimensions represent significant categories in both causal and treatment terms. The last part of this chapter attempts to support this claim with an extended justificatory argument.

## THE DEVELOPMENT OF TYPOLOGICAL VIEWS

Movement in the direction of study of variations among types of lawbreakers and away from analysis of "crime" and "delinquency" is a major trend in criminology. Recent textbooks by Bloch and Geis,[3] Sutherland and Cressey,[4] Clinard,[5] Korn and McCorkle,[6] and Cavan [7] are all structured around the viewpoint that "crime" and "delinquency" represent heterogeneous forms of behavior. They maintain that, within these behavioral grabbags, homogeneous patterns of deviant conduct can be identified, so attention must be directed toward investigation of specific offender types. No single theory of crime or delinquency is going to be sufficient to account for the various forms which these phenomena take, so it is generally argued that causal "theories of the middle range" specific to particular forms of deviant conduct will have to be developed.

Unfortunately, this position has generally been enunciated as an article

[3] Herbert A. Bloch and Gilbert Geis, Man, Crime, and Society (New York: Random House, Inc., 1962), pp. 135–37, 311–43.
[4] Edwin H. Sutherland and Donald R. Cressey, Principles of Criminology (7th ed.; Philadelphia: J. B. Lippincott Co., 1966).
[5] Marshall B. Clinard, Sociology of Deviant Behavior (rev. ed.; New York: Holt, Rinehart and Winston, Inc., 1963), pp. 204–91.
[6] Richard R. Korn and Lloyd W. McCorkle, Criminology and Penology (New York: Holt, Rinehart and Winston, Inc., 1959), pp. 142–56.
[7] Ruth Shonle Cavan, Juvenile Delinquency (Philadelphia: J. B. Lippincott Co., 1962); Cavan, Criminology (2nd ed.; New York: Thomas Y. Crowell Co., 1955), pp. 3–31, 125–250.

of faith, without much effort to push etiological study very far in this direction. Most assertions that criminality is not homogeneous, but that particular patterns of uniform behavior can be observed, are followed by vague, incomplete, anecdotal, and logically ambiguous classification systems. Commonly, someone advances the argument that there are types of offenders, and proceeds to list types like "egocentric, wayward offender," "professional criminal," or "gang delinquent" within which offenders are held to fall. These categories are not well-defined, and are often illustrated by case histories rather than explicit statements of the definitional attributes of the types. It is difficult to visualize research tests of such claims, for it is unlikely that different researchers would classify particular offenders in the same way or within the same types.

There is a sizable body of theory and research which has focused upon single patterns of behavior held to represent offender types. Theories have been stated regarding "embezzlers," "gang delinquents," "automobile thieves," "naive check forgers," and a number of other types of criminals and delinquents. Research investigations have also been conducted regarding a number of kinds of juvenile or adult illegality. However, most studies of narrowly defined types have been unguided by any kind of broad organizing theory, most of the patterns that have been the subject of investigation having been defined *ad hoc*. There are nearly as many versions of specific types as there are persons who have conducted research studies. While the empirical data accumulated from these researches are of great importance, they do not have the same cumulative impact as would a collection of findings structured in terms of a single, over-all theoretical view of the range of offender patterns.

So much for general comments. Let us look more closely at a few of the typological statements in the criminological literature.

### Adult Offenders

One instance of a general statement regarding criminal types is provided by Cavan, who has classified forms of criminal activity in terms of the degree of the individual's withdrawal or exclusion from the control of the dominant social organization. She concludes that there are five major types of criminal behavior and a number of subtypes.[8] The Cavan classification is relatively crude, illustrated in anecdotal fashion by case histories, and unsuitable as a basic structure on which to hang etiological theory. Cavan's distinctions are not clear enough in the first place, and

[8] Cavan, *Criminology*, pp. 20–29. Another recent typological statement which is similarly too broad and general is Albert Morris, "The Comprehensive Classification of Adult Offenders," *Journal of Criminal Law, Criminology and Police Science*, LVI (June 1965), 197–202.

additionally are probably not sufficiently detailed to make each pattern causally homogeneous. For example, within her category of professional criminals there may be several specific patterns of professionalized criminality, each stemming from a different etiological sequence.

The statement on criminal types by Bloch and Geis is open to the same sort of criticism. These authors list as separate types of crime professional criminality, organized crime, homicides and assaults, sex offenses, property crimes, petty offenses, and white collar crime.[9] They provide a discursive treatment of these offender patterns, consequently their classification is not sufficiently developed to serve as a basis for causal theory.

Different problems are encountered with the specific investigations of offenders. Consider a series of studies by Roebuck and his associates, all based on one sample of 1155 inmates in the District of Columbia reformatory, which is sorted into such categories as "Negro armed robbers," "Negro drug addicts," "Negro drinkers and assaulters," "Negro jack-of-all-trades offenders," and "Negro short con men."[10] Roebuck's typology was based on legal categories of offense behavior studied within the framework of *criminal careers*. Prison inmates were sorted into classes on the basis of their over-all crime record as revealed in official records. Thirteen patterns of criminal careers were identified in all.

After this typology was constructed, Roebuck went on to compare single types with the balance of the offender group. Negro armed robbers were compared with the rest of the inmates in order to uncover significant differences between the robbers and the other prisoners. The robbers differed significantly from the remainder of the offenders in 22 of 30 social and personal characteristics examined. In the main, they were from more disorganized home backgrounds and more deteriorated and criminalistic areas of urban communities than were the other criminals. They were also characterized by a kind of short-run hedonism, having no long-term plans and relatively spontaneous and uncommitted attitudes.

Similar results were obtained in the other comparisons. Addicts were

[9] Bloch and Geis, op. cit., pp. 135–404.
[10] Julian B. Roebuck and Mervyn L. Cadwallader, "The Negro Armed Robber as a Criminal Type: The Construction and Application of a Typology," Pacific Sociological Review, IV (Spring 1961), 21–26; Roebuck, "The Negro Drug Addict as an Offender Type," Journal of Criminal Law, Criminology and Police Science, LIII (March 1962), 36–43; Roebuck and Ronald Johnson, "The Negro Drinker and Assaulter as a Criminal Type," Crime and Delinquency, VIII (January 1962), 21–33; Roebuck and Johnson, "The Jack-of-all-Trades Offender," Crime and Delinquency, VIII (April 1962), 172–81; Roebuck, "The Negro Numbers Man as a Criminal Type: The Construction and Application of a Typology," Journal of Criminal Law, Criminology and Police Science, LIV (March 1963), 48–60; Roebuck and Johnson, "The 'Short Con' Man," Crime and Delinquency, X (July 1964), 235–48.

generally younger persons and from family backgrounds more favorable than those of the other inmates. Negro drinker-assaulter inmates were from less criminogenic backgrounds than other prisoners, while jack-of-all-trades offenders turned out to be introverted, "marginal" persons.

These studies have much to recommend them. Roebuck employed techniques to overcome the limitations imposed on research when investigations are restricted to the most recent offense in which an offender has been involved. His attention to career aspects of crime is an important contribution. These reports comprise part of the intellectual capital out of which a theory of crime might be evolved. Nonetheless, there are some problems with this material, among which is the ethnic orientation of this typological system. Ethnic background is probably not an important variable for separating out homogeneous types of offenders. There is little reason to suppose that *Negro* armed robbers or other kinds of criminals are much different from their *Caucasian* counterparts.

The major objection to the methodology utilized by Roebuck and other investigators of specific types is that the inductive discovery of types could go on forever. Since persons can be classified in many different ways, to follow this line of activity indefinitely would mean that causal analysis would be forced to contend with hundreds of specific types of offenders. Perhaps a system of types can be stated a priori, involving a limited number of types which subsume most of the patterns arrived at inductively. Indeed, our major thesis is that formulation of a structure of offender types is possible and highly desirable.

Other recent studies of adult offenders include the investigation of assaultive and nonassaultive criminals by Peterson, Pittman, and O'Neal,[11] and Lemert's several studies of forgers.[12] There have also been several reports on patterns of role behavior among prison inmates, representing still another kind of typological work. Schrag has shown that a pattern of four sets of inmate roles oriented around certain focal issues in the prison community exists in prisons. These role patterns are defined in the argot of prisoners by the labels "square John," "right guy," "outlaw," and "politician."[13] In another report, Sykes has indicated that a number of role patterns exist in a New Jersey institution. The inmate argot identifies these role patterns by such colorful labels as "rats," "gorillas," "center

---

[11] Richard A. Peterson, David J. Pittman, and Patricia O'Neal, "Stabilities in Deviance: A Study of Assaultive and Non-Assaultive Offenders," *Journal of Criminal Law, Criminology and Police Science,* LIII (March 1962), 44–48.

[12] Edwin M. Lemert, "The Behavior of the Systematic Check Forger," *Social Problems,* VI (Fall 1958), 141–49; Lemert, "An Isolation and Closure Theory of Naive Check Forgery," *Journal of Criminal Law, Criminology and Police Science,* XLIV (September–October 1953), 296–307.

[13] Clarence Schrag, "Some Foundations for a Theory of Correction," in *The Prison,* ed. Donald R. Cressey (New York: Holt, Rinehart and Winston, Inc., 1961), pp. 309–57; Schrag, "A Preliminary Criminal Typology," *Pacific Sociological Review,* IV (Spring 1961), 11–16.

men," "merchants," "ball busters," and "hipsters." [14] It appears that most of the roles specified by Sykes parallel those listed by Schrag.

These reports represent important sources of information regarding criminal patterns, so research of this kind is certainly to be encouraged. However, each line of inquiry has proceeded independently of the others, making parallels between the types reported by different workers unclear. As a result, these data do not have the same impact as would findings about a common set of types studied by different researchers.

### Juvenile Delinquents

Before leaving the subject of typological contributions, let us take a brief look at some of those having to do with delinquents.[15] A great many of these have been advanced in the psychiatric and sociological literature. For example, Kinch has reported on 15 different typologies that have been put forth.[16] Although most of these are somewhat ambiguous and generally discursive, and the logic of classification on which most of them are based not clear, Kinch suggests that most of the authors of typologies do commonly agree on the existence of three major types: prosocial, antisocial, and asocial delinquents. Kinch has also reported findings regarding variations in self-images among training school delinquents previously classified as prosocial, antisocial, or asocial offenders on the basis of social background data.[17] A report by Fisher of a study of institutionalized delinquents also suggests the existence of three types of offenders, distinguished from each other in terms of the major reference group orientation of the youths.[18] Psychiatrist Richard L. Jenkins has also identified three basic offender patterns through research in several different studies. He has shown that there are unsocialized aggressive delinquents (asocial), socialized or pseudosocial members of delinquent subcultures, and an emotionally disturbed group in the population of serious delinquents.[19] Additional confirmation of the existence

[14] Gresham M. Sykes, *The Society of Captives* (Princeton, N.J.: Princeton University Press, 1958), pp. 84–108.

[15] A more detailed review of these works is found in Gibbons, *op. cit.*, pp. 33–39.

[16] John W. Kinch, "Continuities in the Study of Delinquent Types," *Journal of Criminal Law, Criminology and Police Science*, LIII (September 1962), 323–28.

[17] John W. Kinch, "Self-Conceptions of Types of Delinquents," *Sociological Inquiry*, XXXII (Spring 1962), 228–34.

[18] Sethard Fisher, "Varieties of Juvenile Delinquency," *British Journal of Criminology*, II (January 1962), 251–61.

[19] Richard L. Jenkins and Sylvia Glickman, "Patterns of Personality Organization Among Delinquents," *Nervous Child*, VI (July 1947), 329–39; Lester E. Hewitt and Jenkins, *Fundamental Patterns of Maladjustment, The Dynamics of Their Origin* (Springfield: Illinois State Printer, 1947); Jenkins and Hewitt, "Types of Personality Structure Encountered in Child Guidance Clinics," *American Journal of Orthopsychiatry*, XIV (January 1944), 84–94.

of these types is found in a study of Cook County, Illinois, juvenile probationers which closely paralleled the investigations by Jenkins.[20]

Clinard and Wade have presented evidence on juvenile vandalism as a subtype of delinquency,[21] while England and several others have implied that middle class delinquency is a relatively discrete form of delinquent behavior.[22] Articles have also appeared on automobile theft by juveniles, and the impression emerges that still another pattern of delinquency has been identified.[23]

Finally, mention should be made of recent subcultural analyses of delinquency in this review of typological contributions. These works will be taken up in detail in Chapter Eleven, but at this point note that the slim volume by Albert K. Cohen which appeared in 1955, *Delinquent Boys,* had the effect of triggering renewed attention by sociologists to working class delinquent groups.[24] Critics of Cohen's argument asserted that it was in need of revision at several points, but one of the main objections was that gang delinquency is not all of one kind. In response to this contention, Cohen and Short presented a classification of types of delinquent subcultures in a 1958 essay.[25] They argued that the gang subculture described in *Delinquent Boys* represents the "parent subculture" or basic form of gang behavior from which a number of variant patterns of gang activity have developed. Another major analysis of subcultural delinquency which was stimulated by the work of Cohen is the "opportunity structure" theory of Cloward and Ohlin.[26] These students of delinquency aver that there are several distinct forms taken by gang behavior, depending upon the social character of the neighborhoods in which the activity develops.

Much the same summary judgment applies to typological works in delinquency as to those directed at adult offenders. Theoretical conten-

[20] Albert J. Reiss, Jr., "Social Correlates of Psychological Types of Delinquency," *American Sociological Review,* XVII (December 1952), 710–18.

[21] Marshall B. Clinard and Andrew L. Wade, "Toward the Delineation of Vandalism as a Sub-Type of Juvenile Delinquency," *Journal of Criminal Law, Criminology and Police Science,* XLVIII (January–February 1958), 493–99.

[22] Ralph W. England, Jr., "A Theory of Middle Class Juvenile Delinquency," *Journal of Criminal Law, Criminology and Police Science,* L (March–April 1960), 535–40; Joseph W. Scott and Edmund W. Vaz, "A Perspective on Middle-Class Delinquency," *Canadian Journal of Economics and Political Science,* XXIX (August 1963), 324–35.

[23] William Wattenberg and James Balistrieri, "Automobile Theft: A 'Favored Group' Delinquency," *American Journal of Sociology,* LVII (May 1952), 575–79; Leonard D. Savitz, "Automobile Theft," *Journal of Criminal Law, Criminology and Police Science,* L (July–August 1959), 132–43; Erwin Schepses, "The Young Car Thief," *Journal of Criminal Law, Criminology and Police Science,* L (March–April 1960), 569.

[24] Albert K. Cohen, *Delinquent Boys* (New York: Free Press of Glencoe, Inc., 1955).

[25] Albert K. Cohen and James F. Short, Jr., "Research in Delinquent Subcultures," *Journal of Social Issues,* XIV, No. 3 (1958), 20–37.

[26] Cloward and Ohlin, *op. cit.*

tious and research investigations have gone on as independent endeavors rather than as related parts of a massed attack upon delinquent etiology. As a result, these works are not clearly related to each other and do not have the cumulative impact of a group of coordinated ventures.

## TOWARD A TYPOLOGICAL PERSPECTIVE

What are the prospects for making the typological orientation something more than a crude heuristic or organizing device? Our view is that the major outlines of a coherent typological structure for causal analysis can be carved out. In the pages ahead, a set of basic assumptions behind a role-career view of offender types will be enunciated; then the ingredients of a role-career analysis will be discussed in some detail. Finally, Chapters Eleven through Sixteen will collate a large body of theoretical contentions and empirical claims regarding offenders within a role-career conceptualization of criminal types. Taken as a whole, this network of arguments and propositions might be termed a criminological theory, although it might be just as well to withhold that label from the presentation to follow. Criminology is already plagued with a number of incompletely formed views to which the term theory has been prematurely applied.[27] These presentations, like the one in this book, are of the nature of "explanation sketches" which identify some of the critical variables implicated in criminality, along with some incompletely formed propositions representing a first stage of theorizing, and lack the substantive detail and logical elegance of mature theories.[28]

## SOME BASIC ASSUMPTIONS

The 17 claims below represent a set of exceedingly broad assumptions that stand as a sample of one sociologist's notions about the causation of crime and delinquency. They constitute, as well, a set of contentions with which most criminologist-sociologists would be in agreement. These statements are listed so as to identify in one place the major premises and hypotheses upon which the more detailed remarks about particular forms of criminality in succeeding chapters are based. A number of these notions about useful ways to approach the understanding of criminality are

[27] One illustrative case of these is "containment theory." See Walter C. Reckless, *The Crime Problem* (4th ed.; New York: Appleton-Century-Crofts, Inc., 1967), pp. 469–83.

[28] William J. Wilson, Nicholas Sofios, and Richard Ogles, "Formalization and Stages of Theoretical Development," *Pacific Sociological Review*, VII (Fall 1964), 74–80.

derived from theories of deviant or criminalistic behavior which have been examined in previous chapters. Some of them are also drawn out of existing data on criminality, so the specific discussions in later chapters should demonstrate the accuracy of some of these propositions.

Some of the first assumptions below are in the nature of basic sociology textbook propositions and may appear pedestrian. Nonetheless, there are different perspectives from which deviant behavior could be examined, and one's presuppositions ought to be dragged out into the open for public scrutiny. Some of the 17 claims are also extremely simple. Take assumption six, which argues that "badness" tends to be specific rather than general in form. In other words, there is no reason to suppose that individuals who are "bad guys" as far as criminality is concerned are also "bad guys" in all other ways. There are no grounds for supposing that offenders also beat their wives and abuse their children, belong to the Communist Party, or verbalize atheistic beliefs. However, the opposite assumption about generic "badness" is often involved in commonsense beliefs about deviants.

The seventeen assumptions are these: [29]

1. The members of a society are the carriers of an organization of social roles, that is, behavior patterns reflecting different social statuses or positions. (In other words, it is meaningful to approach the description of the behavior of individual persons by paying attention to the related but independent component activities or roles making up their behavior.)

2. Social roles are the product of social organization and socialization, that is, of the ongoing structure of society and of learning processes in primary groups. (In other words, the developmental process in human behavior centers around the acquisition, by the person, of a collection of social roles made available to him by the society in which he is found.)

3. Various patterns of social organization and socialization exist in complex societies so that, in turn, a variety of statuses and roles exist in them. There is a variety of nondeviant roles as well as a great many deviant ones (radical, homosexual, criminal, and so forth).

4. All people play criminal or delinquent roles at one time or another, if only symbolically. (In other words, petty violations of law are engaged in by nearly every person in the course of his lifetime. Also, many individuals entertain deviant and criminalistic motives but do not act upon them; thus they play deviant roles symbolically.)

5. Sociologically, "criminals" or "delinquents" are persons who play criminalistic roles heavily and/or who are identified by "society" as criminals or delinquents. (Persons who come to be tagged as offenders by the legal processes

[29] These were originally stated in Don C. Gibbons, *Changing the Lawbreaker*, The Treatment of Delinquents and Criminals, © 1965. Reprinted by permission of Prentice-Hall, Inc., Englewood Cliffs, New Jersey, pp. 44–47.

are frequently ones who are involved in repetitive and serious acts of law violation; but individuals who engage in petty and isolated acts of illegality are also sometimes reacted to as violators. Both of these groups are "criminals" or "delinquents" because they have been so labeled by the official machinery of social control.)

6. Criminal or delinquent behavior is one social role, but not the only one, that persons play. Criminal or delinquent individuals also play roles as "citizen," "father," "employee," and so forth.

7. Among persons identified as criminals or delinquents, there are variations in the character and intensity of the deviant role. These include variations in both (a) actual deviant role behavior and (b) role-related social-psychological characteristics. The illegal acts carried on by offenders vary from one individual to another. Also, some persons have no self-image as a deviant, whereas others exhibit such self-definitions. In turn, among individuals with deviant or non-deviant self-conceptions, variations are exhibited in the particular kind of image held ("tough guy," "right guy," "smart hustler," and so on).

8. Stable patterns of criminal or delinquent roles, involving recurrent forms of deviant activity accompanied by uniform social-psychological role characteristics, can be observed in the population of offenders. In these terms, it can be said that types of criminalistic deviance exist.

9. Although behavioral and social-psychological changes occur in specific criminal or delinquent roles during the development of the role, these changes are limited, orderly, and identifiable. As a result, it is possible to define specific, stable criminal and delinquent role-careers. Offenders do not engage in random and unpredictable patterns of role-behavior; they do not "play the field" of offenses.

10. The specific etiological process that leads to one particular kind of criminalistic role behavior involves a number of causal variables and differs from that which produces another criminal role. In this sense, criminal and delinquent behavior is the product of multiple-causation. At the same time, it is possible to identify the different etiological processes which are implicated in the various forms of criminalistic deviance.

11. The learning of criminal and/or delinquent roles is maximized in a criminalistic society, and the United States is such a society.

12. Much, but not all, criminal and delinquent behavior in the competitive, materialistic American society is societally generated and takes the form of assaults upon property. Property crime is not usually the expression of hidden motives but, rather, of surface ones. (Offenders steal to "make a living" rather than to commit symbolic incest and so on.)

13. Crime and delinquency in complex societies are encouraged in a variety of ways by that complexity. For example, police ineffectiveness is a correlate of a democratic, complex, urban social organization. In turn, ineffectual police work aids in the commission of crime and is an encouragement to criminality. (In a society which demands that law enforcement agents behave according to

strict rules of arrest, search and seizure, interrogation, and the like, many offenders are inevitably going to avoid apprehension or conviction for crimes. Additionally, in a society in which relatively few policemen are employed to maintain surveillance over a large population living in metropolitan communities, the law enforcement persons are not going to be able to observe most illegal acts that occur. As a result, the risk of being apprehended for deviant acts will appear to be slight to many individuals.)

14. Some criminalistic roles are mainly the consequence of social-class variations in socialization and life experiences, along with other social-structural variables. In particular, situations in which legitimate avenues to the attainment of common American goals or values are blocked are importantly involved in certain forms of crime and delinquency.

15. Some criminalistic roles are produced by family and other socialization experiences which are not class-linked or class-specific. Among these are "parental rejection," "deviant sexual socialization," and others. These kinds of experiences occur at all social class levels.

16. The "defining agencies" (police, probation services, courts, and so forth) play a part both in the definition of deviants and in the continuation of deviant roles. The result of apprehension and "treatment" may be quite contrary to the expected result. In other words, although one official function of correctional agencies and processes is the reformation of the offender, the actual outcome is often the isolation of the person, reinforcement of the deviant role, and rejection of society by the offender, the final result being nonreformation.

17. Variations can be seen in societal reactions to criminality of different kinds. Personal offenses and crude, visible attacks upon property are likely to be severely dealt with and punitively handled. Accordingly, embezzlers and similar persons are reacted to differently than gas station stick-up artists or strong-arm robbers. In addition, societal reactions to criminal deviants are based upon other characteristics of the individual than criminal role behavior. Middle-class delinquents, for example, are accorded a societal reaction different from that directed toward working-class individuals involved in similar delinquent behavior. In turn, these reactions have implications for involvement in, and continuation in, criminality.

These contentions commit the user of them to a certain view of crime and delinquency causation. This framework eschews pursuit of the causes of "crime" or "delinquency." Instead, the search is pointed toward discovery of the etiology of particular criminalistic roles. The first six claims enunciate some major ingredients of social role analysis. Propositions seven through nine suggest the major dimensions according to which law violators can be studied as incumbents of criminal roles. Finally, statements ten through seventeen point to some major causal factors in criminality. The causal framework in the package of assumptions emphasizes multiple-causation at the same time it implies that scientific explanations of criminality are attainable. In other words, the argument is that the etiological factors in criminality are numerous, and operate in different patterns of conduct in different ways and with varying degrees of influence. At the same time, these variables are also finite or limited, so that, ultimately, propositions such as "If *A, B, C, D,* and *E* occur, criminality of type *X* will result" can be stated.

These terse propositions represent a skeleton version of a causal presentation. Since the perspective contained in them requires elaboration, let us first take up the role-career portion.

## TYPES AS ROLE-CAREERS

The assumption that the total behavior of individuals can be meaningfully examined as a *pattern* of *social roles* lies at the heart of the sociological analysis of many kinds of behavior. Social roles represent the particular ways in which persons interact with others in terms of various statuses or positions within social systems. Statuses are "jobs" in a social division of labor (social system) involving a pattern of normative expectations or rules that the status incumbent is expected to follow in pursuit of some interactional end or objective. The task of professor in an academic institution is an example of a status, for it involves a set of expectations that any particular teacher will behave in specified ways toward students, colleagues, and the general public. The actual performance activity of a specific professor represents role behavior within this particular status. The core of all this is that the sociological perspective on behavior is not a disguised version of the study of personality systems. Statuses are not labels for characteristics internal to the actor, but are identified in terms of the expectations of persons in the external situation in which the status incumbent is placed. A status and related role activities of any individual are not descriptive of that actor as a totality, but of only a part of the total behavior of the person.

Status and role concepts are easily seen as useful in analysis of social behavior when applied to such activities as school superintendent, physician, and a variety of other occupational or social positions. However, status and role analysis may not be so quickly perceived as relevant to the study of such deviant patterns as homosexuality, narcotics addiction, political radicalism, or criminality. Nonetheless, the fact that criminal and delinquent statuses are often pariahs, involving expectations that persons in these positions will behave in ways evaluated negatively by some social groups, does not alter the fact that criminalistic behavior can be tackled within a status-role perspective. As a matter of fact, there are many statuses and roles in addition to the criminalistic that are negatively defined by some group or groups. Moreover, invidious evaluation of criminal or delinquent statuses is relative to particular group standards. Within associations of offenders, deviant statuses are frequently evaluated positively; the "old-time box man" (skilled safecracker) is deemed an exemplary person by his criminal peers. Illustrations of this kind could be multiplied indefinitely, for many "tough" prisoners in institutions are highly esteemed by other inmates, narcotic users are fondly regarded by other drug users, and so forth.

Criminal statuses and roles constitute only one of many statuses and roles in which real-life persons find themselves. However, it may well be that in many cases criminality becomes what Becker has termed a *master status,* the separate social niches occupied by the offender becoming heavily colored by his involvement in criminalistic role behavior.[30] As one example, the occupational activities of the ex-convict are often so greatly influenced by the "parolee" identity he has acquired that he finds the task of obtaining a job exceedingly difficult.[31] Employment instability as a social consequence of being identified as "bad" and "criminal" may create further distortions in the actor's marital role and other facets of his life as well, so that to be a criminal is to be the occupant of a highly significant status.

Even though deviant statuses may color or affect other statuses, it can hardly be inferred that delinquent or criminal individuals differ in all important ways from nonoffenders. There is little reason to assume that offenders are less patriotic or less committed to family values than nonoffenders, or that criminals differ in total personality structure from nondeviants. This may seem obvious, but a good deal of research has proceeded on the basis of an implicit assumption that the deviant is a generally different person from the nondeviant. Failure of investigators to discover traits which distinguish criminals from noncriminals is probably attributable principally to the invalidity of this built-in assumption about deviants and nondeviants. Those investigations which have gone about in vacuum-cleaner fashion, attempting to sweep up evidence of pervasive differences between the two groups, have failed because they were unguided by explicit theory spelling out the salient factors in which the two groups might differ.

Description of offender roles must include the social context within which behavior occurs. Indeed, the concept of role is relatively meaning-

[30] Howard S. Becker, *Outsiders* (New York: Free Press of Glencoe, Inc., 1963), pp. 31–34.

[31] One revealing investigation of this matter is Richard D. Schwartz and Jerome H. Skolnick, "Two Studies of Legal Stigma," in *The Other Side,* ed. Howard S. Becker (New York: Free Press of Glencoe, Inc., 1964), pp. 103–17.

less when divorced from the network of role-expectations of others. Thus it is not sufficient to indicate that an offender engages in role activity taking the form of burglary; we also need to ask about the social circumstances of that behavior. Were the criminal acts carried on in isolation? Or did that behavior take place within the structure of a group of participating role players (other burglars)? Or, finally, is the activity of the person part of a pattern of responses within a deviant subculture in which deviant acts are encouraged by other individuals? While those behavioral incidents which identify a person as a law violator and run counter to legal statutes are necessary components of any description of offender types, attention must also be paid to components of role behavior additional to the particular form of illegal activity. Some deviant roles, such as embezzlement, are enacted surreptitiously, because nonembezzlement is defined as the appropriate behavior within the system of action in which defalcations occur. Other kinds of criminality represent role activities that are positively evaluated by associates of the offender, even though they may be negatively defined by the larger social organization. Along a somewhat related line, some kinds of criminality grow out of situations in which the victim was initially an interactional partner of the offender, as for example in cases of murder of one's spouse or rape. In other instances the victim has had no prior contact with the lawbreaker, and in still other situations no specific victim can be identified, as in forms of white collar crime, shoplifting, and kindred offenses. All of these matters need to be attended to in a sociological description and analysis of criminality.

Turning to examination of role-incumbents, two basic components of social roles can be identified. Roles include behavioral acts or role behavior, along with role-conceptions, that is, self-image patterns and role-related attitudes. This distinction is illustrated in everyday life when predictions are made about the future conduct of an individual. For example, knowledge that an actor has committed an assault is not sufficient evidence on which to predict that additional episodes of violence will occur in the future. Confidence in such a prediction is enhanced when it is observed that the assaultive individual defines himself as a "tough guy" and regards other persons as "mean" and not to be trusted. Quite a different estimate would be in order with observations that the assaulter acted under conditions of severe personal stress and is now contrite and repentant in posture.

Many other illustrative cases can be found wherein ostensibly similar behavior by separate persons has quite different meanings for the individuals. One cannot assume that every case of criminal role behavior of a common kind is accompanied by similar role-conceptions among all the actors in question. This distinction between role behavior and role-conceptions is closely parallel to Lemert's notions of *primary* and *secondary* deviation discussed in Chapter Nine.[32] Lemert notes that deviant behavior is often primary in character, for it is viewed by the person as atypical on his part, and he lacks a self-image as a deviant. Some deviant roles become secondary in form, the actor ultimately integrating his aberrant activity into his total personality organization. In this process of *sociopathic individuation*, he eventually undergoes a measure of personality reorganization in which deviant behavior becomes a role verbalized by such self-reference statements as: "I am a 'hype'" or "I am a thief" or "I am a 'lush.'" While primary deviation precedes development of secondary deviation, the latter does not always follow from involvement in primary deviancy. One obvious illustration of this point, at least in degree, is the "Square John" inmate in prison who persistently alleges that he is not a "real criminal."

Offender roles can also be analyzed profitably in longitudinal terms as *role-careers*. Many nondeviant roles, such as occupational ones, continue over extremely long periods of time and involve a series of changes of behavior as particular social situations change. A medical career illustrates this point nicely, for this career could be said to originate when initial decisions are made by persons to become doctors and activity is undertaken to implement such choices. Medical school is a further episode in the medical career, and a still further segment is involvement in professional employment as a physician. Medical role-incumbents exhibit behavior patterns that are somewhat different in each stage. They also exhibit role-conceptions that are not identical in each of these periods.[33] Nonetheless, it is meaningful to treat these varied behavior patterns and role-conceptions as parts of a long-term career, for they "hang together" in ways which are obvious. These are cumulative events in which advanced stages of occupational involvement are built upon experiences occurring in earlier parts of the occupational history.

Although the notion of careers is most familiar in occupational analysis, it is readily apparent that other roles, including deviant ones, can also be approached in this manner. The alcoholism career extending over several decades, in which the drinker becomes progressively more involved in deviant drinking as well as other altered social relationships flowing out of his alcoholism, comes to mind as one illustration of a complex deviant career pattern. In the area of criminality, the collection of life experiences beginning with petty delinquent episodes carried on by gang members in slum areas stands as an example of an offender career. With advancing

[32] Edwin M. Lemert, *Social Pathology* (New York: McGraw-Hill Book Co., Inc., 1951), pp. 73–98.
[33] Howard S. Becker, Blanche Geer, Everett C. Hughes, and Anselm L. Strauss, *Boys in White* (Chicago: University of Chicago Press, 1961).

age, this career line leads into more systematic involvement in utilitarian thefts, while still later it culminates in a sustained pattern of adult episodes of property crimes interrupted periodically by prison terms. The career is finally terminated by a kind of retirement in which the offender withdraws from active participation in criminality in middle age, as he comes to evaluate continued lawbreaking as too fraught with such hardships as long penal commitments.

Some further observations can be made about deviant role-careers, including the fact that role-careers vary in duration. In some criminal roles, role performance is represented by a single isolated illegal act intruding into an otherwise exemplary life history, while in others involvement in sustained deviance continues over several decades, as in the instance of professional criminals. Although in some ways persons who commit a single, fugitive act of lawbreaking hardly qualify as criminals, many of them do acquire a public identity as violators. Some of them end up in penal institutions and other correctional settings, or encounter other societal reactions directed at them as "bad persons," so that their idiosyncratic acts of deviance do make a difference.

Another point regarding offender roles is that some delinquent patterns lead to adult criminal careers, while others are terminal and do not culminate in adult criminality. In turn, some criminal careers have their genesis in juvenile delinquent behavior, while other forms of adult lawbreaking develop in adulthood and are not touched off by prior delinquent conduct. On this matter, one major argument in favor of a role-career perspective on criminality is that it promises to untangle the web of relationships between juvenile and adult criminality. The durable shibboleth that "the delinquent of today is the criminal of tomorrow" is frequently false, for while some delinquents become adult offenders, others do not.

Some role-careers involve more changes in component episodes of the pattern than do others. Take semiprofessional property offenders as one illustration. This career begins with minor peccadilloes in early adolescence. These frequently lead to more serious forms of delinquency with advancing age, which in turn result in repeated police contacts, commitment to juvenile institutions, "graduation" into adult forms of crime, and more contacts with law enforcement agencies and correctional institutions. Over this lengthy developmental sequence, the social-psychological characteristics of offenders also change. The degree of hostility toward policemen and correctional agents exhibited by the adult semiprofessional criminal is likely to be considerably greater than the enmity demonstrated by that person at an earlier age. The same point holds for other changes in self-image, attitudes, and kindred characteristics.

To summarize, we contend that criminal or delinquent roles usually involve more than a single specific kind of illegal act, but that criminal behavior is *patterned* rather than comprising random behavioral activities. There is some supporting evidence regarding stabilities among deviants, at least with regard to illegal activities. The papers by Peterson *et al.*[34] and by Roebuck[35] are cases in point, as is a report by Frum.[36]

This point of view regarding role-careers and the significant behavioral dimensions along which forms of criminality can be differentiated provides the foundation for a typological analysis of criminality. The discussions of criminal role-careers in the chapters to follow parallel an earlier, abbreviated essay on offender roles which explored the utility of the notions just articulated.[37] In the descriptions of criminal role-careers in Chapters Eleven through Sixteen, offenders are categorized according to the patterns of illegal role-behavior they exhibit and also in terms of the social context within which their deviant acts occur. Offenders are also classified along two additional dimensions having to do with role-conceptions—self-image patterns and role-related attitudes. Finally, observations about temporal changes in deviant roles are provided in a summary characterization of the role-career.

The result of the assumptions and role-career arguments stated above is a set of descriptions of offender roles, in other words, a typology of criminals. The typology contends that lawbreakers can be sorted out so that some are "semiprofessional property offenders," "embezzlers," or "naive check forgers," while others are "nonviolent sex offenders," "professional thieves," or members of some other category. An individual is to be labeled a "naive check forger" or some other role-career incumbent if he shows the pattern of deviant behavior and the social-psychological characteristics specified in the typology. An adequate, comprehensive typology would allow us to place all or nearly all real-life violators within.

In the early stages of development of a criminal typology, descriptions of offender types stand as contentious hypotheses about the real world. The typology makes claims to the effect that real people exist who look like those persons described in the typology. The typology of offenders used in this book is one of these initial ventures into criminal taxonomy, so its empirical status is to some degree indeterminate. There is a body of research evidence that provides direct or tangential support for some of the descriptive claims about offenders, and Chapters Eleven through Sixteen are concerned with study of that material. But at the same time,

[34] Peterson, Pittman, and O'Neal, op. cit.

[35] Roebuck et al., op. cit.

[36] Harold S. Frum, "Adult Criminal Offense Trends Following Juvenile Delinquency," *Journal of Criminal Law, Criminology and Police Science*, XLIX (May–June 1958), 29–49.

[37] Gibbons, op. cit.

some patterns of criminality, such as deviant sexual activities, have been little studied. Accordingly, remarks about these types are more speculative than some of the other characterizations of offenders. In short, the typology utilized here qualifies as both a collation of existing knowledge *and* as a programmatic essay which suggests a number of lines of further research endeavor.

## TYPOLOGIES AND CAUSATION

A criminal typology is a collection of statements which assert that "this is the way offenders are—these are the ways they behave." As such, it says nothing about causation, or "how they got that way." Contentions about the etiology of different criminal role-careers constitute a separate body of hypotheses. The whole package of claims about patterns of criminality and causal factors producing these types would make up a complex theory of criminal behavior. The structure of a typological theory is shown in Figure 4.

In the typological sketches of offender careers in the next few chapters, we will comment about causal factors as well as those which enumerate the behavioral aspects of deviant roles. These remarks will indicate some of the major background characteristics of offender types, organized within four relatively gross categories or dimensions: social class variations, family background patterns, peer group associations, and contacts with defining agencies. These categories arise from the same rationale that underlines the focus upon role-careers.

### Social Class, Family, and Peers

One obvious fact of life which is frequently ignored in discussions of etiological elements in criminality is that the immediate social circumstances in which persons are enmeshed are part of larger patterns of social organization. Individuals are not only members of families and peer associations, they are also situated in distinctive neighborhood and social class locations. These structures impinge upon their conduct, and as a consequence we find offender types distributed in varied ways within social class levels. For example, gang offenders of specific kinds are nearly all working class boys, while joyriders are often from comfortable economic areas, as are naive check forgers and certain other kinds of lawbreakers. Other juvenile and adult types are distributed in still other ways within the class structure of American society. The suspicion arises that these variations are not by chance, that there may be something

OFFENDER TYPOLOGY

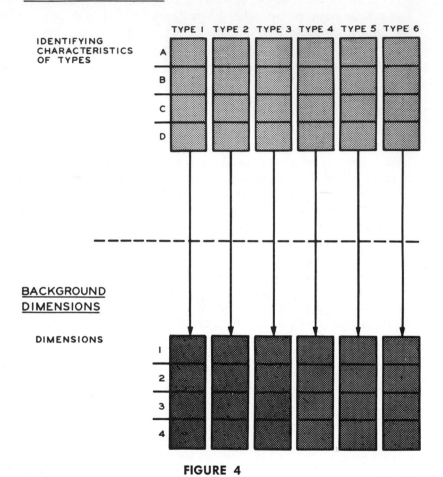

**FIGURE 4**

**The Structure of Typological Arguments**

about the social life of different social class groups that brings forth particular kinds of misbehavior. We will find occasion to return in succeeding chapters to the question of what it is about social stratification which contributes to forms of criminality.

Another elementary fact is that development of a specific person's role-behavior is a direct function of the processes of socialization. Socialization refers to the complex processes of social interaction through which habits, skills, beliefs, and standards of conduct are learned. Not all interaction is equally important to the individual, so the person's conception of self, his attitudes, and the motives he employs in directing his behavior in the world of experience are most likely to be the product of a special kind of interaction—primary group interaction. Family and peer group associations are two kinds of primary groups, and the great attention given by social psychologists to interactional processes within these groups is not accidental.

Whatever else it might be, criminality is learned behavior, so we shall look closely at family and peer groups as sources of causally significant experiences in the development of criminal role-careers. It is possible to identify a plethora of specific family-oriented relationships which enter into different forms of criminality. For one, the family is one of the vehicles through which social class phenomena are expressed, that is, social class values are imparted to persons through family interaction experiences, at least in part. On this point, Walter Miller has argued that the "focal concerns" of lower class society are such as to encourage illegal behavior. He claims that lower class value emphases on "toughness," "having a good time," and related interests bring about deviant activities by many working class males in particular.[38] If this argument is correct, "focal concerns" exert an influence over specific persons only to the extent that they have been communicated through social interaction. The family is one of the major settings in which such learning and communication takes place.

While "class-linked" behavior patterns do exist, individual members of particular social classes vary quite markedly in many aspects of their behavior. Much of this is because of differences in the interactional processes in particular family groups. The values or focal concerns of a social class may be given different emphases in particular families, so the family situation works to condition the impact of class phenomena on individuals.

Families who share a relatively uniform life-style of a particular social class vary from each other in other important ways. Within working class families in which the common values of the class are observed, some parents reject their children, others neglect their offspring, spouses interact in varied ways with each other, and other families carry on still other idiosyncratic forms of existence. There are a number of patterns of criminality closely related to interactional processes and difficulties between family members, particularly between spouses. Incest behavior, assaults, and homicides come readily to mind as cases in point.

[38] Walter B. Miller, "Lower Class Culture as a Generating Milieu of Gang Delinquency," *Journal of Social Issues*, XIV, No. 3 (1958), 5–19; Miller, "Implications of Urban Lower Class Culture for Social Work," *Social Service Review*, XXXIII (September 1959), 219–36.

The comments about the mediating influence of family structure hold as well for peer group associations, so that broad influences of the kind described as class-linked often have their effects upon specific persons through the particular kinds of peer group relationships within which those individuals participate.

Observations about peer group relationships are included in this analysis of offender types in two places. The interactional context of deviant acts, including peer associations, is included as part of offense behavior in the statements about defining dimensions of role-careers. Peer group processes are also included in the body of causally related dimensions. As one illustration, it appears that pressures to engage in white collar criminality are in many cases directed at business employees by their fellow workers. Numerous other illustrations can be uncovered in which the offender's associates have had a large part to play in his deviant behavior.

### Contact with Defining Agencies

What about the causal consequences of contacts with defining agencies? Defining agencies are those official and semiofficial agencies given the responsibility for detection, apprehension, punishment, and rehabilitation of offenders. The discussion of deviant careers and the effects of societal reactions upon them, centering about the contributions of Lemert and Becker, in the preceding chapter suggested that agency contacts may be of major significance. One of the major factors that may drive juveniles toward delinquency as a systematic role revolves around the extent to which the individual has been defined as a "delinquent" and "bad boy" by community organizations. We have already taken note of a study which shows that identified adult criminals may be driven further into criminality as a result of employment difficulties they encounter because of their social stigma.[39] In other cases, contacts with defining agencies or kindred groups may have positive effects, as seems to be the case with amateur female shoplifters or "snitches." Cameron found in a study in Chicago that these women rarely repeated the act of shoplifting after they had been apprehended and compelled by store personnel to admit that they were "thieves" and "criminals." Apparently, the painful social-psychological trauma involved in admitting the deviant nature of shoplifting served to repress these individuals from further behavior of this nature.[40]

[39] Schwartz and Skolnick, *op. cit.*
[40] Mary Owen Cameron, *Department Store Shoplifting* (Doctoral dissertation, Indiana University, 1953); Cameron, *The Booster and the Snitch* (New York: Free Press of Glencoe, Inc., 1964).

Etiological factors of this kind have been given short shrift in research. Customarily, the search for causal variables has paid little or no attention to career processes and agency experiences as career contingencies. However, some years ago, Tannenbaum argued that the effects of official dealings with deviants, ostensibly therapeutic in nature, constitute instead a process of "dramatization of evil." He asserted that the outcome of official handling in the courts and related circumstances was frequently contrary to the announced purposes of such actions. Instead of deflecting the actor away from a deviant career, such experiences alert citizens in the community to the presence of an "evil" person in their midst. Once an individual becomes singled out as "evil," he is likely to be consistently thought of as "bad" in the future, quite apart from how he actually behaves. If his deportment does not change, this validates the original diagnosis in the eyes of the community. If for some reason he does modify his behavior, it is seen as a devious attempt to hide his true nature. Either way, the offender cannot win, so his possibilities for action become narrowly circumscribed. In many instances, the deviant develops sentiments of being unjustly dealt with which operate as rationalizations for his conduct. As a result, the end product of treatment is reinforcement of the very behavior the correctional agents are attempting to reduce.[41] Tannenbaum's thesis is polemic in tone, so there is room for argument concerning the extent to which his dismal implications are warranted. Nonetheless, this provocative hypothesis deserves more attention than it has received. While Lemert and Becker have touched on the effects of societal reactions upon deviants of various kinds, relatively slight work has been done on the specifics of these factors in criminality.[42]

Contacts with defining agencies could have three different results: they could be positive in impact, so as to deflect the deviant away from further misconduct, or they could be harmful in effect, driving the actor into further violations in response to his changed social identity. A third possibility is that such experiences could be of neutral significance, the individual being neither deterred nor harmfully affected by them.

Bits of empirical evidence can be identified which seem to indicate that each of these three possibilities does occur. Cameron's study shows

[41] Frank Tannenbaum, *Crime and the Community* (New York: Ginn and Co., 1938), pp. 19–21; a more general essay on these processes is found in Harold Garfinkel, "Conditions of Successful Degradation Ceremonies," *American Journal of Sociology*, LXI (March 1956), 420–24; see also Erving Goffman, *Stigma* (Englewood Cliffs, N.J.: Prentice-Hall, Inc., 1963); John I. Kitsuse, "Societal Reaction to Deviant Behavior: Problems of Theory and Method," *Social Problems*, IX (Winter 1962), 247–56.

[42] One notable exception is found in the theory of Cloward and Ohlin, where the claims of Tannenbaum are examined and extended to apply to gang delinquents. See Cloward and Ohlin, *op. cit.*, pp. 124–43.

that contacts with defining agencies can lead to deterrence of further deviation, while some findings from the Highfields project seem to point to deleterious consequences of contacts with treatment agencies. The Highfields institution is a small, intensive treatment facility for delinquent boys in New Jersey. As part of a research program associated with that institution, a projective personality test was given to Highfields boys and to inmates of a conventional reformatory in New Jersey at the time of admission and at a later point in their institutional stay. The test results indicated that the reformatory youths moved toward bleaker, darker outlooks on life during their stay in the reformatory, and may have become resigned to further deviation as a life career; the Highfields boys showed movement in an opposite direction.[43] In this case, a double conclusion seems appropriate, to the effect that traditional penal facilities operate in harmful ways as concerns contributions to criminality, but different results can be achieved within an atypical correctional program.

Knowledgeable criminologists are rarely very sanguine about the rehabilitative potential of prison. Indeed, a number of them have estimated that two-thirds or more of the prisoners released from penal institutions return to criminality. If these figures are correct, they certainly imply that correctional institutions play a major role in binding persons to deviant careers. However, a recent, massive investigation by Glaser indicates that these pessimistic judgments about prisoner recidivism are grossly exaggerated, and that recidivists are more likely to make up about a third of all prisoners, rather than comprising a large majority of them.[44] Glaser's detailed study of the workings of the federal prison and parole system demonstrates that, while recidivists in that system are not as common as are men who refrain from further criminality, the whole matter of correctional effects is exceedingly complex. There is not one relationship of criminality, correctional experience, and the like, to reinvolvement in deviance, there are many specific and varied patterns.[45]

It seems clear from these discordant reports on the effect of contacts with defining agencies that there are intervening variables interposed in the situation. The outcome of agency intervention is dependent upon a number of added factors. At least four such variables come to mind, one of which would be *personality variations* among subjects who are the focus of agency concern. There are probably some who, by virtue

[43] Lloyd W. McCorkle, Albert Elias, and F. Lovell Bixby, *The Highfields Story* (New York: Holt, Rinehart and Winston, Inc., 1958), pp. 122–26.

[44] Daniel Glaser, *The Effectiveness of a Prison and Parole System* (Indianapolis: Bobbs-Merrill Co., Inc., 1964), pp. 13–35.

[45] *Ibid.*, pp. 504–13.

of certain personality patterns, would be responsive to even innocuous experiences with agencies and their personnel, whereas others might find such events of no important personal consequence.

A second factor which may condition the effects of these experiences has to do with variations in *societal definitions* of behavior. Consider violations of traffic laws as an illustration. Little public condemnation is attached to this kind of deviance, so the person involved with agencies for this reason runs little risk of societal or agency hostility being directed at him. There are other kinds of criminality defined as serious by agencies but regarded in a more tolerant light by the general public. Persons engaged in these forms of conduct are in a sense insulated from markedly negative repercussions from contacts with agencies because of public tolerance.

Not only do societal reactions vary for different forms of lawbreaking, different segments of the general community react to the same behavior in discrepant ways. Thus a third factor which probably influences the effects of agency experiences has to do with *exposure to antisocial environments*. The person who has grown up in an antisocial subculture in which antipolice attitudes and other hostile sentiments are endemic is not likely to be traumatized by any specific contact with defining agencies. That same individual is immunized against agency pressures by a supportive peer system which assists him in warding off invidious definitions of himself that flow from these agency contacts. On the other hand, a person who is a product of middle class, prosocial social circumstances is much more likely to react to experiences with the police or courts as profoundly important.

Finally, *agency climate* can be advanced as a fourth consideration which influences the impact of agency contacts. Some organizations take a punitive and hostile attitude toward persons who come into their hands, whereas others adopt a more positive posture. It might be expected that the effect of being apprehended by an abusive police officer would be different than results from interaction with a polite and pleasant officer. In the same way, correctional institutions vary in the kind of social atmosphere which dominates them, and may not all act upon offenders who get into them in precisely similar ways. This is suggested in the findings concerning Highfields and a state reformatory.

One thing is certain from this brief discussion: the impact of agency contacts is not the same for all who enter into these contacts. Fragments of tangential evidence can be uncovered which suggest some of the differential effects of agency experiences, but definitive findings gathered through carefully conducted research are sorely needed. The discussion of role-careers in criminality in succeeding chapters will speculate about the part played by these processes in types of offender behavior, which is all that can be done in the face of a paucity of hard evidence.

## CRIMINAL TYPOLOGY: AN ILLUSTRATION

An earlier work by the author presented a typology of nine delinquent role-careers [46] and another involving 15 forms of adult criminality.[47] In the present book, typological descriptions of offender patterns, stemming from the perspective enunciated in this chapter, will be interwoven with other materials on crime causation. In order to close this chapter on a proper note of completeness, let us examine one of the typological characterizations at this point, in order to get the flavor of the role-career approach. The pattern of naive check forger has been selected for presentation below.[48]

### Definitional Dimensions

*Offense Behavior.* Naive check forgers engage in unsophisticated forms of forgery. They normally pass "NSF" ("Not Sufficient Funds") checks on their personal checks, written on their own bank accounts. In some cases, personal checks signed with some fictitious name are passed. But in neither instance does the forger resort to such skilled activities as passing fraudulent payroll checks. Naive check forgers normally have no prior record of delinquency and a record of only minor adult crimes. The naive forger often passes a bad check a number of times; that is, naive forgery is not a "one shot" form of crime.

*Interactional Setting.* Check passing is an activity carried on by the offender acting alone. Checks are passed in liquor stores, supermarkets, and other retail business agencies. Not infrequently the check forger passes "NSF" checks at a business location where he is personally known, such as a neighborhood bar.

*Self-concept.* Naive check forgers do not view themselves as "real criminals." They tend to exhibit stereotyped rationalizations of the form: "You can't kill anyone with a fountain pen" or "No one is hurt by forgery because supermarkets make great profits and don't miss a little money lost through bad checks." Although the forger admits that passing bad

---

[46] Gibbons, op. cit., pp. 75–97.
[47] Ibid., pp. 97–125.
[48] Ibid., pp. 108–10.

checks is outside the range of conventional and acceptable behavior, he argues that there are special circumstances which have compelled him to commit these acts.

*Attitudes.* Naive check forgers exhibit attitudes which are generally prosocial but somewhat atypical of law-abiding citizens. The check forger indicates commitment to conventional work roles and marital activities, but exhibits dissatisfaction, bitterness, and resentment concerning his own participation in such activities. He often shows a pattern of occupational and marital instability which precedes involvement in forgery.

*Role-career.* The role-career of the naive check forger normally begins in adulthood and is not preceded by delinquency. Onset of the role-career is preceded by difficulties in employment, marriage, and general social participation. The check forger gets involved in forgery after he has become significantly isolated from stable social ties. Once check forgery is embarked upon, repeated instances are not uncommon. The forger is often handled informally and outside the framework of criminal courts for his first episodes of forgery. When he is dealt with in a court, he is frequently placed on probation. Probation violation rates are quite high for this class of offender, many of them ultimately making their way into correctional institutions.

### Background Dimensions

*Social Class.* Check forgers are not exclusively from a single economic or class background. However, many would be categorized as middle class, for they have had relatively comfortable economic circumstances and been employed at white collar jobs or similar occupational levels.

*Family Background.* There is little reason to suppose that naive check forgers come from extremely disordered or unconventional family settings. It does not appear that check forgers have experienced severe or atypical parental contacts. Additionally, the adult family background of the check forger is relatively conventional. Many naive forgers are married, but disruptions in marital relationships often play some part in the development of check forgery. It does appear that the marital situation of the check passer has not been entirely harmonious prior to the forgery activities.

*Peer Group Associations.* There is no clearly significant role played by peer group associations in naive forgery. Certainly the forger does not participate in a supportive subculture of forgers. Instead, the naive forger commonly discovers for the first time in prison that other offenders behave in ways similar to his own.

*Contact with Defining Agencies.* Check forgers tend to be dealt with informally for initial violations of the law and then handled in the least punitive way when processed through the courts; for example, they are often placed on probation. Swift and rather dramatic action by defining agencies in the first instance of check forgery might be positive in its consequences. Stated differently, it may be that conventional procedures now employed with check forgers contribute to continuation of this behavior. They may lead the forger to assume that forgery can be carried on with relative impunity. Perhaps a more traumatic and earlier confrontation with the defining agencies would result in a different career outcome in this case.

## SUMMARY

The previous nine chapters, along with the present one, have been directed at the theme that etiological progress in the understanding of criminalistic deviance depends upon reorientation of viewpoints around a typological, role-career framework. It is now time to see whether such an orientation has real promise. The next chapters have that as their major goal. In these, a number of different criminal behavior patterns are examined. The discussion of each includes some attention to the place of these forms of lawbreaking within American social structure. Additionally, the social-psychological concepts which have been nominated as useful in the study of criminal role-careers are to be applied to these patterns of conduct. Chapter Eleven, the first of these chapters, takes up several kinds of property criminals.

# 11

# Introduction to Property Offender Careers

## INTRODUCTION

Acts defined as crimes tend to be those which most grossly offend the major values or sentiments of particular societies. In America, property and material goods are revered, so it is not surprising that a number of forms of conduct centering around violation of property rights have been singled out as crimes. In this and the following chapter, we shall examine a number of different property offender patterns. Chapter Eleven takes up professional thieves, professional "heavy" criminals, and semi-professional property criminals, while Chapter Twelve discusses property offender "one-time losers," automobile thieves, naive check forgers, and amateur shoplifters.

As this chapter unfolds, we shall see that professional thieves develop out of relatively comfortable economic circumstances, while "heavies" and semiprofessionals are often the adult counterparts of urban, slum area gang delinquents. Accordingly, we will have occasion to examine much recent theory and research regarding working class gang delinquency when we take up these two kinds of adult offenders. A major argument in favor of the typological viewpoint is that it tends to illuminate the otherwise murky question of linkages or relationships between juvenile delinquency and crime. Some criminals arise out of delinquency backgrounds, while others do not.

## PROFESSIONAL THEFT AS A WAY OF LIFE

We begin our examination of types of crime with that most colorful and unusual group of offenders made up of persons who call themselves "grifters," "boosters," "carnies," or other argot terms, and are termed "professional thieves" by sociologists. Professional thieves engage in a variety of nonviolent and frequently complex forms of property crime, usually involving some element of the "con" or manipulation of the victim(s). Although some might quarrel with the designation of professional attached to these lawbreakers, they do exhibit a long period of training, complex occupational skills, and a shared set of occupationally oriented attitudes, elements usually regarded as central to professional status.[1] Professional thieves also engage in full-time pursuit of illicit incomes through criminality; "grifting" is a way of life with them. In the discussion to follow, a typological characterization of professional thieves is presented first, followed by some comments about the research evidence regarding thieves, and kindred remarks.

## THE PROFESSIONAL THIEF ROLE-CAREER

### Definitional Dimensions

*Offense Behavior.* Those individuals recognized by other criminals as professional thieves or "grifters" engage in a diverse collection of specific acts of criminality. Some are involved in the "big con," which is an elaborate form of swindle involving a number of players or con men. Other thieves are "short con" men who carry out crimes of lesser duration, which also involve fewer participants and result in smaller profit to the offenders. There are other thieves who shoplift, pick pockets, "hotel prowl," or are involved in related activities. Finally, some thieves are implicated in petty, low-ranked forms of crime, such as "carnival grifting." Cutting through this diversity of behavior, however, is the central element of nonviolent criminality. In many cases "wits" or the ability to manipulate victims counts heavily in successful acts of grifting. Sophisticated, nonviolent conduct is the *sine qua non* of professional theft as a form of criminality.

*Interactional Setting.* Certain kinds of professional theft, such as the "big con," involve a number of participants in a complex, highly staged presentation into which "marks" or victims are drawn by the thieves. Swindles of this kind depend heavily upon larcenous motives on the part of marks. Victims of con games are led to believe that they are in a position to defraud someone else through a "get rich quick" scheme offered by the con man. Something of the same sort is involved in "short con" episodes. However, other forms of professional theft, such as pickpocket behavior, involve victims who are not active participants in the illegal events, as is true also of shoplifting, sneak thieving, and hotel prowling.

[1] Everett Cherrington Hughes, *Men and Their Work* (New York: Free Press of Glencoe, Inc., 1958), p. 33. See Hughes' commentary, pages 78–87, for some problems with the designation of forms of criminality as professional in character.

In most instances, grifters carry out their criminal endeavors in collaboration with one or more confederates. Pickpockets work in groups called "troupes" or "whiz mobs." These associational networks among offenders often extend into the noncriminal segments of their lives, so that many are involved in a generalized pattern of differential association with other thieves. A highly developed and esoteric argot or specialized language is characteristic of thieves and is one of the central features of a criminal subculture of thieves.

*Self-concept.* Professional thieves define themselves as "thieves" or "grifters" and disassociate themselves from other criminals who they regard as amateurs and of markedly lower social standing. Among thieves, status or prestige distinctions are drawn along the dimensions of criminal skills and profit derived from illegality, "big con" men being accorded highest rank. In turn, these persons think themselves the elite of the criminal world. Grifters as a group show self-reference notions in which they judge themselves to be clever criminals in a world populated by devious, scheming, corrupt individuals. In this view, "everyone has a racket," and grifters regard themselves as basically no worse than the "marks" they defraud.

*Attitudes.* Professional thieves exhibit relatively positive attitudes toward most individuals in their social environment. They tend to view the criminal world as made up of thieves like themselves, certain other professional criminals with whom they have interests in common, and the balance of the offender population, whom they regard as amateurs and aliens to their own world. In the view of thieves, the noncriminal population is made up of "marks" who deserve to be victimized because of their larcenous motives, law enforcement persons seen as performing necessary tasks of regulating the affairs of society but representing an occupational hazard to be neutralized through bribes or avoided, and other noncriminal citizens. Thieves tend not to demonstrate extreme hostility toward any of these individuals; instead, they simply regard themselves as different from, and superior to, these others. Grifters take considerable pride in their criminal skills and view themselves as incumbents of professional roles.

*Role-career.* Professional thieves enter into grifting relatively early in life. Some become involved in learning experiences as neophyte grifters in their teens, while others enter into thievery at a later age from occupational backgrounds peripheral to the criminal underworld. Professional theft is a way of life pursued over an extended period of time and in a relatively uninterrupted fashion. Professional grifters are rarely found in prison populations, due to the skilled nature of their criminality. Also, the victims of thieves are frequently reluctant to report being victimized to the police authorities, so many cases of theft go unreported. It is likely that many thieves ultimately retire voluntarily from theft activity as they come to regard the frequent traveling and other features of theft behavior as overly burdensome. Still, professional theft is a form of criminality which probably represents an atypically long career pattern.

### Background Dimensions

*Social Class.* Professional thieves appear to be drawn from a variety of social class backgrounds. Most of them do not seem to be from extremes of poverty, so professional theft is not a form of criminality that commonly draws its members from lower class populations. The evidence on professional grifters suggests that many are inducted into this activity from occupational categories or situations peripheral to the criminal underworld. The recruitment process often involves bartenders, taxicab drivers, bellhops, and kindred occupational types who interact with grifters and various other deviant individuals in the course of their occupations. Such persons begin by playing a tangential and minor role in acts of grifting. Ultimately, many move into full-time involvement in grifting; the end product of the training process through which they proceed is professionalized crime skills.

*Family Background.* It is likely that professional thieves often derive from family backgrounds which are unexceptional in character, but, some may have grown up in somewhat disturbed or deviant family settings. On this point, one line of argument holds that there is a "budding grifter" personality type produced by certain situations of tension between family members. According to this view, the manipulative, devious personalities generated in such situations are individuals who frequently make their way into professional thievery as a life's work. However, probably a good many grifters have grown up in family settings in which they have become alienated from other family members and detached from parental ties relatively early in life. In turn, these actors have come into contact with carnival grifters or other mobile groups of thieves, and have become grifters.

*Peer Group Associations.* There is little basis for supposing that the peer group relationships in which professional thieves were involved before they became grifters have played a significant role in causation of their behavior. Whatever the etiology of professional theft, it does not appear to be a function of any kind of peer influence. However, once an individual is engaged in grifting activity, peer relations take on critical significance. It is impossible to acquire the complex and subtle crime skills of professional theft by any other technique than direct tutelage by other criminals. In addition, the life of professional grifting is a behavior system or subcultural way of life, so differential association with criminal peers is very much a part of this form of crime. Hence the thief is in a situation of constant reinforcement of his deviant self-notions and attitudes through interaction with like-minded individuals.

*Contact with Defining Agencies.* It does not appear as though the contacts that thieves have with law enforcement and correctional agencies act as major forces in their criminality. Thieves do not look upon such organizations with great hostility. One reason for their relatively mild attitudes toward the police and correctional personnel is that they have little contact with such persons. Professional theft is a low risk crime in that grifters are rarely apprehended for their illegal acts. They often enjoy relatively congenial relations with members of defining agencies. Thieves are usually articulate, charming persons, they do not shoot at or assault policemen, and they are not antagonistic toward them. On those infrequent occasions when a grifter "falls" (is arrested) the experience is not likely to be particularly traumatic for him.

### Some Evidence

The greatest portion of the data regarding professional theft concerns the criminal activity in which grifters engage.[2] Police officers have compiled lengthy collections of case material on the *modus operandi* of thieves,[3] while several social scientists have also spent some of their energy cataloguing the details of professional grifting.[4] What emerges from all of these accounts is a picture of criminality, parallel to that sketched above, which demonstrates the esoteric and complex nature of grifting as a kind of crime.

Considerably less is known about the backgrounds and causal situations from which professional thieves derive than is apparent about the criminality in which they engage. Our typological remarks suggested that

[2] Herbert A. Bloch and Gilbert Geis, *Man, Crime, and Society* (New York: Random House, Inc., 1962), pp. 191–215; Walter Bromberg and Sylvan Keiser, "The Psychology of the Swindler," *American Journal of Psychiatry*, XCIV (May 1938), 1441–58; Walter B. Gibson, *The Bunco Book* (Holyoke, Mass.: Sidney H. Radner, 1946); Richard L. Jenkins, *Breaking Patterns of Defeat* (Philadelphia: J. B. Lippincott Co., 1954), pp. 148–58; John C. R. McDonald, *Crime is a Business* (Stanford: Stanford University Press, 1939); David W. Maurer, *The Big Con* (New York: Bobbs-Merrill Co., Inc., 1940); Maurer, *Whiz Mob* (New Haven, Conn.: College and University Press, 1964); Julian R. Roebuck and Ronald Johnson, "The 'Short Con' Man," *Crime and Delinquency*, X (July 1964), 235–48; Edwin M. Schur, "Sociological Analysis of Confidence Swindling," *Journal of Criminal Law, Criminology and Police Science*, XLVIII (September–October 1957), 296–304; Edwin H. Sutherland, *The Professional Thief* (Chicago: University of Chicago Press, 1937).

[3] McDonald, *op. cit.*

[4] Maurer, *op. cit.*; Roebuck and Johnson, *op. cit.*; Sutherland, *op. cit.*

thieves are often recruited from certain occupations in which contact with underworld figures is fairly common and that, in addition, grifters may often be drawn from a cohort of individuals with particular personality patterns. On this first point, Sutherland's report on professional offenders indicated that many of these persons originally were active in occupational pursuits peripheral to criminalistic ones.[5]

The contention that thieves are individuals with "budding grifter" kinds of personality structures has been advanced by psychiatrist Richard L. Jenkins.[6] He suggests that "budding grifters" are specialists in deceit who have developed interpersonal betrayal into a fine art. Rather than experiencing guilt over their devious activities, they exhibit a professional pride in their workmanship and may feel chagrin and humiliation in instances where their manipulative endeavors go awry.

According to Jenkins, the elements or experiences which may contribute to the development of "budding grifter" personalities include the following:

1. Experiences (as of unusual hardship) during the formative period which put a high premium upon material success.

2. Early experiences which force a close self-protective attention to the emotional reactions of intermittently or constantly hostile adults.

3. Early experiences which tend toward the development of distrust and the expectation of betrayal.

4. Attitudes on the part of those emotionally important to the child which sanction unreliability, or which laud deceit or betrayal as an adaptation and means of getting on in the world. In some instances this involves definite teaching or coaching in the art of betrayal.

5. Early and repetitive gain from the use of deceit.

6. Attitudes and experiences which lead to the development of verbal facility, social charm and ingratiating ways.[7]

The kinds of social settings likely to culminate in learning of deceit and reward for its practice include disharmony and marital tension between the parents of the child. In this situation, the parents compete for the allegiance of the child, attempting to win his loyalty and alienate him from the other marital partner. The "budding grifter" learns to turn this situation to his own advantage by playing each parent off against the other.

These claims of Jenkins represent a series of clinical hunches derived from psychiatric practice, rather than hard facts from careful research.

[5] Sutherland, *op. cit.*, pp. 211–14.
[6] Jenkins, *op. cit.*, pp. 148–58.
[7] *Ibid.*, p. 150.

Moreover, the hypothesis advanced in this case is broad, holding that the "grifter" personalities generated by these experiences subsequently make their way into a variety of social circumstances. Jenkins does not argue that all or most of them become professional criminals, so that one might expect to find "budding grifters" at work on used car lots, selling vacuum cleaners or aluminum siding, or in myriad other settings.

At least one corroborative study has revealed that grifters do exhibit unique personality configurations. Roebuck and Johnson have reported that the "short con" men they examined were of above average intelligence, and that most of them exhibited the personality marks of the grifter suggested by Jenkins.[8]

Although facts are hard to come by, it is our estimate that professional theft has always been a relatively uncommon form of criminality in American society. Moreover, there is reason to suppose that grifting is generally on the decline. Certain forms of grifting, in particular, have become nearly obsolete, probably as a consequence of certain broad changes that have occurred in societal conditions in the United States. For one, the practice of the "big con" has probably waned due to changes in banking procedures, the growing sophistication of "marks," and other trends of that sort. Carnival grifting is perhaps a vanishing form of illegality because of the general disappearance of the carnival as a feature of small-town life in this country. Certain other forms of grifting are more hardy and survive to the present, so that "boosting" (shoplifting) and certain "short con" games persist as forms of professional theft. But even these surviving patterns are probably infrequent in comparison to the "garden variety" forms of lawbreaking.

What is the significance of professional theft? Two points stand out in any evaluation of the criminological salience of grifting. First, professional theft is an extreme illustration of the extent to which a pattern of deviant conduct may become elaborated into a complex interactional pattern, behavior system, or subculture, in which the members are bound together by a variety of social ties in addition to their involvement in criminal acts. Moreover, these deviant actors are players in a complex social system in which they are implicated in symbiotic ties with a variety of "noncriminals," including policemen, tipsters, fences, cab drivers, and kindred types. Professional theft is a significant case of deviant conduct transmitted from generation to generation; much of the content of activity originated well before the birthdates of contemporary thieves.

The second observation to be made about criminality, stemming from the study of grifting, has to do with the interconnections of illegality to

[8] Roebuck and Johnson, op. cit., 238–41.

other features of organized social life. For example, Schur has suggested that professional theft cannot be understood apart from consideration of basic values of American society which encourage or condone swindles, frauds, "sharp" business practices, and unethical conduct of various kinds.[9] The United States exhibits a cultural climate in which profit motives, salesmanship, and "something for nothing" interests stand out. The professional thief is a skilled worker who turns this situation of tolerance for devious conduct to his own advantage. Grifters claim that it is difficult if not impossible to grift in England, due to the lesser emphasis upon risk-taking, acquisitive actions in that nation. In the same way, they frequently assert that it is not possible to "con" or victimize an honest man; the mark must have "larceny in his soul" in order to be swindled. In short, the case of professional thieves stands as one of many illustrations of the impossibility of sustaining the clear distinctions between the "good guys" and the "bad guys" in American society. The law violator is no less a product of society than the moral, upright citizen, and both of them have much more in common than they are likely to acknowledge.

## PROFESSIONAL "HEAVY" CRIMINALS

The typological descriptions woven into this section of the book and around which the content of this text is organized suggest the existence of a number of relatively clear-cut types of property offenders. Professional "heavy" criminals who engage in robberies and burglaries of various kinds are distinguished from semiprofessional property offenders and "one-time loser" property criminals who also engage in robberies and related offenses. One major basis for separating these offender role-careers is that the three vary markedly in terms of the criminal expertise demonstrated by the respective role-incumbents.

However, it ought to be made clear at the outset that the distinction between professional "heavy" criminals and semiprofessional property offenders is actually one of degree rather than kind. The dividing line between professional and semiprofessional property offenders is somewhat arbitrary. On the whole, professional "heavies" are highly competent lawbreakers who reap large sums of money from their illegal activities and work at this occupation full time. Semiprofessionals tend to be relatively unskilled, poorly paid for their criminal endeavors, and work at crime in some cases on a part-time basis. Doubtless many offenders would fall clearly into one or another of these types, but there

[9] Schur, op. cit.

would be some criminals who might be difficult to categorize, in that technical skill, amount of profit from crime, and involvement in criminality are matters of degree rather than different qualitative attributes of offenders.

Descriptions of professional "heavy" crime are to be found in some number, including several in the form of the life stories of professional criminals.[10] One useful account of professional crime which might serve as a comparison to other instances would be the famous Brink's robbery which occurred in Boston in 1950. The flavor of professional crime is clearly communicated in the following excerpt from the Federal Bureau of Investigation report regarding its investigation of the robbery:

The Brink's robbery was a product of a combined thought and criminal experience of men who had known one another for many years. The gang spent more than a year in planning the robbery and they started a systematic study of the Brink's organization after it moved to its present site on Prince Street in Boston.

Before the robbery was carried out, all the participants were well acquainted with the Brink's premises. Each had surreptitiously entered the building on several occasions after the Brink's employees had left for the day and they made a study of Brink's schedules and shipments.

The planning for the robbery included several "trial runs" in which the gang members practiced their approach to the building in a truck and their flight over the "getaway" route. The gang abandoned plans to carry out the robbery several times when conditions were not favorable.

During these occasions one gang member was stationed on the roof of a building on Prince Street overlooking Brink's. He signaled the others with a flashlight. The last of these "false" approaches took place on the evening before the robbery.

During the early evening of January 17, 1950, members of the gang met in the Roxbury section of Boston and entered the rear of a Ford stake-body truck which had been stolen in Boston in November, 1949, to be used in the robbery.

Including the driver, this truck carried nine members of the gang to the scene of the robbery. During the trip from Roxbury seven of the men donned Navy-type peacoats and chauffeur's caps. Each of the seven also was given a pistol and Halloween-type mask. Each had gloves and wore either crepe-sole shoes or rubbers so their footsteps would be muffled.

As the men approached the Brink's building, they looked for a signal from the "lookout" on the roof of a Prince Street building. The "lookout" previously had arrived in a stolen Ford sedan.

[10] Everett DeBaun, "The Heist: The Theory and Practice of Armed Robbery," Harpers, CC (February 1950), 69–77; Quentin Reynolds, I, Willie Sutton (New York: Farrar, Straus & Giroux, Inc., 1953); John Bartlow Martin, My Life in Crime (New York: Harper & Row, 1952), Jack Black, "A Burglar Looks at Laws and Codes," Harpers, CLX (February 1930), 306–13; Black, You Can't Win (New York: The Macmillan Co., 1926).

After receiving the "go ahead" signal, seven members of the gang left the truck and walked through a playground which led to the Prince Street entrance to Brink's. Using the side-door key they had previously obtained, the men quickly entered and donned the masks.

Other keys in their possession enabled them to proceed to the second floor, where they took five Brink's employees by surprise. The seven robbers ordered the employees to lie face down on the floor, tied their hands behind them, and placed adhesive tape over their mouths. Before fleeing with the loot, the seven armed men attempted to open a metal box containing the payroll of the General Electric Co., but they had brought no tools and were unsuccessful.

Immediately upon leaving, the gang loaded the loot into the stolen truck. As the truck sped away with nine members of the gang, the "lookout" departed in the stolen sedan. The truck was unloaded at the home of one of the participants in Roxbury that same evening. Some members of the gang made a preliminary effort to count the loot, but they quickly dispersed to establish alibis for themselves.

On the night of the robbery, approximately $380,000 of the loot was removed from the house in Roxbury for security reasons. Additionally, the equipment used in the robbery was taken by a gang member for disposal. On January 18, 1950, another gang member took the remainder of the loot from the house; and several weeks later it was divided among the eleven men.

In addition to the cash and securities, the robbers took four pistols from Brink's. One of these was recovered by a Somerville, Mass., police officer on February 5, 1950. It had been found by a group of boys near the Mystic River in Somerville.

Descriptions of the truck used in the robbery were obtained from persons in the vicinity of the crime scene. Pieces of an identical truck were found at a dump in Stoughton, Mass., March 14, 1950. This truck had been cut up with an acetylene torch.

During the F.B.I.'s six-year investigation thousands of possible suspects were eliminated. Thousands of other persons, possible witnesses and individuals who could furnish background information concerning matters arising in various phases of the investigation were interviewed. Circulars concerning a $100,000 reward offered by Brink's were distributed to all parts of the country and no tip was overlooked.[11]

This illustration of a complex armed robbery parallels in many of its details the *modus operandi* of the "heist" enumerated by a former robber, DeBaun.[12]

In the sections to follow, a typological description of professional "heavy" offenders will be presented, followed by a typological characterization of semiprofessional criminals. As these discussions will indicate, the social backgrounds of both of these types of lawbreakers seem

---

[11] *Seattle Times,* January 11, 1957.
[12] DeBaun, *op. cit.*

relatively similar, so it appears that relatively unskilled offenders and technically proficient ones alike usually develop out of gang delinquent origins. Most of these individuals have lived in urban communities, frequently in slum neighborhoods. Highly skilled professional "heavies" appear to be those former gang offenders of above average intelligence who have been in social situations where they have been able to acquire special skill in criminality, usually through differential association with other professional violators. Semiprofessionals, on the other hand, are the less able deviants, probably of only average intelligence, and have been deprived of criminal learning opportunities.

Following the typological description of these two kinds of offenders, the available theories and evidence regarding their etiological backgrounds will be examined. We shall pay particularly close attention to those recent theoretical contentions regarding working class, subcultural delinquency and to the pieces of research evidence that have been produced regarding these lines of argument.

## THE PROFESSIONAL "HEAVY" ROLE-CAREER [13]

### Definitional Dimensions

*Offense Behavior.* Professional "heavy" criminals engage in armed robbery, burglary, and other direct assaults upon property. They are highly skilled at crime, so although the element of coercion and threat of violence is involved here, actual force is rarely employed. The *modus operandi* of professional "heavy" criminals involves a relatively lengthy period of detailed planning prior to execution of the criminal offense. The actual burglary or robbery is accomplished swiftly, with the offenders employing the element of surprise to avoid the risk of apprehension.

*Interactional Setting.* Most activities of professional "heavy" criminals are carried on as team or "mob" operations. Although robberies can on some occasions be carried out by a single offender, most burglaries and robberies by professionals utilize a number of crime partners. The crime partners are involved in specialized roles; one of the participants may be the "rod man," while another is the "wheel man," a specialist in driving getaway cars.

*Self-concept.* Professional "heavies" define themselves as criminals and as professionals in criminality. They exhibit pride in their specialized skills and view crime as a lucrative and satisfying way of life. Profession-

[13] Don C. Gibbons, *Changing the Lawbreaker,* The Treatment of Delinquents and Criminals, © 1965. Reprinted by permission of Prentice-Hall, Inc., Englewood Cliffs, New Jersey, pp. 102–4.

als draw clear distinctions between themselves and other offenders, whom they regard as amateurs.

*Attitudes.* The attitudes of the professional "heavy" toward the police range from scorn for inept policemen regarded as "clowns" to respect for competent police workers. In either event, the professional does not exhibit great hostility toward the police, who are regarded as necessary persons with a job to do. The professional "heavy" shows somewhat negative attitudes toward conventional work roles, inasmuch as crime seems to him a preferable way of earning a livelihood.

*Role-career.* Professional "heavies" are normally from urban, lower class backgrounds. Most of them began their criminal careers as predatory gang delinquents. This does not mean that most predatory gang offenders become professional "heavies," but rather that "heavies" are selected out of a large group of gang delinquents. The "heavy" usually goes through a process of increasing differential involvement with older professionals from whom he learns necessary crime skills. Persons who engage in professional property offenses tend to continue criminal activities into middle age, whereupon many of them ultimately retire into noncriminal occupations.

### Background Dimensions

*Social Class.* Offenders of this type have usually resided for long periods of time in working class (lower class) neighborhoods in urban areas. They frequently lived as youngsters in deteriorated neighborhoods in which patterns of adult criminality were often readily observable. As adults, some of them have moved into more "respectable," middle class neighborhoods, while at the same time maintaining their previous social ties to working class friends.

*Family Background.* As juveniles, most of these offenders experienced family backgrounds of parental neglect and exposure to delinquency patterns. The family structure was not usually characterized by intense interfamily tension. Family members were on relatively good terms with each other, but the offender commonly was not subjected to close parental supervision. On occasion, this type had experienced a family background in which siblings were also delinquent or involved in criminality. In addition, the parents were on occasion involved in forms of criminality, so that differential association with deviant family members played a significant part in career development.

Adult "heavy" professional offenders are usually involved in stable marital relationships and parental ties to offspring. Involvement in deviant behavior on their part tends not to be disruptive of family relationships, for "heavy" criminals are rarely caught up in the correctional machinery which might create family disorganization.

*Peer Group Associations.* As a juvenile, this type of offender was involved in interaction within the structure of delinquent gangs or differential association with delinquent peers. In some cases these delinquent peers form a recognizable gang, whereas in others they represent a loose confederation of offenders. In either case, the offender exhibited differential avoidance of nondelinquent juveniles in his community. Commonly, this type associated with a group of youths known in the area as troublemakers and delinquents, all of whom shared such characteristics as expulsion from school and unemployment. The peer structure provided him with group support for his hostile and cynical attitudes. The peer structure also provided social rewards for prowess in delinquent acts, in that peers often accorded high status to the most delinquent boys.

Adult "heavy" professional criminals continue to associate differentially with criminal peers. They may number among their friends a large number of other "heavy" professionals. However, these individuals do not usually constitute a stable "mob" carrying on repeated acts of criminality. Instead, "mobs" or groups of lawbreakers are formed on the occasion of a specific criminal offense and disbanded at its conclusion. The constituent members of these "mobs" vary, so that professional "heavies" are only loosely organized into a criminal confederation.

*Contact with Defining Agencies.* This type usually exhibited early involvement with the police. In many instances, his police contacts are considerably more common than indicated by his official record. This type was also well-known to the juvenile court. His record is likely to show several juvenile probation experiences, culminating in placement in a correctional institution. The usual view of persons who dealt with the offender as a juvenile was that he was a "tough kid," lacking in insight and concern over his delinquent conduct. In turn, the offender's usual view of law enforcement and correctional agents was that such persons are "phonies."

The early adult history of this offender is likely to show several commitments to penal institutions. Commonly, some of the criminal skills exhibited by the person were acquired in this learning environment. As the developing professional acquires expertise in deviance and becomes more enmeshed in the world of professional criminality, prison becomes an occupational hazard which he infrequently encounters. Accordingly, the correctional machinery has an insignificant effect upon mature professional "heavy" criminals.

## THE SEMIPROFESSIONAL PROPERTY CRIMINAL ROLE-CAREER[14]

### Definitional Dimensions

*Offense Behavior.* Semiprofessional property offenders engage in strong-arm robberies, holdups, burglaries, larcenies, and similar direct assaults upon personal or private property. They employ crime skills which are relatively simple and uncomplicated. For example, strong-arm robbery does not involve much detailed planning and careful execution of the crime, but rather application of crude physical force in order to relieve a victim of his money. This is referred to as semiprofessional crime, because even though technical skill is not characteristic of these offenders, most of them attempt to carry on crime as an occupation.

*Interactional Setting.* Many of the offenses of the semiprofessional offender are two-person affairs involving an offender and a victim, for example, strong-arm robbery and liquor store and gas station stickups. On occasion, semiprofessionals operate in collections of several crime partners, as in instances of burglary and safe-robbery. In either event, the criminal act tends to be direct and unsophisticated, a complex interactional pattern rarely being involved.

*Self-concept.* Semiprofessional property offenders view themselves as criminals. Additionally, the semiprofessional sees himself as an individual who has few alternatives to criminal behavior and as a victim of a corrupt society in which everyone has a "racket." Thus the semiprofessional is relieved from any sense of guilt regarding his criminality by deflecting blame onto "the system."

*Attitudes.* The attitudes of the semiprofessional offender toward the police tend to be more hostile and antagonistic than is the case with professional "heavies." Doubtless this is in considerable part a function of the greater number of contacts with police agents experienced by this offender. In the same way, the semiprofessional's views of the courts and correctional agents are more hostile than those of the professional "heavy." Semiprofessionals also denigrate conventional occupations as a way of life, holding that "only slobs work." They frequently show a diffuse set of bitter and resentful attitudes toward, not only the police and correctional agents, but their parents, social agencies, and schools.

*Role-career.* Semiprofessional property offenders represent the more

[14] Don C. Gibbons, *Changing the Lawbreaker,* The Treatment of Delinquents and Criminals, © 1965. Reprinted by permission of Prentice-Hall, Inc., Englewood Cliffs, New Jersey, pp. 104–6.

usual outcome of patterns of predatory gang delinquency, as contrasted to the professional "heavy" adult outcome. That is, most adult semiprofessional offenders exhibit juvenile backgrounds of predatory gang behavior, and many juvenile gang offenders continue in criminality as semiprofessionals. As an adult, the semiprofessional rapidly accumulates an extensive "rap sheet," or record of crimes and institutional commitments. Because of the low degree of skill involved in the criminality of the semiprofessionals, the risks of apprehension, conviction, and incarceration are high. Many semiprofessionals spend a considerable part of their early adult years in penal institutions, where they are likely to be identified as "right guys," or antiadministration inmates. It does not appear that conventional treatment efforts are successful in deflecting many of these persons away from continuation in crime. On the other hand, many of them ultimately do withdraw from crime careers upon reaching early middle age.

### Background Dimensions

*Social Class.* See description of professional "heavy" criminals. Semiprofessionals are from similar social class origins.

*Family Background.* See description of professional "heavy" criminals. Semiprofessionals are from similar family backgrounds.

*Peer Group Associations.* See description of professional "heavy" criminals. Semiprofessionals experience similar peer group associations. However, semiprofessionals have usually been restricted in their interactional experiences to associations with other relatively unskilled offenders, so they have not had opportunities to learn the more esoteric or complex crime skills. In addition, semiprofessional offenders usually interact as adults with kindred types of individuals, rather than with professional criminals. That is, the noncriminal endeavors of these persons as they act out their general social roles take place within collectivities of noncriminal citizens or semiprofessional offenders.

*Contact with Defining Agencies.* See description of professional "heavy" criminals. Semiprofessionals experience similar agency contacts, particularly as juveniles. However, adult semiprofessional offenders spend major portions of their lives in penal institutions. Many are recidivists who enter, leave, and reenter prisons, so they are treatment failures. It appears that many of them become progressively more hostile in attitude and fixed in behavior as they undergo these recurrent prison commitments; contacts with defining agencies play a contributory role in the development of their deviant careers.

## Some Evidence

Descriptive data regarding the characteristics and social backgrounds of professional and semiprofessional offenders are available in considerable quantity, so certain contentions in the typological sketches above are well-supported. We have already taken note of a group of biographical and autobiographical reports by offenders regarding their social origins and participation in crime.[15]

Detailed investigations of semiprofessional offenders have been carried out in good number. One early research study of this kind was directed by the Gluecks, who examined the backgrounds and criminal histories of 500 Massachusetts Reformatory inmates who had been released from the institution in 1921–1922. The Gluecks traced individuals up to 1926–1927 and asserted that 80 per cent had not been rehabilitated.[16] This early study seemed to point unequivocally to the conclusion that penal institutions are dismal failures. However, less than half of the group was alleged to have committed felonies or other serious acts of lawbreaking. Recent evidence suggests that prisons are considerably more effective than formerly supposed.[17]

Study of the social backgrounds of these 500 offenders by the Gluecks turned up indications that most of them had developed in disorganized families in slum areas and had experienced relatively wretched life situations. For example, about 75 per cent of the inmates had backgrounds in which other family members were involved in criminality.[18]

A more recent inquiry into the backgrounds of institutionalized offenders was conducted in Wisconsin by Gillin.[19] In his investigation, he compared murderers, sex offenders, and property criminals. Unfortunately, Gillin lumped a variety of types of property criminals within the single category that he compared with sexual offenders and the murderers, and as a result a confused picture of the social origins of property violators is found in his report.[20]

A more theoretically satisfactory piece of work is Hayner's, in which he tested a series of hunches regarding five hypothesized offender types,

[15] See footnote 10. See also Donald MacKenzie, *Occupation: Thief* (Indianapolis: Bobbs-Merrill Co., Inc., 1955); Hutchins Hapgood, *Autobiography of a Thief* (New York: Fox, Duffield, 1930).

[16] Sheldon and Eleanor Glueck, *500 Criminal Careers* (New York: Alfred A. Knopf, Inc., 1930).

[17] Daniel Glaser, *The Effectiveness of a Prison and Parole System* (Indianapolis: Bobbs-Merrill Co., Inc., 1964), pp. 13–35.

[18] Sheldon and Eleanor Glueck, *op. cit.*, pp. 112–13.

[19] John L. Gillin, *The Wisconsin Prisoner* (Madison: University of Wisconsin Press, 1946).

[20] *Ibid.*, pp. 14–16.

one of which was the "heavy." [21] In this study, Hayner examined the case records of inmates in Washington State institutions in order to determine if certain types, including "alcoholic forgers" and "heavies," do exist. "Heavies" were identified as prisoners over 25 years old who had been engaged in robbery or burglary as a crime pattern, so they were apparently semiprofessionals. Hayner discovered that these individuals had frequently attempted to escape from prison, exhibited antisocial personalities, and were defined as "right guys" by other inmates in the prison. The "heavies" had poor work records outside of the institution, were often from families in which other members were delinquent or criminal, and were generally from lower socioeconomic status groups. As a result of this accumulation of unfavorable social characteristics, they were usually given long prison sentences by the paroling agency.

The results of investigations by Schrag and his associates run parallel to the findings of Hayner. Schrag has reported the social characteristics of "antisocial" prisoners who are known as "right guys" in the argot of prison culture.[22] Antisocial inmates are recidivists who show an evolving career pattern in lawbreaking which began with truancy and expressive theft during the adolescent period and developed into semiprofessional property criminality in adulthood. These prisoners show a background of low socioeconomic status and associations with delinquent companions or criminalistic siblings. They often come from relatively warm and stable family backgrounds, but ones which are criminogenic in character owing to the involvement of family members in deviance.

Roebuck conducted still another study which turned up findings compatible with those already enumerated.[23] He investigated the social backgrounds of a group of Negro offenders in the Washington, D.C., Reformatory by comparing these persons with inmates who had engaged in other kinds of criminality. The armed robbers were older than most of the other felons, had grown up in urban areas and in slum neighborhoods, had been inducted into delinquency quite early in their lives, and exhibited average intelligence ratings. Most of them had experienced dismal home conditions in which their families were frequently dependent upon public assistance for support. Most were members of migrant families from the southern region of the country. These characteristics are the

[21] Norman S. Hayner, "Characteristics of Five Offender Types," *American Sociological Review*, XXVI (February 1961), 96–102.

[22] Clarence C. Schrag, "Some Foundations for a Theory of Correction," in *The Prison*, ed. D. R. Cressey (New York: Holt, Rinehart and Winston, Inc., 1961), pp. 346–56; Schrag, "A Preliminary Criminal Typology," *Pacific Sociological Review*, IV (Spring 1961), 11–16.

[23] Julian B. Roebuck and Mervyn L. Cadwallader, "The Negro Armed Robber as a Criminal Type: The Construction and Application of a Typology," *Pacific Sociological Review*, IV (Spring 1961), 21–26.

sort enumerated in the typologies in this chapter, although these specific Negro robbers were perhaps from somewhat more deteriorated social
surroundings than would be true of other samples of semiprofessional
criminals, owing to the fact that the subjects were Negro and, as a
consequence, recipients of special kinds of social and economic dis-
crimination.

Still other reports concerning semiprofessional property offenders which
are germane to this discussion are those by Peterson, *et al.*,[24] and by
Frum; [25] stable deviant careers were discovered in both cases. Collectively,
what all of these investigations indicate is that there is a type of criminal
career which we have labeled semiprofessional property crime. Although
there might be some quibbling about specific items in the characterization
of semiprofessional offenders, the general accuracy of this portrait does
not seem to be in question.

There is a rich body of empirical data regarding the gang delinquency
backgrounds out of which semiprofessional offenders develop, in addition
to evidence on their adult activities. Indeed, a major collection of intellectual currency is found in early, detailed investigations of the gang world
by Thrasher, Shaw and McKay, and others. Until recently, criminologists
have simply made use of this data and failed to continue the sorts of
studies that produced this original lode of factual evidence. But, as we
shall see shortly, a rejuvenation of theoretical and research interest has
occurred in the past decade or so.

The largest single study of gangs ever attempted is Thrasher's pioneering work in Chicago, in which he examined the activities of 1313 boy
gangs.[26] One of his conclusions which has stood relatively unquestioned
to the present is that *"gangland represents a geographically and socially
interstitial area in the city"* (emphasis in the original).[27] By interstitial,
he meant those spaces (interstices) that intervene between sections of the
urban fabric, areas thought to be socially disorganized. Although there
is reason to quarrel with the characterization of gangland as socially
disorganized, rather than differentially organized, it is apparent that
juvenile gangs are most frequently encountered in slum, deteriorated,
working class sections of the city.

Thrasher's work in Chicago was paralleled by many reports of Shaw,

---

[24] Richard A. Peterson, David J. Pittman, and Patricia O'Neal, "Stabilities in Deviance: A Study
of Assaultive and Non-Assaultive Offenders," *Journal of Criminal Law, Criminology and Police
Science*, LIII (March 1962), 44–48.

[25] Harold S. Frum, "Adult Criminal Offense Trends Following Juvenile Delinquency," *Journal
of Criminal Law, Criminology and Police Science*, XLIX (May–June 1958), 29–49.

[26] Frederic M. Thrasher, *The Gang*, abridged and with a new introduction by James F. Short, Jr.
(Chicago: University of Chicago Press, 1963).

[27] *Ibid.*, p. 20.

McKay, and others.[28] Shaw and McKay presented a series of ecological studies which demonstrated that gang delinquency tends to be concentrated in "delinquency areas" of the city, which are also slum neighborhoods characterized by high rates of social breakdown of various kinds. They also contributed a number of detailed descriptions of delinquent *behavior* of urban gangs. These commentaries on delinquent boys indicated that most of them are lacking in personality pathologies, and are the products of learning situations in which criminalistic endeavors are initially learned as forms of hedonistic "fun." As they progress through careers in delinquency, deviant acts come to take on a more utilitarian character, so that many of the boys ultimately acquire the skills and criminal sophistication of semiprofessional offenders.

Finally, in this collection of early work on delinquency, note should be taken of several other ecological investigations of delinquency rates and social conditions in urban areas.[29] These confirm contentions about linkages of gang delinquency to low socioeconomic status and kindred conditions.

## THEORY AND RESEARCH ON DELINQUENT SUBCULTURES

Although gang delinquency has been a subject of persistent interest to sociologists since the 1920's, relatively little theorizing or research was carried out regarding gang misconduct in the interval between the Chicago work discussed above and the 1950's. Publication in 1955 of Albert K. Cohen's *Delinquent Boys* was a signal event, for that volume triggered an impressive resurgence of speculative and empirical attention to delinquent gang activity. A massive body of argument and counterargument has grown out of the initial insights of Cohen. In the same way, a large and valuable collection of research evidence produced in the past dozen years represents research material initially stimulated by

[28] Clifford Shaw, The Jack Roller (Chicago: University of Chicago Press, 1930); Shaw and Maurice E. Moore, The Natural History of a Delinquent Career (Philadelphia: A. Saifer, Publisher, 1951); Shaw, Henry D. McKay, and James F. McDonald, Brothers in Crime (Chicago: University of Chicago Press, 1938); Shaw and McKay, Juvenile Delinquency and Urban Areas (Chicago: University of Chicago Press, 1942); Shaw and McKay, Social Factors in Juvenile Delinquency, Report on the Causes of Crime for the National Commission on Law Observance and Enforcement, Vol. II (Washington, D.C.: U.S. Government Printing Office, 1931).

[29] Bernard Lander, Towards an Understanding of Juvenile Delinquency (New York: Columbia University Press, 1954); David J. Bordua, "Juvenile Delinquency and 'Anomie': An Attempt at Replication," Social Problems, VI (Winter 1958–1959), 230–38; Roland J. Chilton, "Continuity in Delinquency Area Research: A Comparison of Studies for Baltimore, Detroit, and Indianapolis," American Sociological Review, XXIX (February 1964), 71–83; Richard Quinney, "Crime, Delinquency, and Social Areas," Journal of Research in Crime and Delinquency, I (July 1964), 149–54.

the work of Cohen. Clearly, the theoretical contributions of Cohen are contentions of great significance, due to the seminal role they have played in the growth of what is frequently termed *subcultural* theory and research. In the pages below, we shall examine some of the major developments in this area of inquiry, in a roughly chronological order of presentation.

## Cohen and Delinquent Subcultures

In his initial essay on gang delinquency, *Delinquent Boys,* Cohen began by indicating that he was interested in accounting for the emergence of delinquent subcultures in working class areas of American cities.[30] According to Cohen, a delinquent subculture may be defined as "a way of life that has somehow become traditional among certain groups in American society. These groups are the boy's gangs that flourish most conspicuously in the 'delinquency neighborhoods' of our larger American cities."[31] The delinquent subculture revolves around behavior which is *nonutilitarian, malicious,* and *negativistic.* That is, Cohen asserts that much of the stealing and other behavior of gang delinquents is motivated by interests other than rational utilitarian gain, so that gang offenders steal "for the hell of it." The malicious and negativistic character of gang behavior is revealed in a variety of ways, most commonly in observations that gang members reap enjoyment from discomfort they have caused others and find cause for pride in reputations they have acquired for "meanness."[32] Cohen also characterizes subcultural misbehavior in terms of *short-run hedonism,* indicated by a lack of long-term goals or planning on the part of gang members. Finally, *group autonomy* is a hallmark of subcultural deviance, and delinquent gangs are said to be solidary collectivities.[33]

Why did the delinquent subculture develop among lower class boys? In brief, Cohen's answer is that working class gang delinquency represents a social movement among juvenile delinquents. This subculture arose as a solution to *shared* problems of low status among working class youths. In his words, "The crucial condition for the emergence of new cultural forms is the existence, *in effective interaction with one another,*

---

[30] Albert K. Cohen, *Delinquent Boys* (New York: Free Press of Glencoe, Inc., 1955). On the issue of the social class distribution of subcultural gang delinquency, Cohen argues: "It is our conclusion, by no means novel or startling, that juvenile delinquency and the delinquent subculture in particular are overwhelmingly concentrated in the male, working-class sector of the juvenile population" (*Delinquent Boys,* p. 37).

[31] *Ibid.,* p. 13.

[32] *Ibid.,* pp. 25–30.

[33] *Ibid.,* pp. 30–32.

*of a number of actors with similar problems of adjustment*" (emphasis in the original).[34]

The shared problem of low status or esteem among gang boys arises as a consequence of their placement in the social order working class youths experience status threats when they are evaluated in terms of a middle class measuring rod, by which is meant a set of social expectations regarding the characteristics of "good boys." These expectations center about such traits as ambition, individual responsibility, possession of talents, asceticism, rationality, manners and courtesy, and control of physical aggression.[35] The exemplary youth, in the eyes of middle class school teachers and other important citizens, embodies most or all of these social characteristics. But the working class boy has been inadequately socialized in these notions of proper behavior, so he finds himself at a competitive disadvantage in classrooms and other social arenas as he competes with middle class peers for recognition by adults. Again, to cite Cohen: "The delinquent subculture, we suggest, is a way of dealing with the problems of adjustment we have described. These problems are chiefly status problems: certain children are denied status in the respectable society because they cannot meet the criteria of the respectable status system. The delinquent subculture deals with these problems by providing criteria of status which these children *can* meet." [36] These boys who withdraw from such situations of social hurt as the school find their way into the subculture of the gang, which provides them with a social setting in which they can become insulated against assaults upon their self-esteem.

Cohen's original picture of gang delinquency was painted with a broad brush, relatively small areas of factual data being joined with big strokes of speculation. No wonder that a number of critics detected what they felt to be errors in this initial formulation. An early criticism was advanced by Sykes and Matza in the form of some remarks about "techniques of neutralization." [37] They contend that delinquents are at least partially committed to the dominant social order, experience guilt or shame when they engage in deviant acts, and contrive rationalizations or justifications for their acts of lawbreaking in order to assuage guilt feelings. Sykes and Matza then go on to enumerate some of these techniques of neutralization, which include denial of responsibility for one's behavior, denial of injury, and condemnation of the condemners. These

[34] *Ibid.,* p. 59.
[35] *Ibid.,* pp. 84–93.
[36] *Ibid.,* p. 121.
[37] Gresham M. Sykes and David Matza, "Techniques of Neutralization: A Theory of Delinquency," *American Sociological Review,* XXII (December 1957), 664–70.

notions represent a useful contribution in their own right, in that they direct attention to some of the ways in which offenders define the situation so as to exculpate themselves from guilt regarding violations of norms they regard as valid "in principle." However, a close reading of Cohen's theory indicates that he was not inattentive to the delinquent boy's sensitivity to middle class ethical standards; the Sykes-Matza argument is compatible with that of Cohen.

Other defects in the Cohen theory have been noted by Wilensky and Lebeaux.[38] One of the most systematic evaluations of the theory was produced by Kitsuse and Dietrick, who noted several major problems with it.[39] They charged that Cohen failed to make a compelling case for the argument that working class boys care about middle class persons' views of them. Kitsuse and Dietrick maintain that working class boys are not oriented to status in middle class systems. Accordingly, in their view, Cohen's notion of the delinquent subculture as a "reaction formation" is seriously undermined. These same critics also contend that Cohen's description of delinquent subcultures is faulty, in that real-life delinquents are more businesslike in action and less directly malicious toward "respectable" persons than the theory suggests. Finally, they claim that the theory is flawed because it is ambiguous on the issue of how subcultures are maintained once they come into existence. Kitsuse and Dietrick propose an alternative formulation to that of Cohen, arguing that the original motives of delinquent actors for participation in gangs are varied. Once they get involved in the subculture, hostile responses by respectable adults, correctional agents, and others are directed at them. In turn, the offenders reject their rejectors through further deviant conduct. Thus, according to these authors, "the delinquent subculture persists because, once established, it creates for those who participate in it, the very problems which were the bases for its emergence." [40]

Bordua has also raised a series of questions about theories of subcultural delinquency, including the one by Cohen.[41] He notes that, in most of these, the image put forth of the delinquent is markedly different

[38] Harold L. Wilensky and Charles N. Lebeaux, *Industrial Society and Social Welfare* (New York: Russell Sage Foundation, 1958), pp. 187–207.

[39] John I. Kitsuse and David C. Dietrick, *"Delinquent Boys: A Critique,"* *American Sociological Review,* XXIV (April 1959), 208–15.

[40] *Ibid.,* 215.

[41] David J. Bordua, *Sociological Theories and their Implications for Juvenile Delinquency,* Children's Bureau, Juvenile Delinquency, Facts and Facets, No. 2 (Washington, D.C.: U.S. Government Printing Office, 1960); Bordua, "Delinquent Subcultures: Sociological Interpretations of Gang Delinquency," *Annals of the American Academy of Political and Social Science,* CCCXXXVIII (November 1961), 119–36; Bordua, "Some Comments on Theories of Group Delinquency," *Sociological Inquiry,* XXXII (Spring 1962), 245–60.

from that advanced by Thrasher many years ago. While Thrasher's boys were caught up in the attractiveness of delinquent "fun," the delinquents of contemporary theorists are "driven" by stresses and anxieties emanating from a prejudicial and harsh social environment.[42] In addition, Bordua contends that Cohen's theory places undue emphasis upon the non-utilitarian character of gang misconduct. Bordua also suggests that Cohen, as well as a number of other subcultural theorists, has failed to accord sufficient weight to family, ethnic, and certain other social variables in delinquency causation. In particular, he suggests that class-linked family patterns may be the source of much of the stress experienced by delinquent boys. The relatively loosely structured parent-child relationships, absentee fathers, and other common characteristics of many working class families may have much to do with the development of problems and, subsequently, delinquency in lower class boys.[43]

Cohen has responded to some of these criticisms of his work. In a paper with James F. Short, rejoinders to a number of critical points were offered, including the assertion that there is more than one form of working class gang delinquency.[44] Cohen and Short agreed with this view and suggested that lower class subcultures include the parent-male subculture, the conflict-oriented subculture, the drug addict subculture, and a subculture oriented around semiprofessional theft. The characteristics of the parent-male subculture are enumerated in *Delinquent Boys*. Cohen and Short employ the label of "parent subculture" in order to suggest that other gang forms are specialized offshoots from it, thus "it is probably the most common variety in this country—indeed, it might be called the 'garden variety' of delinquent subculture. . . ."[45]

In endeavoring to account for the development of these different subcultural forms in individual neighborhoods, Cohen and Short laid much stress upon an earlier paper by Kobrin.[46] In that essay, Kobrin pointed out that areas vary in the extent to which conventional and criminal value systems are mutually integrated, so that in some areas criminality is meshed with the local social structure. Adult criminals are prestigious citizens, active in local businesses, fraternal organizations, politics, and so on. They serve as local "heroes" or role-models for juvenile apprentice criminals. In other neighborhoods, criminality is individualistic, uncontrolled, and alien to the conventional social organization. We shall see

[42] Bordua, "Delinquent Subcultures."

[43] Bordua, "Some Comments on Theories of Group Delinquency," 249–56.

[44] Albert K. Cohen and James F. Short, Jr., "Research in Delinquent Subcultures," *Journal of Social Issues*, XIV, No. 3 (1958), 20–37.

[45] *Ibid.*, p. 24.

[46] Solomon Kobrin, "The Conflict of Values in Delinquency Areas," *American Sociological Review*, XVI (October 1951), 653–61.

these notions reappearing in the work of Cloward and Ohlin, to which we now turn.

### Delinquency and Opportunity Structures

Chapter Eight has already traced the development of anomie theory originating with Durkheim, through the work of Merton, to the application of this argument to delinquency in the contentions of Cloward and Ohlin. Let us briefly reexamine these latter claims.[47]

This body of theory represents a full-scale alternative rather than some exceptions to parts of the Cohen argument. For Cloward and Ohlin, the raw material for delinquent gangs consists of boys concerned about economic injustice rather than with middle class status. They aver: "It is our view that many discontented lower class youth do not wish to adopt a middle-class way of life or to disrupt their present associations and negotiate passage into middle-class groups. The solution they seek entails the acquisition of higher position in terms of lower-class rather than middle-class criteria."[48]

Cloward and Ohlin argue that working class gang delinquent subcultures are to be understood in the following terms. Lower class boys share a common American value commitment to "success," measured largely in material terms. But these youths are at a competitive disadvantage compared to their middle status counterparts. Either they do not have access to legitimate or conventional means to reach these success goals, or if they do have objective opportunities for achievement, they perceive their chances of success as circumscribed. Accordingly, for many working class boys, a severe disjunction exists between aspiration levels and expectations, or between what they want out of life and what they anticipate that they will receive. Pressures to engage in deviant behavior are generated by this goals-means discrepancy.[49] Cloward and Ohlin summarize their position in the following way:

Our hypothesis can be summarized as follows: The disparity between what lower-class youth are led to want and what is actually available to them is the source of a major problem of adjustment. Adolescents who form delinquent subcultures, we suggest, have internalized an emphasis upon conventional goals. Faced with limitations on legitimate avenues of access to these goals, and un-

[47] Richard A. Cloward and Lloyd E. Ohlin, *Delinquency and Opportunity* (New York: Free Press of Glencoe, Inc., 1960).
[48] *Ibid.*, p. 92.
[49] *Ibid.*, pp. 77–143.

able to revise their aspirations downward, they experience intense frustrations; the exploration of nonconformist alternatives may be the result.[50]

The particular adaptation assumed by working class youths is heavily influenced by the opportunity structures for deviant behavior. Borrowing from the insights of Kobrin, Cloward and Ohlin argue that some lower class areas are characterized by integration of criminalistic and conformist patterns of social organization, whereas others are lacking in stable criminalistic networks. In the organized, criminalistic neighborhood, "criminalistic" gang subcultures develop in which boys are involved in instrumental acts of theft and in careers which often lead eventually to adult criminal behavior. This is the community which produces the "budding gangster." In areas lacking in criminalistic traditions, gang delinquency tends to take the form of "conflict" subcultural behavior in which gang fighting ("bopping" and "rumbles") predominates. Some boys who are failures in both the legitimate and illegitimate opportunity structures disengage themselves from the competitive struggle and withdraw into the "retreatist" subculture of the drug addict.

Reactions to the Cloward and Ohlin theory have generally been extremely favorable. A number of action programs for the prevention and amelioration of juvenile crime have been formulated on the basis of opportunity structure theory.[51] Still, a series of critical comments have been advanced on this theory.[52] It has been noted that the definition of subcultures employed by Cloward and Ohlin limits applicability of their theory to a minority of all delinquents. Critics have contended that much gang delinquency in working class areas is more spontaneous and unstructured than Cloward and Ohlin would have us believe. One authority has termed many of these deviant collectivities "near groups," in order to highlight their shifting membership, ambiguous role definitions, lack of group identifications, and other characteristics.[53] Regarding this objection, it would be possible to liberalize the definition of subcultures without abandoning the major ingredients of the theory.

Bordua and others who have assessed the opportunity structure formulation have also raised questions about its failure to deal system-

---

[50] *Ibid.*, p. 86.

[51] Gibbons, *op. cit.*, pp. 179–82.

[52] Bordua, "Delinquent Subcultures," "Some Comments on Theories of Group Delinquency"; David Matza, review of *Delinquency and Opportunity, American Journal of Sociology,* LX (May 1961), 631–33; Clarence C. Schrag, "Delinquency and Opportunity: Analysis of a Theory," *Sociology and Social Research,* XLVI (January 1962), 167–75.

[53] Lewis Yablonsky, "The Delinquent Gang as a Near-Group," *Social Problems,* VII (Fall 1959), 108–17.

atically with variations in working class family structures, racial factors, and other background variations among different working class groups.[54] The major direction of this body of commentary has been to suggest that real-life social structure in a society such as the United States is exceedingly complex, being comprised of interwoven layers of social variables which are combined in varied ways and produce behavioral outcomes such as delinquency. In short, existing theories of gang delinquency are not yet rich or elaborate enough to encompass the varieties of real-life experience.

### Lower Class Focal Concerns and Delinquency

Walter B. Miller has proposed another explanation of gang behavior which is strikingly at variance with that of Cohen.[55] For Miller, the structure of lower class life plays the dominant role in bringing forth gang delinquency. Delinquency is the product of long established, durable cultural traditions of lower class life, rather than the result of responses to conflicts with middle class values.

In Miller's view, lower class culture is most strikingly embodied by those persons Harrington has described as populating "the other America," that is, the world of rural migrants to urban areas, American Indians, Puerto Ricans, and urban Negroes.[56] These individuals are at the bottom of the social heap, with little prospect of ascending. The culture of this segment of the population can be described by a series of structural elements peculiar to it and by a complex pattern of "focal concerns." [57]

One of the major structural patterns in lower class society is what Miller calls a female-based household, in which the stability of the family unit is provided by one or more adult females. The mother and older daughters play multiple roles, providing economic support for the family unit as well as discharging the household and affectional duties. This kind of family structure results from the practice of serial monogamy,

---

[54] Bordua, "Some Comments on Theories of Group Delinquency," 250–52.

[55] Walter B. Miller, "Lower Class Culture as a Generating Milieu of Gang Delinquency," *Journal of Social Issues*, XIV, No. 3 (1958), 5–19; Miller, "Implications of Urban Lower Class Culture for Social Work," *Social Service Review*, XXXIII (September 1959), 219–36; Miller, "Preventive Work with Street Corner Groups: Boston Delinquency Project," *Annals of the American Academy of Political and Social Science*, CCCXXII (March 1959), 97–106; Miller, "The Impact of a 'Total-Community' Delinquency Control Project," *Social Problems*, X (Fall 1962), 168–91; William C. Kvaraceus and Walter B. Miller, *Delinquent Behavior: Culture and the Individual* (Washington, D.C.: National Education Association, 1959).

[56] Michael Harrington, *The Other America* (New York: The Macmillan Co., 1962). On this matter, see also Jackson Toby, "The Prospects for Reducing Delinquency Rates in Industrial Societies," *Federal Probation*, XXVII (December 1963), 23–25.

[57] These are discussed at length in Miller, "Lower Class Culture as a Generating Milieu of Gang Delinquency."

in which women find themselves involved in repetitive sequences of mate-finding, legal or common-law marriage, and divorce or desertion by the male. One result of this dynamic is that the household may be made up of a number of children, each of whom has been born to the same mother but a different father.

For the male who grows up in the female-dominated family, life is fraught with anxieties about sex-role identification. The young male is assaulted on all sides by verbal assertions that men are "no damn good." From this situation, there flows a concern on the boy's part for becoming a "real man" as quickly as possible. The male adolescent peer group, territorially located in the urban streets, provides the training ground and milieu in which lower class males seek a sense of maleness, status, and belonging.

These elements, along with the pervasive sense of material and social deprivation common to lower class citizens, result in life patterns and experiences organized around what Miller calls focal concerns. Focal concerns or values represent a series of broad themes that condition the specific acts of lower class persons. The focal concerns of lower class society include "trouble," "toughness," "smartness," "excitement," "fate," and "autonomy." Trouble refers to a dominant concern about avoiding entanglements with the police, social welfare agencies, and similar bodies—encounters that are an ever-present possibility in this segment of society—while toughness denotes a concern for continued demonstrations of bravery, daring, and other traits which show that one is not feminine or "soft." Smartness is a label for such things as the ability to dupe or outwit others, live by one's wits, and earn a livelihood through a "hustle" (pimping and the like). Excitement is identified by Miller as a generic concern for seeking out weekend activities which disrupt the monotony of weekday routine jobs, while fate has to do with definitions by lower class citizens that their lives are ruled by forces over which they have little control, that "luck" plays a major part in one's life chances. Finally, autonomy refers to a profound concern about avoiding being controlled or dominated by others.

These structural elements and focal concerns combine in several ways to produce criminality. Those who respond to some of these focal concerns automatically violate the law through their behavior. In situations where lower class persons have a choice of alternative lines of conduct, a deviant form of activity is selected as the most attractive. In summary of this position, Miller's argument is that to be lower class in contemporary American society is to be in a social situation which contains a variety of direct influences toward deviant conduct, one form of which is juvenile delinquency.

Miller's notions have not escaped criticism; [58] the major objections raised to this argument include the following. First, it has been noted that Miller fails to account for the varieties of gang delinquency which other students have posited. Some offenders steal, some "rumble," and some "shoot dope," but we are not given much explanation for these variations. A second quarrel is over Miller's failure to spell out the detailed variations which can be observed in patterns of lower class culture. His characterization seems to be most applicable to certain urban, slum area groups, particularly Negroes, and hardly descriptive of such other lower class groups as residents in Italian or Chinese enclaves. Specifically, the picture of serial monogamy and female-based households is accurate principally for Negroes and does not hold for other low income, disadvantaged groups. A third claim centers about the danger of tautology in the focal concerns used to account for delinquent conduct. Miller is not always careful to distinguish between observations about these interests and evidence of the behavior they are designed to explain. Finally, Bordua has observed that Miller has not effectively refuted Cohen's contention that working class boys are sensitive to middle class standards. [59] In Bordua's view, it is possible that both Cohen and Miller are partially correct. Perhaps many lower class boys do not initially internalize middle class norms as part of their socialization, but when they get into schools and other competitive situations these status-measuring standards are forced upon them. These experiences may then alienate lower class boys, driving them into involvement in delinquent subcultures. The reader will note the similarity of this line of conjecture to that of Kitsuse and Dietrick.

One other observation that should be made about Miller's perspective is one of appreciation. We agree with Bordua, who suggests that the description of lower class focal concerns stands as a detailed ethnography of working class life which fills in some of the descriptive gaps in the Cohen and Cloward and Ohlin statements. [60]

### Other Voices

The three lines of analysis examined to this point are the best-known and influential theories regarding working class delinquency, but other views have been put forth. Bloch and Niederhoffer claim that a cross-cultural perspective on youth behavior is needed in order to correct the

[58] Bordua, "Some Comments on Theories of Group Delinquency," "Delinquent Subcultures."
[59] Bordua, "Delinquent Subcultures," 129–30.
[60] Ibid., 131.

ethnocentric bias in Cohen's theory.[61] They contend that adolescent crises centered about the transition from childhood to adulthood occur in all societies, and ganging is the universal response to these problems. In this sense, lower class delinquent gangs have much in common with middle class ones, and they in turn share many ingredients with peer collectivities in other lands.

Bloch and Niederhoffer make a good deal of sense when commenting on structural similarities among adolescent groups in various locales. However, their thesis is flawed in a number of places by anthropological observations of questionable accuracy, as well as by highly suspect assertions regarding American society, such as the claim that class or status differentials are disappearing in this country.[62] Most important, while they raise some challenges to parts of Cohen's description of gang behavior, the cornerstone of his argument remains undisturbed. This is that serious, repetitive, organized, subcultural delinquency is a particularly peculiar working class phenomenon in the United States, qualitatively different from peer behavior in other strata or in most other cultures. In consequence, more is needed than an adolescent crisis theory in order to account for the particular form taken by working class adolescent conduct.

Another discordant voice is that of Yablonsky, to whose views on "near groups" we have already alluded. The major tenet of his explanation of working class gang delinquency is that the central figures in these gangs are sociopaths. They are socially deficient boys who cannot manage the social struggle as adequately as other lower class youths, but who find in the gang a social structure in which they can survive.[63] Critics of Yablonsky's view have not treated him kindly, charging that he has little or no evidence for the sociopathy hypothesis independent of the aggressive delinquency it is supposed to explain.[64]

One final contribution, which represents something of an antidote to certain theories of delinquency, is that of Matza and Sykes, which stresses the role of "subterranean" values in delinquency.[65] They suggest that the view of middle class culture which emphasizes ascetic devotion to thrift, hard labor at a work task defined as a calling, and so on, is one-sided. There are other respectable but subterranean or unpublicized

[61] Herbert A. Bloch and Arthur Niederhoffer, *The Gang* (New York: Philosophical Library, 1958).

[62] *Ibid.,* p. 175.

[63] Lewis Yablonsky, *The Violent Gang* (New York: The Macmillan Co., 1962).

[64] Solomon Kobrin, review of *The Violent Gang, American Sociological Review,* XXVIII (April 1963), 316–17.

[65] David Matza and Gresham M. Sykes, "Juvenile Delinquency and Subterranean Values," *American Sociological Review,* XXVI (October 1961), 712–19; Matza, *Delinquency and Drift* (New York: John Wiley and Sons, Inc., 1964).

values pursued by large numbers of conventional citizens, such as pursuit of hedonistic fun or tolerance for certain kinds of aggression and violence. Thus the delinquent's search for "kicks," disdain for work, desire for the "big score," and posture of aggressive toughness make him an exaggerated and immature version of many middle class citizens. The substance of these ideas is to remind us that delinquency may have considerable positive appeal to youngsters at all social class levels, including those in the working class, who for one reason or another are indifferent to or alienated from schools, adult role-preparation, and so forth.

### Research on Delinquent Subcultures

These varied lines of explanation for gang delinquency present a bewildering pattern of claims at cross purposes with one another. Each of the theories has a ring of plausibility, at least until the criticisms are heard or we are confronted with one of its theoretical competitors. Clearly, a mass of hard evidence which will allow us to adjudicate among these theoretical contenders is needed. Let us look at some of the data which has been produced on questions of working class delinquency. A word of warning is in order before we turn to this material. The research findings will not magically reduce the argument about gang delinquency to one set of straightforward propositions. Rather, the evidence is likely to make the matter of gang delinquency even more complex, in that it reflects the diversity and richness of real life as experienced by actual deviants.

The first question to be answered is: what do lower class boys do in the way of delinquent conduct? Is subcultural deviance patterned in the ways suggested by Cohen and Short and by Cloward and Ohlin? One report on this matter has been made by Robin, concerning an investigation in Philadelphia in which he studied the official and unofficial police records of over 700 male Negro members of 27 gangs in that city.[66] Most of these youths came to the attention of the police before they were 15 years old. They showed progressive movement toward deviant acts of increasing seriousness which in many cases culminated in adult criminal careers. Robin maintains that although most of these subjects had committed a diversified collection of delinquent acts, about two-thirds had engaged in at least one offense involving physical violence. He interprets this finding as support for the claims of Cloward and Ohlin concerning the existence of a conflict subculture in delinquency.[67]

[66] Gerald D. Robin, "Gang Member Delinquency: Its Extent, Sequence and Typology," *Journal of Criminal Law, Criminology and Police Science*, LV (March 1964), 59–69.
[67] *Ibid.*, 64–65.

Spergel has provided evidence in two separate studies which seems to confirm the Cloward and Ohlin description of different delinquent sub-cultures.[68] His research in Chicago indicated that delinquency and crime tended toward a criminalistic form in a relatively stable Negro slum area, while in a more unstable neighborhood criminality was untrammeled and violent in character.[69] In the New York City investigation, Spergel indicates that conflict behavior was most common in Slumtown, a dis-organized area, while criminalistic delinquency was oriented around theft activities in one relatively integrated neighborhood and around racketeering in another community area heavily populated by Italian-Americans.[70] Spergel's material provides a footnote to the Cloward and Ohlin framework by suggesting that criminalistic delinquency comes in several varieties.

The richest body of recent empirical evidence on gang behavior is found in studies in Chicago by Short and others.[71] One of their investiga-tions was an examination of the delinquent and nondelinquent conduct of about 600 members of Chicago gangs, in which street workers main-tained detailed records of the day-to-day activities of these boys. The findings indicate that most of the offenders are involved in a wide range of deviant and nondeviant acts, rather than in the narrowly-focused patterns suggested by Cloward and Ohlin. Short and his colleagues argue that an undifferentiated "parent delinquent subculture" exists from which more specialized deviant groups emerge. In other words, they suggest that the generic form of gang behavior involves behavioral versatility, and that, from this broad form, cliques and subgroups branch off into more specialized careers in deviant conduct.[72]

A final bit of information on gang behavior is found in a study by Reiss which concerned a group of lower class delinquent males in Nashville.[73] Their activities included participation in a complex structure of relationships with adult homosexuals in which the boys submitted to

---

[68] Irving Spergel, "Male Young Adult Criminality, Deviant Values, and Differential Oppor-tunities in Two Lower Class Negro Neighborhoods," *Social Problems*, X (Winter 1963), 237–50; Spergel, "An Exploratory Research in Delinquent Subcultures," *Social Service Review*, XXXV (March 1961), 33–47; Spergel, *Racketville, Slumtown, Haulburg* (Chicago: University of Chicago Press, 1964).

[69] Spergel, "Male Young Adult Criminality."

[70] Spergel, *Racketville, Slumtown, Haulburg.*

[71] James F. Short, Jr., "Gang Delinquency and Anomie," in *Anomie and Deviant Behavior*, ed. Marshall B. Clinard (New York: Free Press of Glencoe, Inc., 1964), pp. 98–127; Short and Fred L. Strodtbeck, *Group Process and Gang Delinquency* (Chicago: University of Chicago Press, 1965).

[72] Short, *op. cit.*, pp. 103–105; Short, Ray A. Tennyson, and Kenneth I. Howard, "Behavior Dimensions of Gang Delinquency," in Short and Strodtbeck, *op. cit.*

[73] Albert J. Reiss, Jr., "The Social Integration of Queers and Peers," *Social Problems*, IX (Fall 1961), 102–20.

adult fellators in exchange for pay, an interaction pattern they conceptualize as strictly a business transaction.

These seemingly contradictory characterizations of gang delinquency, indicating existence of different subcultures in some but not in others, can perhaps be reconciled. It may well be that gang misconduct takes a number of forms, both in terms of the degree of organization among the deviant actors and in the kind of activity in which they engage. We suggest that relatively crystallized forms of conflict delinquency may be most common in very large cities, and quite uncommon in smaller communities. It is possible that gang structure is influenced by ethnic variables, variations in neighborhood organization and community structure, and other contingencies of this sort. The variability in the descriptive data may be a reflection of the diversity of behavior in the real world of delinquents.

Another research problem attacked recently is the matter of social class correlates of delinquency, neighborhood characteristics and deviant patterns, and related topics. Reiss and Rhodes have thrown much light upon the relationships between delinquent conduct and socioeconomic position.[74] In a study dealing with a large number of juvenile males in the Nashville, Tennessee, metropolitan area, they found that there is no simple or uniform linkage between social class position and delinquency. While those boys most frequently encountered in the population of officially designated delinquents are from the lower class, delinquency life-chances or risks are not the same for all working class youths. Juvenile misconduct is most common in homogeneous lower class neighborhoods and less usual in neighborhoods of mixed social status. Accordingly, Reiss and Rhodes maintain that the behavior of working class boys is conditioned by the social class structure and cultural traditions of the community areas in which they live. Youths whose parents are working class individuals have a high risk of delinquent involvement if they live in areas populated largely by other lower class persons, but they are not so likely to become offenders if they live in neighborhoods of mixed or predominantly middle class socioeconomic status.

A second report on these matters is in the New York City study by Spergel in which he claimed to have identified separate theft, racketeering, and conflict subcultures, each existing in distinct lower class neighborhoods.[75] Spergel describes Slumtown, the locale of conflict behavior, as an area with a Puerto Rican and Negro population suffering from extremely low socioeconomic status and the highest index of social break-

[74] Albert J. Reiss, Jr., and Albert Lewis Rhodes, "The Distribution of Juvenile Delinquency in the Social Class Structure," *American Sociological Review*, XXVI (October 1961), 720–32.

[75] Spergel, *Racketville, Slumtown, Haulburg,* pp. 2–28.

down as shown by public assistance caseloads, venereal disease rates, and other indicators of social liabilities. Haulburg, the community area in which theft behavior predominated, was populated by second generation Americans of European stock and stood highest of the three in measures of socioeconomic status, occupational structure, and absence of social breakdown. Racketville was intermediate between the other two on most of these measures of community structure. These results generally confirm the claims of Cloward and Ohlin regarding neighborhood variations in illegitimate opportunity structures, although there is some ambiguity as to how Spergel identified these neighborhoods and the techniques by which these descriptions were developed.

A number of lines of evidence have also accumulated regarding social-psychological characteristics of gang delinquents.[76] One test of the Cloward and Ohlin formulation regarding delinquents' hypothesized disjunction between occupational aspirations and expectations, in other words, between what boys want and what they expect to get out of life, is found in Spergel's New York City study.[77] He reports that delinquent boys in Slumtown and Haulburg had a marked disparity between aspirations and expectations, while the young Racketville deviants had aspirations and expectations closely in harmony. Thus these results partially confirm the Cloward and Ohlin theory, although it should be noted that Spergel's cases were so few as to require that the findings be interpreted with caution. Elliott has also reported on the question of perceptions of legitimate opportunities on the part of delinquent boys.[78] He found that *both* the middle class and lower class delinquents in his sample perceived their life chances as more limited than did the nondelinquent youths.

The most detailed and comprehensive data regarding position discontent, delinquent norms and values, and related matters, are to be found in the Chicago material of Short and others.[79] On the question of aspirations contrasted to perceptions of opportunities, these findings show that delinquents exhibit greater discrepancies between occupational aspirations and expectations than do nondelinquents. More delinquent boys view educational opportunities as closed to them than do nonoffenders. But these relationships are far from clear, for Negro boys who show the greatest divergence between their aspirations and expectations,

[76] John W. Kinch, "Self-Conceptions of Types of Delinquents," *Sociological Inquiry*, XXXII (Spring 1962), 228–34; Sethard Fisher, "Varieties of Juvenile Delinquency," *British Journal of Criminology*, II (January 1962), 251–61.

[77] Spergel, *Racketville, Slumtown, Haulburg*, pp. 93–123.

[78] Delbert S. Elliott, "Delinquency and Perceived Opportunity," *Sociological Inquiry*, XXXII (Spring 1962) 216–27.

[79] Short, *op. cit.*; Short and Strodtbeck, *op. cit.*

compared to the achievements of their fathers, are at the same time least delinquent. Also, contrary to the hypotheses in the Cloward and Ohlin theory, those boys who had high educational aspirations but poor school adjustment or perceived educational opportunities as relatively closed were less delinquent than those youths with low educational aspirations.[80] Short interprets these results in the following way: "A possible explanation of findings reported in this paper lies in the hypothesis that for our boys, high aspirations are indicative of identification with conventional values and institutions. The stake in conformity thus indexed serves to protect the boys from delinquency involvement."[81]

Short and his colleagues have also examined the question of value commitments of delinquent boys. They find that, contrary to theories which contend that subcultural delinquents are in rebellion against middle class ideals, individual offenders verbalize allegiance to such middle class values as cohesive family life, stable jobs, and conformist behavior.[82] However, the structure of gang life inhibits youngsters from expressing those sentiments openly, so that a state of "pluralistic ignorance" prevails in which gang members see each other in distorted terms. Finally, and most important, Short argues that although gang behavior is not a direct revolt against middle class values or a protest against generalized invidious rankings of the boys by the wider society, status considerations are nevertheless of major importance in comprehending lower class delinquency. He contends that delinquent activities are often a response to a host of real or imagined status threats experienced by boys, and that most of these status deprivations emanate from the more immediate social world, including threats to the boys' status as males, gang members, and so on.[83]

[80] Short, op. cit., pp. 105–15.

[81] Ibid., p. 115. On the question of "insulation" from delinquency, see also Walter C. Reckless, Simon Dinitz, and Ellen Murray, "Self Concept as an Insulator Against Delinquency," American Sociological Review, XXI (December 1956), 744–56; Reckless, Dinitz, and Barbara Kay, "The Self Component in Potential Delinquency and Potential Non-delinquency," American Sociological Review, XXII (October 1957), 566–70; Reckless, Dinitz, and Murray, "The 'Good Boy' in a High Delinquency Area," Journal of Criminal Law, Criminology and Police Science, XLVIII (May–June 1957), 18–25; Dinitz, Kay, and Reckless, "Group Gradients in Delinquency Potential and Achievement Scores of Sixth Graders," American Journal of Orthopsychiatry, XXVIII (July 1958), 598–605; Jon Simpson, Dinitz, Kay, and Reckless, "Delinquency Potential of Pre-Adolescents in High Delinquency Areas," British Journal of Delinquency, X (January 1960), 211–15; Frank R. Scarpitti, Murray, Dinitz, and Reckless, "The 'Good' Boy in a High Delinquency Area: Four Years Later," American Sociological Review, XXV (August 1960), 555–58; Dinitz, Scarpitti, and Reckless, "Delinquency Vulnerability: A Cross Group and Longitudinal Analysis," American Sociological Review, XXVII (August 1962), 515–17.

[82] Short, op. cit., pp. 115–21. For some parallel findings, see Edward Rothstein, "Attributes Related to High School Status: A Comparison of the Perceptions of Delinquent and Non-delinquent Boys," Social Problems, X (Summer 1962), 75–83.

[83] Short, op. cit., pp. 117–27.

## An Evaluation

At this point, the reader may well ask, "What does it all mean?" By way of a brief summing up, these things can be said about gang delinquency. First, it is clear that gang delinquents frequently become adult criminals, although there are many working class deviant youngsters who drift out of delinquency and into conventional life patterns. Second, it is readily apparent that the ecological habitat of gang behavior is the lower class neighborhood of the city. Third, explanations of the development and persistence of gang misbehavior are not very easily evaluated. Most of the formulations examined in the pages above are polemical in tone, putting forth an overdrawn and incomplete version of the mainsprings of subcultural delinquency. The empirical world resists being forced into the patterns represented by existing theories.

The temptation is very strong to take refuge in a fuzzy eclecticism by arguing that all of the variables identified in the different theories play their part in delinquency. But we do not counsel that course of action. Instead, we suggest that while the motivations that lead boys into gang delinquency vary, they are identifiable. A complete census of these psychological sources of involvement in youthful deviance would probably indicate that existing theories have already identified a good many of them. Some lower class juveniles are in gangs because of social status concerns stemming from their placement at the bottom of the social order. For some youths, the pervasive deprivations of lower class life provide the psychological fuel which propels them toward gangs. For others, the status problems which lead toward deviant peer groups are more immediate, centering about the need to be protected by the gang from assaults by other boys, masculinity anxieties, and so on. These different motivational dynamics are of varied importance in separate cohorts of lower class youths, so that boys in Negro slums may face problems different from lower class whites in smaller cities. There is not one route to the gang, there are several.

In addition, the preceding pages have suggested that a series of intervening variables need to be examined if we are to understand how this boy became a delinquent while another one, similar to the first, became an exemplary citizen. One intervening variable alluded to at various points is the influence of variations in family structure. Highly cohesive lower class families probably turn out juveniles with a marked stake in conformity. These boys encounter adversity in the school system and elsewhere, but instead of becoming delinquent they double their efforts in the direction of zealous pursuit of success. Along a somewhat different line, we need to be more sensitive than has been customary to fortuitous factors and feedback processes in delinquency. Conceivably, one of the contingencies which influences the development of delinquent careers on the part of working class boys is the experience of early apprehension by the police, often an almost chance happening. We need also to examine the matter hinted at in several of the essays considered above, that delinquency begets more delinquency. We may well find that, as boys get caught up in flirtations with deviant behavior, they encounter societal rejection which then impairs their adjustment to school and other social institutions, so they are driven further into delinquent conduct. What this adds up to is a picture of delinquency extremely rich in its details. To portray it otherwise would be to do violence to the facts.

## SUMMARY

This chapter has considered three cases of everyman's criminals. That is, we have taken a detailed look at three of the kinds of offenders most people have in mind when they think of crime and criminals. Chapter Twelve continues this study of property offenders, but pays attention to some kinds of illegality which are not so widely attended to as those in this chapter. However, as we shall see, certain of these undramatic forms of criminality may well be more costly in terms of monetary losses to the public than the criminality considered to this point.

# 12

# Additional Property Offender Careers

## INTRODUCTION

The preceding chapter considered three kinds of lawbreaking that the man on the street thinks of as "crime." In this chapter, we turn to some additional forms of illegality involving property that are not so widely known, or are less subject to public denunciation as criminality. Two of these, amateur shoplifting and naive check forgery, are extremely common forms of predatory conduct usually directed at retail stores and other business concerns. The evidence seems to indicate that shoplifting and "bad checks" are normal events in business life, in that merchandisers expect a large volume of this conduct to take place. In turn, they adopt pricing policies which anticipate business losses from thefts and checks that "bounce" (as well as from pilferage by employees). These kinds of lawbreaking have an "iceberg" appearance; those cases reported to the police represent only a fraction of the instances known to store personnel or which occur but are undetected even by the business establishment. A good many of these acts of shoplifting or check forgery are carried on by "nice people" from moderate economic circumstances. They do not fit the image of the slum area "tough guy," which probably has much to do with the infrequent referral of such persons to the police.

Chapter Twelve also takes up the matter of automobile theft—"joyriding"—as still another form of property crime. Joyriders are young adults who steal cars for recreational purposes rather than to "strip" them and sell the parts for profit. Finally, this chapter will be concerned with the property offender, "one-time loser." This role-career is represented by relatively naive and unsophisticated offenders who do not shoplift, forge checks, or steal cars, but steal some amount of property from an individual or from an organization other than a retail store. The label "one-time loser" suggests the nature of this kind of lawbreaking. Large numbers of persons manage to find their way into isolated but frequently serious instances of illegal conduct in which they commit a single burglary or theft. While much deviant behavior of this kind no doubt goes unreported, some is not ignored. Indeed, some culprits involved in this kind of idiosyncratic criminality are to be found in state prisons serving relatively long sentences.

Each of these forms of criminal conduct will be taken up in some detail. However, several general lines of causal commentary regarding much of this behavior might be advanced at this point. In Chapter Nine, we reviewed some of the contentions of Lemert regarding the development of deviant careers.[1] Two sources of deviant conduct which he identifies seem particularly relevant to much of the criminal behavior under discussion. One has to do with value pluralism in the United States, in which groups holding one set of standards find themselves required to conform to another and discordant set of values. Insofar as these persons violate the alien standards, their actions come to be labeled deviant.[2] Lemert offers a number of illustrations of this form of deviance, including the case of "totin'" or petty theft by rural Negro migrants. We suggest that petty thievery is a not uncommon kind of activity which is at least tolerated, if not actually supported, by value preferences in many rural areas in the United States. Thus a good many isolated acts of larceny by amateur or casual offenders may be defined by those individuals as "borrowing," and be fairly commonplace activities. Nonetheless, some of these persons are unlucky enough to be sternly dealt with in the correctional process and receive prison sentences for their actions.

The second etiological hypothesis that Lemert advances centers about "risk-taking," in which individuals get involved in deviant behavior as a result of embarking upon a line of conduct having several potential outcomes, one of which is a deviant form.[3] This kind of nonconforming behavior cannot be called the product of clear-cut motivational elements driving the actor, for the individual did not specifically intend to become involved in deviance at the beginning of the behavioral events. Commenting on the suicide behavior of residents of the island of Tikopia, Lemert says: "This analysis of suicide suggests the more general possibility that there are many instances in which people do not elect deviant solutions to problems but instead initiate lines of behavior which, according to how circumstances unfold, may or may not become deviant." [4] He then goes on to show that, in his research on naive check forgery, he found a number of persons who were not motivated to pass bad checks but simply took chances that a check they authored might not be

[1] Edwin M. Lemert, "Social Structure, Social Control, and Deviation," in *Anomie and Deviant Behavior,* ed. Marshall B. Clinard (New York: Free Press of Glencoe, Inc., 1964), pp. 57–97.

[2] *Ibid.,* pp. 64–66.

[3] *Ibid.,* pp. 71–73.

[4] *Ibid.,* p. 72.

honored, or that they might not be allowed to cover the check if it "bounced." [5]

The major value of these contentions of Lemert regarding the risk-taking origins of deviance is that they warn us against the automatic assumption that criminal conduct is always "motivated," in the sense of being related to relatively long-standing attitudes and psychological concerns of the individual. All too frequently, the presumption is made that criminalistic deviance stems from "antisocial" orientations within the actor which are the product of some set of experiences that occurred much earlier in his life career. Without denying that many kinds of criminality do show such a form, a goodly number of them are probably instances of situational risk-taking that emerge out of ongoing processes.

Likely examples of risk-taking criminality can be identified in abundance. One illustration might be felonious drunken driving in which the offender did not deliberately set out to become intoxicated. It is probable that the majority of episodes in which individuals become involved in a situation they define as being "drunk" represent one of several possible outcomes of social drinking. At the beginning of the drinking activity, the prospect of becoming intoxicated was the eventuality least anticipated by the drinker, so that his drunkenness in this sense was unintentional. With the drunk driver, becoming intoxicated was an unplanned outcome of social drinking. In turn, the individual who drives while in a drunken condition does not intend to drive erratically and certainly does not plan to have an accident or injure anyone. However, with his driving ability impaired by alcohol, these results can eventuate if the driver is "unlucky," that is, if certain contingent events occur. Doubtless most drivers perceive these risks, at least dimly, when they drive while intoxicated.

Another place where risk-taking processes may play a major role in the genesis of deviant behavior is in the assaultive conduct of lower class groups. In Chapter Eleven we examined some of the arguments of Miller regarding the "focal concerns" of lower class culture.[6] One of his hypotheses which has much merit is that the weekly round of activities of working class persons is frequently made up of the unrelieved boredom of weekday work routines, punctuated in dramatic fashion on weekends by the hedonistic pursuit of "fun" and "excitement." These weekend events center about drinking and provocative interaction with others, including members of the opposite sex. Although avid pursuit of fun does not directly lead to deviant or criminal behavior, that is one potential

[5] *Ibid.*, p. 72.
[6] Walter B. Miller, "Lower Class Culture as a Generating Milieu of Gang Delinquency," *Journal of Social Issues*, XIV, No. 3 (1958), 5–19.

outcome of unrestrained hedonism. Flirtatious interaction with another person's wife or girl friend may culminate in a "cutting," that is, a knife-assault. Similarly, when a group of individuals who have been drinking are brought together in close contact, assaultive acts are likely to occur over a variety of interactional difficulties. Again, these kinds of criminality stand as risks in a larger pattern of social class life. They cannot be understood as events which grow out of idiosyncratic but long-standing psychological characteristics of the offenders who commit them.

A third application of risk-taking notions can be made to many of the "one-time loser" property offenders to be examined in more detail later in this chapter. Examination of descriptive materials in probation case files and elsewhere reveals that many of these persons get involved in petty acts of crime as part of a sequence of activities which were not initiated as criminalistic ventures. For example, Skid Road transients often find themselves in the hands of the police as a result of petty burglaries carried out after becoming markedly intoxicated in a drinking bout with alcoholic companions, for falling into a drunken sleep in the bathtub of a cheap hotel, or for other ventures into risk situations. Other minor instances of theft may be a function of situational opportunities, rather than deep-seated motivational elements of the offenders. Many individuals may manage to suspend their normal feelings of condemnation toward crime and steal petty articles of property when the immediate situation appears conducive to such behavior, particularly when the victim is a relatively large and impersonal organization. The processes which operate may have something in common with the activities of campers and picnickers who litter campgrounds with beer cans and rubbish in blatant disregard for fellow campers. These same individuals would probably hesitate to throw beer cans into the yards of neighbors in the residential areas in which they live. They would also give verbal allegiance to the general principle that one should keep picnic grounds clean.

A final application of risk-taking hypotheses can be made to many instances of amateur shoplifting, both by juveniles and adults. Quite probably, the original motive for entering a retail store was either to purchase some item or to "look around," to examine merchandise and possibly buy some of it. Shoplifting actions are emergent as the sojourn through the store takes place. The impulse to pilfer some item develops as the shopper perceives the immediate situation as conducive to stealing—salespersons who might observe him are absent from the particular section of the store. The act of shoplifting by an adult thief may also be related to some immediate budgetary problem, the stolen articles allowing the individual to spend some of his money on things he would not otherwise be able to purchase. In any event, monetary problems of the person do not fully explain his behavior, for such problems do not always lead to thievery. The majority of shoppers with financial difficulties probably never resort to shoplifting, so something more than economic need is involved in this form of criminality.

So much for these general remarks. In the following pages our attention turns to amateur shoplifters, naive check forgers, automobile thief—"joyriders," and property offender, "one-time losers."

## THE AMATEUR SHOPLIFTER ROLE-CAREER

The typological sketch of the amateur shoplifter, or the "snitch," as this person is known in the language of the retail store, is something of a caricature. The description is more or less accurate for the variety of amateur thieves who roam through retail stores, but it is most characteristic of adult, women thieves. Small children and juveniles who steal from stores depart in certain ways from the characterization below.

### Definitional Dimensions

*Offense Behavior.* Amateur shoplifters or "snitches" steal amounts of property which vary in cost, so that some steal petty items and others steal quite costly merchandise. Amateur shoplifters also vary in terms of crime skills, some of them employing "booster bags" and other criminal paraphernalia, while others exhibit only rudimentary techniques of crime. Further, these offenders vary in their degree of involvement in crime, for some steal only once or twice and others are caught up in recurrent acts of deviance. The distinguishing mark of the amateur as contrasted to the professional "booster" is that the former steals merchandise for his own use. The "booster," on the other hand, converts the results of his thievery into cash by selling the stolen goods to other persons.

*Interactional Setting.* Amateur shoplifters carry out their criminal acts in large department stores and variety stores in urban communities. Their deviant activities are enacted by individuals operating alone, as contrasted to professional "boosters" who commonly engage in team operations with other shoplifters.

*Self-concept.* Amateur shoplifters consider themselves to be honest, upright citizens. They do not think of themselves as thieves, nor do they exhibit other sorts of deviant self-image patterns.

*Attitudes.* Amateur shoplifters exhibit prosocial sentiments of an ordinary variety. They verbalize sentiments indicating that they are opposed to crime and thievery, in principle.

*Role-career.* Amateur shoplifters frequently engage in repetitive acts of theft, so their careers are often more than "one-shot" affairs in crime. Most amateur "snitches" are eventually apprehended by store personnel, although few are subsequently reported to the police. Store officials are reluctant to refer other than the most serious cases of shoplifting to the authorities. Instead, store detectives and other employees handle many of the cases informally. The offender is compelled to confess his wrongdoing and promise to refrain from further stealing. The apparent consequence of this kind of handling is to deter the person from further criminality.

### Background Dimensions

*Social Class.* The social class origins of shoplifters are somewhat varied; both lower and middle class "snitches" come to the attention of store personnel. However, it does not appear that amateur shoplifting is class-linked in any important degree.

*Family Background.* The family backgrounds of shoplifters are quite mixed in character, although most store thieves are from relatively common and conventional family backgrounds. Most adult shoplifters are married.

*Peer Group Associations.* There is nothing particularly unusual or striking about the peer associations of amateur shoplifters, either as juveniles or adults. These individuals receive no peer group support or encouragement for criminal acts.

*Contact with Defining Agencies.* As indicated above, most detected cases of amateur shoplifting are handled informally by personnel of the victimized store. The offender is led to confess his criminality and promise not to repeat the behavior. Store officials threaten various dire consequences if they apprehend him again. These experiences are apparently so traumatic in their impact upon the offender that they deter him from further criminality. The principal factor seems to be that criminality is inconsistent with the person's own self-conception. Once he is forced to acknowledge participation in activities discordant with his self-image, he avoids repetition of those actions. The socially-psychologically painful aspects of the confrontation process are such as to make the offender unwilling to experience that process again. In order to avoid the pain, the individual avoids shoplifting.

## Some Evidence [7]

The opening remarks of this chapter indicated that shoplifting is a kind of crime which rarely becomes a matter of public knowledge. Shoplifters are infrequently observed in the act, so those who become known to the victim store or business concern represent only a fraction of those actually involved in stealing from it. Individuals who shoplift are most likely to be apprehended in stores which employ private police or protective personnel. Other factors which condition the likelihood of shoplifters being detected include such things as variations in the operating procedures of store detectives, racial biases of protective officers which lead them to scrutinize more closely the movements of Negroes in the stores, reluctance to confront "respectable" people with accusations of criminality, and special attention to juveniles who are thought to be particularly theft-prone.[8]

Known shoplifters constitute a minority of all thieves who direct their predatory activities at retail stores. In addition, most offenders known to store personnel are not reported to the police, so officially labeled shoplifters represent an even smaller sample of all store thieves. As we shall see below, shoplifters who become publicly identified as criminals through court proceedings are in no sense representative of known thieves or of all shoplifters.

How much shoplifting takes place in the United States? How much money is lost through the criminality of store thieves? A variety of estimates have been advanced, not all in agreement with each other. However, they all indicate that shoplifting is a far from inconsequential kind of lawbreaking. For example, one claim has been made that shoplifters stole $247,000,000 of merchandise from drug and department stores, grocery stores, and variety stores in the United States in 1948.[9] Another contention has been that 12 department stores in New York City suffered over $10,000,000 in shoplifter losses in 1951, while still another authority has argued that over $1,700,000,000 is taken each year by shoplifters from retailers in this nation.[10] A final estimate of the magnitude of shoplifting

[7] Mary Owen Cameron, The Booster and the Snitch (New York: Free Press of Glencoe, Inc., 1964); Loren E. Edwards, Shoplifting and Shrinkage Protection for Stores (Springfield, Ill.: Charles C Thomas, Publisher, 1958); Gerald D. Robin, "The American Customer: Shopper or Shoplifter?" Police (January–February 1964); Robin, "Patterns of Department Store Shoplifting," Crime and Delinquency, IX (April 1963), 163–72.

[8] Cameron, op. cit., pp. 24–32.

[9] Robin, "The American Customer: Shopper or Shoplifter?"

[10] Cameron, op. cit., pp. 9–15.

is derived from a report of the National Commission on Food Marketing, established by Congress. That commission set the annual cost of shoplifting at $300,000,000 per year, or 2 per cent of total sales. The commission survey profiled the average shoplifter as between 18 and 30 years of age, stealing predominantly on Thursday, Friday, or Saturday, between 3 and 6 P.M., and stealing about $3.75 worth of goods. The commission urged that all shoplifters except pregnant women, senile aged, and "kleptomaniacs" be prosecuted.[11]

According to store protective agents, most losses are inflicted on stores by amateur shoplifters or "snitches," rather than professional "boosters," although the average amount stolen is apparently larger in cases of professional shoplifting than in amateur stealing.[12] In general, criminal skills used by professionals exceed those of "snitches," although the latter often show some degree of sophistication in their criminality. Many use "bad bags" (well-worn shopping bags issued by the victim store), are equipped with scissors or razor blades for snipping price tags from stolen merchandise, sometimes carry lists of items they intend to steal, and often plan their offenses in advance.[13]

An important parenthetical note is that even though shoplifting is commonplace, it makes a relatively small contribution to the total losses suffered by stores. Protection agencies estimate that about 75 per cent of all pilferage in stores is the work of employees rather than customer-thieves.[14]

The most detailed study of shoplifters is by Cameron, involving analysis of records on a sample of shoplifters apprehended in a Chicago department store between 1943 and 1950, along with a sample of women charged with "petty larceny, shoplifting" in Chicago courts between 1948 and 1950.[15] Cameron discovered that shoplifters in "Lakeside Company" were generally apprehended for relatively small thefts averaging about six dollars, juveniles stole amounts of merchandise of lesser value than did adults, and male shoplifters were caught with fewer stolen items in their possession than was true of women. About one-fifth of the apprehended adult thieves were men. The much higher number of shoplifting women is attributable to most department store customers being women, as well as the fact that women steal more items than men and thus run a greater risk of being observed.[16]

11 National Council on Crime and Delinquency, NCCD News, XLV (March–April 1966), 1.
12 Cameron, op. cit., p. 56.
13 Ibid, pp. 58–60, 70–84.
14 Ibid., pp. 11–15.
15 Ibid., pp. 24–38.
16 Ibid., pp. 70–88.

Cameron's findings from "Lakeside Company" indicate that the shoplifters are a cross-section of the Chicago population in terms of socioeconomic status, although they are of somewhat lower status than the over all customer group in the store. Negro shoplifters are found in about the same proportion as in the Chicago population, but Negro shoplifters are much more likely to be reported to the police. Moreover, Negro offenders convicted in court tend to receive stiffer penalties than do white shoplifters.[17]

The results reported by Cameron make it abundantly clear that officially recognized shoplifters make up only a small part of all store thieves. She indicates that between 1943 and 1949 the Chicago Police Department tallied an average of 633 women per year charged with larceny of all kinds. At the same time, "Lakeside Company" apprehended about 400 women each year for shoplifting, although only about 10 per cent were turned over to the police. Thus Cameron declares: "One department store, in other words, *arrested* for shoplifting about 60 per cent of the total number of women per year as were officially charged with all types of larceny (including shoplifting) in the entire city of Chicago" (emphasis in the original).[18]

Many factors are involved in the decision to prosecute, including such as refusal of the suspected thief to confess and difficulties of getting speedy court action at any particular time. As already noted, stores are more likely to report Negro offenders to the police, as well as turn over professional "boosters" to the authorities. The result of these decisions is that court cases of store thieves are ecologically concentrated in areas with generally high crime rates and low socioeconomic status, although the total group of known thieves is not so distributed.[19] Shoplifting stands as a prominent example of differential law enforcement, with official rates of shoplifting bearing little relationship to the true distribution of such behavior.

Cameron effectively demolishes hypotheses about shoplifting which would explain this behavior as a result of psychiatric disturbances, compulsiveness, or "kleptomania." The contention that store theft is a compulsive psychiatric aberration is inconsistent with her evidence that most shoplifters stopped stealing after getting caught, even though they had engaged in repetitive acts of criminality up to that point.[20] "Kleptomania" turns out to be nothing more than a social label hung on "nice people"

[17] *Ibid.,* pp. 91–96, 136–44.

[18] *Ibid.,* p. 123.

[19] *Ibid.,* pp. 132–33.

[20] *Ibid.,* pp. 115–17, 154–57; the psychiatric theme concerning shoplifting is expressed in Fabian L. Rouke, "Shoplifting: Its Symbolic Motivation," *NPPA Journal,* III (January 1957), 54–58.

who steal and withheld from "bad people" who are simply "crooks"! It is a social identity akin to that of "sick alcoholic" which is accorded the middle class drinker and denied the Skid Road "drunk." Cameron's own interpretation of her findings is that amateur female shoplifters are women who steal items which their limited budgets will not allow them to buy without depriving other family members. These women have no self-conception of themselves as thieves and offer a variety of rationalizations to "explain away" their deviance. When apprehended by store detectives, they are forced to acknowledge that they are thieves. These women are without any in-group support for their stealing, so they have no way of buffering themselves against social condemnation. Consequently, they refrain from further shoplifting because they cannot accommodate themselves to a revised self-definition as a "thief." [21]

The most important single conclusion from Cameron's data probably has to do with the observation that "normal," respectable people can and do engage in systematic criminality. As Becker has suggested, these findings call into question notions which utilize "middle class morality" as an explanatory variable accounting for conformity of middle status individuals. Most respectable citizens are probably less guided in conduct by a deeply introjected set of values than is sometimes supposed. Instead of being kept on a consistent course of conformity by an internal gyroscope of ethical standards, many reinterpret values to fit particular situations and invoke countervailing rationalizations which allow them to deviate under certain circumstances. Their law-abiding conduct may frequently be due more to fear of being caught and punished than to deeply held values which keep them upright in conduct. [22]

A more recent report on department store shoplifting has been made by Robin. [23] He examined data on all 1584 persons apprehended for shoplifting in three of the five largest department stores in Philadelphia in 1958. Most of his findings run parallel to those of Cameron; for example, he discovered that the stores are both cautious and informal in their handling of detected thieves. Juvenile thieves are almost never turned over to the authorities for official action, while only about one-fourth of the adult shoplifters are prosecuted. [24] Individual thefts that were detected usually involved relatively small losses, about half of them of merchandise valued at less than $10. Juveniles were responsible for smaller losses on the average than were adult thieves. [25] There are some

[21] Cameron, op. cit., pp. 159–70.
[22] Howard S. Becker, review of Mary Owen Cameron, *The Booster and the Snitch, American Journal of Sociology,* LXX (March 1965), 635–36.
[23] Robin, "Patterns of Department Store Shoplifting."
[24] Ibid., pp. 169–70.
[25] Ibid., pp. 167–69.

differences in these two studies. Robin notes that nearly half of the shoplifters in the Philadelphia stores were Negro, although Negroes make up considerably less of the total city population. Women thieves outnumbered male shoplifters, but not so strikingly as in Cameron's materials. Juvenile thieves constituted about 60 per cent of all shoplifters, thus they were more frequent than in Cameron's data.[26]

One major observation that emerges from both Robin's and Cameron's research is that juvenile shoplifting is most commonly *group* activity, while adult thieves usually engage in surreptitious and individualistic thievery.[27] Among juveniles, many of the youngsters act as "aiders" or "abettors" who do not themselves steal, but act as lookouts for their peers. Cameron suggests that adult thieves are probably often persons who engaged in group stealing as adolescents and learned their crime skills in that setting; in other words, the juvenile thieves of today become the adult shoplifters of tomorrow. This may be a dubious hypothesis, for juvenile theft could be a peer-supported kind of conduct which develops out of some temporally circumscribed influences of a "youth culture" and is terminated as youngsters move out of this age period. At any rate, the hypothesis needs more study, for its accuracy is presently indeterminate.

Robin indicates that a major factor influencing the decision to prosecute cases of shoplifting is size of theft, so that very few individuals who pilfer less than $20 worth of merchandise are reported to the police, while nearly all those who steal things valued at over $60 are prosecuted.[28]

Robin's observations also bear upon contentions that amateur shoplifters are driven by psychological aberrations or compulsions to steal. He shows that thefts are markedly more common during the months of October, November, and December than they are at any other time of the year.[29] If compulsions impel individuals toward thievery, rates of stealing should be much the same the year around, for compulsions should not wax and wane with the seasons. Clearly, these fluctuations have more to do with seasonal budgetary strains than with psychological tensions. Along the same line, Robin cites an instance of a power failure in Chicago's Loop area in which, during the 30 minutes of darkness that ensued, thousands of dollars of merchandise was stolen by "normal" persons.[30] Finally, he notes that a study of 698 "food lifters" in Chicago supermarkets in 1951 showed that nearly all were ordinary citizens, mainly housewives, who had enough money in their possession to pay

[26] *Ibid.*, p. 166.
[27] *Ibid.*, p. 170; Cameron, *op. cit.*, pp. 101–4.
[28] Robin, "Patterns of Department Store Shoplifting," 169–70.
[29] *Ibid.*, pp. 170–71.
[30] Robin, "The American Customer: Shopper or Shoplifter?"

for the stolen items found in their custody.[31] These bits of evidence seem to confirm Cameron's argument that amateur shoplifters steal in order to stretch their budgets, doing so deliberately and rationally, after conjuring up rationalizations which allow them to continue to think of themselves as honest, law-abiding citizens. These thieves steal when they evaluate the elements of immediate situations to be most conducive to successful deviance.

## THE NAIVE CHECK FORGER ROLE-CAREER

There is every reason to believe that the writing and passing of "bum checks" is an extremely commonplace and costly form of American crime. The significance of checks in modern society is indicated by Bloch and Geis, who report that over 90 per cent of the money transactions in this country at present take place by means of checks rather than through cash transactions.[32] No wonder that numerous endeavors by professional criminals toward obtaining money through fraudulent checks occur, for forgery and check passing is relatively easy in a cultural situation in which check transactions are normal activities arousing little suspicion. Nearly every adult citizen learns to handle his affairs through checking accounts as a part of growing up. This includes acquisition of simple skills which can easily be turned toward forgery by the amateur offender in need of emergency funds.

The naive check forger discussed below is one of two relatively distinct kinds of check passers. The other is the professional forger who engages in check passing as a means of livelihood and exhibits fairly complicated and well-developed crime skills.[33] Professionals manufacture and pass checks in bunches, frequently in an elaborate fashion involving the printing of impressive looking payroll checks from a nonexisting company. Or professional forgers often pass fictitious checks made to look authentic through the use of a stolen check-printer. Offenders of this kind are not discussed in the commentary on naive forgers. Instead, professional check passers stand as a case of "grifting," a variant of professional thieves. The previous chapter contained an analysis of professional thieves, and the

---

[31] *Ibid.*

[32] Herbert A. Bloch and Gilbert Geis, *Man, Crime, and Society* (New York: Random House, Inc., 1962), p. 202.

[33] Evidence on aspects of professional forgery is found in Edwin M. Lemert, "The Behavior of the Systematic Check Forger," *Social Problems*, VI (Fall 1958), 141–49; David Maurer, "The Argot of Forgery," *American Speech*, XVI (December 1941), 243–50; Julius L. Sternitzky, *Forgery and Fictitious Checks* (Springfield, Ill.: Charles C Thomas, Publisher, 1955); Norman S. Hayner, "Characteristics of Five Offender Types," *American Sociological Review*, XXVI (February 1961), 96–102.

reader is directed back to that section for further remarks regarding professional forgers.

A role-career description of the naive check forger has already been presented in Chapter Ten. That characterization pictured this offender as a person with simple crime skills who thinks of himself in prosocial terms. Check forgery was seen as developing out of certain situations of social stress. The role-career description from Chapter Ten need not be repeated, but the reader is referred back to pages 240–242 for that presentation.

### Some Evidence

Some indication of the widespread nature of forgery was provided in the analysis of Uniform Crime Reports statistics for the United States in Chapter Five. Another measure of the extent of this kind of illegality can be found in reports in the state of California. For example, in 1963, of the 27,222 persons referred to probation departments for consideration for probation, 4668 were charged with forgery and check offenses.[34] But there is every reason to suppose that these known cases are a small fraction of all check violations which occur. For one thing, many instances of behavior which qualify technically as forgery probably go unreported because they are suspected of being accidental in nature. Persons do fairly commonly write checks which unintentionally "bounce" because they have miscalculated the amount of money in their checking accounts. As a result, the demarcation point between mistakes and willful misconduct is hazy. The deliberate or intentional forger has this defense available to employ against the aggrieved merchant. He can assert that the "NSF" check was an accidental miscalculation, and the businessman may well find himself forced to honor this explanation for fear of alienating the customer. That same offended merchant may be deterred from responding to the forger's misconduct as crime out of feelings of identification and sympathy for the actor, particularly if the forger is a person of middle class position and a long-standing customer of the victim's establishment. Finally, the merchant victim of a bad check may be loath to report the case to authorities for fear of getting entangled in time-consuming court appearances, and also out of anticipation that he will then be unable to gain recompensation for the financial loss he has suffered.

One bit of evidence probably symptomatic of the differential handling of forgers comes from the author's own work.[35] Interviews with the mana-

---

[34] State of California, *Delinquency and Probation in California, 1963* (Sacramento: Bureau of Criminal Statistics, 1963), p. 179.
[35] Interview material in the author's personal files.

ger of a suburban chain drug store in the San Francisco area disclosed that this establishment is victimized by large numbers of check forgers each week, even though it takes elaborate steps to prevent such incidents. Nearly all of the checks which "bounce" and are returned to the store by banks are handled informally. The drug store endeavors to collect its losses from the check passers, and in many cases succeeds in so doing. But the store does not always manage to recoup its losses; the manager reported that "chiselers" who pass bad checks for small amounts frequently refuse to make good on them. They predicate their actions on the assumption that the store will not be willing to go through the cumbersome, time-consuming steps required in order to prosecute. These forgers are usually correct in this assumption, for the management rarely engages in formal actions against check passers. Those cases which are prosecuted normally involve a large amount of money lost to the store.

The most detailed and revealing investigation of amateur check forgers now available is by Lemert.[36] His research was designed to investigate the theory that "naive check forgery arises at a critical point in a process of social isolation, out of certain types of social situations, and is made possible by the closure or constriction of behavior alternatives subjectively held as available to the forger." [37] Lemert examined the case records of over 1000 naive forgers in the Los Angeles area and conducted interviews with a sample of these individuals. The subjects had little or no contact with criminal individuals, were nonviolent persons with a marked repugnance for forms of crime other than forgery, and appeared to be likeable and attractive but impulsive individuals. The forgers were predominantly white males, older on the average than other probationers, and with higher intelligence ratings and better occupational status than other offenders.[38]

Lemert's hypothesis about social isolation as the prelude to forgery was borne out by his observations. Most of the check writers had been involved prior to their criminality in unemployment, gambling losses, alcoholic sprees, difficulties in military service, or estrangement from their families. Marital disruptions appear to play a particularly critical role as an isolating experience, for about 40 per cent of the forgers were divorced. In general, Lemert concludes that these various experiences tend to be progressive in character and mutually reinforcing, so that the person caught up in them becomes more and more alienated from conventional social bonds.[39]

[36] Edwin M. Lemert, "An Isolation and Closure Theory of Naive Check Forgery," Journal of Criminal Law, Criminology and Police Science, XLIV (September–October 1953), 296–307.
[37] Ibid., p. 298.
[38] Ibid., pp. 299–300.
[39] Ibid., pp. 301–4.

According to Lemert, the social experiences most of these persons get involved in immediately prior to check forgery are what he terms "certain dialectical forms of social behavior." [40] He means that the individual usually embarks upon a course of action or events having a clear beginning and end, so there is considerable impetus built up to carry the activities through to their conclusion. An alcoholic "spree" is a case in point, in which initial involvement in drinking pressures the actor to continue until he has been intoxicated for a lengthy period of time. In the event that he prematurely exhausts his funds, considerable tension may arise, provoking him to seek some solution which will bring the action pattern to its terminal point.

Lemert argues that the forger finds relief from this situational tension by a social-psychological process of "closure." [41] Check forgery is selected as a way to bring finality to the dialectical events. The choice of check writing comes about in part because less deviant solutions do not suggest themselves to the individual—he feels he cannot borrow money from anyone, or other alternatives are not perceived as open to him. Moreover, forgery is "in the culture," learned as part of becoming an adult, so no special skill is required in order to commit this act. It is also nonviolent in character, and can be rationalized through such arguments as "You can't kill anyone with a fountain pen."

This work by Lemert should be acknowledged as the most significant study of naive forgers which has been accomplished. In addition, the argument should be evaluated for its broader implications regarding models of causation in criminology. Lemert's account of the development of check forgery stands as an illustration of his concept of "situational deviation" which we examined in Chapter Nine. The isolation and closure conception of check forgery can also be offered as an example of a mechanistic or situational explanation of criminality, which Sutherland and Cressey contrast to historical or genetic models of etiology.[42] A situational view of causal dynamics accounts for some kind of behavior in terms of processes operating at the moment of the criminality, as compared to genetic formulations, which look for the roots of ongoing behavior in earlier experiences, often separated by a lengthy interval of time. Although some of the causal elements which contribute to forgery probably are genetic, it is also apparent that check writing cannot be understood without reference to problems of the immediate situation, or to Lemert's dialectical endeavors.

---

[40] *Ibid.*, pp. 303–4.

[41] *Ibid.*, pp. 304–5.

[42] Edwin H. Sutherland and Donald R. Cressey, *Principles of Criminology* (7th ed.; Philadelphia: J. B. Lippincott Co., 1966), pp. 79–80.

There are several other studies of naive forgers which reveal findings parallel to those of Lemert. Gauthier discovered that forgers in Kingston Penitentiary in Canada were older males with above average educational levels and from "good" middle class families.[43] He suggests that these offenders engage in forgery as a technique for relieving inner tensions of the kind proposed by Lemert. Berg's comparison of forgers and other inmates in Southern Michigan Penitentiary turned up similar results: the check offenders had higher intelligence ratings than the other inmates, were older than the other convicts, and were less criminally involved than the other felons.[44] Gillin's report on Wisconsin criminals in that state's prison noted that forgers were from middle income backgrounds and were older and more intelligent than other felons.[45] Several of the case histories cited by Gillin present a picture of check writing that meshes with the isolation and closure formulation. Finally, Hayner has contrasted professional or "con forgers" and naive or "alcoholic forgers" with other prisoner types in the Washington State penal institutions. The naive forgers turned out to have higher than average intelligence.[46] Many were from situations of social isolation—45 per cent of them were divorced. According to Hayner, alcoholic forgers are frequently "dependent" persons. This is a judgment arrived at by examination of case record materials available on the prisoners.

This last contention is worthy of further exploration. The claim that check writers are commonly individuals who are dependent and passive in temperament is one which the author has frequently heard advanced by correctional agents in California and elsewhere.[47] The same argument turns up in the data presented by Hayner. The problem is that such a finding could emerge from case records as an artifact of the belief systems of correctional persons, rather than as an accurate indicator of true characteristics of forgers. In other words, if correctional treatment workers regard check writers as dependent individuals, they may report such observations in case documents, even though the forgers do not fit this characterization. What is needed in this instance is a more carefully controlled kind of inquiry which would search out evidence on the psychological correlates of check writing behavior. The study by Lemert of dependency on the part of alcoholic individuals offers a model of the

[43] Maurice Gauthier, "The Psychology of the Compulsive Forger," *Canadian Journal of Corrections*, I (July 1959), 62–69.

[44] Irwin A. Berg, "A Comparative Study of Forgery," *Journal of Applied Psychology*, XXVIII (June 1944), 232–38.

[45] John L. Gillin, *The Wisconsin Prisoner* (Madison: University of Wisconsin Press, 1946), pp. 167–73.

[46] Hayner, *op. cit.*, pp. 96–102.

[47] For a discussion of this matter, see Gibbons, *op. cit.*, pp. 267–70.

kind of investigation required.[48] In summary, this dependency claim must be regarded at present as a contentious one.

## THE AUTOMOBILE THIEF-"JOYRIDER" ROLE-CAREER

That form of car theft called "joyriding," in which the offenders steal automobiles for short-run recreational purposes rather than to deprive the owner permanently of his property, is an extremely commonplace kind of illegality in the United States. In addition, joyriding behavior is one of several forms of deviance which span juvenile delinquency and adult criminality. Joyriding car theft is very often carried on by persons from about 13 to 20 years of age. Many of these individuals get apprehended and diverted into juvenile courts, thereby becoming "delinquents" in point of legal fact, while others are remanded to criminal courts and acquire the legal status of "criminal." The typological description below is framed in terms which describe relatively young individuals, so that it is a characterization of a "juvenile delinquent" as well as a "criminal." [49] Moreover, the research findings on car thieves reported in the succeeding section refer principally to samples of car thieves from juvenile court or training school situations.

### Definitional Dimensions

*Offense Behavior.* Joyriders steal cars for recreational or joyriding purposes, not to "strip" them or for other profit motives. The customary activity is to steal automobiles by the technique of "hot wiring," ride around in them for a short time, and then abandon the car undamaged. Car thieves are sometimes known in the community as "wild" boys who drink and associate with "wild" girls. However, their delinquent activities tend to center around auto theft and they are not usually involved in other kinds of property offenses.

*Interactional Setting.* Joyriders steal cars within a loosely structured group of fellow joyriders. On any particular occasion, an individual car thief engages in these acts with several other delinquents. Over a series of joyriding incidents, the participants in such acts vary somewhat; on one occasion cars are stolen by boys A, B, and C, whereas another time they are stolen by boys A, D, E, and F. Consequently these boys, A, B,

[48] Edwin M. Lemert, "Dependency in Married Alcoholics," *Quarterly Journal of Studies on Alcohol,* XXIII (December 1962), 590–609.

[49] Don C. Gibbons, *Changing the Lawbreaker,* The Treatment of Delinquents and Criminals, © 1965. Reprinted by permission of Prentice-Hull, Inc., Englewood Cliffs, New Jersey, pp. 88–90.

*C, D, E,* and *F,* do not constitute a well-structured gang, but represent individuals who associate differentially with each other, that is, "birds of a feather." As a group they are likely to be juveniles (or young adults) with adjustment problems in school and elsewhere.

*Self-concept.* These offenders define themselves as nondelinquents or noncriminals and distinguish themselves from "real delinquents" or "real criminals." They are youths who frequently exhibit a considerable psychological investment in self-notions as "tough" and masculine. In general, they regard their delinquent activities as evidence that they are "tough" and "cool."

*Attitudes.* Joyriders exhibit essentially prosocial attitudes, in that they show conventional attitudes toward work and reveal other conventional norms. Their views of the police are not so much hostile as they are notions that the police are stupid and inefficient.

*Role-career.* The role-career of the joyrider begins in adolescence with automobile theft. It may persist over several years and involve a number of instances of joyriding. Repetitive acts of car theft are likely to result in arrest of the offender, adjudication as a delinquent or adult felon, and placement on probation. Some of these youths eventually end up in training schools or reformatories, where they make a reasonably stable adjustment. It appears that most car thieves terminate these actions in the late teenage years and become law-abiding citizens.

### Background Dimensions

*Social Class.* Joyriders are juveniles who specialize in this kind of activity, as distinct from juveniles who occasionally steal cars but whose acts are normally in the direction of predatory theft. Car thieves of the first sort are usually from middle class, comfortable economic backgrounds. They live in single-family dwellings in middle income areas. Their parents are usually white collar or other types of middle class workers.

*Family Background.* The family situation out of which joyriders emerge is one of relatively close supervision and discipline by the parents. However, joyriders frequently indicate a lack of intense interaction with their fathers. It may be that the fathers of the car thieves fail to provide completely adequate models of adult, masculine behavior to their sons. Another not uncommon characteristic of the families of joyriders is a relatively high degree of occupational and residential mobility. This pattern may sometimes contribute to the marginal status of the boy in the community in terms of peer group membership.

*Peer Group Associations.* Joyriders exhibit relatively adequate peer group adjustments. However, although they interact with nondelinquent peers, they exhibit differential association with other car thieves, most of whom have reputations as "wild" and somewhat deviant. To some extent, the joyrider appears to be a marginal member of conventional peer groups.

*Contact with Defining Agencies.* Contact with defining agencies in the case of joyriders seems to confirm the person's status as a "tough" individual in his own eyes. Repeated contacts with the police and courts tend to produce negative attitudes toward these groups. However, these contacts do not usually lead the offender to a commitment to adult patterns of criminality. Instead, the joyrider is sufficiently socialized to conventional norms that he ultimately gets a job, gets married, and assumes the behavior of a conventional law-abiding citizen.

### Discussion and Research Findings [50]

The preceding portrait of the juvenile or young adult joyrider suggests the following causal dynamics. First, car thieves are relatively well-adjusted boys on good terms with most of their peers, particularly fellow joyriders with whom they steal cars. These boys are predominantly middle class youths who have grown up in a family setting which is relatively stable, but creates problems of masculine identity for adolescent males. Further, boys who steal cars often show family backgrounds involving some mild degree of parent-child tension. Out of all middle class males who show social-psychological problems surrounding masculinity, the ones most likely to get involved in automobile theft are perhaps those involved in situations of "marginality" of one kind or another. Marginality is our term for a variety of conditions which prevent the boy from working out his problems of masculinity in nondeviant ways. The pimply lads who have communication difficulties with girls and other persons, the boys who are too small to engage in high school athletics, or the ones with families who show residential mobility in the form of frequent moves within the city, so that the youngsters have difficulties in becoming socially integrated into school life, are the kinds of youths who are candidates for delinquent careers in joyriding. What is suggested is a multifaceted process by which certain middle class boys are drawn into car theft.

This hypothesized etiological background in joyriding is an elaboration

[50] This section is a slightly revised version of Don C. Gibbons, "Problems of Causal Analysis in Criminology: A Case Illustration," *Journal of Research in Crime and Delinquency,* III (January 1966), 47–52.

of a line of analysis regarding "middle class delinquency" first advanced by Talcott Parsons [51] and subsequently enunciated by Cohen.[52] The ingredients of this set of notions have been succinctly summarized by Cohen in the following remarks:

> Because of the structure of the modern family and the nature of our occupational system, children of both sexes tend to form early feminine identifications. The boy, however, unlike the girl, comes later under strong social pressure to establish his masculinity, his *difference from* female figures. Because his mother is the object of the feminine identification which he feels is the threat to his status as a male, he tends to react negativistically to those conduct norms which have been associated with mother and therefore have acquired feminine significance. Since mother has been the principal agent of indoctrination of "good," respectable behavior, "goodness" comes to symbolize femininity, and engaging in "bad" behavior acquires the function of denying his femininity and therefore asserting his masculinity. This is the motivation to juvenile delinquency (emphasis in the original).[53]

Parsons and Cohen both maintain that it is middle class boys who have the most severe masculinity difficulties, owing to the fact that the father works at some distant locale and his son cannot observe him as a role model. The work tasks of the father are also of a relatively abstract and intangible kind, so that the boy cannot easily identify with them.

We have added to this argument the two ingredients of parent-child tensions and marginality to form overarching rubric for a series of specific contingencies which some middle class, adolescent or young adult males encounter. It might be noted that one British student of delinquency has also offered this masculinity hypothesis to account for car thieves that he studied, holding that these boys were from families characterized by fathers who failed to serve as adequate role-models.[54]

Since our remarks so far have been phrased in speculative terms, the question might be asked: How well do these propositions stand up in the face of empirical evidence? Are these contentions about masculine protest, marginality, and the like, true? Unfortunately, unequivocal answers to these questions are not to be found in available research materials. The existing data are only tangentially relevant to the preceding lines of theoretical exposition.

Empirical investigations of car theft conducted to date stand as dramatic illustrations of the poverty of results which comes from studies

[51] Talcott Parsons, "Certain Primary Sources and Patterns of Aggression in the Social Structure of the Western World," *Psychiatry*, X (May 1947), 167–81; Parsons, "Age and Sex in the Social Structure of the United States," *American Sociological Review*, VII (October 1942), 604–16.

[52] Albert K. Cohen, *Delinquent Boys* (New York: Free Press of Glencoe, Inc., 1955), pp. 157–69.

[53] *Ibid.*, p. 164.

[54] T. C. N. Gibbens, "Car Thieves," *British Journal of Delinquency*, VIII, No. 4 (1958), 257–68.

unguided by explicit theory and dependent upon information reported in official records. The record-keeping systems of most official agencies involve only a limited number of facts about offenders, such as age, sex, and official charge for which the person had been apprehended. Not uncommonly, even these sparse items are unreliably or unsystematically recorded. But most important, these fact-gathering procedures are usually insensitive to the accumulation of data on theoretically significant dimensions with which the investigator is concerned. Few facts are recorded on such critical matters as the structure of the social behavior which has resulted in the offender being labeled as a deviant. For example, statements about victims and their relationship to the offender are usually absent from official records. An investigator can draw out of official reports only those facts put there by agency officials, and in many cases he will be lucky if some of these happen to be related to the concepts and categories in which he is interested. This is particularly true of instances where the researcher is investigating some complex dimension or process, such as marginality or Lemert's "isolation" in the case of naive forgery. These are not simple concepts that are equivalents of the common sense categories utilized in correctional record-keeping. This adds up to the inescapable conclusion that significant research of the future will involve testing of specific theories through collection of first-hand observations explicitly linked to concepts in a theoretical argument.

This is not to suggest that existing pieces of inquiry are of no use whatsoever. No such implication is intended, for the evidence at hand is superior to no evidence at all and, in addition, that material does help to delineate promising etiological hypotheses which might be pursued in future studies.

Detailed surveys of the existing information regarding car theft have been made by Savitz [55] and by Jerome Hall.[56] In discussing joyriding forms of car theft as distinguished from those automobile larcenies in which the car is "stripped" or permanently stolen, Savitz notes that many jurisdictions have created special legislation to cover this form of behavior. He notes that early efforts to prosecute joyriders under general larceny statutes were often unsuccessful, because the offenders had not intended to deprive the owners of their automobiles permanently.[57] As a result, an offense usually labeled "Taking a Motor Vehicle Without the Owner's Permission" was invented to cover the activities of joyriders.

[55] Leonard D. Savitz, "Automobile Theft," Journal of Criminal Law, Criminology and Police Science, L (July–August 1959), 132–43. Several older studies of car thieves which are not discussed in this book are noted in Savitz' paper.
[56] Jerome Hall, Theft, Law and Society (2nd ed.; Indianapolis: Bobbs-Merrill Co., Inc., 1952), pp. 233–88.
[57] Savitz, op. cit., p. 132.

Along a somewhat related line, Hall notes that some courts have resorted to administrative procedures through which joyriders were dealt with under a statute which, technically, did not apply to them, rather than under the relevant law covering theft of cars, in order to prevent these persons from being harshly punished for relatively minor criminal acts.[58]

The essays by Savitz and Hall indicate that the crime techniques or *modus operandi* of car thieves are quite varied, some of them employing technically simple tactics of lawbreaking, while others utilize more esoteric skills.[59] Other salient descriptive facts about car theft presented by these authors include the observation that about 90 per cent of the vehicles reported stolen are ultimately recovered, usually undamaged, and usually within a short time interval.[60] Reports of the San Francisco Police Department show that, of the cars stolen in the nine different police districts of that city, more than half were recovered within the same district in which they had been stolen.[61]

Savitz has also enumerated some major characteristics of car thieves which are indicated in available reports and studies.[62] He notes that most of them are young males, usually under 20 years of age, and single. Large cities have the highest rates of automobile theft, probably due in part to anonymity and other features which provide opportunities for vehicles to be stolen easily and with slight risk.

One of the major studies utilizing firsthand evidence regarding joyriders is that of Wattenberg and Balistrieri.[63] These investigators examined the detailed case records of over 200 white boys apprehended by the Detroit police in 1948 for car theft, and compared these youths with several thousand other white youngsters who had been arrested for different delinquencies. Negro car thieves were not studied because they were infrequently encountered, at least by the police, even though Negroes constituted a sizeable portion of the Detroit population.

The major impression that emerges from the comparisons of car thieves with other delinquents centers about the "favored group" status of the former. Car thieves were from neighborhoods rated as "above average" by the police, from uncrowded single-family dwellings, from houses in good physical condition, and from racially homogeneous neighborhoods. They were also from families in which only one parent was employed.

[58] Hall, op. cit., pp. 262–75.

[59] Savitz, op. cit., pp. 139–40; Hall, op. cit., pp. 250–56.

[60] Savitz, op. cit., p. 133; Hall, op. cit., pp. 240–45.

[61] "An Analysis of Auto Thefts and Recoveries by Police District," mimeographed, in the author's files.

[62] Savitz, op. cit., pp. 133–35.

[63] William W. Wattenberg and James Balistrieri, "Automobile Theft: A 'Favored-Group' Delinquency," *American Journal of Sociology*, LVII (May 1952), 575–79.

The car thieves were older boys on good terms with their peers. Although the automobile thieves were rated as rambunctious gang members, the police frequently evaluated these youngsters as "responsive." Finally, the parents' involvement in their sons' recreation was judged to be "occasional" rather than "seldom" or "regular." [64] Wattenberg and Balistrieri interpret this pattern of results as an indication that car thieves are the product of a permissive upbringing which results in an "other-directed" personality structure. These boys are thought to be easily drawn into peer-supported patterns of antisocial conduct; at the same time they are unresponsive to larger social entities and their values. [65]

A second report on juvenile car thieves is found in a study by Browning. [66] He compared 56 car thieves, 63 truants, and 58 control group nondelinquent juveniles. The offenders were Los Angeles County probation wards. Both groups of offenders were from broken homes in greater numbers than were the control group boys. The auto thieves and controls were more commonly from medium income backgrounds than were the truants. Similarly, the car thieves and nondelinquents showed better community and personal adjustment than did the truant youngsters. Considerably more car thieves had backgrounds of residential mobility than did the other two groups; about three-fourths of the car thieves had lived for less than five years at their present addresses. In the main, these findings parallel those of Wattenberg and Balistrieri, particularly with regard to the "favored group" status of car thieves.

Another investigation to be considered is one by Schepses involving boys in the New York state training school at Warwick. [67] Schepses compared 22 boys who were "pure" car thieves, that is, with records solely of vehicle theft, with 59 "mixed" car thieves who had engaged in other delinquencies as well, and 81 control group cases of training school wards charged with offenses other than automobile theft. He observed that, in most cases, joyriding is a group form of deviance, for most of the thieves had been apprehended with at least one other offender or "fall partner." [68]

The other major results turned up in this inquiry involve the following observations. First, car thieves are more frequently white boys, rather

[64] Ibid., pp. 577–78.

[65] Ibid., pp. 578–79.

[66] Charles J. Browning, "Differential Social Relations and Personality Factors of Parents and Boys in Two Delinquent Groups and One Nondelinquent Group" (Doctoral dissertation, University of Southern California, 1954).

[67] Erwin Schepses, "Boys Who Steal Cars," Federal Probation, XXV (March 1961), 56–62; Schepses, "The Young Car Thief," Journal of Criminal Law, Criminology and Police Science, L (March–April 1960), 569.

[68] Schepses, "Boys Who Steal Cars," pp. 58–59.

than Negro or Puerto Rican, than are the control cases, even though
Negro car thieves are fairly common in the Warwick population. This
finding differs from that of Wattenberg and Balistrieri, who encountered
few Negro joyriders in their sample. Car thieves were generally more
intelligent and advanced in reading skills than were the other delinquent
boys. They were also more commonly from comfortable economic circumstances than were the control youngsters. The "pure" automobile
thieves were principally from unbroken homes, while the "mixed" car
thieves and the control group boys were from broken homes in over
half the cases.[69] According to Schepses, the car thieves exhibited a wide
variety of family constellations, in that some had passive fathers, some
had authoritarian parents, while others showed various other family
backgrounds. In his view, theories which allege that a specific kind of
nuclear, middle class family pattern leads to joyriding are incorrect.[70]

One indicator of the differences between the social process which leads
boys into car theft and that which draws youngsters into other forms of
delinquency is found in Schepses' observation that the car thieves were
older at their first court appearance than were the other delinquents. His
materials also indicate some slight tendency for car thieves to make a
poorer institutional adjustment than the other wards; for example, more
of them have records as runaways from the school.[71] Finally, the three
groups differed slightly in post release adjustment.[72]

Dosick has provided some further evidence on automobile thieves,
derived from a study of federal Dyer Act violators.[73] He hypothesized
that car theft takes three general forms—joyriding by juveniles, along with
"short history" and "long history" patterns of car theft among young
adults (17 to 21 years old, predominantly). "Long history" thieves have
engaged in a variety of criminal acts, are criminally sophisticated, and
are enmeshed in delinquent subcultures. "Short history" offenders are
youths who have been less involved in criminality. In Dosick's view, the
young adult car thieves steal cars for "instrumental" reasons, but for
motives which differ between "short history" and "long history" offenders. Among "long history" thieves, cars are stolen for various impulsive
reasons which are usually illegitimate, but "short history" offenders steal
cars as an illegitimate route to legitimate or conventional goals, such
as a new job. Interviews and questionnaire responses on 200 Dyer Act

[69] Ibid.
[70] Ibid., pp. 58–60.
[71] Ibid., pp. 60–61.
[72] Ibid., pp. 60–62.
[73] Martin L. Dosick, "Statement for Presentation to the Subcommittee to Investigate Juvenile
Delinquency, United States Senate, January 17, 1967," mimeographed.

violators generally confirmed these hypotheses. The "long history" car thieves had stolen cars in order to engage in a show of masculine daring and toughness or to obtain other short-run delinquent goals. The "short history" offenders had taken cars in order to go to another area in search of a job, or for other reasons of that kind. More were concerned about upward mobility and other middle class goals than were the "long history" cases. Dosick concluded that: "My data, then, points to some men who stole cars as incidents in delinquent careers, and to other men who took cars to help solve the problem of educational and job-based transition into male adulthood" (emphasis in the original).[74]

Several other studies of violators of federal auto theft laws are available for examination. In one of these, a sample of auto offenders received in federal institutions in 1964 was studied.[75] The researchers discovered that 49 per cent of these lawbreakers had previously been convicted for auto theft, and 20 per cent had stolen two or more cars in their last offense. The reasons for car theft seemed varied, for 52 per cent of the offenders had stolen cars for transportation, 32 per cent had taken them for joyriding, and only 5 per cent had stolen the auto in order to sell or strip it. However, 71 per cent of the offenders under the age of 17 had taken cars for joyriding purposes.

Karacki investigated a group of 632 federal offenders charged with auto theft and compared them with 369 prisoners who had committed other offenses.[76] The car thieves showed greater residential mobility than the other lawbreakers, for 59.3 per cent of them had moved three or more times in the previous five years. More auto thieves had been in military service or confinement prior to their offense than was true of the other inmates. More auto thieves had poor work records than did the other offenders. The institutional adjustments of car thieves were poorer, more of them having been involved in disciplinary incidents, escapes, transfers to other institutions, or close or maximum confinement. The auto thieves showed poorer post release records; 63.8 per cent of them had violated parole in the two years after release, as contrasted to 46.3 per cent of the other prisoners. Karacki was led to conclude that these findings suggest that car thieves are from more unfavorable backgrounds than most other offenders, a conclusion different from most of the claims made about auto thieves.

The observation that emerges most consistently from these studies is

---

[74] *Ibid.*, p. 5.

[75] Federal Bureau of Prisons, *Auto Theft Offenders, 1964*, mimeographed.

[76] Larry Karacki, "Youthful Auto Theft Offender Study," Federal Bureau of Prisons, 1966, unpublished.

the "favored group" character of joyriding. However, these reports are not entirely consistent in this regard, and are even less uniform on such matters as the ethnic backgrounds of car thieves. Most have little to say about specific contentions regarding family patterns in joyriding. At this point, we return to our initial observation that investigations are in order which would test specific hypotheses about automobile thieves, through the use of firsthand data gathering and measures specifically relevant to the dimensions of personality, family life, and so on, identified in the theoretical claims. Not much more can be said about car thieves until such studies are conducted.

## THE PROPERTY OFFENDER, "ONE-TIME LOSER" ROLE-CAREER [77]

As we have seen, casual offenders who do not define themselves as lawbreakers can be found engaging in various kinds of illegality. Some shoplift, some write "bad checks," still others steal cars. There is still another kind of miscreant to be noted, the "one-time loser" property offender who commits isolated acts of petty or major larceny. We commented earlier on the applicability of "risk-taking" notions to these individuals who engage in idiosyncratic instances of lawbreaking. But let us examine these commonly encountered offenders in greater detail.

### Definitional Dimensions

*Offense Behavior.* This category refers to offenders who commit a single property crime, frequently relatively serious in nature, such as grand theft. It excludes embezzlers, who also frequently commit only a single, isolated criminal act. One-time losers normally show little skill in criminality, so arrests are frequent.

*Interactional Setting.* The criminal acts of one-time losers are often carried out by the offender acting alone. In those cases in which several crime partners are involved, all are likely to be amateur offenders.

*Self-concept.* Individuals of this type exhibit noncriminal self-images. The offender usually admits readily that he has been involved in a serious deviant act, but maintains that it was atypical and that he is not a "real criminal." When seen in a correctional institution, he maintains that he is different from most of the inmates in the institution. In turn, he is seen as different by the inmate group. One-time losers are regarded

[77] Don C. Gibbons, *Changing the Lawbreaker*, The Treatment of Delinquents and Criminals, © 1965. Reprinted by permission of Prentice-Hall, Inc., Englewood Cliffs, New Jersey, pp. 106–8.

as "square Johns" by other prisoners, that is, aliens in the criminalistic subculture of the prison.

*Attitudes.* These offenders verbalize prosocial sentiments. In prison, this offender is likely to be planning to resume a law-abiding career upon release. In most cases, he was working at some conventional occupation before arrest. His attitudes toward conventional work roles are the same as those of law-abiding citizens. Similarly, individuals of this type are usually married and exhibit conventional attitudes regarding marital roles.

*Role-career.* The one-time loser property offender usually shows no delinquency record and no prior criminal record other than such minor law violations as drunkenness or disturbing the peace. Such persons are frequently placed on probation, and usually complete the probation period satisfactorily. Some who have committed a property offense involving large financial loss to the victim are sentenced to prison. Their adjustment there is satisfactory, they are infrequently involved in conduct infractions, and they gain early paroles. They complete the parole period satisfactorily and do not reenter the offender population.

### Background Dimensions

*Social Class.* These violators are from several social class levels, but the most common is lower middle class. Many one-time losers are persons who earn modest incomes from skilled or semiskilled occupations and are normally from nonslum areas or relatively rural small towns.

*Family Background.* Most individuals in this type are from relatively stable and conventional family backgrounds. Behavior of this kind cannot be linked to any critical kind of family background situation.

*Peer Group Associations.* There is nothing particularly unusual or striking about the peer associations of one-time losers, either as juveniles or adults. These offenders receive no peer support or encouragement for criminal acts.

*Contact with Defining Agencies.* Contacts with defining agencies are not causally significant except perhaps in a minor but positive way. These offenders have the same interpretation of their criminal acts as do law enforcement agencies. The individual views crime as atypical for him. Although he may develop rationalizations which excuse this atypical, "bad" act, such rationalizations are not powerful enough to counteract other prosocial attitudes. Accordingly, these offenders do not usually repeat their deviant activities, quite apart from any rehabilitative programs in which they might have participated.

## Some Evidence

Supporting evidence for the characterization of one-time loser property offenders is available in some abundance. Analyses of the records of adult probationers show that many were involved in isolated, nonrecurrent acts of illegality. They also show these individuals to be quite conventional in appearance, without antisocial attitudes or criminogenic backgrounds.

One of the most detailed of these studies of probation records has been carried out by England.[78] He examined the records of 500 federal probation cases who had completed the probationary period. Most were white, older, married males. They had been sentenced for a variety of offenses, although nearly half had been convicted of liquor law violations. The remainder had committed a large variety of crimes, but forgery, draft evasion, mail fraud, and assorted kinds of theft were also commonly found. Most of these probationers had records of law-abiding behavior prior to the offense for which they had been placed on probation. About 80 per cent of these individuals had remained free of recidivism for five years after being released from probation. In another study of these persons, England demonstrated that few had received any significant amount of casework on probation, so their successful adjustment must be attributed to general lack of criminal orientation.[79]

In another report concerned with prison inmates in Washington State, Schrag has noted that prosocial "square Johns" are numerous in institutional populations. Many of these "square Johns" are individuals who have been sentenced for some kind of larceny.[80] These felons are lacking in serious records of criminality, they are not from particularly disordered or criminogenic backgrounds, and their actions seem attributable to various kinds of situational stresses.

This material reveals that a goodly number of individuals who might be judged petty lawbreakers by the detached observer nonetheless are

[78] Ralph W. England, Jr., "A Study of Postprobation Recidivism Among Five Hundred Federal Offenders," *Federal Probation*, XIX (September 1955), 10–16; see also England, "What is Responsible for Satisfactory Probation and Postprobation Outcome?" *Journal of Criminal Law, Criminology and Police Science*, XLVII (March–April 1957), 667–76; Don C. Gibbons, "Probation: Theory and Reality," *Canadian Journal of Corrections*, I (January 1959) 10–18; Albert Wahl and Daniel Glaser, "Pilot Time Study of the Federal Probation Officer's Job," *Federal Probation*, XXVII (September 1963), 20–25.

[79] England, "What is Responsible for Satisfactory Probation and Postprobation Outcome?"

[80] Clarence C. Schrag, "A Preliminary Criminal Typology," *Pacific Sociological Review*, IV (Spring 1961), 11–16; Schrag, "Some Foundations for a Theory of Correction," in *The Prison*, ed. Donald R. Cressey (New York: Holt, Rinehart and Winston, Inc., 1961), pp. 346–56; see also Gillin, *op. cit., passim*.

reacted to as fairly serious law violators. Those who encounter certain contingent risks end up as probationers and prison inmates, so the legal consequences of their behavior are far from petty.

## SUMMARY

The lawbreakers considered in Chapter Eleven tend to be those "bad guys" that citizens have in mind when they engage in discussions of "the crime problem." The common man less often thinks of the behavior patterns discussed in this chapter as crime, although some of these activities are serious and costly kinds of illegality. In the next chapter, our attention will turn to some cases of criminality carried on by businessmen and influential citizens. These forms of misconduct, such as white collar crime, are rarely included in the laymen's complaints against lawlessness. Yet, as we shall see, some of these "hidden" forms of crime are much more costly and serious than the total of "garden variety" crimes.

# 13

# Criminality Among "Respectable Citizens"

## INTRODUCTION

Imagine the case of a suburban resident named John Smith who returns home late in the evening from a weekend excursion, only to discover that the lock on the back door of his house has been broken. Imagine further that he surprises a total stranger inside the house, and that the intruder has a cloth bag filled with silverware and other items belonging to the Smith family. What will Smith do now? In all probability he will call the police, for he senses that he is the victim of a "burglary." The police will have no hesitation about arresting the apprehended stranger, for they recognize a "burglar" when they see one. When the offender is convicted of the crime, he will find the condemnation of the community directed at him, for he is clearly a "criminal person." The same could be said of acts of assault, rape, and various forms of property crime, and of the persons who do these things. These are the kinds of behavior seen by nearly everyone as "crimes." These are usually crude, highly visible attacks upon persons or private property carried on by offenders who are undistinguished in appearance and unknown to the victims. Layman, lawyers, and criminologists rarely ask whether these are "really" crimes or whether the actors are "really" criminals. In legal theory, the crimes described here are termed *mala en se*, in that they are seen as behavioral deviations which are uniformly condemned in the community. Criminal laws regarding these activities are viewed as the formal expression of conduct definitions which are "in the mores." Such crimes stand in contrast to those which are *mala prohibita*, that is, actions which are technically illegal but do not offend basic moral values or common public sentiments.

Is this all there is to crime? Are these nondescript persons who carry out crude actions the sum total of our criminals? What about respectable citizens who engage in "antisocial" or "unethical" conduct? What shall we say about "suede shoe" salesmen who use trickery and deceit in order to sell merchandise to unwary customers? What of violations of antitrust statutes, labor-management regulations, or related rules? Should criminologists concern themselves with such things as fee-splitting and abortions carried on by physicians or with embezzlement of large sums of money by trusted employees? Perhaps a sociological conception of crime should be developed which would focus attention on "socially harmful" conduct, such that all of the above forms of behavior would be subsumed under that conceptual umbrella.

The most prominent development in this direction in the past several decades has centered about the concept of "white collar crime." This term was contrived by E. H. Sutherland to refer to violations by businessmen of laws designed to regulate conduct of business affairs. Used in this fashion, the notion of white collar crime appears to direct attention to a relatively homogeneous form of behavior involving actions undertaken by individuals to contribute to the financial success of the organization. They violate the law *for* the firm. However, as we shall see, the term has been loosely defined and indiscriminately employed since it was first introduced.[1] Even Sutherland failed to employ the notion in a consistent way. The net result is that the label is often attached to such actions as embezzlement, which bear little relationship to violations of regulatory provisions in business. Embezzlers are "enemies within" who surreptitiously steal the assets of the organization and make no contribution to the economic health of the business concern. Many other forms of conduct to which the term has been applied have even less in common with the original meaning of the concept.[2]

Blanket application of a single term to unrelated kinds of activity will not do, just as it would not profit us to attempt to analyze all forms of criminality under a single encompassing label, as though these activities had a good deal in common. Some distinctions must be made regarding unlike forms of behavior by respectable people. These disparate acts must be sorted into relatively homogeneous behavioral units if causal progress is to be made. Incidentally, we use the term "respectable people" merely to draw attention to a group of criminal activities which are not often the target of public condemnation, the persons who carry on these actions not being considered as criminals in the common view. In point of legal fact, the behavior under discussion

---

[1] The conceptual anarchy involved in applications of this term has been discussed by Geis. See Gilbert Geis, "Toward a Delineation of White-Collar Offenses," *Sociological Inquiry*, XXXII (Spring 1962), 160–71.

[2] The concept is used in this way in connection with embezzlement in the popular literature. As a case in point, see Norman Jaspan with Hillel Black, *The Thief in the White Collar* (Philadelphia: J. B. Lippincott Co., 1960); see also Frank Gibney, *The Operators* (New York: Harper & Row, 1960). Illustrations of the loose use of the term in the criminological literature can be found in Donald J. Newman, "White-Collar Crime," *Law and Contemporary Problems*, XXIII (Autumn 1958), 735–53; Herbert A. Bloch and Gilbert Geis, *Man, Crime, and Society* (New York: Random House, Inc., 1962), pp. 379–404.

is illegal and those who engage in it are criminals. From a sociological standpoint, one of the most interesting questions about this criminality concerns the reasons why the conduct does not discredit the perpetrators. How do they stay "respectable" while committing crimes?

In the pages to follow, we will examine several categories of criminality conducted by respectable people. First, we will reserve the term "white collar crime" for violations of business regulations or occupational roles carried on as contributory to the business or occupational enterprise. An offense will be said to be a white collar one insofar as it represents violation of a legal rule constructed to govern business affairs or occupational practice, and insofar as the law violation took place as part of the conduct of regular business or occupational activities. By this definition, misrepresentation in advertising is a white collar crime, embezzlement is not. White collar offenses are also distinguished from the common or conventional crimes of persons of comfortable economic circumstances. Acts of murder, manslaughter, rape, or drunk driving by high status individuals need no special label, and these lawbreakers will not be discussed in this chapter. Another general class of criminality is embezzlement, in which employees are involved in stealing from the organization. This is not a white collar crime because it is not lawbreaking which is a part of regular business practice. Finally, we shall separate from these other matters a group of offenses, such as abortion, engaged in by professional persons. These are discussed as "fringe" violations because they are frequently regarded with some condemnation within the professions in which they occur. These are criminal acts which utilize professional skills, but are occupationally deviant, and are often committed by marginal figures within the professional group. They are usually the endeavors of individuals acting alone, rather than organizational events involving a collection of fellow deviants.[3]

# WHITE COLLAR CRIME

## The White Collar Criminal Role-Career

The discussions of criminality in preceding chapters have begun with descriptions of offender role-careers, organized in terms of definitional and background dimensions. In the case of white collar offenders we

[3] These distinctions were first presented by the author in Don C. Gibbons and Donald L. Garrity, "Definition and Analysis of Certain Criminal Types," *Journal of Criminal Law, Criminology and Police Science*, LIII (March 1962), 34–35; they were elaborated in Don C. Gibbons, *Changing the Lawbreaker* (Englewood Cliffs, N.J.: Prentice-Hall, Inc., 1965), pp. 110–16. Geis has commented on this same matter and suggested that embezzlement should be separated from white collar crime. See Geis, *op. cit.*, 170-71.

shall depart from that format. The brief characterization below amalgamates a series of different claims about these lawbreakers into a two-paragraph sketch. In an earlier book, the author presented the following picture of white collar violators:

White collar crime means those criminal acts in which employees steal or violate the law for the benefit of their employer (although the individual employee may benefit from these violations too). Such crimes as embezzlement represent stealing *from* the employer. The employer does not encourage or sanction such activities, and they are not properly classified as white collar crime. . . . The white collar criminal category is comprised of those persons in business and corporate organizations who violate state and federal regulatory statutes. The violations are usually processed by such federal regulatory agencies as the Federal Trade Commission, the Securities and Exchange Commission, and the Attorney General's office. Informal or civil court disposition of these cases is common, because of the difficulties of criminal prosecution. That is, partly because many of these activities are complex in character, it is often difficult to demonstrate that a clear-cut violation of law has occurred.

"Ignorance of the law" is not, in most cases, an important factor in white collar violations. That is, the offenders were involved in activities which they recognized as illegal or probably illegal. What does appear to be significant in these cases is a process in which business and corporate groups have come to define violations of regulatory statutes as acceptable or necessary conduct. Many white collar criminals acknowledge the moral superiority of regulatory provisions over prevailing business ethics, but legitimacy is withdrawn from these regulatory norms on the grounds that violation of such laws is necessary in order to survive in business, in order to regularize competition, and so on. In other words, it is likely that many white collar violators would prefer to conform to the law, but at the same time, they define the economic situation as demanding deviant conduct. If this line of argument is correct, explanations seeking to locate the genesis of white collar criminal acts in the backgrounds and personalities of the offenders would be misguided. Instead, white collar criminals are normal, conventional persons who come to learn definitions of the situation favorable to violation of law in the course of involvement in business or corporate organization.[4]

### Development of the Concept [5]

Relatively inarticulate observations about the criminality of respectable citizens have been made by a variety of sociologists in the past half-dozen decades. Interest in this phenomenon has also been stimulated by

[4] Don C. Gibbons, *Changing the Lawbreaker, The Treatment of Delinquents and Criminals,* © 1965. Reprinted by permission of Prentice-Hall, Inc., Englewood Cliffs, New Jersey, pp. 111–12.

[5] The origins of the white collar crime concept are briefly discussed in Bloch and Geis, *op. cit.,* p. 380.

recurrent reports in the mass media concerning criminality and unethical conduct by businessmen, professionals, and other high status persons. For example, *Reader's Digest* conducted an informal survey in 1941 of illegal or questionable business tactics among auto repairmen, radio repair men, and automobile mechanics which turned up evidence of widespread "crookedness" on the part of these concerns.[6] In the same way, a former retail furniture salesman has revealed some of the hazards the customer runs in patronizing "borax houses" selling inexpensive furniture.[7] However, Sutherland was the sociologist who turned the behavioral deviations of high status persons into an important sociological category.[8]

Sutherland offered several accounts of what he meant by "white collar crime." In one place, he declared: "white-collar crime may be defined approximately as a crime committed by a person of respectability and high status in the course of his occupation." [9] Another time, he specified that: "The white collar criminal is defined as a person with high socio-economic status who violates the laws designed to regulate his occupational activities." [10] The first of these definitions implies that embezzlers are to be included, while the second suggests that they should not be so designated. In yet another discussion, Sutherland mentioned "robber barons" and other rapacious early figures in American commerce and industry as white collar criminals. He declared that Philip Musica, alias Donald F. Coster, who stole a huge sum of money from the McKesson-Robbins drug company while its president, was a white collar criminal, as were other individuals of this ilk, such as Insull, Kruger, and Sinclair. In that essay, he also named abortions, fee-splitting, political graft, and embezzlement as forms of white collar crime.[11]

Many of those who adopted Sutherland's term to their own uses showed an even more cavalier attitude toward precise definitions. No wonder that a number of critics of this concept have warned that objective analysis of criminality could deteriorate into denunciatory comments by the

[6] This survey is summarized in *ibid.,* pp. 393–94.

[7] Lee Nugent, "Here's How I Gyp You," *Saturday Evening Post* (June 29, 1957), 25–76.

[8] Edwin H. Sutherland, "White Collar Criminality," *American Sociological Review,* V (February 1940), 1–12; Sutherland, "Crime and Business," *Annals of the American Academy of Political and Social Science,* CCXVII (September 1941), 112–18; Sutherland, "Is 'White Collar Crime' Crime?" *American Sociological Review,* X (April 1945), 132–39; Sutherland, "The White Collar Criminal," in *Encyclopedia of Criminology,* ed. Vernon C. Branham and Samuel B. Kutash (New York: Philosophical Library, 1949), pp. 511–15; Sutherland, *White Collar Crime* (New York: The Dryden Press, Inc., 1949); Sutherland, "Crime of Corporations," in *The Sutherland Papers,* ed. Albert Cohen, Alfred Lindesmith, and Karl Schuessler (Bloomington: Indiana University Press, 1956), pp. 78–96.

[9] Sutherland, *White Collar Crime,* p. 9.

[10] Sutherland, "The White Collar Criminal," p. 511.

[11] Sutherland, "White Collar Criminality."

criminologist directed at activities which offend his private sensibilities, but have little or nothing in common with crime.[12] The term might be reduced to a pejorative one, rather than a scientific concept.

Although the concept has been loosely defined, it has not been so recklessly employed in actual research studies. The several major investigations of white collar crime have all directed attention at a relatively consistent body of violations of regulatory provisions designed to control business operations. It seems clear that these are the kinds of behavior to which Sutherland intended the term to apply. At any rate, these are the forms of conduct which we think the concept should properly concern.

### Studies of White Collar Crime

*Sutherland's Research.* Sutherland's investigation of the violations of corporations is probably the best-known study of this kind.[13] He examined the corporate life-histories of the 70 largest manufacturing, mining, and mercantile corporations in the United States, which had been in existence for an average of 45 years. He assembled the data on violations of regulations in the categories of restraint of trade, misrepresentation in advertising, infringement of patents, trademarks, and copyrights, unfair labor practices, rebates, financial fraud, and trust violations, violations of wartime regulations, and certain miscellaneous offenses.

Addressing himself to the question of whether these kinds of behavior represent criminality, he answered in the affirmative. Sutherland's argument was that they constitute crimes because the regulations or rules which they violate meet the two basic criteria of crimes. These statutes and regulations involve: *a*) a legal description of acts as socially injurious, and *b*) legal provision of a penalty for violations.[14] Moreover, he notes that many of the regulatory statutes state explicitly that the forbidden acts are "crimes" or "misdemeanors," while many of the laws have logical roots in the common law, so that false advertising is an extension of common law fraud. Sutherland was forced to concede that the criminal status of certain of these activities was in question. In the instance of patent, trademark, and copyright infringements, some forms of infringement are not explicitly defined in federal statutes as crimes, nor are criminal penalties, such as punitive damages, provided in the laws. Sutherland admitted that of 222 decisions on infringements in-

[12] A good resumé of the controversy surrounding this concept can be found in Frank E. Hartung, "A Critique of the Sociological Approach to Crime and Correction," *Law and Contemporary Problems*, XXIII (Autumn 1958), 722–25.

[13] Sutherland, *White Collar Crime.*

[14] Sutherland, "Is 'White Collar Crime' Crime?"; Sutherland, "The White Collar Criminal," p. 511; Sutherland, *White Collar Crime*, pp. 29–55.

cluded in his data, 201 appeared not to constitute acts of criminality.[15]

Records of the corporations regarding violations of law indicated that the 70 had been involved over their organizational lifetimes in 980 violations (including the 201 infringement cases above). The most "criminal" corporation had been implicated in 50 decisions, while the least "criminal" had been involved in a single decision. These organizations had an average of 14 adverse decisions in their careers.

Differential implementation of the law emerged most strikingly from the corporation records, in that only 158 (16 per cent) of the 980 decisions had been reached in criminal courts. In other words, only 16 per cent of these cases were "crimes" in the technical sense that they had been so labeled in a criminal tribunal. Of the rest, 425 had been reached in civil or equity courts, and 397 had been produced informally through commission orders or other procedures.[16] In Sutherland's view, the use of civil or informal, rather than criminal, proceedings against business organizations is related to the high status of businessmen, the general trend away from harsh punishments, and relatively unorganized public resentment regarding these activities.[17]

*The Black Market.* Another major collection of findings regarding white collar crime is in Clinard's study of World War II black market operations.[18] Like Sutherland, he felt compelled to defend labeling as "crime" the violations of rationing and economic control regulations imposed during the war. Clinard argued that nearly all of these rules defined the relevant behavior as offenses and allowed criminal penalties to be utilized in case of violations. However, the criminal status of certain of the behavioral forms which Clinard studied is not clear, as, for example, civil rule violations that were unintentional and to which criminal sanctions were not applied. Additionally, the criminal status is ambiguous in certain violations of administrative orders of governmental agencies, rather than statutory rules, which were handled under contempt proceedings.[19]

However one might label the activities studied by Clinard, the rules that were violated were clearly required during wartime. He makes a convincing case for the importance of these regulations in maintaining an equitable distribution of scarce goods and minimizing the long-term

[15] Sutherland, *White Collar Crime,* pp. 36–38, p. 95.

[16] *Ibid.,* pp. 22–25.

[17] *Ibid.,* p. 46.

[18] Marshall B. Clinard, *The Black Market* (New York: Holt, Rinehart and Winston, Inc., 1952); Clinard, "Criminological Theories of Violations of Wartime Regulations," *American Sociological Review,* XI (June 1946), 258–70.

[19] Clinard, *The Black Market,* pp. 226–63.

costs of the war.[20] He shows that violations of these regulations were so widespread that the war effort was jeopardized on more than one occasion. For example, during a nine-month period in 1944–1945, counterfeit gasoline stamps involving 88 million gallons of gas were discovered, along with stamps for great quantities of rationed sugar and meat.[21] Price ceiling violations, tie-in sales, and mislabeling and quality violations were similarly commonplace.

How are these violations of law to be explained in the face of strong public support for price controls and rationing during wartime? [22] Who were the offenders who engaged in these violations? According to Clinard, the black market offenders were principally conventional businessmen, many of whom were carrying on forms of business conduct closely akin to tactics they had used prior to wartime and the imposition of controls. The major exception, in which conventional criminals were involved, was the counterfeiting of rationing stamps.[23] Clinard attributed these law violations to a combination of factors, one of which was the generally lenient penalties handed out for violations. These were not sufficient to act as a deterrent to illegality.[24] He also maintained that the process of differential association among businessmen, in which group support was provided for hostile attitudes toward the regulations, was a major determinant of lawbreaking. He was also of the persuasion that personality differences among businessmen must have played some part in their behavior, for some disobeyed the laws while others, similarly situated in the world of business affairs, refrained from violations.[25]

*Hartung's Study.* The third investigation in this survey was conducted by Hartung and concerned violations of wartime regulations in the wholesale meat industry in Detroit.[26] Between 1942 and 1946, 122 cases of price violations and other illegal acts were processed by regulatory agencies in Detroit. Only two of the offenders had prior records of criminality, so these were predominantly acts of lawbreaking by respectable businessmen. The offenders paid $132,811 in damages and nearly $100,000 in fines, while a few were given jail terms as well. A major conclusion from this investigation centers about the discrepancy between

[20] *Ibid.*, pp. 1–7.
[21] *Ibid.*, pp. 28–50.
[22] *Ibid.*, pp. 89–114.
[23] *Ibid.*, pp. 156–63.
[24] *Ibid.*, pp. 151–53.
[25] *Ibid.*, pp. 285–389. See also Clinard, "Criminological Theories of Violations of Wartime Regulations," 267–70. In that essay, he indicated that the size of the firm was unrelated to rates of violation.
[26] Frank E. Hartung, "White-Collar Offenses in the Wholesale Meat Industry in Detroit," *American Journal of Sociology,* LVI (July 1950), 25–32.

the generally lenient penalties invoked and the seriousness of the activities, measured in monetary terms and other ways as well.

### Is "White Collar Crime" Crime?

The relatively strict definition of white collar crime embodied in the three studies above and contained in the perspective of this book has come under a barrage of critical attack, separate from that directed at the more omnibus usages of the term. There are those who would exclude study of violations of regulatory statutes in business from criminological attention.[27] Tappan has sometimes been identified as one of these abolitionists, although he has disclaimed some of the views attributed to him. His critical fire has been focused upon those who would make white collar crime the study of "unethical" or "immoral" behavior, much of it outside legal codes. He has declared:

> The author wishes to make it clear here, since there has been some misconstruction of his view in literature on the subject, that he believes white-collar crime, properly and precisely defined, to be not only a legitimate but an important phase of criminological inquiry. He deplores the loosely normative connotations that have been attached to the concept by some of Sutherland's interpreters, and he believes that they have resulted in some confusion so far as needed empirical research in this area is concerned.[28]

Caldwell is another critic of white collar criminologists. Several of his remarks are not entirely clear, but one does have merit. He pointed out that decisions of civil courts and administrative agencies are often arrived at by procedures which have less regard for strict due process than do criminal court proceedings. Consequently, there is occasionally some question as to whether the actions processed in these ways would have been declared criminal if they had been dealt with in a criminal court.[29] These remarks underscore the persistent ambiguity inherent in the phenomenon of white collar crime, even when it is carefully defined.

One of the most well-known attacks on the narrow conception of white collar crime is that of Burgess, which we noted in Chapter Two. In a comment on the research of Hartung, Burgess maintained that meat

---

[27] A good discussion of these criticisms, as well as rejoinders to them, may be found in Donald R. Cressey, Foreword to 1961 edition of Sutherland, *White Collar Crime* (New York: Holt, Rinehart and Winston, Inc., 1961); see also Newman, *op. cit.*

[28] Paul W. Tappan, *Crime, Justice and Correction* (New York: McGraw-Hill Book Co., Inc., 1960), p. 7.

[29] Robert G. Caldwell, "A Reexamination of the Concept of White-Collar Crime," *Federal Probation*, XXII (March 1958), 30–36.

violations were not crimes because the offenders did not define themselves as criminals, nor did the public so regard them. Moreover, he held that the regulations were not supported by the mores, so little social condemnation was directed at the violators. He also said these were not crimes because great numbers of citizens were involved in them.[30] Burgess offered the opinion that these may have been criminal acts in legalistic but not in sociological terms, for: "A criminal is a person who regards himself as a criminal and is so regarded by society. He is the product of the criminal-making process." [31] Most of these factual contentions of Burgess are highly questionable; for example, Hartung notes that many people did, in fact, support price controls in wartime.[32] As we will see later on, there is also evidence that white collar offenders do view themselves as implicated in wrongful and criminal conduct. But even if Burgess had been correct in these assertions about white collar crime, the general conception of crime and criminals he promoted must be declared nonsense. There are countless offenders in prison who do not think of themselves as criminals, although they are so regarded by some citizens. Are we to declare that they are not criminals? What is the "criminal-making process" of which Burgess speaks? Probably the clearest example would be the judicial process through which lawbreakers get tagged as criminals! There seems to be no single process through which law violators are manufactured. In summary, to follow this advice of Burgess' would be to enter a conceptual maze from which one might never escape.

A second complaint that white collar crime is somehow not "real" crime is that of Vold, who has argued that these activities are not condemned by the mores, so they are not resented by the public. Vold has declared: "There is an obvious and basic incongruity involved in the proposition that a community's leaders and more responsible elements are also its criminals." [33] We readily agree that the situation of high-status persons committing acts of criminality does seem incongruous. Vold would have us define these activities out of criminology. But our suggestion would be that the low visibility of such crimes, lack of their social condemnation, and the ability of offenders to maintain positions of social prestige while violating the law all represent critical matters for inquiry, rather than topics to be conceptually jettisoned from criminological study.

[30] Ernest W. Burgess, "Comment," *American Journal of Sociology,* LVI (July 1950), 32–33; Hartung, *op. cit.;* Hartung, "Rejoinder," *loc. cit.,* 33–34; Burgess, "Concluding Comment," *loc. cit.,* 34.

[31] Burgess, "Concluding Comment."

[32] Hartung, "Rejoinder."

[33] George B. Vold, *Theoretical Criminology* (New York: Oxford University Press, 1958), p. 253.

## Some Other Views

Our position that the ambiguities of business violations, differential treatment of these activities, and so on, are fundamental problems for criminological analysis rather than matters to be disposed of by exclusion is shared by a number of others. Newman has argued that we should examine the problems of value conflicts, power relations, social control, and other matters revealed in white collar crime.[34] Aubert has made much the same judgment, advising:

> For purposes of theoretical analysis it is of prime importance to develop and apply concepts which preserve and emphasize the ambiguous nature of the white-collar crimes and not to "solve" the problem by classifying them as either "crimes" or "not crimes." Their controversial nature is exactly what makes them so interesting from a sociological point of view and what gives us a clue to important norm conflicts, clashing group interests, and maybe incipient social change.[35]

Aubert has illustrated the kinds of research which he believes white collar crime demands. In one study of the attitudes of Norwegian businessmen toward regulatory statutes, he found that they held allegiance in principle to law-abiding conduct, but also felt a commitment to the special norms of the business group which defined law violations of business regulations as acceptable behavior. In another case, he examined the character of a new Norwegian law governing the working conditions of domestic help. He found that the law provided criminal sanctions but was practically unenforceable due to the private nature of the violations. The law was a legislative hybrid, designed to pacify several interest groups who were making divergent demands on the lawmakers.[36]

Geis has recently echoed some of these same sentiments with a call for more attention to the analytical problems embodied in white collar crime.[37] Although he contended that the concept of white collar crime is valuable, he noted that a number of improvements in its application are in order. There is a pressing need for separate studies of relatively homogeneous forms of business crime within the encompassing class of white collar offenses. Closer attention to internal variations would involve exploration of forms of corporate organization, patterns of corporate

[34] Newman, op. cit.

[35] Vilhelm Aubert, "White-Collar Crime and Social Structure," American Journal of Sociology, LVIII (November 1952), 266.

[36] Ibid., pp. 268–70.

[37] Geis, op. cit.

ethics, differential involvement of corporation officials in lawbreaking, and so on. The general theme is that white collar analysis has tended to make uncritical generalizations about the behavior of corporations as entities, without sufficient awareness of variations in the internal workings of these organizations.[38] What is needed is not more epidemiological documentation of the extent of white collar crimes; causal analysis is in order, in which the detailed morphology of business crime would be investigated.

Geis made much of the facts regarding the electrical conspiracy case revealed in 1961, for these tell us a good deal about the complex character of lawbreaking in corporate organizations.[39] This was a fantastically intricate pattern of business activity, so we might profit from a look at it.

The electrical conspiracy case refers to an antitrust criminal action taken by the federal government against 29 corporations and 45 corporation officials who had conspired to rig bids on electrical products and carry out other price-fixing schemes. The individual defendants were found guilty, a number were given jail terms, and the fines levied by the court totaled nearly two million dollars. General Electric received a $337,500 fine, while Westinghouse was fined $72,500. Additionally, these concerns are liable to civil actions by victims seeking recovery of the illegal profits.[40]

Smith has devoted detailed attention to the workings of the conspiracy within General Electric. He indicated that the price-fixing was no new innovation, for the circuit-breaker division of General Electric had been involved in price-rigging for about 25 years before the criminal action was filed.[41] In his view, one of the conditions which led to price-fixing in that corporation was the decentralization inaugurated in 1950. The corporation was broken into 27 autonomous divisions made up of 110 small companies, thus reducing surveillance of the corporation from the top of the organizational hierarchy. There were a number of "collusionists" among the corporation executives who looked upon antitrust violations as illegal, but necessary for economic survival and not unethical. Most of them engaged in conspiratorial tactics with reluctance, but felt that the erratic features of the electrical business demanded that they

[38] Ibid., 161–68. Another statement which takes Sutherland to task for uncritical discussions of corporations as "criminal," as though they represented homogeneous entities, is Thomas I. Emerson, book review, Yale Law Journal, LIX (February 1950), 581–85.

[39] Richard Austin Smith, "The Incredible Electrical Conspiracy," Part I, Fortune, LXIII (April 1961), 132–218; Part II, LXIII (May 1961), 161–224. See also John Herling, The Great Price Conspiracy: The Story of the Antitrust Violations in the Electrical Industry (Washington, D.C.: Robert B. Luce, Inc., 1962).

[40] Smith, op. cit., Part I, pp. 132–34.

[41] Ibid., Part I, p. 137.

violate the law in order to stabilize the market. There is little question that they were clearly aware of the illegal nature of their activities, for they took great precautions to conduct their conspiratorial affairs in secrecy and to disguise their activities. At the same time, there were other company officials who refused to engage in price-fixing, holding that such practices were clearly unethical. The picture of the corporation as a monolith of like-minded individuals is undermined by these observations.[42] Examples of corporation officials who were either ignorant of the conspiracy or refused to participate in it were also observed in other of the corporations.[43]

There is more to the explanation of price-fixing in this case than the association of criminally-inclined executives. Smith indicates that there were variations in the extent of lawbreaking in different parts of the corporation, and fluctuations in the degree of criminality within organizational units as well. During several periods of "white sale" waves of discounting prices, pressures to engage in price stabilization became particularly acute. The price-rigging conspiracies were revived at these times after they had been relatively dormant.[44]

In a final comment on this price-fixing case, Smith argued:

The problem for American business does not start and stop with the scofflaws of the electrical industry or with anti-trust. Much was made of the fact that G.E. operated under a system of disjointed authority, and this was one reason it got into trouble. A more significant factor, the disjointment of morals, is something for American executives to think about in all aspects of their relations with their companies, each other, and the community.[45]

### The Ethics of Businessmen

Some other pieces of evidence exist on the question of business ethics, corporate organization, and allied matters. Lane studied patterns of labor relations violations and misrepresentation cases in the New England shoe industry.[46] One of the issues he examined was the question of ignorance of the law as a factor of criminality. His findings suggest that this is not a major consideration, for shoe manufacturing concerns with the largest employee groups were more involved in lawbreaking than those with

42 *Ibid.*, Part I, pp. 134–35.
43 Geis, *op. cit.*, pp. 168–69.
44 Smith, *op. cit.*, Part I, 132–218.
45 *Ibid.*, Part II, p. 224.
46 Robert E. Lane, "Why Business Men Violate the Law," *Journal of Criminal Law, Criminology and Police Science*, XLIV (July–August 1953), 151–65. See this article for further data on the extent of white collar offenses.

fewer workers. This is the reverse of what would be expected if ignorance plays a part in violations, in that large firms can avail themselves of more legal counsel and advice than small ones, and should thus be better able to maintain a law-abiding record.[47] Some support for a differential association interpretation of law violations was found, for Lane observed that violation rates varied from community to community. Moreover, many of the individuals implicated in law violations were also ones who read materials hostile toward governmental regulations. Finally, illegality was more common in smaller manufacturing towns, where businessmen with antiregulatory attitudes might conceivably be in common contact with each other.[48] In another publication dealing at length with the attitudes and values of businessmen, Lane contended that an older business ideology involving such beliefs as the sacredness of private enterprise and the inalienable rights of industry has been undermined, without a newer ethical code taking complete form. Accordingly, hostility toward business regulations may be a transitional stage, to be succeeded by a revised ethical system.[49]

A second study of the ethical standards of businessmen is by Baumhart, involving a sample of 1700 executives in various business organizations in the United States.[50] These officials were given a detailed questionnaire which probed a variety of matters having to do with ethical beliefs and practices in business. Although much of the behavior reported in that study had to do with activities and practices which were not clearly illegal, the responses shed considerable light on the question of antiregulatory attitudes of businessmen as a factor in white collar crime.

Some of the major findings of this study were these: first, most businessmen verbalized sentiments of general concern for ethical business behavior. Nearly all said that businessmen should be concerned with goals additional to profit-making, while 85 per cent declared that a manager who operates solely in terms of his stockholders' interests would be unethical. Only about 20 per cent agreed with the principle of *caveat emptor*, or "Let the buyer beware." Nearly all said that use of call girls as a business tactic or "padding" of expense accounts would be clearly unethical.

However, many of these executives disagreed on the specifics of "ethical" or "unethical" conduct. Moreover, many of them professed a

[47] *Ibid.,* pp. 155–58.

[48] *Ibid.,* pp. 158–61.

[49] Robert E. Lane, *The Regulation of Businessmen* (New Haven, Conn.: Yale University Press, 1954).

[50] Raymond C. Baumhart, "How Ethical are Businessmen?" *Harvard Business Review,* XXXIX (July–August 1961), 6–176.

higher level of ethical aspiration and conduct for themselves than they were willing to concede for the "average businessman." Baumhart argued that the judgments made about the probable behavior of other executives are probably closer to the actual conduct of affairs in business than are the claims these people make about themselves. In other words, it may be that the executives put forth an exaggerated picture of themselves, reporting on the kind of organizational official they would prefer to be rather than the kind they actually represent.[51]

These officials not only expressed considerable cynicism about the ethical behavior of other organizational executives, in addition many of them asserted that unethical practices, many of which are also illegal, were widespread. Although the practices varied from one industry to another, the use of call girls, granting of gratuities, price violations, and dishonest advertising were among those often identified as common in industry.

The responses of the officials in this study suggest that one major influence determining the degree of unethical behavior in organizations is the model of conduct set by those at the top of the executive pyramid. The "behavior of company superiors" was ranked as the most important variable making for ethical or unethical conduct. Baumhart employed an "organization man" kind of theory to interpret these results, arguing that organizations vary in the degree to which individual executives are in differential association with carriers of unethical beliefs or practices.[52] Interestingly, the majority of the persons studied argued that an industry-wide ethical code would be desirable as a means of reducing unethical activities, but they favored systems of code enforcement without "teeth," such as self-policing within the industry. Only about 4 per cent of them thought that a government agency should have charge of enforcing a code of ethics.[53]

### White Collar Crime and Public Opinion

We have seen a common contention advanced that white collar crime is not really crime because the public does not regard it as criminality. We also observed that certain studies of citizen opinion, particularly with regard to wartime rationing and price control regulations, indicated that these laws were supported and violations of them condemned by citizens. More attention is needed on this critical question, as a part of the broader interest in public attitudes toward laws in general. Chapter Two

[51] *Ibid.*, pp. 16–19.
[52] *Ibid.*, pp. 156–57.
[53] *Ibid.*, pp. 166–72.

drew attention to one illustrative case of the kind of research required.[54] Newman examined laymen's views of violations of the Federal Food, Drug and Cosmetic Act of 1938. In this investigation, a sample of citizens was asked to select the punishments thought appropriate in cases of product misbranding and food adulteration. Their selections were then compared to the penalties actually invoked in the cases studied. About 80 per cent of the consumer respondents felt that the penalties for these offenses should have been more severe than the ones which were levied. At the same time, the citizens favored sanctions that were less harsh than those used for such conventional crimes as burglary. In general, their penalty choices were within the range of punishments allowable in existing statutes. Thus it seems that these citizens were generally satisfied with existing legislation, and their dissatisfaction was with the administration of the statutes.

### Concluding Comment

It must be clear that this book is allied with that group of criminological arguments which favor examination of white collar crime. The commentary above has stressed a number of complex problems which will continue to plague investigation of this kind of criminal conduct. For example, we will continue to find instances of business or occupational behavior which are not clearly criminal or noncriminal, owing to the administrative procedures by which the activity was handled, the complexity of the behavior, and other factors. But these difficulties should not be "solved" by excluding them from scrutiny. Instead, careful attention to such matters as clear specification of categories of business behavior should go some distance in allowing us to make progress in the study of white collar crime. A number of the pieces of research cited in the preceding pages stand as models of the kind of inquiry which must be pursued in criminology.

One other point ought to be made before leaving this topic. Throughout most of the preceding passages, we have spoken of business and occupational offenses as making up white collar crime. Nearly all of the empirical evidence on this kind of lawbreaking has centered about the behavior of corporations and large businesses. But there is no logical reason why the deviant acts of professional persons and workers in small-scale occupational settings should not also be studied. One case of this sort of research is provided by Quinney's investigation of prescription

[54] Donald J. Newman, "Public Attitudes Toward a Form of White Collar Crime," *Social Problems*, IV (January 1957), 228–32.

violations among retail pharmacists.[55] He studied the extent and nature of prescription law violations among druggists in Albany, New York. Twenty pharmacists who had been detected in prescription violations were compared with another group of 60 druggists who had not been so involved.

Quinney points out that retail pharmacy combines elements of both a professional and a business pursuit, so the druggist should experience some degree of role strain as a consequence. He identified four role-orientations among the pharmacists he studied: some saw themselves as professionals, some as businessmen, some as involved in both roles, and a few were indifferent to these matters. Prescription violations were significantly related to the role-orientations of the druggists, in that 75 per cent of the business-oriented persons had commited violations, while none of the professionally-oriented had. Generally, the more professionally-oriented the pharmacist, the lower the likelihood of occupational deviance. Quinney contends that the professional orientation of the druggists provided internal social controls which constrained them from deviant activity, while the business-oriented persons were not influenced by these standards. Quinney suggests that the same phenomena of role strains and deviant conduct might be expected to be found in other professions and occupations, such as dentistry, optometry, chiropody, osteopathy, real estate, and accounting, which combine elements of business and profession.

## EMBEZZLEMENT AND EMBEZZLERS [56]

The opening remarks of this chapter characterized embezzlers as "enemies within" who are engaged in financial subversion, rather than organizational warriors who make positive contributions to the business firm or concern. These are furtive and secretive enemies, the extent of their surreptitious deviations almost impossible to identify with much accuracy. Instead, wildly divergent estimates of the total financial cost of employee pilfering and embezzlement have been advanced. But one thing is clear—these employee-thieves are responsible for huge financial losses incurred by the organization.

One indication of the magnitude of this kind of crime has been provided by Jaspan, who noted that thefts and embezzlements by employees may total more than $4,000,000 per day in the United States. He also

[55] Earl R. Quinney, "Occupational Structure and Criminal Behavior: Prescription Violation by Retail Pharmacists," *Social Problems*, XI (Fall 1963), 179–85.

[56] A detailed bibliography of studies on embezzlement can be found in Donald R. Cressey, *Other People's Money* (New York: Free Press of Glencoe, Inc., 1953), pp. 159–66.

indicated that bonded losses from thefts in 1946 amounted to $13,000,000, while in 1957 such losses totaled $35,000,000. The significance of these figures is that only about 10 per cent of the private business firms in the United States are covered by theft insurance, so the total losses must have been greatly in excess of these figures.[57] Jaspan also observed that his own business protective agency unearthed $60,000,000 of employee dishonesty in 1959 alone; again, this kind of deviant activity must be extensive indeed.[58] Jaspan's account on employees who steal is filled with case history documents which seem to show that dishonest workers are an extremely varied bag of individuals who steal out of a diverse set of motives.

Another well-researched statement on embezzlement and theft set the amount of employee larcenies at $500,000,000 in 1956, but also indicated that some experts regard this figure as too low, contending that the losses from employee criminality are probably in excess of one billion dollars per year.[59] One expert has claimed that the total cost of this kind of crime is nearer three billion dollars than these lower estimates. A figure against which to gauge the importance of these amounts is an F.B.I. estimate that the total loss from burglaries, armed robberies, auto thefts, and incidents of pickpocket activity was only about $440,000,000 in 1956. Employees steal at least twice this amount from their employers. This same discussion noted that embezzlement is a crime of growing magnitude, for fidelity insurance losses increased by about 250 per cent between 1946 and 1956, although insurance in force grew only by about 70 per cent. This article pointed out that bank losses through misappropriations of funds have been increasing steadily in recent decades. In 1951, the Federal Deposit Insurance Corporation had 608 reports of defalcations in insured banks, involving 759 employees from various employee levels.[60] These figures would be considerably higher at the present. A final set of estimates of this sort can be taken from Cameron's work on shoplifting. She indicated that 12 department stores in New York City set their losses from shoplifting and employee pilferage combined at ten million dollars in 1951. She also noted that store protection agencies estimate that thefts by employees make up three-fourths of all the "inventory shrinkage" suffered by stores.[61] One writer has argued that the increase in employee criminality is linked to

[57] Jaspan, op. cit., p. 234.

[58] Ibid., p. 10.

[59] "Embezzlers, the Trusted Thieves," Fortune, LVI (November 1957), 142–88.

[60] Marshall B. Clinard, The Sociology of Deviant Behavior (rev. ed.; New York: Holt, Rinehart and Winston, Inc., 1963), p. 268.

[61] Mary Owen Cameron, The Booster and the Snitch (New York: Free Press of Glencoe, Inc., 1964), pp. 9–11.

the changing "scale" of modern societal organization, growing impersonality within organizations, and attenuation of attitudes which hold
wealth to be sacred.[62] Whatever the causes, the findings above indicate
that respectable employees who are involved in stealing from their
employers are legion.

## THE EMBEZZLER ROLE-CAREER [63]

### Definitional Dimensions

*Offense Behavior.* This type involves persons who violate positions of
trust by stealing from an employer, excluding those emoplyees who pilfer
small amounts of merchandise. The embezzler is an employee who converts a large sum of his employer's money to his own uses, usually through
some form of alteration of business records.

*Interactional Setting.* The interactional setting of embezzlement is one
in which the violator ostensibly performs a conventional occupational
task while, in secrecy, he engages in criminal acts. The embezzler takes
great pains to keep his illegal activities minimally visible. Normally, the
criminal actions of the embezzler are unknown to the employer, the
spouse of the offender, and other associates of the deviant.

*Self-concept.* The embezzler exhibits a noncriminal self-image, but
shows relatively elaborate rationalizations for his conduct when discovered in embezzlement. These often include allegations that he was
only "borrowing" the money, not stealing it. It appears that such rationalizations are contrived by the offender *before* he begins to embezzle.
They allow him to square deviant activities with his self-image as a
law-abiding person. When the embezzler is sent to prison upon conviction, he is likely to argue that, unlike the other inmates, he is not a
"real" criminal.

*Attitudes.* The embezzler is characterized by conventional, prosocial
attitudes. The offender indicates that he acknowledges the "bad" character of such acts, but has rationalizations which excuse him from
culpability for these "bad" and "evil" actions.

*Role-career.* The embezzler is normally a person without any delinquent or criminal record prior to involvement in embezzlement. One
reason is, of course, that persons with criminal records are not able to
obtain positions of trust in the first place. A great many detected em-

[62] David Cort, "The Embezzler," *The Nation*, CLXXXVIII (April 18, 1959), 339–42.
[63] Don C. Gibbons, *Changing the Lawbreaker, The Treatment of Delinquents and Criminals*,
© 1965. Reprinted by permission of Prentice-Hall, Inc., Englewood Cliffs, New Jersey, pp. 114–16.

bezzlers are dealt with informally by their employers or by bonding agencies, so that only a small and perhaps biased sample is handled within criminal courts. Those offenders who are convicted and sentenced to institutions tend to make a good adjustment in that setting. Upon release, further violations of the law are unlikely. However, it is probable that many paroled embezzlers find readjustment to civilian society somewhat difficult insofar as their criminal records create impediments for them. A paroled embezzler is likely to have some trouble obtaining another position of trust.

### Background Dimensions

*Social Class.* Embezzlers tend as a group to be persons from relatively comfortable, middle class backgrounds.

*Family Background.* The parental background of the embezzler appears to be of little significance in the explanation of deviation. Embezzlers do not develop out of any specific parent-child interaction pattern. On the other hand, the offender's adult family pattern does have some significance, for some of his "nonshareable" problems, often described as "wine, women, and song" difficulties, relate to patterns of family activity. It is likely that many acts of embezzlement develop as attempts to sustain a standard of living and to live according to a pattern of expectations for which legitimate income is insufficient.

*Peer Group Associations.* The peer associations of embezzlers are of little significance in the development of this behavior. Such offenders do not learn attitudes favorable to embezzlement or how to embezzle from their associates. Peer associations may play some part in embezzlement in that the offender is unable to communicate about certain "nonshareable" problems with his peers.

*Contact with Defining Agencies.* Contacts with the police, courts, and correctional agencies do not seem to be highly significant for embezzlers. In prison, the embezzler is regarded by other inmates as a "square John." He associates differentially with other "square Johns," and such associations tend to reinforce the offender's conception of himself as a law-abiding citizen.

### Some Evidence

The typological description of embezzlers describes individuals who steal relatively large sums of money, often in increments over an extended time period. The typological sketch said nothing about other employees who pilfer small amounts and often steal only once or twice. One major reason for emphasizing the serious cases of embezzlement is that a more complex concatenation of events may be required to produce this form of conduct than is the case in petty thefts. Large-scale embezzlements may be responses to emergency situations faced by the actor, while pilfering may often be spur-of-the-moment behavior. Perhaps workers who carry away small items or petty amounts of cash do not face a major social-psychological problem of reconciling this conduct with their conception of self, for they may be able to dismiss it as innocuous and "not really criminal." The large-scale thief may go through a more elaborate process of contriving face-saving rationalizations. A second reason for the stress on costly embezzlement is that most of the data from which the typological characterization has been drawn are based on major cases of trust violation.

One thing quite clear with regard to embezzlement is that it is a form of illegality which rarely results in criminal prosecution. Hall has suggested that only about 1 per cent of the cases of trust violation are dealt with as criminal actions.[64] He enumerated a number of factors responsible for infrequent prosecution, one of which is the embezzler's deviation in appearance and demeanor from the stereotype of the "crook" or "bad guy." In addition, organizations fear adverse public reactions to "cold-hearted" companies which prosecute their employees. Management often feels some loyalty to the worker, particularly if he is an "old-timer." Along a similar line, the actor's lawbreaking is often related to a dire emergency he faces, so the embezzler is often the beneficiary of sympathetic understanding. Still other factors include costs and uncertainty associated with prosecutions, as well as the difficulties of obtaining restitution. Finally, according to Hall, too much scrutiny of employee behavior may throw unwelcome investigative light into other dark corners and turn up evidence of peccadilloes by management.[65]

Several studies of embezzlers have been conducted, one of which was by Redden.[66] She examined 7629 cases from fidelity insurance company records and classified them into a half-dozen commonsensical categories, including such types as "the little-fellow embezzler," "the grab-and-run-embezzler," and so on.

The best sociological study of embezzlers to date was carried out by Cressey.[67] In his opening comments, Cressey distinguished between investigations of *systematic* and *genetic* causation. Systematic causation refers to a definable conjuncture of events operating at the time of an

[64] Jerome Hall, *Theft, Law and Society* (2nd ed.; Indianapolis: Bobbs-Merrill Co., Inc., 1952), pp. 304–6.
[65] *Ibid.*, pp. 306–12.
[66] Elizabeth Redden, *Embezzlement: A Study of One Kind of Criminal Behavior with Prediction Tables Based on Fidelity Insurance Records* (Doctoral dissertation, University of Chicago, 1939).
[67] Cressey, *Other People's Money.*

offense. It is the person-situation complex in existence just preceding a deviant act; an example might be drinking and quarreling which eventuates in a husband-wife assault case. Genetic causation refers to the prior life experiences which have propelled the individual into his present circumstances. In the case of trust violators, the study of systematic causation asks: "What goes on at about the time a person embezzles?" while genetic investigations probe into the early life experiences which may produce a "budding grifter" or an individual predisposed to thievery.[68] Cressey identified his inquiry as a case of systematic etiology.

Cressey employed the method of analytic induction, in which hypotheses are formulated and then examined in application to a group of embezzlers. These hypotheses are rejected if found defective, until a hypothesis is discovered which accounts for the cases under study.[69] Although the research began as a study of embezzlement, it was quickly changed to an investigation of "criminal violation of financial trust." Cressey discovered that some persons in his group of 133 prisoners from Joliet Prison, Illinois, Chino in California, and the federal penitentiary at Terre Haute, Indiana, who were charged with embezzlement had actually been involved in such offenses as confidence swindles. In order for a subject to be included in the study as a violator of financial trust, he must have accepted a position of trust in good faith and then violated that trust by criminality.[70] Note that "criminal violation of financial trust" is not a category derived from statutory law. It is behavioral, and groups together similar individuals who may have been formally charged with a variety of specific offenses.

Cressey rejected several initial formulations about the dynamics of trust violation, including one that violations occur when employees learn that theft is defined as acceptable behavior within the organization. Another hypothesis which failed the test of evidence was that violations of trust take place when individuals experience financial emergencies. Some offenders had encountered grave financial difficulties earlier in their occupational careers, but had not "solved" these by theft. The final version of Cressey's generalization about embezzlement is: "Trusted persons become trust violators when they conceive of themselves as having a financial problem which is nonshareable, are aware that this problem can be secretly resolved by violation of the position of financial trust, and are able to apply to their own conduct in that situation verbalizations

[68] *Ibid.,* pp. 12–14.

[69] *Ibid.,* pp. 13–17. For criticisms of this method, see Ralph H. Turner, "The Quest for Universals in Sociological Research," *American Sociological Review,* XVIII (December 1953), 604–11; W. S. Robinson, "The Logical Structure of Analytic Induction," *American Sociological Review,* XVI (December 1961), 812–18.

[70] Cressey, *Other People's Money,* pp. 19–26.

which enable them to adjust their conceptions of themselves as trusted persons with their conceptions as users of the entrusted funds or property." [71] The entire process must occur before trust violation takes place.

Two major ingredients in this process can be underscored—the role of *nonshareable* problems in trust violation and the development of justificatory rationalizations *in advance* of the deviant act. Cressey's concept of nonshareable problems is an inclusive label for a plethora of difficulties about which the actor cannot communicate to others, so he cannot resolve them by legitimate means. One kind of nonshareable problem centers about the sort of activity which the layman calls "booze, bookies, and blondes," in which an individual gets entangled in unconventional or discrediting experiences which must be kept hidden from others. Many of Cressey's subjects had nonshareable problems which involved attempts to "live up to one's position," as in the case of bank employees who felt compelled to affect styles of living for which their incomes were not adequate. In general, most of the problems of the trust violators related to status-seeking or status-maintaining behaviors which created financial problems for them.[72]

Cressey's analysis of the role of rationalizations in trust violation represents a major contribution to etiological understanding. His point is that these justificatory arguments must be developed *before* embezzlement can occur, which is markedly different from conventional views of rationalizations. He asserts:

> The rationalizations which are used by trust violators are necessary and essential to criminal violation of trust. They are not merely *ex post facto* justifications for conduct which already has been enacted, but are pertinent and real "reasons" which the person has for acting. When the relationship between a personal non-shareable problem and the position of trust is perceived according to the bias induced by the presence of a rationalization which makes trust violation in some way justified, trust violation results.[73]

The significance of this argument extends well beyond trust violation. It is likely that the process wherein actors develop rationalizations before they engage in deviance also occurs in other forms of lawbreaking. Sykes and Matza have contended that juvenile delinquents contrive neutralizing beliefs which allow them to violate norms which they uphold in principle. These techniques of neutralization precede deviant activities rather than follow from them.[74]

[71] *Ibid.*, p. 30.
[72] *Ibid.*, pp. 33–76.
[73] *Ibid.*, pp. 136–37.
[74] Gresham M. Sykes and David Matza, "Techniques of Neutralization: A Theory of Delinquency," *American Sociological Review*, XXII (December 1957), 664–70.

Critics of Cressey's generalizations have stressed several points thought to be defects in his work. Schuessler has complained that one can hardly imagine an adequate test of the argument, for a cross-section of the general population would have to be examined. In that way, it might be possible to determine whether all individuals who have nonshareable problems and appropriate rationalizations engage in trust violations.[75] Clinard has also expressed disappointment with Cressey's research, arguing that some of Cressey's techniques were questionable. However, his major contention is that the behavioral sequence described lacks predictive meaning. We can only predict occurrence of trust violation at the moment that the complete process has transpired. Clinard contends that other studies could perhaps discover particular personality configurations or social situations which are indicators of the onset of trust violation, and would be operative some time prior to trust violation.[76] But it may well be that Clinard is in error. Perhaps trust violation is a kind of criminality in which genetic and systematic aspects of causation merge into a single process. There may not be any clear-cut personality dynamics that predispose persons to embezzlement, so that the etiology of this behavior may begin with involvement in nonshareable predicaments, and not before. If this is the case, the search for long-term genetic influences or causes would be an illusory goal.

Most of the commentary on embezzlement to date, other than that of Cressey, has emphasized the traits and characteristics of the violator. Little or no attention has been paid to situational contexts which may contribute to trust violation. As a result, we cannot point to much evidence showing the influence of social situations. However, one bit of material regarding the organization of a bank lends itself to speculation in this direction. Argyris has reported that one bank he studied went about hiring employees thought to be "the right type." These workers were passive, quiet, obedient, and careful individuals. Once employed, they avoided each other's conversation and remained on cordial but distant terms. These employees rarely communicated any complaints and opinions about the work situation to their superiors, nor did bank officials endeavor to deal with human relations problems in the bank.[77] Although this research had nothing directly to do with embezzlement, it is not

[75] Karl F. Schuessler, review of *Other People's Money, American Journal of Sociology*, XLIX (May 1954), 604.

[76] Marshall B. Clinard, review of *Other People's Money, American Sociological Review*, XIX (June 1954), 362–63.

[77] Chris Argyris, *Human Relations in a Bank*, Labor and Management Center, Reprint No. 21 (New Haven, Conn.: Yale University, 1954); Argyris, "Human Relations in a Bank," *Harvard Business Review*, XXXII (September–October 1954), 63–72.

difficult to see how such a work situation could contribute to the non-shareable character of employee problems.

Another set of observations on this point has to do with the extremely low rate of employee thefts among postal workers. Embezzlement and thefts in United States Post Offices appear to be very rare, particularly given the opportunities for criminality present in that situation. Hall has indicated that, in 1951, only 531 workers were apprehended for mail theft and only 144 employees detected in embezzlement out of a work force of over a half-million employees. However, 569 of these 675 were prosecuted and convicted. Hall suggested that several factors operate to repress employee crimes, including the plethora of postal inspectors, which maximizes likelihood of detection, and the frequent prosecution of detected offenders, which deters other potential thieves. On the positive side, postal employees have relatively high morale and identification with the postal service, so this may affect their behavior, too.[78] Any organization which desires to repress employee pilfering and embezzlement might pay close attention to these situational variables.[79]

Smigel's study of public attitudes toward stealing from organizations of varied size also has implications for embezzlement control. He discovered that most citizens say they disapprove of stealing from organizations of any size. But when forced to choose the organization from which they would steal with least reluctance, most said they would do so first from large business firms, then governmental agencies, and from small businesses last. Apparently most of these persons were influenced by two considerations—the relative risks of detection and the principle of least evil. They regarded stealing from large businesses as less reprehensible and less harmful than other thefts. One might argue that this willingness to steal from large businesses stems from views which regard such organizations as cold and impersonal.[80] At any rate, these kinds of contentions regarding situational influences in employee theft are worthy of further exploration.

---

[78] Hall, op. cit., pp. 326–30. For a discussion which indicates that postal workers are involved in a good deal of "deviance" which is not criminal in nature, see Dean Harper and Frederick Emmert, "Work Behavior in a Service Industry," Social Forces, XLII (December 1963), 216–25.

[79] One technical discussion of methods of controlling embezzlement in business is Albert E. Keller, Embezzlement and Internal Control (Washington, D.C.: Warner-Arms Publishing Co., 1946).

[80] Erwin O. Smigel, "Public Attitudes Toward Stealing as Related to the Size of the Victim Organization," American Sociological Review, XXI (June 1956), 320–27.

## THE PROFESSIONAL "FRINGE" VIOLATOR ROLE-CAREER [81]

The last group of lawbreaking respectable citizens to be considered in this chapter is that of professional "fringe" violators. This category designates those who engage in law violations in which their professional skills are centrally involved. Their activities are regarded by professional colleagues as unacceptable forms of behavior. Yet at the same time, fringe violators are often involved in symbiotic ties with more law-abiding fellow professionals, so that the deviants perform services for the nondeviants. The doctor-abortionist who gets his referrals from other physicians who are themselves loath to commit abortions is the clearest case of a violator who occupies a marginal or fringe position within a professional group.

### Definitional Dimensions

*Offense Behavior.* Professional fringe violators are members of legitimate professions who employ professional skills in the commission of crimes not regarded as legitimate activities within the profession. Illegal abortions by physicians represent the clearest cases, particularly those instances of "abortion mills" in which the physician is involved in full-time, systematic practice of abortion. Also included would be illegal practices occasionally found among members of the legal profession. This type does not include ordinary crimes committed by persons who incidentally happen to be professional persons.

*Interactional Setting.* Professional fringe violators are normally involved in two-person crimes involving the offender and a "victim." In the instance of abortions, no victim in the usual sense is involved, for the pregnant female has sought out the services of the abortionist. Although fringe violators are regarded by other professionals as engaged in behavior which is beyond the pale, many of these offenders are at the same time abetted in their activities by other professional persons. In the case of abortion, for example, many abortionists commit these illegal acts upon females who have been referred to them by other physicians who are themselves unwilling to perform abortions.

*Self-concept.* Fringe violators regard themselves as legitimate professional persons, not as criminals. Although the offender acknowledges the

[81] Don C. Gibbons, *Changing the Lawbreaker*, The Treatment of Delinquents and Criminals, © 1965. Reprinted by permission of Prentice-Hall, Inc., Englewood Cliffs, New Jersey, pp. 112–14.

illegal character of his actions, he normally offers some explanation or rationalization by which he attempts to square criminality with his non-criminal self-image.

*Attitudes.* Fringe violators exhibit conventional, prosocial attitudes. Many abortionists would argue that they are performing a service which is technically illegal but necessary. They maintain that the proper solution to the problem of abortion would be to modify the legal statutes which define such acts as criminal.

*Role-career.* In the nature of this form of criminality, fringe violators begin their criminal careers late in life. Some of them commit only a single law violation, others engage in several episodes of criminality, still others are involved in systematic criminal practice. Most of these law violations do not result in detection or prosecution. Among offenders who are prosecuted, different outcomes develop. Some desist from further crimes of this kind, whereas in other cases prosecution and incarceration fail to deter the offender from further deviant acts.

### Background Dimensions

*Social Class.* By definition, professional fringe violators are middle income, middle class persons. Law violations of this kind are likely to be differentially common among professional persons in urban areas and less common among rural or small-town professionals.

*Family Background.* Professional fringe violators are in most cases from relatively conventional family backgrounds.

*Peer Group Associations.* Peer associations are relatively unimportant in this type of crime, except insofar as professional peers have failed to maintain the behavior of the offender within professional norms and standards. As suggested earlier, members of professional groups in which these kinds of violations occur tend to be somewhat ambivalent toward certain illegal activities involving professional skills. Lack of strong moral censure for these acts plays some part in the behavior of fringe violators.

*Contact with Defining Agencies.* Fringe violators tend to have few contacts with defining agencies. It appears that, for those professionals who are apprehended, convicted, and sentenced to institutions, such experiences have a relatively neutral impact. Individuals who desist from further law violations are more likely responding to concerns about their standing within the professional group than anything else. It is unlikely that offenders who commit further offenses do so as a consequence of contacts with correctional agents or other defining agencies.

### Some Evidence

Occupational deviations of the fringe variety have been little studied, particularly by sociologists. The professional person who commits these violations has not been subjected to much investigation, so little is known of the occupational career line that leads the doctor into abortion, or other professionals into marginal activities.

One recent study of unethical and illegal activities by lawyers stands as a model of the sort of research needed into fringe violations. Reichstein investigated "ambulance chasing" (solicitation of cases) in personal injury cases in Illinois.[82] Among other things, he discovered that Chicago lawyers are not all in agreement in their opinions of personal injury solicitation, even though such activity is forbidden by Bar Association ethical canons and state law as well. In general, attorneys who worked in small firms or by themselves and served low status clients looked upon solicitation tolerantly, while lawyers from large, successful firms practicing corporation law had unfavorable views of "ambulance chasing." Reichstein also indicated that lawyers who had been brought before the Illinois Supreme Court on disciplinary charges involving solicitation were dealt with relatively leniently. All of this goes to suggest the ambiguous line between proper and improper behavior in the legal profession.

A second inquiry which meshes with the first is that of Ladinsky concerning legal careers among Detroit area attorneys. He pointed out that the lawyers who engage in "solo" work, as contrasted to group practice in a law firm, were usually sifted earlier in their careers into relatively poor law schools. They were barred from entry into high prestige law schools because of ethnic considerations or other variables which influence the selection process. These same "solo" lawyers are the ones who do the "dirty work." The less desirable, poorer paying legal tasks are allocated to them, such as criminal court defense work, personal injury cases, and parallel chores.[83] It is not hard to see how some of these individuals might drift into unethical or illegal practices if their legal

[82] Kenneth J. Reichstein, "Ambulance Chasing: A Case Study of Deviation and Control Within the Legal Profession," Social Problems, XIII (Summer 1965), 3–17.

[83] Jack Ladinsky, "Careers of Lawyers, Law Practice, and Legal Institutions," American Sociological Review, XXVIII (February 1963), 47–54; further evidence on this point is contained in Jerome E. Carlin, Lawyers on their Own (New Brunswick, N.J.: Rutgers University Press, 1962). Carlin's study of 93 Chicago attorneys who were solo practitioners revealed that they were often compelled to engage in "dirty work," such as "fixing" cases, bribing officials, and so on. See also Arthur Lewis Wood, Criminal Lawyer (New Haven, Conn.: College and University Press, 1967).

careers were to deteriorate, in that they are already vulnerable to occupational and financial vicissitudes by virtue of their occupational detachment from the organized practice of law.

On the subject of abortion and abortionists, Schur has provided an admirable summary of the literature on this matter.[84] One question he addressed concerns the extent of abortions in the United States. He noted that the Kinsey investigations indicated that about one-quarter of the married women in that study had experienced at least one induced abortion before they were 45 years of age. Estimates of the extent of abortion in 1955 indicated that at least 200,000, and perhaps as many as 1,200,000, are performed in the United States annually. These abortions are nearly all illegal under existing state laws. The females who are aborted are a cross-section of the population, so that some are married, others are single women, and they are from various economic, religious, and ethnic groups.[85]

Schur pointed out that most state laws permit induced abortions only when necessary to preserve the life of the mother. The practical effect of such statutes is to make abortion nearly always illegal, for pregnancies today almost never endanger the mother's life, due to advances in modern prenatal care. Therapeutic abortions performed in hospitals by physicians are often technically illegal, even though the law enforcement authorities do not usually take action in these cases. A number of abortions are performed in cases where the pregnant woman has contracted German measles, because this experience often results in various malformations, such as cataracts, lesions, and mental abnormality, of the newborn infant. Other abortions are carried out for psychiatric reasons or because pregnancy is the result of rape or incest. However, the rise in number of abortions in German measles cases or for psychiatric or other reasons has not been sufficient to offset the decline of legal abortions to save the life of the pregnant female. Thus the over-all rates of abortions performed in hospitals have declined.[86]

Reduction of legal or quasi-legal abortions stems from the uncertainty surrounding existing police and court procedures. Physicians are not now able to anticipate the consequences which might ensue if they perform an abortion for a reason not recognized as legitimate in existing laws. One device that has been contrived as a way of protecting doctors both from entreaties of patients and prosecution by authorities is the abortion committee in hospitals. The committee makes the decision as to

[84] Edwin M. Schur, Crimes Without Victims (Englewood Cliffs, N.J.: Prentice-Hall, Inc., 1965), pp. 11–66.

[85] Ibid., p. 12.

[86] Ibid., pp. 13–14.

whether a female will be allowed an abortion, so the responsibility is spread around among a number of doctors.[87]

The hospital abortion committee does not completely solve the problem for many doctors, and it certainly does not alleviate the difficulties of the woman with an unwanted pregnancy. She may continue to demand an abortion, even after being refused by the committee. Schur suggested that many of the doctors who find themselves faced with an insistent patient either perform the abortion or refer the person to an abortionist-doctor. The Kinsey findings indicated that most of the women in that study who reported an abortion said they were aborted by a physician.[88]

Evidence regarding the characteristics of doctors who commit abortions is obviously hard to uncover. However, Schur argued that the physicians who practice abortions are frequently marginal figures in one way or another. Some are doctors who have lost their licenses, some are foreign-trained physicians who have not been admitted to practice in this country, while still others may be unsuccessful doctors who are attracted by the lucrative financial aspects of abortion.

One indication of the symbiotic links between these fringe figures and other doctors is in the case of a Baltimore doctor who had performed abortions over a 20-year period, and indicated that he had received referrals from 353 other physicians.[89] Schur indicated that the practice of abortion in American cities appears to be an elaborate *sub rosa* form of medical practice, rather than an ephemeral form of sporadic deviance. Abortion "mills" have been discovered involving doctors in full-time abortion practices, with various assistants and an elaborate network of referral sources including other doctors, drug store personnel, and so on.[90]

## SUMMARY

This chapter has examined several kinds of "hidden crime" involving lawbreaking by respectable citizens. Throughout the discussion, questions and controversies have been noted which point to the need for further research. It is likely that some major changes in criminological analysis will come about as these matters receive more attention in the future. Accumulation of evidence on the pervasive character of criminality and the interweaving of illegal conduct into the fabric of social and economic

[87] *Ibid.,* pp. 18–21.
[88] *Ibid.,* p. 21.
[89] *Ibid.,* pp. 25–31.
[90] *Ibid.,* pp. 31–34. For a detailed account of abortion practices in New York, see Jerome E. Bates, "The Abortion Mill: An Institutional Study," *Journal of Criminal Law, Criminology and Police Science,* XLV (July–August 1954), 157–69.

life will compel us to abandon those comforting notions that crime is restricted to only a relatively few daring "bad guys." The study of criminality turns out to be a major task in sociological inquiry, for law-breaking is often a central feature of the day-to-day activities of citizens everywhere in American society.

Beginning with the next chapter, our attention turns away from property offenses and toward some role-careers involving assaults and other interpersonal actions. Chapter Fourteen is addressed to assaultive and homicidal behavior, while Chapter Fifteen will focus upon patterns of sexual deviation.

# 14

# Murderers and Assaultists

## INTRODUCTION

In this and the following chapter, our attention moves away from property offenders and property crime. We shall take up murder and assaultive behavior in Chapter Fourteen, while in Chapter Fifteen a variety of kinds of sexual criminality will be examined. Both chapters deal with forms of conduct which appear to many laymen to be particularly bizarre, deviant, or unusual activity, as contrasted to the endeavors of thieves, robbers, or business offenders. To those uninformed about criminality, the taking of a human life, violent assault by one person upon another, or coercion of a female into sexual intercourse appear extremely unusual events. The murderer, assaultist, or sexual offender is often presumed to be an individual with markedly idiosyncratic personal characteristics. In the public view, rapists must be "fiends" with pathological personalities, for how else can their actions be explained? Laymen often invoke an explanation of homicides which emphasizes situations of extreme social stress as the mechanism triggering violent acts.

As this chapter unfolds, we shall discover that most murders and assaults depart markedly from the popular image of activities carried on by clever, scheming individuals and involving complex techniques by which persons are killed or assaulted. For every publicized case in which some person contrives a complicated and elaborate scheme for murder, there are countless other cases in which one person kills another on the spur of the moment and in dismal surroundings. From another perspective, if the facts were known to citizens, garden variety homicides and assaults would appear strange and virtually inexplicable. In the eyes of the middle class individual, homicides and assaults would seem to arise out of extremely trivial circumstances. The files of municipal police departments are filled with cases in which one person killed another over a slighting remark or a seemingly innocuous, socially inappropriate action, such as a flirtatious gesture toward the murderer's spouse. Indeed, the mundane character of much assaultive conduct would be a source of bewilderment to individuals who live outside situations in which interpersonal violence is relatively commonplace.

## THE LAW OF HOMICIDE AND ASSAULT

In law, the term *homicide* is generic, referring to the killing of one person by another.[1] Culpable homicides which result in criminal prosecution are differentiated from *justifiable* homicides and *excusable* homicides. Justifiable homicide constitutes those killings performed as a result of legal demands, such as a police officer shooting a fleeing suspect. In this instance, the homicide occurred while the officer was discharging his legal responsibility to pursue the criminal. Another case of justifiable homicide is in occurrences where jail or prison guards kill prisoners attempting to escape from confinement. Excusable homicide is the term for deaths which result accidentally from lawful acts performed by lawful means. The death of a child from medicine administered by the parent in the course of an illness would be treated as excusable homicide.

Culpable homicides for which persons are held criminally responsible are normally differentiated in law into *murder* in the *first* or *second degrees* and *manslaughter*. In turn, these distinctions rest upon degrees of *premeditation* and *malice aforethought*. Premeditation designates intent to violate the law formulated prior to the activity; in other words, a decision to commit a crime, planning the execution of it, and so on. Malice aforethought refers to the simple presence of intent to kill at the time of the act. In order for a person to be convicted of murder in the first degree, both premeditation and malice aforethought must be established. In second degree murder, only malice aforethought must be proved. Statutes define manslaughter as culpable homicide in which neither premeditation nor malice aforethought are present. Manslaughter is unintended or unwitting homicide. Degrees of manslaughter are usually recognized in law, first degree manslaughter designating that in which a fatal outcome to a set of behavioral events could be reasonably anticipated by a prudent person. The accidental death of a passenger in an automobile driven in a reckless manner by an intoxicated driver would be a case in point.

Although relatively clear distinctions are drawn in law among forms of homicide, it should be noted that these are often blurred in judicial practice. There are a host of conditions which influence the decision to process a case of criminality as first or second degree murder or manslaughter, in addition to the similarity of the conduct to legal definition. Many acts of homicide which could be prosecuted as first degree murder

---

[1] For a discussion of homicide law, see Herbert A. Bloch and Gilbert Geis, *Man, Crime, and Society* (New York: Random House, Inc., 1962), pp. 253–58.

are instead processed as second degree murder or manslaughter. For instance, an individual may "cop a plea," that is, agree to plead guilty to a homicide in return for reduction in the charge from second degree murder to manslaughter. Accordingly, one would be unwise to assume that court statistics on first and second degree murder and manslaughter correctly indicate the distribution of cases technically fitting the legal definitions of these terms.

*Assault* in common law and statute law, both in the United States and in England, is usually defined as an attempt to commit a battery, which is the unlawful application of physical force to another person. Assaults can and frequently do culminate in two separate kinds of actions against the offender. The injured party can endeavor to obtain redress in civil action, while the assaulter is also liable to criminal court prosecution for the criminal violation of law. Criminal laws usually distinguish degrees of assault; *aggravated assault* is the most serious form and involves such actions as assault with a deadly weapon or assault with intent to kill. Aggravated assault is a felony carrying more severe penalties than common or ordinary assault. The latter is a misdemeanor which involves lesser punishments.

The kinds of persons who commit homicides or assaultive acts and the situations in which they engage in these are considerably more varied than the categories of murder, manslaughter, and assault recognized in statute law. As a consequence, any meaningful discussion of crimes against persons must pay some attention to the major dimensions along which these vary. Several attempts have been made by students of homicide to provide taxonomies of forms of murder or murderers. Guttmacher has provided one in which he enumerated kinds of murderers.[2] According to Guttmacher, there are normal, sociopathic, alcoholic, and avenging murderers, as well as schizophrenic killers and those who are temporarily psychotic. Still other murderers include homosexuals, passive-aggressive killers, and sadistic murderers. Doubtless the population of killers includes each of these kinds of individuals, but Guttmacher's classification is too anecdotal and descriptive to be of much use in explanations of homicide behavior. Guttmacher's scheme is paralleled by one by Neustatter in which case histories are used to illustrate schizophrenic, hysteric, and mentally defective murderers.[3] Neustatter also contends that there are killers who are paranoiac, epileptic, or suffering from organic brain damage. Other murderers are held to be

---

[2] Manfred S. Guttmacher, *The Mind of the Murderer* (New York: Farrar, Straus and Giroux, 1960), pp. 13–106; for another eclectic discussion of murder, see John M. MacDonald, *The Murderer and his Victim* (Springfield, Ill.: Charles C Thomas, Publisher, 1961).

[3] W. Lindesay Neustatter, *The Mind of the Murderer* (New York: Philosophical Library, 1957).

sadistic, psychopathic, melancholic, or suffering from hypoglycemia. Much the same comment applies to Neustatter's scheme as to Guttmacher's, for both are relatively descriptive and anecdotal.

In the discussion below, no detailed classification of forms of homicide or assault will be offered. Instead, a generalized description of the role-career of a personal offender, "one-time loser" will be presented first. Following this, we shall examine a body of theory and research on homicide and assault. The role-career statement can be likened to a sort of standard against which empirical cases can be contrasted. For example, assaultists come in several varieties, so that certain of them are more similar to the role-career description than are others.

## THE PERSONAL OFFENDER, "ONE-TIME LOSER" ROLE-CAREER [4]

### Definitional Dimensions

*Offense Behavior.* This type includes offenders involved in major crimes of a personal and normally violent nature. Murder, negligent homicide, and serious assaults are the forms of behavior included. Some of these violators have prior records of other assaultive activities so that, strictly speaking, they are not "one-time losers" or first offenders. However, individuals who commit violent acts while in the course of carrying out other criminal offenses, such as those involved in "felony-murder," are not included in this category.

*Interactional Setting.* Personal offender, one-time losers are normally engaged in offenses with a victim who is well-known to the offender, or at least has been in interaction with the violator. Homicide in which the victim is the offender's spouse is the classic case. In instances where the offender and victim are members of the same family group, the criminal act is often the culmination of a long period of tense relationships. In some cases of wife-murder, the offender has been involved in wife-beating for a long time. Finally, he administers a beating to his wife which turns out to be fatal.

*Self-concept.* One-time loser personal offenders exhibit noncriminal self-images. Frequently the violator himself reports his behavior to the police, due to the fact that, after it has occurred, he is contrite, guilt-ridden, and repentant.

*Attitudes.* The attitudes of the one-time loser are conventional and

[4] Don C. Gibbons, *Changing the Lawbreaker*, The Treatment of Delinquents and Criminals, © 1965. Reprinted by permission of Prentice-Hall, Inc., Englewood Cliffs, New Jersey, pp. 116–17.

prosocial. In prison, these persons are designated by other inmates as "square Johns," prisoners who are aliens in the criminal subculture.

*Role-career.* Most personal offenders show no extensive delinquency record or previous patterns of criminality. On occasion, the offender has been involved in minor offenses, such as drunkenness and wife-beating. Criminals of this type receive long prison sentences. When they are released on parole, as many are, their adjustment is normally quite satisfactory.

### Background Dimensions

*Social Class.* One-time loser personal criminals do not come exclusively from one specific social class background. However, rates of homicide and assault are considerably higher among lower class groups than any other in the American population. Furthermore, those who are from lower class backgrounds have often been involved in aggression preceding the major violent episode, partly because of the subcultural approval of interpersonal violence in lower class groups.

*Family Background.* It does not appear that there is a specific family background of parent-child interaction which leads to a "violence prone" personality type. The early family backgrounds of these persons are quite varied. On the other hand, the adult family situation is much involved in the illegal behavior of the person. Cases of extreme violence normally develop out of a marital situation in which tensions have existed for a long time between the victim and the offender.

*Peer Group Associations.* The peer affiliations of the personal offender apparently have little significance in the development of violent behavior.

*Contact with Defining Agencies.* The contacts of the one-time loser personal offender with defining agencies are of neutral significance. The person has the same definition of his behavior as do the defining agencies, and tends to agree that he should be punished for his deviant act. Correctional institutions appear to have little effect, positive or otherwise, upon such individuals.

## FOUR STUDIES OF HOMICIDE

A reasonably full understanding of homicide behavior can be gained from the examination and comparison of four relatively extended studies of homicide. Although these investigations are not strictly parallel in every detail, they do provide evidence on a number of points in common. The first study was by Wolfgang, involving information on all 588 crimi-

nal homicides known to the police which occurred in Philadelphia between 1948 and 1952.[5] Wolfgang's inquiry stands as the most comprehensive single examination of empirical evidence on homicide in the
United States. The second piece of research was by Bensing and Schroeder, concerning 462 homicides in Greater Cuyahoga County (Cleveland), Ohio, between 1947 and 1953.[6] Bullock's examination of all cases
of homicide in Houston between 1945 and 1949 is our third source of
evidence,[7] while Pokorny's replication of Wolfgang's Philadelphia work,
carried on in terms of Houston homicides between 1958 and 1961, is the
final study.[8] In the paragraphs below, the findings of all four investigations will be considered in sections dealing with different aspects of
violent behavior.

### Temporal and Ecological Characteristics

In the Philadelphia study, homicides were found to occur most frequently on weekends: 66 per cent occurred between Friday and Sunday,
while 32 per cent took place on a Saturday.[9] Bensing and Schroeder
found that 62 per cent of the homicides in Cleveland took place on the
same three days,[10] and, similarly, Bullock reported that most homicides
occur on weekends.[11] To locate the occurrence of acts of violence more
specifically, in both the Philadelphia and Cleveland cases these criminal
events were most common between 8 P.M. and 2 A.M.[12] In each of these
cases, the temporal fluctuation in violence appears related to cycles of
weekday labor and weekend leisure pursuits. Proximity of persons, increased use of alcohol, and so on, on weekends serve to increase the
potential for violent outbursts.

Homicides do not occur randomly throughout the urban community,
for Bullock found that over 70 per cent of those in Houston took place

[5] Marvin E. Wolfgang, *Patterns of Criminal Homicide* (Philadelphia: University of Pennsylvania Press, 1958). Wolfgang's volume provides a rich source of materials on homicide in the United States and elsewhere.

[6] Robert C. Bensing and Oliver Schroeder, Jr., *Homicide in an Urban Community* (Springfield, III.: Charles C. Thomas, Publisher, 1960).

[7] Henry A. Bullock, "Urban Homicide in Theory and Fact," *Journal of Criminal Law, Criminology and Police Science*, XLV (January–February 1955), 565–75.

[8] Alex D. Pokorny, "A Comparison of Homicides in Two Cities," *Journal of Criminal Law, Criminology and Police Science*, LVI (December 1965), 479–87; see also Pokorny, "Human Violence: A Comparison of Homicide, Aggravated Assault, Suicide, and Attempted Suicide," *Journal of Criminal Law, Criminology and Police Science*, LVI (December 1965), 488–97.

[9] Wolfgang, op. cit., pp. 96–119.

[10] Bensing and Schroeder, op. cit., pp. 8–10.

[11] Bullock, op. cit., p. 566.

[12] Bensing and Schroeder, op. cit., pp. 8–10; Wolfgang, op. cit., pp. 96–119.

in 18 per cent of the census tracts in that city.[13] Similarly, the Cleveland data show that two-thirds of the crimes took place in 12 per cent of the city of Cleveland.[14] Both of these studies located the urban centers of homicidal acts in predominantly Negro areas characterized by dense populations and overcrowding, physical deterioration, and other manifestations of urban slum conditions.

Wolfgang found that homicides were about evenly divided between the home and places outside the home, in terms of specific locale, which was also true of the Houston homicides investigated by Bullock and Pokorny.[15] Incidents of violence occurring outside of residences were mainly in streets adjacent to taverns or eating places.

### Motives, Situations, and Methods

The private motives within the offender who engages in violence are always difficult to determine, particularly when reliance is placed upon police reports of motives instead of interviews with the culprits. Nonetheless, several of these studies enumerated the most commonly identified motives in police files and other official records. These tell us a good deal about the social situations leading up to acts of violence, which is also true of the information recorded regarding the weapons employed in these behavioral episodes.

In the Philadelphia materials, 37 per cent of the offenses were attributed to altercations of one kind or another, while domestic quarrels accounted for 13 per cent and jealousy was said to be at the base of another 11 per cent. The parties to the crime were close friends in 28 per cent of the cases and family relatives in another quarter of the homicides.[16] Pokorny's evidence for Houston shows the same pattern, with the parties to homicide being close friends or family relations in most instances.[17] The Cleveland homicides were most frequently linked to petty quarrels, marital discord, and sexual disputes.[18] In each of these cases, the circumstances which appear to trigger homicides might well strike the outsider as petty in nature.

These investigations of homicide are not in complete agreement on the question of methods of killing. In Wolfgang's data, stabbing was the leading technique, accounting for 39 per cent of the homicides. Negroes were particularly likely to utilize knives, while white offenders more com-

[13] Bullock, op. cit., pp. 567–69.
[14] Bensing and Schroeder, op. cit., pp. 105–37.
[15] Wolfgang, op. cit., pp. 120–33; Bullock, op. cit., pp. 570–75; Pokorny, op. cit., pp. 481–82.
[16] Wolfgang, op. cit., pp. 185–89, 203–21.
[17] Pokorny, op. cit., p. 483.
[18] Bensing and Schroeder, op. cit., pp. 72–77.

monly beat their victims to death. Women most frequently employed cutting instruments, usually a kitchen knife.[19] In Cleveland, guns accounted for 55 per cent of the homicides, while only 27 per cent were accomplished with knives.[20]

### Racial and Sexual Variations

One of the most striking findings on which all these inquiries are in agreement has to do with the high rates of homicide among Negroes in American cities. Wolfgang found that 73 per cent of the victims and 75 per cent of the offenders in Philadelphia were Negroes, although Negroes made up only 18 per cent of the 1950 population of that city. Homicides were also concentrated among males, for 76 per cent of the victims and 82 per cent of the offenders were males, while males comprised only 48 per cent of the population. Women were infrequently involved in homicide; although females represented only 18 per cent of the offenders, they constituted 24 per cent of the victims. *However, the racial concentration was more marked than the sexual one.* The rate of homicide for Negro males (41.7 offenses per 100,000 population) was many times greater than that for white males (3.4 homicides per 100,000 population). In addition, the homicide rate for Negro females (9.3 per 100,000 population) also exceeded that for white males. Racial lines were crossed in only 6 per cent of the homicides, so Negroes nearly all kill Negroes, while whites nearly all kill other whites.[21] The Cleveland homicides were distributed in the same fashion, for 76 per cent of the offenders were Negro, although only 11 per cent of the Cuyahoga County population was made up of Negroes.[22] Pokorny reported that Houston Negroes made up only 23 per cent of the population of that city, but they contributed 63 per cent of the offenders.[23]

### Age, Social Class, and Criminal Backgrounds

Several of these studies indicated that variations exist in the ages of offenders and victims. Wolfgang noted that killers are generally younger than those killed, for the majority of offenders were between 20 and 30 years of age, while the victims were on the average about five years older.[24] Bensing and Schroeder indicated that most homicides were car-

---

[19] Wolfgang, op. cit., pp. 79–95.
[20] Bensing and Schroeder, op. cit., p. 84.
[21] Wolfgang, op. cit., pp. 31–35.
[22] Bensing and Schroeder, op. cit., p. 41.
[23] Pokorny, op. cit., pp. 480–81.
[24] Wolfgang, op. cit., pp. 65–78.

ried out by relatively young persons, 72 per cent of them between 21 and 45 years of age.[25]

The preceding material on the ecological distribution of homicides makes it clear that this activity is more common among working class groups than any other. Further confirmation of socioeconomic differentials in violence is found in both the Philadelphia and Cleveland studies, wherein rates of homicide for lower class individuals of all ethnic backgrounds were found to exceed those for persons of higher economic status.[26]

The Philadelphia material contains some data on the criminal backgrounds of offenders and victims. Wolfgang indicated that 64 per cent of the offenders and 47 per cent of the victims had a record of prior offenses. Those with criminal backgrounds had usually been involved in earlier incidents of violence, for 66 per cent had been implicated in crimes against persons.[27] Finally, Wolfgang noted that alcohol was present in 64 per cent of the homicide occurrences, and that both parties to the act had been drinking in 44 per cent of the cases.[28]

### Victim-Precipitated Homicide

One of the most important innovations introduced into the study of homicide by these four investigations is the notion of "victim-precipitated homicide" in Wolfgang's inquiry. Victim-precipitated homicide is a term for acts of violence in which the victim initiated the fatal outburst by making the first menacing gesture or striking the first blow. As we have seen, a good many homicides take place between persons who have been in social interaction with each other, but victim-precipitated killings involve more than prior interaction. In the victim-precipitated case, the victim induced his death through his own menacing actions. A separate examination of victim-precipitated homicides by Wolfgang showed that these more commonly involve Negro victims and offenders, with the victim being male while the offender is female. The victim is often the husband of the offender, and he is commonly stabbed in circumstances in which he has been drinking. Finally, the victim frequently had a prior record of assaultive conduct.[29]

[25] Bensing and Schroeder, op. cit., pp. 70–71.

[26] Ibid., pp. 128–29; Wolfgang, op. cit., pp. 36–39.

[27] Wolfgang, op. cit., pp. 168–74.

[28] Ibid., pp. 134–67. On this point, see also MacDonald, op. cit., pp. 18–20. He summarized a series of studies which show that a third or more of the offenders in homicide cases had been drinking prior to the act of violence.

[29] Wolfgang, op. cit., pp. 264–65.

## SUBCULTURES OF VIOLENCE

Bullock's findings in Houston were interpreted in broad terms in the following way: "The basic ecological process of urban segregation centralizes people of like kind, throws them together at common institutions, occasions their association on levels of intimacy, and thereby paves the way for conflicts out of which homicides occur." [30] In other words, the urban community shows concentrations in particular areas of groups who live styles of life that are especially productive of homicides and assaultive acts. This argument has recently been advanced under the rubric of "cultures of violence," in which it is claimed that the life circumstances of certain groups trigger violence as a relatively commonplace outcome of social interaction.[31]

Subcultures of violence made up of groups quick to utilize force in interpersonal relations appear to be centralized in those urban slum areas indicated in the preceding four studies as the places where homicide rates are high. Frequently, these neighborhoods are populated by lower income Negroes, so they are residential ghettos. According to many sociologists, the grinding poverty, unstable nature of community organization, and disorganized character of family life in such areas lead to the emergence of certain lower class values or focal concerns.[32] One of these identified by Miller is "trouble," which refers to suspicion of others and generalized anticipation of difficulty from policemen, welfare agencies, schools, and fellow citizens. Another focal concern is "excitement," which has to do with pursuit of hedonistic pleasures, particularly on weekends, in order to counteract the dullness of weekday pursuits. Given actors with these motivations thrown together in close contact, the potential for violent incidents is heightened. The contention is that this subcultural situation goes far toward accounting for high rates of homicide among lower class citizens. This argument makes it unnecessary to invoke notions of personality pathology to account for homicides.

One interesting bit of evidence on this point comes from a study by Schultz in St. Louis.[33] He reviewed a series of investigations which

---

[30] Bullock, op. cit., p. 575.

[31] One valuable discussion and resumé of the literature on this topic is Frank E. Hartung, *Crime, Law and Society* (Detroit, Mich.: Wayne State University Press, 1965), pp. 136–66.

[32] Miller has provided the richest description of these ingredients of lower class life. See Walter B. Miller, "Lower Class Culture as a Generating Milieu of Gang Delinquency," *Journal of Social Issues,* XIV, No. 3 (1958), 5–19; Miller, "Implications of Urban Lower Class Culture for Social Work," *Social Service Review,* XXXIII (September 1959), 219–36.

[33] Leroy G. Schultz, "Why the Negro Carries Weapons," *Journal of Criminal Law, Criminology and Police Science,* LIII (December 1962), 476–83.

showed that Negroes commonly carry weapons, and that the arrest rates for weapons offenses are much higher among Negroes than whites. He conducted interviews with 50 Negro offenders who had been convicted of charges centering about possession of dangerous weapons. These violators offered a number of reasons for carrying guns—some did so in order to commit crimes, while some alleged that they did so in order to force payment of debts owed them by others. However, 70 per cent declared that they carried weapons because they anticipated attack from others in their environment. Carrying a weapon was a defensive or anticipatory act. Schultz indicated: "This group voiced a chronic concern about being attacked and the need for self-defense and assumed automatically that others in their environment were also carrying weapons, or if not actually carrying weapons, 'acted as if they were.' " [34]

## SOME OTHER STUDIES

Brief note should be taken of several other studies of murder in the United States. One investigation was by Gillin, involving inmates in a Wisconsin prison, in which he observed that 44 per cent of the murderers studied had committed their crime in connection with another offense, while 24 per cent had killed in conjunction with an immediate quarrel and another 32 per cent had murdered someone with whom they had been carrying on a long-standing feud.[35] In addition, he reported on the background characteristics of the incarcerated killers. They were found to be more frequently from rural areas than were the sex offenders or property criminals. More of them had contributed to the support of their families at an early age than had the other prisoners. More killers had foreign-born parents, more were from lower income backgrounds, more had left school prematurely, and more had unsteady employment records than was the case with the other prisoners. Finally, the murderers had less frequently been involved in prior offenses than had the other convicts.[36] These findings add up to a picture of Wisconsin murderers as "Square John" criminals, so that while they were commonly detached and alienated individuals, they were also relatively conventional persons.

Another study of a group of imprisoned murderers was made by Palmer, dealing with 51 offenders in New England penal institutions who

---

[34] Ibid., p. 479.

[35] John L. Gillin, The Wisconsin Prisoner (Madison: University of Wisconsin Press, 1946), pp. 56–60; see also Gillin, "Murder as a Sociological Phenomenon," Annals of the American Academy of Political and Social Science, CCLXXXIV (November 1952), 20–25.

[36] Gillin, The Wisconsin Prisoner, pp. 9–11.

were compared with their noncriminal siblings.[37] He found that most of these murders were unplanned, shooting was the leading technique of homicide, and alcohol was not usually present. One difference between Palmer's data and that of the four studies examined above is that the victims of these murderers were strangers or slight acquaintances in 67 per cent of the cases. The murderers were persons with low educational attainment and low socioeconomic status.[38] Interviews with the mothers of the offenders led Palmer to conclude that the killers had been subjected to uncommonly frequent frustrations in their lives, in contrast to their siblings. However, there is some possibility of error in the observations of the mothers as they attempted to report retrospectively the experiences of their sons.

## HOMICIDE IN OTHER SOCIETIES

One basic fact about homicide is that this crime occurs at markedly varying rates in different countries. In general, African societies have low homicide rates, as do many Asiatic nations and most European countries. The United States is characterized by comparatively large numbers of violent deaths, as are Ceylon, Finland, and a number of other nations. Some indication of worldwide variations in homicide can be gained from computations made in England between 1940 and 1949 of rates per 1,000,000 population. These show England and Wales with a rate of 4.0 and New Zealand with a rate of 7.2, while in the United States rates vary from 13.6 in Massachusetts to 167.3 in Georgia.[39] In all of these cases, we are led to suspect that there is something about the social structure of different nations which influences their homicide rates.[40]

Although detailed data on homicide in other nations are not available in abundance, several revealing investigations have been conducted on this topic. Bohannan has reported on homicide in a number of African societies.[41] He notes that one of the forms of killing in Africa is nonculpable homicide in dangerous but legal institutions. Hunting with poisoned arrows falls into this category, for deaths frequently occur as a consequence of the risk-courting in such activities. These nonculpable homicides have American parallels in such activities as auto racing,

[37] Stuart Palmer, A Study of Murder (New York: Thomas Y. Crowell Co., 1960).

[38] Ibid., pp. 21–37.

[39] Bloch and Geis, op. cit., pp. 259–60.

[40] One analysis of the high homicide rate in Finland is Veli Verkko, Homicides and Suicides in Finland and Their Dependence on National Character (Copenhagen: G. E. C. Gads Forlag, 1951).

[41] Paul Bohannan, ed., African Homicide and Suicide (Princeton, N.J.: Princeton University Press, 1960).

where unintended deaths are caused by the participants. A second form of homicide which is nonculpable is institutionalized killing such as jural homicide (executions) or ritual killings. Finally, culpable homicides occur in African societies in which the offender is held criminally accountable.[42]

One of the most significant facts about African homicide centers about discordant definitions of culpable and nonculpable homicide. Bohannan indicates that thief-killing, witch-killing, and killing of adulterers are often defined by African tribes as nonculpable acts. However, these are regarded as criminal actions in British law which has been injected into African affairs. The conflict between tribal norms and western law is reduced through compromises, so that judges tend to be lenient in the sentences handed down to native killers. In some instances, the charge against the violator is reduced from murder to manslaughter.[43]

Another highly significant finding on African criminality is that homicide rates among natives are extremely low, compared to rates for American Negroes. The Philadelphia Negroes in Wolfgang's study had a rate of 24.6 homicides per 100,000 population during the period between 1948 and 1952, while Bohannan reports that African tribes had rates of less than 12 homicides per 1,000,000 population. These African rates, which are among some of the lowest in the world, demolish effectively any hypotheses which would link high homicide rates of American Negroes to biological or racial factors.[44]

A third observation on African homicide is that the proportion of female offenders in the population of killers is even smaller than that for the United States and other western nations. However, in several African tribes, females comprise 45 to 60 per cent of the victims, while women are homicide victims in only about one-quarter of the cases in the United States.[45]

Bohannan's material points to still another homicide variation from western patterns. In the United States, when a family member is killed, the victim is likely to be a spouse; in Denmark, the victim is likely to be a child; but in African countries, a wide variety of different kinsmen are the victims of homicide. Clearly, this has much to do with the extended family patterns more common in African nations than in western ones.[46]

[42] *Ibid.*, pp. 230–34.
[43] *Ibid.*, p. 233.
[44] *Ibid.*, pp. 236–37.
[45] *Ibid.*, pp. 237–39.
[46] *Ibid.*, p. 242.

Homicide in Ceylon has received the attention of several investigators. Some years ago, Straus and Straus observed that the relatively high rate of homicide in Ceylon is principally the result of killing among the lowland Sinhalese in that country, rather than the Tamil group. The Sinhalese have experienced the most contact with European cultural influences, so they live in a less rigid class structure than the Tamil. According to these investigators, the looser social ties among the Sinhalese are responsible for their greater contribution to the homicide rate.[47]

Wood has engaged in a more recent study of homicide in Ceylon in which two hypotheses were examined and confirmed.[48] The first contended that homicide should be most common in the lowest ranks of an achieved status system, particularly when members of these groups perceive themselves to be externally restrained from achieving their goals. The reader may recognize a good deal of similarity of this argument to the "opportunity structures" notions of Cloward and Ohlin,[49] which hold that lower class youths are disproportionately represented in the population of delinquents because they see themselves as constrained from achieving their goals by an unjust social order. A social structure which theoretically provides open opportunities for all is perceived as hypocritically restricting the life-chances of working class individuals. Wood's second hypothesis was that homicide is more frequent among persons who are alienated, demoralized, and showing reactions of hostility. Evidence in support of both hypotheses was uncovered in this investigation.

Interpersonal relationships between victims and offenders in homicides have been the subject of two studies in Denmark and in India. Svalastoga observed that, in Danish homicides for the periods 1934–1939 and 1946–1951, family members were victims in 57 per cent of the cases, friends and acquaintances were victims in 31 per cent, while strangers were killed in only 12 per cent of the homicides.[50] Along the same line, Driver notes that in Indian homicides the partners to the offense are usually

[47] Jacqueline H. Straus and Murray A. Straus, "Suicide, Homicide, and Social Structure in Ceylon," *American Journal of Sociology,* LVIII (March 1953), 461–69.

[48] Arthur L. Wood, *Crime and Aggression in Changing Ceylon* (Philadelphia: Transactions of the American Philosophical Society, 1961); Wood, "A Socio-Structural Analysis of Murder, Suicide, and Economic Crime in Ceylon," *American Sociological Review,* XXVI (October 1961), 744–53.

[49] Richard A. Cloward and Lloyd E. Ohlin, *Delinquency and Opportunity* (New York: Free Press of Glencoe, Inc., 1960).

[50] Kaare Svalastoga, "Homicide and Social Contact in Denmark," *American Journal of Sociology,* LXII (July 1956), 37–41.

kinsmen or close associates of the same sex, religion, or caste. Prior to the actual killing, the interactional partners have been caught up in situations of heightened enmity flowing out of sexual disputes, arguments about property, or kindred quarrels.[51]

By way of summary, it can be seen that homicide is a form of crime which has a universal flavor; similarities in homicide crop up in various nations around the world. At the same time, some of the data indicate that homicidal activities in different nations take on certain characteristics or the coloration of the host social system.

## PATTERNS OF AGGRESSION

There is a good deal of evidence which points to the existence of two general forms of assaultive conduct. The first is situational or subcultural in character, in which some individuals who reside in certain urban neighborhoods get involved in violence largely in response to the exacerbated tensions and disorder of their social situation. This kind of assaultive conduct bears a close similarity to the homicides occurring in subcultures of violence; indeed, both are the product of the same general social variables.

A second form of criminally aggressive behavior is psychogenic or individualistic in form, rather than subcultural. The evidence indicates that certain kinds of socialization experiences produce individuals with atypically hostile psychological orientations. These persons, variously called "unsocialized aggressives," "psychopaths," or "sociopaths," find their way into the population of offenders as a result of attacks upon others. Many commit property violations as well as assaultive acts, but in any event their conduct is marked by a violent and aggressive posture as a central feature of their personalities. These offenders are from a variety of social class backgrounds, for the conditions which generate them are not class-linked.

In the discussion to follow, we shall first study some findings on the matter of situational assault. Then a typological characterization of the "psychopathic" assaultist role-career will be presented, along with some supporting evidence on this form of criminality.

[51] Edwin D. Driver, "Interaction and Criminal Homicide in India," *Social Forces,* XL (December 1961), 153–58.

## SITUATIONAL AGGRESSION

One of several important studies of assaultive conduct was by Peterson, Pittman, and O'Neal, concerning St. Louis police arrest cases.[52] These investigators determined that most of the apprehended offenders had relatively stable patterns of deviance, so that individuals arrested for crimes of violence had rarely been involved in property crimes earlier in their careers. Conversely, most of the property offenders had avoided use of violence in their criminal careers. The assaultive offenders were from more seriously disrupted homes, and at the same time had higher levels of generalized hostility than did the property criminals.

A more recent investigation of assaultive behavior has been carried out by Pittman and Handy, also centered in St. Louis.[53] They conducted a test of Wolfgang's hypotheses in order to determine if assaults show patterns similar to those for homicide. By and large, the observations about the morphology of assault closely paralleled Wolfgang's analyses of homicide. For example, 132 of the 241 aggravated assault cases investigated in this study occurred between 6 P.M. Friday and 6 A.M. on Monday, most taking place on Saturday. The assaults occurred in a variety of places, but 45 per cent were on streets, while 38 per cent transpired in homes. No seasonal variation in assaultive acts was observed. About one-half of the assaults involved knives, but physical force was more common among white assaultists, while Negro offenders employed weapons. Many of the offenses were reported to the police by the victim and nearly all were cleared by arrest. In only three cases was another crime involved.[54]

Most of the information examined by Pittman and Handy having to do with offender-victim relations in assault duplicated that of Wolfgang. The majority of acts of violence occurred within an offender-victim dyad, in most of the cases the participants were similar in age, most of the parties to violence were "blue collar" workers, interracial assaults were uncommon, and most of the offenders with criminal records had backgrounds of petty criminality. The majority of the assaults developed out of quarrels and arguments immediately prior to the violent outbursts.[55]

---

[52] Richard A. Peterson, David J. Pittman, and Patricia O'Neal, "Stabilities in Deviance: A Study of Assaultive and Non-Assaultive Offenders," Journal of Criminal Law, Criminology and Police Science, LIII (March 1962), 44–48.

[53] David J. Pittman and William Handy, "Patterns in Criminal Aggravated Assault," Journal of Criminal Law, Criminology and Police Science, LV (December 1964), 462–70.

[54] Ibid., pp. 463–67.

[55] Ibid., pp. 467–68.

Another piece of evidence on assaultive offenders has been presented by Roebuck and Johnson.[56] They compared the social backgrounds of 40 Negro felons charged with assault and drunkenness with the backgrounds of 360 other prisoners. The violent offenders had developed out of more rigid, fundamentalist family backgrounds and had more strict, dominating fathers than the other inmates. But they also showed closer primary group ties in childhood and adulthood than the other prisoners, and were from less criminogenic social circumstances.

These investigations seem to add up to a picture of assault carried on in relatively disorganized social settings by individuals who are not particularly bizarre or pathological in personality organization. It is for this reason that this kind of criminality can properly be called situational. For the most part, this material confirms the argument about subcultures of violence advanced in previous pages.

## THE "PSYCHOPATHIC" ASSAULTIST ROLE-CAREER

Chapter Seven included a discussion of etiological hypotheses which link criminality to the existence of certain kinds of atypical individuals called "psychopaths" or "sociopaths." An abundant psychiatric literature holds that there is a clinical entity or personality type called a "psychopath." This kind of person is said to be poorly socialized, unconcerned about the privileges of others, insensitive to social influences, and frequently violent in disposition. According to this view, such persons develop out of certain atypical social backgrounds, and in particular are the product of disordered family experiences. It is a small jump to the corollary contention that psychopaths are inordinately common in the population of criminal deviants, for their personality characteristics are thought to impel them toward lawbreaking or other deviant paths.

Chapter Seven also alleged that customary applications of psychopathy formulations are defective, for the concept is used too loosely in most cases. Specific indicators of psychopathic personality patterns are not usually enumerated. Instead, the term is applied in *ex post facto* fashion to persons already identified as deviants, such as criminals, homosexuals, or political radicals. Used in this way, the concept is circular in definition, and proof of psychopathy turns out to reside in the same deviant conduct which the label is supposed to explain.

Perhaps it would be possible to rescue the psychopathy hypothesis if it were not used to account for all manner of socially aberrant individuals.

[56] Julian Roebuck and Ronald Johnson, "The Negro Drinker and Assaulter as a Criminal Type," *Crime and Delinquency*, VIII (January 1962), 21–33.

In the role-career description below, psychopathic assaultists are described who exhibit a fairly clear and identifiable syndrome of characteristics centering about the use of aggressive and violent gestures in social relations. We retain the term psychopath because the offenders included in this pattern frequently receive this label in correctional diagnostic processes.

### Definitional Dimensions

*Offense Behavior.* Psychopathic assaultists are adults who engage in violent and seemingly meaningless assaults upon others. On occasion, these applications of force are in conjunction with the commission of another crime, but in such cases the assaults are characterized by others as "senseless." The violent actions go well beyond the degree of force which might be required to carry off the criminal act, so the behavior has the appearance of irrationality in the eyes of others. These offenders often show records of juvenile misconduct involving unprovoked assaults upon their peers and, on occasion, upon adults or animals. Acts of extreme cruelty toward other humans or animals are characteristic of such offenders.

*Interactional Setting.* Psychopathic or overly aggressive offenders are "lone wolves." They rarely engage in sustained forms of cooperative criminality, for their involvement in diffuse forms of aggression alienates them from others.

*Self-concept.* These offenders exhibit defiance, a kind of chip-on-the-shoulder attitude, and the view that people are not to be trusted. Because of their suspicion of others, they lash out with the intent of striking the first blow before they are punished or harmed by others suspected of having bad motives. At the same time, psychopathic assaultists show a marked psychological investment in self-notions centering about the view of themselves as "tough" and "manly."

*Attitudes.* The attitudes of psychopathic assaultists make up a collection of diffuse sentiments of hostility toward persons and society.

*Role-career.* These offenders frequently show records of early incarceration as juveniles in correctional institutions. Their adult lives are likely to be filled with recurrent episodes of commitment to penal institutions, along with prison sentences of increasing length. Psychopathic assaultists often become defined as "hopeless" criminals not amenable to treatment, so they are kept in custody for long periods of time.

### Background Dimensions

*Social Class.* Psychopathic assaultists do not come from any single social class background. Instead, such persons are found in several social class groups.

*Family Background.* Although specific family experiences of overly aggressive offenders vary somewhat, in nearly every case some kind of early and severe parental rejection appears to be the prelude to aggressive behavior. As youngsters, psychopathic offenders were usually illegitimate or unwanted pregnancies, rejected and abandoned by their parents at an early age, or underwent severe parental rejection within the home if the offender was not physically separated from his parents. Many have lived for extended periods of time in foster homes, orphanages, and so on, rather than with their natural parents.

*Peer Group Associations.* Intensive interaction with peers is uncommon among overly aggressive offenders because of two factors. First, most aggressive offenders refrain from initiating relationships with peers because they are socially inept and because of their hostile views of people. Second, most eligible peers avoid contacts with aggressive psychopaths because of the potentially violent consequences.

*Contact with Defining Agencies.* As children, overly aggressive offenders exhibit considerable contact with police, courts, and child guidance clinics, and show hostile attitudes toward such agencies and persons. These attitudes are not the product of such experiences, however; they are the result of diffuse feelings of hostility directed toward people generally by the aggressive person. In adult life, psychopathic assaultists continue this career line, spending lengthy periods of time in prison. Parole violation rates are consistently high for such offenders, quite independent of the amount of time spent in incarceration. In prison, these offenders are feared and avoided by other inmates, so they are not central figures in the inmate subculture.

### Some Evidence

Let us examine a few of the important strands of data on psychopathic assaultists. There is a good deal of evidence of the existence of a small band of violent and socially maladjusted individuals in prison designated in the inmate language system as "hard guys," "outlaws," "gorillas," "toughs," or some similar appellation. Sykes has noted that inmates in a New Jersey state prison single out "gorillas" as persons to be avoided, for such prisoners are quick to utilize coercion in order to extract favors from other convicts. Certain other individuals are labeled "toughs" and also avoided due to their touchiness and willingness to employ physical violence in settling minor disputes.[57] Both of these argot roles or inmate

[57] Gresham M. Sykes, *The Society of Captives* (Princeton, N.J.: Princeton University Press, 1958), pp. 84–108.

types look very much like a within-prison variant of psychopathic assaultists. Much the same picture emerges from studies by Schrag, in which asocial prisoners called "outlaws" by their peers have been reported. "Outlaws" have been imprisoned for a variety of offenses, but have frequently employed violent and bizarre techniques of criminality. They exhibit records of excessive recidivism, and are usually the product of backgrounds of early and severe parental and social rejection.[58] Garrity has observed that "outlaws" exhibit very high rates of parole violation which seem little influenced by the amount of time spent in custody.[59] These reports all appear to be concerned with roughly the same kind of offender, so the different labels of "outlaw," "gorilla," "hard guy," and "tough" are apparently simply a reflection of regional variations in prison argot.

There is an abundance of revealing data on the childhood social backgrounds of overly aggressive persons.[60] The specific socialization experiences which such individuals have undergone vary considerably, but one recurrent thread throughout these case histories is early and severe parental rejection. For example, Jenkins examined a goodly number of aggressive children, nearly all of whom had been abandoned by their parents or suffered some other severe form of rejection, including repeated physical assaults by their parents. As a consequence, they developed into relatively unsocialized individuals who engaged in myriad forms of aggression against human and animal targets.[61]

Another detailed study of aggressive youngsters was conducted by Bandura and Walters, involving delinquents who were not as poorly socialized or aggressive as those reported in the psychiatric literature.[62] These boys had been singled out by school authorities or juvenile court workers as aggressive because they had engaged in frequent fights with other children, or for other reasons of that sort. According to Bandura

[58] Clarence Schrag, "Some Foundations for a Theory of Correction," in The Prison, ed. Donald R. Cressey (New York: Holt, Rinehart and Winston, Inc., 1961), pp. 346–56; Schrag, "A Preliminary Criminal Typology," Pacific Sociological Review, XLI (Spring 1961), 11–16.

[59] Donald L. Garrity, "The Prison as a Rehabilitation Agency," in The Prison, ed. Cressey, pp. 375–78.

[60] R. L. Jenkins and Lester E. Hewitt, "Types of Personality Structure Encountered in Child Guidance Clinics," American Journal of Orthopsychiatry, XIV (January 1944), 84–94; Jenkins, Breaking Patterns of Defeat (Philadelphia: J. B. Lippincott Co., 1954), pp. 9–28; Albert J. Reiss, Jr., "Social Correlates of Psychological Types of Delinquency," American Sociological Review, XVII (December 1952), 710–18; John W. Kinch, "Self-Conceptions of Types of Delinquents," Sociological Inquiry, XXXII (Spring 1962), 228–34; Fritz Redl and David Wineman, The Aggressive Child (New York: Free Press of Glencoe, Inc., 1960); Leonard Berkowitz, Aggression (New York: McGraw-Hill Book Co., Inc., 1962); Albert Bandura and Richard H. Walters, Adolescent Aggression (New York: The Ronald Press Co., 1959).

[61] Jenkins, op. cit.

[62] Bandura and Walters, op. cit.

and Walters, children on this end of a continuum of aggressive behavior are the product of relatively stable and intact homes. Their early socialization has been of such a quality as to produce dependency needs on their part. However, they have cold and indifferent fathers who fail to nurture these dependency needs, and instead are encouraged to solve their problems by themselves. Additionally, the youngsters are encouraged in aggressive actions by parents who take some pride in the ability of the child to fight successfully with other children. These same parents tend to be relatively lax in the demands and restrictions they impose upon their children. A developmental chronology in these cases begins with adequate early socialization of the child which leads to the development of dependency yearnings on his part, and then to frustration of these by the father in particular. The aggressive child is then allowed to express hostility outside the home and restrictions are not imposed on him within the home setting. At some point, he gets into difficulties with the schools or juvenile courts as a result of aggressive acts.

Unfortunately, longitudinal studies which follow these kinds of persons from childhood through adult life are not available. We lack information on the effects upon them of commitment to guidance clinics, training schools, reformatories, or kindred experiences. But it seems likely that these life events serve to exacerbate the hostile perspectives of the offender, so that he becomes cumulatively more aggressive and hostile as he encounters a variety of kinds of social rejection. Accordingly, the psychopathic assaultist is probably something more than the aggressive child grown up, for his adult behavior is also influenced by these career contingencies.

## SUMMARY

This chapter represents half of our analysis of forms of crime against persons. The foregoing pages have shown that interpersonal violence is many-faceted; there are a number of forms which it takes. In the same way, the etiological influences behind assaultive acts are diverse. This picture of assaultive behavior will be paralleled by the admixture of behavioral forms taken up in the next chapter. Chapter Fifteen concerns sexual deviation in its many varieties. We will see that sexual misconduct ranges from very pedestrian and unexceptional actions to some extremely violent and bizarre deviant behavior.

# 15

# Patterns
# of
# Sexual Deviation

## INTRODUCTION

Sociological analyses of criminality have not devoted equal attention to all forms of lawbreaking. Much work has been done on property crimes at the same time that little has been said about other illegality, particularly sexual misconduct. This relative inattention to sexual criminality probably stems from an impression that this behavior is the result of causal factors of a different sort from those identified in social-structural explanations of property violations. Sexual deviation does not seem to fit conveniently within the usual frames of reference of the sociologist, so it is systematically ignored.

Sociologists have done a fair amount of work on certain matters having to do with sexual behavior, but have had relatively little to say about sexual deviations of one kind or another.[1] This silence regarding patterns of deviant sexual activity can be linked to inattention to the basic question of sexual socialization in social psychology. In other words, we have little to say about deviant conduct because we lack a socialization model concerning sexual development against which to measure departures from "normal" sexual socialization.

Consider the claim that sociological theorizing regarding deviant behavior is incomplete in that it fails to include sexual crimes and sexual deviation in a systematic way within contemporary theory. As a case in point, one of the best-known and most widely used textbooks on "the sociology of deviant behavior" devotes only 16 pages out of more than 600 to sexual deviation.[2] A review of contemporary criminology textbooks turns up similar results, giving sexual offenders short shrift or no attention at all, even though sexual deviants represent a significant group of

[1] This point has been made regarding homosexuality by Howard S. Becker, in his review of Hendrik M. Ruitenbeek, ed., *The Problem of Homosexuality in Modern Society* (New York: E. P. Dutton and Co., 1963) in *American Journal of Sociology* LXX (July 1964), 130.

[2] Marshall B. Clinard, *Sociology of Deviant Behavior* (rev. ed.; New York: Holt, Rinehart and Winston, Inc., 1963), pp. 240–56.

real-life criminals. On this topic, Barnes and Teeters,[3] Tappan,[4] Taft and England,[5] Caldwell,[6] Cavan,[7] Johnson,[8] and Sutherland and Cressey [9] are all silent, or nearly so. Bloch and Geis,[10] Korn and McCorkle,[11] and Reckless [12] devote some space to sexual criminals, but their remarks are somewhat tangential to the question of causation. For example, Korn and McCorkle report on a number of fallacious beliefs about sex offenders,[13] including the notions that there are a large number of homicidal sex fiends abroad in the land, sexual deviants are usually recidivists, and sexual criminals usually progress from minor to increasingly more violent and serious crimes. Other misconceptions center about the belief that "sexual psychopaths" exist as a clinical entity, that these offenders are oversexed, that effective methods for treating them are known, and that recently passed laws aimed at sexual offenders are effective.

There is some evidence of growing interest in sociological analysis of sexual misconduct. Wheeler's critique of sex offense statutes contains a number of insights regarding the sociological analysis of sexual behavior and sexual deviation.[14] He hints at several provocative hypotheses concerning social interactional backgrounds out of which certain forms of sexual deviation may develop.[15] McCord, McCord, and Verden have reported upon the family backgrounds of sexual deviants in one of their siftings of the Cambridge-Somerville Youth Study data.[16] Reiss has

---

[3] Harry Elmer Barnes and Negley K. Teeters, *New Horizons in Criminology* (3rd ed.; Englewood Cliffs, N.J.: Prentice-Hall, Inc., 1959), pp. 96–105.

[4] Paul W. Tappan, *Crime, Justice and Correction* (New York: McGraw-Hill Book Co., Inc., 1960).

[5] Donald R. Taft and Ralph W. England, Jr., *Criminology* (4th ed.; New York: The Macmillan Co., 1964), pp. 247–70.

[6] Robert G. Caldwell, *Criminology* (2nd ed.; New York: The Ronald Press Co., 1965).

[7] Ruth Shonle Cavan, *Criminology* (2nd ed.; New York: Thomas Y. Crowell Co., 1955), pp. 220–23.

[8] Elmer H. Johnson, *Crime, Correction, and Society* (Homewood, Ill.: The Dorsey Press, 1964).

[9] Edwin H. Sutherland and Donald R. Cressey, *Principles of Criminology* (7th ed.; Philadelphia: J. B. Lippincott Co., 1966).

[10] Herbert A. Bloch and Gilbert Geis, *Man, Crime, and Society* (New York: Random House, Inc., 1962), pp. 282–309.

[11] Richard R. Korn and Lloyd W. McCorkle, *Criminology and Penology* (New York: Holt, Rinehart and Winston, Inc., 1959), pp. 158–67.

[12] Walter C. Reckless, *The Crime Problem* (4th ed.; New York: Appleton-Century-Crofts, Inc., 1967), pp. 226–54.

[13] Korn and McCorkle, op. cit., pp. 162–66.

[14] Stanton Wheeler, "Sex Offenses: A Sociological Critique," *Law and Contemporary Problems*, XXV (Spring 1960), 258–78.

[15] Ibid., pp. 277–78.

[16] William McCord, Joan McCord, and Paul Verden, "Family Relations and Sexual Deviance in Lower-Class Adolescents," *International Journal of Social Psychiatry*, VIII (Summer 1962), 165–79. It should be noted that this is a somewhat defective study. For one thing, some relatively novel definitions of "sexual deviance" are employed, so that juvenile masturbators are labeled as "perverted" deviants. Also, no data are provided regarding the adult outcomes of these juvenile patterns, so it is not entirely clear as to what kinds of persons are the subject of attention here.

illuminated the topic of adolescent sexual deviation through a thoughtful examination of American values, adolescent status structure, and related variables.[17] He notes a number of ways in which contemporary values and adolescent status ambiguity contribute to patterns of sexual behavior. He also directs attention to the varied societal definitions of adolescent sexual conduct which are related to age, racial, socioeconomic, and other variables. We shall have occasion to examine other cases of this sort as this chapter unfolds.

Unfortunately, these recent works are exceptions to the major point that the developmental processes by which persons come to be homosexuals, exhibitionists, child molesters, or to engage in other forms of sexual conduct, have been ignored by sociologists. One common tendency in the study of deviance and criminology has been to default on the etiological issues regarding sexual deviation by turning this matter over to psychiatrists. For example, this kind of behavior is often attributed to "compulsions" which are supposed to drive the deviant. Sex offenders are seen as persons whose actions are not rationally motivated, so they are thought to lie outside the purview of sociological commentary.[18] But we need to discontinue practices of this kind. Sexual conduct, deviant or otherwise, is learned behavior. As such it is no less "sociological" than most of the other phenomena to which we direct our curiosity.

## SEXUAL SOCIALIZATION

What about socialization theory? What have social psychologists had to say regarding sexual socialization, by way of a model of "normality" against which to contrast deviant sexual behavior and roles? One summary of the social-psychological state of interest in sexual issues has been made by Child. He declares:

But while socialization variables are thus shown by elimination to have great importance as antecedents to adult sexual behavior, we do not yet have an

[17] Albert J. Reiss, "Sex Offenses: The Marginal Status of the Adolescent," *Law and Contemporary Problems*, XXV (Spring 1960), 309–33.

[18] An incisive analysis of the compulsive hypothesis has been made by Cressey. See Donald R. Cressey, "The Differential Association Theory and Compulsive Crimes," *Journal of Criminal Law, Criminology and Police Science*, XLV (May–June 1954), 29–40. Cressey notes that offenders to whom the label "compulsive" is attached, such as "kleptomaniacs," are motivated in the same way that other criminals are motivated. They select places in which to carry out their acts, plan their crimes in advance, and behave in other ways indicating deliberate, rational thought. Cressey suggests that application of the "compulsive crime" label most frequently occurs when the subject is not able to verbalize about his behavior in terms of motives that are current, popular, and sanctioned in society.

adequate scientific basis for stating the exact relationships involved. Nor do we have as yet an adequate basis for judging the extent to which variations in adult sexual behavior are to be ascribed directly to variables in sexual socialization, and to what extent they are instead to be considered as indirect effects of variables originally pertinent to other systems of behavior.[19]

A review of contemporary social psychology textbooks bears out Child's negative report, for most of these books systematically ignore the subject of sexual socialization,[20] while others devote only a few pages to patterns of sexual behavior.[21] However, the beginnings of socialization theory in the area of sexual behavior can be discerned. In the remarks to follow, we shall sketch a framework of analysis which will orient our subsequent discussions of sexual deviance.

From what sources shall a conception of sexual learning be drawn? The most well-known approach to sexual development is in psychoanalytic theories.[22] These arguments stress the assumed role of instinctual sources of sexual motivation in behavior and advance a number of claims about early life experiences and sexuality which are difficult or impossible to test scientifically. Accordingly, we must look elsewhere for directions regarding sexual socialization theory. Some psychiatrists, such as Harry Stack Sullivan, have offered interpretations of sexual behavior which are rooted in learning theory and symbolic-interactional perspectives on human behavior.[23] Similarly, psychiatrists have conducted studies of sexual conduct which provide behavioral data that lend themselves to

---

[19] Irvin L. Child, "Socialization," in *Handbook of Social Psychology*, II, ed. Gardner Lindzey (Cambridge: Addison-Wesley Publishing Co., Inc., 1954), p. 667.

[20] The following were examined for material on sexual socialization: S. Stansfeld Sargent and Robert C. Williamson, *Social Psychology* (2nd ed.; New York: The Ronald Press Co., 1958); Theodore M. Newcomb, *Social Psychology* (New York: Holt, Rinehart and Winston, Inc., 1950); Jack H. Curtis, *Social Psychology* (New York: McGraw-Hill Book Co., Inc., 1960); Muzafer Sherif and Carolyn W. Sherif, *An Outline of Social Psychology* (rev. ed.; New York: Harper & Row, 1956); Tamotsu Shibutani, *Society and Personality* (Englewood Cliffs, N.J.: Prentice-Hall, Inc., 1961); Kimball Young, *Social Psychology* (3rd ed.; New York: Appleton-Century-Crofts, Inc., 1956); Robert E. L. Faris, *Social Psychology* (New York: The Ronald Press Co., 1952); Solomon E. Asch, *Social Psychology* (Englewood Cliffs, N.J.: Prentice-Hall, Inc., 1952); David Krech, Richard S. Crutchfield, and Egerton L. Ballachey, *Individual in Society* (New York: McGraw-Hill Book Co., Inc., 1962); Paul F. Secord and Carl W. Backman, *Social Psychology* (New York: McGraw-Hill Book Co., Inc., 1964).

[21] Richard Dewey and W. J. Humber, *The Development of Human Behavior* (New York: The Macmillan Co., 1951), pp. 168–70, 464–79; Alfred R. Lindesmith and Anselm L. Strauss, *Social Psychology* (rev. ed.; New York: Holt, Rinehart and Winston, Inc., 1956), pp. 553–60, 680–86.

[22] For examples of psychoanalytic theory applied to sex offenders, see Bernard Glueck, Sr., "Sex Offenses: A Clinical Approach," *Law and Contemporary Problems*, XXV (Spring 1960), 279–91; Clifford Allen, *A Textbook of Psychosexual Disorders* (London: Oxford University Press, 1962).

[23] Harry Stack Sullivan, *The Interpersonal Theory of Psychiatry* (New York: W. W. Norton and Co., Inc., 1953), pp. 263–96.

social psychological interpretations; that is, these materials can be understood in interactional terms.[24]

Manford Kuhn has offered some observations which suggest the directions which a symbolic interactional view of sexual behavior would take. He points out that sex acts, sexual objects, and sexual partners are *social objects* which have meaning to persons because social meanings have been assigned to them through language and communication. The physiology of man does not explain his behavior, sexual or otherwise. Kuhn asserts that sexual roles are social, so that while physiology sets limits upon the role-behavior which is possible, it is the learning process which creates sexual motives, designates partners, and determines the kinds of behavior to be engaged in to reach sexual objectives.[25]

These observations of Kuhn offer a starting point for development of a social-psychological theory of sexual socialization and sex roles. Patterns of sexual behavior—sex roles—are learned.[26] Regarding patterns of sexual action, it is clear that there is a wide range of stimuli having the potential to call out sexual responses, so individuals could react, in theory at least, in ways they define as sexual (ejaculation, and so on) to such varied stimuli as heterosexual intercourse, homosexual mouth, genital, or anal contacts, animal contacts, burglary of dwelling units, firesetting, and a plethora of seemingly "non-sexual" stimuli. Nearly all of the potential sexual stimulus-response patterns are actually observed in any large population of adults. All of the varied forms of sexual role-behavior are learned through some kind of socialization experience.

One major observation is that the relatively permanent sexual role-behavior adopted by individuals is largely a function of their sexual self-concepts. For example, evidence from the Kinsey studies shows that many males experience homosexual contacts at some point in their lives, but do not adopt homosexuality as an adult, preferred pattern of sexual adjustment.[27] On this same point, studies by Ward and Kassebaum and by Giallombardo in two women's prisons indicate that a number of the prisoners become involved in a transitory pattern of homosexual activity,

[24] Irving Bieber, Harvey J. Dain, Paul R. Dince, Marvin G. Drellich, Henry G. Grand, Ralph H. Gundlach, Malvina W. Kremer, Alfred H. Rifkin, Cornelia B. Wilbur, Toby B. Bieber, *Homosexuality* (New York: Basic Books, Inc., 1962).

[25] Manford H. Kuhn, "Kinsey's View of Human Behavior," *Social Problems*, I (April 1954), 123.

[26] A general review of existing writings and research in the anthropology and sociology of sex is Winston Ehrmann, "Social Determinants of Human Sexual Behavior," in *Determinants of Human Sexual Behavior*, ed. George Winokur (Springfield, Ill.: Charles C Thomas, Publisher, 1963), pp. 142–63.

[27] Alfred C. Kinsey, Wardell B. Pomeroy, and Clyde E. Martin, *Sexual Behavior in the Human Male* (Philadelphia: W. B. Saunders Co., 1948); for a review and critique of the Kinsey studies, see "Sexual Behavior in American Society" issue, *Social Problems*, I (April 1954). This issue contains a series of papers centered around the Kinsey studies.

becoming known by the other prisoners as "jail house turnouts." [28] The interesting thing is that most of these women continue to define themselves as heterosexual in sexual posture and apparently return to heterosexual patterns of response upon release from prison. Impressionistic observations from male prisons suggest that similar, temporary homosexual liaisons occur among male inmates without leading to homosexuality as a preferred sexual role outside of prison walls. Reiss' data regarding delinquent boys who "play the queers" indicate that these youths participate in homosexual mouth-genital contacts without their adult heterosexual roles being impaired.[29]

The proper question regarding sexual socialization does not ask how persons come to engage in certain forms of overt behavior. Rather, the major thrust of the preceding remarks is to suggest that we would do better to ask how actors come to define themselves as "normal" (and subsequently engage in heterosexual acts). In the same way, we need to inquire as to how persons adopt role-conceptions of themselves as "gay," "dikes," "sexually inadequate," and so on, and thereafter come to engage in various forms of deviant conduct.

In a very general way, it appears that individuals get a self-image of themselves as "normal," heterosexual males or females out of a variety of sex role experiences beginning early in life. Probably the most critical are those which contribute to the development of a stable, *generalized* conception of self as male or female. That is, the specific sexual conception of self and the sexual response preferences that develop represent the relatively natural outgrowth of acquisition of a broad set of cultural definitions centering around gender roles.

The kinds of experiences involved in normal sexual socialization are those in which parents consistently deal with the child within the guidelines of culturally prescribed parent-child interactional norms. The clinical literature on sexual behavior indicates that an atmosphere of tolerance for forms of sexual experimentation, such as masturbation, and an open-minded and "natural" posture by parents regarding sexual matters have important consequences for the degree of sexual adjustment adopted by the individual. The literature suggests that "deviant" sexual adjustment patterns, particularly homosexual ones, are commonly the product of atypical socialization experiences in which he is dealt with in sexually inappropriate ways, or fails to acquire an appropriate pattern of identi-

[28] David A. Ward and Gene G. Kassebaum, "Homosexuality: A Mode of Adaptation in a Prison for Women," *Social Problems*, XII (Fall 1964), 159–77; Ward and Kassebaum, *Women's Prison* (Chicago: Aldine Publishing Co., 1965); Rose Giallombardo, *Society of Women* (New York: John Wiley and Sons, Inc., 1966).

[29] Albert J. Reiss, Jr., "The Social Integration of Queers and Peers," *Social Problems*, IX (Fall 1961), 102–20.

fication with his parents. This clinical material shows that a number of markedly unconventional, "seductive" parent-child experiences sometimes occur which lead to markedly deviant sexual role-conceptions and behavior patterns.

Sexual learning is unduly complicated and fraught with danger in American society, due to the peculiar nature of American sexual values which define sexuality as evil or "dirty" and not to be discussed openly. According to Gagnon, there is a pronounced lack of consensus in the United States regarding sexual behavior and sexual experiences. For the most part, value agreements concerning sexuality are evolved between such sexual pairs as husbands and wives largely in terms of subtle cues and gestures rather than explicit communicational dialogues. As a result of this secretive and unshared character to sexuality, parents are required to work out by themselves solutions to parent-child interactional concerns in the sexual area.[30] Because sexuality is a forbidden topic, parents normally fail to provide their children with a vocabulary for interpreting and integrating sexuality and allied matters, and widespread "nonlabeling" occurs. In turn, Gagnon holds that "given this framework of repression and avoidance by parents, it is not surprising that the child gets the bulk of his sexual information, though not his attitudes, through peer relationships." [31]

Our discussion so far suggests that we should look for clues regarding the plethora of sexual difficulties in which Americans are enmeshed in the general area of early interactional experiences. Such distortions of sexuality as frigidity might be traced to overly repressive parent-child experiences, and impotency or sexual fears are probably linked to identifiable interactional experiences. Idiosyncratic socialization experiences are probably frequently at the heart of homosexual role behavior carried on by individuals heavily involved in that kind of sexual activity. It is also likely that some markedly atypical experiences, including seductive interaction, contribute to the development of instances of violent sexual conduct on the part of adult males in which the victim is mutilated, beaten, and otherwise abused by the offender. In brief, the long-term sexual activity of the adult is conditioned by early interactional experiences. These lead to particular sexual self-notions which, in turn, result in adoption of some specific sexual role pattern such as that of "homosexual."

[30] John H. Gagnon, "Sexuality and Sexual Learning in the Child," *Psychiatry,* XXVIII (August 1965), 212–28; see also Daniel G. Brown and David B. Lynn, "Human Sexual Development: An Outline of Components and Concepts," *Journal of Marriage and the Family,* XXVIII (May 1966), 155–62.

[31] Gagnon, *op. cit.,* p. 223.

It is probable that some forms of sexual behavior, particularly deviant ones, emerge out of adult life experiences. Moreover, in some cases, it is likely that the person's sexual self-image emerges *after* some initial, exploratory playing of a new sex role. For example, exhibitionism and child-molesting are carried on by individuals who have gone through a conventional socialization experience and are "normal" in sexual orientation. But in later life certain of these persons have undergone alterations in family relationships or other experiences which culminate in self-concept changes toward notions of "inadequacy." Their behavior appears to be related to these relatively current experiences and is not traceable back to initial sexual socialization.

A parallel line of argument is that investigation of homosexual behavior might profit from attention to the risk-taking, processual conceptualization of the development of deviant careers advanced by Lemert.[32] It may be that homosexual roles sometimes grow out of situations in which tentative and exploratory flirtations with homosexual activities lead to social identification of the person as a "queer" or "fairy." This altered social identity cuts the person off from reentry into the world of "normals," so he is prevented from reestablishing his heterosexual self-image. It is conceivable that a "mechanistic" causal pattern operates here, instead of the commonly assumed genetic process in which early life experiences result in early sexual identities which then determine adult role-behavior.

On the point of mechanistic or situational causation, Wheeler holds that a good deal of the behavior which might be labeled as "normal" rape, in which force is employed in sexual intercourse but mutilation and other aberrant actions are absent, is carried on by "normal" individuals.[33] These instances of deviation often develop out of a pattern of interaction in which the "victim" is initially a willing and voluntary participant in the actions. The activities of the two interactional partners become "rape" only at a later point, when the offender's sexual demands exceed the expectations of the "victim," as for example when he requests anal intercourse with the "victim." Some evidence is at hand to indicate that cases of "pedophilia" (child-molesting) are carried on by relatively "normal" individuals who have come to develop feelings of sexual and interpersonal inadequacy out of relatively recent life events.[34] There are several obvious ways in which deteriorated relationships between marital partners might contribute to genesis of this kind of behavior. Finally,

[32] Edwin M. Lemert, "Social Structure, Social Control, and Deviation," in *Anomie and Deviant Behavior,* ed. Marshall B. Clinard (New York: Free Press of Glencoe, Inc., 1964), pp. 57–97.

[33] Wheeler, *op. cit.*

[34] Saul Toobert, Kenwood F. Bartelme, and Eugene S. Jones, "Some Factors Related to Pedophilia," *International Journal of Social Psychiatry,* IV (Spring 1959), 272–79.

data on father-daughter incest contain indications that this activity is carried on by males with relatively conventional sexual orientations. Involvement in sexual behavior with "inappropriate" partners seems related to unavailability of more appropriate sexual partners, due to illness of the spouse, social and physical isolation of the family unit, and related factors. In some cases, seductive interaction between father and daughter may contribute to development of incestuous acts, as may covert collaboration of the wife in the relationship, as she encourages the father to refrain from sexual acts with her and "winks at" sexual contact between him and his daughter.

Some of the broad outlines of a social-psychological perspective on sexual development have now been established. These guidelines will be used in the pages to follow, where we shall also elaborate upon learning processes in normal and deviant sexual conduct. The nature of some of the causal hypotheses to be advanced is hinted at by the foregoing, but in subsequent pages these etiological contentions are to be elaborated in more detail.

## SEX AND LAW IN AMERICAN SOCIETY

One thing readily apparent to any literate citizen in the United States is the schizoid character of American social structure as it has to do with sexual conduct.[35] The major cultural heroes of American society include the Hollywood actress sex symbol who serves as an erotic object in the fantasies of millions of males. This society couples a kind of *Playboy* mentality and an emphasis upon youthfulness, eroticism, and sexual attractiveness with laws which strive to restrict the display of sexual conduct to marriage. Even there, laws of various states attempt to regulate the particular forms of sexual activity in which marital partners may engage. In short, sexual behavior occupies a central place in the scheme of American values, coexistent with puritanical sentiments which would severely circumscribe the citizen's opportunities to engage in sexual activity.

American criminal laws regarding sexual misbehavior are extremely ubiquitous. In general, these laws endeavor to regulate: *a*) the degree of consent in sexual acts, *b*) the nature of the sexual object, *c*) the nature of the act, or *d*) the setting in which the act occurs.[36] Wheeler argues that these statutes embody conflicting aims, for some express the moral

---

[35] One discussion of this theme can be found in Bloch and Geis, *op. cit.*, pp. 286–87.
[36] Wheeler, *op. cit.*, pp. 258–59.

condemnation of the community, such as laws directed at homosexuals. Others are concerned with sex acts viewed as socially harmful, while still others endeavor to control individuals thought to be psychopathological in personality organization.[37] This situation of large numbers of laws directed at sexual behavior means that nearly all sexual acts other than specific forms of heterosexual intercourse in marriage are forbidden by law.

Of course, the fact that criminal laws are extremely broad-gauged in definition does not mean that the majority of persons who violate them are dealt with as criminals. Quite the contrary, for a great many forbidden acts are voluntarily engaged in within situations of privacy and go unobserved and unreported. Laws against fornication would be a case in point, for it is doubtful that more than a negligible share of the adult fornicators ever become subjected to the criminal law.

American sex laws are not without critics; it has been widely argued that these statutes improperly and unwisely extend the concern of criminal law to innocuous matters of private morality, such as homosexual acts between consenting adults. The critics would revise these prohibitions to narrow the kinds of behavior they proscribe to those which are unequivocally harmful to society. Another feature of sex laws in the United States which make them open to criticism is that they are extremely inconsistent from one jurisdiction to another. As examples, adultery laws vary between different states both in definitions of adultery and in penalties associated with these acts; mutual masturbation is a criminal offense in some states and not in others; penalties for consensual homosexual acts range from fines or jail sentences to life imprisonment. Clearly, the uniformity criminal law is presumed to contain is missing in the case of sex statutes.[38]

Existing laws defining sex offenders have several major implications for the study of causation. First, the etiological task cries out for some kind of taxonomy of sex offender patterns which will allow us to reduce the variety of criminal activities to an orderly set of types amenable to explanation. One example of such a classification is by Bloch and Geis, who propose a three-fold system involving offenses against minors, offenses employing violence, and offenses which offend moral sentiments

[37] *Ibid.*, pp. 259–61.

[38] An excellent summary of American laws, with particular emphasis on the variations in these laws, is Morris Ploscowe, "Sex Offenses: The American Legal Context," *Law and Contemporary Problems*, XXV (Spring 1960), 217–24; see also Karl M. Bowman and Bernice Engle, "A Psychiatric Evaluation of Laws of Homosexuality," *American Journal of Psychiatry*, CXII (February 1956), 577–83; Karl M. Bowman, "Review of Sex Legislation and Control of Sex Offenders in the United States of America," in *Final Report on California Sexual Deviation Research*, State of California, Department of Mental Hygiene (Sacramento: State of California, 1954), pp. 15–40; John Drzazga, *Sex Crimes* (Springfield, Ill.: Charles C Thomas, Publisher, 1960).

of the community.[39] We shall see a number of other efforts to evolve meaningful systems for categorizing sex offenders in the pages that follow. Our commentary will be organized around a number of descriptions of offender role-careers which are designed to identify homogeneous patterns of sexual criminality.

The second causal consequence which flows out of existing criminal statutes is that an adequate formulation concerning sexual criminality will have to be sufficiently multifaceted and complex to explain extremely disparate kinds of behavior. Some kinds of criminality represent behavior patterns which differ little or not at all from conventional patterns of sexual behavior, such as statutory rape, which involves consenting individuals both of whom are sexually although not chronologically mature. In this case, the explanatory problem is in accounting for social contingencies which result in some persons falling into the hands of the police, rather than accounting for personal idiosyncracies of the offenders. At the polar extreme from this kind of illegality stand bizarre and violent incidents of sexual crimes. Since these actions are probably not carried on by individuals who are the product of normal sexual socialization, a strikingly different explanation of behavior must be uncovered.

In the remarks to follow on patterns of sexual deviancy, six types of offender behavior will be identified. We shall take up statutory rapists, aggressive rapists, violent sex offenders, nonviolent sex offenders (child-molesters and exhibitionists), incest cases, and homosexuals. Role-career descriptions will be provided for all of these types.

Before turning to examination of role-careers, let us take an overview of several major studies of sex offenders.[40] A summary presentation of these pieces of research should be useful in acquiring a sense of sex offenders in the aggregate. Moreover, most research in the past has been oriented to inductive discovery, rather than being informed by a body of theory which focused the inquiry. These investigations have not endeavored to test propositions about sex offender role-careers, so they are difficult to interpret in typological terms.

## STUDIES OF SEX OFFENDERS

One older study of sex offenders concerned deviants referred to Bellevue Hospital in New York for psychiatric investigation.[41] The researchers

---

[39] Bloch and Geis, op. cit., pp. 283–84.

[40] For a somewhat incoherent but rather complete summary of studies, see Benjamin Karpman, *The Sexual Offender and His Offenses* (New York: The Julian Press, Inc., 1954).

[41] Benjamin Apfelberg, Carl Sugar, and Arnold Z. Pfeffer, "A Psychiatric Study of 250 Sex Offenders," *American Journal of Psychiatry*, C (May 1944), 762–70.

indicated that these criminals had been involved in a wide variety of sex crimes, including incest, forced sexual relations, child-molesting, and homosexual acts. Most of the offenders had prior records of criminality, but this is to be expected in view of the special character of the sample. Another of these older investigations concerned Wisconsin prisoners.[42] Gillin reported that of the 279 sex offenders incarcerated in the institution, 127 had been convicted of rape, 25 had been charged with statutory rape, while the remaining 127 had committed a wide variety of other sex offenses. The sex offenders as a group were predominantly from backgrounds of low socioeconomic status, had poor school records and relatively low intelligence, poor marital ties, and generally bland personalities.

A third report on sex offenders has been made by Guttmacher concerning 172 persons referred to a court-connected psychiatric clinic in Baltimore.[43] Some of the major findings in this material are that Negroes were underrepresented in the group of sex offenders, while persons of low intelligence were overrepresented. Slightly over one-half of the offenders were categorized as showing "neurotic character disorders." This is not surprising, given the kind of sample involved in this study.[44]

Ellis and Brancale have examined a somewhat more representative sample of sex offenders in an investigation in New Jersey.[45] As a result of legislation passed in 1949 in that state, all persons charged with rape, sodomy, incest, lewdness, indecent exposure, dealing in obscene material, indecent communications to females, or carnal abuse were to be referred to the New Jersey Diagnostic Center.[46] This study reported on the characteristics of the first 300 persons sentenced to the center. These offenders were a mixed bag of individuals, for 20 per cent had committed statutory rape, 17 per cent had been involved in sex relations of other kinds with minors, 29 per cent had engaged in exhibitionism, and 16 per cent had been apprehended for homosexuality. Only 3 per cent of the offenders had been involved in forcible rape, while incest cases made up only 4 per cent of the group. Clearly, the majority of sex offenders who fall into the hands of the police and courts in New Jersey are relatively petty or nonviolent individuals.[47] In comparing the center commitments with

[42] John L. Gillin, The Wisconsin Prisoner (Madison: University of Wisconsin Press, 1946), pp. 11–13, 88–131.

[43] Manfred S. Guttmacher, Sex Offenses (New York: W. W. Norton and Co., 1951).

[44] Ibid., pp. 58–104.

[45] Albert Ellis and Ralph Brancale, The Psychology of Sex Offenders (Springfield, Ill.: Charles C Thomas, Publisher, 1956); for a summary of this study, see Brancale, Ellis, and Ruth R. Doorbar, "Psychiatric and Psychological Investigations of Convicted Sex Offenders: A Summary Report," American Journal of Psychiatry, CIX (July 1952), 17–21.

[46] Ellis and Brancale, op. cit., pp. 11–12.

[47] Ibid., p. 31.

inmates at the state prison, the former appeared to include many more relatively petty deviants, while the prison received the more disordered or violent individuals.

Some major characteristics of the sex offenders were that about one-half were under 30 years of age, nearly one-half were single, 44 per cent had less than eighth grade educational attainment, and nearly 70 per cent were from low income backgrounds.[48]

The Ellis and Brancale data lend themselves to two general conclusions. First, it appears that the vast majority of sex offenders are petty criminals who are relatively normal in personality structure. They do not fit the "sex fiend" image in any important way. For example, only about 5 per cent of these offenders had employed force in their crimes. Additionally, 78 per cent were diagnosed as "normal," "mildly neurotic," or "severely neurotic," while only 3 per cent were judged psychopathic. Over one-half of these violators were deemed to be sexually inhibited, with 72 per cent of the exhibitionists and 66 per cent of the child-molesters being so classified. These findings are markedly at variance with sex fiend notions currently held by citizens in American society.[49]

The second major impression from this study is that apprehended sex offenders tend to be socially disadvantaged individuals of generally low intelligence and economic position. It looks as though persons identified as sex offenders are often picked out of the population because of their social backgrounds, rather than as a direct result of their criminality. In this sense, the case of apprehended sex offenders parallels that of property offenders, many of whom appear unluckier than other persons, rather than distinctly more criminalistic than nonoffenders.

Another large-scale study in sexual deviation was carried on in the 1950's in California.[50] That study noted that felony sex crimes in 1952 constituted only 2.5 per cent of all reported felonies in that state. Of the 3705 felony sex crimes in 1952, 1941 were cases of forcible or statutory rape, while 1764 were other kinds of sex offenses. Extreme force and violence was rare, even in felony crimes, so that only 9 per cent of the persons prosecuted in San Francisco on rape charges were convicted of forcible rape. The investigators reported that most of the sex offenses known to the police in California were petty misdemeanor offenses.[51] On the basis of these data, they concluded: "These data therefore show that the majority of all convicted sex offenders commit socially-offensive

[48] *Ibid.*, p. 12.
[49] *Ibid.*, pp. 26–63.
[50] State of California, Department of Mental Hygiene, *Final Report on California Sexual Deviation Research.*
[51] *Ibid.*, pp. 94–98.

but nondangerous acts, and the majority of all convictions occur at the level of misdemeanors." [52]

Other findings from this research included the observation that incarcerated sex offenders had less extensive records of prior criminality than other kinds of criminals, and also showed lower parole violation rates than other prisoners.[53] In a separate part of this study, a group of violators who had been placed in Metropolitan State Hospital as "sexual psychopaths" were examined. These individuals were a somewhat varied collection of sex deviants, but most had been sexually involved with children. A group of these offenders were classified by the clinical staff either as *minor sexual deviants* who had histories of commonplace sexual acts or *major sexual deviants* who employed aggression and force in their criminality and were characterized by compulsive pursuit of bizarre sexual activities. The researchers subjected these persons to psychological testing, using the Minnesota Multiphasic Personality Inventory. They found that a scale of 21 items from that personality inventory did separate the two groups of deviants: the major sexual deviants generally had different scores on this scale than the minor deviants. This evidence appears to confirm the findings of other studies which show that many sex offenders are relatively normal individuals, but that some relatively disturbed individuals who commit atypically deviant sexual acts are to be found in the population of sexual criminals.[54]

The most recent study of sex offenders, as well as the most complex and detailed investigation to date, is by the Kinsey-founded Institute for Sex Research, Inc.[55] The report of that investigation is nearly 1000 pages in length, representing a vast compendium of findings on sexual deviants. However, the study is impressive negatively as well, for it demonstrates the relative paucity of results from inductive, fact-gathering inquiry. This work was not guided by a set of theoretical propositions around which evidence was gathered. Instead, it endeavored to discover significant facts about sex offenders through examination of great amounts of descriptive information.

This study dealt with a sample of 1356 convicted sex offenders, principally from prisons in Indiana and California, who were interviewed during 1941–1945 and 1953–1955. These sex offenders were compared to a sample of 888 prison inmates who had been convicted of nonsexual offenses and a control group of 477 noncriminal citizens.[56]

[52] *Ibid.*, p. 99.
[53] *Ibid.*, p. 100.
[54] *Ibid.*, pp. 136–47.
[55] Paul H. Gebhard, John H. Gagnon, Wardell B. Pomeroy, and Cornelia V. Christenson, *Sex Offenders* (New York: Harper & Row, 1965).
[56] *Ibid.*, pp. 27–53.

The range of activities engaged in by the sex offenders was considerable; the researchers found it necessary to categorize them and their actions in several major dimensions. The sexual offenses were classified in terms of the sex of the victim or co-participant, so that heterosexual and homosexual behaviors were recognized. In addition, sexual actions were divided into those which were forced as opposed to those consensual in nature, while the victims or co-participants were categorized as children, minors (persons between 12 and 15 years of age), and adults. Combinations of these dimensions yielded 12 possible types of behavior, but patterns of forced homosexual relations were excluded because they were rarely encountered among the offenders. Finally, the researchers sorted sex offenders into three additional incest types based on age of victim or co-participant, as well as into two other categories, peepers and exhibitionists. In all, 14 types of sex misbehavior were singled out for study.[57]

The general strategy in this research centered about examination of a number of kinds of experiences in the lives of each of the individuals involved in the 14 kinds of sexual activity. Facts were reported regarding early life experiences, masturbation, sex dreams, heterosexual petting, premarital coitus, marital experiences, extramarital coitus and postmarital coitus, animal contacts, criminality of the offenders, and a number of other matters. While much of this factual and statistical material tends to obscure more than it reveals, some significant facets of sexual misconduct do emerge from this information. For example, almost none of the heterosexual offenders against children said that they preferred young girls as sex objects, so their behavior appears to be more the result of situational contingencies than pathological motivation.[58] Regarding heterosexual acts with minors or adults, the data indicate that the victim was frequently active in initiation of the sex behavior, and that the offenders were quite normal and conventional persons.[59] Another finding was that those who used force in heterosexual offenses against adults were not markedly unconventional individuals, save with regard to their willingness to utilize coercion in achieving sexual ends.[60] Finally, the investigators reported that exhibitionists and peepers were meek, sexually inadequate persons rather than sex fiends.[61] We shall have occasion to refer to more of this material when we examine offender role-careers in greater detail.

[57] Ibid., pp. 10–11.
[58] Ibid., p. 66.
[59] Ibid., pp. 83–102.
[60] Ibid., pp. 177–206.
[61] Ibid., pp. 358–99.

## PATTERNS OF SEXUAL CRIMINALITY

Our earlier comments indicated that sex offenders are a mixed bag of deviants who need to be sorted out into behavioral types. The studies discussed above also pointed to variability among these criminals, so that classificatory efforts have repeatedly been involved in these investigations. There are doubtless various ways of classifying sex offenders which could be recommended as having merit. However, we will treat as relatively distinct types six forms of sexual deviation. In general, our distinctions between offenders are drawn in terms of character of the sexual acts and role of the victims in the behavior. Statutory rapists and aggressive rapists represent two categories similar in the sense that relatively "normal" heterosexual conduct is involved in both, but different in the degree of force and coercion employed in attaining sexual ends. We hold that these two kinds of offenders are fundamentally different from violent sexual assaultists who exhibit idiosyncratic and bizarre sexual motives centering about violence and cruelty. In turn, nonviolent offenders who engage in child-molesting or exhibitionism differ from the preceding three types, both in terms of their behavior and in the sexual inhibitions which characterize them. Of course, nonviolent offenders also vary from the others in the sense that they are likely to be defined as "perverted" or in other ways markedly unusual by members of the general public. Their behavior is of a kind hard to identify with, either because the activity appears very peculiar or the victims seem markedly inappropriate as sexual objects. Incest behavior is a fifth kind of sexual deviancy which appears to be the product of a relatively specialized form of motivational process and background situation. Finally, we shall single out male homosexuals as a sixth group, but it should be recognized that, within the category of homosexuals, important variations exist in sexual behavior, participation in homosexual subcultures, and so on. The six types discussed here are viewed as sufficiently homogeneous to warrant separate discussion, although more detailed differentiations are possible within the role-career categories.

## THE STATUTORY RAPIST ROLE-CAREER [62]

### *Definitional Dimensions*

*Offense Behavior.* Persons in this category are adult males who engage in sexual intercourse with minor females. The "victim" is a willing and voluntary participant in the sexual activities.

[62] Don C. Gibbons, *Changing the Lawbreaker: The Treatment of Delinquents and Criminals,* © 1965. Reprinted by permission of Prentice-Hall, Inc., Englewood Cliffs, New Jersey, pp. 122–23.

*Interactional Setting.* Statutory rape cases develop in a variety of ways. Some offenders are persons such as sailors apprehended "shacking-up" with a minor female in a downtown hotel, for example. Other cases involve adult males who have been carrying on a long-term relationship with a minor female and have been apprehended for sexual acts with that person. In either instance, the essential character of statutory rape is that two individuals have entered into a cooperative, voluntary sexual relationship which happens to be illegal because of the age of the female. The girl in cases of statutory rape which result in detection is usually dealt with in a juvenile court.

*Self-concept.* Statutory rapists regard themselves as law-abiding citizens. They usually view themselves as unlucky persons who were simply doing what everyone else is doing, but got caught. There is, of course, considerable truth in that claim.

*Attitudes.* The attitudes of statutory rapists tend to be conventional and prosocial.

*Role-career.* These persons usually are without any prior record of delinquency or adult criminality. They are essentially law-abiding citizens who have fallen into the hands of the police and courts for technically illegal but culturally widespread acts. Many apprehended and convicted statutory rapists are placed on probation, where they are good risks. Those sent to correctional institutions make good adjustments and tend to play the role of "square Johns" in the institution.

### Background Dimensions

*Social Class.* There is little reason to suppose that statutory rape is a class-linked form of behavior. However, there may be some tendency for law-enforcement agencies to take more stringent actions against detected lower class offenders than against other statutory rapists.

*Family Background.* The family backgrounds of statutory rapists are usually normal and conventional, lacking in any kind of major interactional problems among family members.

*Peer Group Associations.* The peer group affiliations of statutory rapists are conventional. They are usually involved in peer associations in which sexual activities are highly regarded, but this is in no way an atypical peer group value.

*Contact with Defining Agencies.* Contacts with defining agencies are relatively neutral in effect. Some offenders probably feel some degree of hostility toward the police and courts because they view themselves as merely "unlucky" rather than deviant. But it is doubtful that this hostility leads to any reorganization of the person's self-image or to continuation in criminality.

### Discussion

Evidence on the characteristics of statutory rapists is contained in several of the studies discussed earlier. The investigation by Gebhard, *et al.*, contains a number of findings which generally confirm the role-career description above. These investigators report that the median age of men convicted of heterosexual offenses with minor partners (females between 12 and 16 years of age) was 25 years of age. Four-fifths of these individuals were first offenders, while very few were pathological persons. In most cases, the "victim" did not discourage the sexual activity, and in most cases, she failed to report the sexual behavior to anyone. Instead, the complaint against the offender was originated by a third party.[63]

Much the same picture emerges regarding offenders involved in heterosexual acts with adults. Most of the female "victims" were under 25 years of age, and three-fifths were under 18 years of age.[64] No very unusual characteristics on the part of the offenders emerge from the data, so that the authors were moved to conclude: "One is left with the over-all impression of an uneducated, opportunistic, and basically goodhearted soul who takes his pleasure where he finds it and lets the future take care of itself." [65]

## THE AGGRESSIVE RAPIST ROLE-CAREER

### Definitional Dimensions

*Offense Behavior.* Aggressive rapists are persons usually charged with "rape" rather than "statutory rape" when apprehended. They employ varying degrees of force to coerce a physically adult female into sexual activity. The amount of force utilized varies in cases of aggressive rape, and, in addition, interpretations of the offender and the victim regarding the coercion involved in the event frequently differ. Aggressive rapists often argue that they have been convicted on a "bum beef" in that the victim was actually more cooperative than she was willing to admit. At any rate, aggressive rape differs from statutory rape because the sexual activity was not freely entered into by both participants. In most instances of aggressive rape, the sexual activity centers about heterosexual intercourse. Occasionally, aggressive rapists compel the victim to

63 Gebhard, *et al., op. cit.,* pp. 83–105.
64 *Ibid.,* pp. 106–32.
65 *Ibid.,* p. 132.

engage in other sexual acts, such as fellatio, which are commonly defined as "perversions" but are nonetheless fairly commonplace forms of sexual behavior among "normal" persons. In short, this behavior is deviant principally because force is employed by the offender, for the ends pursued by the criminal are relatively conventional.

*Interactional Setting.* Aggressive rape is a form of criminality which often represents a disruption of ordinary interactional patterns. In a good many cases, aggressive rape is the end result of a pattern of social intercourse between a "victim" and an offender which began with voluntary involvement of the two persons in some kind of social activity. An example of this kind of sequence would be a "pickup" in a cocktail bar. Initially, the two individuals engage in drinking and both anticipate that the evening will end on a sexual note. But as events unfold, the offender makes sexual demands which exceed the expectations of the "victim," so coercion is employed. At that point, fornication is converted into "rape." Aggressive rape also sometimes involves instances in which persons unknown to the victim seize her and force her into sexual acts, but this kind of rape probably occurs less frequently.

*Self-concept.* Aggressive rapists do not define themselves as criminals. While they acknowledge that they have been involved in a criminal act, they offer a variety of arguments designed to minimize the seriousness of their behavior, such as the contention that the victim acted in provocative and seductive ways toward them. These offenders view their acts of deviance as essentially alien or unimportant aspects of their conduct.

*Attitudes.* The attitudes of aggressive rapists are relatively conventional, save perhaps for a relative insensitivity to the feelings of the victim.

*Role-career.* Aggressive rapists show backgrounds of little or no prior criminality. If they have been involved in earlier episodes of lawbreaking, these are usually relatively petty offenses. It does not appear that rapists are particularly prone to parole violation and recidivism. Instead, most of them serve long prison sentences and are released, whereupon they are absorbed back into the population of law-abiding citizens.

### Background Dimensions

*Social Class.* Aggressive rapists are commonly lower class or lower middle class individuals. Apparently the general disposition to employ force in interpersonal relations is most common in this social stratum, so aggressive rape is a manifestation of class-linked toleration of violence.

*Family Background.* Aggressive rapists are not from markedly unusual family situations, although some do show backgrounds of relatively early alienation from family bonds. This estrangement from conventional social ties probably contributes to the willingness of the offender to infringe upon the rights of others in the area of sexual conduct.

*Peer Group Associations.* The peer group relationships of the aggressive rapist do not appear to contribute in any marked way to the development of this behavior, at least in the sense of effecting the genesis of sentiments in favor of rape. Of course, in instances of gang rape, the stimulus of group contacts immediately preceding the rape probably contributes something to these episodes.

*Contact with Defining Agencies.* Experiences such as imprisonment apparently have a relatively neutral effect upon these offenders. It does not seem likely that these contacts impel them in the direction of further involvement in criminality.

### Discussion

Data directly relevant to the role-career description above are hard to obtain, particularly in the case of contentions about the interactional processes leading up to rape. Unfortunately, criminologists have devoted insufficient attention to systematic collection of information concerning the social nature of the behavior which becomes subject to attention by social control agencies. This deficiency in the literature of criminology is particularly apparent in the area of sexual misconduct. We are in need of a good deal more descriptive material which would indicate the kinds of social circumstances in which incest, rape, and other sexual offenses occur.

One bit of data regarding rape comes from a study by Pacht, Halleck, and Ehrmann.[66] These investigators examined 1605 offenders who had been committed to the Department of Public Welfare in Wisconsin for psychiatric diagnosis. The Wisconsin Sex Crimes Law requires a psychological investigation in all cases of rape, attempted rape, or indecent sex behavior with a child. Slightly less than half of these offenders were judged to be "not deviated" in psychological makeup. Additionally, these researchers indicated that, of the persons committed to prison, only 17 per cent subsequently violated parole. These findings lend confirmation to the picture of the aggressive rapist which portrays him as a person without marked pathology.

The New Jersey study by Ellis and Brancale also contributes to an

---

[66] Asher R. Pacht, Seymour L. Halleck, and John C. Ehrmann, "Diagnosis and Treatment of the Sexual Offender: A Nine-Year Study," *American Journal of Psychiatry,* CXVIII (March 1962), 802–08.

understanding of rape behavior.[67] They reported that in 66 of the 300 cases examined at the diagnostic center, some degree of force had been involved in the sexual offense. They suggest that reports of coercion in rape cases are sometimes exaggerated because the victim frequently endeavors to minimize her own complicity in the offense. This same study noted that sexual assaultists and rapists had relatively low recidivism rates in comparison to petty sex offenders.

The inquiry into sex offenses by Gebhard, *et al.*, also contains some material germane to the case of aggressive rapists. The heterosexual aggressors in that study who had been involved with minors (females between 12 and 16 years of age) were relatively young men. Many were somewhat impulsive persons from relatively disorganized backgrounds. The heterosexual aggressors against adult females were relatively nondescript individuals who were unusual only in the sense that they had utilized force in sexual activities.[68]

A recent study by Amir represents a beginning of the kind of research needed on rape and other sexual offenses.[69] That investigation dealt with 646 cases of forcible rape that occurred in Philadelphia in 1958 and 1960. It examined the social backgrounds of the 646 victims and 1292 offenders, as well as the circumstances surrounding the acts of forcible rape.

The findings of the research show that most forcible rapes were intraracial events, rather than acts occurring between persons of different racial background. Rapes were significantly more frequent among Negroes than whites, for the rape rates were 12 times higher among Negro than white females. Of course, these observations ought to be treated with some caution, in that they may reflect differentials in crime reporting and law enforcement practices, as well as real racial variations in forcible rape.

Most of the forcible rape offenders in this report were between 15 and 25 years of age, while the majority of victims were also young women. Most of the offenders were unmarried, which was also true of the victims. However, Amir rejected any sort of demographic imbalance explanation of rape, for the sex ratio of unmarried persons in Philadelphia was not unbalanced. Most of the offenders and victims were from lower income backgrounds, and goodly numbers of them were unemployed. About half of the rapists had prior records of criminality, while about a quarter of the victims had been in difficulties with the law or acquired tarnished reputations.

Amir discovered no appreciable relationship between rape and season

[67] Ellis and Brancale, *op. cit.*, pp. 32–37.
[68] Gebhard, *et al.*, *op. cit.*, pp. 155–206.
[69] Menachem Amir, "Forcible Rape," *Federal Probation*, XXXI (March 1967), 51–58.

of the year. However, marked variations existed in the distribution of forcible rapes by days of the week, for most occurred on the weekends, particularly on Saturday. The peak hours for rape were from 8:00 P.M. to 2:00 A.M. Alcohol appeared to be a factor in only about one-third of the cases.

Most of the rapists and their victims lived within the same general area of the community, and the acts of sexual assault occurred within this same neighborhood. About half of the offenders and victims had been involved in a primary relationship with each other before the sexual assault, so these findings seriously undermine the stereotype of the wild-eyed rapist who assaults a total stranger.

The types of coercion or violence employed in the rape incidents were classified and tabulated. In 15 per cent of the incidents, no force was used, while in another 29 per cent roughness was employed by the offenders. Brutal beatings or choking accompanied forcible rapes in only about 30 per cent of the cases. Here again, forcible rape seems to depart from some of the public stereotypes about this behavior. The other side of the coin concerns resistance on the part of the victim. Amir found that the victims were submissive and put up no resistance in over half of the rape incidents. The rapists subjected the victims to "sexual humiliation" (fellatio, cunnilingus, or repeated intercourse) in only about a quarter of the cases. Multiple rape by two or more offenders was involved in 276 of the 646 rape cases.

One point which Amir makes relevant to the typological characterization of rapists is that, in 122 of the incidents, the rape appeared to be victim-precipitated. That is, the victim deported herself in such a way as to encourage sexual assault. She had agreed to engage in intercourse but had later recanted, or she had acted in a sexually provocative manner.

Taken on balance, these findings are supportive of the typological description of aggressive rape. This kind of criminality apparently departs from conventional sexual conduct mainly in the sense that threats or force are utilized. The participants in aggressive rape do not appear to be pathological types. The strong suggestion emerges from Amir's research that forcible rape may be an occasional legal outcome of situations in lower class areas where casual and transitory sexual episodes are commonplace. Quite probably, a large number of sexual liaisons take place which are not very different from the forcible rapes.

Richard Jenkins has offered a set of theoretical contentions regarding rape and other sexual assaults in American society which is congruent with the above findings.[70] He maintains that the bulk of sexually as-

[70] Richard L. Jenkins, "The Making of a Sex Offender," in Criminology: A Book of Readings, eds. Clyde B. Vedder, Samuel Koenig, and Robert E. Clark (New York: The Dryden Press, 1953), pp. 293–300.

saultive conduct in the United States involves fairly minor degrees of force employed by relatively normal persons. At the same time, he claims that there is another end of the scale of violence, involving pathological actors who engage in unprovoked sexual assaults of a bizarre and extraordinary kind. We shall turn to these offenders in the following section.

Jenkins' central thesis is that American society involves the association of violence with sexuality, so that themes or motives which join eroticism and cruelty are often learned in sexual socialization. The results of this kind of socialization frequently show up in mildly sadistic acts which do not become subject to official attention. If Jenkins is correct, one would expect such incidents to be reported by marital partners fairly regularly. However, when these associations with sexuality occur in persons hostile to others, a potential rapist can be observed. According to Jenkins, the extreme example of hostility and sadistic orientations to sexual behavior can be recognized in lust-murderers. Jenkins contends that aggressive rapists are not a particularly unusual or aberrant group of individuals. He avers: "The difference between the law-abiding man and the rapist lies typically not in a difference of sex impulse, but in a difference of inhibition and consideration for the personality of others." [71]

One piece of confirmatory evidence bearing upon this claim that aggression and sexuality are often joined in American society comes from a study by Kirkpatrick and Kanin of dating behavior on a college campus.[72] Over half of the girls interviewed in that study said that they had been offended by sexual aggression directed at them in the previous year. Moreover, the 162 girls who were the targets of aggression reported 1022 such episodes of gratuitous force. Nearly one-quarter of the girls claimed that their dates had endeavored to coerce them into sexual intercourse.

## THE VIOLENT SEX OFFENDER ROLE-CAREER

We have already seen that sex offenders taken *en masse* represent an extremely variegated group of criminals. Within this class of lawbreakers, there are a good many who direct their attention to adult females. But even this subgroup is heterogeneous, for, as we have observed, statutory rapists are unlike aggressive rapists in a variety of ways. Scattered among the offenders who engage in sex offenses against mature females is a third and much smaller group of lawbreakers referred to here as violent sex offenders. They are actors who carry out such violent actions against

[71] *Ibid.*, p. 295.
[72] Clifford Kirkpatrick and Eugene Kanin, "Male Sex Aggression on a University Campus," *American Sociological Review*, XXII (February 1957), 52–58.

female victims that homicides often result from their behavior. There is no denying that the offenders described below exist in some number, for newspapers periodically report incidents of criminality which fit this characterization, and a reading of case-history materials in penal institutions turns up persons who fit this role-career description. Nonetheless, the role-career commentary below must be treated as speculative and contentious, for no detailed evidence has been collected on offenders of this kind. Some indication of the nature of this criminal pattern can be obtained from a work by de River which contains of series of extremely disagreeable photographs of victims of these crimes, but de River's book has few other redeeming features. It does not contain evidence on the causal backgrounds out of which these offenders develop.[73] The studies of sex offenders we have examined above are also of little use as far as violent sex offenders are concerned, for these investigations made no attempt to separate out such lawbreakers for special attention. Instead, violent sex offenders have been intermingled with more conventional murderers and sex offenders.[74]

### Definitional Dimensions [75]

*Offense Behavior.* Violent sex offenders engage in attacks upon female victims which are ostensibly sexual in character. The assault is usually accompanied by acts of extreme and bizarre violence, such as slashing of the victim, cutting off of breasts, and other activities. This behavior is in no sense conventional statutory rape in which the "victim" is a willing participant in sexual intercourse but below the age of consent. Neither is this conventional aggressive rape, for violent sexual offenders employ extreme forms of aggression against a victim, sometimes culminating in homicide. In some cases, normal sexual acts are not part of the actions of the person.

*Interactional Setting.* Violent sex assaults are two-person affairs between a victim and an offender. Victims are chosen in several ways. Some are casual pickups, others are ambushed or surprised by the offender; in either case, the victim has not been in interaction with the offender for any lengthy period of time prior to commission of the criminal act.

*Self-concept.* Violent sex offenders think of themselves as noncriminal,

[73] J. Paul de River, *The Sexual Criminal* (2nd ed.; Springfield, Ill.: Charles C Thomas, Publisher, 1956); see also Drzazga, op. cit.

[74] Gebhard, et al., op. cit., pp. 197–205.

[75] Don C. Gibbons, *Changing the Lawbreaker: The Treatment of Delinquents and Criminals,* © 1965. Reprinted by permission of Prentice-Hall, Inc., Englewood Cliffs, New Jersey, pp. 118–19.

law-abiding citizens, but are likely to exhibit some self-awareness that they are "different" from other persons.

*Attitudes.* The attitudinal structure of violent sex assaultists is conventional, except in the rather private area of sexual attitudes. These are attitudes which are not highly "visible" or likely to be noticed prior to commission of a violent sex act.

*Role-career.* Most violent sex assaultists have no delinquency record or history of involvement in criminality. On occasion, the violent sex offender has been involved in episodes of "peculiar" conduct, such as minor stabbings of females. The offender is normally apprehended after the commission of the crime, convicted, and sentenced to prison. He is normally incarcerated for a lengthy period of time, so recidivism is unlikely in many cases.

### Background Dimensions

*Social Class.* Violent sex criminals seem not to be the product of any single social class background. The etiological factors which lead to this form of criminality are not class-linked in any important way.

*Family Background.* Although there is considerable confusion about the causal backgrounds which lead to this form of behavior, certain patterns of parent-child interaction are significantly involved. It is likely that the violent sex assaultist is the product of a family pattern of repressive sexual notions, seductive mother-son interaction, or similar conditions.

*Peer Group Associations.* Patterns of peer group interaction have no specific significance for behavior patterns of this kind.

*Contact with Defining Agencies.* This violator's contacts with defining agencies are apparently of neutral significance. Such contacts appear not to be harmful, but neither does any treatment seem to have an impressively positive effect.

### Discussion

The need for a typological orientation to sex offenders which would divide this heterogeneous population into meaningful units, as well as for an improved form of sexual socialization theory from which deviant departures could be studied, is readily apparent in the case of violent sex offenders. Research investigations of these persons are not available, and the direction an explanation of their behavioral development should take is not clear. However, the role-career description above hints at some notions which might be entertained about these lawbreakers as hypotheses for investigation. The thrust of these claims is that violent sex offenders probably grow up in family environments which are simultaneously seductive and repressive. The developing person acquires out of this situation a basic heterosexual orientation centered about the expression of conventional erotic motives. This orientation is further aroused or stimulated by a variety of sexually provocative overtures of the mother. Case history documents often note such experiences as the mother sleeping with the son or bathing with him long after he has become a physically mature young male. It would be surprising if the offender could repress completely any feelings of sexual arousal that emanate from these experiences. At the same time, the youth is prevented from overt demonstrations of arousal, partly because of the incest taboo which strongly forbids sexuality directed at the mother. The mother in many cases probably verbalizes about sexual responsiveness in ways which treat it as dirty, evil, and something not to be openly acknowledged. This sort of interactive process may well produce individuals who are carriers of combined themes of lust and aggression in pronounced form. Their hostility-charged sexual actions represent the extreme form of the erotic-aggressive syndrome described by Jenkins and noted earlier in this chapter.

## THE NONVIOLENT SEX OFFENDER ROLE-CAREER

Probably the most abhorred sexual offender, in the eyes of both the general public and prison inmates, is that person who engages in exhibitionism or child-molesting. These individuals are regarded as "perverts," due to their involvement in sexual activities which depart strikingly from conventional heterosexual intercourse with adult partners. In the role-career sketch below, exhibitionists and child-molesters (pedophiles) are described as one pattern of criminality. Even though the specific acts of lawbreaking in which they engage differ, both child-molesters and exhibitionists share a good many characteristics in common.

### Definitional Dimensions [76]

*Offense Behavior.* This category includes offenders involved in exhibitionism, child-molesting, and related offenses, such as peeping or making lewd telephone calls. A comment is in order regarding the term "nonviolent." It is true that, on occasion, the victims of child-molesters are

[76] Don C. Gibbons, *Changing the Lawbreakers: The Treatment of Delinquents and Criminals,* © 1965. Reprinted by permission of Prentice-Hall, Inc., Englewood Cliffs, New Jersey, pp. 119–21.

killed by the offenders. However, this is frequently the result of a panic reaction in which the person fears that the victim will report him, and is not an act motivated by interest in homicidal behavior or violence. Thus persons in this category who commit homicides differ in two ways from violent sex offenders. The former commit sex acts against physically immature victims and show no basic motivational component of violent and aggressive interests. The point should be underscored that the majority of acts of child-molesting are restricted to fondling of the child, are psychologically insignificant events as far as trauma to the victim is concerned, and do not culminate in violence of any sort.

*Interactional Setting.* The interactional settings in which these crimes occur vary somewhat. In the case of exhibitionism, "victims" are usually persons unknown to the offender, chosen somewhat randomly. Exhibitionism tends to occur at places where female observers are likely to be present—schools, parks, and so on. In child-molesting, some victims are unknown to the offender and chosen rather randomly, but others are youngsters well-known to the deviant—neighborhood children, children of friends, children of relatives, and so on.

*Self-concept.* The self-image of the nonviolent sex offender is noncriminal in form. Some offenders vehemently deny that they are "real" criminals. Some also deny that they did, in fact, commit the acts for which they are imprisoned. Others admit that they are engaged in the acts for which they have been charged, but for reasons quite different from the apparent ones. Child-molesters, for example, sometimes contend that the victim initiated the sexual activity. Denial of involvement in sex crimes and avowal of righteous religious sentiments is a common characteristic of nonviolent sex criminals.

*Attitudes.* The attitudes of nonviolent sex offenders are for the most part conventional and prosocial.

*Role-career.* Most criminals in this category are without delinquency records or backgrounds of other criminal activities. Persons engaged in this kind of sexual deviation are usually apprehended, convicted, and sentenced to long prison terms. Those released on parole appear to get reinvolved in such activities in a number of cases.

## Background Dimensions

*Social Class.* This form of crime is not class-linked, so that such offenders come from a variety of social class origins.

*Family Background.* It does not appear that the early parental backgrounds of nonviolent sex offenders are of major significance. These background experiences may play some contributory role in that the offender is characterized by a timid, retiring personality which resulted from early experiences. However, it appears that the more significant family variables by far have to do with the adult marital situation of the offender. In most cases, a pattern of long-term sexual inadequacy on the part of the individual seems to precede involvement in sex crimes, particularly exhibitionism and child-molesting. Sexual inadequacy appears to be part of a larger constellation of husband-wife characteristics in which the husband is dominated by a physically and socially more aggressive spouse. The husband has been troubled by the "man or mouse" question, in which he has experienced chronic, nagging doubts about his adequacy as a male.

*Peer Group Associations.* Peer group interaction patterns are not of major importance in development of this kind of behavior, except insofar as the person's associations have contributed to his sense of inadequacy through joking or ridicule directed at him. Such experiences may play a contributory role in development of behavior patterns of this kind, but they do not play a central part in such activities.

*Contact with Defining Agencies.* Nonviolent sex offenders rather frequently get into the hands of the defining agencies. These organizations tend to share the same extremely negative views of such offenders as do citizens generally. Doubtless such notions are communicated to the offender, so that he experiences considerable difficulty in preserving any kind of self-image as a "normal" person. In prison, nonviolent sex offenders are assigned the status of "ding" and "rapo," terms referring to the lowest social positions occupied by inmates. All of these experiences create difficulties for the criminal, but it is also probable that he would encounter great problems of identity protection even if he were to receive rather different reactions from the defining agencies, given the general scorn, revulsion, and hostility directed at him by the general public.

### Discussion

For the most part, evidence which can be marshalled concerning the role-career description of nonviolent sex offenders congeals into a consistent picture. However, this is not entirely the case: Gebhard and Gagnon have presented some findings concerning male sex offenders against very young children in which the subjects were relatively young adult males.[77] This does not square with other accounts which report that pedophiles are usually older men.

[77] Paul H. Gebhard and John H. Gagnon, "Male Sex Offenders Against Very Young Children," *American Journal of Psychiatry*, CXXI (December 1964), 576–80.

An investigation some years ago by Apfelberg, Sugar, and Pfeffer noted that child-molesters were the oldest group among six different kinds of sex offenders held for psychiatric examination at Bellevue Hospital in New York. This same study reported that exhibitionists showed inferiority feelings of a variety of kinds, including concerns about sexual adequacy.[78] The more recent work of Gebhard and others revealed that sex offenders against children infrequently had serious records of prior criminality, and that those with previous involvement in lawbreaking had usually been involved in sex offenses. These investigators also pointed out that about 60 per cent of the victims were known to the offenders before the sex acts had occurred.[79] This inquiry also uncovered evidence of hetero-sexual difficulties on the part of exhibitionists. These offenders were described as sexually inadequate, such that their acts of exhibitionism served as affirmations of masculinity.[80] "Peeping Toms" also appeared to be inhibited individuals with inadequate heterosexual lives.[81] Bernard Glueck examined a number of homosexual pedophiles in Sing Sing Prison and compared these offenders with incarcerated rapists and a general sample of other inmates. He contended that the homosexual child-molesters exhibited attenuated heterosexual interests, and also showed self-images centering about feelings of inadequacy.[82] The New Jersey study discussed earlier also turned up evidence that exhibitionists and child-molesters are sexually inhibited individuals, rather than hyper-sexed "fiends."[83] Toobert and others subjected a large group of San Quentin Prison pedophiles to the Minnesota Multiphasic Personality Inventory, with the result that the child-molesters appeared more distrustful, effeminate, and passive than the control group prisoners.[84] These researchers contended: "Most typically the pedophile is a person who is sexually dissatisfied, who has rather strong religious interests, who feels inadequate in his interpersonal relations, who expresses a good deal of guilt, and who is highly sensitized to the evaluations of others."[85] Conn observed that a group of exhibitionists placed on probation were un-

[78] Apfelberg, Sugar, and Pfeffer, op. cit.

[79] Gebhard, et al., op. cit., pp. 54–82.

[80] Ibid., pp. 380–99.

[81] Ibid., pp. 358–79.

[82] Bernard C. Glueck, Jr., "Psychodynamic Patterns in the Homosexual Sex Offender," American Journal of Psychiatry, CXII (February 1956), 584–90; see also N. K. Rickles, Exhibitionism (Philadelphia: J. B. Lippincott Co., 1950); Alex J. Arieff and David B. Rotman, "One Hundred Cases of Indecent Exposure," Journal of Nervous and Mental Disease, XCVI (November 1942), 523–28.

[83] Ellis and Brancale, op. cit., pp. 41–44.

[84] Toobert, et al., op. cit.

[85] Ibid., p. 278.

commonly meek, passive, sexually inhibited males who were married to domineering, aggressive, "castrating" females.[86]

The innocuous character of child-molesting has been the subject of comments by Bender and Blau [87] and by Gagnon.[88] In both cases, it was observed that the sexual experiences usually had slight effect upon the victim and, moreover, the children frequently played an initiatory role in the sexual activities.

The final group of research observations about nonviolent sex offenders has to do with the outcast status of these persons among other prisoners in correctional institutions. Studies of prison communities have indicated that most convicts avoid social contacts with a large group of fellow prisoners known in the inmate argot as "dings." Many of these outcasts are assigned this pariah status because of their bizarre or unpredictable patterns of behavior. Those "dings" who receive the special label of "rapos" are nonviolent sex offenders held in contempt by other prisoners, due to the nature of their sexual crimes.[89] One investigation of "rapos" by Martin confirmed the commonplace assertion by inmates that nonviolent sex offenders are the major recruits into the prison religious program. Martin observed that "rapos" frequently verbalized religious sentiments in the institution and were most frequently involved in attendance at church.[90]

## THE INCEST OFFENDER ROLE-CAREER

Criminal statutes in the United States which define the offense of incest show a good deal of variation from state to state. Intercourse between father and daughter, mother and son, and brother and sister are prohibited everywhere, but some states extend the meaning of incest to sexual intercourse between first cousins, while others do not. Brothers and sisters of half blood are sometimes included within the purview of incest legislation, as are fathers and adopted daughters. There are other states which do not prohibit sexual relations between these kinds of individuals, at the same time that some forbid such pairs of individuals

86 J. H. Conn, "The Psychiatric Treatment of Certain Chronic Offenders," Journal of Criminal Law and Criminology, XXXII (March–April 1942), 631–35.

87 Lauretta Bender and Abram Blau, "The Reaction of Children to Sexual Relations with Adults," American Journal of Orthopsychiatry, VII (October 1937), 500–18.

88 John H. Gagnon, "Female Child Victims of Sex Offenses," Social Problems, XIII (Fall 1965), 176–92.

89 Clarence C. Schrag, Social Types in a Prison Community (Master's thesis, University of Washington, 1944); Peter G. Garabedian, "Social Roles and Processes of Socialization in the Prison Community," Social Problems, XI (Fall 1963), 139–52.

90 Walter T. Martin, The Religious Attitudes of the Prison Sex Offender (Master's thesis, University of Washington, 1944).

to marry. These statutory variations are of little importance in one major respect, for, in practice, father-daughter incest is almost the sole form of forbidden sexual intercourse which results in prosecution as "incest." This is not to say that sexual intercourse never occurs between mothers and sons or between siblings. These acts occur but are rarely reported, unlike father-daughter incest. In the latter case, the mother often acts as complainant against the father, while in other instances the daughter becomes pregnant and is induced to identify her father as the person responsible for her pregnancy.

### Definitional Dimensions

*Offense Behavior.* Incest offenders are normally fathers who have been charged with sexual intercourse with a daughter. Most commonly, the daughter is an adolescent or older, so that the sexual acts between the two consist of sexual intercourse. The deviant character of the behavior resides in the inappropriateness of the sexual partners, rather than in the behavior itself.

*Interactional Setting.* Acts of intercourse between father and daughter tend to develop in situations of physical and social isolation, where the daughter represents the only sexual partner available to the father. Not infrequently, the daughter is a relatively willing participant in the sexual activity, in which case the behavior may extend into a number of sexual incidents over time. In many cases, the father and mother have become estranged although they continue to live in the same household. In some instances, the sexual activity between father and daughter is apparent to the mother, who tolerates the situation in order to avoid the sexual demands of the father.

*Self-concept.* Incest offenders lack criminalistic self-images, and often deny their involvement in incest. Some offer justificatory arguments for their conduct in which they contend that they were motivated to engage in incest for reasons other than erotic ones. They assert that they were carrying out a parental obligation to educate their children, or advance other claims of this sort. In prison, incest offenders are sensitive to the low esteem in which they are held by other prisoners.

*Attitudes.* The attitudes of incest offenders are relatively conventional. These lawbreakers do not verbalize criminalistic attitudes.

*Role-career.* Incest offenders do not exhibit extensive records of criminality before being apprehended for incest. Most of them refrain from further involvement in crime after release from prison. However, they tend to receive exceedingly long prison sentences, due to the general abhorrence of such behavior in American society.

## Background Dimensions

*Social Class.* These individuals are predominantly from lower class backgrounds. The conditions of physical and social isolation which contribute to attenuation of internalized prohibitions against incest tend to be most common in lower class populations.

*Family Background.* There apparently is no important link between early life family experiences and incest behavior. However, the adult life family situation in which incest occurs plays a directly contributory role in this form of deviance. Incest offenders are frequently in marital situations marked by tension and social distance between the husband and wife. On occasion, the offender's spouse is physically disabled so as to be incapable of fulfilling the offender's sexual demands. Distorted interactional patterns in families in which incest occurs lead the law-breaker to focus upon a daughter as a sexual substitute for the wife.

*Peer Group Associations.* The peer associations of the incest violator do not play any direct part in this behavior. However, isolation from the controlling influence of peers does sometimes contribute to the genesis of this behavior.

*Contact with Defining Agencies.* The experiences of the incarcerated incest offender with correctional agencies do not appear to impair his ability to refrain from recidivism upon release. For one thing, the long prison sentences these persons serve have the effect of altering their family situation, making repeated episodes of incest unlikely. That is, the offender serves a long prison term, during which time his female children grow into adulthood and leave the parental family. By the time the offender is released from prison, there are no children remaining at home with whom he might resume incestuous activities. Although the paroled incest case returns to the community heavily stigmatized, he often goes back to a situation of social isolation from others, so their hostile views are of little import to him.

## Discussion [91]

A number of pieces of evidence on incest confirm the characterization of this role-career in the preceding section. Riemer has reported on a number of father-daughter incest cases in Sweden.[92] He indicated that incest occurs most frequently among agricultural laborers or other simi-

[91] A review of materials on incest can be found in R. E. L. Masters, *Patterns of Incest* (New York: The Julian Press, Inc., 1963).

[92] Svend Riemer, "A Research Note on Incest," *American Journal of Sociology*, XLV (January 1940), 566–75.

larly disorganized groups of industrial workers. The typical life history of these persons shows that they came from broken homes or experienced early separation from their family due to tensional relationships with their parents. Entry into the labor market early in life restricted their educational attainment. As a consequence, their adult life showed frequent job changes and employment instability. Shortly preceding the episode of incest, these persons had been involved in marked employment difficulties or other disruptions of social routine. Riemer contended that the incest offenders had been in situations of sexual frustration prior to occurrence of the crime, in that their wives had become incapacitated or had refused to engage in intercourse. Riemer held that incest is thus due to indifference toward social responsibilities on the part of the actor, joined with extreme sexual frustration. The choice of a sexual partner outside of the family was limited, so while the offender had no special sexual interest in his daughter, she was the only sexual partner available to him.

A study of Illinois offenders by Weinberg involved predominantly father-daughter incest cases.[93] He argued that the offender's behavior is a manifestation of personal instability and retarded emotional development. According to Weinberg, incest offenders are of two general types. Some show schizophrenic characteristics; they are involved in such ingrown family relationships that they have difficulty in relating effectively to persons outside of the family. The second type of incest violator exhibits "psychopathic" characteristics, and has insufficiently internalized guilt and aversion toward sexual relations with family members. This latter individual was involved in relatively disorganized family relationships in which effective social constraints against incest were absent. Throughout Weinberg's analysis, case materials are presented which point to the role of social isolation and family disorganization as major precipitating factors in the onset of father-daughter incest.

Lustig and others have conducted research on incest and the family constellations in which it takes place which also emphasized the disorganized character of family situations in which incest occurs.[94] In the same way, Kaufman and others have studied a small group of incest cases involving fathers and daughters in which this portrait of family patterns also emerges.[95] The fathers in these cases were lower class indi-

93 S. Kirson Weinberg, *Incest Behavior* (New York: Citadel Press, 1955).

94 Noel Lustig, John W. Dresser, Seth W. Spellman, and Thomas J. Murray, "Incest," *Archives of General Psychiatry*, XIV (January 1966), 31–40.

95 Irving Kaufman, Alice L. Peck, and Consuelo K. Tagiuri, "The Family Constellation and Overt Incestuous Relations Between Father and Daughter," *American Journal of Orthopsychiatry*, XXIV (April 1954), 266–77; see also Hector Cavallin, "Incestuous Fathers: A Clinical Report," *American Journal of Psychiatry*, CXXII (April 1966), 1132–38.

viduals involved in poverty, alcoholism, and employment instability, so that they resembled the individuals described by Riemer. The sex offender research of Gebhard and others reported that prisoners who had been convicted of incest with children were ineffectual, nonaggressive, dependent individuals who drank heavily and were employed sporadically.[96] Much the same pattern of personal characteristics and social situations was uncovered in the case of incest offenders involved with minor or with adult daughters.[97]

## THE MALE HOMOSEXUAL ROLE-CAREER

Those persons who engage in acts of sexual conduct with members of the same sex represent one of the most widely discussed groups of deviants in American society. There has been no shortage of commentary directed at homosexuals, ranging from objective analyses on one extreme to denunciatory attacks upon the homosexual cast in moral terms on the other. At the same time, there has been a paucity of attention paid to homosexuality by sociologists, so a major share of the literature is psychiatrically-oriented and has been produced by psychiatrists.

In the pages to follow, our attention will focus exclusively upon male homosexuals. This is not to say that female homosexuals are uncommon in the United States, for there is reason to believe that lesbians are about as numerous as male homosexuals. But the fact is that nearly all arrests of individuals for homosexual conduct involve males. Although the police have considerable difficulty in apprehending male homosexuals, they would encounter even greater obstacles were they to attempt to round up a large number of lesbians. Homosexual acts among women are carried out in private places to which the police do not have access, and so are less "visible" than acts of male homosexuality. Additionally, there is probably a general disposition to disbelieve in the possibility of homosexuality among women, so agents of social control do not feel compelled to ferret out such persons. This situation is in contradistinction to male homosexuality, which the police go about detecting through a variety of techniques, such as vice squad work by plainclothesmen who make themselves available for homosexual advances and then arrest the offender who makes such overtures.

All types of hypotheses have been advanced to account for homosexual behavior. One prominent school of thought contends that homosexuality is constitutional in nature, having its base in physiological

[96] Gebhard, et al., op. cit., pp. 207–29.
[97] Ibid., pp. 230–71.

factors. This same line of argument often holds that homosexuals represent a fairly distinct personality type.[98] Bergler is a prominent exponent of the view that homosexuality is always the result of a neurotic distortion of personality structure.[99] It is noteworthy that persons who advance this contention tend to be emphatic in stating the claim without offering much persuasive evidence in its support.

There is a growing body of opinion which asserts that homosexuality is the outcome of certain kinds of sexual socialization, rather than the product of faulty biology. Kardiner has averred that male homosexuality develops in family settings in which individuals develop incapacitating fears of females and kindred characteristics conducive to homosexual involvement.[100] This social perspective has also been enunciated by Clara Thompson [101] and by Cory,[102] among others. This frame of reference will be followed in the role-career description below, after which some evidence consistent with a social learning approach to homosexuality will be examined.

### Definitional Dimensions

*Offense Behavior.* Male homosexuals get into the hands of the police or the criminal courts under a variety of charges, but frequently for a misdemeanor offense such as "lewd conduct" or "disorderly conduct," owing to difficulties the police encounter in making arrests for specific illegal sexual acts. However, the offender becomes the subject of official attention because he is presumed to be involved in homosexuality. The specific sexual acts committed by these individuals are quite numerous, encompassing a variety of masturbatory acts, oral and anal contacts, as well as other sexual responses.

*Interactional Setting.* Adult male homosexuals exhibit a good deal of variation in regard to the social context in which their illegal acts are conducted. Some engage in transitory episodes of homosexuality with male "hustlers" and other casual sexual partners, while others are found in differential social and sexual association with members of a homosexual subculture. Those homosexuals who "cruise" for casual pickups run the greatest risk of detection, for they are the ones most often en-

---

98 One example of this thesis can be found in Herbert Greenspan and John D. Campbell "The Homosexual as a Personality Type," *American Journal of Psychiatry*, CI (March 1945), 682–89.

99 Edmund Bergler, *Homosexuality: Disease or Way of Life?* (New York: Hill and Wang, Inc., 1956).

100 Abram Kardiner, "The Flight from Masculinity," in *The Problem of Homosexuality in Modern Society*, ed. Hendrik M. Ruitenbeek (New York: E. P. Dutton and Co., Inc., 1963), pp. 17–39.

101 Clara Thompson, "Changing Concepts of Homosexuality in Psychoanalysis," in Ruitenbeek, *op. cit.*, pp. 40–51.

102 Donald Webster Cory, *The Homosexual in America* (New York: Greenberg, Publisher, 1951).

countered by vice squad detectives. They are also the ones most in danger of being assaulted by "rough trade" sexual partners.

*Self-concept.* Many adult homosexuals who have been engaged for any length of time in homosexuality define themselves as homosexuals and as "gay." However, most regard themselves as noncriminals who are unfairly harassed by the social control agencies. Many would argue that they are engaged in a form of deviance which is not harmful either to themselves or to "society."

*Attitudes.* The attitudes of homosexuals are for the most part conventional and prosocial, the only major exception being that they exhibit tolerance and positive attitudes toward homosexuality.

*Role-career.* Adult male homosexuals often compile a lengthy record of arrests for homosexually-related charges during their lifetimes. However, most of them show little or no involvement in crimes of other kinds.

### Background Dimensions

*Social Class.* These individuals are not from one particular social class background. Homosexuals can be discovered at all social class levels in American society.

*Family Background.* Although adult homosexuals have experienced somewhat mixed family background patterns, it does appear that certain kinds of sexual socialization and parent-child relations are inordinately common in their life histories. In particular, maternal domination is a frequently reported pattern in the family origins of these offenders.

*Peer Group Associations.* The peer associations of homosexuals do not appear to play an important contributory role in the genesis of their behavior. However, for adult members of homosexual subcultures, differential association with homosexual peers operates as a major social support in the offenders' attempts to establish a *modus vivendi* with the "straight" or nonhomosexual society.

*Contact with Defining Agencies.* Encounters which adult homosexuals have with policemen and other social control agents are not very congenial. But it is likely that their attachment to this role-career is more conditioned or influenced by considerations other than the effects of societal reactions as mediated through defining agencies.

### Some Research on Homosexuality

In our view, the research of Bieber, *et al.*, represents the most revealing etiological study of male homosexuality.[103] This investigation involved

103 Bieber, *et al., op. cit.*

a sample of 106 homosexuals undergoing psychoanalytic treatment in metropolitan New York City, along with a sample of 100 nonhomosexual "controls." The data of the study consisted of observations on these persons recorded on questionnaires by the psychiatrists treating them.[104]

Bieber and his associates reported that most of these homosexual subjects were the product of peculiar family backgrounds. In particular, nearly 70 per cent had been reared by "close-binding-intimate" (CBI) mothers who accorded them preferential treatment. These same mothers were over-controlling in their dealings with their sons, while many also behaved seductively toward their sons.[105] The authors concluded: "A seductive CBI configuration emerges from these data. Such mothers overstimulated their sons sexually within the context of an overclose, overintimate relationship, and at the same time, through antisexual attitudes, prohibitions, and demasculinizing behavior toward their sons, compelled them to conceal all manifestations of sexuality. Thus, the sons were caught in a double-bind: *maternal seductiveness—maternal sexual restriction*" (emphasis in the original).[106]

The remaining homosexual subjects in this study showed a variety of relationships with their mothers. The researchers observed that the fathers of most of the homosexuals were detached, hostile, minimizing, and openly rejecting figures.[107] The most frequently observed family pattern was a triangular system involving the homosexual, a close-binding mother, and a detached-hostile father dominated by the mother. At the same time, these families showed a good deal of structural variation, so departures from this pattern were observed.[108]

These researchers inquired into the developmental backgrounds of the homosexual subjects. They observed that many were excessively afraid of injuries in childhood, growing up dependent upon their mothers and isolated from their peers. A number of them showed early involvement in homosexual conduct.[109]

One interesting part of this study concerned evidence of heterosexual inclinations on the part of many of the homosexuals. These persons reported that they had made attempts to engage in heterosexual intercourse and also had experienced dreams with heterosexual content.[110]

These investigators concluded that their findings add up to a picture of homosexuality as an adaptation to hidden but incapacitating fears of

[104] *Ibid.*, pp. 21–29.
[105] *Ibid.*, pp. 44–84.
[106] *Ibid.*, p. 53.
[107] *Ibid.*, pp. 85–117.
[108] *Ibid.*, pp. 140–72.
[109] *Ibid.*, pp. 173–206.
[110] *Ibid.*, pp. 220–54.

the opposite sex. In their view, homosexuality is a pathological alternative to heterosexuality.[111]

One confirmatory study which noted parallel results to those of Bieber, et al., has been conducted by McCord, McCord, and Verden.[112] The "feminine" deviants in that study who were homosexually oriented were from families dominated by repressive, authoritarian mothers. Their mothers were also sexually anxious, while their fathers were physically punitive. Somewhat similar findings were put forth in an investigation of homosexual children by Bender and Paster.[113] More recently, Gebhard, et al., have claimed that homosexual offenders are frequently from disordered families. They also maintained that their subjects usually began their homosexual activities at a relatively early age.[114]

Evelyn Hooker has probably accumulated the most detailed body of descriptive data on homosexuals and their sexual patterns.[115] In one of her reports, she observed that male homosexuals engage in varied and changeable forms of sexual activity, so that categorizations of such persons as "fellators," "insertees," "passive," or "active," oversimplify the real world.[116] Her most critical set of observations concerns the psychological adjustment of homosexuals. Hooker has shown that a group of 30 overt male homosexuals apparently did not vary in psychological well-being from a sample of nonhomosexuals.[117] This finding is markedly at variance with the frequently stated opinion that homosexuals are neurotic or in some other way abnormal.

The organized world of homosexuals in American society has been the subject of fictional treatment [118] as well as objective scrutiny by social researchers. The latter includes observations by Cory and LeRoy [119] and

[111] Ibid., pp. 303–19.

[112] McCord, McCord, and Verden, op. cit.

[113] Lauretta Bender and Samuel Paster, "Homosexual Trends in Children," American Journal of Orthopsychiatry, XI (October 1941), 730–43.

[114] Gebhard, et al., op. cit., pp. 272–357.

[115] Evelyn Hooker, "Male Homosexuality," in Taboo Topics, ed. Norman L. Farberow (New York: Atherton Press, 1963), pp. 44–55; Hooker, "Male Homosexuals and Their Worlds," in Sexual Inversion, ed. Judd Marmor (New York: Basic Books, Inc., 1965), pp. 83–107; Hooker, "An Empirical Study of Some Relations Between Sexual Patterns and Gender Identity in Male Homosexuals," in Sex Research: New Developments, ed. John Money (New York: Holt, Rinehart and Winston, Inc., 1965), pp. 24–52; Hooker, "The Adjustment of the Male Overt Homosexual," Journal of Projective Techniques, XXI (March 1957), 18–31.

[116] Hooker, "An Empirical Study of Some Relations Between Sexual Patterns and Gender Identity in Male Homosexuals," loc. cit.

[117] Hooker, "The Adjustment of the Male Overt Homosexual," loc. cit.

[118] John Rechy, City of Night (New York: Grove Press, 1963); Hubert Selby, Last Exit to Brooklyn (New York: Grove Press, 1964).

[119] Donald Webster Cory and John P. LeRoy, The Homosexual and His Society (New York: Citadel Press, 1963).

by Reinhardt.[120] Leznoff and Westley studied the homosexual community in a Canadian city and observed the existence of both "secret" and "overt" homosexuals.[121] Helmer's description of the homosexual subculture in New York City also pointed to the existence of an organized set of social relations among homosexuals in that city.[122] All of these materials agree that American cities include a component population group of homosexuals who frequent "gay bars," restaurants catering to "gay" individuals, and clothing stores which feature particular lines of apparel. The homosexuals who patronize these "gay" enterprises also restrict much of their social interaction to other homosexuals. Finally, the behavior patterns of "hustlers" who sell sexual services to homosexuals have been described by Reiss [123] and by Raven.[124]

## SUMMARY

This chapter has endeavored to illuminate a number of questions concerning patterns of sexual criminality in American society. Throughout this discussion, we have commented upon the dearth of attention which has been paid to these forms of lawbreaking. At a number of points, our analysis has been hampered by the lack of solid empirical works upon which we might draw. It is to be hoped that sociological inquiry will become more concerned with sexual deviation so that future discussions of such matters will be able to marshal a larger body of supporting evidence which can be concentrated upon the discussion. In particular, more research informed by a role-career or typological perspective on sexual offenders is surely in order.

Our efforts to comprehend the variety of forms of criminal conduct are not yet finished. Certain major patterns of criminality remain to be examined. In particular, drug addiction, chronic drunkenness, and organized crime have to be considered. Chapter Sixteen is addressed to these forms of lawbreaking.

[120] James M. Reinhardt, *Sex Perversions and Sex Crimes* (Springfield, Ill.: Charles C Thomas, Publisher, 1957), pp. 17–77.

[121] Maurice Leznoff and William A. Westley, "The Homosexual Community," *Social Problems,* III (April 1956), 257–63.

[122] William J. Helmer, "New York's Middle-Class Homosexuals," *Harpers,* CCLXVI (March 1963), pp. 85–92.

[123] Reiss, "The Social Integration of Queers and Peers," *loc. cit.*

[124] Simon Raven, "Boys Will Be Boys: The Male Prostitute in London," in Ruitenbeek, *op. cit.,* pp. 279–90.

# 16

# Other Criminal Careers

## INTRODUCTION

This chapter will bring our discussion of crime causation to a close, for succeeding chapters turn to matters of judicial and correctional processing of offenders. Unlike preceding chapters, which discussed relatively compatible collections of lawbreakers, this one takes up some disparate forms of criminality. Specifically, Chapter Sixteen is concerned with organized crime, drug addiction, and petty crime, such as drunkenness. These patterns of behavior are brought together here since they did not fit within preceding sections. However, it should not be supposed that this chapter is oriented around some relatively unimportant "tag ends" of deviant behavior. Quite the contrary, for the kinds of illegality discussed here involve important costs of various kinds, either to general society or to the person involved in these patterns of lawbreaking.

## ORGANIZED CRIME

### Organized Crime and American Society

The flamboyant cowboy-gunfighter is frequently alleged to be a unique cultural type, found only in the United States and symbolizing a variety of cultural values. Yet *vaqueros* and other kinds of cowboys are common in South America. A better candidate as a unique American type would be the gangster engaged in racketeering or provision of illicit services to the general public. Various authorities have pointed out that organized criminals embody major cultural values in their activities and differ hardly at all from their fellow citizens with regard to the ends they pursue. The gangster and the businessman are both engaged in single-minded pursuit of material success, so they differ from each other principally in terms of the services they render and the techniques by which they ply their trade.[1]

The image of organized criminals or gangsters conveyed by such as the television program "The Untouchables" is of evil malefactors against whom the police are relatively powerless. These "bad guys" are pictured as involved in extortion, violence, and other crimes directed against an innocent public which is exorcized by such behavior but at the same time intimidated by these malevolent figures.

There are two fundamental flaws in this conception of organized crime. Gangsterism has normally involved collusion among the criminals, police, and city officials. Cooperation rather than conflict among these groups has been commonplace, so the notion of society at war with its internal enemies in the shape of gangsters is more of a caricature than anything else.[2]

The second error in popular views of organized crime is that they imply that this criminality exists *in spite of* the wishes of the public, rather than *as a consequence* of citizen demands for illegal goods or services. Someone has to pay hoodlums to engage in union-busting and similar violence; someone must be willing to purchase sexual intercourse in order for prostitution to succeed as a business; customers must be found for illegal liquor if bootlegging is to flourish; and at least two persons are required in gambling, one of them a citizen who wishes to place a bet or draw a card. In short, organized crime exists to provide for the satisfaction of widely demanded, but legally prohibited, activities or products.

The cultural roots of organized crime have been incisively identified by Bell.[3] He has argued:

Americans have had an extraordinary talent for compromise in politics and extremism in morality. The most shameless political deals (and "steals") have been rationalized as expedient and realistically necessary. Yet in no other country have there been such spectacular attempts to curb human appetites and brand them as illicit, and nowhere else such glaring failures. . . . Crime as a growing business was fed by the revenues from prostitution, liquor and gambling that a wideopen urban society encouraged and which a middle-class Protestant ethos tried to suppress with a ferocity unmatched in any other civilized country.[4]

---

[1] See Alfred R. Lindesmith, "Organized Crime," *Annals of The American Academy of Political and Social Science*, CCXVII (September 1941), 119–27; Herbert A. Bloch and Gilbert Geis, *Man, Crime and Society* (New York: Random House, Inc., 1962), pp. 220–21.

[2] For some commentary on this matter, see Robert K. Merton, *Social Theory and Social Structure* (rev. ed.; New York: Free Press of Glencoe, Inc., 1957), pp. 72–82.

[3] Daniel Bell, "Crime as an American Way of Life," *Antioch Review*, XIII (June 1953), 131–54.
[4] *Ibid.*, p. 132.

This theme has been echoed by Tyler, who notes that American attempts to suppress "immorality" have provided the seed bed out of which organized crime has grown.[5] On this point, he indicates that:

Our puritanism creates a whole range of illegal commodities and services, for which there is a widespread demand. Into the gap between what people want and what people can legally get leaps the underworld as purveyor and pimp, with gaming tables, narcotics, and women. Puritanism gives the underworld a monopoly on a market with an almost insatiable demand.[6]

The thrust of this kind of commentary is to emphasize that organized crime is not some kind of alien "sickness" afflicting an otherwise healthy social organism. Instead, organized criminality is as natural a part of society as various kinds of socially esteemed behavior. Three basic groups of citizens are bound together in the complex comprising organized crime: the criminals who engage in organized crime, the police and city officials with whom they are in collusive cooperation, and the citizens who purchase the services of racketeers, gamblers, and kindred types.

### Trends in Organized Crime

Although organized criminality has been in existence for a long time, most students of this problem identify passage of the Volstead Act (the Eighteenth Amendment) as the signal experience which led to pronounced growth of organized crime after 1920 in the United States.[7] During the 14 years of Prohibition in which consumption of alcohol was outlawed, gangsters such as Al Capone were prominent figures in every American city. These organized criminals in the 1920's and 1930's earned lucrative sums from bootlegging, labor racketeering such as strike-breaking, and prostitution.

The organized crime of this period was noteworthy for its grossness, among other things. Prostitution was carried on in houses of prostitution within organized vice districts, so it was highly visible in character. Similarly, physical violence predominated in labor racketeering. Allsop has indicated that, during the 14 years of Prohibition, at least 700 gang murders occurred as a consequence of intergang conflicts.[8] Probably

---

[5] Gus Tyler, ed., *Organized Crime in America* (Ann Arbor: University of Michigan Press, 1962).
[6] *Ibid.*, p. 48.
[7] For a history of organized crime, see Bell, *op. cit.*; Bloch and Geis, *op. cit.*, pp. 222–28.
[8] Kenneth Allsop, *The Bootleggers and Their Era* (Garden City, N.Y.: Doubleday and Co., Inc., 1961), p. 14; see also Alson J. Smith, *Syndicate City* (Chicago: Henry Regnery and Co., 1954).

no period in American history exceeded this one in terms of violent lawlessness. The television and movie image of the Prohibition era gangster in odd clothing, equipped with a submachine gun, racing through the streets in an open black touring car with machine gun blazing, is based on fact, even though other elements of this picture are not accurate.

Prostitution as carried on in American cities in early decades of this century provides a clear illustration of the symbiotic linkages between elements of the population involved in organized crime. Prostitution was almost exclusively conducted in segregated "red light" districts. These areas of the city, usually near the downtown section, were filled with houses of prostitution peopled by a madam and a collection of prostitutes. Clients either found their way there by themselves or were delivered to the vice district by taxicab drivers. The fact that prostitution was the major activity of the area was an open secret.

The prostitutes who worked in houses were employees, for they turned their earnings over to the madam and were paid a share of their total earnings in wages. The metropolitan police were involved in the regulation of this business, rather than its suppression. In return for tolerating the vice operations, and in payment for their actions in controlling unruly clients and other contingencies of this sort, the police extracted a sizeable share of the proceeds from the persons operating the prostitution outlets. This "payoff" was then redistributed among various policemen, politicians, city officials, and other citizens.

Public attitudes were frequently tolerant during these years of organized prostitution in vice districts. Arguments were advanced regarding positive social functions prostitution was alleged to perform. Prostitution was held to be a stimulant to business through attracting visitors to the city, or it was contended that it provided an outlet for sex deviants who would otherwise rape "decent" women. Reform campaigns would occasionally direct negative attention to prostitution, so a call for police suppression would sporadically be heard. On these occasions, conventional police practice was to stage token raids of houses of prostitution. A few days later, business would be back to normal, with prostitution running at full speed.

Part of the mythology of organized prostitution was that girls were forcibly abducted into sexual bondage by "White Slavers," thus the prostitute was seen as a female who had been physically coerced into a fate worse than death! The truth is that prostitutes usually engaged quite voluntarily in this activity. Most saw that work career as less obnoxious and more lucrative than the alternatives open to them, such as waitress or sales clerk positions. Once involved in the practice of prostitution, the girls became caught up in an occupational pattern in which they were periodically moved from one community to another in order to provide variety to the customers of the houses.[9]

In a number of ways, organized crime in the United States mirrors the changes which have occurred in the host society. Take prostitution as an example. Although vice districts can still be found in some American cities, prostitution has generally undergone radical changes in form. The decline of political corruption in American cities, particularly since World War II, has meant that organized prostitution in segregated vice districts has been suppressed by the police. Prostitutes no longer work in large whorehouses with a dozen or so fellow employees. The new forms of prostitution involve individual women who act as "pickups" and "hustle" out of cocktail bars, other kinds of independent street-walkers, or "call girls" who engage in sexual transactions involving relatively large amounts of money. This kind of prostitution is much less visible to the general public. Moreover, this form of vice activity does not depend upon police collusion for its success. It creates some complicated law enforcement problems for the police which were not encountered in the days of organized vice districts.[10]

Daniel Bell is one observer who has noted the changes in the shape of organized crime in the United States. He contends that organized prostitution and industrial racketeering have declined, while other forms of criminality have flourished. According to Bell, "in the last decade and a half, industrial racketeering has not offered much in the way of opportunity. *Like American capitalism itself, crime shifted its emphasis from production to consumption*" (emphasis in the original).[11] He contends that organized crime has become more "civilized" and technologically complex in recent decades. Wire-service betting on horseracing, with its telegraph communication of race results, network of bookies, and arrangements for "lay-off" betting in which gamblers share the risks of financial losses, illustrates this transition nicely. Organized criminals have profited from the increasing subtlety of crime and have become more respectable figures.[12]

Bell sees the future as one in which organized crime will be less prominent as the social sources for it are eroded away. He avers:

[9] One description of this operation on the West Coast can be found in Robert Y. Thornton, "Organized Crime in the Field of Prostitution," *Journal of Criminal Law, Criminology and Police Science*, XLVI (March–April 1956), 775–79.

[10] See Jerome H. Skolnick, *Justice Without Trial* (New York: John Wiley and Sons, Inc., 1966), pp. 96–111.

[11] Bell, op. cit., p. 152.

[12] Geis has also remarked upon the decline of violence as a style among organized criminals. Gilbert Geis, "Violence and Organized Crime," *Annals of The American Academy of Political and Social Science*, CCCLXIV (March 1966), 86–95.

With the rationalization and absorption of some illicit activities into the structure of the economy, the passing of an older generation that had established a hegemony over crime, the general rise of minority groups to social position, and the break-up of the urban boss system, the pattern of crime we have discussed is passing as well. Crime, of course, remains as long as passion and the desire for gain remain. But big, organized city crime, as we have known it for the past seventy-five years, was based on more than these universal motives. It was based on certain characteristics of the American economy, American ethnic groups, and American politics. The changes in all these areas means that it too, in the form we have known it, is at an end.[13]

In this passage Bell sounds the death knell for labor racketeering, extortion, prostitution, and certain other kinds of organized crime. It seems clear enough that these kinds of organized crime are diminishing in importance. However, the newer forms of organized lawbreaking, particularly gambling and narcotics traffic, are likely to be with us for a good long time. Bell's forecast seems less valid for these kinds of organized criminality.

Evidence regarding current patterns of organized crime has been uncovered in greatest detail by two investigative committees of the United States Senate. The first of these was the Committee to Investigate Crime in Interstate Commerce, commonly known as the "Kefauver Committee" and chaired by the late Senator Estes Kefauver. This group, investigating organized crime in the late 1940's, found widespread evidence of gambling and other forms of racketeering in a number of American cities.[14] More recently, the Select Committee on Improper Activities in the Labor or Management Field, often designated as the "McClellan Committee" and led by Senator John L. McClellan, turned up a vast amount of information about corrupt practices in American labor unions. This committee uncovered a large number of instances in which gangsters and racketeers were influential in the conduct of union affairs.[15]

The most recent survey of organized crime in the United States is presented in the report of the President's Commission on Law Enforcement and Administration of Justice.[16] The commission indicates that estimates of the amount of money spent on illegal gambling in the United

---

[13] Bell, op. cit., p. 154.

[14] Estes Kefauver, Crime in America (Garden City, N.Y.: Doubleday and Co., Inc., 1951); see also Morris Ploscowe, ed., Organized Crime and Law Enforcement, two vols. (New York: The Grosby Press, 1952); Marshall B. Clinard, Sociology of Deviant Behavior (rev. ed.; New York: Holt, Rinehart and Winston, Inc., 1963), pp. 273–84.

[15] Robert F. Kennedy, The Enemy Within (New York: Harper & Row, Publishers, 1960).

[16] The President's Commission on Law Enforcement and Administration of Justice, The Challenge of Crime in a Free Society (Washington, D.C.: U.S. Government Printing Office, 1967), pp. 187–209.

States range from $7 to $50 billion per year. Loan sharking is alleged to be a widespread form of organized crime, although no figures are offered regarding the profits involved. Narcotics traffic was held to result in $21 million in profits per year to importers and distributors of drugs. The commission also claims that organized criminals have reinvested much of their money in legitimate businesses, so that these are indirectly controlled by gangsters. Finally, labor racketeering is said to remain an important form of organized crime. According to the commission, organized crime can be found in all sections of the nation, in small cities as well as in large ones.[17]

### Mafia: Myth or Reality?

One of the most widely held notions among the mass audience in the United States is that organized crime in this country is under the control of a national and international criminal conspiracy, ruled from Sicily and known as the Mafia. In this view of things, Italian-American criminals such as Frank Costello, Albert Anastasia, and Joey Adonis are linked to "Lucky" Luciano and other members of the Mafia hierarchy in Sicily. The Kefauver Committee gave great credence to this hypothesis; on the basis of testimony before his committee, Senator Kefauver contended: *"A nationwide crime syndicate does exist in the United States of America, despite the protestations of a strangely assorted company of criminals, self-serving politicians, plain blind fools, and others who may be honestly misguided, that there is no such combine"* (emphasis in the original).[18] Kefauver's discussion of this claim is somewhat equivocal, for he went on to indicate that the nationwide syndicate is elusive and furtive in character. Nonetheless, he continued by asserting: *"Behind the local mobs which make up the national crime syndicate is a shadowy, international criminal organization known as the Mafia, so fantastic that most Americans find it hard to believe it really exists"* (emphasis in the original).[19]

Supporters of the Mafia interpretation of organized crime make much of a supposed "summit meeting" of gangsters held in 1957. In November of that year, 58 persons from all over the United States converged on the Apalachin, New York, residence of Joseph Barbara, a wealthy beverage distributor. These 58 individuals all drove expensive automobiles, carried extraordinarily large sums of money on their persons, had extensive criminal records, and were of Italian extraction. They explained

[17] *Ibid.,* pp. 188–91.
[18] Kefauver, *op. cit.,* p. 12.
[19] *Ibid.,* p. 14.

their presence at the small village of Apalachin as guests of a barbecue—an explanation which surely lacks the ring of plausibility! Twenty of these persons were subsequently convicted in a federal court in December, 1959, of conspiring to obstruct justice by lying about the purpose of their meeting. However, this conviction was overturned by an appellate court in 1960 on the grounds that the federal government had failed to prove that any improper conduct had taken place at that meeting. Hence this whole affair is sufficiently ambiguous to be interpreted either as support for the Mafia argument or contrary to that contention.

That the Mafia existed as a corrupt quasi-political organization in certain parts of Sicily is not debated, for a number of investigators have thrown light upon that phenomenon.[20] What is at issue is the body of claims advanced by such persons as Harry Anslinger, former Director of the Federal Bureau of Narcotics, to the effect that an international Mafia controls the traffic in narcotics, gambling, and other forms of organized crime in America. Allen is another who has stridently enunciated this view of the Mafia and organized crime,[21] while it is also favored by Sondern [22] and by Reid.[23]

The report of the President's Commission on Law Enforcement and Administration of Justice contains a modified version of the Mafia argument which is probably closer to the truth. This description portrays the system of organized crime as made up of a number of loosely coordinated regional syndicates. According to the commission, organized crime in America has the following features:

Today the core of organized crime in the United States consists of 24 groups operating as criminal cartels in large cities across the Nation. Their membership is exclusively Italian, they are in frequent communication with each other, and their smooth functioning is insured by a national body of overseers. To date, only the Federal Bureau of Investigation has been able to document fully the national scope of these groups, and FBI intelligence indicates that the organization as a whole has changed its name from the Mafia to La Cosa Nostra. . . .

In individual cities, the local core group may also be known as the "outfit," the "syndicate," or the "mob." These 24 groups work with and control other racket groups, whose leaders are of various ethnic derivations. In addition, the

20 For accounts of the Sicilian Mafia, see Norman Lewis, The Honored Society (New York: G. P. Putnam's Sons, 1964); Giovanni Schiavo, The Truth About the Mafia (New York: Vigo Press, 1962).

21 Edward J. Allen, Merchants of Menace—The Mafia (Springfield, Ill.: Charles C Thomas, Publisher, 1962).

22 Frederic Sondern, Jr., Brotherhood of Evil: The Mafia (New York: Farrar, Straus and Giroux, 1959).

23 Ed Reid, Mafia (New York: Random House, Inc., 1952).

thousands of employees who perform the street-level functions of organized crime's gambling, usury, and other illegal activities represent a cross section of the Nation's population groups. . . .

The highest ruling body of the 24 families is the "commission." This body serves as a combination legislature, supreme court, board of directors, and arbitration board; its principal functions are judicial. Family members look to the commission as the ultimate authority on organizational and jurisdictional disputes. It is composed of the bosses of the Nation's most powerful families but has authority over all 24. The composition of the commission varies from 9 to 12 men. According to current information, there are presently 9 families represented, 5 from New York City and 1 each from Philadelphia, Buffalo, Detroit, and Chicago.

The commission is not a representative legislative assembly or an elected judicial body. Members of this council do not regard each other as equals. Those with long tenure on the commission and those who head large families, or possess unusual wealth, exercise greater authority and receive utmost respect. The balance of power on this nationwide council rests with the leaders of New York's 5 families. They have always served on the commission and consider New York as at least the unofficial headquarters of the entire organization.[24]

Those who argue against the Mafia theory begin by stipulating that Italian-Americans are inordinately frequent among organized criminals in the United States. However, they maintain that organized crime consists of a number of loosely coordinated regional syndicates in the United States, rather than a single network of criminal associations. They would not be entirely convinced of the accuracy of the President's Commission description of an all-powerful "commission." Furthermore, critics of the Mafia hypothesis suggest that organized crime and participation of Italian-Americans in it is an indigenous feature of American life. Daniel Bell is one of these disbelievers.[25] He has argued that heavy involvement of Italians in organized crime must be seen as a consequence of the late arrival of Italian immigrants into the United States. Most of them came to this country after the beginning of the present century, and found many of the routes to upward mobility and wealth which earlier immigrants had encountered closed to them. Many of these individuals turned to illicit avenues of mobility, such as bootlegging, others found their way into relatively unconventional occupations which offered the promise of success, such as boxing, while still others entered urban politics. The latter were frequently aided by the criminals, who provided much financial support for Italian political hopefuls. As a result of these de-

[24] The President's Commission on Law Enforcement and Administration of Justice, op. cit., pp. 192–95.
[25] Bell, op. cit.

velopments, a number of Italian-Americans did rise to positions of political importance in city government, at the same time that others became prominent in criminal mobs and gambling. Within the Italian-American community, gangsters and mobsters were viewed with a good deal of respect and admiration, for their careers represented "success," albeit through somewhat unconventional means. All of this is a far cry from a nationwide conspiracy controlled from Sicily. Moreover, as Bell's remarks quoted earlier noted, this interlocking structure of Italian politicians and criminals is probably on the wane with the assimilation of Italian-Americans into more conventional opportunity structures.

Schiavo is another student of the Mafia who contends that those who have put forth this argument regarding American organized crime are deluded.[26] He contends that the Mafia did exist in Sicily, but virtually disappeared after 1927 when the Italian dictator, Mussolini, forcibly disbanded it. Moreover, Schiavo argues that there is no evidence showing the existence of either an American or an international Mafia in control of organized crime.

What shall we make of these divergent claims about the Mafia? In our view, the burden of proof lies with those who contend that an international conspiracy controls organized crime in America. At best, the Mafia theory is a piece of plausible conjecture, based on such inferential support as the concentration of Italian-Americans in organized crime. It is also a useful set of ideas, for it aids the Bureau of Narcotics and other of its advocates to gain public support for their activities. But none of those who assert belief in this notion have succeeded in adducing direct evidence of a Mafia. There is good reason to argue that the facts will ultimately show that organized crime is an American way of life, managed by local or regional criminal "power structures" bound together into loose and relatively informal larger organizations or associations. Presumably, the Apalachin gathering represented a meeting of members of this criminal structure.

### Gambling in the United States

The discussion earlier in this chapter suggested that gambling and other forms of consumptive activity have emerged as prominent contemporary forms of organized crime. Let us examine some facets of gambling in America in more detail.[27]

[26] Schiavo, op. cit.

[27] A useful review of materials on gambling is Robert D. Herman, *Gambling* (New York: Harper & Row, Publishers, 1967); for an analysis of gambling in Nevada, where it is legal, see Wallace Turner, *Gamblers' Money* (Boston: Houghton-Mifflin Co., 1965).

Although facts regarding the extent of gambling in this country are difficult to ascertain, all the available estimates indicate that gambling is "big business." For example, Kefauver suggested that over 50,000,000 adult Americans gamble in some way or another and spend $30,000,000,000 per year in this activity. Of this sum, $6,000,000,000 was said to represent the profit to syndicates and gambling entrepreneurs. This figure is greater than the annual profits of all the largest industrial enterprises in this nation combined.[28] A similar staggering estimate of the profits in gambling has been offered by Cook, who asserts that this activity nets $10,000,000,000 per year in profits to those who control gambling.[29]

What accounts for the involvement of hordes of Americans in gambling? On a general level, Bloch has argued that gambling of various kinds meets some deepseated human needs.[30] Among other things, it introduces an element of hope into lives otherwise filled with failure and despair. The chance of winning through gambling offers the working class person an opportunity to demonstrate some mastery over his life. Furthermore, Bloch contends that gambling finds a particularly tolerant audience in the United States, for it is little different in principle from various kinds of socially approved forms of risk-taking and tampering with fate, such as stock market speculation.

Some concrete observations of this contention regarding the social functions of gambling have been made by Zola.[31] He studied horse-race betting in a lower class bar and discovered that this behavior represents a method by which the working class person can "achieve" and gain some recognition by "beating the system" and demonstrating that one's fate is not solely a matter of "luck." The horse-players who had highest status among their peers were those who at least occasionally won and employed betting systems, handicapping techniques, and so on.

Gambling serves other social functions as well. The persistence and popularity of "numbers" or "policy" gambling in urban areas is due in part to the fact that this form of gambling operates as a kind of welfare aid. Although the numbers player has a slight likelihood of winning when he places a wager on some number(s) which he predicts will turn up in a drawing of some sort, when he does occasionally win his earnings allow him to purchase goods and services he could not otherwise obtain. Policy winnings make possible enjoyment of hedonistic pleasures that

[28] Herbert A. Bloch, "The Dilemma of American Gambling: Crime or Pastime?" in *Crime in America,* ed. Bloch (New York: Philosophical Library, 1961), p. 335.

[29] Fred J. Cook, "Gambling, Inc.," *The Nation,* CXCI (October 22, 1960), 260. This special issue of *The Nation* was devoted to a lengthy and revealing essay on American gambling by Cook.

[30] Bloch, op. cit.

[31] Irving Kenneth Zola, "Observations on Gambling In a Lower-Class Setting," in *The Other Side,* ed. Howard S. Becker (New York: Free Press of Glencoe, Inc., 1964), pp. 247–60.

he cannot obtain through "legitimate" welfare services provided by local or state government. Thus numbers profits make the difference between a life of dull monotony and one which contains an occasional moment of novelty and pleasure. It is not surprising to find that local residents of urban slum areas have relatively sanguine views of policy gambling.[32]

In their detailed examination of the workings of the numbers racket in Chicago's "Black Belt" area, Drake and Cayton indicated that it was one of the major businesses in that neighborhood, providing employment for a good many local residents. Their analysis documented the linkages between organized crime and the police. The Chicago Negroes prominent in policy enjoyed high status as "race leaders" and "race heroes" in the community.[33]

In those locales where the playing of numbers is commonplace, it is often bound up with magical practices and other elaborations. McCall has shown that numbers and hoodoo religion are intertwined in Negro communities, so that the players' choices of numbers on which to bet are made in terms of superstitions, religious omens, and so on.[34]

These kinds of observations about gambling in the United States suggest that it is likely to persist as one of the more enduring forms of organized crime in America. In a society of growing affluence which at the same time produces a marked sense of alienation in a goodly number of citizens, gambling may well continue to serve as an outlet for numerous frustrations and hostilities.[35]

## DRUG ADDICTION

Those persons who exhibit "vices" in which they ingest chemicals of various kinds arouse a variety of indignant and hostile sentiments on the part of the general public in the United States.[36] Witness the furor in recent years over LSD and other hallucinatory drugs which resulted in the passage of criminal laws making the use of such substances illegal in California and certain other states. At the same time, citizen attitudes

[32] One detailed account of the numbers racket is St. Clair Drake and Horace R. Cayton, *Black Metropolis* (New York: Harcourt, Brace and World, Inc., 1945), pp. 470–94.

[33] *Ibid.*

[34] George J. McCall, "Symbiosis: The Case of Hoodoo and the Numbers Racket," in Becker, *op. cit.*, pp. 51–66.

[35] For one case illustration of this point, see William Barry Furlong, "Out in the Bleachers, Where the Action Is," *Harper's* CCXXXIII (July 1966), 49–53.

[36] For some data on public attitudes toward drug addicts, see Elizabeth A. Rooney and Don C. Gibbons, "Social Reactions to 'Crimes Without Victims,'" *Social Problems*, XIII (Spring 1966), 400–10.

are clearly far from consistent on these matters. A case in point is marijuana, for "pot" smoking is a criminal act which is widely regarded as particularly dangerous and immoral. The fact is that marijuana is relatively innocuous, for it is not addictive in character, it is not accompanied by harmful physiological effects upon the user, and it does not produce bizarre or exaggerated behavior. Marijuana use stands in marked contrast to tobacco smoking or consumption of alcohol, both of which are associated with distinctly harmful physical effects upon the person engaged in them. Yet alcohol and tobacco are not illegal, nor are they viewed as "vices."

Doubtless there are a number of reasons behind the rise of "drug fiend" stereotypes, in which users of marijuana, opiates, or certain other drugs have become the target of hostile public attitudes and efforts to "criminalize" their behavior through passage of laws proscribing the use of these substances. Becker has identified the Federal Narcotics Bureau, acting in the role of *moral entrepreneur*, as a major force in promulgating hostile views of addicts.[37] Federal and state narcotics enforcement personnel have been the principal source from which definitions of the seriousness of drug use and of the drug addict have been derived, so these groups have contributed heavily to current attitudes.

In the years since passage of the Harrison Narcotic Act of 1914, making the possession of opium derivatives illegal in most circumstances, drug use has become a subject of considerable scientific interest and investigation. There is at present a voluminous literature on drug use of various kinds. Our discussion will touch only briefly upon most of this material.[38]

First, how frequent is use of illegal narcotics in the United States? Although detailed and highly accurate statistics are impossible to obtain, various estimates of the magnitude of this phenomenon have been made. Clausen contends that there are probably not less than 50,000 opiate users (persons who consume opium derivatives) nor more than 100,000 such persons in the United States. He notes that most of them are concentrated in metropolitan areas within New York, Illinois, and California, with others gathered in Washington, D.C., Detroit, St. Louis, Dallas, and a few other metropolitan areas.[39] The American Medical Association

---

[37] Howard S. Becker, *Outsiders* (New York: Free Press of Glencoe, Inc., 1963), pp. 121–46.

[38] Valuable summaries of this literature can be found in Edwin M. Schur, *Crimes Without Victims* (Englewood Cliffs, N.J.: Prentice-Hall, Inc., 1965), pp. 120–68; John A. Clausen, "Drug Addiction," in *Contemporary Social Problems*, ed. Robert K. Merton and Robert A. Nisbet (2nd ed.; New York: Harcourt, Brace and World, Inc., 1966), pp. 193–235; Clinard, *op. cit.*, pp. 292–317; Alfred R. Lindesmith, *The Addict and the Law* (Bloomington: Indiana University Press, 1965); Earl Rubington, "Drug Addict as a Deviant Career," *The International Journal of the Addictions*, II (Spring 1967), 3–20.

[39] Clausen, *op. cit.*, p. 205.

claimed in 1956 that there are about 540,000 persons who use marijuana in this country, along with another 60,000 who are opiate addicts.[40] By contrast with any other Western nation for which figures are available, the United States is clearly the only country which has a narcotic "problem." Yet it should be emphasized that the majority of these drug users are marijuana smokers, most of whom do not graduate into opiate addiction. Although American opiate addicts are more numerous than those in other countries, they constitute a numerically small portion of all criminals in the United States.

Drug *use* should be distinguished from drug *addiction*, for the latter represents a special case of the former. Drug addiction involves three elements: an overpowering compulsion to take a drug, development of a need for increased dosages of the drug over time, and psychic dependence upon the drug.[41] Using this definition, marijuana is not an addicting drug, while opiates are markedly addicting in character. Individuals can engage in sporadic smoking of marijuana without developing any pronounced craving for the drug or tolerance to it. Opiate users, on the other hand, exhibit compulsive use of the drug, tolerance, and also exhibit an *abstinence syndrome*. That is, persons who have become involved in continued use of opiates invariably experience a marked degree of physiological distress involving lacrimation, cramps, tenseness, sweating, and other physical responses when withdrawn from opiate use. It is the opiate addict who furnishes the model on which public views of narcotic use are based, for he is the individual who has a "habit" which becomes progressively more costly as he requires increased dosages of heroin or other opiates in order to feel "normal." The opiate addict is also the subject of books and movies such as *The Man With the Golden Arm*, where he is portrayed as experiencing physical agony when unable to acquire drugs in order to maintain his "habit." It is the opiate user rather than the "pot" smoker who engages in petty theft, prostitution, and other forms of criminality in order to maintain a supply of narcotics. No wonder criminologists tend to minimize the seriousness of marijuana and to lay major stress on opiate addiction. In the sections to follow, we shall pay most attention to the opiate addict role-career, with only passing concern for marijuana use.

The opiate addict role-career outlined below describes *criminal* addicts, that is, individuals normally from slum backgrounds who are the subject of law enforcement agency attention. But a footnote to that discussion is in order concerning narcotic addicts who escape the criminal label and correctional processing. A relatively large number of physicians and

[40] Bloch and Geis, *op. cit.*, p. 356.
[41] Clausen, *op. cit.*, pp. 195–98.

other medical personnel are narcotic addicts. Winick claims that the addiction rate among doctors is one in 100 physicians, compared to a rate of one addict among 3000 citizens in the general population. He studied nearly 100 doctors who had been drug addicts and found that their addiction was attributable to a number of factors, one of which is relatively easy access to narcotics. These addict-physicians also exhibited role-strain, in that many were relatively unenthusiastic about medical careers. They were also frequently passive individuals with self-images centering about omnipotent views of themselves. According to Winick, doctors of this kind are the ones most likely to find medical practice particularly stressful and seek some relief from occupational pressures in drug use.[42]

## THE OPIATE ADDICT ROLE-CAREER

### Definitional Dimensions

*Offense Behavior.* Most criminal opiate addicts are young men who specialize in the use of narcotics as deviant behavior. Many begin by experimenting with marijuana as juveniles, progressing in turn to occasional use of heroin or other opium derivatives, and ending by becoming heavily involved in addiction. Many of them engage in other criminal acts, particularly forms of petty property crime or "hustling" (pimping, and so on), but only to obtain funds to purchase drugs.

*Interactional Setting.* Juvenile and young adult drug users are not normally members of large delinquent gangs. While drug users are sometimes recruited from delinquent gangs, involvement in patterns of "heavy" drug use normally results in expulsion of the user from more conventional delinquent peer groups or voluntary withdrawal of the addict from such groups. Narcotic users are often viewed by other delinquents as undependable and bizarre personalities. Drug users are often members of an addict subculture, which sometimes takes the form of a "cat" culture. Differential association with other drug users occurs for several reasons. Association with narcotic addicts involves a system of mutual aid in which users inform each other about sources of drugs, means to obtain narcotics by illicit means, and so on.

*Self-concept.* The narcotic user usually exhibits a self-image as a drug addict rather than as a "delinquent" or "criminal." He maintains that use of drugs is no more deviant than the various other "kicks" resorted to by noncriminals, such as drinking or smoking. The narcotic addict

[42] Charles Winick, "Physician Narcotic Addicts," *Social Problems*, IX (Fall 1961), 174–86.

views himself as a person who has plenty of justification in his life circumstances for drug use. He argues that he should be allowed to use narcotics and that, if he were, there would be few problems either for himself or society. Some narcotic addicts view themselves as "cats," individuals who are "cool" and able to make a living through various forms of "hustle." In turn, "cats" evidence considerable disdain for "squares" or noncriminal persons.

*Attitudes.* The attitudes of the heroin user take the form of allegations that he is being harassed by a society which provides few satisfying experiences for persons of his kind. The narcotic user has negative attitudes toward work, but his principal antagonism is directed toward the police. This is, of course, understandable in view of the fact that the addict experiences considerable contact with the police, which he defines as harassment, and is continually under surveillance by narcotic agents.

*Role-career.* Narcotic addicts are sometimes juveniles who began their delinquent careers as members of conventional gangs but ultimately branch off from such groups as they become caught up in narcotic use. On other occasions, the drug user drifted into narcotic use outside the framework of conventional gangs. The juvenile drug user often continues in drug use into adulthood and becomes an adult, criminal drug user.

### Background Dimensions

*Social Class.* Drug users are usually from urban, slum area, lower class backgrounds. They appear to be recruited from those in lower class areas who have the most pronounced feelings of low status, lack of opportunity, and inability to extricate themselves from situations of extreme stress and unpleasantness.

*Family Background.* Drug users tend to be from lower class families in which close parent-child ties are absent. Family life tends to be relatively meaningless and unimportant for the drug user.

*Peer Group Associations.* Narcotic addicts normally associate differentially with other addicts. They usually learn the use of drugs and norms defining narcotics as pleasant from interaction with other addicts. When the "budding addict" becomes seriously involved in drug use, he usually withdraws into almost exclusive isolation from nonaddicts and into interaction with other users. This interaction has important consequences for his continuation in drug use, for these persons share a set of norms which define narcotic use as acceptable and suggest that cures for addiction are nonexistent.

*Contact with Defining Agencies.* Drug users experience numerous contacts with defining agencies during the course of their deviant careers.

On one hand, it does not appear that involvement in programs of conventional treatment in which the user is incarcerated, withdrawn from dependence upon narcotics, and given psychiatric treatment has any pronounced rehabilitative effect. Instead, drug users tend to resume drug habits quickly upon release from treatment. But, on the other hand, it does not appear that contact with defining agencies plays any direct role in drug relapse. Such contacts have only a neutral impact upon drug users.

### Discussion

This role-career description stands as a set of propositions about opiate users. But what of the supporting evidence for this characterization? Let us examine some of the data at hand regarding opiate addicts.

In the years since passage of the Harrison Act, certain major trends have occurred regarding the social characteristics of addicts. In earlier decades, only about 10 per cent of the addicts received at the U.S. Public Health Service Hospital, Lexington, Kentucky, which treats drug users, were Negro, while in recent years about two-fifths of the addict patients have been Negroes. While two decades ago only about 10 per cent of the addicts were under 25 years of age, in recent years over one-third of them were under 25 years of age.[43]

Present-day criminal drug addicts tend to come from certain urban social areas in largest numbers. These are neighborhoods which show a concentration of indices of social breakdown—high crime and delinquency rates, high rates of prostitution and illegitimacy, high infant mortality, and large numbers of broken homes. They are also areas of marked population density, with a great deal of population turnover among the heterogeneous groups who live there.[44]

One major study which documents the wretched character of the neighborhoods from which addicts come was carried out by Chein and others in New York City.[45] Their evidence shows that, in addition to the social and physical deterioration characteristic of these areas, two cultural themes pervade the social life of high delinquency-high addiction neighborhoods. The residents commonly exhibit negative perspectives on life, along with a deep-seated sense of futility.[46]

Although delinquency and drug addiction are commonplace in such

[43] Clausen, op. cit., p. 206.

[44] Ibid., pp. 210–11.

[45] Isidor Chein, Donald L. Gerard, Robert S. Lee, and Eva Rosenfeld, *The Road to H* (New York: Basic Books, Inc., 1964), pp. 47–77.

[46] Ibid., pp. 78–108.

communities, they are not causally related. Juvenile street gangs are not active in the spread of drugs through a process of differential association. Some drug users may have been in gangs at an earlier point in their lives, but dropped out of gang life when they became involved in drug use. Addicts are poorly regarded by delinquent gang members, for they are viewed as unreliable and are thus shunned. Contrary to current stereotypes of the addiction process, most juvenile drug users are *not* initiated into drug use by adult "pushers." Instead, they usually began using drugs at the urging of a peer.[47]

Recent studies have shown that young opiate addicts have frequently begun the use of drugs by experimenting with marijuana.[48] Chein and his associates assert that 86 per cent of the young adults they studied had begun by smoking marijuana, most frequently around the age of 15.[49] At first glance, this would seem to indicate that marijuana use is a prelude to opiate addiction. In a sense this is true, but what is not revealed by these observations is that a great many individuals in slum areas and elsewhere who smoke marijuana never progress to opiate addiction. Thus marijuana smokers who become opiate addicts represent a small subclass of all marijuana users.

Opiate addiction cannot be explained solely in terms of the socio-economic and physical deficiencies of slum areas and the ideological themes of futility and negativism found there. Residents of such areas demonstrate a variety of life patterns; some are criminals, many are noncriminals, and fewer are drug addicts. There must be something additional to the factors identified so far which diverts some youths into drug addiction. That factor is widely held to be a pattern of disordered and inadequate home life which produces persons with pronounced personality pathology. These individuals are in the market for the special solution to life's problems promised by heroin.

This psychogenic contention about addicts is found in the theoretical work of Cloward and Ohlin. They contend that drug users make up a special subculture of "retreatists" who are "double failures." These youths have not managed to find a niche for themselves either in the world of nondelinquent conformists or the delinquent street gang. Presumably, such boys are "double failures" because they are crippled by personality deficiencies which alienate them from more normal youngsters.[50] Support for this view of the addict is found in the Chein, *et al.*, study, for

[47] *Ibid.*, pp. 3–16.
[48] Clausen, *op. cit.*, pp. 213–16.
[49] Chein, *et al.*, *op. cit.*, p. 149.
[50] Richard A. Cloward and Lloyd E. Ohlin, *Delinquency and Opportunity* (New York: Free Press of Glencoe, Inc., 1960), pp. 178–86.

these investigators report that users are youths with a variety of personality problems. These pathologies fall into four major groupings:
ego pathology, narcissism, superego pathology, and problems of sexual
identity.[51] These personality attributes are not the by-product of involvement in deviant behavior. The personality disturbances preceded
drug use and were the outgrowth of situations of family pathology. The
drug users who were compared with nonusers from the same neighborhoods much more commonly came from homes marked by absence of
a father figure, conflict between the marital partners, and inadequate
parental standards.[52]

Another study which turned up similar findings was conducted by
Roebuck, dealing with 50 Negro addicts in the District of Columbia
Reformatory who were compared with a large group of nonaddict
inmates. According to Roebuck, the users were predominantly "passive-
dependent-dependent" personalities who had grown up in home situations of maternal dominance. However, it should be noted that the
addicts in this study were from social and economic backgrounds more
favorable in some ways than those from which the nonaddicts came.[53]

Further confirmation of many of the claims in the role-career description of addicts can be found in a Chicago study by Finestone. The drug
users in his research were young Negro males who had become enmeshed in a "cat" culture, centered about pursuit of hedonistic pleasures
and supported by a variety of illicit, nonviolent "hustles," such as
pimping.[54]

Nearly all of the commentary to this point has dealt with *male* opiate
addicts, and for good reason. Although it has been estimated that female
addicts outnumbered males before passage of the Harrison Act, in recent
decades women users have comprised less than 20 per cent of all addicts.
Regarding female drug users, Chein and his associates have indicated
that they show much the same pattern of disordered home life, low
socioeconomic status, and so on, as male opiate users.[55]

Drug addiction is perhaps the most pronounced case of criminality in
which recidivism is extremely common. This high rate of relapse into
drug use is noted in the addict's assertion: "Once an addict, always an
addict." Estimates of the relapse rate for addicts treated in the major

[51] Chein, *et al., op. cit.,* pp. 193–226.

[52] *Ibid.,* pp. 251–75.

[53] Julian B. Roebuck, "The Negro Drug Addict as an Offender Type," *Journal of Criminal Law,
Criminology and Police Science,* LIII (March 1962), 36–43.

[54] Harold Finestone, "Cats, Kicks, and Color," *Social Problems,* V (July 1957), 3–13; the reader
is also directed to examine the narrative on New York juvenile addicts by Rice. See Robert Rice
"Junk," *New Yorker,* XLI (March 27, 1965), 50–142.

[55] Chein, *et al., op. cit.,* pp. 299–319.

specialized treatment facilities, such as the hospital at Lexington, Kentucky, note that at least 75 per cent and perhaps 95 per cent or more of the treated addicts relapse into drug use.[56] Miserable social circumstances, intensified personality problems, and stigmatization of the addict come together to make it extremely difficult for the treated addict to maintain his commitment to the role of nondeviant.[57]

One claim in the role-career description had to do with the association of drug use and other forms of criminality. O'Donnell recently carried out an investigation of this question in which he examined the criminal activities after release from treatment of nearly 300 addicts who had been patients at the U.S. Public Health Service Hospital at Lexington.[58] The follow-up data on these users was compared with results from other studies of the criminality of addicts. O'Donnell's major conclusions were that addicts have increasingly been recruited from the ranks of persons with prior criminal records in recent decades. These persons commit more crimes after becoming addicted than they would have otherwise. But the fact remains that many addicts do not have criminal records, either before or after becoming addicted.[59]

O'Donnell reached the same conclusion at which other investigators have arrived, that drug addiction per se does not produce criminality. Rather, petty thievery and other forms of instrumental criminality represent secondary consequences of addiction to which the addict is driven because of the illegality of drug use. Presumably, if the user were not a target of law enforcement agents but free to ingest drugs if he so chose, he would not be involved in criminality to support his addiction.

## ALCOHOLISM AND AMERICAN SOCIETY

No statistics are required to demonstrate that drinking of alcoholic beverages is extremely widespread in the United States. That is a fact obvious to any adult American, although the precise extent of drinking may not be so clear. One detailed indication of the ubiquity of alcohol comes from a study by Mulford involving a nationwide sample of persons over 21 years of age.[60] Nearly three-fourths of these persons reported

[56] Schur, op. cit., p. 146.

[57] For a study of the relapse process in drug addiction, see Marsh B. Ray, "The Cycle of Abstinence and Relapse Among Heroin Addicts," in The Other Side, ed. Howard S. Becker (New York: Free Press of Glencoe, Inc., 1964), pp. 163–77.

[58] John A. O'Donnell, "Narcotic Addiction and Crime," Social Problems, XIII (Spring 1966), 374–85.

[59] Ibid., p. 385.

[60] Harold A. Mulford, "Drinking and Deviant Drinking, U.S.A., 1963," Quarterly Journal of Studies on Alcohol, XXV (December 1964), 634–50.

themselves as drinkers, so that it appears that upwards of 80,000,000 adult Americans consume alcoholic beverages. Of these drinkers, 11 per cent said they were "heavy drinkers," while 10 per cent admitted that they had experienced difficulties in managing their drinking behavior.

These exceedingly commonplace drinkers, ranging over a spectrum from moderate drinkers to chronic alcoholics, are the subject of a massive literature dealing with the chemical, biological, psychological, legal, and sociological facets of drinking. For example, the *Quarterly Journal of Studies on Alcohol* is devoted entirely to reports and discussions on aspects of alcohol behavior. There is also an abundance of books which have dealt with various features of drinking.[61] In this text, we shall have to be content to peruse only a small sampling of this storehouse of material.

Drinking behavior is of interest to criminologists for several reasons, but the most important is that arrests for drunkenness are extremely common in the United States. Police arrest figures for 1965 indicate that of 5,031,393 arrests reported to the Federal Bureau of Investigation, 1,535,040 were for drunkenness.[62] "Skid Road" alcoholics, who contribute most of these arrests, represent "garden variety" offenders constituting a major class of lawbreakers. We should probably add to this figure for drunk arrests some sizeable part of the arrests for vagrancy and disorderly conduct, offenses which frequently involve excessive drinkers. In addition, drunkenness is associated with other forms of criminality such as petty thievery and, less frequently, homicidal actions.[63]

The report of the President's Commission on Law Enforcement and Administration of Justice contains some information about drunkenness arrests in the United States. The commission indicates that not only are arrests for drunkenness and allied offenses exceedingly common, many offenders are chronic repeaters, turning up repeatedly in arrest statistics over an extended period of time. The commission also notes that communities vary markedly in their policies with regard to arresting drunks. In a comparison of Washington, D.C., St. Louis, and Atlanta, widely discrepant figures emerge regarding the percentage drunk arrests comprise of all arrests. In Washington, 76.5 per cent of all arrests in 1965 were for drunkenness, disorderly conduct, and vagrancy, while 76.7 per

[61] One good summary of much of this material is Clinard, *op. cit.*, pp. 318–61. For a representative sample of essays which touch on a number of dimensions of alcohol behavior, see David J. Pittman and Charles R. Snyder, eds., *Society, Culture, and Drinking Patterns* (New York: John Wiley and Sons, Inc., 1962).

[62] Federal Bureau of Investigation, *Uniform Crime Reports for the United States, 1965* (Washington, D.C.: U.S. Government Printing Office, 1966), p. 114.

[63] Marvin E. Wolfgang and Rolf B. Strohm, "The Relationship between Alcohol and Criminal Homicide," *Quarterly Journal of Studies on Alcohol*, XVII (September 1956), 411–25.

cent of the total arrests in Atlanta were for these reasons. In St. Louis, on the other hand, which had a tolerant policy toward drunks, only 18.9 per cent of all arrests were for these offenses.[64]

Two basic types of alcoholics can be discerned, one of which is a "criminal" drinker while the other is usually a nonoffender. The latter is represented by the chronic drinker, usually of middle class origin, who is found in such private alcoholism treatment settings as "Alcoholics Anonymous" or psychiatric counseling, or has been processed through civil court commitment into a public treatment organization. These individuals are often tagged with labels such as "inebriate" or "alcoholic," so they are not stigmatized as "criminals."

The evidence regarding middle class alcoholics indicates that their drinking has been solitary activity, often conducted in surreptitious fashion so as to avoid detection by associates. Jellinek and other investigators have identified a process of involvement in alcoholism through which these persons go, starting with social drinking which leads progressively to more pathological forms of drinking. These phases in the drinking career usually extend over a 15 or 20 year period. This alcoholic career is one of gradual change from *primary* to *secondary* deviation; the middle class alcoholic does not adopt a self-orientation as a "lush" or "alcoholic" until he reaches an advanced stage of this pattern.[65] The noncriminal alcoholic also endeavors to drink at the same time that he discharges the role obligations of his conventional roles as a parent, employee, and so on, although at some point his drinking begins to have serious ramifications for successful performance of these roles. Along a related line, several researchers have turned up evidence showing that families in which this kind of alcoholism develops go through several stages of adjustment. The role structure of the family unit undergoes changes as the members adapt to the presence of an alcoholic in their midst.[66] The personality characteristics of middle class alcoholics have been studied, as illustrated in Lemert's investigation of "dependency" on the part of married alcoholics. In that analysis, measures of dependency among alcoholics were obtained from observations on domination of the person by his spouse, economic dependence of the alcoholic on others, and dependence imputed to the person by his wife. Indications

---

[64] The President's Commission on Law Enforcement and Administration of Justice, op. cit., pp. 233–37.

[65] E. M. Jellinek, "Phases of Alcohol Addiction," in Pittman and Snyder, op. cit., pp. 356–68.

[66] Joan K. Jackson, "The Adjustment of the Family to the Crisis of Alcoholism," *Quarterly Journal of Studies on Alcohol*, XV (December 1954), 562–86; Edwin M. Lemert, "The Occurrence and Sequence of Events in the Adjustment of Families to Alcoholism," *Quarterly Journal of Studies on Alcohol*, XXI (December 1960), 679–97.

of dependency existing prior to the onset of drinking problems was uncovered in about two-fifths of the cases.[67]

The middle class alcoholic does sometimes become involved with law enforcement agencies and the courts on charges of "public intoxication." But it is the second type of alcoholic, the denizen of "Skid Road," who is of most concern to criminologists.[68] In the folklore of American society, these individuals are sometimes thought to be similar to middle class alcoholics. They are seen as persons who have experienced a "fall from grace" in which they eventually drifted to the "Skid Road" area of homeless men and drinking as a life-career. According to this romanticized version of "Skid Road" alcoholism, we should expect to find numerous ex-professors, lawyers, and other persons of that sort whose drinking resulted in their social degradation. But most "Skid Roaders" originated out of humble backgrounds and have been isolated from conventional patterns of social life for most of their adult lives. They show a career in alcoholism which differs in important ways from the pattern of middle class problem drinkers.

## THE "SKID ROAD" ALCOHOLIC ROLE-CAREER

### Definitional Dimensions

*Offense Behavior.* "Skid Road" alcoholics are individuals whose lives center about drinking. They show patterns of multiple arrests for "public intoxication," "vagrancy," "disorderly conduct," and kindred offenses.

*Interactional Setting.* "Skid Roaders" are frequently involved in drinking activities and other social endeavors in "bottle clubs" made up of fellow drinkers. Many of them engage in forms of socialization and mutual aid with other alcoholics, although "Skid Road" also contains drinkers who are isolates and social rejects.

*Self-concept.* These individuals view themselves not as "criminals," but as persons who drink as their major life activity.

*Attitudes.* "Skid Roaders" are characterized by generally prosocial

---

[67] Edwin M. Lemert, "Dependency in Married Alcoholics," *Quarterly Journal of Studies on Alcohol,* XXIII (December 1962), 590–609.

[68] In the literature on alcoholism, the homeless men area of the city is referred to as both "Skid Road" and "Skid Row." The label "Skid Road" originated in Seattle and preceded the term "Skid Row." As used initially, "Skid Road" had reference to logging roads constructed of small logs laid side by side, over which larger logs were "skidded" to a loading area. The term was applied to the area of homeless men and transients because a good many of the residents of that area were heavy drinking loggers.

attitudes. However, they exhibit disinterest in stable occupational or marital ties or other conventional social activities. These individuals look upon the police as persons to avoid, but do not see the police in markedly hostile terms. In general, "Skid Roaders" are reconciled to recurrent contacts with law enforcement persons, jail personnel, or public alcoholic treatment agency workers.

*Role-career.* The "Skid Road" alcoholic usually becomes involved in this kind of alcoholism relatively early in life, as he severs his connections with his family and other conventional social ties. "Skid Road" life becomes a pattern of day-to-day drinking, interrupted from time to time as the alcoholic is sentenced to a short jail term. The "Skid Roader" repeatedly passes through a correctional "revolving door." This role-career is eventually terminated when the drinker dies from tuberculosis, cirrhosis of the liver, or other hazards related to a life of alcoholism.

### Background Dimensions

*Social Class.* These individuals are usually from relatively lower class origins.

*Family Background.* These offenders are often from relatively conventional family backgrounds, although they commonly become estranged from their parental family as young men. Many "Skid Roaders" have never been married, while others were at one time married. The latter have customarily been isolated from their spouses for a long time through divorce or desertion.

*Peer Group Associations.* The early life peer group ties of these drinkers are apparently not of major importance in the genesis of their deviant behavior. However, the peer ties which many of these drinkers establish with other "Skid Roaders" have considerable influence upon them. These social ties provide reinforcement for many of the offender's attitudes about drinking, treatment agencies, and other matters.

*Contact with Defining Agencies.* These alcoholics have numerous contacts with the police and other defining agents. Their interactions with policemen tend not to be laden with hostility, either on the part of the officers or the drinkers. Policemen normally regard "Skid Roaders" more as nuisances than as "bad guys." The policeman who patrols a "Skid Road" beat is often seen by the drinker as something of a friend, even though he does occasionally arrest the alcoholic. Not uncommonly, the beat patrolman acts to promote the welfare of the drinker, as when he removes him from an alley during a cold night, thus preventing the alcoholic from freezing to death. In a similar way, the alcoholic takes a relatively bland view of judges and other correctional agents, for he sees them as duty bound to interfere with his drinking. The pronounced recidivism of these offenders is due to factors other than harmful effects of correctional processes.

### Discussion

Suporting evidence for the characterization of the "Skid Roader" above can be found in a number of studies, one of which is by Pittman and Gordon.[69] In that investigation, detailed data was gathered on 187 chronic police case inebriates in the Monroe County Penitentiary in Rochester, New York. The sociocultural profile of these persons indicated that they were older than males in the general population, with a mean of 47.7 years of age. A high percentage of the inebriates were Negroes, while Irish and English comprised the largest nationality groups. Nearly 60 per cent of the alcoholics had been married at some time, but almost none were living with their spouses at the time of the study. These offenders were from disadvantaged social backgrounds, for 70 per cent had not gone beyond grammar school, while 68 per cent were unskilled workers. The majority of these individuals showed backgrounds of great residential instability. Most of them had been arrested many times, so they had a mean number of 16.5 arrests.[70]

Pittman and Gordon reported that the alcoholics they studied were products of early family life situations marked by inadequate socialization. According to these investigators, "Skid Roaders" were ill-equipped by virtue of their backgrounds to embark upon stable adult lives.[71] As a result, most had experienced unsatisfactory marriages and had failed in their occupational endeavors.[72] Many of them then became caught up in "Skid Road" life, and a number of them had been institutionalized for lengthy periods of their lives. On "Skid Road" they turned to daily wine drinking, often with small groups of other alcoholics.[73]

Another study which produced results similar to those of Pittman and Gordon is by Grote, concerning "inebriates" who were alcoholics handled in civil court proceedings and "arrested drinkers" who had been criminally processed.[74] Grote found that these two groups of individuals in Oakland, California, were dissimilar types of alcoholics. The "inebriates"

[69] David J. Pittman and C. Wayne Gordon, *Revolving Door* (New York: Free Press of Glencoe, Inc., 1958).

[70] *Ibid.*, pp. 16–58.

[71] *Ibid.*, pp. 78–93.

[72] *Ibid.*, pp. 109–24.

[73] *Ibid.*, pp. 59–77.

[74] Lois P. Grote, *Inebriates, Arrested Drinkers, and Other Offenders: An Exploratory Study* (Master's thesis, San Francisco State College, 1962).

were from relatively stable, middle class origins, while the "arrested drinkers" were "Skid Roaders" from lower class backgrounds. The "arrested drinkers" were concentrated in three tracts in Oakland which make up the homeless man area.[75]

A third report of this sort compared workhouse inmates incarcerated for drunkenness with a group of alcoholic patients in a volunteer clinic. The workhouse inmates were "Skid Roaders" who differed in marked ways from the volunteer patients, for the former were either unmarried or divorced, had begun drinking early in their lives, and had been isolated from conventional social ties for a long time.[76]

The social life of "Skid Road" has also been the subject of sociological attention. Jackson and Connor have investigated this matter in Seattle, where they report that "Skid Road" is populated by two groups of residents, nonalcoholics and alcoholics. The alcoholic group is further divided into types recognized in the argot of the drinkers, for they speak of such persons as "bums," "characters," "winos," "rubby-dubs," and "lushes." "Bums" and "characters" violate group norms about drinking or exhibit bizarre forms of behavior. "Winos" and "lushes," on the other hand, are those alcoholics who band together in social groups devoted to drinking and forms of mutual aid.[77] Peterson and Maxwell have also analyzed the social life of "Skid Road" and have shown that many alcoholic residents are involved in a rich, albeit deviant, interactional network of social ties.[78]

## SUMMARY

This chapter has brought a variety of materials together concerning organized crime, drug addiction, and alcoholism. At this point, analysis of offender types has been completed, and the remainder of the book turns to the correctional processing of lawbreakers.

One point ought to be made before we begin consideration of correctional responses. The things done to criminals within correctional organizations are normally thought of as different from causation, that is, from the factors which get these persons into the correctional machinery. In

[75] *Ibid.,* p. 65.

[76] Francis E. Feeney, Dorothee F. Mindlin, Verna H. Minear, and Eleanor E. Short, "The Challenge of the Skid Row Alcoholic," *Quarterly Journal of Studies on Alcohol,* XVI (December 1955), 645–67.

[77] Joan K. Jackson and Ralph Connor, "The Skid Road Alcoholic," *Quarterly Journal of Studies on Alcohol,* XIV (September 1953), 468–86.

[78] W. Jack Peterson and Milton A. Maxwell, "The Skid Road 'Wino,'" *Social Problems,* V (Spring 1958), 308–16.

this view, causal processes are restricted to matters we have already reviewed. But as we will see in the pages to follow, correctional reactions directed toward lawbreakers may often operate as influences which impel some of these persons toward further involvement in criminality. Quite probably, the study of etiological influences cannot be neatly restricted to just those experiences which have occurred to offenders before they became the subjects of penological handling.

The mass of material we have studied to this point makes it abundantly clear that criminality comes in many forms. We should not be surprised to find that the correctional and punitive reactions toward it have been of many varieties as well. Chapter Seventeen surveys some of the dispositions which have been made of offenders in past eras, as well as actions taken against them in contemporary society. Chapters Eighteen through Twenty-one will also look at features of correctional experiences which offenders encounter in prisons, probation, and other settings.

# 17

# Variations in Correctional Dispositions

## INTRODUCTION

This chapter takes up some matters originally introduced in Chapters Three and Four dealing with the processing of offenders by the police, courts, and related agencies. Chapter Seventeen is concerned with an overview of the various dispositions that can be made of lawbreakers who have been convicted in a criminal court. The chapter is divided into two parts, the first dealing with the ways in which criminals have been disposed of in earlier historical periods, the second having to do with contemporary correctional proceedings. The remaining chapters of the book will take up various facets of current correctional procedures in greater detail.

## A BRIEF HISTORY OF CORRECTIONAL PRACTICES

During the long complex history of correctional actions against criminals, all manner of reactions have been employed at one time or another. Offenders·have been subjected to death or torture, social humiliation such as the pillories and stocks, banishment and transportation, imprisonment, and financial penalties. In general, responses toward lawbreakers were originally retributive in form, criminals being compelled to make amends to their victims in some way. Later, restraint and punishment became the principal form of reaction to deviants, and this approach is still dominant in western societies and elsewhere in the world. Most recently, a rehabilitative philosophy has begun to emerge in which it is held that some form of corrective action should be taken against criminals to deflect them from deviant pathways.

Large-scale societal devices and procedures for dealing with criminals are of recent origin. For example, the prison system of the United States, in which over 200,000 adults are incarcerated at any one time, developed within the past 100 years. The entire world population numbered only about 450,000,000 in 1650, although it exceeds three billion at present.

Thus, until the last several centuries, individual societies were generally small in size and characterized by uncodified and informal techniques of social control. In this sense, the history of corrections extends only over the past several centuries.[1]

Some formalized legal codes and state administered procedures of justice can be uncovered in ancient times. The earliest known system of laws was the Code of Hammurabi, developed by King Hammurabi of Babylon in the eighteenth century B.C. This code was exceedingly complicated, designed to regulate a wide variety of human affairs. Concerning crime, the ruling principle of the code was the retributive *lex talionis,* or "an eye for an eye, a tooth for a tooth." Death was a frequently employed means of dealing with lawbreakers, as was mutilation and monetary compensation. Mosaic law and the legal codes of the Roman Empire are other cases of formalized legal codes and criminal proceedings in antiquity.

In small, preliterate societies, both past and present, secular offenses not thought to offend the spirits were handled as private wrongs. These acts were usually left to family or clan groups to settle as they saw fit, commonly by means of retaliatory blood feuds.[2] For example, the Germanic conquerors of Rome were organized into tribal groups in which retaliation by victims was seen as a hereditary right which could be exercised by the offended family if it so chose. This was a system of private vengeance in which the society played a secondary role. Eventually, blood feuds were replaced by retaliation in the form of pecuniary compensation. The Teutonic tribes of Northwest Europe at the beginning of the Christian era took vengeful retaliation upon offenders by extracting monetary compensation. Still, the injuries for which persons were forced to make compensation were regarded as private matters. The Germanic groups recognized only a limited number of tribal crimes, as contrasted to private wrongs.[3] In the same way, until about the twelfth century, England was divided into shires presided over by sheriffs who assisted in obtaining compensation from violators to be paid to injured parties.

[1] The history of correctional practices is reviewed in Edwin H. Sutherland and Donald R. Cressey, *Principles of Criminology* (7th ed.; Philadelphia: J. B. Lippincott Co., 1966), pp. 305–64; Richard R. Korn and Lloyd W. McCorkle, *Criminology and Penology* (New York: Holt, Rinehart and Winston, Inc., 1959), pp. 358–414; Harry Elmer Barnes and Negley K. Teeters, *New Horizons in Criminology* (3rd ed.; Englewood Cliffs, N.J.: Prentice-Hall, Inc., 1959), pp. 285–347; U.S. Bureau of Prisons, *Handbook of Correctional Institution Design and Construction* (Washington, D.C.: U.S. Bureau of Prisons, 1949), pp. 16–25; Elmer H. Johnson, *Crime, Correction, and Society* (Homewood, Ill.: The Dorsey Press, 1964), pp. 317–50.

[2] Regulation of private feuding by the larger society is discussed in E. Adamson Hoebel, *The Law of Primitive Man* (Cambridge, Mass.: Harvard University Press, 1954).

[3] For an account of changes in Germanic legal systems, see Korn and McCorkle, *op. cit.,* pp. 384–88.

During the twelfth century in England, the crown gradually assumed control over administration of justice, so compensation began to be paid to the King rather than to the wronged party. As the crown intruded into the regulation of these matters, a system of punishment slowly began to emerge. Briefly defined, punishment involves pain or suffering produced by design and inflicted upon a member of a group by that group or society in its corporate capacity. Punishment is directed at persons viewed as having wronged the group as well as the victim. As we shall see, punitive policies developed and flourished well before the emergence of a clear-cut philosophy of punishment which rationalized this posture toward offenders.

The forms of punishment most common in Europe in the middle ages and in the period up to the nineteenth century involved various kinds of corporal punishment or banishment; imprisonment is a relatively recent invention. European jails in the middle ages were places for the confinement of prisoners awaiting trial or punishment, rather than custodial institutions in which punishment was meted out. These jails were frequently maintained in castle towers and similar locations, managed by private citizens, and were usually wretched places in which persons of both sexes and all ages were indiscriminately thrown together. In the sixteenth and seventeenth centuries, offenders were often sentenced to labor in the galleys as another form of punishment, but this was more of an expedient for providing laborers in the ships than a conscious effort to contrive a kind of imprisonment as punishment.

Houses of correction established in England in the 1500's constitute forerunners of imprisonment as a form of punishment. A house of correction known as "Bridewell," opened in London in 1557, was used for incarceration of vagrants and other idle persons. This was a congregate institution, as were other English houses of correction, so the inmates were not maintained in separate cells. Those vagrants, unemployed persons, orphans, and other individuals kept therein were put to work at various kinds of labor, and their services were frequently contracted out to private citizens. Institutions of this kind were constructed in some number on the European continent in the 1600's and 1700's. The most famous of these was a workhouse at Ghent, Belgium, opened in 1773. This institution featured individual cells and certain other characteristics to become common in modern prisons. Some other prototypes of modern correctional institutions were found in Italy in the 1700's. However, prisons and penitentiaries in which offenders are incarcerated for extended periods of time and subjected to various punitive or corrective measures did not become widespread until the nineteenth century.

Banishment has been utilized at various points in human history as a technique for dealing with malefactors. One of the most prominent examples was England, which transported as many as 100,000 criminals from that country to America between 1597 and 1776. After England was compelled to discontinue transporting offenders to this country, criminals were banished to Australia; from 1787 to 1875, over 135,000 lawbreakers were disposed of in that manner.[4] Many of these criminals eventually became influential citizens in Australia and, along with other Australians, were ultimately successful in forcing England to discontinue the policy of transportation. Banishment to other lands and penal colonies has also been employed by France and other nations at various times in the past.

Capital punishment was another procedure for handling offenders which was widely used in Europe in past centuries. For example, England had only about 17 capital crimes in the early 1400's, while by 1688 the number of capital offenses had increased to 50, and by 1780 there were 350 separate crimes carrying the death penalty. Between 1327 and 1509, six statutes were enacted which carried the death penalty; between 1509 and 1660, 30 more capital crimes were defined; and from 1660 to 1819, 187 additional capital offenses were created. Moreover, creation of new capital offenses at an accelerated pace during the eighteenth century was not an empty ritual, for large numbers of executions were carried out in accordance with this legislation. Many of these executions were of persons convicted of property crimes, so these penalties were grossly severe by contemporary standards. Life was cheap and society had little hesitation in spending that of criminals. The excesses of this period eventually ran their course, for by 1830 the number of capital offenses had been reduced back to only 17.

As noted earlier, punitive responses to offenders grew in advance of tightly reasoned philosophies of punishment. The first full-blown argument in defense of punishment is found in the classical school of thought which developed out of the writings of Locke, Hume, Voltaire, Montesquieu, Rousseau, and others.[5] The most prominent classical theorist was the Italian nobleman Cesare Bonesana, Marchese de Beccaria (1738–1794), while others involved in this school of thought were Blackstone, Eden, and Romilly in England. Beccaria's book, *An Essay on Crimes and Punishment*, written in 1764, grew out of his agitation regarding widespread abuses and inequities in prevailing legal practices. He was disturbed by the secret accusations, inadequate defense of accused persons,

---

[4] Barnes and Teeters, op. cit., pp. 294–305.

[5] A summary of classical, neoclassical, and positivist views on punishment can be found in George B. Vold, *Theoretical Criminology* (New York: Oxford University Press, 1958), pp. 14–40. The rise of classical views is discussed briefly in Barnes and Teeters, op. cit., pp. 322–27, while it is discussed in detail in Leon Radzinowicz, *A History of English Criminal Law and its Administration from 1750*, 3 vols. (New York: The Macmillan Co., 1948–1957).

arbitrary and capricious exercise of powers by judges, and barbarous penalties commonplace in the Europe of his time.

The classical position on punishment revolved around a conception of men as rational animals who deliberately and willfully chose the courses of action they pursued. According to this view, the ruling principle by which men orient their behavior was *hedonism,* or pursuit of pleasure and avoidance of pain. Criminals were seen as individuals who made a conscious choice to behave in a lawbreaking manner, but could be coerced into conformity. Nondeviant behavior was to be obtained through application of a finely calculated measure of suffering; the offender would make a hedonistic decision to refrain from crime in the future. Beccaria endeavored to introduce order into the punitive system and to modify the situation in which offenders were frequently punished in a harsh and violent fashion well beyond the quantity of suffering required to tip the hedonistic balance toward law-abiding conduct. He was also concerned about ending the practices through which some more fortunate law violators escaped punishment altogether. Many of Beccaria's suggestions for reform of punishment were embodied in the French Penal Code of 1791, as well as in the revisions of correctional practice in nineteenth century England.[6]

The reader may recall that the classical position on punishment and criminality was discussed in Chapter Six, where it was noted that the initial reforms in criminal law which grew out of classical arguments made little provision for discretionary handling of lawbreakers. The French Penal Code of 1791 ignored individual differences among kinds of criminals and treated adults and minors, intelligent persons and mentally defectives, sane persons and psychotics, as all equally competent to stand trial. All were held equally responsible for their criminality. Subsequent revisions in punitive theory, usually identified as neoclassical, were such as to grant judges some freedom to modify sentences on the basis of extenuating circumstances. Neoclassical reforms also made exceptions in correctional practices for children and incompetents.[7] By and large, contemporary criminal laws and procedures are neoclassical in form, in that their underlying behavioral presumptions are the same as those in neoclassical thought. Additionally, the penalty structure built into criminal codes in western societies has remained relatively unmodified in the past century. Such developments as probation and parole have served to introduce a measure of variability into correctional practice without making any fundamental changes in neoclassical punitive philosophy.

[6] Radzinowicz, op. cit.
[7] Vold, op. cit., pp. 24–26.

Another distinct philosophy of punishment arose in the latter part of the nineteenth century in the positivist school of thought associated with Lombroso, Ferri, Garofalo, and others. The views of Lombroso have already been noted in Chapter Six. He and his followers were of the persuasion that criminality is caused by a multiplicity of factors, including biological in some cases. The positivist position denied that offenders were responsible for their deeds, thus claiming that a punitive posture toward them is unjustified. Instead, lawbreakers were to be treated if they were treatable, while those who could not be reclaimed from criminality were to be maintained in segregation from their fellow men.

Vold has argued that modern criminology is positivist in form, in the sense that criminologists contend that criminality can and should be studied by the methods of science. Contemporary criminology is also positivist in that some version of behavioral determinism is contained within the theoretical assumptions of most criminologists.[8] Positivism is involved in contemporary correctional methods as well, but to a lesser extent; the rehabilitative endeavors which have grown here and there are allied with behavioristic conceptions of criminality. Most correctional workers involved in treatment activities are followers of a positivist perspective on criminality. However, it would be a mistake to suppose that the "new penology" which endeavors to rehabilitate offenders rather than punish them is very much in evidence in the United States and elsewhere.[9]

Returning to historical developments in correctional practice, we should note that penitentiaries are an American invention which arose in the early years of American history.[10] The first forerunner of the modern prison was the Walnut Street Prison opened in Philadelphia in 1776, under the urging of Pennsylvania Quakers. This institution was followed by the Pennsylvania Prison at Cherry Hill, opened in 1829. These penitentiaries operated on the *solitary system*. The Pennsylvania system prisons, as they are often called, were characterized by a distinct architecture intended to allow for physical isolation of prisoners from each other. Inmates were kept in single cells in which they took their meals, engaged in individual forms of labor, exercised, and contemplated the error of their ways. This prison program and architecture attracted a

[8] *Ibid.*, pp. 39–40.

[9] The undeveloped state of a treatment-oriented correctional practice is discussed in Don C. Gibbons, *Changing the Lawbreaker* (Englewood Cliffs, N.J.: Prentice-Hall, Inc., 1965), pp. 190–96.

[10] Brief discussions of the historical origins of American prisons can be found in Barnes and Teeters, *op. cit.*, pp. 328–47; Johnson, *op. cit.*, pp. 335–44.

good deal of attention from European observers. Many were persuaded that this system was reformative in character, and as a result a number of solitary institutions were created in Europe.

However, the Pennsylvania system had a major competitor in the United States. Auburn Prison in New York was opened in 1819, followed a few years later by Sing Sing Prison in the same state. These institutions provided the architectural model for nearly all penitentiaries and reformatories constructed in the United States until the last several decades. The Auburn-Sing Sing system was sometimes referred to as a *silent system*. These prisons were walled institutions in which inmates were incarcerated in cells in multi-tiered cell blocks. The prisoners worked together and took their meals in a common dining room. However, nearly total silence among convicts was maintained within a repressive regime featuring striped uniforms, lock-step marching, and severe punishment for violations of rules.

Advocates of the Auburn-Sing Sing model of prison architecture and program won out in the United States. Until a decade or so ago, nearly all prisons and reformatories constructed in this country were based on the same general physical plant design. These places are surrounded by high walls on which guard towers are placed at various points, they include a number of multi-tiered cell houses with inside cells housing one or more prisoners, and they have dining halls and work areas in which inmates are handled in congregate fashion. Most of these institutions had additions made in a relatively haphazard fashion, with new cell houses or other buildings occasionally built within the original walled area in order to alleviate the pressures of a growing inmate population. As a consequence, these foreboding-looking penal institutions are actually difficult places in which to maintain close security over prisoners, and escapes from them are fairly common.

The rapid growth of prisons in this country is indicated in a publication of the American Correctional Association.[11] That report shows that, of the 90 state penal institutions for males in the United States in 1957, 15 were constructed before 1850, while 52 were opened before 1900. Only 16 new institutions were built between 1930 and 1957. Many of these facilities are large in size, for 48 of the 90 institutions had inmate populations exceeding 1000. Eighteen of the penal facilities held over 2000 inmates; of these, San Quentin Prison in California, Joliet-Statesville Prison in Illinois, and Southern Michigan Prison at Jackson each held over 4000 prisoners.

[11] American Correctional Association, *State and National Correctional Institutions of the United States of America, Canada, England and Scotland* (New York: American Correctional Association, 1957). Minimum security institutions and farms were not counted in these tabulations.

Over the decades since the beginnings of imprisonment in the United States, institutions have gradually become less severe and more humane places. The lock-step, rules of silence, physical punishments for rule infractions, isolation of recalcitrant prisoners in "the hole," strict limits on visiting privileges of inmates, and so on, have been abandoned or eased. These changes in prison life represent humanitarian reforms designed to lessen the pains of imprisonment.[12] Prisoners in contemporary prisons are allowed to listen to radios in their cells, see movies regularly, are allowed a goodly number of visitors per month, are fed well, and receive good medical and dental care. In these ways, doing time has been made less painful. However, some authorities maintain that little has been done to relieve the psychological "pains of imprisonment" which inevitably accompany the experience of doing time.[13] We shall have more to say about this question in a later chapter.

Several other major developments in correctional practices should be noted in passing. For one, probation has become a widely-used technique for handling juvenile offenders and many relatively petty adult criminals. Probation in this country originated with the work of a Boston shoemaker, John Augustus, who interceded with the courts to take on the informal supervision of offenders in that city in the middle of the nineteenth century. Probation ultimately became a state-sponsored program with passage of enabling legislation in Massachusetts in 1878. In the past century, probation services have become standard in all of the states and in the federal correctional system. Parole programs have also become commonplace in the United States within the last century; currently, about 95 per cent of all adult offenders sentenced to institutions are eventually released under supervision on parole.

Innovations of various kinds continue to be attempted in correctional work. In recent years, halfway houses to which parolees are released from prisons have been suggested as a device for curbing parole failure. Along a somewhat related line are work-release programs developed in some county jails, in which prisoners work at conventional jobs during the day and return to the jail at night. Still other innovations can be found in private correctional endeavors such as Synanon, a residential treatment facility for drug addicts. These activities are the subject of extended discussion in later chapters where attention turns to contemporary correctional programs.

---

[12] On the rise of humanitarianism, see Johnson, op. cit., pp. 322–28; Gibbons, op. cit., pp. 130–34.

[13] Gresham M. Sykes, The Society of Captives (Princeton, N.J.: Princeton University Press, 1958), pp. 63–83.

## VARIATIONS IN CONTEMPORARY DISPOSITIONS [14]

Criminals in the United States and other western societies are disposed of in one of several major ways. A few who have committed felonies are executed, but most felons are imprisoned or placed upon probation. Those guilty of lesser crimes are put on probation, fined, or sentenced to relatively short terms in jail. While the major outlines of criminal handling are clear to all, the details are not so apparent. Some of these specifics of correctional handling, such as variations in use of imprisonment as a disposition, are examined below.

The enormous size of the correctional workload in the United States is revealed in figures of the President's Commission on Law Enforcement and Administration of Justice. Table 12 shows data the commission ob-

### TABLE 12
### Some National Characteristics of Corrections, 1965 [15]

|  | AVERAGE DAILY POPULATION OF OFFENDERS | TOTAL OPERATING COSTS | AVERAGE COST OF OFFENDER PER YEAR | NUMBER OF EMPLOYEES IN CORRECTIONS | NUMBER OF EMPLOYEES TREATING OFFENDERS |
|---|---|---|---|---|---|
| Juvenile corrections |  |  |  |  |  |
| Institutions | 62,773 | $ 226,809,600 | $3613 | 31,687 | 5,621 |
| Community | 285,431 | 93,613,400 | 328 | 9,633 | 7,706 |
| Adult felon corrections |  |  |  |  |  |
| Institutions | 221,597 | 435,594,500 | 1966 | 51,866 | 3,220 |
| Community | 369,897 | 73,251,900 | 198 | 6,352 | 5,081 |
| Misdemeanant corrections |  |  |  |  |  |
| Institutions | 141,303 | 147,794,200 | 1046 | 19,195 | 501 |
| Community | 201,385 | 28,682,900 | 142 | 2,430 | 1,944 |
| Total | 1,282,386 | $1,005,746,500 | ———— | 121,163 | 24,073 |

[14] A valuable, up-to-date survey of contemporary correctional dispositions in the United States is The President's Commission on Law Enforcement and Administration of Justice, The Challenge of Crime in a Free Society (Washington, D.C.: U.S. Government Printing Office, 1967), pp. 159–85; see also The President's Commission on Law Enforcement and Administration of Justice, Task Force Report: Corrections (Washington, D.C.: U.S. Government Printing Office, 1967).

[15] President's Commission on Law Enforcement, The Challenge of Crime, p. 161.

tained in a nationwide survey of the correctional caseload. The offenders listed as being in institutions were in jails, reformatories, penitentiaries, and other custodial facilities. Individuals listed in the community were offenders on probation or parole.

Correctional work represents a major employment category, as Table 12 indicates. However, one should not suppose that the 121,000 persons employed in this activity in 1965 were principally involved in rehabilitation and treatment. Only 24,000, or 20 per cent of the correctional workers, were engaged in some treatment capacity in institutions or the community. The time of the remaining 80 per cent was taken up with custodial or maintenance tasks.[16]

### Capital Punishment

No other penological issue provokes as much acrimonious controversy as the debate over capital punishment. The death penalty is violently opposed by some and stoutly defended by others as a necessary device for dealing with criminals. Although the death penalty is not widely used anywhere in the world today, it arouses intense feelings in nearly everyone. Those who oppose its use find the death penalty indefensible even when used sparingly, for they view it as barbarous and immoral. Defenders of capital punishment hold that it is required if certain kinds of crimes are to be deterred.[17]

In general, capital punishment is commonly authorized in most nations in cases of homicide. However, there is considerable variation around the world in the specification of crimes which constitute capital homicides. In the United States, all states which employ capital punishment do so in the instance of first-degree murder, that is, premeditated and intentional homicide. In addition, treason, espionage, and rape carry the death penalty in federal law. Kidnapping is a capital offense in 30 states, treason carries the death penalty in 24 states, and rape is so defined in 21 states, while persons can be executed for robbery in nine states, for arson in five, and for burglary or train wrecking in four states. Although the death penalty is used widely nowhere, it is employed more frequently in the United States than elsewhere. For example, 632 persons were executed in England and Wales between 1900 and 1940. Between 1930 and 1960, 3724 executions were held in the United States. Even though the American population is much larger than that of England and Wales, the relative number of executions was still far

[16] Ibid., p. 162.

[17] A useful sourcebook on capital punishment is Thorsten Sellin, ed., Capital Punishment (New York: Harper & Row, Publishers, 1967).

greater in the former. Of these American executions, 3225 were in cases of murder, 434 were for rape, 23 for armed robbery, 18 for kidnapping, 11 for burglary, and 13 for other crimes. Only 31 of these executions were for federal offenses, and only 31 involved female offenders.

There are some pronounced patterns in capital punishment in the United States. Of the 3724 executions between 1930 and 1960, nonwhites were executed in 50 per cent of the murders, 90 per cent of the rapes, and 46 per cent of the other offenses. One of the principal arguments against capital punishment is that it is highly discriminatory in character, so that those offenders who are from lower income backgrounds and disadvantaged ethnic groups are the ones most likely to be executed. Capital punishment is also more common in some sections of the country than in others—60 per cent of the executions occurred in the 17 southern states. All but two of the executions for rape and all of the burglary executions took place in southern states. This contrast is also revealed by the observation that only one execution occurred between 1940 and 1960 in New Hampshire, while the state of Georgia took the lives of 358 individuals. These figures partially reflect regional variations in occurrence of capital offenses, but the southern states also show a greater willingness to snuff out the lives of criminals.

One trend in capital punishment in the United States has been toward a reduced number of executions. Table 13 shows the number of persons executed in individual years since 1952; it can be seen that capital punishment has been infrequently employed in recent decades. In the period from 1930 to 1934, the average annual number of executions in this country was 155, while in the 1956–1960 period, the yearly average was 57, and between 1962 and 1966, the average was 18.

Other developments in capital punishment include the slight trend toward abolition of the death penalty; nine states were without capital

## TABLE 13
### Executions, United States, 1952–1966

| YEAR | NUMBER OF EXECUTIONS | YEAR | NUMBER OF EXECUTIONS |
|------|----------------------|------|----------------------|
| 1952 | 88 | 1960 | 57 |
| 1953 | 62 | 1961 | 42 |
| 1954 | 82 | 1962 | 47 |
| 1955 | 76 | 1963 | 21 |
| 1956 | 65 | 1964 | 15 |
| 1957 | 65 | 1965 | 7 |
| 1958 | 48 | 1966 | 1 |
| 1959 | 49 | | |

punishment in 1965. The death penalty has also become permissive rather than mandatory, in that it is optional in capital cases except in the District of Columbia. The number of capital crimes has also been reduced in the United States. There are currently 12 capital offenses in the 50 states combined, while 14 states have only one capital crime, two offenses carry the death penalty in eight states, and only nine states have six or more capital crimes. Executions have also become private events rather than public spectacles, and the techniques of executions have become relatively swift and painless.[18] The most widely-used means of carrying out the penalty is electrocution.

Arguments against capital punishment are several, including the ethical position that the practice is morally wrong. Opponents of the death penalty stress its inequitable features, pointing to the large proportion of lower class and nonwhite individuals who are executed. In addition, abolitionists note that execution is irrevocable and cannot be undone once it is carried out. Doubtless there have been cases of persons wrongfully convicted and executed.

Enemies of the death penalty contend that the major argument for its use, its presumed deterrent effect, is erroneous. If capital punishment reduces the occurrence of capital offenses, its impact should be observed in comparisons of crime rates. Instead, statistical studies show that yearly homicide rates are about the same for contiguous states which are socially and economically similar, even though the death penalty is used in one state and not in another. The long-term trends in homicide rates are also similar in adjoining states even though some use capital punishment and others do not. In cases where the death penalty has been introduced, abolished, or reintroduced in a state, the homicide rate has not fluctuated as proponents of capital punishment suggest it should. Finally, the rates of homicide involving policemen are no higher in states without capital punishment than in states which employ the death penalty.

### Imprisonment

Although most American citizens go through their lives without ever seeing the inside of a correctional institution, imprisonment befalls more persons in the United States than in most other nations. Bloch and Geis note that the imprisonment rate in this country is about 120 persons out of each 100,000 population. In other words, each year about this number of individuals can be found serving time in penal institutions. When

[18] Sutherland and Cressey, op. cit., pp. 314–17.

the number of persons serving time is calculated to include lengthy jail sentences, the rate of imprisonment increases to 178 persons per 100,000. By contrast, the imprisonment rate in England and Wales is 65 persons, and in Japan 89 persons, per 100,000 population.[19] The number of adult prisoners in state and federal prisons and reformatories in recent years is shown in Table 14.

## TABLE 14
### Prisoners in State and Federal Prisons and Reformatories *

| YEAR | FEDERAL INSTITUTIONS | STATE INSTITUTIONS | TOTAL | RATE PER 100,000 POPULATION |
|------|------|------|------|------|
| 1960 | 23,218 | 189,907 | 213,125 | 118.7 |
| 1961 | 23,696 | 196,453 | 220,149 | 120.8 |
| 1962 | 23,944 | 194,886 | 218,830 | 118.3 |
| 1963 | 23,128 | 194,152 | 217,280 | 115.7 |
| 1964 | 21,709 | 192,647 | 214,356 | 112.4 |
| 1965 | 21,040 | 190,111 | 211,151 | 109.6 |

* Prisoners on December 31 of each year.

One thing not revealed by the figures in Table 14 is the high turnover of prisoners in institutions. For example, during 1964, 75,096 new prisoners were received in state prisons. Thus, of the 192,647 persons in these places at the end of the year, about 40 per cent had not been there one year earlier. Over an extended period of time, this high population mobility means that a sizeable segment of the population experiences penal commitment. Another point about Table 14 is that it does not include delinquents incarcerated in juvenile facilities. On April 1, 1960, 45,695 youngsters were in custody in juvenile institutions in this country.

A large number of custodial institutions is required for all of these persons who are incarcerated. According to an American Correctional Association publication, there were 118 state prisons and reformatories for males in the United States in 1957, along with 29 women's institutions and 117 honor farms or camps. The federal penal system involved an additional six penitentiaries, four reformatories, four juvenile and youth institutions, seven correctional institutions, four camps, one detention facility, and a medical center. State juvenile facilities included 75 training schools for boys, 56 schools for girls, and 29 camps.[20]

Some indication of the magnitude of incarceration in the larger states

[19] Herbert A. Bloch and Gilbert Geis, Man, Crime, and Society (New York: Random House, Inc., 1962), p. 517.
[20] American Correctional Association, op. cit.

can be obtained from statistics for California. The population of that state in July, 1965, was approximately 18,602,000. On December 31, 1965, California had 26,325 adult prisoners in state penal institutions.[21] In addition, 6377 juvenile delinquents were in Youth Authority institutions as of that date.[22] At about the same time, county and city jails held 16,233 persons in custody, while an additional 9763 were in county and city operated camps. Of the 25,996 county and city prisoners, 16,897 were sentenced offenders serving time in these places.[23] Clearly, in states such as California, the local and state governments represent major employers, for large numbers of correctional workers are required to keep all of these prisoners occupied at various tasks.

### Other Dispositions

As we have noted, probation and other dispositions are widely employed at present as alternatives to incarceration. Unfortunately, recent statistics on the extent of probation as a form of disposition are not available. The U.S. Bureau of the Census discontinued collection of these data in 1946. However, statistics for 1945 indicated that probation was utilized across the country in 31.6 per cent of major offenses. Probation was granted in only 13.0 per cent of the serious crimes in Iowa, but was employed in 64.6 per cent of the instances in Rhode Island. The trend is apparently toward greater use of probation, for in 1935 probation had been employed in only 28 per cent of the serious cases of crime. Data from New York State show that probation was granted in 34.6 per cent of the felony cases in 1945, but in 39.8 per cent of the cases in 1951.[24] In the same way, evidence indicates that probation was employed in 32.8 per cent of the felony cases in California in 1945, but in 44.2 per cent in 1955. In both 1964 and 1965, probation was granted in California in 50.8 per cent of the felony cases.[25]

Some further details on utilization of probation and other dispositions are available from detailed statistics gathered in California. Convictions were given to 84.2 per cent of the felony defendants before the courts in 1965 in that state, while 62.3 per cent of them were convicted through pleas of guilty or *nolo contendere*.[26] Probation was not granted to these

[21] State of California, *Crime and Delinquency in California, 1965* (Sacramento: Bureau of Criminal Statistics, 1966), p. 134.

[22] *Ibid.,* p. 197.

[23] *Ibid.,* p. 131.

[24] Paul W. Tappan, *Crime, Justice and Correction* (New York: McGraw-Hill Book Company, 1960), pp. 559–60.

[25] State of California, *op. cit.,* p. 80.

[26] *Ibid.,* p. 67.

convicted offenders at the same rate throughout the state. As few as 4 per cent were placed on probation in one county, while in another 70.6 per cent of the convicted persons received probation. Probation granting also varies in terms of the offenses for which persons are charged. Table 15 indicates the sentences imposed on felony defendants in California in 1965.[27]

### TABLE 15
### Sentences Imposed on Felony Defendants, California, 1965

| OFFENSE | IMPRISONMENT | PROBATION | JAIL | OTHER * |
|---|---|---|---|---|
| Murder | 94.8 | 2.6 | — | 2.6 |
| Manslaughter | 51.3 | 42.3 | 1.7 | 4.7 |
| Manslaughter, vehicle | 11.2 | 79.4 | 6.9 | 2.5 |
| Robbery | 63.4 | 20.1 | 1.9 | 14.6 |
| Assault | 18.7 | 56.5 | 19.9 | 4.9 |
| Burglary | 25.4 | 46.0 | 18.4 | 10.2 |
| Theft, except auto | 13.9 | 56.3 | 24.8 | 5.0 |
| Auto theft | 17.5 | 41.1 | 25.4 | 16.0 |
| Receiving stolen property | 14.2 | 62.4 | 17.7 | 5.7 |
| Forgery and checks | 26.6 | 53.6 | 16.6 | 3.2 |
| Rape | 16.8 | 63.3 | 12.2 | 7.7 |
| Lewd and lascivious conduct | 28.0 | 70.5 | 0.4 | 1.1 |
| Other sex offenses | 11.8 | 76.2 | 9.5 | 2.5 |
| Narcotics and dangerous drugs | 25.4 | 65.6 | 2.8 | 6.2 |
| Deadly weapons | 23.6 | 41.5 | 29.8 | 5.1 |
| Drunk driving | 5.1 | 81.7 | 10.0 | 3.2 |
| Failure to render aid | 5.0 | 81.4 | 9.1 | 4.5 |
| Escape | 59.9 | 6.5 | 30.8 | 2.8 |
| Bookmaking | 0.6 | 85.2 | 6.2 | 8.0 |
| Contributing | — | 75.2 | 22.0 | 2.8 |
| All other | 7.9 | 63.3 | 21.5 | 7.3 |

* Includes transfer to Youth Authority jurisdiction.

Table 15 contains few surprises, for it is apparent that California courts are loath to grant probation in homicide cases and instances of gross and coercive crime such as robbery, while nonviolent offenses frequently culminate in probation. The low percentage of sex offenders imprisoned might be of some surprise to the laymen, but these figures probably reflect the fact that the majority of sex offenses are innocuous, petty acts.

[27] *Ibid.*, p. 81.

This discussion of contemporary dispositions of offenders would not be complete without some mention of decisions in the cases of juveniles. The subject of juvenile handling was touched upon in Chapter Three, where we noted that police throughout the United States settle informally most of the delinquency cases they encounter in the community. As a consequence, juveniles who end up in the juvenile courts represent only a fraction of all those known to the police or other groups in the community. Some further details regarding the juvenile correctional machinery are available from reports in the state of California. In 1965, the police in that state reported 277,649 arrests of juveniles, of which 21.6 per cent were for major law violations, while the remainder were on charges of minor law violations or "delinquent tendencies." The police reported 45.7 per cent of the total cases to juvenile courts, referring 72.4 per cent of the major law violations and only 39.5 per cent of the "delinquent tendencies" instances.[28]

The fact that a youngster is referred to a juvenile court does not mean that he will become officially labeled a "juvenile delinquent" or be incarcerated. In the California referrals in 1965, 49.6 per cent of the cases were closed at intake or turned over to other agencies, while an additional 13.6 per cent were placed on informal probation. Petitions, the juvenile court parallel of indictments or informations, were filed in only 36.8 per cent of the cases.[29] The sorting processes in which individuals are disposed of in various ways continues beyond the petition-filing stage, for while 35,614 petitions were filed in juvenile courts, only 6174 youths were committed to the California Youth Authority in 1965.[30] The other juveniles were either assigned to probation supervision or incarcerated in county operated institutions. These statistics indicate that there is a pronounced shrinkage of cases at every point from initial police contact of juveniles through institutionalization of some of them in state training schools.

## SUMMARY

This chapter has been concerned with the different events which occur to offenders after they have been convicted or adjudicated in the courts. In the next chapter, our attention turns to an examination of the social workings of the agencies and institutions to which these individuals

[28] *Ibid.,* p. 144.
[29] *Ibid.,* p. 163.
[30] *Ibid.,* p. 197.

are consigned. We shall discover that most of them operate in ways which are not accurately described in organizational charts or brochures which enumerate the purposes or workings of these structures. In particular, we shall find that prisons and other correctional institutions often constitute social communities which function at cross-purposes with their official aims.

# 18

# Correctional Social Organization

## INTRODUCTION

The preceding chapter indicated that, as societies have grown in size and complexity, particularly in the past few centuries, relatively permanent organizational structures have been invented for dealing with law-breakers. Some of these, such as prisons, are physically separated from the societies they serve, while such others as police agencies or probation organizations exist within the community and impinge more directly on the activities of citizens. In either case, these law enforcement and correctional devices represent prominent social forms in modern societies.

In the past decade or so, sociologists have begun to subject these structures to research scrutiny, so that at present a large and growing literature exists regarding the subject we shall call "the sociology of correctional organizations."[1] This term refers to that body of sociological work which attempts to discover the social processes and patterns characteristic of correctional organizations. The sociologist approaches prisons and other custodial institutions, as particular cases of "total institutions," or as a subtype of the larger class of formal, complex organizations.[2]

Analysis of the social workings of legal and correctional agencies encompasses a wide variety of organizations, not all of which are discussed in this chapter. Inquiries into the social structure of the police represent one case of the sociology of correctional organizations, but the police have already been dealt with in Chapter Three. Studies of social values and attitudes regarding crime have been reported in Chapter Two,[3]

[1] The growth of this area of interest is reflected in Don C. Gibbons, "Bibliography on the Sociology of Correctional Organizations," mimeographed. This collection of materials on prisons, police, and other correctional organizations runs to nearly 200 titles, most of which have appeared in the past decade or so.

[2] For a discussion of the characteristics of "total institutions," see Erving Goffman, "On the Characteristics of Total Institutions: The Inmate World," and "On the Characteristics of Total Institutions: Staff-Inmate Relations," in The Prison, ed. Donald R. Cressey (New York: Holt, Rinehart and Winston, Inc., 1961), pp. 15–106.

[3] Arnold M. Rose and Arthur E. Prell, "Does the Punishment Fit the Crime? A Study in Social

while the question of social stigma resulting from legal handling has also been examined earlier.[4] This chapter is devoted to sociological aspects of prisons, training schools, and other custodial institutions, as well as probation and parole agencies.[5]

The various correctional devices extant in modern society have not all been subjected to equal research treatment by sociologists: some of them, such as jails and certain police systems, have been generally ignored. We shall take note of various gaps and deficiencies in the literature on correctional social organization at various points in the material to follow.

## PRISON SOCIAL ORGANIZATION

In a number of ways, prisons are unlike any other kind of institution or organization in modern society. They are foreign to the experience of most citizens, for few individuals other than prisoners and their keepers ever see the inside of a prison. Although it is possible to describe life in a penal institution to persons who have not been in one, such a description can hardly portray all the atmosphere of the place. Such descriptions fail to capture the noises of clanging cell doors; the mean, harsh, "grey" flavor of institutional living, even in the most humane penitentiary; and many of the other elements which make life in the penal institution unique as a human experience. Nonetheless, the pages to follow will endeavor to provide some glimpses of social life behind prison walls, beginning with an examination of similarities and variations among prisons.

### Prison Similarities and Variations

One characteristic shared by all prisons is that they are places where one group of men devote their attention to managing a group of captives. Prisoners do not enter penitentiaries voluntarily; they are forcibly brought there and restrained by prison workers whose main product is social order among inmates. Prisons also resemble each other in the sense that inmates who enter them are roughly similar from one state to another,

---

Valuation," *American Journal of Sociology*, LXI (November 1955), 247–59; Elizabeth A. Rooney and Don C. Gibbons, "Social Reactions to 'Crimes Without Victims,'" *Social Problems*, XIII (Spring 1966), 400–410.

[4] Richard D. Schwartz and Jerome H. Skolnick, "Two Studies of Legal Stigma," in *The Other Side*, ed. Howard S. Becker (New York: Free Press of Glencoe, Inc., 1964), pp. 103–17.

[5] This chapter is a revised and expanded version of material which first appeared in Don C. Gibbons, *Changing the Lawbreaker* (Englewood Cliffs, N.J.: Prentice-Hall, Inc., 1965), pp. 189–227.

so prisons everywhere work with much the same raw material. Reformatories and penitentiaries show much the same kind of architecture in the United States, most of them being walled institutions with inside cell blocks and other features of the Auburn-Sing Sing physical plant. Most inmates depart from penal facilities through the device of parole. Finally, prisons are devoted to the same general functions—they are all concerned with administering some punishment to lawbreakers while keeping them securely in custody, and with certain other aims.

There are some important differences among penal institutions which probably condition the kind of social structure which grows in them. For one, prisons vary considerably in size of physical plant and inmate population. As noted in Chapter Seventeen, American prisons range in size from some holding several hundred men to several with over 4000 men.

Although the Auburn-Sing Sing style of architecture is the most commonly encountered in the United States, there are some penal institutions in this country which have been constructed along different lines. A major variant in physical design is the so-called "telephone pole" physical plan, in which all of the institutional buildings are connected to one central corridor. This architectural style evolved relatively recently, and has provided the model for most of the newer institutions in this country. One major advantage of this kind of physical plant is that control over inmates does not demand the inordinate amount of time and energy devoted to that task in the older Auburn-Sing Sing kind of prison, with its hodge-podge of poorly designed and poorly located structures.

Penal institutions also vary in regard to the financial resources they are able to call upon for implementation of their programs. For example, some states pay guards extremely low wages, while in some other states correctional officers receive fairly reasonable salaries. Another variation among prisons has to do with the kind of administrative organization within which they are placed. In some states, a Department of Corrections or similar agency exercises continued jurisdiction over the individual institutions, and usually provides a degree of stability to the correctional program. In other areas, prisons are autonomous operations subjected to the vicissitudes of political interference.

Custodial institutions show some differences in terms of the kinds of inmates with which they deal. Reformatories usually handle relatively young prisoners, most of them under 25 years of age, while prisons and penitentiaries hold an older, more mature offender population. In all likelihood, institutions with youthful populations are subjected to more violent and erratic behavior by inmates than is true of those places with an older convict population. Certain states, such as California, have moved far in the direction of establishing diversified institutions, each holding a relatively homogeneous group of prisoners. Thus the institution at Chino holds minimum security inmates, while Folsom Prison is restricted to dangerous, criminally mature offenders. In many states with a smaller total population of prisoners, one prison handles the entire heterogeneous mixture of felons.

It is likely that penal institutions mirror various features of the societies in which they are found. Accordingly, the student of prison life might expect to find variations in these places from one country to another. Indeed, several studies of European prisons have turned up discrepancies between them and American institutions.[6] Similarly, Cressey and Krassowski have identified some features of Soviet labor camps which are not found in American institutions.[7]

### Prisons and the "Host" Society

Prisons are sometimes seen as "total institutions" in which all of the prisoner's life events occur. This label implies that penal facilities exist in isolation from the society they serve, but such a view is partially in error. Most of the day-to-day concerns of prisoners center about life inside the walls, and they are painfully aware that they have been isolated from other citizens. Yet convicts are not completely cut off from contact with the outside world. Visitors and tours frequently pass through the institution. Inmates are allowed to listen to radios and read newspapers so that they do not lose complete contact with the world outside the prison. They sometimes seize upon such devices as riots and disturbances to dramatize their complaints against the institution to an audience in the free community.

Prisons are less than "total" in another sense, since the persons who run these places are restrained by interests outside the institution. What kinds of restraints operate on prison administrators? It appears that the citizens in whose name prisons are maintained are generally ignorant and diffident about these places. One study of public knowledge about correctional practices in California indicated that most citizens were unaware of the bases on which persons are committed to prisons, as well as being ignorant of the number, variety, or character of penal institutions in that state. Most of the laymen knew that executions take place

[6] Terence and Pauline Morris, *Pentonville* (London: Routledge and Kegan Paul, Ltd., 1963); Hugh J. Klare, *Anatomy of Prison* (Baltimore: Penguin Books, 1962); Thomas Mathiesen, *The Defences of the Weak—A Sociological Study of a Norwegian Correctional Institution* (London: Tavistock Publications, 1965).

[7] Donald R. Cressey and Witold Krassowski, "Inmate Organization and Anomie in American Prisons and Soviet Labor Camps," *Social Problems*, V (Winter 1957–58), 217–30.

by means of gas at San Quentin Prison, but they showed little awareness of most other facets of the correctional program.[8]

Although laymen do not appear to have any sustained or informed interest in penitentiaries, it would be a mistake to suppose that the public plays no part in the programs of prisons. Various community groups which have an interest in penal operations function as pressure groups that endeavor to influence institutional programs. For example, social worker associations pressure the prison to establish therapy programs, while various industry and labor organizations attempt to force the institution to curtail manufacture of goods which compete with products of private industry. Prison phenomena, such as the widespread idleness endemic in American institutions, cannot be understood without taking into account the activities of outside pressure groups of this sort which have forced institutions to restrict themselves to production of "states-use" goods.

The interest groups which intrude themselves into prison policies are such a mixed collection that different ones often press for conflicting ends. Correctional administrators are sometimes able to manage the disruptive potential of these claims on the system because much of the activity of these groups is intermittent in character. Administrators sometimes deal with interest groups by "giving" one institution to one group and another to a different pressure group. In other words, treatment is stressed in one facility in order to reduce agitation from welfare workers, while a repressive regime is established in a second prison to assuage proponents of punitive themes.[9]

### Prison Programs

A brief sketch of the workings of the prison as revealed in casual observations would include some of these elements. The prison is nominally under the control of an administrator, usually called a warden or superintendent. He is assisted by one or more associate wardens responsible for the custodial or treatment programs of the institution. The custodial staff is by far the largest group of employees, comprised of a captain of the guards and his lieutenants, along with the guards. The latter are sometimes called "correctional officers" by administrators and are usually termed "bulls" or "screws" by the inmates.

[8] Don C. Gibbons, "Who Knows What about Correction?" *Crime and Delinquency*, IX (April 1963), 137–44.

[9] For a discussion of correctional interest groups, see Donald R. Cressey, "Prison Organizations," in *Handbook of Organizations*, ed. James G. March (Chicago: Rand McNally and Co., 1965), pp. 1030–32.

A second group of prison employees consists of a business manager along with various clerical persons and bookkeepers. These individuals have the task of managing the flow of goods and supplies into and out of the prison community.

The third group of workers in the modern prison is made up of those individuals presumed to be working at the rehabilitation of the prisoners. Most prisons have some kind of classification office which gathers detailed facts about newly arrived prisoners. This information is then used in making custodial assignments and other program decisions about inmates. Institutions also maintain a school program and a number of teachers who attempt to continue the education of some of the convicts. A variety of vocational training is often found in modern penal facilities, so that some prisoners learn typewriter repair or other skills of that kind. However, the bulk of the inmates work during the day in various kinds of prison industries which have no vocational consequences for them. Prisoners assist in the kitchen, make clothing or shoes for other state institutions, manufacture road signs and license plates, or engage in related kinds of prison labor. Supervisory employees are responsible for these activities, along with guards who also maintain surveillance of the inmates during the day. Social workers are employed by the institution to engage in various kinds of "helping" activity with the convicts.

Correctional administrators often distribute descriptions of their prisons which imply that these are orderly, efficient, coherent systems in which the various facets of correctional activity converge upon the inmate to convert him into a law-abiding citizen. But how accurate is the official description of the prison? Recently accumulated evidence on the social workings of penal organizations indicates that the official view of penal operations is more fiction than fact.

### Prison Social Structure

The general description of prison organization that follows is drawn from the existing literature and should be viewed as most descriptive of maximum security prisons, and as more or less accurate for institutions that vary in the ways suggested in the preceding pages.

Prisons are often thought of by members of the general public as autocratic in form.[10] Custodial officers *give orders* and inmates *obey* them. Prisoners are seen as totally managed persons whose opportunities for self-direction and independent action are almost completely circumscribed. Penal institutions are also commonly regarded as monoliths with

[10] For an analysis of prisons as autocracies, see Norman A. Polansky, "The Prison as an Autocracy," *Journal of Criminal Law and Criminology*, XXXIII (May–June 1942), 16–22.

a singularity of purpose in which all responsibilities of members of the system are clearly and specifically defined. Prisons are well-oiled, smooth-running, people-punishing, and people-changing social machines. In this view, there is clarity and consensus among all prison employees, from the warden down to the guards. All these individuals are in agreement regarding their tasks of maintaining, disciplining, and sometimes treating inmates. Prisons are frequently believed to be models of autocratic and rational bureaucratic structures.

There are major distortions in this image of prisons, for they normally depart rather markedly from this monolithic model. Cressey has devoted a good deal of attention to a discussion of the organizational cross-currents built into modern prisons.[11] He has pointed out that, as basic concepts of prison purposes and institutional management have changed, new activities have been added to the institutional operation, but without being integrated with the earlier forms of administrative structure. Accordingly, nearly all modern penal facilities have three principal administrative hierarchies, relatively independent of each other, and devoted to keeping, serving, and using inmates. In other words, prisons have a number of employees who maintain custody over prisoners, another group which supervises inmates in their work activities, and a third collection of workers who endeavor to rehabilitate the prisoners.[12] Of course, in many institutions, that part of the system supposed to be devoted to treatment is a very small segment of the organization, but at least a token effort to develop a rehabilitative program has been made in many penal institutions in recent years. Cressey also notes that in the general shift in the past century, away from the view that persons are sent to prison *for* punishment to the perspective which regards imprisonment alone as punishment enough, "mere incarceration" has not been consistently defined. Over the decades, prisons have vacillated from repressive regimes to periods in which they have been loosely run and less punitive and harsh in character. Still, most contemporary prisons continue to place prisoners in some degree of physical discomfort, so "mere incarceration" tends to refer to a mean existence unrelieved by many of the diversions of normal living.[13]

The somewhat contradictory ingredients of the mandate under which modern prisons operate has been summarized by Cressey in the following terms:

... at present there are three popular and sanctioned reactions to crime in contemporary American society. One is hostility, with insistence that the crimi-

[11] Cressey, "Prison Organizations," pp. 1023–70.
[12] *Ibid.*, p. 1024.
[13] *Ibid.*, pp. 1026–30.

nal be made to suffer in prison, whether the suffering is physical or psychological. Another reaction is one of humanitarian concern that the punishments in prisons not be too harsh, severe, cruel, or inhuman. A third is inquiry designed to secure comprehension of the social and psychological processes in criminal behavior, so that control can be based on knowledge.[14]

The charge to the prison that it maintain secure custody over prisoners so they cannot escape, and at the same time refrain from brutalizing the inmates, creates grave difficulties for the institution. One basic fact is that the prisoners are not in the institution voluntarily and do not accord legitimacy to the official norms or prescriptions of the organization. The situation of prisoners is different from that of persons in a military autocracy, for in the latter case most members of the system have internalized the authority of the rules, albeit somewhat grudgingly. Most are motivated to conform to military regulations and procedures, even though they may regard conformity as personally unpleasant. The same cannot be said for many (but not all) prison inmates.

Autocratic rule over hostile and uncooperative inmates could theoretically be obtained at a price. Prisoners could be isolated from each other, physically abused and coerced, and put under continual and pervasive surveillance by guards. In theory, they could be maintained under conditions of marked anomie and demoralization. However, these possibilities do not exist in actual fact, for prison officials are expected to deal with their charges in a humane fashion. They are obligated to minimize the physical and social isolation of inmates, rather than maximize it, and are forbidden to abuse physically or coerce prisoners. These are very real limitations, for institutions do come under periodic scrutiny by the outside world. In addition, constant surveillance of prisoners by correctional officers to detect rule violations is impossible for two reasons: most prisons are not physically constituted in such a way as to allow continual supervision and observation of convicts, and there are not enough observers. Although guards comprise the largest single class of employee, they are greatly outnumbered by the prisoners.[15]

In theory, officers are expected to maintain social distance from prisoners and give orders which inmates are presumed to obey because they are powerless to do otherwise. But as indicated earlier, prison guards do not have techniques of physical coercion available to obtain com-

[14] *Ibid.*, pp. 1029–30.

[15] For one incisive commentary on the limits of "total power" iin prisons, see Gresham M. Sykes, *The Society of Captives* (Princeton, N.J.: Princeton University Press, 1958), pp. 40–62; Sykes, "The Corruption of Authority and Rehabilitation," *Social Forces*, XXXIV (March 1956), 257–62; Clarence Schrag, "Some Foundations for a Theory of Correction," in Cressey, *The Prison*, pp. 338–39.

pliance from recalcitrant prisoners. Moreover, physical force would be self-defeating in the long run as a technique for managing convicts even if it were legitimized. Guards are grossly outnumbered by inmates, so extensive use of force would produce convict reprisals, uprisings, and other negative consequences.

One technique contrived for control of uncooperative prisoners has been to urge them to put themselves into voluntary isolation from other convicts, to "do your own time," and pursue incentives and privileges as rewards for conformity. In turn, if an inmate violates rules, privileges are withdrawn from him.[16] However, this mechanism has severe limitations. Deprivation of privileges tends to have little effect within the harsh environment of institutions because the prisoners are already severely deprived. They are cut off from sexual relations and many kinds of freedom of action as to choice of clothing, companionship, and so on. To be denied the privilege of attending a movie tends not to be viewed as a severe loss. Incentives such as reduction of the inmate's sentence for good behavior have been redefined by the prisoners as "rights" rather than rewards, so the administration tends to tamper with "good time" credits only in extreme cases. Furthermore, they are accorded to the inmate at the start of his sentence, rather than at points in his institutional career as rewards for appropriate institutional conduct. Thus they do not operate as important incentives, and are normally awarded routinely to nearly all inmates except those who have had extremely troublesome and violent institutional careers.

The modern prison must find some way of maintaining a reasonable degree of order without extreme physical coercion and manipulation of meaningful rewards for conformity. The solution of this problem of how to keep the peace with and among uncooperative inmates takes the form of "corruption of authority" in many prisons.[17] Corruption of authority assumes several forms. One refers to liaisons, relationships, "deals," and other informal *sub rosa* ties which develop between inmates and administrators and are not defined as legitimate or proper within the formal definitions of prison procedures. Penal administrators and prisoner "elites" enter into informal relationships which provide special privileges to these leaders. In turn, they take over the job of coercing other inmates into minimally disruptive behavior. As Korn and McCorkle have indicated, "far from systematically attempting to undermine the inmate

[16] Richard A. Cloward, "Social Control in the Prison," in Cloward, Donald R. Cressey, George H. Grosser, Richard McCleery, Lloyd E. Ohlin, Gresham M. Sykes, and Sheldon L. Messinger, *Theoretical Studies in Social Organization of the Prison* (New York: Social Science Research Council, 1960), pp. 20–48.

[17] Sykes, *The Society of Captives*, pp. 52–62.

hierarchy, the institution generally gives it covert support and recognition by assigning better jobs and quarters to its high-status members providing they are 'good inmates.' In this and other ways the institution buys peace with the system by avoiding battle with it." [18] Being a "good inmate" in this context means refraining from direct assaults upon the administrative system. It *does not* mean "doing your own time," for elites interfere with other inmates, control them, and demand special privileges and favors from less powerful prisoners. They are covertly aided in these activities by the prison administration, which pretends not to see this interaction among the convicts.

A second form of corruption of authority extends to inmate-guard relationships generally, in which correctional officers obtain a measure of cooperation and obedience from inmates by discretionary action in which they overlook some conduct infractions. In turn, in a *quid pro quo* relationship, inmates are expected to create a minimum of visible trouble for the correctional officers. In other words, the guard persuades convicts to behave by allowing them to deviate from rules in certain situations. This form of authority corruption stems from several factors. Correctional officers are not immune from general pressures to be "good guys." They probably find it difficult to associate with inmates on extremely distant and aloof terms, for they quickly discover that prisoners are quite ordinary humans and not monsters. More important, discretionary actions represent the most obvious available technique by which inmate disorder can be kept to a minimum by the guard. The officer without a club of some sort must persuade and cajole. Discretionary action represents the "carrot" by which he obtains a modicum of conformity to major rules and regulations.

In the public view, the job of correctional officer is fit for simpletons who need only to follow explicit orders. In reality, it is probably one of the more difficult occupational tasks in American society. The job demands a high order of skill in manipulating and managing men. The officer must use discretion, but at the same time must be alert to the dangers of being drawn into situations where he buys cooperation from prisoners at too great a price. He must avoid being lured into *sub rosa* relationships in which he takes contraband into or out of the institution or performs other illicit services for inmates. Discretion up to a point is required of the guard, but there is considerable risk that he will be manipulated by convicts into discretionary actions beyond the tolerance point of his superiors. If he uses too much discretionary judgment, he

[18] Lloyd W. McCorkle and Richard Korn, "Resocialization Within Walls," *Annals of the American Academy of Political and Social Science*, No. 293 (May 1954), 91.

may be fired or punished in some other way. To complicate his situation further, appropriate action must be worked out by each officer himself, for the most part unguided by advice and instruction from anyone else. Cressey has suggested that in prisons of either custodial or therapeutic orientation, the guard faces a situation in which his superiors are not able to give him explicit directions as to precisely how and in what way he is to function in his discretionary role.[19]

For reasons of this kind, prisons might be more accurately defined as partially disorganized, rather than model autocracies. They exhibit less than complete organizational consensus among employees, and tend to show defective communication patterns. Orders are supposed to move down a chain of command to guards, where they are implemented, while information on which decisions are made moves up the command line. But distortions often occur in message flow, particularly in the feedback of explanations behind orders to such low ranking members as custodial officers. Consequently, prisons frequently show a degree of guard alienation from the institutional program.[20] Officers either do not understand the bases on which decisions and orders are formulated or they disagree with these directives. This lack of internal consensus among employees regarding goals of the system is found in prisons of various kinds, but is particularly severe in treatment oriented prisons, where the guards are often more similar to the inmates than they are to the higher administrators. Because they tend to view therapy operations as a threat to sound custody, they are in accord, although for different reasons, with the prisoners' negative definitions of treatment programs.

### "Treatment Oriented" Prisons

The problems of prisons discussed to this point seem generic to treatment and custodial institutions alike. But there are some additional difficulties which seem to be peculiar to therapy oriented prisons.[21]

The discussion of treatment in modern penitentiaries should begin by noting that the rehabilitative function has not been widely adopted or implemented in American prisons to date. As Schnur has indicated, it does not make much sense to ask whether the "New Penology" oriented

[19] Donald R. Cressey, "Contradictory Directives in Complex Organizations: The Case of the Prison," *Administrative Science Quarterly*, IV (June 1959), 1–19.

[20] Schrag, *op. cit.*, pp. 336–38.

[21] Organizational differences between "punitive oriented" and "treatment oriented" prisons are discussed at length in Cressey, "Prison Organizations," pp. 1033–54; see also Johan Galtung, "The Social Functions of a Prison," *Social Problems*, VI (Fall 1958), 127–40; Galtung, "Prison: The Organization of Dilemma," in Cressey, *The Prison*, pp. 107–45.

around rehabilitation is a success, for the "New Penology" still exists for the most part mainly in textbooks.[22] Schnur pointed out that, around 1958, about 27,000 persons were employed in state and federal penal facilities to manage some 165,000 inmates—a ratio of one employee for every six prisoners. Only small numbers of these employees were assigned to activities that could be called treatment; most were custodial officers. Moreover, only a small proportion of the persons designated as treatment personnel were actually involved in therapy activities. According to Schnur, "more people, however, are employed to shuffle papers than to implement the new penology." [23] For example, only 23 psychiatrists were available full-time to treat 165,000 inmates, so the ratio of prisoners to psychiatrists was 7026 to 1. If each convict received the same amount of psychiatric help, he would get 82 seconds of therapy per month.

A more recent study of the same general kind has been reported by Johnson.[24] He found in a 1961 survey of 47 state correctional systems that persons with M.S.W. degrees were employed in only 14 states. Eighteen states indicated that no "social workers" were employed in their programs. Additionally, in those remaining states reporting utilization of social workers, this occupational category was defined so broadly as to include persons who did not have training in social work practice and techniques. The definition of social work was stretched to subsume a variety of institutional activities not conventionally thought of as social work.

Although the rehabilitative function is not yet widespread or fully developed, enough prisons have begun to move in this direction to provide some indication of the organizational difficulties which arise with injection of treatment into institutional workings.

Addition of the treatment role has introduced views into the institution to the effect that a coercive, restrictive social climate is inimical to therapy. Prisoners are in need of opportunities to ventilate hostility, work out new patterns of adjustment, and so on. Prisons have come to be regarded as serving ends similar to those presumed to characterize mental hospitals, with guards enjoined to be receptive, passive, and relaxed. Significantly, this new view is not usually shared by all members of the employee group. Such notions have frequently been brought into the

[22] Alfred C. Schnur, "The New Penology: Fact or Fiction?" Journal of Criminal Law, Criminology and Police Science, XLIX (November–December 1958), 331–34; for some evidence suggesting that the "New Penology" has not been fully implemented in England either, see Terence Morris, "In the Nick," and Alan Little, "The Borstal Boys," The Twentieth Century (London,) CLXX (Winter 1962), 22–34, 35–42.

[23] Schnur, op. cit., 332.

[24] Elmer H. Johnson, "The Present Level of Social Work in Prisons," Crime and Delinquency, IX (July 1963), 290–96.

institution by top administrators who attempt to impose them upon the custodial force. However, a large segment of the guard group is made up of veterans of the "old order" who have served for many years under a straightforward custodial system. These officers are supported by the force of tradition in their belief that the "old ways" are better, and tend to be unreceptive to rehabilitative declarations by recently arrived administrators. Nonetheless, correctional institutions attempting transformation into treatment oriented systems do exhibit a more relaxed, less coercive social climate than the more traditional penal facilities. Although there are serious questions regarding the extent to which prisons can be converted into therapeutic communities, efforts to do so weaken the authoritarian order of the institution and disrupt relations among employees.

The most usual outcome of introduction of treatment into an institution is an uneasy marriage of custodial and therapeutic activities, and security considerations often prevail in the operation of the organization.[25] In other cases, the rehabilitative goal pervades many facets of the prison in the face of resistance by some employee holdouts. The specific pattern which emerges probably depends in the main on how the treatment function is brought into the prison. If it is introduced by hiring middle level employees such as social case workers, but is not supported by the warden and his aides, the common consequence is to find it perverted in practice to serve custodial ends. Psychiatrists are used in such institutions to "cool out" threatening inmates rather than to conduct therapy. In the same way, the treatment recommendations of other workers are subordinated to custodial decisions. The custodial force is able to control communication within the organization, so the therapists are kept ignorant of, and removed from, the important operations of the prison. They are reduced to a form of prison "window dressing."[26]

The outcome of the custody-treatment quarrel differs where the warden and other top level administrators have introduced rehabilitation as an end, or give allegiance to this goal. In this case, treatment workers are more influential in the operation of the institution and make important policy decisions. But again, the situation tends to be an uneasy one in which functional harmony is less than complete. No clear format has yet been devised which spells out the nature of an effective therapy program operating within the limits of necessary security provisions. Treatment oriented penitentiaries tend to lack unambiguous definitions

---

25 Donald R. Cressey, "Limitations on Organization of Treatment in the Modern Prison," in Cloward, et al., op. cit., pp. 78–110.

26 Harvey Powelson and Reinhard Bendix, "Psychiatry in Prison," Psychiatry, XIV (February 1951), 73–86.

of the specific manner in which rehabilitative agents are to operate. As a consequence, many of these employees come to see themselves as rescuers, helpers, and protectors of inmates, rather than as rehabilitators. The worker who identifies his task as one of helping inmates sometimes comes to conceptualize his job as involving protection of convicts from the custodial force. He begins to see himself as a mediator between offenders and guards rather than a coworker with the correctional officer with whom he shares a common task. This kind of role-performance probably exacerbates the treatment-custody conflict in prisons. It has been argued that the therapy agent who views his task as rescuing and helping inmates plays into the hands of the prisoners. He lends covert support to that group's attempts to "reject the rejectors" or deflect blame away from themselves and onto "society." [27]

The treatment oriented prison creates special difficulties for the guard force. Not only are correctional officers told to maintain order without being given clear instructions as to how they are to accomplish this goal, they are also told to behave in ways which contribute to therapy. As Cressey notes:

It is clear that in treatment-oriented prisons, directions to guards regarding their relationships with inmates are likely to be confusing and contradictory. There are to be no rules to enforce, but the guard is to enforce "understandings" to the extent necessary for the prison to achieve the minimum degree of orderliness it needs. There is to be no punishment, but guards are to report nonconformists to a central board for hearings, during the course of which punishments are ordered, in the name of justice. Guards are to "relax" but they are not to relax "too much." [28]

From this description by Cressey, it appears that correctional officers in the treatment prison are pulled at from several different sides, so that they are "damned if they do, and damned if they don't." Such a state of affairs could hardly add to the attractiveness of this kind of occupation.

From the discussion so far, it is evident that administrations of most prisons do not present a united front to the inmate group. Points of ambiguity exist within the organizations, conflicts between different administrative groups lie barely hidden and sometimes blossom into overt interorganizational conflict, and other difficulties characterize prisons. Little has been said so far about the inmate group. What is the nature of social life among prisoners in maximum security prisons?

[27] McCorkle and Korn, op. cit., 88–89.
[28] Cressey, "Prison Organizations," p. 1058.

## The Inmate Social System

One common but exaggerated view of convicts is that they are an aggregate of persons all in opposition to the administrative regime. In the laymen's view, inmates are assumed to be a collectivity of "wild beasts" from whom the guards have much to fear, continually engaged in attempts to escape and carrying on a variety of violent activities among themselves. Something of this same conception of the inmate group can be found in the sociological literature as well. Sykes and Messinger have described an "inmate code" of normative prescriptions said to exist in all prisons.[29] By implication, allegiance to this code characterizes most convicts. The code consists of a collection of conduct definitions centering around directives to refrain from interfering with inmate interests, avoid quarrels and conflicts with other prisoners or go "no rap" with one's fellow convicts, be strong in the face of administrative pressure and punishment, and so on. The code defines the model convict, from the inmates' perspective, in terms which contrast markedly with the staff version of the good inmate. Prisoners are expected to cooperate with each other in overt and covert defiance of institutional expectations.

Several hypotheses have been advanced to account for this code. Sykes and Messinger maintain that the most likely explanation is functional, in which the code is seen as serving to reduce the "pains of imprisonment" in custodial institutions.[30] These pains of incarceration include deprivations of liberty, goods and services, heterosexual relations, and autonomy which are experienced as psychologically painful by offenders. According to these authors, "as a population of prisoners moves in the direction of solidarity, as demanded by the inmate code, the pains of imprisonment become less severe." [31] A compatible thesis is advanced by McCorkle and Korn, who hold that the code and prisoner solidarity in opposition to the authorities permits the inmate to "reject his rejectors" instead of himself.[32] That is, convicts are supported by their peers in a set of definitions and attitudes which hold that society is at fault for their criminality, so they are not forced to turn blame inward upon themselves. Much the same argument has been advanced by Cloward.[33]

[29] Gresham M. Sykes and Sheldon L. Messinger, "The Inmate Social System," in Cloward, et al., op. cit., pp. 5–19.

[30] Ibid.

[31] Ibid., p. 16.

[32] McCorkle and Korn, op. cit., 88–89.

[33] Cloward, "Social Control in the Prison."

There is no question that an inmate code exists in prisons and that psychological pains accompany the experience of incarceration. But that does not necessarily mean that the code is solely the product of pressures of confinement.[34] It is conceivable that it exists in prisons in part because some prisoners bring it into the institution from the outside. There are several pieces of evidence which support a "diffusion" interpretation of inmate norms. Wheeler has shown that role-conflict and discrepancies in role-expectations between inmates and administrators are less than complete.[35] He found that prisoners had different expectations regarding the behavior of other inmates than did guards, but there were some offenders with views similar to those of correctional officers who approved of violations of inmate definitions. Wheeler also suggests that some of the conflict between prisoners and authorities is more apparent than real. His data show that prisoners judge other inmates to be more hostile to treatment and other institutional activities than they are in fact. This discrepancy between private sentiments and estimates of group views appears related to the greater visibility of the most antisocial persons in the prison. Individual prisoners gauge the degree of antiadministration sentiment among other offenders from observation of a biased sample of the total inmate group.

Wheeler has contributed a second kind of evidence supporting a diffusion interpretation of the inmate code. His findings from a number of Scandinavian prisons show that the pains of imprisonment are found in these places, but there is no clear parallel to the inmate code or prisoner solidarity observed in American institutions.[36] Wheeler's interpretation of these results is that most prisoners in Scandinavian institutions enter from a society which contains a lower incidence of antiauthority attitudes than the United States. Conversely, in American prisons, many offenders bring into the institution antisocial attitudes which are widespread among lower class groups.

Observations regarding social types or argot roles in prisons also lend support to diffusion hypotheses regarding the inmate code.[37] Schrag has shown that a pattern of four sets of inmate roles oriented around certain focal issues exist in the prison community. These role patterns are

[34] One bit of evidence in support of the functionalist thesis is Charles R. Tittle and Drollene P. Tittle, "Social Organization of Prisoners: An Empirical Test," *Social Forces,* XLIII (December 1964), 216–21. This investigation was conducted in the U.S. Public Health Service Hospital which holds drug addicts.

[35] Stanton Wheeler, "Role Conflict in Correctional Communities," in Cressey, *The Prison,* pp. 229–59.

[36] Stanton Wheeler, "The Comparative Analysis of Prison Social Structure," paper read at meetings of the American Sociological Association, September 1962.

[37] Schrag, *op. cit.,* pp. 309–57; Schrag, "A Preliminary Criminal Typology," *Pacific Sociological Review,* IV (Spring 1961), 11–16; Sykes, *The Society of Captives,* pp. 84–108.

identified in the argot of inmates by such labels as "square John," "right guy," "outlaw," "ding," "rapo," and "politician," but Schrag has retitled these with more neutral terminology. Similarly Sykes' report on the New Jersey state prison indicates that the inmates recognize the existence of different behavioral roles in their midst and employ argot labels such as "center man," "hipster," "gorilla," "real man," and "ball buster" to designate these inmate patterns. It appears that a group of basic patterns of inmate adjustment arise in prisons, so that while the inmate terminology for these varies from one prison to another, the patterns are similar.

According to Schrag, prosocial inmates (square Johns) consistently define role requirements in terms of the legitimate norms of the civilian community of law-abiding citizens, whereas antisocial inmates (right guys) perceive role requirements in terms of the norms of prisoner society. The latter are loyal to other convicts and engage in minimal contact with prison officials. Pseudosocial prisoners (politicians) shift their allegiance between legitimate norms and prisoner standards and engage in interaction with both inmates and administrators. Asocial inmates (outlaws) are rebels against both legitimate norms and prescriptions and the standards of inmate society.

Schrag has summarized a series of studies which demonstrate that these role patterns are of primary importance in understanding inmate behavior within prisons. Among other observations, he notes that each role type is the product of a relatively distinct constellation of background experiences. Prosocial offenders are usually involved in crimes of violence or naive property offenses. Their behavior appears to be the product of situational stress rather than long-term conditions of family instability or other kinds of disorganization. On the other hand, antisocial inmates are highly recidivistic, frequently involved in crime careers which started at an early age, and usually from urban, slum area backgrounds. They are gang delinquents "grown up." Pseudosocial inmates have engaged in sophisticated and subtle property crimes involving manipulation of other persons, rather than the use of coercion and violence. They tend to develop out of relatively stable and comfortable economic backgrounds. Asocial prisoners have been involved in violent, bizarre forms of crime, and closely resemble descriptions of "sociopaths." In most cases, such individuals seem to be the product of backgrounds of early and severe parental rejection.

In addition to differences in social background, Schrag notes other correlates of these role patterns. Social participation within the institution varies among these different types, as does the inmates' responses to such prison experiences as treatment programs or punishment. To take one example, prosocial inmates associate differentially with other pro-social prisoners and engage in frequent contacts with staff members. Prosocial convicts also make considerable use of the various treatment programs in the prison, in contrast to other types who shun such activities.[38]

The important point regarding social types, the inmate code, and the functional and diffusionist arguments is this: there are many prisoners who engage in some form of antiadministration, proinmate code activity, and these are usually called "right guys." There are others who cooperate with the authorities, uphold conventional norms, and reject the inmate code, and are termed "square Johns." Antisocial inmates are usually from lower class backgrounds with long prior records and previous institutional commitments, whereas "square Johns" often show no prior criminal pattern or history of previous incarceration. If the pains of imprisonment lead to emergence of a prisoner code and allegiance to the code by inmates, how are prosocial "square Johns" to be explained? Certainly it could be argued that the first-offender, situational criminal would be the most traumatized by prison, while the recidivism-prone, crime-wise, working class prisoner should be less likely to experience a prison sentence as severe social rejection. The diffusionist view is that allegiance to an inmate code by certain offenders is the continuation, inside the walls, of a pattern of "rejection of the rejectors" which originated at a much earlier point in their careers. In many cases, the point of origin probably lies in early experiences with the police, juvenile courts, and so on. Elements of the inmate code represent institutional manifestations of hostility to the police and other attitudes widespread in lower class society. The first offender experiences the pains of imprisonment and societal rejection, but his preprison experiences and involvement in prosocial reference groups outside the walls serve to insulate him from developing any serious loyalty to the inmate code. In addition, insofar as the situational first offender is a novice in crime, he is likely to be rebuffed in any attempt to play the role of "real criminal" among the antisocial inmates in the prison.

A recent effort to unravel the threads of prison social life has been made by Irwin and Cressey, who suggest that some elements of institutional culture are indigenous to penal facilities, while other facets of prison life are examples of "latent culture" brought in from outside the

[38] One of the studies which Schrag draws upon in this discussion of role types is that by Garabedian in a maximum security prison in a western state. See Peter G. Garabedian, "Social Roles in a Correctional Community," *Journal of Criminal Law, Criminology and Police Science,* LV (September 1964), 338–47; Garabedian, "Social Roles and Processes of Socialization in the Prison Community," *Social Problems,* XI (Fall 1963), 139–52.

walls.[39] They suggest that the penitentiary must be seen as made up of three subcultures among inmates, a "prison culture," a "criminal subculture," and a "legitimate" or conventional system. Some prisoners, oriented toward "making out" *inside* the institution, are often persons who have spent most of their lives in custodial facilities. They participate in conniving and other antiadministration interaction, endeavor to obtain "bonaroos" (special clothing) and other material goods, and are members of a "convict" subculture. "Thieves" are the members of the "criminal" subculture oriented toward the society of lawbreakers *outside* the prison. They exhibit values centered about toughness, courage, and so on, but these are not indigenous to the institution. Instead, they are values which are widespread in general society. "Thieves" tend to remain aloof from participation in the conniving and machinations of convicts, for they prefer to "do their own time" and "go no rap" with other prisoners. The latter term refers to deliberate noninvolvement with criminal peers in the institution. Members of the legitimate subculture, "do-rights," are those "square John" individuals who remain outside of the groups of antisocial prisoners.

The thrust of this analysis by Irwin and Cressey, as well as of much of the other material discussed above, is that the prison life which emerges among inmates is significantly influenced by characteristics which these individuals import into the institution. This diffusionist view is favored in this book, and we shall see further evidence supporting this argument in the discussion of women's prisons to follow.

### Women's Prisons

Although there is a fairly large collection of works dealing with various administrative aspects of women's prisons, few sociological investigations of these places have taken place.[40] One obvious reason for the lack of attention to women's institutions is that they are relatively few in number. In many states, no prison for females exists autonomous from the state prison, due to the small number of felons of that sex to be incarcerated.

Two studies of women's prisons have recently been reported, with findings which are quite similar for the two institutions. One investigation concerned the Federal Reformatory at Alderson, West Virginia,[41] while

[39] John Irwin and Donald R. Cressey, "Thieves, Convicts and the Inmate Culture," *Social Problems*, X (Fall 1962), 142–55; see also Julian Roebuck, "A Critique of 'Thieves, Convicts and the Inmate Culture,'" *Social Problems*, XI (Fall 1963), 193–200.

[40] One early study is Ida Harper, "The Role of the 'Fringer' in a State Prison for Women," *Social Forces*, XXXI (October 1952), 53–60.

[41] Rose Giallombardo, *Society of Women* (New York: John Wiley and Sons, Inc., 1966).

the other had to do with the state prison for women at Corona, California.[42]

Giallombardo's research in the federal facility turned up evidence that role problems and administrative conflicts similar to those noted for men's institutions are seen in women's prisons.[43] Many workers in the federal reformatory were hostile to the therapy program which had been introduced a short time earlier. The correctional officers were held to ambiguous role requirements, for they were charged with the responsibility of carrying out counseling without the requisite knowledge for the task. Giallombardo indicates that:

In the new program, with its emphasis on freedom and understanding, the correctional officers were to counsel and to use friendliness and firmness to secure compliance from the inmates. This meant that they had to accept some expressions of aggressive behavior which might be distasteful to them. Their confusion was further intensified because they were expected to control some forms of aggression by suppression just as they had in the earlier program.[44]

Although therapeutic notions had gained entry into the institution and created problems for many of the workers, the rehabilitation program had not yet become the primary institutional activity. Maintenance and custodial concerns continued to be the primary determinants of organizational operation.[45]

Both studies of women's prisons provide information on the pains of imprisonment in such places.[46] Loss of liberty and autonomy was keenly felt by prisoners in both institutions. Most inmates in Alderson were from places quite distant from the prison, so they rarely received visitors. The Corona women were particularly troubled by the forced separation from their families, in that 68 per cent were mothers and 59 per cent had minor children.[47] Inmates in both places regarded themselves as being markedly deprived of various material goods which make life tolerable in free society, but this was particularly true in the federal facility. In that reformatory, prisoners were dressed in shabby, ill-fitting prison clothing, including brown or white panties cut in the pattern of men's boxer shorts.[48] Although the women prisoners in these two places did not feel themselves physically threatened by other inmates, they

---

[42] David A. Ward and Gene G. Kassebaum, *Women's Prison* (Chicago: Aldine Publishing Co., 1965).

[43] Giallombardo, *op. cit.*, pp. 39–56.

[44] *Ibid.*, pp. 47–48.

[45] *Ibid.*, pp. 57–91.

[46] *Ibid.*, pp. 92–104; Ward and Kassebaum, *op. cit.*, pp. 1–29.

[47] Ward and Kassebaum, *op. cit.*, pp. 14–16.

[48] Giallombardo, *op. cit.*, pp. 95–98.

did find life in a one-sex society quite disagreeable. At Alderson, the inmates complained of the "bitchiness" of other prisoners, contending that most of them were untrustworthy, predatory, and prone to "penitentiary darby," that is, involvement in malicious gossip. The women in Corona seemed to have relatively little allegiance to an inmate code of loyalty among prisoners.[49]

One other pain of imprisonment in women's prisons is deprivation of heterosexual relations. All of these psychological problems of imprisonment influence the kind of social life which emerges among female felons, but the last seems particularly critical to an understanding of inmate life.

A large number of inmate social types were observed at Alderson, including "snitchers," "inmate cops," "squares," "jive bitches," and "homeys." [50] The first involves women who interfere with the lives of other prisoners, "squares" are prosocial inmates, "jive bitches" are troublemakers, and the last type consists of women from the same geographical area. "Connects" are inmate connivers, "boosters" are women who steal food and other goods, and "pinners" are lookouts who assist in illicit activities among other prisoners.

The most significant grouping of inmates in both prisons was centered about homosexual activities. Ward and Kassebaum estimate that about half of the prisoners had been involved in at least one homosexual episode during their stay at Corona.[51] In both places, "lesbians" or "true" homosexuals were distinguished from "penitentiary turnouts" ("jail house turnouts" in Corona).[52] "True" homosexuals were women who had been involved in homosexual activity prior to incarceration. Both studies suggest that patterns of sexual activity make up a variety of social-sexual roles, but the basic division is between "butches" or "stud broads" and "femmes." "Butches" are masculine-appearing women who are the active or aggressive partners in sexual activity, while "femmes" play a feminine, passive role in sexual episodes. More of the true homosexuals take the "stud broad" role than do the "jail house turnouts," but some of the latter engage in "butch" behavior.[53]

The evidence in both investigations indicates that prison homosexuality on the part of "jail house turnouts" is a transitory pattern of behavior representing an adjustment to prison life that is usually eschewed upon release. The investigators contend that disruptions of conventional sex

[49] Ward and Kassebaum, op. cit., pp. 30–55.
[50] Giallombardo, op. cit., pp. 105–32; "snitchers" are also common in Corona. See Ward and Kassebaum, op. cit., pp. 32–37.
[51] Ward and Kassebaum, op. cit., p. 92.
[52] Ibid., pp. 95–98; Giallombardo, op. cit., pp. 105–32.
[53] Ward and Kassebaum, op. cit., p. 104.

roles attendant upon a prison commitment lead most women to involvement in a sexual-affectional dyadic relationship which buffers them against pains of prison life. However, the difficulties of prison life for women arise out of the sex-role definition of women in American society, so that Giallombardo avers:

The deprivations of imprisonment may provide necessary conditions for the emergence of an inmate system, but our findings clearly indicate that the deprivations of imprisonment in themselves are not sufficient to account for the form that the inmate social structure assumes in the male and female prison communities. Rather, general features of American society with respect to the cultural definition and content of male and female roles are brought into the prison setting and function to determine the direction and focus of the inmate cultural systems.[54]

### Prison Social Change

We have observed in a number of places in the last chapter and the present one that American prisons have gradually been modified from extremely repressive, punitive institutions to relatively humane places, and in some cases treatment programs have been adopted as well. In general, the changes wrought in prison life have been relatively crescive or unplanned, so that penitentiaries have drifted with the tide of broad trends in American life. These alterations have occurred over an extended time period, so reform leaders would be difficult to identify at any specific point in time. Much of the history of penal change has also been cyclical in character, in which humanitarian developments have been repudiated only to be followed by further humanitarian modifications. This ebb and flow of changes in prison systems has followed closely the shifting fortunes of state political parties.

However, it is possible to single out some instances of deliberate or planned correctional social change, the most prominent case being in California.[55] In that state, since 1943, an orderly and planned series of major improvements has been made in the penal system. These modifications have produced a correctional system generally acknowledged to be the most progressive, treatment oriented in the United States.

Planned correctional social change, insofar as it occurs at all, tends to take place unobtrusively. In the past two decades, a good deal of public attention has been focused upon prison riots and disturbances which were particularly prominent in the early 1950's. These cases of prisoner in-

[54] Giallombardo, op. cit., p. 187.
[55] A history of correctional change in California is found in Joseph W. Eaton, Stone Walls Not a Prison Make (Springfield, Ill.: Charles C Thomas, Publisher, 1962).

surgency have been viewed as attempts by the captives to obtain penal reforms. Although disturbances do not always produce modifications in correctional practices, they have had that result in at least some instances.

The wave of prison riots in this country began in 1952, with major uprisings in the Southern Michigan Prison at Jackson and the New Jersey State Prison at Trenton,[56] followed by riots in Idaho, Illinois, Kentucky, Louisiana, Massachusetts, New Mexico, North Carolina, Utah, Ohio, California, Oregon, and Washington, among other states.

A kind of *morphology of prison riots* seemed to be common to these incidents—most of them followed the same general pattern. Prison revolts were preceded by extended periods of uneasiness and tension, often described by prisoners and employees in such expressions as "The joint is 'hot,' it's going to 'blow up.'" Some event, such as a rumor that an inmate had been beaten by the guards, served as the spark to ignite these tensions and touch off widespread destruction of property, seizure of hostages, and occasionally assaults upon staff members and convicts. After some days of internal disorder in the prison, inmate leaders emerged to make demands for correctional reforms, including better food, improved medical care, segregation of sex offenders, and modifications in sentencing and parole practices. The offenders who stepped forward to act as leaders and spokesmen were frequently drawn from the "outlaw" group of violent and asocial persons, while the "right guys" remained in the background.[57] Moreover, many of the prisoners' grievances appeared to be invented after the riot, rather than prior to its inception.[58] Negotiations between convicts and state officials usually resulted in promises of improvements in the penal program, at which point the inmates returned to their cells and the riot ended. On some occasions, the leaders were eventually prosecuted by the state and agreements which the correctional authorities had entered into were repudiated.

What was responsible for the unprecedented wave of rioting in prisons in the early 1950's? The American Prison Association produced a report on these disturbances, alleging that they were due to such evils as inadequate financial support for prison programs, inadequate and untrained staffs, widespread idleness, a shortage of well-trained leadership,

---

[56] Details of the Michigan riot are reported in John Bartlow Martin, *Break Down the Walls* (New York: Ballantine Books, 1954), while a popular treatment of the New Jersey disturbances can be found in Peg and Walter McGraw, *Assignment: Prison Riots* (New York: Holt, Rinehart and Winston, Inc., 1954).

[57] Frank E. Hartung and Maurice Floch, "A Social-Psychological Analysis of Prison Riots: An Hypothesis," *Journal of Criminal Law, Criminology and Police Science*, XLVII (May–June 1956), 55.

[58] Lloyd E. Ohlin, *Sociology and the Field of Corrections* (New York: Russell Sage Foundation, 1956), pp. 23–24.

overcrowding of prisoners in institutions of excessive size, and poor
sentencing and parole practices.[59] These factors closely parallel the
grievances identified by inmates. Certain of the prison uprisings, particularly those in the southern United States, do seem to fit this explanation. For example, a series of protest actions occurred at the Louisiana
prison at Angola in 1951, culminating in the slashing of heel tendons by
several dozen prisoners. A subsequent inquiry into conditions in that
institution turned up evidence of severe abuses against inmates which
closely fitted the list above. The public outcry which followed these dis-
closures resulted in construction of a new prison in that state.[60]

A number of authorities have criticized this "intolerable conditions"
argument as an explanation of all riots. Ohlin has noted that conditions
were generally worse in many states where riots had not taken place,
while the prisons that had suffered disturbances had begun to move in
the direction of improved penal practices.[61]

The alternative view of prison riots is a "disequilibrium" one, in which
it is argued that disturbances stem from disruptions in the stability of
inmate-administration relations in institutions. Floch and Hartung offer
this kind of explanation for "collective" riots, which they distinguish from
uprisings due to brutal conditions.[62] They assert that protests and incidents grow out of the nature of the maximum security prison, with its
overcrowding and kindred features along with the aggregation of a
heterogeneous mixture of prisoners, and from the destruction of the semiofficial pattern of informal inmate self-government which occurs when a
new reform administration takes over. When reform comes to the "con-
run" institution described above, authorities endeavor to "tighten up"
the organization by removing prisoners from positions of power and
influence. These moves overlook the fact that the inmate leaders have
been a stabilizing force in the prison, enforcing order among other
prisoners in exchange for privileges from the administrators. As a result
of their fall from power, the leaders turn their attention to subversive
ends. They stir up dissatisfaction among other convicts which smolders
until finally triggered by some dramatic incident. These leaders then
emerge during and after the riot as the champions of "mistreated prisoners," so they appear to be revolutionaries striving for a better way of
life. But the fact is that the leaders are really seeking a return to the
older ways of life, rather than penological reforms.

[59] Committee on Riots, *Prison Riots and Disturbances* (New York: American Prison Association, 1953).

[60] Reed Cozart, "What Has Happened to 'America's Worst Prison'?" *Federal Probation*, XIX (December 1955), 32–38.

[61] Ohlin, op. cit., p. 23.

[62] Hartung and Floch, op. cit., 51–57.

Ohlin has offered some similar hypotheses regarding prison unrest, but he also contends that these disturbances were most common in penitentiaries where reform efforts were only embryonic.[63] Prisons where progressive aims had been translated into programs of education and therapy experienced fewer incidents than those places where tightening of security and removal of inmate leaders from influential positions represented the major reforms achieved. Ohlin also maintains that disturbances were fairly common in institutions characterized by decentralization of authority, for in these cooperation between administrative units in the prison had broken down. The effect of these conditions was to produce disruptions in the established expectation system which controlled relations between staff and inmates. Channels for airing of grievances were closed off, leading to an increase of disciplinary incidents. Efforts on the part of authorities to repress such incidents by increasing controls over prisoners then led to heightened tension among staff and inmates. The end product of this circular build-up of tension was often a prison riot. A chronology of events of this kind seems to have touched off an insurrection in the Oahu Prison.[64]

Prison uprisings have continued since the 1950's, but less frequently than in the previous decade. Some measure of protest and resistance probably represents an inevitable price that must be paid if penological reforms are to occur in institutions.

One final comment is in order concerning prison disturbances. There are some ominous signs that outbreaks of violence and disorder in the future will often be of a different kind than those of the 1950's. In several cases in California in recent years, racial antagonisms between white and Negro prisoners have developed to the point where one state institution was in danger of a full-scale racial war of prisoners against their fellow inmates. A number of observers have suggested that racial hostilities have hardened among both whites and Negroes in American society in the past few years, as a consequence of economic and civil rights gains by Negroes which seem to threaten the social status of whites. These prejudiced attitudes apparently become exacerbated in the close confines of prisons, particularly because these places contain sizeable numbers of extremists of both races, such as Muslims and American Nazis. It may well be that the problem of working out some *modus vivendi* concerning interracial interaction constitutes the major pain of imprisonment for individual prisoners, black and white alike.[65]

63 Ohlin, op. cit., p. 24.
64 Richard H. McCleery, "The Governmental Process and Informal Social Control," in Cressey, The Prison, pp. 149–88; see also Sykes, The Society of Captives, pp. 109–29.
65 This point was brought to my attention by John Irwin.

## TRAINING SCHOOL SOCIAL ORGANIZATION

Since the focus of this book is upon adult lawbreaking, only those patterns of juvenile delinquency which are career forerunners of criminality have been discussed. For the same reason, our commentary on the social workings of correctional agencies is principally concerned with adult institutions and organizations. However, some mention should be made of the social structure of training schools, if only because many adult lawbreakers begin their institutional experiences in these places. A brief sketch of the traditional form of social organization in state training schools will be presented, after which some recent research evidence on these institutions will be examined.

Most state training schools are smaller in population size than prisons. In many states, the boys' schools handle a few hundred boys or less, and the girls' schools are even smaller. The administrative staffs of juvenile facilities are also usually smaller than in adult institutions. Training schools normally show a physical structure quite different from that of prisons and reformatories. They are usually unwalled institutions made up of a number of dormitory buildings euphemistically called "cottages." Groups of several dozen or more juveniles, or "wards" as they are often called, inhabit these dormitories, and much of the social life of the institution goes on within these structures. Training schools also include an assortment of other buildings, such as a school, trade training shops, barns and other farm buildings, and so on. Juvenile institutions more closely resemble residential academies or schools than prisons, although many of them are more rundown and deteriorated in appearance. Escapes, or "rambles," as they are often called, are frequent from training schools, partly because of the ease of escape from such places.

The superintendent of the training school traditionally has been the product of the political "spoils system," such as an ex-county sheriff or similar person to whom a political debt is owed. It goes without saying that he has often been a singularly unimpressive figure, ill-trained for the job of maintaining and managing a custodial institution. The rest of the staff tends to be divided into two general groups. The first includes work supervisors, teachers, and sometimes social case workers, who deal with the inmates in one connection or another during the day. Also included in this group are the kitchen personnel, clerks, and similar workers. The second general group of employees in the school is made up of cottage supervisors or cottage parents. They have the major responsibility of managing the wards at night and during those times of the day when the inmates are not involved in some formal program. The cottage workers have the greatest amount of interaction with the wards and the most difficult experiences with them. Prevention of runaways and other disturbances of the institutional routine is usually their responsibility.

Training schools in the past have usually operated a minimal treatment program. Most inmates have been placed in a school program or some kind of vocational or other work experience. Occasionally they receive some kind of individual therapy from a social case worker, but this tends to be a relatively infrequent event.

The overriding concern in juvenile institutions has revolved around prevention of escapes and large-scale disturbances. Staff members regard runaway behavior as serious indeed, for even though most fugitives are quickly apprehended and normally do not create any incidents in the surrounding community, the community reacts negatively to escapes. Consequently, the juvenile institution which acquires a reputation for frequent escapes usually receives a good deal of hostile and highly vocal criticism. In turn, runaways come to be defined as extremely serious by the employees.

Juvenile facilities share certain structural shortcomings with their adult counterparts. In both places, uncooperative individuals must be restrained in some way, but a number of potentially effective control techniques are not available to the authorities. Although the training school personnel can keep their charges "in line" by occasional beatings and other kinds of physical coercion, they must be circumspect in the use of force. There is a very real danger that word will get out to the community if beatings become a regular part of the disciplinary program of the school. Cottage parents who utilize physical aggression as a main technique of control are also in some danger of reprisals. The worker may be physically able to intimidate any individual ward, but may not emerge the victor in a fight with a half-dozen or more inmates. This is not to say that corporal punishment is never used in juvenile institutions. Coercion which transcends the official rules is employed, but tends to be relatively mild in form and used as a supplement to other control devices.[66]

The tactic commonly employed to deal with uncooperative boys parallels the arrangements in adult prisons. The institutional staff enters into tacit bargains with certain inmate leaders in the dormitories. These older, physically mature, sophisticated juveniles operate "kangaroo courts" in which they coerce other, weaker youths into docile behavior. In addition to keeping order and preventing "rambles," these toughs often use their

[66] Sethard Fisher, "Social Organization in a Correctional Residence," *Pacific Sociological Review*, IV (Fall 1961), 88.

power to force other inmates into homosexual practices, obtain money from them, and victimize them in other ways.

As these remarks suggest, there is a prisoner social system in juvenile institutions. A kind of inmate code characterizes most training schools. This is a juvenile parallel of that found in prisons, centering around the same kinds of antisocial norms as the adult counterpart, and antiadministration and antitreatment in content. It prescribes "playing it cool" as model behavior for wards; they are expected to do their time as pleasantly as possible, without entering into meaningful relationships with staff members.

A pattern of role-types also exists in juvenile institutions. The system tends to be relatively simple, based on differences in physical prowess and criminal sophistication. Two major role types emerge in training schools, "toughs" or "dukes" and "punks." The former are juveniles who have been in the institution for a relatively long time, have extensive delinquency records, and are physically superior to other inmates. The second group is made up of boys who are physically immature and are often less sophisticated offenders.

The preceding comments are consistent with a body of impressions about state training schools presented some years ago by Deutsch.[67] He traveled around the country looking at a large sample of these institutions, at the end of which tour he reported that ten "deadly sins" characterized most of them. These ten faults included regimentation, institutional monotony in the form of unvaried diets and the like, mass handling of inmates without regard to individual needs, and partisan political domination. Additionally, he listed public penury, isolation, complacency, excessive physical and mental punishment, Babelism, and enforced idleness as other deficiencies. Babelism was his term for various semantic reforms that are common in corrections, in which "the hole" is renamed the "adjustment center" but the character of the punishment program not changed, the recreation program is retitled "mass treatment," or the name of the institution is changed from Boys' Industrial School to Brown Mountain School for Boys.

Ohlin and Lawrence have recently discussed the treatment problems which arise in such places as training schools where interaction occurs among hostile "clients" and group norms define the model inmate as one who is "playing it cool," that is, refraining from significant involvement with therapeutic agents.[68] Their remarks parallel the earlier ones of

[67] Albert Deutsch, "A Journalist's Impressions of State Training Schools," Focus, XXVIII (March 1949), 33–40.
[68] Lloyd E. Ohlin and William C. Lawrence, "Social Interaction Among Clients As a Treatment Problem," Social Work, IV (April 1959), 3–13.

Topping, who noted that treatment of "pseudosocial" delinquents (gang offenders) is complicated by the group interaction which develops among these offenders in institutions.[69] She reported that many of them exhibit a classical "crime-punishment" orientation in which they see themselves as serving time to pay their societal debt. Many of these same youngsters disavow any conception of themselves as having problems or in need of therapy. In both of these investigations, some procedures which might circumvent some of these difficulties are suggested, including development of treatment efforts centered within cottage units in order to utilize the inmate social organization in therapy.

The social structure of a boys' training school in Colorado has been described by Barker and Adams.[70] Rigid interactional and communication barriers between inmates and staff members are reported, along with a pervasive spirit of authoritarianism in which the offenders do not identify with the values and goals of the staff. The authors also note the existence of a status order among the inmates, heavily structured around displays of physical toughness and victimization of peers. They speculate that this system may be the result, at least in part, of widespread insecurities among delinquent boys regarding masculinity.[71]

Polsky has provided a detailed description of the social structure among inmates through a study of the boys residing in a cottage within a private correctional institution.[72] He reports a diamond-shaped status system in which a few boys have very high or low rank among their peers, with the largest group falling into a middle range. Polsky maintains that this system is independent of the particular youths who fill it in any particular period, for it persists relatively unaltered over time, even though cottage residents enter and leave the system. Departure of a leader, for example, produces competition, conflict, and jockeying among inmate aspirants for the position, followed by reestablishment of equilibrium. According to Polsky, the status types in the cottage include "toughs" and "con artists" at the apex of the order, "quiet types" in the middle range, and "bushboys" and "scapegoats" on the bottom of the system. The latter are subjected to unrelenting physical and psychological attacks by those higher in the pecking order. Probably the most sig-

[69] Ruth Topping, "Treatment of the Pseudo-Social Boy," American Journal of Orthopsychiatry, XIII (April 1943), 353–60.

[70] Gordon H. Barker and W. Thomas Adams, "The Social Structure of a Correctional Institution," Journal of Criminal Law, Criminology and Police Science, XLIX (January–February 1959), 417–22.

[71] Ibid.

[72] Howard W. Polsky, "Changing Delinquent Subcultures: A Social-Psychological Approach," Social Work, IV (October 1959), 3–15; Polsky, Cottage Six (New York: Russell Sage Foundation, 1962).

nificant of Polsky's observations is that the inmate system is abetted by the institutional staff. He notes: "Thus, the theme of aggression with all its authoritarian overtones is structurally configurated in the cottage. Under its roof the cottage parents join the older boys in scapegoating the defenseless low-status boys—the sneaks, punks, and the sick. The latter 'deserve' the beatings because of *their* provocativeness and 'unfitness.' The unwritten compact of cottage parents and toughs makes it unbearable for the 'deviants' because they are blamed for everything." [73]

A recent examination of a training school in California indicates that even in that state, where treatment goals have been emphasized in state institutions for several decades, training schools place primary emphasis upon regimentation of youngsters in the interests of controlling them.[74] In this environment, therapeutic activities are subordinated to custodial ends. As part of this study, Fisher observed the social structure among inmates.[75] He found that both the wards and supervisors rank and victimize certain boys and, moreover, the low-ranked boys in the eyes of officials are also the low-status inmates in the ward hierarchy. Staff workers often interpret disruptive behavior by low-status boys as evidence of psychological maladjustment rather than as flowing out of the social structure and interactional patterns among offenders. Low-ranked, victimized inmates are defined as "mess-ups," implying that they willfully engage in disapproved behavior out of psychological tensions. Instead of attempting to undermine the inmate system, the authorities react to boys in its terms, so that institutional rewards are differentially accorded to boys with high status among their peers.

Some attention has been given to organizational problems which develop in training schools upon introduction of rehabilitation as a major goal. One of the earliest warnings of the potential problems was sounded by Jenkins,[76] who indicated that treatment clinics are likely to become mere institutional window-dressing if they are simply grafted on to a custodial program and unconnected to the rest of the institution. They become reduced to making diagnostic and treatment recommendations which are diverted to custodial ends or are systematically ignored. To be effective, clinical operations must be heavily centered around the cottage groups and cottage personnel.

More recently, Weber has identified a number of areas in which conflict arises between professional and nonprofessional personnel in

[73] Polsky, *Cottage Six*, p. 133.

[74] Carl F. Jesness, *The Fricot Ranch Study* (Sacramento: State of California, Department of the Youth Authority, 1965), pp. 8–17.

[75] Fisher, *op. cit.*, 87–93.

[76] R. L. Jenkins, "Treatment in an Institution," *American Journal of Orthopsychiatry*, XI (January 1941), 85–91.

institutions where treatment is introduced.[77] One major problem which
he identifies, and which is also noted by Ohlin,[78] centers around the
role-difficulties which develop for cottage workers. Their authority position is often reduced or undermined with the introduction of treatment
goals. They are likely to feel that their prestige has been lowered with the
entry of professional personnel into the program. Redefinition of the role
of the cottage worker also occurs, and he is expected to run a quiet
and well-disciplined dormitory and to contribute to therapy. But because
he is not given clear instructions as to how he is to accomplish these
ends, he experiences much the same role-dilemma noted earlier for prison
guards. Weber and others have suggested that a number of negative
consequences develop from introduction of "rehabilitation" into previously custodial institutions.[79] Staff cooperation is reduced and replaced
by conflicts between professional and custodial personnel, defensive
reactions develop among cottage workers, and other difficulties arise.
Inmates manipulate these conflicts to their own ends by playing competing groups against each other.

The most ambitious research on training schools to date dealt with
six juvenile institutions in a comparative fashion.[80] These training schools
varied in size, several being very small institutions while others had
inmate populations of well over 100 boys. Some of the schools were
private institutions, others were state schools. These facilities also varied
in terms of program, ranging from institutions favoring obedience and
strict conformity by boys to treatment oriented, milieu operations. The
researchers supposed that variations in size might influence the social
structure of the institutions, as would the different auspices under which
these places are operated. State schools should be under greater pressure
from the general public. Finally, the investigators hypothesized that the
treatment oriented schools would be more conflict-ridden than the strictly
custodial plants.

In general, the findings supported these contentions. Among other
things, the institutions varied in terms of the leadership "styles" of their
executives. The staff members exhibited different perspectives on de-

[77] George H. Weber, "Conflicts Between Professional and Non-Professional Personnel in Institu-
tional Delinquency Treatment," Journal of Criminal Law, Criminology and Police Science, XLVIII
(May–June 1957), 26–43; see also Weber, "Emotional and Defensive Reactions of Cottage
Parents," in Cressey, The Prison, pp. 189–228.

[78] Lloyd E. Ohlin, "The Reduction of Role-Conflict in Institutional Staff," Children, V (March–
April 1958), 65–69.

[79] Weber, "Emotional and Defensive Reactions of Cottage Parents"; Mayer N. Zald, "Power
Balance and Staff Conflict in Correctional Institutions," Administrative Science Quarterly, VII
(June 1962), 22–49.

[80] David Street, Robert D. Vinter, and Charles Perrow, Organization for Treatment (New York:
Free Press of Glencoe, Inc., 1966).

linquents, the workers in custodial schools viewing boys as more willful than did employees in treatment institutions. Rather marked variations in the level of staff conflict existed from school to school, with greatest staff conflict in the rehabilitation oriented institution in which a high degree of staff *interdependence* existed. That is, in the milieu treatment school, staff members representing different segments of the school program were in frequent communication with each other and were involved in much joint decision-making.

## PROBATION AND PAROLE ORGANIZATION

Parole and probation agencies can justifiably be discussed together, even though there are some important differences between them. The major dissimilarity is that parole involves more serious, criminalistic offenders than does probation; the former handles persons processed through institutions, whereas the latter does not. Penal commitment represents the harshest penalty outside of capital punishment, so it tends to be used with the most difficult and intractable law violators, whereas probation is a disposition commonly reserved for persons lacking in criminalistic orientation. Even though parole and probation differ in this way, both deal with offenders in the community, and certain organizational features seem to be common to both of them.

Our commentary on parole is mainly concerned with adult systems, in that juvenile parole programs are nonexistent or only slightly developed in many states. In particular, the notes on the general organization of parole should be read as a description of adult systems.

### The Structure of Parole and Probation

Parole programs in the United States have developed out of changes in criminal laws which have established indeterminate sentences for offenses within the limits of minimum and maximum statutory penalties. Although criminal codes vary from one state to another, they have the same general structure. They allow for alternative penalties for convicted offenders, so that individuals can be placed on probation or committed to institutions. The maximum periods of incarceration are specified in statutes, but prisoners can be released at various points prior to expiration of their maximum sentences. Paroling authorities have been established to determine when inmates should be released from the penitentiary, to serve the remainder of their sentence under supervision in the community.

The paroling function is structured in different ways in the various states. In some, *ex officio* boards made up of government officials serve as the paroling agency; individuals who have major governmental responsibilities elsewhere make release decisions "on the side." The more common arrangement, particularly in the larger states, involves an agency called the "Board of Prison Terms and Paroles," "Adult Authority," or some similar label. A group of persons is appointed by the state governor, usually for fixed terms of office, and then given the full-time task of deciding about release of prisoners to parole. Normally no qualifications are required for service on the board, but members are commonly drawn from corrections, law enforcement, legal, or academic backgrounds. In some states operating under this pattern, the board discharges two functions. It acts as a quasi-judicial board, setting release dates for prisoners, and also administers the parole supervision organization. These boards establish policies for parole supervision and employ and supervise parole agents as well. However, recent correctional thinking has tended to define these as incompatible functions, so certain states, such as California, have removed the administrative task from the paroling agency and placed it within the correctional department.

In theory, decisions to release or not to release an inmate are based upon such criteria as his behavioral change and favorable prognosis for success on parole.[81] In fact, they tend not to be made in this fashion. For one thing, parole boards are often limited in the degree to which they can determine release dates by statutory minimum sentences which require that persons convicted of certain crimes spend no less than some specific period in prison. Minimum sentences are frequently set by the board near the beginning of the prisoner's stay in the institution, so they are determined before a sufficient period of time has elapsed to estimate the person's response to therapy. In addition, parole boards are often made up of members ill-trained to estimate the rehabilitative prospects for inmates. Indeed, the knowledge on which such decisions must be based is not at hand, so no paroling authority, however assembled, could make accurate judgments of this kind. Finally, boards have to contend with factors other than the needs of the prisoners. In particular, they must be sensitive to public pressure which demands that certain offenders be kept in prison for long periods of time. The decision to release a sex offender who will return to a small community from which he was convicted is frequently more contingent upon estimates of the level of community tolerance than the needs of the offender.

[81] One of the few studies of parole board decision-making is Don M. Gottfredson and Kelley B. Ballard, Jr., "Differences in Decisions Associated with Decision Makers," *Journal of Research in Crime and Delinquency*, III (July 1966), 112–19.

The prisoner is paroled if the board judges that such a decision will provoke only a slight amount of "heat."

For reasons of this kind, parole decisions are normally intuitive. They also tend to be based on a mixture of considerations—the nature of the offense, the needs of the offender, and reactions of the general public. They are usually not as individualized as parole theory would lead one to suppose. Instead, paroling agencies develop informal precedents, and prison terms handed out for various offenses average out to a fairly specific figure, such as three years, with little variation around that average. Any marked departure from this standard becomes the focus of inmate grievances. Prison unrest and disturbances sometimes occur as inmates try to reestablish the former precedent in response to shifts in parole policies.

Variations are also seen in the structure of probation services. In some states, probation is an operation grafted on to parole services, and probation is sometimes shunted aside because of the heavy work demands of parole. As a consequence, few offenders are placed on probation. In a number of states, such as California, probation is county operated, with individual probation services in the various counties. Each of these is autonomous and managed by county supervisors or commissioners.

One variation between probation and parole, in addition to patterns of placement within governmental systems, has to do with involvement of probation officers in selection of offenders to be placed under their control. Parole agents receive their "clients" from the institution, without any option to select or reject in terms of some set of eligibility criteria. But in both adult and juvenile probation services, the workers play a major role in the selection process. In juvenile operations, they compile information about youths undergoing court hearings. This collection of data, called the "social investigation," is a principal source of evidence on which adjudication and disposition of cases is based. Similarly, in adult probation, convicted offenders are referred to probation agents for "presentence investigation." The presentence report prepared by the officer becomes, in turn, a major consideration in disposition of the case. This report normally includes a statement of sentence recommendations by the officer which are customarily followed by the judge in his decision.

### On Being a Probation or Parole Officer

Much of the literature on probation and parole implies that workers in these operations are highly-trained professionals who administer intensive and valuable therapy to correctional "clients." But several "time and motion" studies of probation officers indicate that they are harried by clerical tasks and huge case loads which prevent them from rendering much professional help. For example, Diana investigated the kind and amount of assistance given to juvenile probationers in the Allegheny County (Pittsburgh), Pennsylvania, juvenile court.[82] He found that the average number of contacts between probationers and probation officers was about five within a 16-month period. Moreover, these were for the most part quite superficial, only about 14 per cent of the wards receiving any sort of case work treatment. Diana also found an inverse relationship between frequency of probation contacts and later criminality; offenders who had the least interaction with officers were less recidivistic than boys who had received more frequent assistance. What this probably indicates is that there are many juveniles placed on probation who are not seriously delinquent, need little supervision from probation agents, and turn out to be "self-correctors." Accordingly, the officer tends to work with more serious offenders, ignoring the "low risk" cases in his case load.

Another study parallel to that of Diana turned up similar findings. England found that a group of adult probationers had a recidivism rate of only 17.7 per cent, but that this low rate was unrelated to treatment.[83] Most of the offenders received only routine surveillance and superficial help from the probation officers. In England's view, the generally high success rates for probation as a form of disposition are to be attributed principally to most of the persons placed upon probation being essentially "prosocial" and not in need of intensive resocialization.

A study by Hengerer of several juvenile probation departments suggests that most of what goes on in probation is something other than treatment.[84] The workers examined in that study spent most of their time in writing reports, driving from one place to another, and similar operations. They had large case loads and little time to provide therapy to their wards.

The role-dilemmas of probation and parole officers have been closely examined by Ohlin, Piven, and Pappenfort.[85] These authors indicate that probation and parole services have traditionally been assigned a

[82] Lewis Diana, "Is Casework in Probation Necessary?" *Focus*, XXXIV (January 1955), 1–8.

[83] Ralph W. England, Jr., "What is Responsible for Satisfactory Probation and Postprobation Outcome?" *Journal of Criminal Law, Criminology and Police Science*, XLVII (March–April 1957), 667–76; see also his "A Study of Postprobation Recidivism Among 500 Federal Offenders," *Federal Probation*, XIX (September 1955), 10–16. See also a more recent report which presents similar findings regarding federal probation work: Albert Wahl and Daniel Glaser, "Pilot Time Study of the Federal Probation Officer's Job," *Federal Probation*, XXVII (September 1963), 20–25.

[84] Gertrude M. Hengerer, "Organizing Probation Services," *National Probation and Parole Association Yearbook*, 1953, pp. 45–59.

[85] Lloyd E. Ohlin, Herman Piven, and Donnell M. Pappenfort, "Major Dilemmas of the Social Worker in Probation and Parole," *NPPA Journal*, II (July 1956), 211–25.

number of not entirely compatible functions. Probationers and parolees are supposed to be supervised, assisted, and treated, but at the same time officers are expected to collect fines, "protect society" in various ways, and perform other tasks having little to do with helping offenders. These agents must contend with persistent suspicion and hostility directed at them and their charges by the police and other groups in the community. Because of this antagonism, agencies often come to be as much concerned about shielding the organization from criticism as they are about protecting clients. Thus officers spend some of their time giving speeches to citizen groups in which they argue for the merits of their services, agitate for greater financial support, and defend their agencies against charges of "softness," "coddling," and so on.

Several other specific consequences follow from the uneasy status of probation and parole in the public eye. First, the "public relations" orientations that develop frequently mean that occupational mobility in these agencies is more dependent upon "public relations" talents than on technical competency. Organizational "con men" ascend to supervisory positions in the operation. Second, two main kinds of workers, "punitive" and "protective" agents, have developed. The former carry guns, regard themselves as law-enforcement officers rather than rehabilitative agents, are not trained in social service work, and define their responsibilities as principally those of protecting society. They attempt to coerce their charges into appropriate behavior, and punish noncooperative cases by revoking their parole or probation status. The "protective" agents sometimes have had training in corrections and regard themselves as responsible for treatment, but vacillate back and forth from protecting the public to helping clients.

Additional role-problems have cropped up in parole-probation agencies in recent years following the recruitment of large numbers of "welfare workers" into these systems. Officers trained in social work enter these fields expecting to protect clients and to treat them as they would in other welfare settings. They come prepared to apply "generic" principles in this setting. However, they soon discover that there are difficulties with treatment in corrections not covered by their training. Social work education is not much concerned with the special problems of dealing with captive, hostile persons. These subjects differ markedly from the conventional volunteer client who seeks help. The probation-parole social worker also finds that his training has not equipped him to deal with authority problems. He is not prepared to function within the special structure of corrections as both a representative of the punitive social control system and as a helper. In addition, the agent discovers that he lacks the knowledge to understand different client types or deal effectively with these types.

The agent trained in social work also discovers discrepancies between probation-parole settings and traditional images of the welfare agency. For one thing, the rules of client supervision, such as those forbidding probationers or parolees from using alcohol, differentiate correctional settings from noncorrectional ones. There are other restraints on the kinds of decisions that workers can make, and the needs of the client must frequently be subordinated to these demands. The correctional social worker may experience considerable identity conflict because these agency rules and procedures force him to act in ways which depart from the conventional picture of his professional role.

According to Ohlin and his associates, the outcome of inadequate educational preparation and the discrepancies encountered between correctional and conventional welfare agencies is varied in form. Some workers solve these dilemmas by getting out of correctional work or out of social work entirely. Others stay in probation-parole, but with different "styles" of work adjustment. Those in relatively autonomous systems may be able to deport themselves in a fashion close enough to their notion of the welfare worker role to preserve a "social worker" identity. In more restrictive agencies, the agent may try to evade demands he regards as "unprofessional," such as collection of fines, and thereby retain a social worker role-conception. But this arrangement is difficult to sustain over a long period of time, and is also productive of a marginal and ambivalent self-identification. Some workers become reconciled to the peculiarities of restrictive correctional settings, and redefine themselves as some special kind of social worker. They gradually lose interest in, or contact with, the general social welfare literature and social worker organizations.

Several recent studies have appeared which lend support to this picture of the probation-parole agent and his occupational problems. In one of these, nearly 400 probation officers from various parts of the United States filled out a questionnaire asking about tasks which they felt to be appropriate or inappropriate.[86] Most qualified as "professionals," in that 88 per cent possessed bachelor's degrees, while 16 per cent had completed master's degrees. Most of these officers agreed that various referral services and counseling activities are appropriate probation responsibilities. But these same agents demonstrated a good deal of disagreement and confusion about various law enforcement and super-

[86] Dale E. Van Laningham, Merlin Taber, and Rita Dimants, "How Adult Probation Officers View Their Job Responsibilities." *Crime and Delinquency*, XII (April 1966), 97–108.

visory actions. Some felt that the officer should assist the sheriff in arresting an absconding probationer, some thought he should make surprise home visits or contact the probationer's employer to check on work behavior, or engage in other surveillance activities. Some of the officers said that they felt obliged to order probationers to pay their bills, refrain from hanging around pool rooms, or even go to church or marry their pregnant girl friends. At the same time, many of the workers regarded these as inappropriate responsibilities. Nonetheless, supervisory actions in which an offender is coerced into a line of conduct are often required of probation officers, even though they may regard these as alien to their "helping" role.

Gross inquired into the occupational activities of the 84 juvenile probation officers in Minnesota.[87] These workers are representative of the newer breed of "welfare worker," for 94 per cent of them had some college training, 90 per cent had bachelor's degrees, and 23 per cent had master's degrees. Some indication of the extent to which these individuals had become dissociated from social welfare can be found in their reading habits. About half asserted that they subscribed to *Federal Probation,* a correctional journal available without charge, but very few subscribed to social work publications. In a similar vein, 83 per cent said that they read *Federal Probation,* while much smaller numbers read any other professional journal.

The officers in this study were also asked to indicate the factors they weighed most heavily in their recommendations about disposition of offenders. The agents contended that the juvenile's potential for more delinquent activity was the most important factor, while the need for psychotherapy and other considerations of that kind were less important.

More research on the decision-making behavior of probation and parole workers is surely in order, for little data is at hand on this question. One other investigation of this kind has been made by Alexander, regarding juvenile probation officers.[88] She asked a group of agents who worked with female delinquents to choose girls they thought had a good or poor prognosis for nondelinquent behavior, and she endeavored to discover the characteristics which differentiated these two groups of delinquent girls. Alexander indicates that delinquents regarded as having a favorable prognosis tended to be of better economic status than the poor prognosis cases, and were more commonly Caucasian girls, while

[87] Seymour Z. Gross, "Biographical Characteristics of Juvenile Probation Officers," *Crime and Delinquency,* XII (April 1966), 109–16.

[88] Francesca Alexander, "A Preliminary Report on a Pilot Investigation of Some Social-Psychological Variables Influencing the Probation Officer," paper delivered at the Pacific Sociological Association meetings, 1964.

the poor prognosis delinquents were more often Negroes. The good prognosis cases were thought to be the products of situational causation, while girls judged to be poor risks were seen as emotionally troubled.

## SUMMARY

This chapter has provided an overview of the social workings of correctional organizations. Much of the commentary has suggested a fairly dismal outlook for therapeutic endeavors in corrections, for it appears that agencies which press in this direction are beset by all kinds of difficulties. Yet the prospects for treatment may not be entirely bleak. In any event, the matter of rehabilitation has only been addressed tangentially up to this point. In the next chapter, our attention will turn to a more direct and detailed study of the nature of "people-changing" activities that might be directed at lawbreakers.

# 19

# Treatment
# of
# Offenders

## INTRODUCTION

We have observed at a number of points that the rehabilitative philosophy regarding handling of lawbreakers is a relatively recent development. For most of human history, offenders have been made to suffer in order that society might extract retribution from them or potential law violators might be deterred from that course of action. The notion that punishment might also prevent recurrence of deviant behavior by the person being punished, due to his desire to avoid pain, has also been around for some time. But the view that the correctional processes should strive to reform, resocialize, modify, or remake the criminal in some way, so that he will refrain from further lawbreaking, is of recent origin.

Since the therapeutic perspective is a late development, a number of indications of its immaturity can be found. These shortcomings can be seen in the correctional literature, such as *Federal Probation*, where rehabilitative hypotheses or ventures are discussed. For one thing, the treatment point of view is hardly more than a broad orientation to offenders which stresses that something positive should be done to miscreants, but in which details are not spelled out. As we shall see in this chapter, programs designed to rehabilitate criminals or delinquents are frequently confused with activities directed at other goals. Contemporary correctional therapy programs are often based on vague assumptions about the etiology of lawbreaking or causal formulations that are empirically questionable. Finally, rehabilitation has been talked about a good deal more than it has been implemented in correctional practice. Accordingly, in this and the following chapter, we shall be hard pressed to discover much firm evidence about the efficacy of any tactic of treatment.

The contemporary student of criminology might look back on earlier practices as "barbaric" or "senseless." But, at any point in time, the things done to offenders "make sense" because they are buttressed by images of man which rationalize the practices. In earlier times, when life was mean and harsh, early death from natural causes a common occurrence, and life expectancy short, societies had little hesitation in putting deviants to death. We have already noted that the classical views of punishment in the late 1700's were predicated upon a conception of men as willful hedonists, so that criminals were seen as individuals who had made deliberate decisions to be bad. Such persons could be deflected from criminality by judicious application of some kind of pain. The classical picture of the willful law violator has lingered, remaining the most fashionable orientation to offenders among both laymen and correctional workers. This image of the willful criminal lies behind endeavors which try to correct criminality by processing offenders through regimented programs involving work training or allied activities. Defenders of these maintain that, when criminals are forced to conform to rules, or are compelled to work regularly, they learn "good habits," and these experiences will carry over to their lives outside of penal institutions.

Aside from the neoclassical ideas about criminality, two markedly different images of lawbreakers serve as the underpinnings of modern-day treatment proposals and practices. One holds that offenders are psychologically "sick" persons who need the services of a psychiatrist, while the other argues that law violators are no less "normal" than citizens generally. A number of tactics have been contrived around these two perspectives, and most of this chapter will be devoted to an examination of these different approaches.[1]

## THE DEVELOPMENT OF TREATMENT

In Chapter Seventeen, we saw that humanitarian gestures made toward offenders during the past century have modified the conditions of punishment. Prisoners have been incarcerated under more relaxed and humane conditions than was once the case. In most modern prisons, inmates are well fed, their medical needs are served, they are allowed a goodly number of visits, receive an unlimited number of letters, see movies and listen to radios in their cells, and so on. Youths in training schools are allowed to move about the institutional grounds quite freely, are usually protected from severe abuse by staff members or other wards, go into the community to engage in athletic events, are allowed home visits or leaves from the school, and so on. All of these developments, and many others as well, are examples of humanitarian reforms.

We are enthusiastically in favor of humanitarian moves. In our view,

---

[1] The discussion of treatment in this chapter is an abbreviated version of the analysis of treatment theory and therapeutic programs found in Don C. Gibbons, *Changing the Lawbreaker* (Englewood Cliffs, N.J.: Prentice-Hall, Inc., 1965).

offenders are still dealt with in ways which are overly harsh, so humanitarianism could go still further. However, the point needs to be made that humanitarianism is often confused with treatment. Not infrequently, citizens and correctional workers assume that enlightened processing of lawbreakers must have therapeutic consequences. But the hope that good food and other forms of humane handling will cause deviants to mend their ways is naive, for these actions are not directed at the factors which have drawn individuals into criminality. Treatment has to do with specific efforts designed to modify social-psychological characteristics of persons, rather than with humane handling of them.

Korn and McCorkle have incisively stated the case for maintaining the distinction between humanitarianism and therapy. They point out:

> It is the tragedy of modern correction that the impulse to help has become confused with treatment and seems to require defense as treatment. One of the more ironic difficulties with this position is that when one makes "rehabilitation" the main justification for humane handling of prisoners one has maneuvered oneself into a position potentially dangerous to the humanitarian viewpoint. What if humane treatment fails to rehabilitate—shall it then be abandoned? The isolated survivals of flogging and other "tough" techniques which still disgrace American penology remain to remind us that this is no mere academic question. The bleak fact is that just as the monstrous punishments of the eighteenth century failed to curb crime, so the more humane handling of the twentieth century has equally failed to do so.[2]

The confusion about what is and is not treatment extends to other programs, in addition to those developed to relieve the grimness of correctional experiences. Most modern institutions provide a variety of school activities and vocational training operations for inmates. These are sometimes pointed to as "treatment" in contrast to other operations identified as "custodial." However, these services, which have been created to implement the growing emphasis on rehabilitation as a correctional goal, represent *adjuncts* to treatment.

Endeavors such as education or vocational training are different from humanitarian acts, but they are not treatment programs. For example, the rationale behind inmate classification programs involves more than simply an interest in reducing the severity of serving time. The justification is that thorough investigation of the inmate's background is a prerequisite for effective treatment and custodial decisions. As a consequence, well-developed classification programs collect a mass of information about newly arrived prisoners which is presented in a document called the

[2] Lloyd W. McCorkle and Richard Korn, "Resocialization Within Walls," *Annals of The American Academy of Political and Social Science*, No. 293 (May 1954), 94–95.

"Admission Summary." This record becomes the basis for various institutional decisions made about these persons. But classification is only the starting point of treatment. Classification activities produce diagnoses and recommendations about what should be done with the prisoner, while implementation of the therapy recommendations constitutes treatment.

Other programs, such as vocational or educational training, religious activities, recreational participation, or prerelease planning, are all examples of adjuncts to treatment, because none deal directly with some therapy problem presented by the prisoner. Vocational experiences may improve the rehabilitation potential of the offender subjected to such a program, to the extent that he acquires good work habits and vocational skills. But vocational training is likely to have some impact only when accompanied by some kind of direct resocialization experience in which the inmate comes to modify his negative attitudes toward work. Criminals engage in lawbreaking, not because they are unemployed or unemployable, but because they embrace attitudes which devalue the importance of conventional work careers. If this is the case, offenders may be helped to a successful law-abiding adjustment by receiving some vocational aid, but only insofar as their perspectives on work are changed through involvement in therapy.

Let us now examine the theories of treatment which have grown up in corrections.[3] One basic fact about rehabilitative theory is that it has been heavily larded with psychogenic contentions which picture the offender as psychologically disturbed or "sick." In this view, the criminal is a parallel of the neurotic or psychotic individual, save that his personality pathology is expressed in an illegal fashion. This perspective sees offenders as analogous to machines which are wired in a defective manner. The therapeutic corollary is that lawbreakers need to be "rewired" by a psychiatrist or some other psychiatric technician who can delve inside their psyches.

This approach to law violators, which divides the world into "bad guys" who are also "sick," and "good guys" (correctional workers and other citizens) who are emotionally healthy, has been dominant in the rehabilitative theories with which correctional agents have operated.[4] The view remains vigorously alive, even though evidence examined in Chapter Seven and succeeding chapters runs counter to psychogenic arguments. The major thrust of the findings uncovered by sociologists

[3] Gibbons, op. cit., pp. 6–12.

[4] See Stanton Wheeler, "The Social Sources of Criminology," Sociological Inquiry, XXXII (Spring 1962), 139–59, for a discussion of some of the reasons why sociological theories have played an insignificant part in most correctional programs.

is that the large majority of law-violating deviants are relatively well-socialized and "normal."

Some major improvements are in order in the operating principles upon which treatment is based. Closer links must be forged between the etiological facts about criminality and the assumptions upon which strategies of therapy are based. In other words, the treatment implications of the findings reported in Chapters Eleven through Sixteen need to be spelled out. If many lawbreakers are relatively normal individuals, but with group-supported antisocial attitudes and positive self-images of themselves as "thieves" and so on, rehabilitative theories are going to have to be contrived which take these matters into account.

Existing versions of treatment theory are deficient in other ways, in addition to their inattention to sociogenic variables in deviant behavior. Much of this theory fails to acknowledge variations among types of lawbreakers. It seems clear enough from Chapters Eleven through Sixteen that offenders constitute a disparate collection of individuals. While there are many "normal" criminals and delinquents, these persons are not all alike in attitudinal or self-image terms. Different tactics of therapy may be in order for various of these patterns. There are persons who fit the psychiatric picture of the abnormal offender, so psychotherapeutic activities may be called for in these cases. In summary, much of the treatment theory now in existence is based on overly simplified assumptions about law violators. If rehabilitation is to become a major goal of corrections, a more detailed form of treatment theory must be developed. We shall return to this matter in more detail later in this chapter.

## SOME NEGATIVE VIEWS ON TREATMENT

Not everyone is sanguine about the prospects of rehabilitating offenders, nor is the therapeutic orientation everywhere applauded. There are many criminologists and sociologists who question whether it is possible to treat most offenders, however laudable that goal might be. Full-blown efforts at treatment will cost a great deal more money than has so far been invested in rehabilitation. Correctional skeptics see little justification for supposing that financial support for therapeutic programs will be forthcoming in the decades ahead. The pessimists on this issue also contend that law enforcement and correctional processes which single out offenders for attention inevitably stigmatize these persons, severely constricting their opportunities for law-abiding conduct. Once they are publicly identified as "bad" persons, this label stays with them and drives them into secondary deviance; they reorganize their lives around their status as "outsiders." Even if lawbreakers did not encounter these liabilities that ensue from being dealt with as criminals or delinquents, therapy would be difficult to accomplish because it requires offenders to take on negative views of themselves or to engage in self-rejection. The psychological price is too high for most law violators, who tend instead to reject their rejectors. Instead of blaming themselves for their predicament, they deflect blame onto "society." The offender who adopts the posture of a person with a grievance against society is hardly a likely candidate for therapy.

Although there is a ring of plausibility to many of these contentions about obstacles to rehabilitation, it is too early to tell whether such hypotheses are entirely accurate. Most of these arguments are speculative and conjectural, rather than the result of empirical research. But if these hypotheses turn out to be correct, they will probably apply most forcefully to treatment endeavors within penal institutions. Perhaps offenders can be resocialized, but less easily within walls than in other circumstances. The description of maximum security prisons in Chapter Eighteen suggested that it is very difficult at best to restructure these places in such a way as to carry on effective treatment within them. Security requirements of prisons are such that little time is available for activities other than counting, cell-searches, and so on. Prisoners must be regimented and ordered about if they are to be controlled. In addition, the inmate social system places the prisoner who shows signs of "reform" under great pressure. For these and other reasons, penal institutions strike many observers as most unlikely locations for therapeutic endeavors. There may be a good deal to recommend in a correctional program in which the offender's penal career would be divided into dissimilar episodes. The law violator might be placed in a prison for a time in order to satisfy demands that he be punished, and while there simply serve time under relatively humane conditions. The treatment effort might not be mounted until he is released from the institution. Such a program would reverse the current order of things, in which most of the therapeutic attack upon the individual goes on within walls.

Assume for a moment that workable treatment strategies could be developed which do convert lawbreakers into law-abiding citizens. There are a number of social scientists concerned about the ethical implications these programs would involve. These critics concede that tactics could be contrived to resocialize offenders, suggesting that these might bear some similarity to "brainwashing" techniques used by the Chinese against prisoners in the Korean war. But the question arises, do these tactics constitute "cruel and unusual punishment"? Most offenders would possibly find compulsory participation in therapeutic sessions which assault their self-esteem and sense of personal worth to be more painful than any of the other pains of imprisonment. There can be little doubt that intensive treatment programs do cause the participants some anguish. By way of illustration, the Synanon organization, which will be discussed in some detail later in this chapter, subjects members to a good deal of unpleasant social interaction in order to get them to refrain from drug use. The usual assumption that serving time in a custodial institution is unpleasant, while participating in therapy is a benign experience, is faulty. The question of whether society is justified in subjecting persons to psychological distress in the name of treatment is fundamental, although it has only begun to be given any serious attention.[5]

## THE NATURE OF TREATMENT [6]

We have argued earlier that treatment consists of some kind of explicit activity designed to alter or remove conditions operating on offenders which are responsible for their behavior. What is the nature of these conditions to which therapy is directed? Our view is that criminal and delinquent activities are a function of *definitions of the situation* entertained by persons who engage in these acts. Definitions of the situation refer to individuals' self-concepts and attitudes toward criminality and kindred matters, that is, the belief systems and interpretive frameworks by which they "make sense" out of sensory perceptions and direct their behavior. In short, actors behave as they do because of their definitions of the situation. If offenders are to be directed toward law-abiding behavior, certain of their definitions must be altered. Certain aspects of their self-images, atttitudes, and beliefs must be modified.

Examples of definitions of the situation characteristic of lawbreakers are provided in abundance in Chapters Eleven through Sixteen. As one instance, we noted that Cressey's research on financial trust violation indicated that individuals engage in embezzlement when they define themselves as having "nonshareable problems" and *after* they have managed to construct a set of justificatory arguments or rationalizations for trust violation.[7] The material on semiprofessional property offenders

[5] Some discussion of this point can be found in David Sternberg, "Legal Frontiers in Prison Group Psychotherapy," *Journal of Criminal Law, Criminology and Police Science,* LVI (December 1966), 446–49.

[6] These matters discussed in this section are analyzed in greater detail in Gibbons, *op. cit.,* pp. 136–43.

[7] Donald R. Cressey, *Other People's Money* (New York: Free Press of Glencoe, Inc., 1953).

argued that these persons are involved in criminality, at least in part, because they think of themselves as having little opportunity to earn money in conventional ways, and because they regard themselves as victims of a corrupt society. The analysis of joyriding auto thieves hypothesized that they engage in this form of law violating out of personal concerns about masculinity.

Some further observations can be made about the definitions of the situation expressed by offenders. Although definitions are located inside individuals, some are widely shared while others are idiosyncratic. Earlier chapters have noted that some criminalistic definitions are common within certain social class groups, others are restricted to the members of such smaller collectivities as peer groups, and some are novel views held by isolated individuals.

Definitions of the situation also vary along a time dimension, so that some are acquired early in life from socialization experiences and remain with the individual throughout his lifetime, while others are of extremely short duration. Some interpretive beliefs arise out of specific interactional events and have an extremely short life span. Most homicides stand as examples of short-lived definitions. These events usually involve a quarreling husband and wife or other pairs of individuals in intense social interaction with each other. Homicide is often the culmination of a violent and drunken quarrel in which the killing of the victim was inadvertent. In these cases, conventional definitions prohibiting murder are suspended temporarily rather than replaced by new attitudes.

Temporal variations in definitions of the situation mean that some are more difficult to modify than others. In extreme examples, certain definitions are so central a part of the personality configuration of the person as to be unamenable to modification. The beliefs of "overly aggressive" offenders that other persons are basically mean and untrustworthy represent major anchorage points of their personalities, so they are extremely difficult to alter. At the other extreme, some definitions are of recent origin, tenuously held by the offender, and as a consequence rather easily modified. "One-time losers" are individuals with transitory definitions favorable to criminality.

One general comment which needs little repetition is that offenders are characterized by various patterns of definitions rather than a uniform set of attitudes and beliefs which set them off from noncriminals or nondelinquents. The typological descriptions in Chapters Eleven through Sixteen elaborated upon the different views exhibited by lawbreakers. Because definitions vary, as do the experiences producing them, no single kind of therapy activity can be expected to accomplish the rehabilitative task.

## VARIATIONS IN TREATMENT TACTICS [8]

The various treatment procedures for dealing with law violators can be lumped into two major categories, *a*) psychotherapies, and *b*) environmental therapies. The first group of strategies proceed from psychogenic assumptions that offenders are emotionally troubled to some degree, so their psyches must be altered. Psychotherapeutic programs endeavor to reveal the inner workings of the person so his problems can be dissolved. In general, psychotherapeutic approaches center about the individual, with less concern for his group affiliations or social circumstances.

Environmental treatment activities operate from a different perspective on offenders. They assume that lawbreakers are relatively normal individuals who exhibit antisocial conduct definitions related to their interactional experiences and social relations. Consequently, environmental tactics are directed at groups of deviants, rather than at individuals.

These major categories of treatment involve a number of subtypes. Let us take a glance at some of these variations.

### Psychotherapies

"Depth" psychotherapy has often been advocated as an appropriate strategy for treatment of criminals. In this view, law violators are regarded as persons whose behavior is a function of cognitive elements buried deep within the "inner layers of personality." These deep-seated tensions are dimly perceived by the individual, or may be unperceived by him, but can be made apparent by a skilled psychiatrist. Once the actor becomes cognizant of the bases of his behavior, the way is opened for him to change himself. The reader will recognize this as the brand of intensive individual therapy widely urged for mentally disordered individuals. It is the kind of therapy which has been portrayed in countless movies and television plays.

Group psychotherapy is another kind of treatment closely parallel to individual "depth" psychotherapy. The major difference between the two is that in group psychotherapy, a therapist endeavors to bring about "insight" and "catharsis" on the part of a number of patients who meet together, while "depth" psychotherapy goes on in dyads made up of a

[8] Variations in treatment procedures are discussed at greater length in Gibbons, *op. cit.*, pp. 142–88.

patient and a therapist. Although individual and group forms of "depth" psychotherapy have frequently been suggested as ideal tactics for use in correctional treatment, they are rarely used in fact. More than anything else, the great shortage of trained psychotherapists in correction works against use of these procedures.

"Client-centered therapy" is another pattern of psychotherapy utilized quite regularly in handling offenders.[9] This kind of counseling is predicated on a picture of clients as persons who have problems of social adjustment. However, they are seen as normal individuals who can be aided toward working out their social difficulties in a relatively short time without intensive probing psychotherapy. As a general set of procedures for dealing with persons in trouble, client-centered therapy is used by probation officers and other correctional employees with their clients. This kind of treatment is quite similar to "reality therapy" advocated by psychiatrist William Glasser.[10] These procedures are used in correctional practice when probation officers strive to get check forgers to adopt nondeviant solutions to their problems or try to persuade individual predatory delinquents to adopt new perspectives on work, the police, and so on.

### Environmental Programs: Group Therapy

One of the most prominent trends in the mental health field and corrections since World War II has been the rise of group forms of treatment. For a variety of reasons, dissatisfaction has developed with individual therapy as the sole tactic for dealing with offenders or mental patients. The suggestion has been voiced from a number of quarters that group treatment offers more promise in rehabilitation of deviants. Much of the commentary on group endeavors implies that this is a single form of therapy, even though it is variously labeled "group psychotherapy," "group therapy," "guided group interaction," or "group counseling."

Let us hasten to note that there are two distinct kinds of therapy involving the "group" label. *The first, group psychotherapy, is essentially individual therapy in a group setting, while the second is "group" therapy in the true sense, and is designed to change groups, not individuals.* The aims of these two programs differ, the role of the therapist differs, the nature of the group activities differ, and still other contrasts can be identified.[11]

9 Carl R. Rogers, *Client-Centered Therapy* (New York: Houghton Mifflin Co., 1951).

10 William Glasser, *Reality Therapy* (New York: Harper & Row, Publishers, 1965).

11 Donald R. Cressey, "Contradictory Theories in Correctional Group Therapy Programs," *Federal Probation*, XVIII (June 1954), 20–26.

The outlines of true group therapy have been sketched in the following terms by the author in another book:

This treatment stratagem focuses upon groups as the "patient." It assumes that specific persons exhibit unfavorable attitudes, self-images, and the like because of the associational network in which they are involved. Because the person's interactional associates are extremely meaningful to him, any attempt to change the person without altering those groups with which he associates is likely to fail. Accordingly, group therapy proceeds on the premise that entire groups of persons must be recruited into therapy groups and changed. In addition, it is argued that treatment in which an individual's close associates are participants is likely to have more impact upon a specific person than some other form of treatment. Group therapy encourages the participants to put pressure on each other for behavioral change and to get the group to define new conduct norms. In a real sense, individual participants in group therapy are at the same time patients and therapists. The person who is formally designated as a therapist frequently comes to play a secondary role in the therapeutic process as it develops over time. In summary, group therapy represents a kind of primary group relationship in which behavioral change is attempted through the same mechanisms by which attitude formation and behavioral change take place in conventional primary groups.[12]

The individuals to whom group therapy is directed are viewed as aberrant persons who need to gain insight into their peculiarities. Group therapy (group counseling, guided group interaction) proceeds out of quite different premises, for the therapy subjects are viewed as normal individuals who can be changed through manipulation of group relations. Cressey has lucidly identified the principles underlying group therapy in the following terms:

1. If criminals are to be changed, they must be assimilated into groups which emphasize values conducive to law-abiding behavior and, concurrently, alienated from groups emphasizing values conducive to criminality. . . .

2. The more relevant the common purpose of the group to the reformation of criminals, the greater will be its influence on the criminal members' attitudes and values. . . .

3. The more cohesive the group, the greater the members' readiness to influence others and the more relevant the problem of conformity to group norms. . . .

4. Both reformers and those to be reformed must achieve status within the group by exhibition of "pro-reform" or anticriminal values and behavior patterns. . . .

5. The most effective mechanism for exerting group pressure on members will be found in groups so organized that criminals are induced to join with noncriminals for the purposes of changing other criminals. . . .

[12] Gibbons, *op. cit.,* p. 151.

6. When an entire group is the target of change, as in a prison or among delinquent gangs, strong pressure for change can be achieved by convincing the members of the need for change, thus making the group itself the source of pressure for change.[13]

The principles of group therapy can be found operating in a number of ongoing correctional programs and allied structures. For example, Alcoholics Anonymous is a voluntary, nongovernmental organization devoted to rehabilitation of alcoholics which operates in ways parallel to those outlined by Cressey. Alcoholic individuals join groups of ex-alcoholics as a way of refraining from drinking. These groups of reformed drinkers strive to get new members to take on new norms against drinking, both by exerting group pressure and by rewarding them with group approval. As the ex-alcoholic continues in this inter-action, he is eventually expected to lend his support to new recruits in their efforts to stay sober. As he succeeds in these efforts, his own self-image as a reformed drunk is strengthened and reinforced.

Detached worker programs, or street worker programs as they are also called, are a second illustration of group relations principles in action. These operations have centered upon delinquent gangs in urban neighborhoods. Street workers are employed who are usually fairly young persons with social backgrounds similar to those of the gang youths with whom they work. The worker tries to become an associate of a particular fighting gang, with an eye toward drawing the members into nondelinquent recreational activities, community services, or other non-deviant patterns of behavior. The detached worker also attempts to woo the boys over to more positive work attitudes and other prosocial sentiments. Part of his role involves rendering of assistance to delinquent youths, such as helping them obtain jobs or aiding them in getting readmitted to school.[14]

Group therapy programs have also been tried in a number of institutional settings. In some of these, the professional treatment agents have conducted group treatment sessions with inmates, oriented along group

[13] Donald R. Cressey, "Changing Criminals: The Application of the Theory of Differential Association," *American Journal of Sociology*, LXI (September 1955), 118–19; see also the more general statement by Cartwright on which Cressey's model is based: Dorwin Cartwright, "Achieving Change in People: Some Applications of Group Dynamics Theory," *Human Relations*, IV, No. 4 (1951), 381–92.

[14] See as illustrative of this approach James R. Dumpson, "An Approach to Anti-Social Street Gangs," *Federal Probation*, XIII (December 1949), 22–29; P. L. Crawford, D. I. Malamud, and J. R. Dumpson, *Working with Teen-Age Gangs* (New York: Welfare Council of New York City, 1950); Walter Bernstein, "The Cherubs are Rumbling," *New Yorker*, XXXIII (September 21, 1957), 129–59; John M. Gandy, "Preventive Work With Street Corner Groups: Hyde Park Youth Project, Chicago," *Annals of The American Academy of Political and Social Science*, No. 322 March 1959), 107–16; Stacy V. Jones, "The Cougars, Life With a Brooklyn Gang," *Harper's*, CCIX (November 1954), 35–43.

relations lines. A variant of group treatment called "group counseling" has been suggested as a useful way of mobilizing resources of the institution in the rehabilitative task by using lay persons, such as guards, as therapists.[15]

Doubtless the task of treating prisoners effectively through group methods within the confines of a custodial institution is fraught with problems. Inmates often attempt to make a sham performance in therapy groups by pretending that they have acquired new perspectives and attitudes from the group interaction. Many employees have antagonistic feelings toward these rehabilitative ventures, for they fear that the freedom allowed prisoners will undermine the security of the institution. Finally, the correctional administrator has a difficult time finding meaningful rewards which he can bestow upon individuals who seem to have truly changed in their orientations toward criminality. The warden cannot release inmates when he regards their prognosis as favorable to law-abiding adjustment; the prisoners must wait for the decisions of a parole board. For reasons of this kind, we should not be surprised to find that group treatment programs which have been subjected to research evaluation have not achieved dramatic results.

### Environmental Programs: Milieu Management

Milieu management is a form of treatment not too different from group therapy; indeed, the latter is often included as part of the former. Milieu programs usually go on in institutions where efforts are made to coordinate all parts of the operation to the goal of rehabilitation. The developers of milieu programs try to construct "therapeutic communities" which provide opportunities for inmates to experiment with law-abiding social living. Similarly, milieu treatment institutions try to insure that all events which occur to the prisoners will be therapeutic. In a conventional prison, such an operation might take the form of group therapy augmented with regularized work experiences. In this same institution, custodial officers might carry out counseling. The guards would also be dissuaded from expressing views that psychiatrists are "head shrinkers" or "bug doctors" and the caseworkers immature "college boys," and from other acts which have a negative effect upon treatment.

The Highfields Project in New Jersey is a clear example of milieu management.[16] The delinquent subjects in that program were placed in

[15] Norman Fenton, An Introduction to Group Counseling in State Correctional Service (New York: The American Correctional Association, 1958); Fenton, ed., Explorations in the Use of Group Counseling in the County Correctional Program (Palo Alto, Calif.: Pacific Books, 1962).
[16] Lloyd W. McCorkle, Albert Elias, and F. Lovell Bixby, The Highfields Story (New York: Holt, Rinehart and Winston, Inc., 1958).

a small institution holding about two dozen boys, where they were subjected to a treatment diet of "guided group interaction" in the evenings. In addition, these youths were given opportunities to work for pay during the daytime at a nearby mental institution. They were not compelled to work, and could be fired if they did not perform adequately. The developers of this system regarded delinquent boys as normal youngsters with antisocial attitudes and delinquent self-images. The boys tended to denigrate the importance of conventional work careers and regard other conforming behavior patterns with scorn. The entire program of guided group interaction, along with the related work experiences and peer interaction, was directed toward pressuring the delinquents toward new perspectives and improved work skills.

The private organization called Synanon, which deals with drug addicts, is a second illustration of milieu management.[17] In that program, newly admitted persons are subjected to a harsh form of group therapy, so that they come to reject their former selves as addicts. At the same time, they are given a good deal of psychological comfort by the ex-addict peers with whom they live in a Synanon residence. Synanon residents work at maintenance tasks in the residence facility or at a Synanon industry, such as a service station. The residential program as a whole is calculated to prepare the ex-addict for eventual return to free society completely cured. To date, however, the majority of Synanon members have either remained within one of the Synanon institutions or become employed as executives of a new Synanon facility.

The supporters of Synanon contend that this kind of treatment represents the model for the future, while Synanon members have been particularly immodest in praise of this program. It is fairly clear that Synanon has managed to keep a good many persons "clean" (free from drug use) for extended periods of time.[18] But we ought to be cautious in looking for a correctional panacea in this operation. Those not so optimistic about general applicability of the Synanon model to corrections have raised a number of questions.[19] This is a private operation rather than governmental, and voluntary rather than coercive. Thus the question arises as to the ease with which this format might be imposed upon such places as prisons, with their collections of hostile and noncooperative inmates. However, the most important limitation on the

[17] Lewis Yablonsky, *The Tunnel Back: Synanon* (New York: The Macmillan Co., 1965); Yablonsky, "The Anticriminal Society: Synanon," *Federal Probation*, XXVI (September 1962), 50–67; Daniel Casriel, *So Fair a House: The Story of Synanon* (Englewood Cliffs, N.J.: Prentice-Hall, Inc., 1963).

[18] Rita Volkman and Donald R. Cressey, "Differential Association and the Rehabilitation of Drug Addicts," *American Journal of Sociology*, LXIX (September 1963), 129–42.

[19] David Sternberg, "Synanon House—A Consideration of Its Implications for American Correction," *Journal of Criminal Law, Criminology and Police Science*, LIV (December 1963), 447–55.

Synanon structure as a general guide for corrections has to do with the aims of official correctional devices. These are designed to achieve "rehabilitation" of lawbreakers so that they will eventually reenter free society as conventional citizens. Regardless of whether this goal is achieved, it is different from the one Synanon seems to pursue. As Sternberg has pointed out, Synanon appears to offer *protection* of addicts rather than reintegration into society.[20] Persons who succeed in the Synanon system tend to become members of an ex-addict social system, living in a Synanon residence, and working for the organization. In short, they become professional ex-addicts. There are serious doubts about the extent to which official corrections can or will be remade in the direction of long-term protection of offenders.

Another version of milieu management has been developed by Korn and McCorkle as a prescription for converting conventional penal institutions into treatment milieus.[21] Their program involves systematic frustration of the inmate in his attempts to "beat the system" by manipulating officials. The offender is prevented from developing exploitive techniques by which he can do "easy time." The aim of this organization of effort would be to bring prisoners to the ultimate realization that they have much to gain by living within conventional rules, first in the prison and later in the free community.

A final case of milieu therapy can be seen in an experimental treatment program at Fricot Ranch, a training school for boys in California.[22] One of the cottages in this institution was singled out as the target of an intensive milieu effort. A series of coordinated experiences running throughout the day was established in order to obtain behavioral change on the part of the wards.

As the importance of a coherent, positive institutional climate for achievement of treatment ends becomes generally acknowledged, it is likely that other milieu efforts similar to those described here will be created in prisons and training schools.

### Environmental Programs: Environmental Change

This last form of treatment is one in which attempts are made to change various features of natural social environments, such as urban community areas. Environmental modification strives to bring about

[20] *Ibid.*

[21] Richard R. Korn and Lloyd W. McCorkle, *Criminology and Penology* (New York: Holt, Rinehart and Winston, Inc., 1959), pp. 540–52.

[22] Carl F. Jesness, *The Fricot Ranch Study* (Sacramento: State of California, Department of the Youth Authority, 1965).

such results as an improvement in community social organization, so it is not as individual-centered as other therapeutic endeavors. Environmental operations are frequently pointed at social agencies and non-criminals as well as offenders. Yet their ultimate aim is to modify the antisocial sentiments of citizens and thereby reduce rates of criminality.

Most of the environmental change efforts to date have been preventive in orientation, geared to curtailing budding delinquent careers before they get underway, so that rehabilitation of persons already known to be law violators is a secondary goal of these efforts. Most cases of environmental change have had to do with delinquency, rather than adult criminality.[23]

Consider some examples of environmental change. One of the earliest was the Chicago Area Project.[24] The goals and assumptions of that project, which operates in certain Chicago working class, high delinquency neighborhoods, are as follows:

> The Chicago Area Project operates on the assumption that much of the delinquency in slum areas is to be attributed to lack of neighborhood cohesiveness and to the consequent lack of concern on the part of many residents about the welfare of children. The Project strives to counteract this situation through encouraging local self-help enterprises through which a sense of neighborliness and mutual responsibility will develop. It is expected that delinquency will decline as youngsters become better integrated into community life and thereby influenced by the values of conventional society rather than by those of the underworld.[25]

The kind of delinquency theory on which this project operates contends that delinquency and criminality in working class neighborhoods flow out of the unavailability of conventional routes to American success goals, and are thus a response to economic and social frustration. The area project also presumes that lower income areas are to a degree "disorganized," in that they are characterized by value conflicts and lack of social cohesion. Criminal persons exist side by side with law-abiding citizens, and many social ties unite the deviants with the conformists. The area project attempts to bring about cohesiveness in the neighborhood through establishment of a neighborhood center, staffed principally by indigenous leadership. Thus the Chicago Area Project

[23] For a summary of many of these, see Helen L. Witmer and Edith Tufts, The Effectiveness of Delinquency Prevention Programs, U.S. Children's Bureau Publication No. 350 (Washington, D.C.: U.S. Government Printing Office, 1954).

[24] Witmer and Tufts, op. cit., pp. 11–17; Solomon Kobrin, "The Chicago Area Project—A 25-Year Assessment," Annals of The American Academy of Political and Social Science, No. 322 (March 1959), 19–29.

[25] Witmer and Tufts, op. cit., p. 11.

tries to develop an "antidelinquency society" in slum neighborhoods so that pressures toward delinquency and criminality will be reduced.

The "Midcity Project" in Boston is a more recent example of environmental change, also directed principally at reduction of delinquency.[26] This program was multifaceted, including efforts to improve the degree of coordination and cooperation between existing social agencies in the community. "Chronic-problem" families in the area were provided a variety of kinds of assistance so as to make them less dependent upon social agencies. Detached workers were also employed to work with delinquent gangs.

The Midcity Project was a demonstration effort, designed to serve as an illustration of the usefulness of a "total community" approach to delinquency. Unfortunately, the project did not achieve a significant reduction in misbehavior, although it did accomplish some other important ends. Community social organization was improved, so it is possible that the project might have a delayed effect on delinquency in the long run.

The most ambitious program of environmental change to date has been the multimillion dollar "Mobilization for Youth" operation in a lower east side neighborhood in New York City.[27] That undertaking was based upon the "opportunity structures" theory of Cloward and Ohlin which we examined in Chapter Eleven. Those investigators contended that working class, subcultural delinquency is the product of disjunction between the goals of lower class youths and their opportunities to achieve these through legitimate or conventional pursuits. Mobilization for Youth involves 30 separate "action" programs in the four major areas of work, education, community, and group services. All these devices and structures are pointed at the task of opening up or increasing the law-abiding opportunities for success and achievement in slum neighborhoods. For example, an "Urban Youth Service Corps" provides employment for unemployed, out-of-school youths, while a "Youth Jobs Center" serves as an employment office and tries to find permanent jobs for youngsters. Several devices have been conjured up as techniques for improving school performance of the youths, while efforts have also been made to strengthen the existing community social agencies.

Research evaluation of this program has not yet been undertaken, so its results are unknown. Moreover, given the many components included

---

[26] Walter B. Miller, "The Impact of a 'Total Community' Delinquency Control Project," *Social Problems*, X (Fall 1962), 168–91.

[27] *A Proposal for the Prevention and Control of Delinquency by Expanding Opportunities* (New York: Mobilization for Youth, Inc., 1961); see also *A Report on Juvenile Delinquency* (Washington, D.C.: Hearings of the Subcommittee on Appropriations, 1960), pp. 113–16.

in this operation, it may become exceedingly difficult to untangle the specific contribution, if any, that each part has made to an end result, such as reduced rates of deviant behavior. At least one critic of Mobilization for Youth has suggested that undertakings of this kind are destined to produce only slight results unless major changes are made in the general employment structure of American society. In other words, programs of this sort are involved in preparing persons for conventional jobs which are either relatively unrewarding or, in many cases, nonexistent.[28] This point holds for other federally funded efforts to create employment and other kinds of legitimate opportunities which have been carried on in a number of other cities in the United States, following the model of Mobilization for Youth.

## TYPES OF TREATMENT AND TYPES OF OFFENDERS

Most of the literature on treatment contains singular treatment prescriptions of some kind. Group therapy or some other form of handling is recommended for all offenders as though they all exhibit much the same problem for rehabilitative action. It has sometimes been acknowledged that different types of law violators require different kinds of attention, but the implications of this view have not been spelled out in detail until recently.

The most detailed theoretical attempt to match diagnostic types of offenders to varied forms of therapy has been made by the author.[29] This is not the place to review this argument in detail, but a few comments about it are in order. It endeavored to show that the population of lawbreakers is made up of individuals who run the entire gamut of human variations. Many criminal or delinquent persons are quite normal and well socialized, but have acquired subcultural standards which emphasize hostility toward the police or other antisocial perspectives. There are other criminalistic individuals who are relatively stable and unconventional and not members of deviant subcultures, but who have adopted illegal problem-solving techniques. Naive check forgers or joyriders are illustrative of this group. Finally, several different kinds of offenders are relatively aberrant individuals, such as violent sex offenders

---

[28] Robert Arnold, "Mobilization for Youth: Patchwork or Solution?" *Dissent*, XI (Summer 1964), 347–54. Another pessimistic report on this kind of program can be found in James C. Hackler, "Boys, Blisters, and Behavior: The Impact of a Work Program in an Urban Central Area," *Journal of Research in Crime and Delinquency*, III (July 1966), 155–64.

[29] Gibbons, *op. cit.*, pp. 228–82.

or psychopathic assaultists. The data presented in Chapters Eleven through Sixteen regarding offender careers indicated the nature of these variations in detail.

The several forms of treatment identified previously are not equally applicable to the 21 offender patterns discussed in this book. Group therapy is a more likely tactic for certain of these role-careers than for others, and, in the same way, psychotherapeutic approaches make sense for some of these patterns and not others. Accordingly, the author has developed some fairly detailed programmatic recommendations about the therapy forms which ought to be fitted to different criminal role patterns. For example, the suggestions regarding naive check forgers center about use of client-centered therapy, either in probation or in prison settings. The hypothesis is advanced that check forgers might respond to a kind of "shock therapy" early in their correctional careers, in which they might be placed in jail for a short sentence of a few weeks or a month. Following this sentence, they might be released on probation, where they would receive intensive counseling. This initial jail term would serve as a dramatic warning about the consequences which come from acts of check forgery. Currently, check forgers are repeatedly placed on probation. They often violate the conditions of probation, apparently in part because they regard writing "bad checks" as innocuous behavior which can be engaged in without much risk. But eventually these persons exhaust the patience of the courts and the probation officials, and find themselves in prison. Recidivism on the part of these actors might be reduced by tactics of this kind.

The treatment hypotheses advanced by the author are based upon role-career variations among lawbreakers. Group therapy or milieu forms of therapy are suggested for semiprofessional property offenders, drug addicts, joyriders, aggressive rapists, and certain other types. Intensive psychiatric treatment is indicated for nonviolent sex offenders, incest cases, male homosexuals, violent sex offenders, and psychopathic assaultists. A program of minimal treatment is recommended for statutory rapists and for "one-time loser" property or personal offenders.

These program guidelines represent a collection of speculative judgments about therapy strategies which appear to bear some relationship to the different characteristics of offender role-types. At this point in the development of correctional treatment, evidence on the efficacy of particular tactics with specific criminal or delinquent groups is not available. Actual treatment ventures of this sort are exceedingly scarce. However, one effort in this direction is underway in the state of California in the Community Treatment Project. That experiment is studying the use of community-based treatment as an alternative to incarceration of relatively serious delinquents in institutions.[30] The research subjects have been sorted into nine diagnostic types, classified in terms of levels of interpersonal maturity. The youngsters have been designated as asocial aggressives, asocial passives, immature conformists, cultural conformists, manipulators, acting-out neurotics, anxious neurotics, cultural identifiers, or as exhibiting situational emotional reactions. Different techniques for therapeutic management of each of these nine patterns are outlined.[31]

Doubtless a good deal will eventually be learned about treatment and types of offenders from this and other research now underway in California and other states. If therapeutic goals are to become truly significant in corrections, studies of this sort will be needed in great quantity. The evidence now at hand concerning the results of treatment is fragmentary and incomplete, revealing little about the effects of therapy and almost nothing about the merits of specific tactics for particular kinds of lawbreakers. We turn to an examination of this data in Chapter Twenty.

[30] Marguerite Q. Warren and Theodore B. Palmer, *Community Treatment Project: An Evaluation of Community Treatment for Delinquents, Fourth Progress Report* (Sacramento: State of California, Department of the Youth Authority, 1965).

[31] John E. Riggs, William Underwood, and Marguerite Q. Warren, *Interpersonal Maturity Level Classification: Juvenile* (Sacramento: State of California, Department of the Youth Authority, 1964).

# 20

# The Results of Treatment

## INTRODUCTION

What happens to individuals after they are placed on probation? Do they continue to engage in criminality? What are the effects of a penal commitment? Do offenders refrain from further lawbreaking after they have been given some kind of attention in an institution? These are the kinds of questions which this chapter will endeavor to address.

Unfortunately, the answers that appear here will have to be tentative and partial, given the paucity of good evidence on the effects of correctional practices. Correctional agencies have rarely been involved in systematic gathering of statistics on the post-treatment careers of persons whom they process. Data which deal with the effects of specific kinds of correctional intervention are even more uncommon. Controlled experiments on the effectiveness of treatment tactics can be conducted; indeed, some have already been carried out. But to date, few of these experimental studies of correctional actions have been undertaken.

The correctional agencies of the state of California have produced the majority of detailed, sophisticated studies of correctional efforts. Both the California Youth Authority and the Department of Corrections have operated research departments for a number of years, so more is known about the workings of California corrections than of any other state system. Accordingly, we shall make heavy use of California studies in the pages to follow.[1]

There are a variety of reasons for the scarcity of empirical studies of the effects of correctional actions, not the least of which is lack of financial support, which prevents funding of research on a sustained basis. Concern for evidence about programs has been premature until relatively recently, in view of the lack of therapeutic activities in the past. Let it also be noted that evaluative research is not always enthusiastically

[1] A summary of studies in progress in the California Youth Authority can be found in Department of the Youth Authority, *The Status of Current Research in the California Youth Authority* (Sacramento: State of California, 1966).

supported, so that even supporters of treatment sometimes have ambivalent feelings about this kind of investigation. The problem with careful and objective research is that it sometimes turns up unpalatable findings! As an illustration, consider the case of a Catholic-operated training school for girls with which the author is affiliated. The prominent citizens who donate money to that institution frequently volunteer remarks to the staff of the following kind: "You are doing wonderful work here." A careful research study of this training school might produce dysfunctional results if it showed that the institution is achieving only modest rather than complete success with the delinquent wards it processes. Perhaps the affluent sponsors would be less willing to contribute to the program if they had a more accurate perspective on the workings of the place.

## THE OUTCOME OF CORRECTIONS

### Probation

We have already observed in Chapter Eighteen that adult probation departments generally show results of the kind in which three-fourths or more of the probationers are "successes," in that they apparently refrain from further criminality. At the same time, studies of probation departments indicate that little or no counseling occurs, so the high success rates must be explained some other way.[2] The explanation appears to be that probation departments select out prosocial, "square John" kinds of offenders for placement at the same time that they divert more troublesome lawbreakers toward prisons. These prosocial individuals are "self-correctors" who deter themselves from repeated criminality.

Probation success rates vary somewhat from one jurisdiction to another, depending upon the variations in proportions of offenders sent to penal institutions. In California, where probation is granted to relatively large numbers of more serious criminals, failure rates are higher than in many other states.[3] The greater use of probation accounts for the seemingly anomalous situation in which probation violation rates are quite high in a state with well-developed probation services.

[2] See Ralph W. England, Jr., "What is Responsible for Satisfactory Probation and Post-Probation Outcome?" *Journal of Criminal Law, Criminology and Police Science,* XLVII (March–April 1957), 667–76; England, "A Study of Postprobation Recidivism Among 500 Federal Offenders," *Federal Probation,* XIX (September 1955), 10–16.

[3] State of California, *Delinquency and Probation in California, 1965* (Sacramento: State of California, Bureau of Criminal Statistics, 1966), *passim.*

## Juvenile Institutions

The efficiency of training schools in arresting progress of deviant careers is largely conjectural, in that careful follow-up studies of these places are hard to find. However, one study has been carried out in California, a state which has a juvenile correctional system widely acknowledged to be the most advanced in this nation.[4] The results of that investigation are not encouraging and surely do not lead to much confidence in the operations of training schools in other states. In this research, 4000 delinquent wards discharged from the Youth Authority in 1953 and 1958 were examined. Less than 20 per cent of the female wards acquired any sort of criminal record in the five year follow-up period after discharge, so the girls most commonly become "successes." Quite different paths are followed by boys. About 22 per cent of the male wards had been discharged from Youth Authority custody as a result of being sent to prison. Another 22 per cent were sentenced to prison within five years after discharge, while another 26 per cent received one or more nonprison sentences (fines, jail, and/or probation). Thus only 30 per cent of the boys managed to remain free from detected criminality.

State training schools in California vary in a number of ways. Some hold young, relatively prosocial youngsters, while others work with older, more sophisticated delinquents. These institutions have different treatment programs as well. Not surprisingly, the different schools show somewhat varied results. One recent follow-up investigation tabulated parole violations by boys from different facilities in the first 15 months after release.[5] Parolees from the two reception centers showed a violation rate of 40 per cent, while the rate for Fricot Ranch releases was 43 per cent and for Fred C. Nelles School boys it was 60 per cent. Boys from Paso Robles School had a violation rate of 57 per cent, while those from camps showed a rate of 36 per cent. Parolees from Preston School of Industry behaved differently than parolees from Youth Training School, Deuel Vocational Institution, or Soledad Prison. Beverly and Guttmann assert that these different outcomes are the consequence of $a$) selection factors which influence commitment policies, and $b$) variations in institutional treatment influences.

[4] Carolyn B. Jamison, Bertram M. Johnson, and Evelyn S. Guttmann, An Analysis of Post-Discharge Criminal Behavior (Sacramento: State of California, Department of the Youth Authority, 1966).

[5] Robert F. Beverly and Evelyn S. Guttmann, An Analysis of Parole Performance by Institution of Release, 1956–1960 (Sacramento: State of California, Department of the Youth Authority, 1962).

## Prisons

Most studies of populations of offenders in adult institutions show that large numbers of these persons have previously been in trouble with the authorities. Furthermore, these surveys note that incarcerated offenders often show prior records of institutionalization.[6] These figures fail to indicate the proportion of prison inmates who succeed on parole. The fact that prisoners have often been in custody before does not necessarily mean that most inmates fail on parole. Instead, it may be that many of them succeed upon release at the same time that a group of chronic failures flow into, out of, and back into the penitentiary.

### TABLE 16
#### California Parole Violators Returned to Prison, 1954–1965

|      | NEW COMMITMENTS | TECHNICAL RETURNS | TOTAL VIOLATIONS |
|------|-----------------|-------------------|------------------|
| 1954 | 10.8 | 9.7 | 20.5 |
| 1955 | 7.6 | 8.7 | 16.3 |
| 1956 | 8.5 | 7.4 | 15.9 |
| 1957 | 9.4 | 8.7 | 18.1 |
| 1958 | 11.0 | 13.1 | 24.0 |
| 1959 | 10.0 | 11.2 | 21.2 |
| 1960 | 11.9 | 12.8 | 24.7 |
| 1961 | 10.9 | 16.9 | 27.8 |
| 1962 | 11.0 | 17.1 | 28.1 |
| 1963 | 10.4 | 21.6 | 32.0 |
| 1964 | 8.4 | 21.2 | 29.6 |
| 1965 | 8.9 | 22.4 | 31.3 |

One indication of post-release adjustments made by inmates can be obtained from California statistics.[7] These figures are found in Table 16, where the percentages of parolees returned to prison as parole violators are shown. These are divided into parole violations resulting from new commitments due to crimes committed on parole and returns due to technical violations of parole rules. As can be seen in Table 16, the increase in parole violations since 1954 has largely been produced by changes in policies regarding technical violations.

Daniel Glaser's recent survey of the federal prison system indicates

---

[6] Edwin H. Sutherland and Donald R. Cressey, *Principles of Criminology* (7th ed.; Philadelphia: J. B. Lippincott Co., 1966), pp. 541–46.

[7] State of California, *Crime and Delinquency in California, 1965* (Sacramento: State of California, Bureau of Criminal Statistics, 1966), p. 136.

that prisoners frequently make adequate parole adjustments.[8] Glaser noted that the notion is frequently expressed that two-thirds of those who are imprisoned subsequently recidivate. However, one study of federal prison parolees in 1943 and 1944 showed that only about 25 per cent were returned to prison within five years. Glaser also reviewed a collection of surveys which indicate that only about one-third of the parolees from state institutions are returned to penitentiaries within five years after release.

Glaser has identified some major variables associated with parole success or failure. These include age—younger prisoners more often violate parole. Parolees who had been confined in juvenile institutions, left home at an early age, or had records of repeated property crime were the ones who most commonly failed on parole.[9]

The investigation of the federal prison system by Glaser provides a rich source of materials on the workings of penitentiaries. Among other things, this study showed that treatment personnel in institutions were not violently disliked by the inmates, but neither were they accorded much respect or positive feeling. Thus their therapeutic impact upon convicts may be negligible.[10] Glaser also suggests that training in vocational skills is less important as an influence upon parole behavior than habituation of inmates to regularity in employment. Personal attention directed by supervisors to prisoners is an important contributor to rehabilitation.[11] Glaser presents 91 conclusions from his research, and the reader is urged to examine these on his own.

To this point, little has been said about the effectiveness of various forms of treatment. Thus we might ask: "How useful is psychiatric therapy or some other kind of intervention?" Let us look at the available evidence regarding the relative potency of different strategies applied to offenders.

## PSYCHIATRIC TREATMENT

We have noted at other points that the psychiatric orientation turns up in a variety of places in criminology. Psychogenic formulations are exceedingly popular as causal explanations. The treatment corollary of these views, which contends that most offenders need psychiatric aid, has

---

[8] Daniel Glaser, *The Effectiveness of a Prison and Parole System* (Indianapolis, Ind.: Bobbs-Merrill Co., Inc., 1964), pp. 13–35.

[9] *Ibid.*, pp. 36–53.

[10] *Ibid.*, pp. 134–39.

[11] *Ibid.*, pp. 504–13.

enjoyed widespread popularity. Whatever the reasons for allegiance to these notions, it cannot be said that they are supported by much evidence. Instead, most of the research data at hand runs counter to psychiatric claims. Lawbreakers who have been subjected to psychotherapy rarely seem to respond favorably to this experience.

One investigation which casts doubt upon psychiatric treatment has been carried out by Adamson and Dunham,[12] who examined the history of the Wayne County (Detroit) Clinic for Child Study. From 1924 to 1948, the clinic staff was heavily augmented with additional psychiatric professionals, so its effects upon wards should have become more prominent if psychotherapy is effective. But follow-up study of boys who had been in court in 1930, 1935, 1940, and 1948 showed almost no reduction in the proportions of treated youths who got into further trouble. In 1930, 45 per cent of the boys were later arrested by the police, as contrasted to 39 per cent of those who had been in the clinic in 1948. The markedly increased costs of clinic operation were not accompanied by decreased recidivism. Adamson and Dunham were led by these results to the conclusion that psychiatric therapy is inappropriate for the hard-core, working class delinquents at which it was directed.

A second study of psychotherapy took place in California in the form of the Intensive Treatment program at San Quentin and Chino prisons.[13] That operation was an experimental undertaking involving treatment groups which received intensive individual and group psychotherapy, along with control groups processed through the regular institutional program. The theory which informed this project was that most violators are psychologically troubled, so they were thought to need psychotherapy. Results of the program showed no important differences in parole adjustment between the treated and untreated prisoners. Here again, it appears that psychiatric treatment is inappropriate for many of the kinds of inmates found in prison.

A third case of psychotherapy is the PICO (Pilot Intensive Counseling Organization) project which concerned treatment and control groups of prisoners at Deuel Vocational Institution in California.[14] California Youth Authority wards between 17 and 23 years of age were the subjects of the program. The treated subjects were given intensive, individual interview therapy similar to "depth" psychotherapy. They were given

[12] LaMay Adamson and H. Warren Dunham, "Clinical Treatment of Male Delinquents: A Case Study in Effort and Result," *American Sociological Review*, XXI (June 1956), 312–20.

[13] California Department of Corrections, *Second Annual Report, Intensive Treatment Program* (Sacramento: State of California, Department of Corrections, 1958).

[14] Stuart Adams, "The PICO Project," in *The Sociology of Punishment and Correction*, ed. Norman Johnston, Leonard Savitz, and Marvin E. Wolfgang (New York: John Wiley and Sons, Inc., 1962), pp. 213–24.

individual therapy several times per week, along with some group therapy. The control group wards received regular institutional attention, and therefore much less counseling. The individuals in the project were also sorted into "amenable" and "nonamenable" categories before they were introduced into the research experiment. Cases judged to be amenable to treatment were characterized by a level of anxiety which would make them likely to respond to therapy, while the nonamenables were assessed as lacking this prerequisite for treatment. The experimental and control groups both involved a mixture of amenable and nonamenable offenders.

The therapists in this experiment were trained in clinical psychiatry or psychiatric social work. They administered therapy to their assigned subjects for a period averaging about nine months per ward. Each treatment worker worked with a case load of about 25 inmates.

The impact of this program was measured in several ways, but the major criterion of failure was "return to custody" or parole violation. The treated amenables showed the best post-release performance, followed by the control group amenable prisoners. Surprisingly, the treated nonamenable inmates made the poorest post-release records. They apparently got worse rather than better as a result of treatment. The researchers concluded that the treated amenables acquired adjustment skills from the program, and the treated nonamenables may have been given the wrong kind of therapy.

Another California program, reported by Guttmann, had to do with the effects of short-term psychiatric treatment on youths in two training schools.[15] Treatment and control groups of boys were established at Fred C. Nelles School and the Preston School of Industry. In both places, the treatment wards were processed through a Psychiatric Treatment Unit, staffed by psychologists, psychiatric social workers, and a psychiatrist, where the boys were given individual interview therapy. Youths at the two schools were not identical, for the Preston inmates were generally older than the Nelles wards, and other differences concerning personality characteristics were reported by workers at the institutions.

The evidence indicates that the Nelles parolees subjected to intensive treatment had lower violation rates than control group boys from the same school, but at Preston the controls showed less recidivism than the treated boys. Guttmann suggests that the discrepant results may stem from differences in the organizational climate of the two facilities. At Nelles School, the Psychiatric Treatment Unit was new, and a kind of thera-

[15] Evelyn S. Guttmann, *Effects of Short-Term Psychiatric Treatment on Boys in Two California Youth Authority Institutions* (Sacramento: State of California, Department of the Youth Authority, 1963).

peutic milieu with high staff morale and other positive features existed. The Psychiatric Treatment Unit at Preston was the focus of considerable hostility from staff members. Consequently, boys in the special treatment program received invidious handling from staff members and other inmates. Thus it is likely that certain features of the general training school structure worked against psychiatric intervention at Preston.

Supporters of psychiatric treatment for lawbreakers can derive little comfort from most of the results reported above. Still, clinical observations based on small samples occasionally turn up in which it is suggested that psychotherapy is effective with some offenders. For example, Conn has presented some observations which appear to indicate that non-violent sex offenders can be aided toward law-abiding conduct by individual therapy.[16] As we have noted above, psychiatric intervention did seem to have some impact upon certain of the subjects in these experiments. What this may mean is that psychiatric therapy is useful when employed with a restricted sample of offenders, while these efforts are dissipated when directed at other types of violators. If so, future applications of psychiatric strategies will need to pay more attention to the selection of cases to receive this kind of aid.

In all likelihood, lawbreakers amenable to psychiatric tactics are similar to those law-abiding citizens who respond to these experiences. Amenable patients tend to be relatively middle class individuals who are voluble and introspective, able to engage in psychiatric interaction. Individuals of this kind are likely to be most frequently encountered among "square Johns," rather than in groups of hostile, defiant "right guys." The latter have slight appreciation of notions about psychological distress, and do not apply these kinds of hypotheses to themselves. They are loath to define themselves as "crazy" and to enter into relationships in which they pour out their inner thoughts to a psychiatrist. Many of them would probably have difficulty in articulating their feelings about themselves even if they were motivated to do so.

## ENVIRONMENTAL TREATMENT

### The Highfields Project

The experimental program at Highfields in New Jersey, involving a milieu form of treatment and guided group interaction, has already been described in Chapter Nineteen. Two different efforts have been made to

---

[16] J. H. Conn, "The Psychiatric Treatment of Certain Chronic Offenders," *Journal of Criminal Law and Criminology,* XXXII (March–April 1942), 631–35.

measure the impact of this experience upon the boys processed through the institution.[17] In the first, Highfields boys were compared with a group of youths who had been dealt with in Annandale Reformatory, where they were given conventional institutional handling. The Annandale inmates had been incarcerated before the Highfields institution had opened, but were judged to be similar to individuals that Highfields processed, so they were felt to be a good control or comparison group. Recidivism comparisons for the Highfields and Annandale boys showed that 18 per cent of the former violated parole in the first year after release, as contrasted to 33 per cent of the Annandale boys who failed on parole. Highfields youths performed better over extended periods of parole, so fewer of them were violators within two, three, or five years after release.[18]

The second evaluation of Highfields, carried out by Weeks, also compared Highfields wards with comparable boys who had been sent to Annandale Reformatory. He found that 63 per cent of the Highfields boys completed treatment and remained in the community for at least a year, contrasted to 47 per cent of the Annandale boys who succeeded on parole.[19] Weeks observed little difference between white boys from Annandale and Highfields, but the Negro wards from these two places behaved quite differently upon release. Nearly 60 per cent of the Negro boys from Highfields were successful upon release, but only 33 per cent of the Annandale boys stayed out of further trouble.[20]

In one assessment of the Highfields program, Jenkins contends that the guided group interaction experience pressures "adaptive" delinquents to reexamine their self-attitudes, gets them concerned about their delinquency, and makes them anxious about their prospects for law-abiding conduct. Upon release from the program, many of them endeavor to stay out of trouble, while the Annandale experience turns out boys who have resolved only to avoid getting caught in the future. According to Jenkins, the program at Highfields has added effects upon Negro boys, in that they encounter social acceptance in that setting instead of the social rejection that they find outside the institution.[21]

These results from the Highfields program make it clear as to why this experiment has attracted widespread attention and been emulated in

[17] H. Ashley Weeks, *Youthful Offenders at Highfields* (Ann Arbor: University of Michigan Press, 1963); Lloyd W. McCorkle, Albert Elias, and F. Lovell Bixby, *The Highfields Story* (New York: Holt, Rinehart and Winston, Inc., 1958).

[18] McCorkle, *et al., op. cit.,* p. 143.

[19] Weeks, *op. cit.,* p. 42.

[20] *Ibid.*

[21] Richard L. Jenkins, "Treatment Considerations with Delinquents," in Weeks, *op. cit.,* pp. 149–56.

other correctional innovations. But excessive optimism about Highfields as a model for widespread correctional reform ought to be tempered by the observation of McCorkle, Elias, and Bixby that the institution achieved its most noticeable results when it remained small in size. They report that when the facility had more than about 18 or 20 boys in it, aggressive and hostile interpersonal incidents became noticeable.[22] It may be that conventional institutions made up of large dormitories filled with 50 or more wards cannot easily be converted into duplicates of Highfields.

### Group Counseling, California

California has been quick to respond to such treatment innovations as Highfields. One case in point has to do with experimental group counseling programs which were established in several Youth Authority institutions.[23] At Paso Robles School, where the wards live in 50-boy living units, one of the dormitories was organized to provide small group counseling once a week, involving groups of six to eight boys. Another dormitory held community meetings four times per week in an attempt to develop a therapeutic milieu within the unit, while a third dormitory provided a program combining small group counseling and community meetings. One living unit served as a control in which a conventional pattern of surveillance and discipline was maintained.

In the second institution, Youth Training School, the four living units holding 50 boys each were divided up, so that two held small group counseling sessions once a week and the other two served as controls, with regular institutional programs.

The findings from this experiment are much less impressive than those from Highfields. The parole violation rates for groups released from these different dormitories at Paso Robles ranged from 68 to 79 per cent within the 30-month period of supervision on parole, while violation rates ranged from 50 to 63 per cent for groups released from Youth Training School. In both cases, wards who had been in the experimental program did no better on parole than the untreated boys. The major result of the experimental undertaking was to improve the institutional climate in those living units where counseling or group meetings were held—assaults were reduced and staff-ward communication patterns improved.

The failure of group counseling in these two facilities can be explained

[22] McCorkle, et al., op. cit., pp. 166–67.
[23] Joachim P. Seckel, *Experiments in Group Counseling at Two Youth Authority Institutions* (Sacramento: State of California, Department of the Youth Authority, 1965).

by reference to the social structure of training schools. Apparently treatment activities did not sufficiently alter the custodial orientation of the institutions, which places a premium upon orderly behavior by wards and also encourages these individuals to "play it cool." More substantial alterations are probably required in institutional living before inmates can be drawn into meaningful treatment experiences.

Another effort at intensive group treatment is currently underway in California in the Intensive Treatment Program at Chino.[24] An experimental group isolated from the rest of the correctional facility has been structured in the form of a therapeutic milieu. Staff members in that unit are involved in unconventional role-patterns, in that they wear no uniforms and perform both treatment and custodial assignments. The therapy subjects participate in daily community meetings of prisoners and staff and in social therapy groups of a dozen or so men five times per week.

One novel feature of this Intensive Treatment Program is that some of the inmates have been given new roles to play; they have been nominated as "social therapists." The inmate therapists are prisoners who have been in the program for some time and have shown evidence of behavioral change. In the role of social therapists, they engage in the same activities as the civilian treatment workers.

Evidence on the Intensive Treatment Program which has accumulated to date is positive in nature.[25] Inmates who have gone through the milieu program show better parole adjustment than prisoners in the regular institutional program. However, the contrast is most marked regarding those offenders who have gone through the intensive program in the later stages, when inmates have been serving as therapists and the control subjects.

### The Fremont Experiment [26]

Another milieu venture in California, the Fremont Program, was a short-term residential treatment project carried on at the Southern Reception Center Clinic of the Youth Authority. The experiment dealt with

[24] Dennie L. Briggs, "Convicted Felons as Social Therapists," Corrective Psychiatry and Journal of Social Therapy, IX (3rd Quarter 1963), 122–27; Briggs and John M. Dowling, "The Correctional Officer as a Consultant: An Emerging Role in Penology," American Journal of Correction, XXVI (May–June 1964), 28–31.

[25] James Robison and Marinette Kevorkian, Intensive Treatment Project, Phase II, Parole Outcome: Interim Report (Sacramento: State of California, Department of Corrections, 1967).

[26] Joachim P. Seckel, The Fremont Experiment: Assessment of Residential Treatment at a Youth Authority Reception Center (Sacramento: State of California, Department of the Youth Authority, 1967).

16 to 19 year old males, committed from Southern California, who were eligible for a work-therapy program. After diagnostic processing at the clinic, the eligible offenders were placed either in the Fremont Program or a regular institutional program through random assignment. The Fremont wards stayed a fixed period of five months in the program, while the control boys were incarcerated for nine months on the average.

The Fremont boys were subjected to a treatment diet of small group therapy, large group forums, half-day work assignments at the clinic, school classes, home visits, and field trips to various places of interest in the community. This represents a rather rich and varied therapeutic program by contrast to the more usual institutional experience.

Unfortunately, the experimental outcome was not similarly impressive when contrasted to regular institutional handling. The experimental and control group youths showed no statistically significant differences in recidivism after two years of follow-up exposure to parole. In addition, no differences were discovered in the seriousness of post-release offenses in which they engaged, so the experimental cases showed no improvement in that respect either.

One bright feature in the report on this experiment is that parole adjustment was better for boys who had gone through the program at a time near its inception than for those who had proceeded through it at a later point. No differences of this sort emerged in the control group. The researcher speculated that this result may have been a reflection of high staff turnover in the Fremont operation in its later stages. If this be so, the results may be more indicative of efficacious treatment tactics than first appearances suggest, in that a stable and continuous program might turn out improved youngsters.

### The Fricot Ranch Study

One of the most elaborate ventures into milieu treatment within a state correctional system took place recently at Fricot Ranch, a California Youth Authority institution.[27] Fricot Ranch is a training school which holds boys from eight to fourteen years of age.

The conventional form of training school life which the Fricot Ranch project was designed to circumvent has been indicated by Jesness:

When admitted to an institution for delinquents, boys bring with them delinquent values, a hostile attitude toward authority, and a rejection of conven-

[27] Carl F. Jesness, *The Fricot Ranch Study* (Sacramento: State of California, Department of the Youth Authority, 1965).

tional goals. The normal tendency of young boys in institutions is to cluster into informal groups, erect subtle barriers toward administrative efforts to reach them, and to maintain value systems at odds with the rehabilitative aims of the school. New boys coming into the school program participate in these natural groupings and are apt to undergo an experience which tends to reinforce their delinquent value system. While they may conform outwardly to the school program, no basic modification of delinquent attitudinal patterns takes place. When released, they once again seek associations and engage in behavior congenial to their delinquent character and values.[28]

On the administrative side of traditional training school organization, obsessive concern for maintenance of custody and security results in a situation in which the wards are rewarded for "playing it cool." The authorities endeavor to get boys to show outward signs of conformity, with little attention directed at the boys' attitudes. Staff members overlook victimization patterns among wards as long as the older, domineering youths keep order among their peers. In this kind of situation, little or no treatment takes place.

The design of the Fricot Ranch project involved a 20-boy experimental lodge and a regular, 50-boy living unit. The experimental unit was planned to provide intensified contacts between group supervisors and wards, and offer other therapeutic experiences. Boys were randomly assigned to the treatment and control units.

Results of the Fricot Ranch project are at the same time encouraging and discouraging.[29] Wards who had been in the experimental unit and were exposed to parole for 12 months showed a violation rate of 32 per cent, as against the failure rate of 48 per cent for the control subjects. These differences continued for wards from the two units who had been exposed to parole for 15 months. But the failure rates for wards who had been released and exposed to parole for longer periods were the same for both experimental and control boys. In other words, participation in the intensified program at Fricot Ranch had a retarding effect upon recidivism, so that treated wards stayed out of further trouble for longer periods than did the control subjects. But about 80 per cent of both the treated and control boys failed on parole sometime within a three-year follow-up period.

The boys who went through the Fricot Ranch experience were subjected to a variety of kinds of examination in addition to the parole follow-up observations. Jesness indicates that anxious, neurotic boys and

[28] *Ibid.*, p. 4.
[29] *Ibid.*, pp. 85–90.

immature, aggressive youths gained most from the Fricot program, while more mature delinquents were less affected by it.

The Fricot Ranch study has provided the model for another experiment of this kind currently in progress at Preston School of Industry. However, no data are yet available on the results of that project.

### Community Treatment

A recent development in corrections has centered about treatment of offenders in the community, rather than in a correctional institution. Lawbreakers who would normally be sent to a custodial institution have been dealt with in the community instead. One well-known program of this kind was the Provo Experiment in Utah.[30] In this operation, delinquent boys on probation were sent for several hours daily to "Pinehills," an institution somewhat similar to Highfields, where they received some counseling and other aid. However, these youths remained in the community and lived at home, so their program is an alternative to incarceration.

Another community treatment effort is now underway in California, in Sacramento, Stockton, and San Francisco.[31] Two kinds of intervention are involved; in one, differential treatment units consisting of a supervisor, treatment agents, and a work supervisor counsel wards who have been sorted out into interpersonal maturity diagnostic types. Guided group interaction units patterned after the Provo Experiment are administering group treatment to wards in the second kind of intervention. Youths in the community treatment experimental groups are to be compared with matched control subjects who have been institutionalized.

The findings to date on this project indicate several things. First, experimental subjects from Stockton and Sacramento who have been exposed to parole for 15 months show a parole violation rate of 29 per cent, while the control group cases have a violation rate of 48 per cent. These results strongly suggest that community treatment stands as an effective alternative to institutionalization.

Another observation from this program is that 75 per cent of all wards processed through reception centers met the eligibility criteria for in-

---

[30] Lamar T. Empey and Jerome Rabow, "The Provo Experiment in Delinquency Rehabilitation," *American Sociological Review,* XXVI (October 1961), 679–95; the recidivism rates for youths dealt with in this program appear to be significantly lower than for comparable boys who were committed to training schools. See The President's Commission on Law Enforcement and Administration of Justice, *Task Force Report: Corrections* (Washington, D.C.: U.S. Government Printing Office, 1967), p. 39.

[31] Department of the Youth Authority, *op. cit.,* pp. 22–27.

clusion in the community project, even though many were not assigned to it. Clearly, training school commitment may be employed too often as the disposition made of offenders.

## PAROLE PROGRAMS

Theories of parole usually suggest that parolees ought to receive a good deal of attention and guidance. But the fact is that most parole agencies are understaffed and have case loads so large that almost no positive assistance is rendered to parolees. When these excessive case loads are made the subject of discussion, the companion claim is frequently made that parole violations could be markedly reduced if staffs were increased and case loads reduced.

One effort to test this hypothesis was made in California in the SIPU (Special Intensive Parole Unit) Project.[32] Small case loads in which parolees received intensive counseling were contrasted with regular, large case loads where releasees got minimal assistance. The result of this experiment was that parolees who experienced the intensive care did no better on parole than those who had been in regular case loads.

Another suggestion which has recently caught the attention of many has centered about the use of halfway houses in parole, so that parolees would not have to undergo an abrupt change from incarceration to freedom.[33] One research investigation of halfway houses has been made in the case of a facility for narcotic addicts in Los Angeles.[34] The results do not provide much support for enthusiastic views of halfway houses, in that about the same proportion of halfway house subjects and control group cases completed a year on parole without using drugs.[35]

According to Geis, the halfway house was a failure for several reasons. The residents were assigned to the place, and were not voluntary subjects. They received no rewards for participation in the program and were compelled to conform to restrictions not enforced with the control subjects. Finally, the period of stay in the halfway house was apparently too short.[36]

[32] Walter T. Stone, "Administrative Aspects of the Special Intensive Parole Program," pp. 126–31; Bernard Forman, "Report on the Special Intensive Parole Unit-Research Investigation by the Division of Adult Paroles, Adult Authority, State of California," pp. 132–39, in *Proceedings of the American Correctional Association, 1956;* Ernest Reimer and Martin Warren, "SIPU: Relationship Between Violation Rate and Initially Small Caseload," *NPPA Journal* (July 1957), pp. 222–29.

[33] For example, see Robert F. Kennedy, "Halfway Houses Pay Off," *Crime and Delinquency,* X (January 1964), 1–7.

[34] Gilbert Geis, *The East Los Angeles Halfway House for Narcotic Addicts* (Sacramento, Cal.: Institute for the Study of Crime and Delinquency, 1966).

[35] *Ibid.,* pp. 138–86.

[36] *Ibid.,* pp. 245–54.

## SUMMARY

The evidence examined in this chapter does not support some of the optimistic claims which have been made about rehabilitation. At the same time, many dismal views which contend that treatment cannot be accomplished fail to receive much backing from these findings. Probably the major thrust of these data is to point to tactics and strategies which offer promise of modest success in the form of reduced recidivism.

Most of the treatment efforts discussed in this and the previous chapter had to do with corrective techniques designed to divert persons who are already lawbreakers into nondeviant pathways. More complex and direct attacks could be mounted against the social structure from which lawbreakers emerge. What are the prospects for elimination of criminogenic influences in social organization? Could a markedly different and less criminalistic society be arranged in decades to come? These are the kinds of questions which our concluding chapter will consider.

# 21

# The Challenge of Crime

## INTRODUCTION

This concluding chapter has a futuristic orientation in which the prospects for eventual reduction or eradication of crime in American society are discussed. The major document providing the focus for the chapter is the publication of the President's Commission on Law Enforcement and Administration of Justice. This report, titled *The Challenge of Crime in a Free Society*, was published in 1967, the culmination of over a year's effort and study by the presidential commission and its staff.[1] The commission report represents the most comprehensive and searching study of crime in American society ever undertaken by the federal government. The list of over 200 commission recommendations for control and prevention of crime constitutes a detailed and ambitious program of wider scope than any other set of guidelines offered. Accordingly, the document deserves detailed attention in this book.

In a great many ways, the contents of the commission report parallel the substance of this book. In both, crime is portrayed as a complex problem made up of many different kinds of lawbreaking. Criminality is a phenomenon of truly staggering proportions. Moreover, it is behavior which is a reflection of some central features of American society. In a certain sense, a society gets the kind and amount of crime it deserves. A social system which frustrates the legitimate yearnings of many of its citizens must expect many to direct their frustration at that society. Lawbreaking will be markedly reduced only when sources of antisocial sentiments are reduced or removed.

If these claims are correct, we should be wary of facile proposals for the cure of crime through remedies which aim to come down hard on various groups in society. If the history of correctional responses to criminals tells us anything, it points to the futility of efforts to meet crime by intimidation of a few apprehended offenders. The experiences of European nations in the eighteenth century indicate the futility of venge-

[1] The President's Commission on Law Enforcement and Administration of Justice, *The Challenge of Crime in a Free Society* (Washington, D.C.: U.S. Government Printing Office, 1967).

ful, retaliatory gestures towards lawbreakers. Crime was not noticeably reduced by barbarous penalties levied against thieves, robbers, and other "enemies of society." Crime control demands more than token gestures which offer up a few severely punished offenders as proof that "crime does not pay."

The President's Commission report eschews those palliatives and proposed solutions which would escalate the hostility between society and its criminals. The commission does not take refuge in a few simple proposals to "get tough" with law violators. The report points to major renovations in American social structure, rather than at some minor tinkering.

How can the lengthy President's Commission report best be discussed? The most sensible course of action would be to present the summary section of that publication in the pages immediately below. Let us examine this summary statement, after which we shall take up some additional observations about the challenge of crime.

## SUMMARY OF THE PRESIDENT'S COMMISSION REPORT [2]

This report is about crime in America—about those who commit it, about those who are its victims, and about what can be done to reduce it.

The report is the work of 19 commissioners, 63 staff members, 175 consultants, and hundreds of advisers. The commissioners, staff, consultants, and advisers came from every part of America and represent a broad range of opinion and profession.

In the process of developing the findings and recommendations of the report the Commission called three national conferences, conducted five national surveys, held hundreds of meetings, and interviewed tens of thousands of persons.

The report makes more than 200 specific recommendations—concrete steps the Commission believes can lead to a safer and more just society. These recommendations call for a greatly increased effort on the part of the Federal Government, the States, the counties, the cities, civic organizations, religious institutions, business groups, and individual citizens. They call for basic changes in the operations of police, schools, prosecutors, employment agencies, defenders, social workers, prisons, housing authorities, and probation and parole officers.

[2] *Ibid.,* pp. v–xi.

But the recommendations are more than just a list of new procedures, new tactics, and new techniques. They are a call for a revolution in the way America thinks about crime.

Many Americans take comfort in the view that crime is the vice of a handful of people. This view is inaccurate. In the United States today, one boy in six is referred to the juvenile court. A Commission survey shows that in 1965 more than two million Americans were received in prisons or juvenile training schools, or placed on probation. Another Commission study suggests that about 40 per cent of all male children now living in the United States will be arrested for a nontraffic offense during their lives. An independent survey of 1,700 persons found that 91 per cent of the sample admitted they had committed acts for which they might have received jail or prison sentences.

Many Americans also think of crime as a very narrow range of behavior. It is not. An enormous variety of acts make up the "crime problem." Crime is not just a tough teenager snatching a lady's purse. It is a professional thief stealing cars "on order." It is a well-heeled loan shark taking over a previously legitimate business for organized crime. It is a polite young man who suddenly and inexplicably murders his family. It is a corporation executive conspiring with competitors to keep prices high. No single formula, no single theory, no single generalization can explain the vast range of behavior called crime.

Many Americans think controlling crime is solely the task of the police, the courts, and correction agencies. In fact, as the Commission's report makes clear, crime cannot be controlled without the interest and participation of schools, businesses, social agencies, private groups, and individual citizens.

What, then, is America's experience with crime and how has this experience shaped the Nation's way of living? A new insight into these two questions is furnished by the Commission's National Survey of Criminal Victims. In this survey, the first of its kind conducted on such a scope, 10,000 representative American households were asked about their experiences with crime, whether they reported those experiences to the police, and how those experiences affected their lives.

An important finding of the survey is that for the Nation as a whole there is far more crime than ever is reported. Burglaries occur about three times more often than they are reported to police. Aggravated assaults and larcenies over $50 occur twice as often as they are reported. There are 50 per cent more robberies than are reported. In some areas, only one-tenth of the total number of certain kinds of crimes are reported to the police. Seventy-four per cent of the neighborhood commercial

establishments surveyed do not report to police the thefts committed by
their employees.

The existence of crime, the talk about crime, the reports of crime, and
the fear of crime have eroded the basic quality of life of many Americans. A Commission study conducted in high crime areas of two large
cities found that:

43 per cent of the respondents say they stay off the streets at night
because of their fear of crime;

35 per cent say they do not speak to strangers any more because of
their fear of crime;

21 per cent say they use cars and cabs at night because of their fear
of crime;

20 per cent say they would like to move to another neighborhood
because of their fear of crime.

The findings of the Commission's national survey generally support
those of the local surveys. One-third of a representative sample of all
Americans say it is unsafe to walk alone at night in their neighborhoods.
Slightly more than one-third say they keep firearms in the house for
protection against criminals. Twenty-eight per cent say they keep watch-
dogs for the same reason.

Under any circumstance, developing an effective response to the problem of crime in America is exceedingly difficult. And because of the
changes expected in the population in the next decade, in years to come
it will be more difficult. Young people commit a disproportionate share
of crime and the number of young people in our society is growing at
a much faster rate than the total population. Although the 15- to 17-
year-old age group represents only 5.4 per cent of the population, it
accounts for 12.8 per cent of all arrests. Fifteen and sixteen year olds
have the highest arrest rate in the United States. The problem in the
years ahead is dramatically foretold by the fact that 23 per cent of the
population is 10 or under.

*Despite the seriousness of the problem today and the increasing chal-
lenge in the years ahead, the central conclusion of the Commission is
that a significant reduction in crime is possible if the following objectives are vigorously pursued:*

First, society must seek to prevent crime before it happens by assuring
all Americans a stake in the benefits and responsibilities of American
life, by strengthening law enforcement, and by reducing criminal opportunities.

Second, society's aim of reducing crime would be better served if the system of criminal justice developed a far broader range of techniques with which to deal with individual offenders.

Third, the system of criminal justice must eliminate existing injustices if it is to achieve its ideals and win the respect and cooperation of all citizens.

Fourth, the system of criminal justice must attract more people and better people—police, prosecutors, judges, defense attorneys, probation and parole officers, and corrections officials with more knowledge, expertise, initiative, and integrity.

Fifth, there must be much more operational and basic research into the problems of crime and criminal administration, by those both within and without the system of criminal justice.

Sixth, the police, courts, and correctional agencies must be given substantially greater amounts of money if they are to improve their ability to control crime.

Seventh, individual citizens, civic and business organizations, religious institutions, and all levels of government must take responsibility for planning and implementing the changes that must be made in the criminal justice system if crime is to be reduced.

In terms of specific recommendations, what do these seven objectives mean?

## 1. Preventing Crime

The prevention of crime covers a wide range of activities: Eliminating social conditions closely associated with crime; improving the ability of the criminal justice system to detect, apprehend, judge, and reintegrate into their communities those who commit crimes; and reducing the situations in which crimes are most likely to be committed.

Every effort must be made to strengthen the family, now often shattered by the grinding pressures of urban slums.

Slum schools must be given enough resources to make them as good as schools elsewhere and to enable them to compensate for the various handicaps suffered by the slum child—to rescue him from his environment.

Present efforts to combat school segregation, and the housing segregation that underlies it, must be continued and expanded.

Employment opportunities must be enlarged and young people provided with more effective vocational training and individual job counseling. Programs to create new kinds of jobs—such as probation aides, medical assistants, and teacher helpers—seem particularly promising and should be expanded.

The problem of increasing the ability of the police to detect and apprehend criminals is complicated. In one effort to find out how this objective could be achieved, the Commission conducted an analysis of 1,905 crimes reported to the Los Angeles Police Department during a recent month. The study showed the importance of identifying the perpetrator at the scene of the crime. Eighty-six per cent of the crimes with named suspects were solved, but only 12 per cent of the unnamed suspect crimes were solved. Another finding of the study was that there is a relationship between the speed of response and certainty of apprehension. On the average, response to emergency calls resulting in arrests was 50 per cent faster than response to emergency calls not resulting in arrest. On the basis of this finding, and a cost effectiveness study to discover the best means to reduce response time, the Commission recommends an experimental program to develop computer-aided command-and-control systems for large police departments.

To insure the maximum use of such a system, headquarters must have a direct link with every onduty police officer. Because large scale production would result in a substantial reduction of the cost of miniature two-way radios, the Commission recommends that the Federal Government assume leadership in initiating a development program for such equipment and that it consider guaranteeing the sale of the first production lot of perhaps 20,000 units.

Two other steps to reduce police response time are recommended:

[1] Police callboxes, which are locked and inconspicuous in most cities, should be left open, brightly marked, and designated "public emergency callboxes."

[2] The telephone company should develop a single police number for each metropolitan area, and eventually for the entire United States.

Improving the effectiveness of law enforcement, however, is much more than just improving police response time. For example, a study in Washington, D.C., found that courtroom time for a felony defendant who pleads guilty probably totals less than 1 hour, while the median time from his initial appearance to his disposition is 4 months.

In an effort to discover how courts can best speed the process of criminal justice, the known facts about felony cases in Washington were placed in a computer and the operation of the system was simulated. After a number of possible solutions to the problem of delay were tested, it appeared that the addition of a second grand jury—which, with supporting personnel, would cost less than $50,000 a year—would result in a 25-per cent reduction in the time required for the typical felony case to move from initial appearance to trial.

The application of such analysis—when combined with the Commission's recommended timetable laying out timespans for each step in the criminal process—should help court systems to ascertain their procedural bottlenecks and develop ways to eliminate them.

Another way to prevent crime is to reduce the opportunity to commit it. Many crimes would not be committed, indeed many criminal careers would not begin, if there were fewer opportunities for crime.

Auto theft is a good example. According to FBI statistics, the key had been left in the ignition or the ignition had been left unlocked in 42 per cent of all stolen cars. Even in those cars taken when the ignition was locked, at least 20 per cent were stolen simply by shorting the ignition with such simple devices as paper clips or tinfoil. In one city, the elimination of the unlocked "off" position on the 1965 Chevrolet resulted in 50 per cent fewer of those models being stolen in 1965 than were stolen in 1964.

On the basis of these findings, it appears that an important reduction in auto theft could be achieved simply by installing an ignition system that automatically ejects the key when the engine is turned off.

A major reason that it is important to reduce auto theft is that stealing a car is very often the criminal act that starts a boy on a course of lawbreaking.

Stricter gun controls also would reduce some kinds of crime. Here, the Commission recommends a strengthening of the Federal law governing the interstate shipment of firearms and enactment of State laws requiring the registration of all handguns, rifles, and shotguns, and prohibiting the sale or ownership of firearms by certain categories of persons—dangerous criminals, habitual drunkards, and drug addicts. After 5 years, the Commission recommends that Congress pass a Federal registration law applying to those States that have not passed their own registration laws.

## 2. New Ways of Dealing with Offenders

The Commission's second objective—the development of a far broader range of alternatives for dealing with offenders—is based on the belief that, while there are some who must be completely segregated from society, there are many instances in which segregation does more harm than good. Furthermore, by concentrating the resources of the police, the courts, and correctional agencies on the smaller number of offenders who really need them, it should be possible to give all offenders more effective treatment.

A specific and important example of this principle is the Commission's recommendation that every community consider establishing a Youth Services Bureau, a community-based center to which juveniles could be referred by the police, the courts, parents, schools, and social agencies for counseling, education, work, or recreation programs and job placement.

The Youth Services Bureau—an agency to handle many troubled and troublesome young people outside the criminal system—is needed in part because society has failed to give the juvenile court the resources that would allow it to function as its founders hoped it would. In a recent survey of juvenile court judges, for example, 83 per cent said no psychologist or psychiatrist was available to their courts on a regular basis and one-third said they did not have probation officers or social workers. Even where there are probation officers, the Commission found, the average officer supervises 76 probationers, more than double the recommended caseload.

The California Youth Authority for the last 5 years has been conducting a controlled experiment to determine the effectiveness of another kind of alternative treatment program for juveniles. There, after initial screening, convicted juvenile delinquents are assigned on a random basis to either an experimental group or a control group. Those in the experimental group are returned to the community and receive intensive individual counseling, group counseling, group therapy, and family counseling. Those in the control group are assigned to California's regular institutional program. The findings so far: 28 per cent of the experimental group have had their paroles revoked, compared with 52 per cent in the control group. Furthermore, the community treatment program is less expensive than institutional treatment.

To make community-based treatment possible for both adults and juveniles, the Commission recommends the development of an entirely new kind of correctional institution: located close to population centers; maintaining close relations with schools, employers, and universities; housing as few as 50 inmates; serving as a classification center, as the center for various kinds of community programs and as a port of reentry to the community for those difficult and dangerous offenders who have required treatment in facilities with tighter custody.

Such institutions would be useful in the operation of programs— strongly recommended by the Commission—that permit selected inmates to work or study in the community during the day and return to control at night, and programs that permit long-term inmates to become adjusted to society gradually rather than being discharged directly from maximum security institutions to the streets.

Another aspect of the Commission's conviction that different offenders with different problems should be treated in different ways, is its recommendation about the handling of public drunkenness, which, in 1965, accounted for one out of every three arrests in America. The great number of these arrests—some 2 million—burdens the police, clogs the lower courts and crowds the penal institutions. The Commission therefore recommends that communities develop civil detoxification units and comprehensive aftercare programs, and that with the development of such programs, drunkenness, not accompanied by other unlawful conduct, should not be a criminal offense.

Similarly, the Commission recommends the expanded use of civil commitment for drug addicts.

### 3. Eliminating Unfairness

The third objective is to eliminate injustices so that the system of criminal justice can win the respect and cooperation of all citizens. Our society must give the police, the courts, and correctional agencies the resources and the mandate to provide fair and dignified treatment for all.

The Commission found overwhelming evidence of institutional shortcomings in almost every part of the United States.

A survey of the lower court operations in a number of large American cities found cramped and noisy courtrooms, undignified and perfunctory procedures, badly trained personnel overwhelmed by enormous caseloads. In short, the Commission found assembly line justice.

The Commission found that in at least three States, justices of the peace are paid only if they convict and collect a fee from the defendant, a practice held unconstitutional by the Supreme Court 40 years ago.

The Commission found that approximately one-fourth of the 400,000 children detained in 1965—for a variety of causes but including truancy, smoking, and running away from home—were held in adult jails and lockups, often with hardened criminals.

In addition to the creation of new kinds of institutions—such as the Youth Services Bureau and the small, community-based correctional centers—the Commission recommends several important procedural changes. It recommends counsel at various points in the criminal process.

For juveniles, the Commission recommends providing counsel whenever coercive action is a possibility.

For adults, the Commission recommends providing counsel to any criminal defendant who faces a significant penalty—excluding traffic and similar petty charges—if he cannot afford to provide counsel for himself.

In connection with this recommendation, the Commission asks each State to finance regular, statewide assigned counsel and defender systems for the indigent.

Counsel also should be provided in parole and probation revocation hearings.

Another kind of broad procedural change that the Commission recommends is that every State, county, and local jurisdiction provide judicial officers with sufficient information about individual defendants to permit the release without money bail of those who can be safely released.

In addition to eliminating the injustice of holding persons charged with a crime merely because they cannot afford bail, this recommendation also would save a good deal of money. New York City alone, for example, spends approximately $10 million a year holding persons who have not yet been found guilty of any crime.

Besides institutional injustices, the Commission found that while the great majority of criminal justice and law enforcement personnel perform their duties with fairness and understanding, even under the most trying circumstances, some take advantage of their official positions and act in a callous, corrupt, or brutal manner.

Injustice will not yield to simple solutions. Overcoming it requires a wide variety of remedies including improved methods of selecting personnel, the massive infusion of additional funds, the revamping of existing procedures and the adoption of more effective internal and external controls.

The relations between the police and urban poor deserve special mention. Here the Commission recommends that every large department —especially in communities with substantial minority populations—should have community-relations machinery consisting of a headquarters planning and supervising unit and precinct units to carry out recommended programs. Effective citizen advisory committees should be established in minority group neighborhoods. All departments with substantial minority populations should make special efforts to recruit minority group officers and to deploy and promote them fairly. They should have rigorous internal investigation units to examine complaints of misconduct. The Commission believes it is of the utmost importance to insure that complaints of unfair treatment are fairly dealt with.

Fair treatment of every individual—fair in fact and also perceived to be fair by those affected—is an essential element of justice and a principal objective of the American criminal justice system.

## 4 Personnel

The fourth objective is that higher levels of knowledge, expertise, initiative, and integrity be achieved by police, judges, prosecutors, defense attorneys, and correctional authorities so that the system of criminal justice can improve its ability to control crime.

The Commission found one obstacle to recruiting better police officers was the standard requirement that all candidates—regardless of qualifications—begin their careers at the lowest level and normally remain at this level from 2 to 5 years before being eligible for promotion. Thus, a college graduate must enter a department at the same rank and pay and perform the same tasks as a person who enters with only a high school diploma or less.

The Commission recommends that police departments give up single entry and establish three levels at which candidates may begin their police careers. The Commission calls these three levels the "community service officer," the "police officer," and the "police agent."

This division, in addition to providing an entry place for the better educated, also would permit police departments to tap the special knowledge, skills, and understanding of those brought up in the slums.

The community service officer would be a uniformed but unarmed member of the police department. Two of his major responsibilities would be to maintain close relations with juveniles in the area where he works and to be especially alert to crime-breeding conditions that other city agencies had not dealt with. Typically, the CSO might be under 21, might not be required to meet conventional education requirements, and might work out of a store-front office. Serving as an apprentice policeman—a substitute for the police cadet—the CSO would work as a member of a team with the police officer and police agent.

The police officer would respond to calls for service, perform routine patrol, render emergency services, make preliminary investigations, and enforce traffic regulations. In order to qualify as a police officer at the present time, a candidate should possess a high school diploma and should demonstrate a capacity for college work.

The police agent would do whatever police jobs were most complicated, most sensitive, and most demanding. He might be a specialist in police community-relations or juvenile delinquency. He might be in uniform patrolling a high-crime neighborhood. He might have staff duties. To become a police agent would require at least 2 years of college work and preferably a baccalaureate degree in the liberal arts or social sciences.

As an ultimate goal, the Commission recommends that all police personnel with general enforcement powers have baccalaureate degrees.

While candidates could enter the police service at any one of the three levels, they also could work their way up through the different categories as they met the basic education and other requirements.

In many jurisdictions there is a critical need for additional police personnel. Studies by the Commission indicate a recruiting need of 50,000 policemen in 1967 just to fill positions already authorized. In order to increase police effectiveness, additional staff specialists will be required, and when the community service officers are added manpower needs will be even greater.

The Commission also recommends that every State establish a commission on police standards to set minimum recruiting and training standards and to provide financial and technical assistance for local police departments.

In order to improve the quality of judges, prosecutors, and defense attorneys, the Commission recommends a variety of steps: Taking the selection of judges out of partisan politics; the more regular use of seminars, conferences, and institutes to train sitting judges; the establishment of judicial commissions to excuse physically or mentally incapacitated judges from their duties without public humiliation; the general abolition of part-time district attorneys and assistant district attorneys; and a broad range of measures to develop a greatly enlarged and better trained pool of defense attorneys.

In the correctional system there is a critical shortage of probation and parole officers, teachers, caseworkers, vocational instructors, and group workers. The need for major manpower increases in this area was made clear by the findings from the Commissions' national corrections survey:

Less than 3 per cent of all personnel working in local jails and institutions devote their time to treatment and training.

Eleven States do not offer any kind of probation service for adult misdemeanants, six offer only the barest fragments of such services, and most States offer them on a spotty basis.

Two-thirds of all State adult felony probationers are in caseloads of over 100 persons.

To meet the requirements of both the correctional agencies and the courts, the Commission has found an immediate need to double the Nation's pool of juvenile probation officers, triple the number of probation officers working with adult felons, and increase sevenfold the number of officers working with misdemeanants.

Another area with a critical need for large numbers of expert criminal justice officers is the complex one of controlling organized crime. Here, the Commission recommends that prosecutors and police in every State and city where organized crime is known to, or may, exist develop special organized crime units.

## 5. Research

The fifth objective is that every segment of the system of criminal justice devote a significant part of its resources for research to insure the development of new and effective methods of controlling crime.

The Commission found that little research is being conducted into such matters as the economic impact of crime; the effects on crime of increasing or decreasing criminal sanctions; possible methods for improving the effectiveness of various procedures of the police, courts, and correctional agencies.

Organized crime is another area in which almost no research has been conducted. The Commission found that the only group with any significant knowledge about this problem was law enforcement officials. Those in other disciplines—social scientists, economists and lawyers, for example—have not until recently considered the possibility of research projects on organized crime.

A small fraction of 1 per cent of the criminal justice system's total budget is spent on research. This figure could be multiplied many times without approaching the 3 per cent industry spends on research, much less the 15 per cent the Defense Department spends. The Commission believes it should be multiplied many times.

That research is a powerful force for change in the field of criminal justice perhaps can best be documented by the history of the Vera Institute in New York City. Here the research of a small, nongovernmental agency has in a very short time led to major changes in the bail procedures of approximately 100 cities, several States, and the Federal Government.

Because of the importance of research, the Commission recommends that major criminal justice agencies—such as State court and correctional systems and big-city police departments—organize operational research units as integral parts of their structures.

In addition, the criminal justice agencies should welcome the efforts of scholars and other independent experts to understand their problems and operations. These agencies cannot undertake needed research on their own; they urgently need the help of outsiders.

The Commission also recommends the establishment of several regional research institutes designed to concentrate a number of different disciplines on the problem of crime. It further recommends the establishment of an independent National Criminal Research Foundation to stimulate and coordinate research and disseminate its results.

One essential requirement for research is more complete information about the operation of the criminal process. To meet this requirement, the Commission recommends the creation of a National Criminal Justice Statistics Center. The Center's first responsibility would be to work with the FBI, the Children's Bureau, the Federal Bureau of Prisons, and other agencies to develop an integrated picture of the number of crimes reported to police, the number of persons arrested, the number of accused persons prosecuted, the number of offenders placed on probation, in prison, and subsequently on parole.

Another major responsibility of the Center would be to continue the Commission's initial effort to develop a new yardstick to measure the extent of crime in our society as a supplement to the FBI's Uniform Crime Reports. The Commission believes that the Government should be able to plot the levels of different kinds of crime in a city or a State as precisely as the Labor Department and the Census Bureau now plot the rate of unemployment. Just as unemployment information is essential to sound economic planning, so some day may criminal information help official planning in the system of criminal justice.

### 6. Money

Sixth, the police, the courts, and correctional agencies will require substantially more money if they are to control crime better.

Almost all of the specific recommendations made by the Commission will involve increased budgets. Substantially higher salaries must be offered to attract topflight candidates to the system of criminal justice. For example, the median annual salary for a patrolman in a large city today is $5,300. Typically, the maximum salary is something less than $1,000 above the starting salary. The Commission believes the most important change that can be made in police salary scales is to increase maximums sharply. An FBI agent, for example, starts at $8,421 a year and if he serves long and well enough can reach $16,905 a year without being promoted to a supervisory position. The Commission is aware that reaching such figures immediately is not possible in many cities, but it believes that there should be a large range from minimum to maximum everywhere.

The Commission also recommends new kinds of programs that will require additional funds: Youth Services Bureaus, greatly enlarged misdemeaniant probation services and increased levels of research, for example.

The Commission believes some of the additional resources—especially those devoted to innovative programs and to training, education, and research—should be contributed by the Federal Government.

The Federal Government already is conducting a broad range of programs—aid to elementary and secondary schools, the Neighborhood Youth Corps, Project Head Start, and others—designed to attack directly the social problems often associated with crime.

Through such agencies as the Federal Bureau of Investigation, the Office of Law Enforcement Assistance, the Bureau of Prisons, and the Office of Manpower Development and Training, the Federal Government also offers comparatively limited financial and technical assistance to the police, the courts, and correctional authorities.

While the Commission is convinced State and local governments must continue to carry the major burden of criminal administration, it recommends a vastly enlarged program of Federal assistance to strengthen law enforcement, crime prevention, and the administration of justice.

The program of Federal support recommended by the Commission would be directed to eight major needs:

(1) State and local planning.
(2) Education and training of criminal justice personnel.
(3) Surveys and advisory services concerning the organization and operation of police departments, courts, prosecuting offices, and corrections agencies.
(4) Development of a coordinated national information system for operational and research purposes.
(5) Funding of limited numbers of demonstration programs in agencies of justice.
(6) Scientific and technological research and development.
(7) Development of national and regional research centers.
(8) Grants-in-aid for operational innovations.

The Commission is not in a position to recommend the exact amount of money that will be needed to carry out its proposed program. It believes, however, that a Federal program totaling hundreds of millions of dollars a year during the next decade could be effectively utilized. The Commission also believes the major responsibility for administering this program should lie within the Department of Justice.

The States, the cities, and the counties also will have to make substantial increases in their contributions to the system of criminal justice.

## 7. Responsibility for Change

Seventh, individual citizens, social-service agencies, universities, religious institutions, civic and business groups, and all kinds of governmental agencies at all levels must become involved in planning and executing changes in the criminal justice system.

The Commission is convinced that the financial and technical assistance program it proposes can and should be only a small part of the national effort to develop a more effective and fair response to crime.

In March of 1966, President Johnson asked the Attorney General to invite each Governor to form a State committee on criminal administration. The response to this request has been encouraging; more than two-thirds of the States already have such committees or have indicated that they intend to form them.

The Commission recommends that in every State and city there should be an agency, or one or more officials, with specific responsibility for planning improvements in criminal administration and encouraging their implementation.

Planning agencies, among other functions, play a key role in helping State legislatures and city councils decide where additional funds and manpower are most needed, what new programs should be adopted, and where and how existing agencies might pool their resources on either a metropolitan or regional basis.

The planning agencies should include both officials from the system of criminal justice and citizens from other professions. Plans to improve criminal administration will be impossible to put into effect unless those responsible for criminal administration help make them. On the other hand, crime prevention must be the task of the community as a whole.

While this report has concentrated on recommendations for action by governments, the Commission is convinced that governmental actions will not be enough. Crime is a social problem that is interwoven with almost every aspect of American life. Controlling it involves improving the quality of family life, the way schools are run, the way cities are planned, the way workers are hired. Controlling crime is the business of every American institution. Controlling crime is the business of every American.

Universities should increase their research on the problems of crime; private social welfare organizations and religious institutions should continue to experiment with advanced techniques of helping slum children overcome their environment; labor unions and businesses can enlarge their programs to provide prisoners with vocational training;

professional and community organizations can help probation and parole workers with their work.

The responsibility of the individual citizen runs far deeper than cooperating with the police or accepting jury duty or insuring the safety of his family by installing adequate locks—important as they are. He must respect the law, refuse to cut corners, reject the cynical argument that "anything goes as long as you don't get caught."

Most important of all, he must, on his own and through the organizations he belongs to, interest himself in the problems of crime and criminal justice, seek information, express his views, use his vote wisely, get involved.

In sum, the Commission is sure that the Nation can control crime if it will.


## WILL THE CHALLENGE BE MET?

We should note that this book is a kind of miniature President's Commission report. That is, many of the observations and recommendations summarized above parallel those in earlier chapters of this book. This book and the commission report both stress the heterogeneity of crime and criminals. Both suggest that crime is common in American society, although only a fraction of it becomes officially known. The manifold difficulties under which law enforcement, judicial, and correctional agencies labor are identified in both. The commission report recommends a number of correctional programs which have been noted in Chapters Nineteen and Twenty, and it stressed that a variety of tactics will be needed due to the variations among lawbreakers. The commission report has been more direct and outspoken in its recommendation that millions of dollars be expended in a war on crime.

The war on crime proposed above would be waged on many fronts. Programs to eradicate poverty would be teamed with efforts to employ science in the service of law enforcement. Sizeable sums of money would be pumped into correctional endeavors.

During the past decade, the existence of an "other America" of urban ghettos populated by Negroes, American Indians, and other disadvantaged groups has been widely acknowledged.[3] Social critics such as Harrington and James Baldwin [4] have directed attention at the poverty and social injustice in American life, and at their consequences, one of which is believed to be widespread criminality and other forms of social

[3] Michael Harrington, *The Other America* (New York: The Macmillan Co., 1962).
[4] James Baldwin, *The Fire Next Time* (New York: Dial Press, 1963).

disorganization. Jackson Toby has argued that the prospects for reducing delinquency rates in industrial societies are not favorable, unless massive changes are wrought in modern life.[5] He avers that delinquency will continue to be a major problem for some time, in part because the sociocultural gulf between adolescents and adult citizens appears to be widening, and because traditional agencies of socialization and social control have become less effective. Toby also contends that the sting of economic deprivation has increased, so that residents of the "other America" have become more resentful of their place in life. Sentiments of this kind are echoed in the work of Cloward and Ohlin, who attribute the delinquency of lower income youths to their lack of legitimate opportunities for success.[6]

These allegations about poverty and its consequences have led to establishment of a number of programs directed at eradication of poverty.[7] The Federal government has already invested large sums of money in a variety of endeavors which provide employment and other kinds of assistance to lower class citizens of many kinds. As we noted in Chapter Nineteen, the privately-funded Mobilization for Youth project in New York City was the prototype of federal efforts directed at delinquents in a number of American cities.

It would be premature to declare that this war on poverty has been a failure, but neither has it been a success. The federal poverty agencies have yet to develop a completely satisfactory structure of organization.[8] However, the more important point is that poverty efforts to date have been more in the nature of token skirmishes than full-scale campaigns. Most of these activities have provided help for only a limited number of youths, and in many cases the employment assistance has been only temporary in character. As Arnold has noted with respect to Mobilization for Youth, disadvantaged youths need to be trained for new careers, but efforts also must be made to generate new jobs of a permanent and rewarding kind for them.[9] The kind of crime prevention implied in the President's Commission report calls for nothing less than massive changes

---

[5] Jackson Toby, "The Prospects for Reducing Delinquency Rates in Industrial Societies," *Federal Probation*, XXVII (December 1963), 23–25.

[6] Richard A. Cloward and Lloyd E. Ohlin, *Delinquency and Opportunity* (New York: Free Press of Glencoe, Inc., 1960); see also the discussion of these claims by Cloward and Ohlin, Baldwin, Harrington, and others in Don C. Gibbons, *Changing the Lawbreaker* (Englewood Cliffs, N.J.: Prentice-Hall, Inc., 1965), pp. 183–87.

[7] See the issue, "Antipoverty Programs," of *Law and Contemporary Problems*, XXXI (Winter 1966).

[8] Richard H. Leach, "The Federal Role in the War on Poverty Program," in *ibid.*, 18–31.

[9] Robert Arnold, "Mobilization for Youth: Patchwork or Solution?" *Dissent*, XI (Summer 1964), 347–54.

in the economic system of this nation.[10] Poverty cannot be removed by minor tampering in the way of temporary or low-paying jobs. At the time that this book is being written, the nation is involved in a costly real war into which funds are being poured which might otherwise be used in the fight against poverty, wretchedness, and criminality. It is for reasons of this kind that the question about meeting the crime challenge must be regarded as moot.

The reforms and improvements which the commission report calls for in law enforcement, correctional systems, and research will all require great sums of money.[11] Judging from past experiences in which state or federal commissions have reported on the shortcomings of correctional or enforcement agencies, dramatic identification of such problems has not always brought about a prompt and positive response. For example, the history of American prisons is generally a dismal one in which gross scandals which have come to light have often failed to produce any sustained pressure for change. But the President's Commission report may be more difficult to ignore than its predecessors. Perhaps the 1970's will be that decade in which the United States began to win a war against crime.

[10] One cautious view of the war on poverty can be found in S. M. Miller and Martin Rein, "Will the War on Poverty Change America?" Trans-action (July–August 1965), 17–23.

[11] For a recent statement on the need for correctional research, see Robert H. Fosen and Jay Campbell, Jr., "Common Sense and Correctional Science," Journal of Research in Crime and Delinquency, III (July 1966), 73–81.

# Index

Briggs, Dennie L., 525
Brill, A. A., 144
Bromberg, Walter, 143, 249
Bronner, Augusta F., 141, 152
Broom, Leonard, 5, 24, 135, 176
Brown, Daniel G., 373
Browning, Charles J., 305
Bullock, Henry A., 350-354
Burgess, Ernest W., 38
Burgess, Robert L., 208, 322
Burt, Cyril, 152

**C**

Cadwallader, Mervyn L., 43, 219, 261
Caldwell, Robert G., 321, 368
Cameron, Mary Owen, 236, 237, 289,
   290-292, 330
Campbell, Jay, Jr., 551
Campbell, John D., 401
Capwell, Dora F., 154
Carlin, Jerome E., 340
Cartwright, Dorwin, 504
Casriel, Daniel, 506
Catlin, George E. G., 174
Cavallin, Hector, 399
Cavan, Ruth Shonle, 217, 218, 368
Cavan, Sherri, 196
Cayton, Horace R., 418
Chambliss, William J., 26-28
Chein, Isidor, 423-425
Child, Irvin L., 370
Chilton, Roland J., 179, 263
Christenson, Cornelia V., 380-381, 384,
   387, 390, 395, 400, 404
Cicourel, Aaron V., 94
Clark, John P., 111
Clark, Robert E., 123, 388
Clarke, Alfred C., 186
Clausen, John A., 419, 420, 423, 424
Cleckley, Hervey, 158
Clinard, Marshall B., 13, 19, 175-176,
   179, 180, 181, 183, 186, 194, 217, 222,
   275, 284, 319-320, 330, 336, 367, 374,
   412, 419, 427
Cloward, Richard A., 124, 175-180, 215,
   222, 237, 268-269, 272, 274-275, 277,
   358, 424, 461, 467, 550
Cohen, Albert K., 4-5, 8, 124, 135, 176,
   180-181, 185, 187, 189, 200-201, 222,
   263-265, 267, 272, 274, 302, 317
Cole, Stephen, 179
Conn, J. H., 395-396, 522
Connor, Ralph, 432
Cook, Fred J., 62, 417
Cort, David, 331

Cory, Donald Webster, 401, 404
Coser, Lewis A., 174-175
Cottrell, Leonard S., Jr., 5, 24, 135, 176
Cozart, Reed, 476
Crawford, P. L., 504
Cressey, Donald R., 7, 20-21, 25, 35-37,
   43, 91, 93, 120-121, 124, 129-130, 132,
   152-153, 160, 181, 186, 200, 203, 205-
   210, 217, 220, 261, 297, 310, 321, 329,
   333-336, 364, 368-369, 436, 446, 453,
   456-457, 459-460, 461, 463, 465-466,
   471, 477, 499, 502-504, 506, 518
Crutchfield, Richard S., 370
Cumming, Elaine, 60
Cumming, Ian, 60
Curtis, Jack H., 370

**D**

Dain, Harvey J., 371, 402-404
Darwin, Charles, 126
Davenport, C. B., 135
De Baun, Everett, 253, 254
De Fleur, Melvin L., 208
Demerath, Nicholas J., 183
Dentler, Robert A., 111
de River, J. Paul, 390
Deutsch, Albert, 51, 480
Dewey, Richard, 370
Diana, Lewis, 487
Diethelm, Oskar, 159
Dietrick, David C., 266, 272
Dimants, Rita, 489-490
Dince, Paul R., 371, 402-404
Dinitz, Simon, 163, 186, 278
Donnelly, Richard C., 24
Doorbar, Ruth R., 378
Dosick, Martin L., 306-307
Dowling, John M., 525
Drake, St. Clair, 418
Drellich, Marvin G., 371, 402-404
Dresser, John W., 399
Driver, Edwin D., 359
Drzazga, John, 376
Dubin, Robert, 176
Dugdale, Richard L., 135
Dumpson, James R., 504
Dunham, H. Warren, 143, 520
Durkheim, Emile, 174-176, 180, 268
Dynes, Russell R., 186

**E**

Eaton, Joseph W., 25, 184, 474
Edell, Laura, 60

# SUBJECT INDEX

## A

Abortion, 32-33, 341-342
    attitudes toward, 32-33
*Adamson* decision, 54
Aggression, 359-365
    situational, 360
Aggressive rapist, 384-388
    described, 384-386
    research on, 386-388
Alcoholic offenders, dependency, 168, 428-429
Alcoholic, "Skid Road," 429-432
    described, 429-431
    research on, 431-432
Alcoholism, 426-432
    extent of, 427-428
    middle-class, 428-429
Anomie, 174-181, 268-269, 274-275
    in American society, 176-178
    in gang delinquency, 179-181, 268-269, 274-275
    in a military prison, 178-179
Assault, laws on, 347
Automobile theft, 298-308
Automobile thief, "joyrider," 298-308
    described, 298-299
    research on, 300-308

## B

Bail, 80-82
    alternatives to, 81-82
    criticisms of, 80-81
Body type and crime, 132-134
Brink's robbery, 253-254
Broken homes, 210-211
Burglars, types of, 13-14

## C

California Personality Inventory, 162-164
Capital punishment, 438, 444-446

Cartographic school, 120-121
Chicago Area Project, 508
Child-Parents Relationship Scale, 155
Civil law, 19-20
Classical theory, 119-120, 438-439
Community Treatment Project, California, 511-512, 528-529
Compulsive crime, 291-294, 369
Conduct norms, 35-37
Correctional institutions, number of, 447-448
Correctional practices, 435-451, 493-530
    contemporary, 443-451
    history of, 435-442
Correctional social organization, 453-491
Correctional treatment, 493-530
    by offender types, 510-512
    forms of, 501-510
    humanitarian reforms, 494-495
    nature of, 499-500
    opposition to, 497-498
    research on, 515-530
        juvenile institutions, 517, 520-528
        parole, 529
        prisons, 518-519
        probation, 516
        psychiatric therapy, 519-522
Courts, 73-88
    arraignment, 77
    federal, 74-75
    indictment, 76
    jury trials, 84-88
    preliminary hearing, 76
    problems of, 77-80
    procedures in, 75-77
    state, 73-74
Crime:
    definition of, 5, 37-39
        legal, 35-37
        sociological, 35-37
    differentiae of, 21-23
    economic costs of, 98-99

# U

# V

# W